Shiloh

SHILOH

Conquer or Perish

Timothy B. Smith

University Press of Kansas

Published by the University Press of Kansas (Lawrence, Kansas 66045), which was organized
by the Kansas Board of Regents and is operated and funded by Emporia State University,
Fort Hays State University, Kansas State University, Pittsburg State University,
the University of Kansas, and Wichita State University

Library of Congress Cataloging-in-Publication Data

Smith, Timothy B., 1974–

Shiloh : conquer or perish / Timothy B. Smith.

pages cm. — (Modern war studies)

Includes bibliographical references and index.

ISBN 978-0-7006-1995-5 (cloth) — ISBN 978-0-7006-2347-1 (paperback)

ISBN 978-0-7006-2039-5 (ebook)

1. Shiloh, Battle of, Tenn., 1862. I. Title.

E473.54.S635   2014

973.7'31—dc23

2014019701

British Library Cataloguing-in-Publication Data is available.

Printed in the United States of America

10 9 8 7 6 5 4 3 2 1

To
Kelly, Mary Kate, and Leah Grace
and
Mom and Dad

CONTENTS

Illustrations follow page 274.

LIST OF MAPS

PREFACE

Shiloh holds a special place in my heart. My parents began taking me there when I was seven, and since then I have had the privilege of visiting, working at, and living on the Shiloh National Military Park. Many memories stand out, not the least of which are working for the National Park Service and living for several years in park housing right on the battlefield. Leading tours with the likes of Charles P. Roland and John F. Marszalek were special treats as well. Another fond memory is standing with Shiloh historians Wiley Sword and James Lee McDonough, along with others such as present Fort Donelson National Battlefield superintendent Brian McCutchen, at Albert Sidney Johnston's death site(s) on the afternoon of April 6, 2012, exactly 150 years to the time of his death. Ironically, while I had numerous ancestors inside Vicksburg (and that battlefield definitely holds a special meaning to me), I had no one at Shiloh. But it is still my most beloved battlefield.

Perhaps that is the reason I have spent a good deal of my historical career studying the battle and battlefield. Over the years I have written nearly a score of articles and chapters in books, published two volumes of essays, coedited the famous Cunningham manuscript, and written or edited four other books on Shiloh's battle and battlefield. Yet I could never bring myself to write a full battle history—until now. Fortunately, those detailed essays and articles have been extremely helpful in fashioning this more general narrative, and readers who desire more specifics on my thinking in the present book should consult those earlier texts.

Why another book on Shiloh? Foremost, the literature on the battle, while respectable, is not nearly as exhaustive as that of Gettysburg or even other battles. There have been, to be sure, a number of volumes that treat the battle in various ways, from novels to guides and many in between, but there have only been four major academic studies to date, by historians Edward Cunningham, Wiley Sword, James L. McDonough, and Larry Daniel. The freshest research is that of Daniel (Cunningham's was written in the 1960s though only published in 2007), and it is now nearly twenty years old.[1]

There is plenty new to say. Even with the major books already in print, I hope to add several major attributes in this present study. One is a new way of organizing the battle. Civil War buffs and even some historians regularly comment about how fluid and confusing Shiloh was. Veteran Manning Force rightly commented, "A combat made up of numberless separate encounters of detached portions of broken lines, continually shifting position and changing direction in the forest and across ravines, filling an entire day, is almost incapable of a connected narrative." Another veteran, Lewis M. Hosea, added a particularly adept view of the confusion of Shiloh:

> It was impossible for commanders of large bodies to obtain a comprehensive view of the field so as to perceive and provide intelligently for the varying exigencies of the battle as it progressed. They could only guess the swaying movements of the fight by sounds of musketry and the chance reports of messengers, who could locate nothing by fixed monuments. Nor could the men in ranks, or even regimental officers, see beyond a limited distance; and the direction of enfilading or turning movements could be discovered only by the course of bullets among the trees or the tearing of the ground by solid shot or shell.[2]

Obviously, we have a little better overall understanding today than the men on the ground had in the midst of the fighting, but Shiloh is still confusing. By tying the action to the terrain and using physical features to organize the battle into phases and sectors within those phases, however, I hope readers will come away from this book with a clearer understanding of how the action unfolded in time and space. I also hope readers will gain an understanding of just how important terrain was at Shiloh; it was, in my mind, one of the two chief determining factors (the other being Ulysses S. Grant) of victory and defeat. William T. Sherman later summed up the terrain's significance: "On any other [ground] we surely would have been overwhelmed."[3]

Another major goal of this book is to spend nearly as much time on the second day's fighting as on the first. We already know there was heavy action on the second day, with one Illinoisan writing that the fighting "commenced at day break & lasted with one continual stunning roar until 4 P.M." Yet most historians have given the second day less attention; indeed, each of the main studies on Shiloh gives the second day less than 10 percent of its text. Attendant to this lack of examination is the idea that the second day was a done deal and really did not matter. In examining this second day in detail within the context of the overall battle, I argue that it was not a done deal and that it was much more important to the central battle than is often thought.[4]

Last, Shiloh was not fought in a vacuum, and there were numerous social ramifications of the battle. Whereas other historians, particularly Larry Daniel, have sought to place the battle in its correct political and economic context, I chose to use my limited space not in rehashing what has already been argued and published but in examining other social aspects of Shiloh. Thus, I have put much emphasis on the soldiers themselves, letting them tell the story through their own words, and on the local population and how the battle affected them. I hope readers will come away with a heightened sense of just how important Shiloh was to the civilians in the area and to the Civil War's strategic situation.

M any people have aided me in the process of writing this book. The many archivists at the various repositories were extremely helpful in providing materials in a timely and friendly manner. Historian friends also provided material they came across, especially Bjorn Skaptason and Chris Slocombe. Others offered items from their private collections, including Wiley Sword, who made a large quantity of letters and documents available to me, and Van Hedges, David Raith (descendant of Julius Raith), and Stephen E. Williams. Superintendent John Bundy and his staff at the Shiloh National Military Park deserve special mention. As a ranger there several years ago, I had the good fortune to discuss the battle daily with many of them. The current staff made my many research visits worthwhile, including Ashley Berry, Joe Davis, Heather Henson, Paul Holloway, Chris Mekow, Jim Minor, Tom Parson, and Charlie Spearman. Chief ranger Stacy Allen made the entire park's collection available to me, and we had numerous enjoyable (and lengthy) discussions both in person and on the telephone, as well as via email, on the finer points of the battle.

I have been extremely fortunate to have had several historians read the manuscript for me, including my mentor, John F. Marszalek. His attention to detail and grammar was extremely helpful. Several historians affiliated or formerly affiliated with the Shiloh National Military Park also read the manuscript and made wonderful suggestions. Tom Parson and Jim Minor, both at the Corinth Civil War Interpretive Center and experts on Shiloh, read the manuscript and offered several revisions, as did former ranger and current Abraham Lincoln Bookshop historian Bjorn Skaptason. Stacy Allen is a wealth of knowledge on Shiloh, and his detailed comments helped me fine-tune the manuscript, especially in terms of timing issues. I would venture to say there is not a lot that Marszalek, Parson, Minor, Skaptason, and Allen collectively do not know about Shiloh, and their assistance is very much appreciated. Any remaining errors of fact or interpretation are strictly my own.

Working with the University Press of Kansas has once again been a joy. Editor in chief Mike Briggs is extremely good at what he does, and he shepherded this project through the process with great skill and care. Kelly Chrisman Jacques ushered the manuscript through production into book form with equal skill and care. Mike Kehoe similarly attended to all marketing issues, and the rest of the stellar staff at the press are equally gifted and caring about their authors. Copyeditor Karen Hellekson edited the manuscript with great precision.

My family has been a constant source of support and love, and I praise and thank God daily for them and all the many other blessings in my life. My parents continue to support my various efforts; my dad once again aided me in the research for this volume. Life would not be complete without Kelly, Mary Kate, and Leah Grace. I can only hope dedicating this book to them and my parents will express in some small way my love for them.

Timothy B. Smith
Adamsville, Tennessee

PROLOGUE

Today, the area around Pittsburg Landing on the Tennessee River is a majestic national park, groomed to beautification and maintained to high standards by the National Park Service. Tens of thousands of visitors from all across the world visit the park annually. It was not always that way, however, and in the spring of 1862 it was merely home to a hard-luck population that would soon have their world torn apart.

The area that would become the Shiloh battlefield has been continuously inhabited for centuries, with the first known population leaving earthen mounds to mark their gathering places. That early population obviously declined, to be replaced by descendents who became the Chickasaw people, but by the early decades of the 1820s white men had begun to settle there as well. Statehood came to Tennessee in 1796, but the wilds of western Tennessee were not fully opened until treaties with the Chickasaw allowed a deluge of settlers into the area around 1820. Created in 1819, Hardin County became the southernmost county astride the river, although only a small strip of land west of the river was included. Yet that small strip was destined for national prominence.[1]

Most early settlement in the county took place east of the river, where the county seat of Savannah grew on the east bank, but some families began to move to the west side as the years passed. The state granted land west of the river to locals beginning in 1832, when John Chambers took 200 acres at a small landing site on the west side that would eventually become known as Pittsburg. Chambers did little with his land and in fact lost his claim, and it was not until 1843 that Thomas B. Stubbs took the same 200-acre grant. By that time, other men had gained grants to parcels inland from the landing—settlers such as Larkin Bell (October 1836), Peter Spain (February 1840), Robert Grissom (June 1840), and John J. Ellis (June 1841). Jason Cloud and Jacob Wolfe also took grants later in the 1840s, and other families moved to the area after

buying some of the original granted land. Wolfe, for instance, sold land
to John Rhea (also spelled Rea and Rey) and James M. Jones. Those
secondhand owners likewise sold portions of their titles to still others,
such as John C. Fraley, who bought a plot from Jones in January 1860.
These families, whose names would become so famous in history, were
soon joined by others taking additional grants, including Lewis Wicker
(May 1849) and Nancy Stacy (January 1851).[2]

The inhabitants soon forged a small society, with social, religious,
and economic bonds tying them together as a community. The settlers
built a Methodist Episcopal church as early as 1835, naming it, ironically, Union. It stood near the crossing of two roads that had developed,
the main road southwestward into Mississippi and the road that paralleled the river on the west side. Unfortunately, the tug of sectionalism
caused by slavery affected even the isolated people west of the river
when the Methodist denomination split over the issue in 1844. Baptists
did the same thing around the same time, and Presbyterians would do
likewise a little later. The split affected the community as political per-
suasions melded into religious and social concerns. There was enough
antislavery feeling to keep the Union church in operation at least for a
time while the proslavery Methodists moved farther inland on the road
running southwestward and built a new church in 1851 on land John J.
Ellis donated for a school and new church. Unable to think of a fitting
name, the Methodists allowed the local schoolmaster, A. J. Poindexter,
to name it, and he chose the Hebrew term Shiloh. Its meaning—a gathering place with a connotation of peace and tranquility—was fitting for
the new church.[3]

As the population on the western side of the river grew, more ac-
commodations began to appear, including a few cabins and a store on
Stubbs's land on the river. Pittser "Pitts" Miller Tucker soon opened
a store and a ferry at the landing site, playing to a river clientele with
a tavern as well. The landing eventually became known as Pittsburg
Landing, and business grew as river traffic increased, a result of mechanization being instilled into the isolated region by the industrial revolution. Still, the isolated county only grew slowly. The county population was merely 8,000 by 1848. Other landings along the river, such as
Crump's, Brown's, and Hamburg, also grew, with small communities
developing around each one. Yet Pittsburg Landing soon became the
most important, supplying residents in northern Mississippi where a
small town emerged in the mid-1850s at Corinth. The landing was suf-

ficiently deep to allow commerce even in the highest of floods, making it ideal for almost year-round use. Major roads radiating outward from the landing area ran to all points of the compass.[4]

The Pittsburg Landing community continually grew so that by 1860 some thirty or forty different families lived nearby. Many of the first-generation settlers had died or moved away; John Rhea died of a heart attack in 1848 while fetching water from the spring that still bears his name. Other initial landowners such as Jacob Wolfe, John J. Ellis, and Jason Cloud were likewise no longer around, nor were the Tucker brothers, including Pitts, who by this time had moved southward to Corinth, Mississippi. A few of the earliest settlers such as Lewis Seay still inhabited the area, but new owners including Joseph Duncan, Daniel Davis, and William C. Barnes had also moved in.[5]

Most of these men worked the land as best they could, but there was also an assortment of skilled workers such as shoe and boot maker W. T. Stratton, weaver Patsy Fiffs, carpenter George McCrary, and well digger Charles Hopkins. Zachariah Pickins listed his occupation on the 1860 census as a squatter. John W. Sowell wrote that he was a "farmer and officer," apparently in some type of militia or local police force. These families were thoroughly Southern, having mostly been born farther east in Tennessee or in one of the other slaveholding states. No one in the voting district had been born in a free state, although Thomas Walker in a neighboring district hailed from England.[6]

These farmers had a hard time trying to make a living on land ill suited for agriculture. One resident later admitted, "A more unprofitable spot of land, perhaps, could not have been selected . . . for a battleground, . . . with less loss to the county." There were a few early slaveholders such as John C. Rhea and Thomas W. Poindexter, but no plantation agriculture existed in this area west of the river; only eight people in the voting district owned twenty-three slaves in 1860, an average of three slaves each. Joseph Duncan and John C. Fraley each owned one, Lewis Wicker, Dudley Jones, and W.G. Wood owned two each, and Margaret Shelby owned three. James J. Fraley and R. G. Wood were the largest owners, with five and seven, respectively. In addition, these farmers owned horses, cows, and mules or oxen, with the larger landowners such as M. G. Wood, J. G. W. Hagy, H. A. Pettigrew, J. A. Perry, Lewis Seay, and Mary Howell owning more than the others. Swine and sheep were also major commodities, with John C. Fraley having upwards of sixty pigs. These farmers grew mostly corn, while some branched out into wheat, peas, and sweet and Irish potatoes. A few such as M. G. Wood, R. G. Wood, Lewis Seay, and H. A. Pettigrew grew cotton, but it was not a major cash crop. Only three farmers raised tobacco. Others produced beeswax and honey, and most had some type of orchard.[7]

As would be expected of an isolated frontier community, most of these farmers lived in crude log cabins set within their cleared farm fields. Most cabins contained only one room and a loft, but it had to accommodate the entire family and at times a few live-in hands. Only the Cantrell house near Lick Creek had any superiority. One observer noted that it was a "white, frame dwelling-house of some pretension for that region." In addition to their cabins, many locals had outlying buildings such as barns, outhouses, and well houses, although the numerous fresh springs in the hills and hollows allowed for an abundance of fresh water. The fields were fenced—not to keep animals in but to keep them out of their crops. The locals allowed their animals to roam the open range, which had the effect of clearing much of the nearby woods of heavy undergrowth. A definite community aspect thus developed around the Shiloh area, with most of the inhabitants worshiping together at Shiloh Church, trading at the landing store, attending each others' burials in the church or family cemeteries, and sons wooing neighbors' daughters. For example, Manse George wooed and wed Nancy Bell, daughter of Sarah Bell, who lived on the next ridge along the road running parallel with the river.[8]

Whether regarded as idyllic or not, this small frontier community was not so isolated as to be immune from larger national politics. When Tennessee began to talk of secession, the people of Hardin County voted twice against leaving the Union, although what secession sentiment there was resided west of the river. War nevertheless erupted, but these isolated country folk saw or heard little of it through the first year. War talk mainly concerned what was happening farther north and recruitment activities in the area. Then in the spring of 1862, war came to these people, and it came with a vengeance.[9]

The inhabitants of Shiloh stood front and center in the path that armies would take. Their unenviable position, although they were isolated and of little importance, was attributable to the growing phenomenon that was the industrial revolution. The transportation and communication revolutions between the 1820s and 1840s resulted in mechanization of transportation on water and land, with steamboats and railroads developing swiftly and efficiently. By 1860, both would indwell the United

States and change how war was perceived and fought. Thus, while most of the initial year's fighting occurred far to the north, by the spring of 1862 the Federals, utilizing steamboat transportation on the Tennessee River, were pursuing their goal of breaking key Confederate railroads that crossed at Corinth, Mississippi.

Between those two key transportation byways was a twenty or so mile stretch of land on which the fate of the nation would partially be determined. That is exactly where the unfortunate inhabitants of the Shiloh region lived.[10]

Shiloh

1

"A Grand Design"

Majestically, it flows even today in its great valley, draining two-thirds of the North American continent and providing shipping, sustenance, and livelihood for millions of Americans. But it was even more important 150 years ago. The Mississippi River, affectionately termed the Father of Waters, has long been a staple of American strength, might, and economic power, and its possession has caused normally level-headed men to make significant decisions and choices they normally would not make, or even need to make. To control the river and its great valley, nations would go to war.

After its discovery by Europeans, the river dominated the minds of explorers, settlers, and even kings thousands of miles away in a giant chess game of strategy and intellect. European nations battled with one another over its control and that of its major tributaries such as the Missouri, Ohio, and Red. Of utmost importance was its great port, New Orleans. Once the United States became a force in North America, its leaders likewise vied for control of the river. Thomas Jefferson more than doubled the small nation's size when he bought the land it drained, Lewis and Clark became American conquerors when they explored the valley and its tributaries, and Andrew Jackson became a legitimate American hero when he defended the great valley at New Orleans.[1]

Yet the river and its valley were destined for more tension as North and South divided, this time breaking it up not by east and west factions on either bank, as had long been the case, but in north and south demarcations. The upper region was not about to let its great trade route flow through another country, and both sides quickly jockeyed for position. Both the Mississippi and Louisiana secession conventions passed ordinances as early as January 1861 that said they "recognize[d] the right of the free navigation of the Mississippi River," and Braxton Bragg easily saw the importance of the river valley, early on remarking that the river was "of more importance to us than all the country together." Many northwestern states passed resolutions stating they would fight the creation of a new nation that would hinder travel on the great river, but perhaps William T. Sherman, destined to be one of the major actors in the growing Civil War, summed up the Northern feeling best. He remarked, "To secure the safety of the navigation of the Mississippi River I would slay millions. On that point I am not only insane, but mad. Fortunately, the great West is with me there."[2]

When secession came, the stage was set for major military operations in the Mississippi Valley as both sides, acting in part according to the famed but debated Anaconda Plan, sought to control the great river and its tributaries. The fighting would be long and hard, requiring over two years of battles and countless thousands of lives at places such as Vicksburg, Fort Donelson, and New Orleans. The largest and perhaps most significant battle in this complex and lengthy struggle over the river valley, however, would come ironically at an insignificant location not even on the river itself, but along one of its tributaries: Shiloh.[3]

Ironically for the Confederacy, the Mississippi River and other transportation corridors posed a major problem. Flowing as it did southward from Union territory, the river provided a wide, trusted, and year-round axis of advance into the middle of the Confederacy. Realizing that the river would likely be fought over, Confederate strategists quickly began to build defenses that would, they hoped, keep the valley safely in Confederate hands. A makeshift defensive line emerged all across the Confederacy, but the major problem spot was the area between the Appalachian Mountains and the Mississippi River. A vast expanse of over 400 miles, the western Confederacy also contained other major transportation routes, also aiming like daggers into the chest of the Confederacy. Most significant were the Tennessee and Cumberland rivers, which were actually tributaries of the Ohio, which was itself a tributary of the Mississippi. Railroads likewise pierced the western Confederacy's defensive line, most notably the Louisville and Nashville Railroad. The Cumberland Gap on the eastern portion of this line also offered a route of invasion.[4]

With such a defensive challenge, Confederate leaders thought they had three things on their side in 1861. One was a reliance on fixed for-

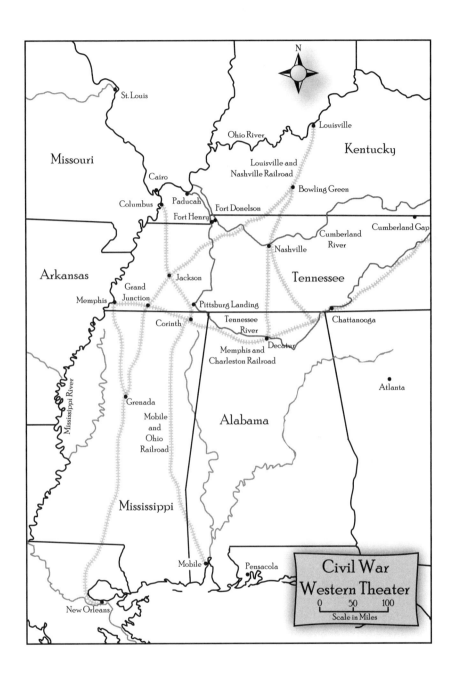

N

St. Louis

Missouri

Ohio River

Kentucky

Louisville

Cairo

Louisville and
Nashville Railroad

Columbus

Paducah

Bowling Green

Fort Donelson

Fort Henry

Cumberland Gap

Nashville

Cumberland
River

Arkansas

Jackson

Tennessee

Grand
Junction

Memphis

Pittsburg Landing

Corinth

Tennessee
River

Chattanooga

Memphis and
Charleston Railroad

Decatur

Atlanta

Grenada

Alabama

Mobile
and
Ohio
Railroad

Mississippi

Mobile

Pensacola

Civil War
Western Theater

0   50   100

Scale in Miles

New Orleans

tifications, something the United States had depended on for its entire history. Confederate politicians and military leaders, most notably Tennessee's governor, Isham G. Harris, began to build fortifications along these rivers and railroads. Second was Kentucky, which early on declared its neutrality, offering a buffer zone along the long and vulnerable Tennessee border. Third was Albert Sidney Johnston, who resigned his position as commander of the United States Department of the Pacific in California and offered his services to his friend Jefferson Davis. Johnston was perhaps the most regarded commander in the old army, with one Texan writing, "Gen. J. was tall, dark, and stern-looking, I think the *grandest* looking man I have ever seen." He had served in Texas and against the Mormons in Utah, and many in the Mississippi Valley petitioned Jefferson Davis to utilize him in their most important theater. "I hoped and expected that I had others who would prove generals," Davis remembered, "but I knew I had *one, and that was Sidney Johnston.*"[5]

Johnston went to work with a will and soon fashioned a semblance of a line across the western expanse. While his command also included the area to the west, his main concern was east of the Mississippi River. Johnston placed Leonidas Polk at Columbus, Kentucky, after that general invaded Kentucky and broke its neutrality in September 1861. Around this area was fought the small battle at Belmont, Missouri, on November 7 against a lower-level Union general, Ulysses S. Grant. Johnston's line continued to the east to the command of Lloyd Tilghman and his small forts on the Tennessee and Cumberland rivers, Fort Henry and Fort Donelson. Later a third fort was situated on better ground on the Tennessee River, Fort Heiman. Farther eastward, Johnston himself made his headquarters in southern Kentucky at Bowling Green, where eventually a small force under William J. Hardee garrisoned that place and defended against any Union movement down the rail line toward Nashville. Farther to the east, another small Confederate force under George B. Crittenden and Felix K. Zollicoffer defended the Cumberland Gap region from any Union incursions into East Tennessee.[6]

All three of these major factors in which the western Confederates placed their trust failed. Fixed field fortifications, especially along rivers, proved too easily turned and captured. Likewise, with Polk's invasion of Kentucky, it was no longer a buffer zone and Federal forces soon flooded into the state. Even Albert Sidney Johnston was not the major asset many, including Jefferson Davis, had envisioned. In fact, by early 1862, after a series of debacles on the twin rivers, many politicians and Confederate leaders were calling for his removal. Jefferson Davis was Johnston's friend, but he had not done him a favor when he assigned him to command Department Number Two, the vast and indefensible area straddling the Mississippi Valley. Though not by choice, Davis gave Johnston pitifully few troops with which to defend the region. Johnston was thus in a no-win situation. He needed to be a miracle worker to fulfill the expectations of him.[7]

The major cause for concern over Johnston came with the surprising Federal victories early in 1862. With more men, and the ability to pick their avenue of advance while Johnston had to defend all points, the Federals had only to find capable leaders to break Johnston's line. Abraham Lincoln tried a number of officers in the west, including John C. Fremont, but finally settled on Henry W. Halleck for the Mississippi Valley command. Old Brains, as Halleck was later termed, was certainly capable of the planning a department command entailed. He was at the time America's foremost military thinker, having translated Jomini's famous work and compiled his own entitled *Elements of Military Art and Science* (1846). The other major western department, the Department of the Ohio, had a continual revolving door of commanding officers, including Fort Sumter's famed Robert Anderson, William T. Sherman, who openly argued that the war in the west would take hundreds of thousands of lives and years to complete and was labeled crazy, and Don Carlos Buell.[8]

Small actions resulted, including Wilson's Creek, Belmont, and Mill Springs, but most attention remained on the Mississippi Valley, where Halleck confronted Leonidas Polk's bastion at Columbus. Polk labeled it "well-nigh impregnable," while Halleck termed it the "Gibraltar of the West." It was in fact so defensible that Halleck and his commanders began to think of alternatives to get around it. Although it is not known exactly who came up with the idea, all sources nevertheless pointed to the same idea of breaking the Confederate line to the east and bypassing Columbus. The plan emerged of using the parallel Tennessee River rather than the Mississippi River as the southward axis of advance. The idea soon caught on at Halleck's headquarters. Slowly brought back into service after a rest, William T. Sherman later told how he, George W. Cullum, and Halleck were plotting strategy on a map one night in December 1861. Halleck asked the engineer Cullum to draw the Confederate line in his department, which he did from Columbus to Forts Henry and Donelson and on to Bowling Green. Then Halleck asked, "Where is the proper place to break it?" The response was, "*Naturally* the center." Halleck took a blue pencil and drew a line perpendicular to the Confederate line at the center. Sherman marveled at how "it coincided nearly with the general course of the Tennessee River." Halleck informed his men, "That's the true line of operations."[9]

For all his intuitive brilliance, however, Halleck would not reap the glory for his plan; it would instead go to a little-known subordinate, Ulysses S. Grant. Unlike many who suffered through the war years, Grant came out of the conflict changed for the better. He went into the war as a failure, barely able to provide adequately for his family. Fortunately, Grant's home congressman from Galena, Illinois, Elihu Washburne, was watching over him, gathering for Grant a brigadier general's star and putting him in position to achieve great triumphs.[10]

Opportunity was all Grant needed. Even as action increased along the Confederate defensive line, most notably at Mill Springs on January 19 where George H. Thomas broke Johnston's right flank, Grant investigated the twin rivers and their Confederate fortifications. When he mentioned a plan to take Fort Henry to Halleck, he was rebuffed. The "crestfallen" Grant nevertheless continued to plan even as Halleck warmed to the idea that had already been congealing in his mind. Halleck ultimately allowed Grant to make the attempt on February 1, and Grant set off the next day.[11]

The next fifteen days made Grant a national hero. He promptly neutralized Forts Henry and Heiman on February 6, with the navy carrying the majority of the load. Before Halleck could recall him, Grant sent word he was heading to take Donelson as well. Although he moved slower than he had planned thanks to rough, wintry weather, he did so by February 16, nabbing not only the fort but also the majority of the garrison, some 14,000 troops. Grant confronted mediocre Confederate generals such as Gideon Pillow, John B. Floyd, and Kentuckian Simon Bolivar Buckner, but in the process of taking both rivers and three forts, Grant became a hero, mainly with his "no terms except unconditional and immediate surrender" response to Buckner. Americans took to calling him "Unconditional Surrender Grant" because of his initials "U. S." Similarly, after hearing that Grant calmly smoked a cigar during the fighting, admirers sent him boxes of cigars, no doubt unwittingly promoting the throat cancer that would eventually take his life years later.[12]

In the larger context, Grant had outflanked both ends of the Confederate line. Of obvious importance was the almost immediate fall of Nashville, Tennessee's capital. The debacle at Donelson doomed the city, and Johnston later wrote how he "determined to fight for Nashville at Donelson, and gave the best part of my army to do it." Similarly, the fall of Nashville and Federal control of the Cumberland River doomed Bowling Green. With Federal troops now as close to the city as Hardee and Johnston were, Johnston had to withdraw to keep from becoming trapped north of the Cumberland River. He issued the necessary orders to retreat as early as February 8, just two days after Fort Henry fell, obviously thinking Donelson was also doomed: "The slight resistance at Fort Henry indicates that the best open earthworks are not reliable to meet successfully a vigorous attack of iron-clad gunboats." Ironically, it was Grant's field army that doomed the fort, and news of the Donelson disaster reached Nashville after glorious accounts of victory. The mood of the city quickly changed, ushering in looting and crime. Making it worse, Hardee and Johnston marched through on February 17, and with them went all normality. One surgeon watched in horror, writing in his diary how "very many persons left the city in vehicles—many on cars—the Gov. & Legislature decamped—Nashville was a panic stricken city." Federal troops soon arrived—first gunboats, then a division of Buell's army hurriedly sent to Grant to reinforce the army at Donelson. An upstaged Buell reported that William "Bull" Nelson landed "before I was aware of it."[13]

Yet Grant's victorious actions netted him trouble as well. Elated at the victories, Halleck nevertheless thought he had to rein in his newly crowned hero. Halleck and Grant seemed to speak different languages, especially when military protocol was concerned, and Halleck thought Grant was a sloppy administrator and commander, even if he did win battles. Halleck wanted things done by the book, and of course he had written the book. The many stories of "the want of order and discipline" in Grant's army after Fort Donelson particularly concerned Halleck. Thus Halleck pounced when a breakdown in communication occurred and news arrived of Grant's going into a different department. He took his concerns all the way to general in chief George McClellan, who gave Halleck permission to remove Grant if needed. Halleck even cheaply mentioned that Grant was reputedly up to his old habits, which the prewar army officer McClellan knew full well meant that Grant was back on the bottle. Grant was thus shocked when he received orders on March 4 to put the tactical army under the command of Charles F. Smith and to return to Fort Henry to act as the strategic commander of upcoming operations. Halleck added a biting scold: "Why do you not obey my orders to report strength and positions of your command?"[14]

Many in Grant's army came to his support, with the general receiving a combined letter from W. H. L. Wallace, Leonard F. Ross, Adolph Schwartz, and John A. McClernand, among others. The officers wrote, "We have heard with deep regret of your having been deposed from your authority as Commander in the field of the forces in this district," and went on to say, "you have slain more of the enemy, taken more prisoners and trophies, lost more men in battle, and regained more territory to the Union than any other leader." Others took up for Grant as well, including eventually Lincoln himself. Halleck reinstated him.[15]

Although the fall of Donelson, its substantial garrison, and Tennessee's capital all fittingly gathered attention in the press, it was perhaps the flanking of the other end of the Confederate line that was of more strategic importance. Grant's twin river victories also outflanked Columbus, Kentucky, which the Confederates soon evacuated. The effects were immediate for Nashville, but it would be several weeks before Polk actually left Columbus. Evacuate he did, however, leaving the grand Gibraltar blocking the Mississippi Valley in Union hands.[16]

While the behind-the-lines Union bickering was taking place, other, more important actions were going forward. Halleck backed down on the Grant issue, but he won another dispute with fellow department commander Buell. Both Halleck and Buell had been pestering McClellan and the War Department that there needed to be a unified command out west, and each recommended himself to be that commander. Halleck was able to claim that it was in his department that most of the victories were being won, and he argued that the Tennessee River was "now the great strategic line of the Western Campaign." Halleck even went so far as to tell McClellan, "You will regret your decision against me on this point." Ultimately, Halleck's insistence paid off; Lincoln made him the new Department of the Mississippi commander on March 11, with Grant commanding the Department of West Tennessee (with the army by the same name, although it is commonly referred to by its more famous and later name, Army of the Tennessee) and Buell commanding the Department of the Ohio.[17]

With the shift of power to Halleck, the scene of future action also shifted from middle Tennessee back to Halleck's Mississippi Valley. In fact, once Nashville fell, all eyes turned to the Tennessee River and its path deep into Confederate territory. Grant, for example, wrote of his plans immediately after Fort Henry fell, telling Halleck that he intended to capture Fort Donelson and then to return to the Tennessee for future operations: "I shall regard it [Fort Donelson] more in the light of an advance grand guard than as a permanent post." Geography also played a major role in the decisions. Unlike the Cumberland River, which made a shallow sweep into Confederate-held territory in middle Tennessee, the Tennessee River had a much longer arc and thus a much deeper sweep that extended all the way into the cotton states themselves: northern Mississippi and Alabama. Because the river flowed generally south to north across the entire state of Tennessee, it provided Federal armies a good avenue into those Deep South states. Obviously the taking of Fort Henry had turned Columbus and made it untenable, but now that the campaign and the operations against Fort Donelson were over, Halleck began to ponder how far southward to advance along the Tennessee before crossing back over to the Mississippi River for continued operations along that line. Looking ahead, Halleck could see where the problem was: the site where the Tennessee River made a great turn eastward away from the Mississippi Valley. Nearby was the crossing point of two major Confederate railroads. Halleck thus reported to Washington as early as March 6 that Confederate general P. G. T. Beauregard was present and using those railroads to concentrate at Corinth, Mississippi. He ominously warned, "He will make a Manassas out of it."[18]

By this time the Federals were privy to ample information about the Tennessee River. Lieutenant Ledyard Phelps had led three timberclads, the *Tyler, Lexington,* and *Conestoga,* southward along the Tennessee River immediately after Fort Henry fell, destroying boats, supplies, and bridges. He also located a nearly completed Confederate ironclad at Cerro Gordo, with valuable timber and iron strewn along the bank, ready to be used. Phelps ultimately reached Florence, Alabama, but was turned back there by shoals. He returned with a vast array of intelligence and information about major Unionist feeling in the area.[19]

Other Federal expeditions followed in the coming weeks. One such voyage precipitated a small fight with a land force on the west side of the river on March 1. The timberclads *Tyler* and *Lexington* were patrolling the Tennessee River south of Savannah when they found an enemy force on a high bluff about nine miles south of town. They learned that the Confederate force was situated on the eighty-foot bluffs at Pittsburg Landing. One anxious soldier aboard the boats remembered the initial confrontation: "The engines slowed down," the soldier on the *Tyler* remembered, "the wheels revolving just sufficiently to hold the vessel nearly motionless against the current." Lieutenant William Gwin, the gunboat's commander, appeared "in complete uniform, with his sword by his side." Gwin peered through his field glasses as a puff of cannon smoke from the heights appeared. A moment later, a shell flew directly over the *Tyler* and splashed in the water astern. The *Tyler* and *Lexington* promptly returned fire.[20]

The artillery was Gibson's Louisiana Battery, supported by Colonel Alfred Mouton's 18th Louisiana. They told a local farmer they intended "to put a stop to these Yankee Gun Boats coming up the river [and] that they intended to sink every one of them." The gunboats opened fire on the bluff and the troops, prompting the farmer who lived just inland from the landing to think it "best to move the women folks farther off." The farmer related that the Louisianans soon had the same idea: they "came running back with their cannon saying their cannon balls could not even knock off the paint from the gun-boats." At least the Confederates hit the timberclads; Lieutenant James Shirk on the *Lexington* remembered that the enemy artillery "was exceedingly well directed," and one of the Illinoisans wrote that the fire peppered the smokestacks and pilothouse, "marks which she bore to the close of the war." To make sure all was silenced, Gwin sent four boats full of sailors and soldiers ashore at the landing; all the soldiers hailed from the onboard 32nd Illinois. The troops moved inland and burned one of the three small cabins that had been used by the enemy, but the Louisianans held their ground at the wood line. The Federals scrambled back to the boats while the gunboats provided covering fire. While ashore, one Federal interestingly captured a drum labeled, "Captured from the Yankees at Manassas." Not to be outdone, the Louisianans peppered the gunboats with more musketry. Gwin wrote that his boats were "perfectly riddled with balls," but the Confederates soon retired again under the heavy naval fire.[21]

The Federal gunboats were but the first wave of Union vessels that soon ascended the Tennessee River. Halleck had decided the true line of operations was southward on the Tennessee, with the goal to break the Confederate railroads in the area. Two major Confederate railroads traversed the tristate area, the east–west Memphis and Charleston and the north–south Mobile and Ohio. Both were critical to the Confederate war effort. Jefferson Davis's first secretary of war, Leroy Pope Walker, described them as the "vertebrae of the Confederacy." Halleck wanted both cut. Over time, the necessity of taking their crossing point also emerged, with Halleck's officers writing as early as late February that "Corinth, the junction of the Mobile with the Memphis Railroad, becomes an important objective point." Halleck thus pointed his command under Smith toward the great bend in the Tennessee River in northern Mississippi and Alabama. Halleck also ordered Buell at Nashville to move to Savannah, allowing him to march overland instead of moving by water, as Halleck had suggested. Still, as unified commander, he was concentrating his forces by the book.[22]

What would become known as the Army of the Tennessee thus snaked its way southward on the Tennessee River, covered by land expeditions out of Fort Henry. All available forces had concentrated at Fort Henry for the trip, causing one of many uninformed soldiers to record he would "march in the morning no telling where." Although there were several days of loading and waiting before all finally moved, they eventually did. One Federal wrote his siblings, "We had a nice time coming up the river. . . . Our fleet was large composed of 104 vessels, a grand sight I assure you." An Indianan wrote, "The Tennessee is a beautiful river, interspersed with islands here and there. . . . The houses along the river present a lonesome deserted appearance, showing that secession has laid its blighting hand on this fair country. The houses have none of that homelike, thrifty appearance of the farm cottages of the North. Whites are scarce, but darkies are in plenty." Those locals who showed themselves, one soldier recalled in his diary, "seem delighted to see us, swinging their hats and handkerchiefs." Yet not all were so friendly. In addition to fog that stopped all river traffic at times, Confederates periodically fired into the boats from ashore. One such incident resulted in the death of one Federal and the wounding of several more, one mortally. On another occasion, Colonel Silas Baldwin landed troops from his 57th Illinois and arrested several townspeople at Clifton, thinking they had fired the shots. It was later learned that Confederate cavalry had done the deed, but Baldwin had already taken the prisoners up the river.[23]

Life aboard the boats was pure misery. One Illinois soldier described "tedious travel of more than a week in the boats." An Ohioan wrote his friend, "You may probably think that riding on a steamboat is fun, well it is a nice place to ride in warm weather but on a boat where there is nearly two thousand men on board and then stay on it over a week is one of the most unpleasant places to live yet and added to this yet we had nothing but river water to drink which is not fit for a hog to drink." "In consequence of which," he added, "we have nearly or about all got the same complaint that old Mrs. Ashby had." The 18th Illinois was so exasperated that they acquired whiskey and "became beastly intoxicated." Brigade commander Richard Oglesby had to send part of the 8th Illinois to stop it and "ordered all of the whiskey throwed over Board." Conversely, a Missourian described how "we were constantly having our blankets, clothing, faces and hands burnt by the shower of sparks from the funnels." Others were more in awe; one member of the 7th Illinois wrote his sister, "What would you think to see 100 steamboats loaded with soldiers, guns, horses and wagons, all going one way, and at last stopping at one place, then have to wait more than two days, before your own boat could get into land, there being so many ahead of it?" Perhaps the only enjoyable part was to "hear the music of brass bands, and fife and drum" on the boats. A few of the vessels had calliopes, and those fortunate enough to be on board marveled at the music. "A person plays upon it as he would on a piano or on an organ," one Federal wrote; "it has keys but the music is made by steam." Officers were, of course, better situated; John W. Foster of the 25th Indiana described a pleasant time playing chess aboard his transport. Still, a nasty feud between division commanders John A. McClernand and Stephen A. Hurlbut developed over rank and the use of particular vessels.[24]

Three gunboats, the timberclads *Lexington* and *Tyler* as well as the ironclad *Cairo,* guarded the transports, some 174 boats in total. One Federal infantryman wrote home, "Think of 50 steamboats, 3 gunboats, and 50,000 troops with numerous splendid bands of music and banners flying all in sight and moving at one time." The supply effort was just as astounding. Charles F. Smith notified his superiors, "We need coal very much. Two barges filled with it arrived this morning, but the two gunboats here consume nearly or quite two-thirds of the quantity brought— say 8,000 out of 12,000 bushels." He also stated that hospital facilities were crowded on the only hospital boat, the *City of Memphis.* Lacking enough vessels to perform all the duties, Smith sent many boats back and forth to Fort Henry. Later, Grant wrote of needing coal because "the unusual stage of water for the last few weeks has washed away all the wood for steamboat purposes, so that coal must be relied on entirely." Later he complained, "It is with great difficulty that quartermasters at Paducah and Cairo can be impressed with the magnitude of our wants in coal and forage."[25]

The first boats arrived at Savannah on March 8, with the 40th Illinois apparently the first regiment in town. Charles Smith initially made Savannah the army's principal forward base. The Federals found the place to be "a quiet, sober looking old town, with a single street, a square brick court house, a number of buildings scattered along the street, with some pretty and rather stylish residences in the suburbs," according to W. H. L. Wallace, a brigade commander in McClernand's division. Indianan S. W. Fairfield gave a detailed view of the town to his wife, describing a street perhaps three quarters of a mile long. He found mostly one-story buildings, and only a few were "respectable." Most were log buildings; a few frame structures were painted white and red. Many buildings were very old, prompting him to write, "I think Noah's Ark must have landed on the top of the hill & the lumber used in manufacturing some of them." Fairfield also described a few lovely gardens, the brick courthouse, a two-story church, and a brick church that "looks as though it had been built in the year *One* & the bricks baked in the sun." In all, he found the town to be about half the size of his own hometown—and similarly "half as pretty."[26]

The Federals were mostly greeted in Hardin County with a warm welcome, mainly because die-hard Confederates had evacuated the area upon the Federals' arrival. In fact, many of the local Unionist citizens quickly came to town selling items and trading goods with the soldiers. Many who had been hiding to keep from being forced into the Confederate army were so pleased to see the Federals that they joined the ranks of the Illinois and Ohio units. One Federal described the touching scenes of "boys a bidding their fathers and mothers farewell, and brothers and sisters adieu, and the husband his wife and family." Those too old to join up simply rejoiced. An Illinoisan told of one "old gray headed man who . . . when he saw the Boats come up he went down with the tears rolling down his cheeks and greeted them as hard as he could." The most helpful civilian was William H. Cherry, who lived in an ornate mansion on the bluff of the river. He informed the Federal commanders of what was happening in the area and sent messengers for them, one all the way to Waynesboro. He also opened his home to the generals.[27]

The majority of the Federals were not as fortunate and did the best they could on the transports. One wrote in his diary of the impressive scene: "A beautiful sight in the evening to see all the fleet lighted up." Those fortunate enough to get onto dry ground, however, began to explore the area. David Claggett of the 25th Kentucky wrote in his diary: "I went into the town and visited some young ladies (misses Irwin) and had a heap of fun and got a splendid dinner." Leonard Ross's Illinois brigade took a more ominous tour, crossing Horse Creek east of town and patrolling amid heavy rain some eight miles to the east without finding anything except a thoroughly flooded creek, which delayed their return.[28]

Despite the tedium, Smith began to contemplate his next move, mindful of Halleck's orders not to spark an engagement before Buell's troops arrived and were available to help. Obviously, Corinth was the major goal, but he explained to Halleck that Corinth's defenses "induced me not to attempt to cut the communication at that place, as that would inevitably lead to a collision in numbers that I am ordered to avoid." He added, "Hence my efforts [will be] north of Purdy and east of Corinth." His soldiers were also ready, and they had confidence in Smith's military way and striking looks. "He is an old man with a beard as white as snow," Charles Cowell wrote in his diary. "He is a military man."[29]

Smith soon began his operations despite the sickness growing in the Union ranks. The wet weather and what Grant described as "alternate days of rain and sunshine, pleasant and very cool weather," in addition to the troops' confinement on the transports for days on end, caused many health problems. One Illinois soldier wrote of "the water which does not agree with our men at all." Even C. F. Smith was not well. While shuttling from a steamboat to a small rowboat, the general skinned his shin. It hurt terribly, but Smith continued his duties despite the pain. Sherman later described it as a "mere abrasion," but it quickly became, also in Sherman's words, "swollen and very sore."[30]

Despite the injury, Smith continued the initiative. Protected by the gunboats, Lew Wallace's division of two brigades commanded by Morgan L. Smith and John M. Thayer landed on March 12 at Crump's Landing and Williams's Landing, just north of Crump's. Widow Elizabeth

Crump still lived there, and Wallace made his headquarters at her house just atop the bluff. The locals continued the warm welcome even on the west side of the river, with women waving their handkerchiefs, although the Federals seemed to be less than impressed: "All the inhabitants dress in butternut colored clothes and the women chew tobacco, smoke pipes, and rot their teeth with snuff." Despite the surroundings, portions of the division moved inland toward the Mobile and Ohio in the wee hours of March 13. Wallace at Crump's with Smith's brigade sent Thayer and his infantry and artillery westward to Adamsville to cover Major Charles Hayes of the 5th Ohio Cavalry, who ranged far out ahead and managed to cause some damage to the railroad at Beach Creek north of Purdy around 10:00 A.M. Constantly watched by Confederate scouts, Hayes soon returned. Wallace wrote that he had felt "a little uneasy" about his cavalry and that his infantry was also suffering from a terrible rainstorm moving through the area, but all were soon safe again on their transports at the landing. Two days later, Smith ordered Wallace to encamp his miserable division. They did so on March 17, his two brigades scattering to the west with a third newly formed brigade eventually moving as far as Adamsville on April 1 to guard against any Confederate advance from that direction.[31]

William T. Sherman commanded another raid. Ever since his early shelving because of false charges of insanity, he had eagerly supported Grant's Henry and Donelson campaign and pestered Halleck to get a field command thereafter: "When am I to go? I prefer General Smith's column." Halleck had allowed Sherman to join the column with a brand new division made of four green brigades, and Sherman was philosophical and appreciative; he told his division that their expedition was "a part of a grand design, devised by the same mind that planned the victories of Forts Henry and Donelson, and led to the evacuation of Columbus and Nashville without a blow." Obviously that mind was Halleck, whom Sherman called "the directing genius" of the campaign.[32]

Sherman was learning on the job, as was his green division. Although he had seen the carnage of Bull Run, Sherman had to weld together a division of totally green troops with some quirky commanders—as if Sherman himself was not quirky enough. One such regimental commander was Thomas Worthington of the 46th Ohio, whom Sherman described as "a strange character." He was far older than almost anyone else on the expedition, having graduated from West Point in 1827.

Worthington seemed to think he was an expert on all things military. Sherman remarked that he was "older than General Halleck, General Grant, or myself, . . . [and] claimed to know more of war than all of us put together." The Ohioan quickly tested his new and tarnished division commander, moving out of line while in column on the river between Fort Henry and Savannah and actually speeding to Savannah ahead of the rest of the division, arriving a day earlier. When Sherman arrived, he found Worthington "flying about giving orders, as though he were commander-in-chief." Stephen G. Hicks of the 40th Illinois was another excited commander who had arrived early, to Sherman's chagrin, and likewise had to be corralled. Sherman was definitely having problems getting his inexperienced colonels to understand regular military ways.[33]

Despite such issues in his division, Sherman made his movement on March 14 with what he called the First Division. This time the target was the Memphis and Charleston Railroad in Mississippi. Smith wondered whether an advance to the south might work better; the high water would affect an operation toward Iuka much less than one toward Purdy. Aware of the importance of Pittsburg Landing, with one of Sherman's staff officers reporting they were fired on as they passed, Sherman asked Smith to send a division to hold that position "as a precautionary measure" while he continued southward. Sherman reasoned that with Confederates having been at the landing, they might return once Sherman moved upriver and "embarrass our return." Stephen A. Hurlbut's division soon took position at the landing, although most of the troops remained on their transports for the time being. Only three companies of the 4th Illinois Cavalry debarked and scouted inland, where they encountered a small band of Confederate cavalry about four miles to the southwest.[34]

Accompanied by the *Tyler,* Sherman moved on, his men crowded into nineteen transports, the artillery disassembled and stored below deck. He landed his cavalry, five companies of the 5th Ohio Cavalry under Major Elbridge G. Ricker, at Tyler's Landing around 7:00 P.M. on March 14 and sent them southward into Mississippi four hours later with a local guide and equipped with axes, crowbars, and other necessary items to break up the railroad. Sherman then followed with his four infantry brigades. One member of the 40th Illinois described the operation, including moving out of the bottom and up "lofty rough pine hills which were quite difficult to ascend." Rain and even snow soon soured the soldiers' attitudes even more, and Sherman began to worry about the success of the operation despite an apparent clearing during the night. The clearing was only temporary; the rains returned and pummeled the troops—so much so that Sherman cancelled his two rearward brigades' movements. The longer it rained, the worse it became. Sherman noted that "ravines became rapid torrents, creeks became as rivers, and streams such as the Sandy were utterly impassable." Members of the 77th Ohio who built a fire on some of the highest ground in a valley were astonished to see the water rise so fast to extinguish it. Sherman especially became alarmed when he received word from his transports that the river was rising six inches an hour.[35]

Colonel Manning Force of the 20th Ohio (later to be part of Lew Wallace's division) noted that the river rose so fast that the boats had only a small "strip of land" to tie up to while he and his Ohioans were detailed to form a perimeter and detain any citizens they encountered. Meanwhile, Sherman began to have second thoughts, sending some of his artillery back to the boats. The guns eventually had to be dragged under water across some bottoms, then taken apart and ferried to the transports at the submerged landing. Meanwhile, the head of Sherman's infantry column, the brigade commanded by Stephen Hicks, stopped at a creek when the water topped the bridge and an attempt to build a second one failed. Sherman realized that speed was his chief asset and it would take too long to continue the slow process of building bridges all along the way. Moreover, word from the cavalry arrived that they were stalled as well, having lost their railroad wrecking tools to the high water and almost losing some of the men and horses. Major Ricker had conversed with his officers and decided that "farther progress would endanger the command, without any possibility of executing your orders," he told Sherman. They turned back, and so did Sherman, confident that "no human energy could have overcome the difficulty." By the time Sherman returned to his transports and his men waded to the boats across the now-submerged landing, the river was well on its way to rising fifteen feet in twenty-four hours.[36]

After getting his men back aboard the transports, Sherman tried again to find the Confederates, steaming southward to Chickasaw where Gwin "politely offered me the use of his gunboat." Sherman shelled the area but elicited no response from the Confederates, whereupon he turned northward. Sherman's depiction of Tyler's Landing as "submerged from the bank back to the bluff" was a good description of most all the landings in the area. Along the route, Sherman reported, "the whole shore [was] under water from Chickasaw down to Pittsburg."[37]

Significantly, that landing proved to be the only one large and deep enough to handle boat traffic even in the high water. Sherman thus decided to stay there, because Hurlbut's division was already on site, and he sent his troops inland on March 16 after he himself made a quick trip to Savannah to report on his actions. The leading elements of the Federal force, composed of a portion of the 5th Ohio Cavalry, had a slight skirmish around Shiloh Church while both divisions climbed the steep hill. Hurlbut's troops soon held the area where the main roads divided just half a mile out from the landing, with the 41st Illinois and half of Burrows's Ohio Battery blocking one road leading to the Snake Creek bridge, while the 44th Indiana and the other artillerymen manned the main Corinth road. The troops also stumbled upon the remnants of the March 1 fight, with the 28th Illinois finding the partially unburied Confederates. The 32nd Illinois also found their own dead from the fight and reburied them. One Illinoisan noted that "the faces of some of them were not entirely covered," and another Illinoisan added, "Buzzards were feasting on the remains." "A sorrowful moment it was for the little company," remembered one of the Illinoisans. Meanwhile, Sherman requested Smith send him "a couple thousand sacks of corn, as much hay as you can possibly spare, and if possible a barge of coal." He reported that he would try to get as much corn as he could find locally until he could be supplied, sending "a steamboat under care of the gunboat to collect corn from cribs on the riverbank."[38]

Once on firm soil, Sherman took a detailed look around the high ground at Pittsburg Landing and liked what he saw; it "admits of easy defense by a small command, and yet affords admirable camping ground for a hundred thousand men," he told Smith. An Indianan wrote that "Pittsburg once had three houses, a dwelling, a smithshop and a store in one end of which I presume was a grocery." An Ohioan added that in addition to the cabins, the only things there were "old rebel fortifications." With the divisions landed, a large portion of the Army of the Tennessee was thus ashore at Pittsburg Landing by mid-March 1862, with Sherman the de facto commander at the forward base while an increasingly ill Smith remained at his headquarters at Savannah. Sherman initially made his headquarters in the small cabin on the high ground overlooking the landing before moving farther out to allow more room for other divisions. Yet as more men arrived, more supplies were also needed. Sherman soon described an "immense fleet" jutting out into the river three layers deep, alternating their unloading times at the landing: "The only drawback is that at this stage of water the space for landing is contracted too much for the immense fleet now here discharging." Work thus began on a new landing to the north. Sherman wrote on March 18, "Colonel McArthur has arrived, and is now cutting a landing for himself." Meanwhile, the wait affected the common soldiers crammed aboard the boats. "Today we lay on the Boat all day," one Illinoisan wrote, "not being able to go ashore on account of so many boats." In all, the men of the 14th Missouri spent seven days onboard their transports; the 7th Illinois was on its transport *Fairchild* a total of thirteen days.[39]

Much has been written in the century and a half since about Sherman's initial and Smith's official choice of Pittsburg Landing as the army's campsite. Some historians have faulted the two generals for placing their army in a trap on the same side of the river as the enemy, and on the opposite side from its nearest reinforcement. Some have even blamed Grant, although the decision was clearly Smith's at this point; Grant was not even on site. Certainly, if the idea was to garrison the area, the army would have been safer on the east bank, but the prevailing thought was to continue the forward movement, ultimately to Corinth. There would only be a few days of waiting until the advance progressed again. Having the army unload on the west bank thus seemed reasonable, as it saved a major crossing later. Although they did not know it yet, the Federal officers had also inadvertently placed the army in a highly defensible area: "hard to assail, easy to defend."[40]

Thus the Federals were content to wait until the river fell to manageable levels, and until Buell could combine with Smith. Yet while waiting, a significant change occurred. Halleck sent Grant to retake command of the expedition. Despite two weeks of sickness, probably caused by Halleck more than anything, Grant soon moved southward and arrived at Savannah on March 17. He immediately improved, telling Sherman he was already feeling better "at the thought of again being along with the troops." The troops felt good about the move as well; one Indianan wrote, "They say Genl Grant has come & if that is so we shall soon be doing something." Grant quickly became oriented to the deployments and Confederate positions, although he admitted to Halleck that news of Albert Sidney Johnston being on the scene "was very much against my expectations." Grant's return relegated Smith to his division, and he resumed command despite still being bothered by his leg injury. Meanwhile, the confident Federals continued to watch and wait, shipping regiment after regiment southward for the great battle all knew was looming.[41]

2

"TIME IS PRECIOUS AND MUCH NEEDED"

In 1860, Corinth, Mississippi, would not have impressed anyone. Barely six years old itself, the town was settled in a bog that was dominated on its fringes by tepid creeks and ridges. "Corinth is built upon low lands and clay soil, so that in wet weather the place may very properly be denominated a swamp," one observer noted; Ambrose Bierce described the town as "the capitol of a swamp." Even worse to some observers, Corinth had not one but two rail lines passing through it. Merchants and travelers reveled in the commerce the railroads brought, but there were no doubt others who loathed the huge locomotives that made such a noise and belched such infernos.[1]

By 1861, the small and insignificant town of Corinth had suddenly become a place of immense importance. As war came, military strategists and politicians suddenly realized that these commerce railroads were now important military prizes. One Alabamian correctly wrote home that were it not for the railroads, Corinth "would never have been noticed." Despite the sickness prevalent there, Corinth initially became one of Mississippi's major troop induction centers, and thousands of Confederate soldiers concentrated there as Jefferson Davis's government and military officials continually called for more troops. Given its access to the east, most of Corinth's initial trainees went to the Virginia front, but more soon replaced them and the process began anew. "Cars are continually arriving and going off bringing and taking off troops," one soldier wrote.[2]

Corinth soon took another leap in importance. Because of the railroads that crossed there, making it, in William Hardee's words "the center of the railroad communications," Corinth and its rail lines were shortly in the crosshairs of the Union invasion. Federal planners were already discussing the need to neutralize Corinth as early as February, George McClellan himself discussing with Halleck on February 24 the occupation of the town. Halleck agreed, planning to send Grant "up the Tennessee, and endeavor to destroy the railroad connections at Corinth." Writing to secretary of war Edwin M. Stanton in March that he was attempting to break the railroads on either side of Corinth, Halleck added, "We must take Corinth before we can seriously injure his communications." Thus, as the Federal armies moved southward, building up strength for their next objective of taking the railroads, and as the Confederates struggled to concentrate their forces to meet them, almost all began to realize a huge battle was shaping up somewhere near Corinth. Indeed, Henry Halleck informed one of his generals in March, "There will probably be a big battle somewhere in that vicinity."[3]

Knowing full well that the Federals would move on Corinth, the Confederate high command began to concentrate around the town after the fall of the defensive line in northern Tennessee and southern Kentucky. Yet just getting there was complicated at best. Two large rivers completely commanded by Federal gunboats separated Johnston's two wings, and with Nashville gone, Johnston had to give up all the transportation, supply, and psychological effects of holding the state capital. His troops thus marched into the city, some of the men sleeping on the steps of the capitol building, but then moved right on southward, leaving the city in what one surgeon described as a "scramble": "All sorts of vehicles in use—stout men walking off with sides and hams—Irish women tottering under the same. Some persons secured large amounts." Johnston quickly withdrew across the Cumberland River at Nashville, removing one obstacle, but he was still within the bowl of the larger Tennessee River, whose arc went much deeper into the South. To concentrate all his troops, Johnston had to remove himself from within the bowl of the river, which meant days of marching, a hazardous crossing potentially amid Union gunboat harassment, and giving up huge swaths of Tennessee. But it had to be done. Johnston had to connect with his left wing now withdrawing from Columbus.[4]

That wing had a much easier time withdrawing than did Johnston, and it had a new commander as well. Jefferson Davis had sent a sick

P. G. T. Beauregard westward in February to serve as Johnston's second in command, and after a conference in early February at Bowling Green, Johnston had sent Beauregard to Columbus via Corinth to oversee his left. The Creole took command and called on the governors of the Deep South states for more men, but Columbus was untenable and Polk evacuated on March 2. Polk withdrew southward along the Mobile and Ohio Railroad into western Tennessee, with many of the troops under Frank Cheatham garrisoning the railroad line at Union City, Humboldt, and Jackson. Much of the heavy ordnance and supplies, as well as a portion of the infantry under Alexander P. Stewart, went to the next stop on the Confederacy's Mississippi River defense tier—Island Number 10, where a garrison set up a defense to block the river around New Madrid. Eventually many of Beauregard's forces, now quickly organized into high-sounding names of "grand divisions," moved into southwestern Tennessee and north Mississippi around Corinth, waiting on Johnston's wing to arrive.[5]

Johnston's retreat was problematic. He marched out of Nashville to the southeast, an odd direction if he intended to join Beauregard behind the Tennessee River's great bend. Johnston had no choice, however, as he had no pontoon boats to build a bridge. He had to rely on the existing railroad bridges, one of which was at Florence. However, Florence was at the head of navigation on the Tennessee River, where Union gunboats and potentially an enemy army could get to his troops as they were hamstrung crossing the river. Phelps and his gunboats had moved to the rocky, shallow water at Muscle Shoals earlier in February, illustrating how the Federals could hamper Johnston's retreat through Florence. The next bridge eastward at Decatur would, Johnston hoped, give him safe passage across because Federal gunboats could not maneuver that far up the river.[6]

Moreover, Johnston had to gather all the troops he could during his retreat, starting with the "fugitives from Donelson" and Crittenden's troops, who were falling back from their defeat at Mill Springs in January. Hardee's growing number of troops, some 17,000 by early March, thus made their way southward, stopping at points to remove large caches of supplies south of Nashville. Also in tow was the Tennessee state government in the form of Governor Isham G. Harris, now ousted from his capital. More tension developed as Johnston slowly crossed the Tennessee River in northern Alabama; getting his wheeled vehicles across the railroad bridge was troublesome because "of the great dif-

ference in the length of axels." Johnston had to slowly load and transport the artillery and wagons over by train. Still, he soon crossed the
river and prepared to burn the Florence bridge to keep his flank secure,
thereby putting the army safely behind the barrier for the time being
and on the Memphis and Charleston Railroad, which could take them
anywhere they were needed.[7]

Historians have often debated when and where the decision was made
to make Corinth the concentration point for the Confederate armies.
Much of the confusion comes from the Johnston/Beauregard relationship, which had to be carried on over long distances with elaborate
codes. Although Johnston was in command of the theater, Beauregard
wielded significant power. After all, he was the hero of Fort Sumter and
Manassas, and even these Westerners were hailing him as the savior
of the nation: "The country looks hopefully—oh! How hopefully—to
you in the hour of its deepest trials here," wrote James T. Trezevant
after Beauregard's arrival. An Alabamian similarly wrote, "Beauregard
is here! We rely upon his valor and discretion—where he leads we will
follow." And who was Johnston? Yes, he had been deemed the hero of
the Confederacy, and still was in Davis's eyes, but many others had begun to have their doubts. In a matter of weeks, Johnston had lost much
of Kentucky and most of Tennessee except the extreme western part,
and he had fallen back into the northern tier counties of the gulf cotton
states. Even his own son later wrote how the South was "in a delirium
of rage and terror." One Kentucky congressman, E. M. Bruce, wrote
President Davis of Johnston: "His errors of omission, commission, and
delay have been greater than any general who ever preceded him in any
country." Even the vast majority of the Tennessee delegation in the Confederate congress—all but one member—called for Johnston's removal.
Johnston no doubt understood their concern, stating to Colonel Edward
W. Munford: "With the people there is but one test of merit in my pro-
fession, that of success. It is a hard rule, but I think it right." Perhaps
that was part of the reason Johnston listened to his second in command
so much; he admitted to Bragg that he had "lost the confidence of his
army." Still, the chief opinion that mattered was Jefferson Davis's, and
he was not shaken in his confidence, at least outwardly. When told by
that Tennessee delegation that Johnston was no general, Davis replied,
"If he is not a general, we had better give up the war, for we have no

general." Privately, Davis wrote Johnston, "It would be worse than useless to point out to you how much depends on you."[8]

Beauregard's later writings probably fueled the debate as well. In his report on Shiloh, he included pointed statements about how Johnston "was called on" to send troops toward Corinth and how "the call on General Johnston was promptly complied with." While there is much evidence of Beauregard pushing the idea, with Johnston writing that Beauregard "has been urging me on," Johnston was probably already thinking in those terms well before Beauregard's call. He wrote to Judah Benjamin, the Confederate secretary of war, on February 25: "The defense of the [Mississippi] valley appears of paramount importance, and, consequently, I will move this corps of the army, of which I have assumed the immediate command, towards the left bank of the Tennessee . . . in order to enable me to co-operate or unite with General Beauregard for the defense of Memphis and the Mississippi." Johnston also later promoted the same idea in a letter to Jefferson Davis. No matter who made the decision, and it was likely made out of the obviousness of the situation, Corinth quickly became the strategic focus that had to be defended.[9]

As a result, the majority of both wings began concentrating at Corinth, with Hardee bringing in his troops from central Kentucky via northern Alabama. One of his soldiers later wrote, "Push now became the order of the day, everything and everybody seemed to be in a hurry." Another of Johnston's tired soldiers similarly wrote home, "Having marched through ¼ of Ky. All of Tenn. Part of Alabama and 30 miles into Miss, you may be assured that we were some what leg weary." At the same time, Polk shuttled many of his Tennesseans down the rail line while others, such as those under Alexander P. Stewart, came eastward from garrisons along the Mississippi River. None of it was easy. Polk's units endured a harrowing train pileup on the Mobile and Ohio, during which train after train collided into the rear of the next on the night of March 18. Soldiers who saw what would happen yelled "jump off," and one Kentuckian remembered, "We jumped off and some of us ran through the ditches and some fell into them and we had quite a time of it." Despite the problems, each column left contingents along the line in either direction for security and for protection of the railroads.[10]

Yet the strategic concentration in the west included more than just Johnston's and Beauregard's troops. As soon as the Tennessee River's defense was breached at Fort Henry, the Confederate high command, on

February 8, began scrambling to send reinforcements to the area. High-level communications took place between Richmond, Johnston and Beauregard in Kentucky, and other departmental commanders such as Braxton Bragg at Pensacola and Mansfield Lovell at New Orleans. Soon the war department issued orders for a major concentration in west Tennessee and north Mississippi and Alabama to defend the rail lines south and east of the Tennessee River. Gone was the policy of trying to cover almost every part of the Confederacy; as the crisis developed, less important areas had to be given up. "By thus subtracting something from other points, where the pressure is not so great," secretary of war Judah Benjamin wrote, "we hope to enable him [Johnston] to defend his lines until the new levies ordered from all the States shall be in condition to take the field."[11]

It was certainly a gamble to concentrate all available forces in the west, but when Davis made the decision, he went all out. Johnston likewise looked for soldiers anywhere, even unsuccessfully attempting to obtain slaves to take logistical positions and free up soldiers for duty. He admitted, "A single brigade may determine the fate of a battle." Johnston needed larger numbers than a single brigade, though, and Davis soon provided them. Braxton Bragg and his gulf coast garrison were called from Pensacola, with many of his troops moving northward on the critical Mobile and Ohio Railroad. "It is not proposed to leave any force at all at Pensacola—a weak garrison would inevitably be captured," Benjamin wrote Bragg. It was a miserable trip for most despite one Southerner's declaration that this was the "best road in the South." In all, twelve of Bragg's regiments in addition to assorted other battalions and batteries eventually made their way into the army assembling at Corinth, with Bragg himself moving there on February 28. The others moved northward in late February and early March, arriving in time to cover the railroads east and north of Corinth.[12]

Mansfield Lovell at New Orleans provided fully as many troops as Bragg. Ordered to send his best troops, Lovell first forwarded the 13th Louisiana and then Daniel Ruggles's brigade of Louisianans toward Columbus before changing the destination in the fluid situation. In all, nine regiments, three battalions of infantry, and four artillery batteries made their way northward toward Corinth, rendezvousing at Grand Junction, Tennessee, before moving to forward areas. Louisiana governor Thomas O. Moore also sent the Crescent Regiment and Orleans Guard battalion and artillery, all state militia. These state units were ninety-day troops, but the need was so great that they joined the volunteers in moving north. Unfortunately, some of the Louisianans enjoyed the trip too much, including several of the 11th Louisiana who "loitered behind with out leave." The company commander asked that they be arrested and returned to the regiment. Ruggles, who was not well himself because of a recent bout with typhoid fever, wrote that "the brunt of winter was upon us and the troops unaccustomed to such exposure suffered severely."[13]

The Louisianans made quite a show when they reached Corinth. One prideful member of the Orleans Guard wrote, "Our arrival at the camp was hailed with a thousand hurrahs, and joy reigned throughout the camps when they learned that we were the Orleans Guard." Beauregard himself came out to see the men he knew so well, having joined the unit as a private. "He appeared greatly moved at seeing us," one Louisianan remembered, proudly noting that Beauregard had not mingled with any other troops since his arrival.[14]

It was a portion of these new troops that confronted the initial Federal advances. Part of Ruggles's force, the 18th Louisiana, fresh up from the gulf, tangled with the gunboats at Pittsburg Landing on March 1. Others under Alabama general Adley Gladden covered the Purdy area and matched wits with Lew Wallace when his division landed and attempted to break the railroad in mid-March. Gladden kept heavy cavalry scouts out and notified his superiors concerning his "information of the utmost importance." Bragg planned a counteroffensive, although he was having enough trouble just finding quarters: "Can your quartermaster secure me some place to cover my head," he wrote, "as my tents are all behind?" Ruggles shifted troops in that direction as well, telling the senior officer near Iuka, James R. Chalmers, "If necessary empty the mail train in the morning coming West and bring forward a Regiment to Bethel." The entire threat turned out to be more minimal than they thought, with Bragg telling portions of his divisions to suspend a movement northward from Corinth to reinforce Gladden and allowing Polk to stop a similar movement southward from his position near Jackson. Bragg also sent Chalmers's Mississippians back eastward to Iuka, and it was a good thing. Sherman was the next of the one–two punch—in exactly that direction. Fortunately for the confused Confederates, mother nature turned him back.[15]

Even the far off trans-Mississippi forces under Earl Van Dorn and Sterling Price were called on for help, although timing played a crucial role against Johnston's plans for full concentration. It took quite a while to gather the necessary rolling stock to transfer so many troops, and what the commanders gleaned was not the best, with many soldiers reporting a miserable trip on open flat cars or filthy boxcars. The sheer distances involved in Van Dorn's movement simply did not allow for success in the given time frame. Likewise, the Confederate concentration came before conscription but around the time that many of the original twelve-month troops' terms expired, and those who rejoined wanted a furlough. Johnston and Beauregard had to resort to yet another call on the governors of the local states to send forward any troops they could.[16]

Perhaps the biggest timing issue facing Johnston, however, was that the Federals chose this most inopportune moment to show themselves in the Corinth area. With the Confederate focus on the Purdy and Eastport areas, the Federal landing in the center at Pittsburg came as a surprise. The only small respites amid the bad news were the arrival of rifled muskets through the blockade and the massive rains of mid-March slowing the Federal advance and allowing Beauregard to gather more troops around Corinth. Despite the slowdown in activity due to the weather, the net result was that the Federals were in a critical area, seemingly to stay. In fact, when Sherman landed at Pittsburg on March 16, he was closer to Corinth than was Johnston at Decatur, Alabama. Still, Johnston's situation was what it was, and he could not do anything about it until his wings were concentrated. Conversely, the longer he waited, the stronger the enemy would grow. Johnston had no good choices.[17]

By the last week in March, the Confederate concentration was reaching massive proportions. Many of the various state regiments camped near one another, especially before assignment to brigades and divisions, and one Alabama soldier wrote home of the mass of men: "We are part of a grand army whose tents are pitched on the ridges all about us as far as we can see through the woods: at reveille we hear bands of music in every direction: some so far off as to be almost inaudible; by this we know that our force is considerable." Others elaborated on the music, writing of the most festive songs such as "Bonny Blue Flag" and "Dixie," with one describing "the reverberation of melody as it passes from hill to hollow." Another marveled that "the whole world seemed to have pitched tents at this place." Johnston and Beauregard had to organize such a collection that Bragg termed "the mob we have, miscalled soldiers," and Johnston left it to what one of Polk's soldiers called "the dashing little Beauregard" to systematize the command. One Louisianan described the process as being "brigaded, divisioned and corpsed."[18]

Beauregard opted for the corps system, each component becoming a corps within the new army. In doing so, he hoped that the trained officers would be able to influence more of the men as well as make the enemy think there were more Confederates than there actually were. Johnston's three divisions under Hardee, Crittenden, and Pillow were whittled down, as were the mediocre generals, to two small three-brigade divisions named corps, with Hardee commanding one and Crittenden the other. Polk's corps from Columbus was formed into two divisions under Charles Clark and Benjamin Cheatham. Bragg's men from Pensacola became one division of a corps he commanded, with Jones Withers moving up to command the division of three brigades. Ruggles's troops from New Orleans made a second division for Bragg, also with three brigades. Each brigade had a battery attached rather than having artillery combined into larger battalions. Each corps did have an artillery chief, however: Francis Shoup, Smith Bankhead, and James Hallonquist. Eventually there would also be an overall cavalry commander, James M. Hawes. Because the goal was to defend the Mississippi Valley, Johnston and Beauregard styled their force the Army of the Mississippi.[19]

There were problems. Vaulting everyone up a notch on the ladder by utilizing the corps system created the need for additional generals and their staffs. Beauregard reported he needed as many as ten brigadier generals, and Polk requested four for his corps alone, noting, "I should have them immediately." Another level was added when division structures were implemented. Daniel Ruggles, for instance, left the command of his brigade to Patton Anderson so he could command the division. Senior colonels who were nearly as raw as their regiments commanded many of the brigades. Eventually the army would get some generals such as John Bowen, but far too few to be of service in the coming campaign. Because of the confusion, Bragg had Daniel Ruggles and presumably others "call at his office every morning between the hours of 10 and 11 o'clock until matters connected with this army are properly organized."[20]

In addition, there is evidence of concern among the corps commanders about serving under Johnston. Francis Shoup, then on Hardee's staff,
described the corps commanders being "nervous about going into battle
with him in command." Johnston was the overall commander, both of
the strategic theater and of the tactical army, if he so chose, but considering the cloud he was under, and with the added complexity of a second in command like P. G. T. Beauregard, Johnston was himself having
second thoughts about his command situation. Johnston met with Beauregard soon after his arrival at Corinth on March 24 and "proposed,
after our staff officers had retired," Beauregard remembered, "to turn
over the command of the united forces to me." Johnston wished to move
into the shadows as departmental commander, keeping his headquarters
father south and letting Beauregard command the army in a tactical
battle. "It was one of the most affecting scenes of my life," Beauregard
confessed years later. The Louisianan declined, however, citing several
reasons such as his still-lingering sickness. Beauregard, after all, had
just endured throat surgery before arriving out west and was not fully
recovered. Johnston seemed relieved, according to Beauregard, who
wrote that Johnston rose and warmly shook his hand, saying, "Well,
be it so, General! We two together will do our best to secure success."
Word of the offer nevertheless soon leaked out; Kentucky Confederate
governor George W. Johnson wrote Johnston that he had heard a rumor
that he "intend[ed] to yield to the senseless clamors of fools and pre-
tenders, and to give up the command of the army at the very crisis of
our fate." He added, "You must not do this. I beg that you will not do it,
both for your own fame and the good of our country."[21]

Although most of the men knew whom they were serving with, the
larger components had never served with one another, nor had the generals or their staffs. One of Beauregard's staff officers, Alexander R.
Chisolm, later lamented, "Very few of the officers were known to me
either by name or sight." Johnston and Beauregard thus had to develop a
working relationship, as did the various corps commanders with their superiors. The various staffs had to be appointed, assimilated, or reworked
to care for the larger army, and they had to learn to work together. To
aid in all the organization, Johnston appointed Braxton Bragg, an able
administrator, to the army chief of staff position in addition to commanding his corps. Welding together an almost totally green army (only
around 17 percent had seen any combat, as opposed to over 50 percent
in the Federal army) took time, however, and there was a critical short-

age of that commodity. The unwieldiness of the organization was also a factor; by early April, Bragg had upwards of 14,000 men in his corps, and Polk had around 9,000 troops. Hardee had even fewer as a result of creating the similarly small reserve corps. Hardee and Crittenden did not even have division structures; they were simply termed a corps of several brigades.[22]

Then there was the problem of the officers themselves, some of whom were confused at best and incompetent at worst. Many of the generals endured a learning curve while operating in new territory. Braxton Bragg, for instance, had trouble finding any reference to Chamberlain (near Monterey) on any of his maps and had to find a very old map to locate the position. Other officers were just plain incompetent. George Crittenden was under a cloud for drunkenness at Mill Springs, and he did not seem to worry about hiding it or his further use of alcohol. As March turned to April, chief of staff Bragg sent Hardee to investigate the command. He found ample evidence of Crittenden's drunkenness and arrested him, placing S. A. M. Wood in temporary command of the corps until a new commander could be appointed. Hardee also arrested brigade commander William H. Carroll for "drunkenness, incompetency, and neglect of his command," and reported "a most wretched state of discipline and instruction." Johnston thus had to have a competent commander to get the reserve corps whipped into shape quickly, and he settled on former vice president and 1860 presidential candidate John C. Breckinridge, who commanded one of the brigades. Despite not being West Point trained, Breckinridge was nevertheless the ranking general in the division and took command on April 3, placing his own Kentucky brigade under Colonel Robert P. Trabue of the 4th Kentucky. Newly minted brigadier John Bowen was the only other option, but he had not seen any more fighting than Breckinridge. Johnston had to gamble with such inexperience, although the other corps commanders were not much better, often degrading the others' troops. Although Beauregard spoke highly of Bragg's regiments, describing them as "a fine corps of troops," an unsatisfied Bragg issued strict orders to close all "grog-shops and drinking saloons" in the area. He observed the other corps of the army and wrote his wife, "I thought my Mobile Army was a *Mob*." He was quick to lay blame: "The good Bishop sets the example, by taking whatever he wants."[23]

Lower-level officers were potential problems as well; one Alabamian wrote of an infantry officer who seemed "quite determined that his head shall not burst, if we are to judge from the amount of gold lace he wears around it." Many officers, he noticed, would not speak to a private except "to order him to duty." The Alabamian added a blanket complaint: "Just put a man who has never enjoyed a good character or good social position at home into an office, however unimportant and if it does not make him a fool, then I will agree to write him down as a most noble exception." Sometimes the haughtiness of officers developed into open mutiny. The illness-struck 17th Alabama, sent to Bethel under Gladden, balked at the order to move to Corinth during heavy rains and without their possessions. Gladden had them put under arrest, which was lifted so they could move the next day. The officers were then again put under arrest in their new brigade under John K. Jackson. Only an open apology by the officers, the intersession of Patton Anderson, and the appointment of the Alabamians' colonel, Thomas H. Watts, as Jefferson Davis's attorney general quieted the matter.[24]

The amalgamation of so diverse a group of soldiers was truly a challenge. In addition, the army contained a good number of foreigners, including British, Irish, German, and other European nationalities. Although the major foreign infusion came from French-speaking areas of Louisiana, some soldiers of Prussian descent were almost royalty. Leon von Zinken of the 20th Louisiana was a former Prussian officer and the son of a general. In addition, the level of training varied, with several of Johnston's generals hailing from West Point while others were totally civilian and had never spent any time in the military. Conversely, there were a good number of younger West Point–trained colonels commanding individual regiments—men such as Charles Wickliffe of the 7th Kentucky, Joseph Wheeler of the 19th Alabama, Jean Mouton of the 18th Louisiana, John H. Kelly of the 9th Arkansas Battalion, and John C. Moore of the 2nd Texas. Others such as William Bate, George Maney, and John H. Clanton were Mexican War veterans.[25]

State pride also played a role in developing cracks in Confederate unity. Mississippi colonel Andrew K. Blythe wrote fellow Mississippian Charles Clark, begging for aid in getting transferred out of their brigade of Tennesseans, which Blythe labeled "this Irish association." He complained at Bethel Station that his regiment was kept amid the Tennesseans and were on doleful duty watching "a few damned traitorous Tennesseeans and guard[ing] a contemptible depot." "Prize us out," Blythe begged, "and we will deem it one of those favors never to be forgotten." The members of the 11th Louisiana were likewise not happy at being "lashed on to the tail of a Tennessee rabble—for those with whom we are placed are little better." Even worse, their brigade commander was Tennessean Robert Russell, whom they knew from the fight at Belmont. Charles Johnson of the Louisiana regiment wrote of him as "the chap that run so in the battle of Belmont." Similarly, the 1st Arkansas in Gibson's brigade desired to be brigaded with other Arkansas units, but the change was never made. Making the state issues more convoluted, some units had Northerners in them, such as Company G of the 15th Tennessee, made up of men from southern Illinois.[26]

The greenness of the troops was also of particular concern. Many of them had come directly from their mustering camps, and some had never even fired their weapons. A few were suddenly transferred to other branches, such as the twenty infantrymen who were detailed to Stanford's Mississippi Battery so the guns could be properly worked. In this case, however, the newcomers were not that far behind the regular artillerymen; the members of Stanford's Battery had not yet even fired their cannons. Bragg labeled the army "an heterogeneous mass, in which there was more enthusiasm than discipline, more capacity than knowledge, and more valor than instruction." Indeed, few of the enlistees knew how to act like soldiers, but Bragg had his remedy. He declared the death penalty for pillaging, telling his force that "men capable of such acts may swell our numbers, but will never add strength to our armies. They would do less harm by serving in the ranks of the enemy." Beauregard took a somewhat more calm approach and issued detailed orders for the command, telling them about the time-honored traits of military combat that were no doubt foreign to these new citizen soldiers. "Field and company officers are specially enjoined to instruct their men, under all circumstances, to fire with deliberation at the feet of the enemy," Beauregard wrote. "They will thus avoid overshooting, and, besides, wounded men give more trouble to our adversary than his dead, as they have to be taken from the field." He also cautioned officers to keep their men from "useless, aimless firing." Beauregard asked them not to employ firing by file, which "excites the men and renders their subsequent control difficult," but to fire by wing or company. He added many other details dealing with medical care as well as requiring soldiers to remain in the ranks; roll calls should be made immediately before and after a battle. In all, it was a curious set of orders that should not have even been necessary, except for the fact that these were not soldiers at all, but armed civilians going off for their first time to do battle. One Alabamian summed it up well when he wrote the men were "perfectly careless about things generally."[27]

The area's infrastructure was not much better. The Confederacy's meager railroad system was becoming dilapidated even this early in the war. Bragg noted how "wood and water stations are abandoned" and that because of a lack of pay or Union sympathies many of the workers had quit and the rest were overworked. An inspection ordered by Beauregard in early March showed "no police organization whatever" on the Mobile and Ohio and an inefficient one on the Memphis and Charleston. In addition, Unionism in southwestern Tennessee and northern Alabama and Mississippi proved to be a problem. One Alabamian wrote, "these Union fellows in this County are lying quite low at present for we watch them closely but I almost know they report to the enemy all of our movements and the number of our force." Even the loyal Confederate citizenry was not that productive. Braxton Bragg, never one to look at the positive side of things, was appalled at the lack of organization he found behind his lines. "The whole country seems paralyzed," he wrote, "and the difficulties of operation become infinitely greater thereby. Nothing is brought to us for sale, and it is most difficult to procure supplies." Bragg also bemoaned the citizens' "unrestrained habits of pillage and plunder." He also realized that the local people sided with the enemy "who certainly do them less harm than our own troops." And the Federals noticed: "They say that the rebel Cavalry are going around making all take the oath to support the Confederacy, and the next day come and draft them in." Union general Lew Wallace reaped the benefit of such Confederate behavior: "I have colonized about one hundred refugees, escaped from the wrath of the rebels, exiles for their loyalty." An observant Federal concluded, "the miserable thing is stinging itself to death."[28]

Other problems emerged as well, such as poor equipment that the negative Bragg described as "lamentably defective" and the poor transportation which he characterized as "deficient in quantity and very inferior in quality." The 2nd Texas illustrated the point well. They had left Texas on March 12 and arrived at Corinth on April 1. In this short period, their shoes had worn out and John C. Moore, commanding the regiment, reported, "many who had left camp with worn-out shoes became totally barefooted." So deficient was the artillery wing of the army that Beauregard called on planters to donate their plantation bells to be melted down and cast into cannon. The churches responded as well, but Beauregard told at least one priest that he would not accept his church's bell except under the direst conditions. Only then would he take the church bells and "rebuke with a tongue of fire the vandals who in this war have polluted God's altar." Then too, some regiments were just completing their organization, such as the 26th Alabama receiving its final four companies on March 31 and only then officially being designated a regiment instead of a battalion. Even on April 3, however, the men did not know their numerical designation. Thus, the Confederates were a hodgepodge of troops and material, but at least they were a large group. By early April Johnston had concentrated nearly 50,000 troops at and around Corinth, with more on the way, eager to do battle with the invading Federals. The scenes around Corinth said as much. One soldier described "our main line of Briggades are now over 4 miles long making a citty of tents almost equal to Orleans . . . I can here at one blast neare 100 bands playing." Another overawed recruit wrote, "the scenery is truly great here to one that never saw an army before. The hills for several miles around are covered with tents resembling hills of snow."[29]

Logically, the concentration of such large numbers in a small area had a distinct effect on the local citizens. One soldier wrote that "all the women and children have left," but others tried to maintain their normal lives. One local judge, Walter A. Overton, expressed the general disdain. "A regiment of soldiers have camped on my land," he wrote in his diary, "and there is no telling how much damage they are doing it. . . . They are cutting all the timber off of it and burning all the rails. If they stay long they will ruin it." Some were supportive if not understanding, one Confederate writing of a conversation he had with an old woman while obtaining buttermilk from her. "She was as old as your mother," he told his wife. The lady wanted to know why the army "came a way down here to fight the yankees." He told her it was a "trap laid to catch them in." The soldier added: "the old feeble patriot dropped her head in an attitude of prayer & said God Bless the trap."[30]

Using Major William M. Inge's home as his quarters, Albert Sidney Johnston daily observed the growing crisis amid the frequent spring rainstorms. "Skirmishes are frequently occurring and a general engagement Cannot be many days in advance," one Louisianan at Corinth wrote home, "so close are matters getting that no one is permitted to leave except on sick furlough." One of the major precautions was entrenching the town. "Intrenchments are going up all along the line," one soldier wrote, "and we hold ourselves in hourly expectation of battle." Braxton Bragg had started the entrenchments when he arrived in March. His engineers found a suitable line of hills on the eastern and northern approaches, and his soldiers as well as slaves dug a series of rifle pits with larger earthworks commanding the roadways in and out of Corinth. Johnston and Beauregard liked what they saw when they arrived, and work continued as the army gathered. Everyone dug, even the blue bloods of New Orleans. One of the Louisianans grumbled at clearing sites for camps and dubbed the lack of food "Camp Starvation." He admitted, "many a botch did we at first make, for the use of such implements was never made known to us by practice at least." But work he did, another Louisianan marveling at seeing aristocratic planters "working with spade and shovel on the fortifications. They went at it a great deal more willingly than many of our regiment who had been used to it all their lives."[31]

In the haste to concentrate his forces, defend Corinth's railroads, and organize an effective fighting force, Albert Sidney Johnston also thought about going on the offensive. Obviously, waiting had its advantages. The longer the army worked together, the more effective and stronger it would become. But the Federals were seemingly not going to give Johnston time to regroup. Several times he called his men into ranks during the latter portion of March, only to discover it had been a false alarm. Delay also meant that the Federal army would grow larger as well. Johnston's scouts kept him well informed as to how many enemy boats had passed certain points on the river and that they were congregating at Savannah and Pittsburg. The local citizens in the area also provided good warning; Chalmers reported that "the women and children in that region [Hamburg] on the river were warned by the enemy to leave." There were brigade-sized reconnaissances as well, such as when Chalmers led his Mississippians northward from their forward station at Monterey. Then there was the factor of Buell's eventual arrival, with Johnston's scouts such as Philip D. Roddey east of the Tennessee River watching carefully. In the long run, Johnston could find himself in a situation where he had gained nothing by waiting, and perhaps even lost ground. Perhaps Braxton Bragg summed it up best in a letter to his wife: "I hope we will save the Mississippi, though time is precious and much needed."[32]

Johnston thus put his army on alert on April 1 to be ready "for a field movement and to meet the enemy within twenty-four hours." He also issued countersigns to be used for the next several days. Although some of his troops played tricks on each other on this "all fools day," Johnston was the epitome of seriousness. It was a good thing; events began to occur in the first days of April that eventually spurred Johnston to go on the offensive. The most pressing was news that Buell was much closer to a linkage with Grant than Johnston had previously thought. That intelligence caused Johnston concern, and in an effort to fight one enemy army at a time, he began to consider attacking Grant at Pittsburg Landing before Buell arrived.[33]

It was the birth of the offensive that would result in Shiloh.

3

"The Plains of Shiloh"

William T. Sherman was a busy man in the latter half of March and the first warmer days of April. He wore many hats, including advisor to Grant, commander of his division, commander of the advance base, and commander of the continuing operations probing forward to break the Confederate railroads. Such roles illustrated Grant's confidence in him; few other people would have garnered such freedom. Indeed, Grant wrote to him immediately upon arriving at Savannah on March 17 that he had ordered all the troops there to report to him so he could "organize them into brigades, and attach them to divisions as you deem best." With Sherman in command at Pittsburg, Grant remained at Savannah waiting for Buell to arrive, headquartered in the lush mansion owned by local slaveowner and Unionist William H. Cherry. Cherry's wife, however, was pro-Confederate.[1]

In order to cover Savannah when the rest of the army departed, Grant kept a brigade stationed there under post commander Walter Q. Gresham, a member of the Indiana legislature. As colonel of the 53rd Indiana, Gresham had arrived with his regiment at Savannah and requested permission to move on to Pittsburg. Grant held him back because of sickness in the regiment. Eventually, Grant collected two other regiments at Savannah, the 53rd Illinois and 14th Wisconsin, and united them into a brigade for Gresham. A few companies of cavalry were also attached, but Gresham was not happy. Grant would not allow him to join the main army, but as post commander, he also found himself sitting on numerous court-martial trials.[2]

Gresham's troubles were minor compared to those of Grant, who had a host of issues to deal with in the days after he retook field command. Most of these emanated from Henry Halleck, who continually harped on Grant's troops' lack of discipline. The decisions Grant had to

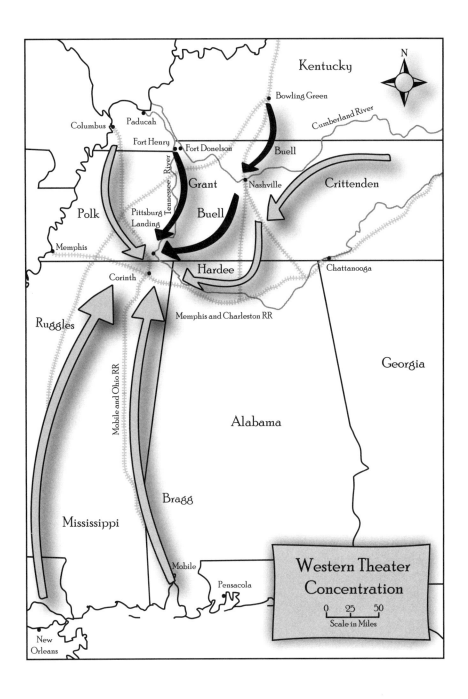

Kentucky

Bowling Green

Cumberland River

Columbus

Paducah

Fort Henry

Fort Donelson

Buell

Crittenden

Nashville

Grant

Buell

Polk

Pittsburg
Landing

Tennessee River

Memphis

Hardee

Chattanooga

Corinth

Memphis and Charleston RR

Ruggles

Mobile and Ohio RR

Georgia

Alabama

Bragg

Mississippi

Mobile

Pensacola

New
Orleans

N

Western Theater
Concentration

0   25   50
Scale in Miles

make on the spot dealing with local civilians were also a major concern and resulted from Halleck's continual prodding about pillaging locals. Although their policy would later change, the Federals in March 1862 were careful in their dealings with local Tennesseans. Few if any were harmed. One civilian living just below the campsite wrote, "There were many tales told of how the women and children would be mistreated which never happened." Some locals even traded with the Federals, with an Illinoisan describing "the Natives [who] bring in corn bread & a few chickens, but there is so many [soldiers] to buy that we hardly ever get any." The encamping army also provided guards for locals around the Pittsburg Landing area. One Ohioan recounted the exchange between civilians and army officials: "Can I get a guard, sah?" Asked if he was loyal, the citizen replied, "Oh, yes, sah: I am a loyal man, sah." Others watched as the local inhabitants went about their daily business, one Illinoisan writing of "a negro woman ploughing with one old horse, & a small one horse plough. She just skimmed the ground, & didn't plough more than 2 inches & yet it is as good as the soil will bear." All the while, her master "sat on his porch and watched and talked to the Union soldiers." Southern women particularly attracted attention from the soldiers; one Iowan wrote on March 20: "Saw 4 women, quite a reirity." An Illinoisan similarly wrote, "I have not seen but one or two girls since I landed at Savannah that was any ways near passable. they ware rather good looking, but some how they are all pot-gutted, young and old, why it is so I cannot tell." An Iowan related, "The people are very ignorant we see wimin standing looking at us bare footed and chew there tobacco with the greatest gusto." When the need occurred, however, the Federals could also be firm. Sherman reported, "I allow no citizen or solider to pass our outer line, and as but few live within our lines, I think they are utterly at a loss." Colonel Kilby Smith of the 54th Ohio summed up the people as "a strange compound of extreme ignorance with very considerable refinement of manner and conversation."[3]

Amid these meager surroundings, the Federal army eventually built up its force at Pittsburg Landing, with boats frequently arriving with more troops. The boats had to be cleaned periodically from all the men having spent days on board. One Indianan wrote home that he was having several boats cleaned, "which I assure you they very much needed." But dirty boats were worth the cargo they carried. Steamboats continually landed at Pittsburg with additional regiments and batteries, with one Illinoisan writing home that boats were "more or less going every day." One staff officer recorded, "I thought we had men enough under arms to clean out the Confederacy and half of Europe." The landing thus bustled with activity, as additional troops, with mounds of supplies, methodically made their way to the riverbank and then up the long slopes to the high ground, where they went into camp.[4]

Some were impatient to move on quickly. A new officer on Sherman's staff, John Taylor, continually asked his general why not go out and attack the enemy. "Never mind, young man," Sherman replied. "You will have all the fighting you want before this war is over, and it will come fast enough for you after awhile." Sherman's words would ring true.[5]

The terrain on which the Federal army camped was perfect for their purposes of a staging area, and that was all they ever intended it to be. Unknown to them, it would also eventually be where a major battle was fought, and in that realm, it served the Federals even better. One Union soldier went so far as to write, "Nature had done her share in the making of an almost impregnable position," and a Federal colonel similarly wrote, "You might search the world over and not find a more advantageous field of battle." Federal commanders did not know it quite in those terms yet, but this staging area and campground provided them very defensible terrain. William Preston Johnston went so far as to describe the ailing Smith's decision to place the army on the west bank of the river as "the dying gift of the soldierly C. F. Smith to his cause."[6]

Any understanding of the Battle of Shiloh has to start with an understanding of the terrain on which it was fought. The dominant terrain feature was the Tennessee River. The river was 300 to 400 yards wide at Pittsburg—far too broad to ford in such a rainy spring as this one. While at times fordable in the dry summers, the river formed a wide eastern boundary to what would become the Shiloh battlefield. Yet lesser watercourses flowing into the river played a far greater role than the Tennessee in shaping the battlefield. Two major creeks flowed into the Tennessee River on either side of Pittsburg Landing, setting the basic parameters of the staging area. A wide—and at flood stage daunting—Snake Creek, with steep banks along the high ground nearer Pittsburg, emptied into the river half a mile north of the landing. Water frequently backed up into the creek; it could only be crossed at bridges, and oftentimes in the spring not even there. Snake Creek flowed in a large loop at the northern end of the campsite, but its major tributary actually had more of an effect on the western boundary. Owl Creek flowed from southwest to northeast, meeting Snake Creek just as it began its giant loop to the north. Owl Creek was similarly substantial so that it could not be forded just anywhere, although because it was farther up the watershed it was not as affected by the river's rises and falls. The swampy bottoms of Snake and Owl creeks thus formed the northern and western boundaries of the Federal staging area. Similarly, several miles to the south, Lick Creek formed the southeastern boundary, flowing into the Tennessee River some two miles south of Pittsburg Landing. Like Snake Creek, Lick was deep and wide and generally flowed parallel to Owl Creek, from southwest to northeast. It was also susceptible to the river's backwater, especially in the spring, making it similarly difficult to cross except by bridge.[7]

With the Tennessee River and the three creeks forming the basic parameters of the campsite, what Beauregard described as a cul-de-sac thus emerged on the high ground tucked between the parallel-flowing Owl and Lick creeks and capped by the Tennessee River and Snake Creek. The area surrounding the high ground was all low and marshy, overgrown with briars, heavy timber, and vegetation. Most of the habitation and agriculture took place on the high ground, and the Federals camped there as well. Often described as a triangle, the base lay along the gap between Owl and Lick creeks with the apex in the great bend of Snake Creek; the river and Owl Creek formed the sides. As defined by a cul-de-sac, there was only one way in and out of what one participant called "the plains of Shiloh," with the exception of the three bridges on the three respective creeks, which themselves could not all be traversed at various times of the year. The three-mile gap between Owl and Lick creeks, the base of the triangle, was the only way large bodies of men could enter or exit the area quickly.[8]

While the three major creeks and the river served to form the parameters of the Federal staging area, a series of perpendicular secondary creeks actually had more of an effect on the Union defense. Four smaller creeks on the high ground, two running parallel eastward and two running parallel westward, would come to dominate the fighting itself. On the western half of the cul-de-sac, Shiloh (also known as Oak) and Tilghman (also known as Brier) branches ran southeast to northwest roughly parallel with each other a little over a mile apart. Both flowed into Owl Creek from the high ground in the center. Conversely, Dill and

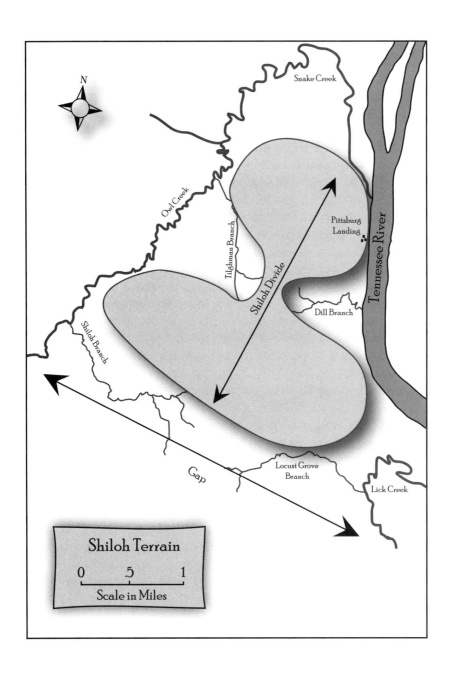

N

Snake Creek

Owl Creek

Tilghman Branch

Shiloh Divide

Pittsburg
Landing

Tennessee River

Dill Branch

Shiloh Branch

Gap

Locust Grove
Branch

Lick Creek

Shiloh Terrain

0   5   1

Scale in Miles

Locust Grove branches also paralleled each other at about the same distance but running west to east, except that Locust Grove Branch flowed into Lick Creek while Dill flowed directly into the river. Emanating from natural springs, the headwaters of all four creeks, or what Don Carlos Buell later described as the "interlocking" nature of these creeks' headwaters in the form of feeder branches, spread out like fingers on a hand. They lay relatively close to one another on the high ground in the center, forcing those on opposite sides to tumble down in opposite directions. Thus, at two points on the battlefield, a relatively east-to-west line of creeks covered the width of the triangle, with only the gap between the headwaters of each set offering any level ground. Moreover, each creek was deeply cut, with the floodplains becoming deeper and deeper the closer to the river or major creeks they flowed. Locust Grove and Dill branches on the eastern side of the field ran through ravines with almost vertical sides, and Tilghman and Shiloh branches had difficult terrain as well. In addition, a series of other smaller ravines bordered the river between the various branches.[9]

The result was a sloping effect on each side of the battlefield, down which each side's creeks poured, leaving in the center a long and high ridge that acted like a smaller version of the continental divide. Ulysses S. Grant mentioned "the ridge which divided the waters of Snake and Lick creeks," and this "Shiloh divide" ran in a southwest-to-northeast direction from the center of the triangle base all the way to Pittsburg Landing and the cap of the cul-de-sac. This divide, spawning Tilghman, Shiloh, Locust Grove, and Dill branches as well as many smaller watersheds from its abundant natural springs, varied in width. Coming up, as Buell stated, "boldly to the river at the landing," thus forming the high bluffs overlooking Pittsburg Landing and Snake Creek, it grew narrower where the headwaters of Dill and Tilghman branches ate away at it. It widened once more, only to be eaten away again by the next set below, Shiloh and Locust Grove branches. No wonder Grant wrote that "the ground on which the battle was fought was undulating," while Buell described the high ground as "undulating table-land, quite broken in places, elevated a hundred feet or thereabout above the river."[10]

An observant Buell also remarked that Tilghman and Dill branches "divide[d] the table-land into two main ridges." The Shiloh divide can thus be viewed as an hourglass, with the northern half of the glass much smaller than the southern half. The Dill and Tilghman watersheds that ate away at the ridge caused the narrower portion in the center, and it was on the southern half of the hourglass that the majority of the Battle of Shiloh would rage.[11]

Adding to the difficulty of the terrain was the cover. Most of the battlefield, somewhere between 80 percent and 90 percent, was timber, mostly hardwood such as oak, hickory, elm, poplar, sweet gum, and dogwood. The dogwoods, along with fruit trees in several farmers' orchards, were beautiful in spring while blooming, emphasizing that winter was over. Yet those areas of beauty were few and far between, as most of the field was open timber or covered with heavy undergrowth. Most of the latter came in creek bottoms and cut over fields, while much of the higher land was continually cleared of the thickest undergrowth by the farmer's roving animals or yearly fires set purposefully to manage the undergrowth and insects. Grant described the battlefield as "heavily timbered, with scattered clearings, the woods giving some protection to the troops on both sides. There was also considerable underbrush."[12]

The most notable man-made features were the roads, if they could be called that. Most were mere dirt paths, a maze of connecting trails, but there were also five major roads. These too were very primitive. The main road in and out of the area was the Corinth Road from Pittsburg Landing southwestward toward the Mississippi town, twenty-two miles distant. Although there were several roads meandering toward Corinth south of the battlefield, the Corinth road wandered out the Shiloh divide between the headwaters of Dill and Tilghman branches before crossing the forks of Shiloh Branch on bridges.[13]

Because the bogs of Shiloh Branch were too difficult to handle in wet weather, locals created an additional road a little to the east. The Eastern Corinth Road left the main Corinth Road (sometimes now referred to as the Western Corinth Road) after it passed through the headwaters of Dill and Tilghman branches and ran down the Shiloh divide between the headwaters of Shiloh and Locust Grove branches. Once on the high ground south of those creeks, the road joined the Bark Road and eventually the Corinth Road south of Shiloh Branch. The Bark Road ran east to west along the elevated hills south of Locust Grove and Shiloh branches.[14]

The primary north and south road on the eastern side of the battlefield was the River Road, more formally known as the Hamburg-Savannah Road. It ran from Hamburg, four miles south of Pittsburg Landing on the river, across Lick Creek to a junction with the Bark Road. From there it crossed Locust Grove Branch and ran up onto the high ground and across the eastern side of the battlefield, just inland from the huge ravines bordering the Tennessee River. The River Road crossed the Corinth Road at the neck of the hourglass on the Shiloh divide between Tilghman and Dill branches and eventually ran off the high ground, crossing Snake Creek at the north end of the cul-de-sac and then moving on to Crump's Landing.[15]

Thus, most of the major roads ran relatively north and south. The only major east-and-west road on the campsite proper (the Bark Road was south of the southernmost creeks) was the Hamburg-Purdy Road. It left the River Road atop the high ground in the southeast corner of the triangle and crossed the Eastern and main Corinth roads in the process of running westward toward the bridge that carried it over Owl Creek. From there, it continued on to Purdy.[16]

In addition to the roads were other man-made features. The occupying Federals were less than impressed with the improvements of this cul-de-sac. One officer described Shiloh Church as "the rude structure in which, within four months past, the voices of the 'poor white trash' of Tennessee mingled in praise to God." An 18th Missouri soldier described the landing: "This Pittsburg took its name from a man that kept a one horse store at the place." A 15th Illinois captain heard a farmer describe the area's soil: "In this part of the state the land was not so good for cotton as in other parts of the state. He had cotton on hand and the reason he had not sold it was because the secesh had made a law that whoever sold cotton to come North should be hanged." Daniel Clark of the 15th Illinois was disappointed because he wanted to see "a large Southern plantation." As it was, the Federal army squatted on the land in mid-March, when there was not even much planting taking place.[17]

By this time, there were few inhabitants still in the vicinity to do any work. Early during the landing and initial camping phases in mid-March, at least one Federal wrote home that farmers "have begun to do their spring work," but that work soon waned as the encampment became larger. "No farming going on and probably will not be this season," wrote one Illinoisan in April. Another Illinois Federal noted, "I have seen but one house for more than a week and the people that lived in it are gone." Another noted, "The country here is thinly settled when the families are all at home, and now it is almost deserted. From the river to our picquets, a distance of four miles, there is but one family living—the balance having been frightened away by our gun boats." He told how the gunboats had periodically thrown a few shells into the woods before the army's arrival, one of which "went through a house 3 miles from the river." Isaac Pugh, in command of the 41st Illinois, noted the absence of civil authorities, who also fled: "There is not a justice of the peace or clerk of the court in the whole country." Others noted the dilapidated nature of the area. "The man in whose field we drill owns 1600 acres of land," one Illinoisan wrote, "has been here sixteen years and lives in a little log house that has never been chinked up or plastered. The cracks between the logs are covered with long shingles."[18]

The Army of the Tennessee was thus encamping in a vast frontier wilderness. And they thought it was only a staging area to prepare for the farther advance into Mississippi.

It was on this sparsely inhabited flatland above the river and the creeks that the Federal army camped, awaiting Buell and the movement to Corinth. From the time the first man stepped foot on dry land at Pittsburg, however, the Federal high command was not willing to merely sit and wait. Still intent on breaking the railroad without a major fight, Sherman admitted that the necessary landing at Pittsburg created a situation in which "there can be but one point of attack, and that is Corinth." He thought he could skirt toward the railroad near Farmington: "It may be still that the interruption of the road without a general engagement could be successfully accomplished." Sherman thus began yet another raid southward, but he asked that Hurlbut's new division take a position inland a bit "so as to defend Pittsburg." Hurlbut thus became the first full division to encamp. Eventually, the division went into camps in an arc, holding the major crossing of the Hamburg-Savannah and Corinth roads at the neck of the hourglass, with James Veatch's Illinois and Indiana troops on the right and Charles Cruft's Indiana and Kentucky troops that had once been a part of Buell's Army of the Ohio on the left in farmer Jason Cloud's large field. Isaac Pugh's Illinois and Iowa troops, soon to be under Nelson Williams when the 3rd Iowa joined the brigade after the initial landing, formed a line in front of the other two brigades, covering both roads. A somewhat disliked Hurlbut himself made his headquarters in the double log cabin owned by Jason Cloud; because of his alleged drunkenness, his soldiers openly ridiculed him as he rode by. Others were disliked as well, including Williams of the 3rd Iowa. One of his Federals admitted that he was "thoroughly disliked and distrusted."[19]

With the major road crossing secure, Sherman's men moved out on
their mission. He quickly found more Confederates than he bargained
for, mostly members of small squads roaming the country. "The cavalry
of the enemy is scattered all over the country in small bands," Sherman
reported up the chain on March 16, later adding, "Every road and path
is occupied by the enemy's cavalry, whose orders seem to be to fire a
volley, retire, again fire and retire." While the 5th Ohio Cavalry under
Lieutenant Colonel Thomas T. Heath "scouted from Dan to Beersheba,"
one of the troopers noted, Sherman moved his division forward, led by
the just-arrived 6th Iowa's colonel John A. McDowell, brother of famed
Manassas Union commander Irwin McDowell. He was now senior officer in the brigade, taking over from Stephen Hicks, with whom Sherman had earlier grown displeased. The other three brigades followed
behind, but Heath soon ran into Confederate cavalry near Pea Ridge and
returned in the wee hours of March 17. Sherman realized a movement
on land would be no easier than on water and reported to Grant, "A dash
cannot be made. I have tried it twice."[20]

Sherman accordingly went into permanent camp far enough out to
leave room for the rest of the army. Thus, the greenest division was the
farthest out on the high ridges overlooking Shiloh and Locust Grove
branches near the log Shiloh Church. Sherman was careful to cover
the approaches onto the high ground, however, posting John McDowell's brigade on his right covering the crossing of Owl Creek at the
Hamburg-Purdy Road. To cover the main entrance into the vast army
camp, Sherman placed two brigades astride the main Corinth Road
near what Sherman variously referred to as the Shiloh Meeting House
or the Shiloh Chapel. Ohio lawyer and state senator Ralph Buckland's
Ohio troops camped on the west side, and sixty-two-year-old mail
agent and sheriff Jesse Hildebrand's three Ohio regiments encamped
on the east side. Hildebrand made his headquarters at the church itself. Sherman sent his fourth brigade under David Stuart farther to the
east to cover the Hamburg-Purdy Road's crossing of Lick Creek; there
the two Ohio and one Illinois regiments guarded the crossing of the
creek, the 55th Illinois putting their tents up in the rows of peach trees
in an orchard near the Cantrell house. Despite such care for security,
Sherman's men bridged the creeks in preparation for moving toward
Corinth. Buckland's brigade worked to build two additional bridges
across Shiloh Branch, laboring on them up to April 5. Security did not
hinder occasional arguments about campsites, either, such as when

one Federal saw the 15th Illinois and 6th Iowa's colonels "jawing each other."[21]

While Sherman watched the front and even made additional forays out toward Pea Ridge, other divisions arrived at the new base. Charles F. Smith's troops, their commander ill aboard the *Hiawatha,* landed on March 19. After some of the units camped at the landing, the brigades went into permanent camp farther back along the Hamburg-Savannah Road, precisely where Sherman's brigades had camped before moving farther inland. Jacob Lauman's Iowa brigade (under the 2nd Iowa's colonel James Tuttle while Lauman commanded the division for the injured C. F. Smith) camped closest to the landing. Thomas Sweeny's Illinois and Iowa men—Sweeny had just arrived and took command of the reorganized brigade—camped farther out, and Scotsman John McArthur's Illinois, Ohio, and Missouri regiments camped on the high ground overlooking the Snake Creek swamps.[22]

Moving John McClernand's division to Pittsburg caused the most concern. McClernand had been promoted to major general, which gave him rank over Sherman and perhaps Smith, who by seniority took command of the advance when he arrived. McClernand soon caused problems, complaining that Smith was in command at Pittsburg (on Grant's order) when he, McClernand, should hold the command. "This order is evidently founded upon the idea that Genl. Smith is my senior and hence ranks me," McClernand wrote to Grant. McClernand and Smith even argued over who was entitled to the distinction of having their division called the first division. McClernand nevertheless soon became the advance commander. He enjoyed the politics of command, savoring the brass bands that serenaded him at his headquarters. Grant was not so enthused. He did not wish McClernand to be in charge and inquired about McClernand's rank compared to Smith's. He also made trips to Pittsburg every day to command in person and hurried staff officer John Rawlins, in charge of the army office at Savannah, to close down the Savannah headquarters to move to Pittsburg. Grant would only wait to meet Buell in a few days, and then he would move southward.[23]

John McClernand's veteran division was accordingly the last to encamp at Pittsburg, moving from Savannah on March 21. After unloading at the landing and spending one night there, the three brigades camped in the middle of the others as a support for Sherman. Richard Oglesby's Illinois and Iowa brigade camped in the wide expanses of Jones Field, while William H. L. Wallace's all-Illinois unit set up camp

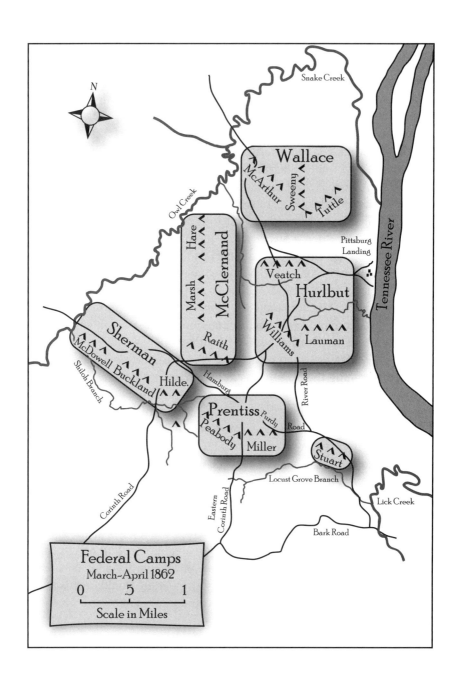

N

Snake Creek

Wallace

McArthur   Sweeny   Tuttle

Owl Creek

Hare

Marsh   McClernand

Veatch

Pittsburg
Landing

Hurlbut

Williams

Lauman

Sherman

Raith

McDowell   Buckland   Hilde.

Tennessee River

Shiloh Branch

Hamburg

River Road

Prentiss   Purdy

Peabody   Miller

Road

Stuart

Corinth Road

Eastern
Corinth Road

Locust Grove Branch

Lick Creek

Bark Road

Federal Camps
March–April 1862

0   5   1

Scale in Miles

just inland from the field, carving out a parade ground from the woods across the road from their camps. Leonard F. Ross's Illinois brigade camped farther to the south on the edge of a large, flat field "used as the review ground," where the Illinois soldiers relished a fresh spring only a quarter of a mile away. McClernand let everyone know that he was the ranking officer on site; one of his captains in the 45th Illinois described going into camp at "Camp McClernand," and Adolph Engelmann of the 43rd Illinois reported that McClernand told them, "We were the pattern for the example of the rest of the Army."[24]

By March 21, four of the army's five divisions were on site at Pittsburg (Lew Wallace was at Crump's Landing), setting up camps and settling into drill and leisure. More troops kept arriving, however, and Grant soon saw the need to create a sixth division. At Halleck's specific request, Benjamin Prentiss entered the theater and took command of the new division on March 26. His first regiment, the 25th Missouri, arrived in camp on March 29. Soon there was a brigade organized out of Missouri, Michigan, and Wisconsin troops, which was put under the senior colonel, Everett Peabody of the 25th Missouri. These troops camped to the west of the Eastern Corinth Road, near Sherman's division. As more troops arrived, an additional brigade took form under the senior colonel Madison Miller of the 18th Missouri. This brigade of Illinois, Missouri, and Wisconsin troops camped just north of Peter Spain's field, from which they cleared some underbrush to create a drill ground. The 18th Wisconsin did not arrive until April 5 and pitched their tents after dark, east of the road in line with Peabody. Another unit, the 16th Iowa, arrived at Pittsburg late on April 5 and camped at the landing, intending to join the brigade the next day. The 15th Iowa, 15th Michigan, and 23rd Missouri were likewise en route, with the Michigan and Missouri regiments also arriving on April 5. Together, they were intended to give Prentiss a third brigade and were to camp in the gap between Miller and Stuart's now detached brigade down along Locust Grove Branch. Other units made their way to Savannah and Pittsburg as well, as did siege batteries and a pontoon bridge.[25]

As these troops went into camp, concern seemed to be more about supply than defense, with Sherman asking Grant to send "the best quartermaster you can." The sheer number of wagons allotted to each regiment—twenty-seven wagons and two ambulances, according to Manning Force—illustrated the early-war naïveté of the army and how much it should carry with it. Many of the Federals had black servants as well, which eased their workload but created more mouths to feed; Ephraim Dawes of the 53rd Ohio wrote, "My Paducah contraband is still with me and has gained for himself the reputation of being the best 'nigger' in camp." Likewise, the officers seemed more intent on comfort than security. Despite specific orders from Sherman to the contrary, the three regiments of Hildebrand's Ohio brigade camped facing three different directions, with the 53rd Ohio far ahead of the other two in Rhea Field to be near Rhea Spring, south of Shiloh Branch. Sherman had stated emphatically that "convenience of water may be considered, but must not control the position of the camp." Apparently Colonel Jesse Appler chose to disregard those orders, and the Ohioans were the only unit camped outside the protective barrier of creeks and rivers.[26]

Officers caused other problems. A general order had to be issued to keep regimental officers out of local cabins. The order only allowed brigade commanders to take cabins as headquarters if "they should occupy grounds contiguous to their brigades." Grant also began to take a stand on women in the camp, writing his wife, Julia, on April 3, "It will be impossible for you to join me at present. There are constantly ladies coming up here to see their husbands and consequently destroying the efficiency." He began to think of publishing a restricting order, calling it "ungallant but necessary." Other officer-related disruptions emerged as well; brigade commanders Leonard F. Ross and Richard J. Oglesby went on leave, and the 21st Missouri's colonel, David Moore, the 12th Illinois's colonel, Augustus Chetlain, and brigade commander John McArthur were all soon under arrest for various actions. Similarly, senior colonels in each brigade and newly appointed generals such as Jacob Lauman (now commanding a brigade in Hurlbut's division) moved to new commands. Grant told Lauman he had to "take all the new Brig Genls away from their old command, at least temporarily." The ripple effects were drastic; Lauman and his staff were not happy, and they returned to their old campsites for meals even as late as April 5. Similarly, Lauman's promotion necessitated an election for a new colonel in the 7th Iowa. The most notable change was in Charles F. Smith's command. His leg injury was becoming such a problem that he had to turn over command of his division to William H. L. Wallace, who had been transferred to command Smith's first brigade. Thus, by seniority in rank, Wallace would become the temporary division commander on April 4. The devout Christian general wrote his wife, "I feel a good deal of embarrassment in attempting to fill the place of such a man as General Smith." Wallace's old brigade went to Carroll Marsh, the brigade's senior colonel. That few of these officers were trained military men—Grant and Sherman being the exceptions—was also a concern. None of the division commanders besides Sherman had any West Point training; most were politicians and lawyers. Only a few of the lower-level commanders had any academy or Mexican War training either; those that did included Colonel Joseph Woods of the 12th Iowa, Julius Raith and Adolph Engelmann of the 43rd Illinois, and Marcellus Crocker of the 13th Iowa. The confusion continued on down the ranks, too. One bewildered Illinoisan wrote on March 25, "We even do not know who is in command, some say Smith of Paducah, some say Grant is not relieved or removed, but is in Command here."[27]

Various other issues also faced the Federals that early April. Language was at times a problem. Many foreign nationalities were represented, and entire regiments were given commands in languages other than English, mostly German. Sherman described much of the army as "green as militia, some regiments arriving without arms or cartridges." Grant described them as "entirely raw, and many of the men had only received their arms on the way from their States to the field." He added that many were "hardly able to load their muskets according to the manual," and that the officers were equally ignorant of their duties. Battery E of the 1st Illinois Artillery was a good example. Its commander reported that they received their horses only ten days before the battle, had been encamped only a week, and had only three days of drill. They had never even fired their pieces, yet were part of Sherman's division on the front line of the army.[28]

These problems were considered minor because the Federals believed they had time to work out these issues before moving on to Corinth. Perhaps the most obvious sign that the Federal high command feared no battle at Shiloh was that there were no entrenchments thrown up to guard the campsite. Despite Halleck sending tools to entrench, Grant and Sherman decided "drill and discipline were worth more to our men than fortifications." Grant did send engineer James B. McPherson to locate a line for entrenchments, but the army was already camping on ground that McPherson deemed the best location. To scouting Confederates, such negligence seemed astounding. Bushrod Johnson, commanding a Confederate brigade under Cheatham near Bethel, wrote in his journal, "Are they not fortifying?" Years later, Manning Force explained the situation: "The army had many things yet to learn, and the use of field fortifications was one of them."[29]

The most detrimental issue for the Federals, however, was a complete reorganization of artillery and cavalry on April 4 and 5. Batteries and cavalry battalions assigned on the brigade level were swapped around and concentrated at the division level, which necessitated assigning new commanders and physically changing campsites. The men of Peter Wood's Chicago Light Artillery were not happy about moving from Wallace's division at Crump's Landing to Pittsburg; they knew that in a fight, the new division artillery commander, Ezra Taylor, would put them "in the most dangerous position he can find." It was an interarmy rivalry: the Chicago artillery had performed better than Taylor's own Chicago battery at Donelson, and they knew Taylor was out for revenge. More importantly, the army was in the middle of the change on April 6. Obviously the highly confident commanders did not know they were about to be attacked; they would not have made so many changes had they known, but the result was confusion in the ranks when the Battle of Shiloh erupted.[30]

Sickness was also prevalent, as were lice, also known as graybacks, which one Iowan admitted was "till this time the most relentless foe we had met in real battle." Grant himself had been battling diarrhea and malaria, and a good number of the army was sick despite the presence of civilian nurses sent from the Northern states. Many men were just plain homesick or discouraged. Rumors also abounded, one saying that Beauregard had sent word to Grant "to get out of here, or he will take us all." Grant had supposedly told Beauregard to try, as it would "save his men of a weary march." More personally, Isaac Parks of the 52nd Illinois dispelled a rumor that he had died: "It was telegraphed there [at home] that I was killed at Donelson but I don't believe it."[31]

Despite everything, the idea that the Federals were totally negligent of security is a myth. Orders went out to arrest any civilians "found lurking in the neighborhood country, unless they are on their own farms and at their own work, when they must be encouraged and protected." The Federal division commanders also had each of the major roads leading into the Federal camping area covered, including the Snake Creek Bridge, which the two Wallaces covered on each end and which high water at the time made impassable; even then, the two Wallaces communicated to get their newly assigned cavalry familiar with the roundabout roads between the two. Although other crossings into the camp area existed and remained unguarded at fords and mills, particularly on Owl Creek, the major avenues were indeed covered. In addition, several of the commanders kept civilian scouts out combing the area. Lew Wallace had men operating from Crump's Landing, and Sherman had scouts keeping him informed, the most famous being L. H. Naron, whom Sherman christened Chickasaw. The Federal commanders also continually patrolled and scouted. Grant even sent a patrol northward to gather a stash of Confederate bacon at Nichol's Landing near Clifton. Such caution sometimes led to minor skirmishing. On one occasion, a Federal picket located the enemy, who challenged with "Halt! Who comes there?" A major replied that it was "the advance guard of the Grand Army of the United States." "The hell you say!" was the reply, and a volley of musketry sent the pickets bounding toward home.[32]

Despite the problems and overconfidence, the Army of the Tennessee soon had a thriving campsite, with one Illinoisan describing "a kind of roar or hum" in the camp rather than actual noise. "Oh, what an Army," another Illinoisan wrote his mother. "I may travel any direction for miles & find nothing but tents & men." To keep everyone less confused, many painted the regimental number and state on the sides of their massive Sibley tents. The amenities were also ample, including water to drink and with which to bathe, room to spread out, and fields in which to drill, train, and play. The weather was also warming, with the first meager hints of spring appearing late in March. Although one Ohioan wrote that "the citizens say this is the most backward spring they ever knew," the Federals welcomed the change. One Iowan wrote that "the peach trees have been in bloom for sometime and the grain fields look finely." The dogwoods soon put on their sparkling white blooms, although an Ohioan complained, "The woods is nice and green but there are no girls here and that spoils the whole thing." The warming weather had a positive effect on the troops' health and morale. W. H. L. Wallace noted that "the sick boys are all getting well and the doctors have scarcely anything to do." The men also received smallpox vaccines. James Black of the 49th Illinois wrote that the troops were "beginning to have some life about them again," many playing euchre and some even playing "town ball."[33]

The staging area at Pittsburg was thus perfect for the army's needs. All the Federals had to do, they thought, was wait for Buell to arrive and prepare for the advance on Corinth.

With everything hinging on Buell's appearance, Grant and Halleck both looked with eagerness toward his arrival. "Push forward your troops as rapidly as possible," Halleck wrote Buell, "so that we can cut their railroad communications." Grant pushed Buell as well, writing as early as March 19 that he was "feeling a little anxious to learn your whereabouts." Buell made quick time to Columbia, with the senior division commander, Alexander McCook, leading the way. Crowds of slaves welcomed the marching troops, with one Indianan writing that "gangs of slaves were seen at work upon almost every plantation." John Hight of the 58th Indiana remembered, "The roadsides were lined with negroes in their best attire eagerly watching the 'Yankees' pass." Buell had the first division to Columbia by March 10, but then his march slowed to a crawl. The divisions congregated at Columbia while Mc-Cook's engineers worked to rebuild the bridge over the Duck River. One Indianan wrote, "Today is Sunday and I hear the Sunday schools ringing across the river in Columbia. It puts one in mind of home Sweet home." Buell was not so sentimental but rather impatient; he was still waiting on March 23. He wrote Halleck of his delay, declaring that because he was extending the telegraph line with his progress, Grant should start the line toward him from Savannah, which he did.[34]

At least one of Buell's division commanders was not willing to allow broken bridges to delay his advance. Wishing to be in the lead, Bull Nelson obtained permission to take the advance if he could get across the river. Nelson immediately told his favorite brigade commander, Jacob Ammen, to cross the river at daylight on March 29. Ammen had tried to resign from the army while sick, but Nelson would not let him, urging Buell to deny the resignation: "Col. Ammen is a little sick and when sick has the blues," Nelson wrote, adding that he was the "most valuable officer in this division." Ammen asked if the bridge would be ready, to which Nelson responded, "No." Ammen asked about boats. Again, no, but Nelson told him, "The river is falling; and d——n you, get over for we must have the advance and get the glory." Sure enough, Ammen led the way as the division snaked across a ford in the falling river now just a few feet deep. Ammen described how "the men are ordered to make bundle of pantaloons, drawers, &c., attach it to bayonets, and wade the stream." They ferried artillery ammunition boxes over in boats and put tents and other items in the bottom of wagons to lift the ammunition above the water. With cavalry stationed in the river to direct the way and break the current and artillery prolonge ropes to catch anyone who was swept away, the men crossed on that "cold and disagreeable day."[35]

By April 1, Buell's divisions were again making progress. They were already two days out of Columbia and moving at intervals of about six miles through Mount Pleasant. They moved across the Buffalo River at Henryville and then on to Waynesboro, where Ammen reported "small Union flags on some houses; women ask to let the band play some old tunes—Yankee Doodle, &c. The music makes them weep for joy." Food was scarce while marching through what one Indianan called "a wild and broken country," causing some to feast on parched corn they found along the way. One soldier reflected, "The way we eat corn that night and next would have done credit to any horse." The troops were also fascinated by the snakes, which they killed. At least one good omen cheered them as they marched: one Indianan noted "a very large eagle soaring above us." Despite the inconveniences, lead elements of Nelson's division arrived at Savannah on April 3, hurried by news of Grant's army being split with part of it on the west side of the river. Although the rest of the division did not arrive until a couple of days later, on April 5, Nelson was adamant about crossing over to Pittsburg, but Grant told him he had "plenty of men to whip them." One Federal wondered whether Grant wanted to fight the enemy alone and reap all the glory. The division thus went into camp at Savannah in what one described as the "dirty little river town." Grant welcomed them in, telling Ammen he would send boats the next week to ferry them to Pittsburg: "There will be no fight at Pittsburg Landing; we will have to go to Corinth, where the rebels are fortified." Buell remained in the rear with his last division, which left Columbia on April 3. With everyone across the Duck River, he swiftly moved to the head of the column, reaching Savannah about sundown on the evening of April 5.[36]

Buell's arrival caused further concerns about rank. He had just been promoted to major general, along with Smith, Lew Wallace, McClernand, and others. Obviously there needed to be one commander, and that one man was Halleck, but because he was in St. Louis, he could not exercise tactical control in the event of an attack. Halleck alerted Grant that Buell would retain his separate command at all times unless the Confederates attacked. In that case, Halleck ordered Grant, "You are authorized to take the general command."[37]

No one was looking for a Confederate attack, however. Buell was more interested in supplies, cautioning Grant that his command needed food and forage after their difficult march through barren and hilly country. For his part, Grant wrote that he would remain in Savannah on April 6 to meet Buell and then move his permanent headquarters down to Pittsburg.[38]

A lot would eventually happen before Grant succeeded in doing so.

4

"I Would Fight Them If They Were a Million"

Albert Sidney Johnston watched his army's deteriorating situation from his quarters at the Inge house in Corinth. Although he kept official headquarters at the Tishomingo Hotel and later at the Corona College, much work and even more thinking was done at the generals' quarters downtown. Johnston weighed all the intelligence gathered from the continual patrols, reconnaissances, and pickets and was beginning to think of an offensive, now knowing for certain that Buell and Grant were closer to linking up than he and Van Dorn. Then came a communication that changed the attitude of all involved. Frank Cheatham, who had taken over command from Adley Gladden at Bethel Station on March 28, sent an urgent wire to Polk, who took it to Beauregard, who sent it on to Johnston with the endorsement, "Now is the moment to advance and strike the enemy at Pittsburg Landing." Cheatham was guarding the railroad and keeping an eye on Lew Wallace's division at Crump's Landing, and it seemed there was a major movement under way toward Bethel. It was actually Wallace's reaction to Cheatham's probes, but Cheatham interpreted the movement as an advance, which would take numbers away from Grant's main army. Perhaps Johnston should strike now, when his own numbers would be the highest he could possibly hope to have and when Grant's were the lowest. It was a crucial gamble, but Johnston had been gambling for several weeks now.[1]

Cheatham's message arrived in Corinth around 11:00 P.M. on the night of April 2, and Johnston walked across the street to Bragg's headquarters with Thomas Jordan, whom Beauregard had sent to Johnston with the note. Busy staff officers came in and out of the room on various errands while the two conversed with Bragg still in his nightshirt. They ultimately hammered out cursory orders to get the army in motion, although it was haphazard. Beauregard later wrote that the plan went forward "incomplete and imperfect as were our preparations for such a grave and momentous adventure." Beauregard and his staffers contended for decades that Johnston displayed nervousness and concerns that the army was not yet capable of such a move and that there was no reserve. His argument persuaded Bragg for a time, to which Thomas Jordan responded that Breckinridge's troops could be brought together from their details along the railroad to the east into a reserve corps. Johnston finally acceded and approved a rough version of a circular order read aloud by Jordan. Orders soon went out for the Confederate army late on April 2 to ready itself to march out of Corinth the next morning at 6:00 A.M.[2]

With the decision made to advance and attack Grant, the Confederate high command went into action to prepare for battle. Knowing they would fight at Pittsburg Landing, they tried to locate inhabitants as well as officers and men who had garrisoned the area before the Federal landing; any intelligence about the nature of the ground would be helpful. Staff work was crucial, and verbal orders soon went out, with more formal written orders following the next morning at 1:40 A.M. Beauregard and Johnston met together early on April 3, when Beauregard drew a more detailed plan of attack on the top of a table. A deficiency in maps prevented a more detailed discussion, but they also talked with the three corps commanders in Corinth (Breckinridge was at Burnsville). All but the critically sick thus prepared to march out of Corinth; Cleburne, for example, ordered forward "only those who was able to march 25 miles in a day and toate his knapsacks gun 50 rounds of catridges and 5 days rations of provisions." One common soldier reported, "The watchword here is Victory or Death."[3]

The logistical effort needed to get the army moving so quickly was enormous. One Alabama regimental commissary officer described his ordeal of butchering beeves and being ordered to have five days' rations prepared at once on April 2. "I was at work till 11 O'clock P.M. when I found everything gone and 2 or 3 Co's yet to be furnished," he grumbled. At dawn he went to the brigade commissary, filled his wagons, and returned to his regiment by 11:00 A.M. He had two days' rations for the troops by 1:00 P.M., then turned to getting the other three days' rations in wagons for the march northward. He labored for hours to "get their 3 days raw rations on wagons and my books posted in time to get off with them," he wrote, but the regiment was long gone by the time he finished. Having had no food all day, he decided to wait until the next morning to leave but then could not obtain a pass. It was April 7 before he was able to leave. Sometimes all the hard work seemed for nothing. A member of the 22nd Alabama reported, "The wagon overturned and we lost three days' rations." One commissary admitted the pay for such a job was good at $140 a month, but concluded, "I had rather be a private."[4]

More ominously, the contentious issue of unity of command surfaced again in the planning. Evidently Beauregard thought that even the tendering of the command, even if declined, won for him a greater say in how things should be done. As a result, Beauregard began to take over much of the planning and decision making for the attack. One of Bragg's staff officers, David Urquhart, later wrote, "It was well understood at the time throughout that army, that the whole plan of operations was Gen. Beauregard's, and in fact, that all which concerned the army from the time of its collection at Corinth, was arranged at and proceeded from Gen. Beauregard's headquarters." He added, "Further, that essentially, he exercised the command of the army." Johnston's son later argued that Johnston himself made the actual critical decision to attack, leaving how it was to be done to Beauregard.[5]

The Confederate plan itself provided a clear example of the confusion. Johnston wrote to Jefferson Davis on April 3 and possibly again the next day, outlining in cipher how the attack would proceed. After noting that Buell was coming close to a junction with Grant, Johnston laid out the attack formation as a linear assault, with Polk on the left, Hardee in the center, and Bragg's large corps on the right; Breckinridge would form the reserve. The deployment was perfect for what Johnston intended: driving around the Union left flank and pushing Grant's army into the creek swamps northwest of Pittsburg Landing. Johnston's orders to the army said as much: "In the approaching battle every effort should be made to turn the left flank of the enemy so as to cut off his line of retreat to the Tennessee River and throw him back on Owl Creek, where he will be obliged to surrender." The high command also warned the corps commanders, "Every precaution must also be taken on our part to prevent unnecessary exposure of our men to the enemy's gunboats." Obviously, those gunboats loomed large in the Confederate psyche.[6]

The orders the commanders received were totally different from anything Johnston had envisioned. Although the same basic idea of turning
the left flank was still desired, the deployment of the army was significantly altered. "Special Order No. 8" was issued under Johnston's
name, but Beauregard fashioned it and Jordan wrote it on the basis of
notes Beauregard had written during the night on the back of telegrams,
envelopes, and "loose scraps of paper." It was an almost incomprehen-
sibly curious order, based on Napoleon's order of battle at Waterloo,
which Jordan had in front of him as he wrote out the official version.
Bragg later termed the original plan "admirable—*the elaboration simply execrable.*"[7]

After a complex set of orders in which two wings of the Confederate army were to march northward on parallel routes and then weave
together into one formidable army at Mickey's—something the green
troops and officers would be hard pressed to perform—the attack formation itself called for a column of corps stacked one behind the other
instead of the linear formation Johnston had envisioned. Beauregard
wanted Hardee's corps, which would lead the march because it was the
most accustomed to making long marches, to take position in a line of
battle about a mile long, as near to the enemy camps as possible without being detected so they could attack in total surprise. About a thousand yards behind Hardee would be Bragg's corps in line of battle. Next
would come Polk's troops behind Bragg. Cheatham was sent orders at
Bethel to concentrate at Purdy and defend against the expected attack
before marching to join Polk's corps on the route northward. Breckinridge's reserve corps would bring up the rear.[8]

There was, as might be expected, much confusion in soldiers' final
letters to loved ones. Johnston's brother-in-law and aide William Preston wrote home, "I am with your uncle who commands our troops. . . . I
may not see you again." One Alabaman spoke for many when he wrote,
"I am in a hurry and everything in Confusion." Cheatham at Bethel
received Beauregard's puzzling orders to defend and then march, and
sent word back: "I do not entirely comprehend it." He did not recognize
any of the road names Beauregard used, and he did not know how long
he was to defend before marching. As a result, Cheatham's division,
consisting of Bushrod Johnson's and William Stephens's brigades, did
not depart Purdy until the morning of April 5.[9]

Much confusion has also attended the proposed day of attack. Many
historians claim that Johnston and Beauregard intended to attack on

April 4. One of Beauregard's staff officers, Alexander R. Chisolm, wrote on April 22, "Oh that the attack had been made the day it was intended two days previous (the 4th), we would have secured the fruits of our victory." Yet Johnston and Beauregard did not leave Corinth until the morning of April 4. Historian Wiley Sword argued that Beauregard did not leave until 11:15 A.M. Likewise, Breckinridge's corps did not receive orders to march until the late afternoon of April 3, with the orders telling him to leave the Burnsville area on the morning of April 4. If the Confederate high command ever counted on an April 4 attack, the plan was no doubt scrapped much earlier than normally cited, perhaps as early as the evening of April 3 and certainly by early April 4. There is sufficient evidence that Beauregard was already waffling as early as April 3. Jacob Thompson, former secretary of the interior and an aide to Beauregard, wrote his wife early on April 3 that he was in the process of "drawing up the instructions to the Generals [——] what they shall do." Significantly, he added, "Genl Beauregard has not yet determined the hour at which he will start." Later, he wrote, "If we stay over tonight, I may write you again." Other pieces of evidence exist as well; a Louisiana officer left behind in Corinth and listening for the sound of the battle noted on April 5 that the army was to attack "at daylight this morning." Whenever the Confederate attack was to start, it had a muddled beginning to a critical gamble.[10]

Confusion only grew as the Confederate army began to march northward. At the delayed target time of 10:00 A.M., April 3, the streets of Corinth were so clogged that hardly anyone could move. When units did begin to advance, they were out of order or had to wait for those supposed to be ahead of them. Even worse, generals interpreted their orders differently. Daniel Ruggles became so confused that it cost the Confederates several hours. His orders read to move at a certain time "tomorrow." Jordan had written these orders late on the night of April 2 but mistakenly put the date as April 3. Ruggles did not receive the orders until 2:30 A.M. the next morning, and he interpreted the message as saying he should leave the next day, April 4. Beauregard also noted, "The leading Command mistook 12M of the order for starting, for 12 at night." Beauregard particularly blamed Polk, whose troops were not even in town. Historian T. Harry Williams concluded that a sick and absent-minded Beauregard simply forgot to send Hardee an order to move. In addition, there were also confusing last-minute decisions concerning who should or should not go. Bragg made the decision to leave Bain's (Vaiden) Mississippi Battery, attached to Gibson's brigade, at Corinth because it was "not ready for field service." A few of the men nevertheless went along and manned a section of Stanford's Battery, which also hailed from Carroll County, Mississippi. W. W. Carnes's Tennessee Battery was also held back. Much of William H. Carroll's former brigade, the 17th, 29th, and 37th Tennessee, remained to guard the Iuka and Burnsville area. Blount's Alabama and Desha's Arkansas battalions also stayed behind, as did the unarmed 51st Tennessee, with a member writing his wife, "We was orde out thar but we could not git guns serfisen to fite with and we did not go." A disappointed officer in the 11th Louisiana was detailed to stay because someone had to command the sick and regimental camp at Corinth, and his company happened to be the only one with a full complement of officers.[11]

Despite the problems, the Confederate army at Corinth began to move northward on the afternoon of April 3. Local citizens watched as the troops filed out. Johnston himself watched from his quarters, providing flags to regiments without any standard. Most, however, were now supplied with the Confederate national flag as well as an assortment of other state and regimental banners such as the Texans' Lone Star flag and the Louisianans' Pelican flag. There were even corps flags: Polk's a red St. George's cross on a blue background, Bragg's blue St. Andrew cross on red that became known as the Confederate battle flag, and Hardee's "white medallion on a blue field." On the march, staff officers paraded the flags in front of the other corps "so that it could be recognized on the battle field." Military music was just as colorful; one witness described the "measured tramp, tramp of moving troops, the bugle, fife, and drum" and the bands that played such songs as "The Girl I Left Behind Me." The soldiers were thus excited at going on the offensive: "Their long-restrained ardor burst into a blaze of enthusiasm," one soldier remembered.[12]

Johnston himself left Corinth on the morning of April 4. Unbeknownst to him, Mrs. Augusta Inge had put two sandwiches and a piece of cake in his coat pocket. As he stepped out of the door, he paused, softly talking to himself, "Yes, I believe I have overlooked nothing." He was quiet and introspective on the trip, according to George Baylor of his staff, only showing any fire when he pronounced he intended to "hit Grant, and hit him hard." Even Major Inge joined the advance, volunteering as an aide on the staff of Mississippi general Charles Clark. Beauregard and his staff met Johnston and Bragg at Monterey around 2:30 P.M. on the afternoon of April 4; all of them were cheered as they passed the marching troops. Johnston, Beauregard, and their staffs remained at Monterey throughout the night, coordinating the growing chaos of the advance and establishing a large depot ultimately envisioned to contain 200,000 rations. Food was also shipped as close to the field of battle as possible.[13]

Meanwhile, the army marched northward. Two corps marched out the westernmost road, known as the Purdy Road as it moved northward out of Corinth. Farther northward, it became known as the Ridge Road (also known as the Bark Road past Mickey's) because it was mostly a high, dry path that followed high ground. As it neared Shiloh, the road followed the high ridge between Lick and Owl creeks, or the Shiloh divide that split the terrain. At noon on April 3, Hardee led the advance on this route, with Cleburne's brigade leading the corps. The corps covered several miles that afternoon and bivouacked off the road beside a spring for the night. Polk did not know that Hardee had left the road and marched on past, thus upsetting the order. The mistake was corrected the next morning, and Hardee moved on despite heavy rains entering the area on April 4. Behind Hardee followed the one division of Polk's corps, Charles Clark's. This later Mississippi governor was a Mexican War colonel in the 2nd Mississippi Infantry and a large plantation owner noted for his propensity to drink. He had no issues this day, however, and his troops kept a half-hour interval between the corps until the minor mix-up during the night. Polk's other division under Cheatham was at Bethel Station and Purdy watching Lew Wallace, and after sending its baggage to Corinth left Purdy on the morning of April 5 to join the corps on the Ridge Road. The march grew increasingly troublesome for all because of developing rains; one ordinance officer reported that an ammunition wagon became stuck numerous times "and had to be unloaded once before we could get it out."[14]

The column on the eastern route, which passed out of Corinth to the northeast, was not doing much better. Bragg and his massive corps led the march on the afternoon of April 3, but one Alabamian described the chaos in his diary: "We then countermarched by left flank and moved back in the same direction that we had come. We finally took the Monterey road and proceeded[.] I could see thousands of soldiers moving in different directions marching and counter marching." After

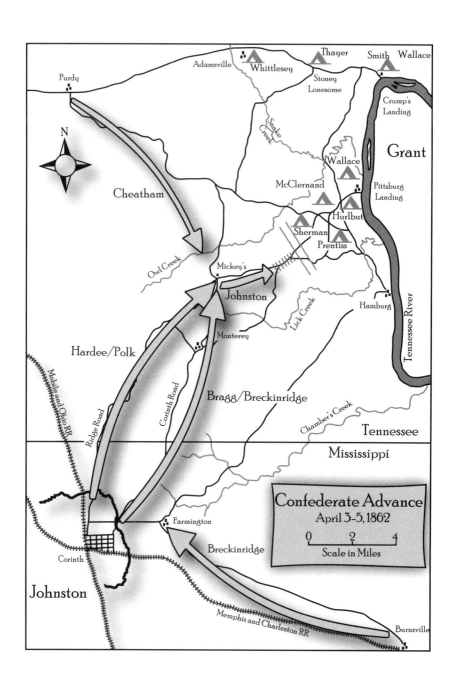

Purdy

Adamsville

Whittlesey

Thayer

Smith   Wallace

Stoney
Lonesome

Crump's
Landing

N

Snake Creek

Grant

Cheatham

Wallace

McClernand

Pittsburg
Landing

Sherman

Hurlbut

Owl Creek

Prentiss

Mickey's

Johnston

Lick Creek

Hamburg

Monterey

Hardee/Polk

Corinth Road

Bragg/Breckinridge

Mobile and Ohio RR

Ridge Road

Chamber's Creek

Tennessee River

Tennessee

Mississippi

Farmington

Corinth

Breckinridge

Confederate Advance
April 3-5, 1862

0   2   4
Scale in Miles

Johnston

Memphis and Charleston RR

Burnsville

bivouacking for the night, the corps moved forward the next morning, their path leading through the small village of Monterey, which sat on high ground where the advance, James Chalmers's and Randall Gibson's brigades, fell in. Confusion reared up again at Monterey as Bragg was to shift his divisions westward to the Ridge Road, thus setting up the merging of wings at Mickey's. Bragg changed the plan, however, causing Polk to wait at the wrong place. To ease the confusion, Bragg called all his division and brigade commanders together at his tent on the night of April 4 to go over the battle plan. "The order of battle was read to them," Bragg noted, "and the topography of the enemy's position was explained, as far as understood by us." The general officers thus had the plan drilled into their heads. John K. Jackson described it as "gradually sweeping around by a protracted wheel of the whole line to the left." Yet the lack of adequate communication created additional problems, such as Gibson's brigade at Monterey not knowing of the advance and wondering aloud what all the commotion and marching was about. Gibson later admitted that he was "as ignorant of the military at that time as it was possible for a civilian to be," but even the most basic communication from his superiors would have done wonders for his knowledge. The naive Gibson unfortunately compounded the problem when he asked Bragg in front of Johnston about the lack of explanation. Johnston then queried the corps commander about why Gibson had not been informed of the advance, and Bragg became furious. Adding to the confusion was the foul weather, causing the men to make "coffee out of water that was so thick with mud, that it looked and tasted like it had milk in it." The execution of a "deserter from Texas" near Monterey did not help either. Only the cheering Tennesseans were joyful, with one member of the 2nd Tennessee writing, "We bivouack in Tennessee once more!!"[15]

The final column on the eastern road was Breckinridge's, and despite all the problems already emerging, he was having the most trouble. The Kentuckians were no doubt excited about moving north; one Mississippian wrote that their bands played "Old Kentucky Home" every night "and many of them weep like children." The troops spent most of the night of April 3 cooking rations, and Breckinridge's brigades finally began their movement around daylight on Friday April 4, moving northeastward of Corinth from Burnsville. The troops had little idea what was about to take place. One Mississippian wrote, "we fell into ranks

& took up line of march. We knew not where." Breckinridge's three brigades began to straggle badly as a result of the horrid roads and the rain that was plaguing the rest of the army to the northwest. "Mud and water was knee deep at every step," remembered one Kentuckian, and many infantrymen had to be detailed to go to the rear to aid stalled vehicles. By 9:00 P.M., the three brigades had nevertheless made their way nearly twenty miles through Farmington and almost to Monterey. Johnston cautioned Breckinridge, "It is desirable that this should be done as soon as possible, having a due regard to an orderly march." The roads were such a problem, however, that Johnston finally ordered Breckinridge to change his line of march from the main Monterey–Pittsburg road across Lick Creek at Atkins's Mill to the drier Ridge Road.[16]

As the tiring troops slogged along that rainy April 4, they used their ingenuity to devise any way they could to stay dry. One Mississippian wrote, "I made me a scaffold and sit there til day." Despite the weather, the army's leadership still hoped to be in position to launch the attack on the morning of April 5. Johnston met with Beauregard and Bragg around 5:00 P.M. on April 4 at Monterey, discussing the enemy position and commanders. The latest intelligence indicated that Grant was in command, with divisions under Smith, McClernand, Wallace, and Sherman—four divisions of thirty-two regiments and twelve batteries. The Confederates estimated no more than 25,000 Federals. Prisoners brought in from a small skirmish tended to support their views, and Johnston pushed ahead with his decision to offer battle the next morning after an early march into position. A meeting later in the evening around 7:30 P.M., this time with Breckinridge in attendance, continued along the same lines despite Breckinridge reporting that his wagons and artillery were stuck in the mud. In the haste to launch the attack the next morning, Johnston told him to "cut a new road for your column."[17]

Yet dawn on April 5 only brought more trouble. While Hardee was nearing his position, the others were having terrible problems to the rear. Perhaps as foreboding, as Trabue's brigade passed through Monterey, they saw a blacksmith turning out pikes to arm men with no muskets. Such a realization must have shaken any confidence the men retained. Even worse, the heads of Polk's and Bragg's corps, on different roads, were nearing Mickey's, but neither had cleared the junction. This would take more time—something Johnston did not have to spare if he was going to hit Grant hard that day.[18]

Albert Sidney Johnston had ridden to Monterey on the morning of April 4, where he and Beauregard both spent the night in preparation for the battle to begin the next morning. He endured continual rain and at times even hail-producing thunderstorms. During the night, Johnston sent staff officer George Baylor to Beauregard asking "if we had not better postpone the attack until Sunday, on account of the rain." Beauregard replied that he thought time was of the essence, and they needed to attack on Saturday. Accordingly, both were among the troops throughout the rainy predawn hours of April 5, with one soldier reporting that Beauregard stood on a stump, hat in hand, motioning his troops onward. Johnston continually urged them forward as well: "Men, did you keep your cartridges dry? Look well along your guns and fire low." The weather caused more delays, however; a heavy storm system moved through the area that morning, pelting the troops as they stood in ranks or column, unable to move because of the mud and darkness. "It was as dark as Erebus," one Confederate noted, "and raining tremendously." A few tried to move on but could only succeed in "wading, stumbling and plunging through the mud and water a foot deep."

By daylight, the troops were able to move again. Hardee went into position by midmorning, and Withers's division followed. Johnston saw no additional troops coming into line, however. He impatiently asked Bragg where his other division was, but Bragg was unable to provide an answer. Finally, after noon, Johnston rode rearward to find the junction at Mickey's totally blocked by Polk's troops. They had passed through Mickey's and were blocking the road because Polk thought that both of Bragg's divisions were to his front. Johnston's patience snapped: "This is perfectly puerile," he barked, "This is not war!" He soon recovered, though, and quickly had Polk's men and wheeled vehicles moved to the side of the road so that Ruggles could proceed. Ruggles cleared Mickey's by 2:00 P.M., allowing Polk to follow to his correct position. A still-straggling Breckinridge finally brought up the rear, arriving near Mickey's later that afternoon, but he found the junction still so clogged that he had to halt for hours and then take a "neighborhood road to the right of Mickey's house." By the time all this was done, April 5 was nearly gone, and the only fighting that took place that day was among the Confederate corps commanders blaming each other for the delay. Most blamed Polk, and Beauregard later wrote of "quite a controversy about that march, between Gen'ls Bragg & Polk, which I checked as soon as I heard of it." William Preston Johnston later declared that Polk held his own: "The plucky old bishop unhorsed his accusers right on the spot." For his part, Daniel Ruggles believed not a word of it, writing years later, "I was not 'unhorsed' myself."[19]

Confusion and jealously reigned among the intermediate-level general officers as well. S. A. M. Wood had earlier had a spat with Patton Anderson while in Florida, when Wood received promotion over Anderson, whom Bragg described as "his senior, and much his superior as a soldier." Similarly, less than two months before, division commander Jones Withers had described Braxton Bragg, his corps commander, as "self willed, arrogant & dictatorial." More urgently, on the eve of battle, Hardee decided to create at least one division in his corps and awarded Thomas Hindman control of both his own brigade and Wood's. Hindman's brigade fell to the command of the senior colonel, Robert Shaver. Johnston made other changes as well, including on the brigade level when he sent George Maney and his 1st Tennessee (only five companies, as the others had been left in Chattanooga) from Chalmers's brigade to Stephens, making Maney the senior colonel and thus the commander. The orders came late on April 5, and Maney would have to march to Polk's corps the next morning before going into action. Similarly, Colonel A. J. Lindsay took formal command of the 1st Mississippi Cavalry the day before the battle, and Colonel John G. Coltart arrived to command the 26th Alabama while the regiment was camped at Monterey. In perhaps the biggest surprise, Lieutenant S. W. Cayce was promoted on April 5 to command of the 21st Alabama. It was a tough job for these officers, suddenly thrust into new commands with new superiors and subordinates on the eve of battle.[20]

Lower-level confusion within the army emerged as well. The 17th Louisiana was in a state of flux, with its colonel, S. S. Heard, under arrest for not controlling his men and command falling to its major, an ill Charles Jones. Similarly, fresh from service in Virginia, the 2nd Tennessee under William Bate arrived late after a march from Corinth and went into position in rear of Cleburne's line, some 500 yards to the left rear to watch that open flank near the Widow Howell's place. The men had not left Corinth until the late afternoon of April 4 and had to make a long night march to be in position by 10:00 A.M. on April 5. They could have opted for sixty-day furloughs for reenlisting, but they trudged forward. Similarly, the major of the 21st Alabama, Frederick

Stewart, learned his resignation had gone into effect on March 31, but he remained with his regiment and marched to Shiloh. Others were joining the column as well, such as S. A. M. Wood, who rejoined his brigade from Burnsville on April 3, taking over for the senior colonel, William K. Patterson, while it was en route.[21]

Even with all the confusion, nothing caused the Confederate high command more concern than a series of skirmishes that took place as the army neared its attack position. Colonel James H. Clanton's Alabama cavalry covered the Confederate march northward, and one official described him as "gallant to rashness." His rashness caused problems when the advance met part of Ralph Buckland's brigade of Sherman's division, out training on April 4. The Federals investigated, and soon Clanton's Alabama horsemen surrounded Company B of the 72nd Ohio. A free-for-all occurred in a heavy rain, with Clanton chasing a "major in his own picket lines ran him out again and brought him back in a prisoner," wrote one of Clanton's officers. Federal cavalry soon drove the Alabamians back to Hardee's main line, but the chasing horsemen suddenly came on Cleburne's brigade full of infantry and artillery. Federal commander Elbridge G. Ricker reported, "When passing the brow of a hill our advance was opened on by three or four pieces of artillery, at least two regiments of infantry, and a large cavalry force." Ricker wisely withdrew, but Sherman was "enraged at what he designated indiscreet conduct." He heard the ruckus and immediately went out with two more regiments of infantry. Night soon ended the affair, and the Confederates somehow dodged discovery.[22]

The little skirmish nevertheless produced major reverberations. Numerous Federal units were called out to form a line in the rain, including some as far back as Hurlbut's, Wallace's, and McClernand's divisions. Only the 49th Illinois seemed to think the wet jaunt was worth it; James A. Black wrote in his diary about his less-than-respected lieutenant colonel: "We enjoyed seeing the Col. (Pease) get his good clothes wet." Four or five Confederate prisoners were brought to Sherman's camps and locked in Shiloh Church. "As we had never seen one," a 57th Ohio soldier remembered, "that evening we thronged around the church and talked through the cracks between the logs with them, and a bold, defiant lot of fellows we found them." More importantly, Grant hurried upriver from Savannah upon hearing news of the fighting, not wanting McClernand to command any major action. Grant soon met W. H. L. Wallace and James B. McPherson, who informed him that they had ridden to Sherman's camps and all was quiet now. In the process of moving back to the landing, Grant's horse fell in the slippery mud and onto its rider's leg, badly bruising Grant's ankle. The swelling was so bad that Grant's boot had to be cut off, and for the next few days he was on crutches and hobbled wherever he went. Similarly, the skirmish also had an effect on the Confederate high command. When thirteen Union prisoners were brought to Beauregard and Johnston at Monterey that evening, Beauregard began to think that the element of surprise was gone. Still, some good news came when one of the captured Federals, Major Leroy Crockett of the 72nd Ohio, viewed the Confederate army advancing to the attack. He "saluted them in genuine military style," one Louisianan remembered, and remarked, "This means a battle," adding, "They don't expect anything of this kind back yonder." Thomas Jordan and engineer Jeremy Gilmer further interrogated Crockett "with the least possible semblance of so doing" and learned that the Union army was not expecting an attack and had no earthworks for defense.[23]

Unbelievably, the Federals had missed this sign. Despite the skirmishes and other indications, such as large numbers of rabbits and squirrels rushing through their picket line on Saturday morning (about the time Hardee was taking his position just to the southwest) and dogs that came with the Confederate army meandering into the Federal camp, Sherman just could not—or would not—perceive the danger. He later admitted, "I did not believe that he designed anything but a strong demonstration." Neither he nor Prentiss could fathom the idea that the entire Confederate army was advancing on them, and their actions would later cause much embarrassment. In the most noted episode, Sherman overcompensated with sarcastic remarks when alerted by the 53rd Ohio's colonel, Jesse Appler, that Confederates were on his front. Sherman was evidently already aggravated with Appler because the 53rd Ohio in a recent review had done "miserably—just as poor as was possible for men to do," according to the regiment's adjutant, Ephraim Dawes. Now with reports of confrontation from the regiment's colonel, Sherman told a courier, "Tell Colonel Appler to take his d——d regiment to Ohio. There is no force of the enemy nearer than Corinth." Obviously Sherman knew there was enemy presence closer than Corinth, but he had been burned once by seemingly crying wolf in Kentucky, and he was not about to make that mistake again.[24]

Clearly the Federal commanders seemed unworried about any attack, despite the signs and even reports from civilian scouts. "He acted as if unconcerned," the scout Chickasaw wrote of Sherman when he reported the Confederate army's advance. Sherman even sent Grant the famed message, "I do not apprehend anything like an attack on our position," prompting Grant to send Hallack in St. Louis the equally famous message, "I have scarcely the faintest idea of an attack (general one) being made upon us, but will be prepared should such a thing take place." The division commanders only strengthened their pickets and advised greater caution.[25]

Even as Sherman and Grant were sending those fateful messages, however, Johnston's army, shielded by the cover of Hardee's troops and pickets farther to the front, was stacking up behind Hardee's line, preparing for the attack that would take place the next morning. Bragg's corps eventually went into line a thousand yards behind Hardee on the slope of an elevated ridge on which the Bark Road ran to the east. Bragg was on site aligning the brigades according to markings on the trees made by staff officers, placing Daniel Ruggles's division on the left of the line and Jones Withers's division on the right. Because of the distance between Hardee's right and Lick Creek and the need to fully plug the gap, Adley Gladden's brigade of Withers's division filed forward and extended Hardee's line. Behind Bragg was Polk's corps, Charles Clark's division in front and Cheatham's division, fresh from Purdy, behind. Polk himself ranged ahead to keep the correct interval from Bragg's troops and met Ruggles forming his division. To the rear of Polk, Breckinridge's three reserve brigades filed into columns of brigades as well.[26]

Thus situated, the Confederate army was within a mile of the Union camps, and some reported "a momentary expectation of a conflict." Most were nevertheless in good spirits. One member of Stanford's Battery in Polk's Corps wrote in his diary that the weather "cleared off and [it] was a fine evening." The calm of the night allowed a rest for all except those on picket duty. A proclamation from Johnston himself buoyed them further. Johnston declared that they were fighting for their homes, women, and way of life. "With such incentives to brave deeds and with the trust that God is with us," Johnston wrote, "your generals will lead you confidently to the combat, assured of success." One member of the 7th Kentucky reported these words "made a deep impression on all the men," and a Mississippian declared it to be the "best written and most thrilling address I have ever seen." He remembered that an unwise but "enthusiastic shout went up from the entire line."[27]

Johnston had written the buoyant address days before, but now on the evening of April 5 his patience was further tested when he happened on a gathering of his corps commanders at Beauregard's headquarters. Although historians have often called this a council of war, it was in fact a chance meeting of the generals, and Hardee was not even there. He had taken position with his front line of troops only a mile out from the Union camps. It was fortunate that Johnston arrived because the consensus among the generals was that the army should withdraw to Corinth. The instigator was Johnston's second in command, Beauregard, who had drawn up the plan in the first place. While Beauregard was talking to Bragg, he sent word to Polk to come to his headquarters. Later, an ailing Breckinridge happened up as well. Beauregard was already displeased with the corps commanders, particularly Polk, and Polk began to defend his actions in what became a "warm discussion." Beauregard argued that "our success depended upon our surprising the enemy" and "this was now impossible, and we must fall back to Corinth." Then Johnston appeared, something Beauregard had not counted on. One of a watching group of staff officers gathered nearby remembered, "We could hear the low, earnest discussion of our superiors, but could not distinguish the words spoken."[28]

Beauregard had some good arguments on his side. After returning from riding Hardee's line, he reported the men cheering, as occurred with the other corps as well. The soldiers had also been firing their weapons in the wet weather to see if their powder was dry, and one Texan admitted that several men on picket had requested permission to fire their guns off, which was "followed by a fusillade by the whole regiment." The firing became so loud that Colonel John A. Wharton was placed under arrest for not keeping his men quiet. He appealed to Johnston to be allowed to go into the fight and was released. Johnston's aide and brother-in-law, William Preston, recorded in his diary that he even heard a cannon fired at sunset. Drums could also be heard in the enemy camps; one cavalryman wrote in his diary, "We can hear the enemy's drums distinctly." Captain William H. Ketchum, commanding an Alabama battery, remembered "hearing the tattoo from their different camps." He reported that the closeness made him think all the more: "I deemed it prudent to keep my horses in harness all night." Because of the closeness to the enemy, the delay, and the noise produced, as well as the hunger of the troops, Beauregard argued that the enemy knew of their presence. He stated the Federals would be "intrenched to the eyes." Bragg agreed.[29]

Johnston would have none of it, and Polk supported him. As historian Charles Roland has pointed out, Johnston took firm control at the critical moment that military philosopher Carl von Clausewitz wrote always preceded a battle. Johnston argued that the troops had marched twenty difficult miles through awful terrain and even worse weather. To withdraw now would severely damage morale. One watching staff officer noted Johnston "seemed to terminate [the meeting] a little abruptly," dictating, "Gentlemen, we shall attack at daylight tomorrow." As he turned and walked away, he confided to a staff officer that Polk was a true friend and also uttered his most famous words: "I would fight them if they were a million. They can present no greater front between these two creeks than we can, and the more men they crowd in there, the worse we can make it for them." To another he confided, "I intend to 'hammer 'em!'"[30]

Some generals still had questions, however. As he walked away, Bragg told Captain Samuel Lockett of his staff to reconnoiter the Federal left before dawn the next morning. Daniel Ruggles confided to a staff officer that he feared Johnston's idea of turning the enemy left would not work. The enemy "would not swing that way," he said, but would instead endeavor to retreat toward their gunboats. As Johnston himself left the gathering and made his way to his own headquarters farther to the rear near Stephens's brigade of Polk's corps, he continued to buoy himself with strong talk, perhaps seeking the approval of his staff officers. Polk later reported that Johnston "coveted [the opportunity] for vindicating his claims to the confidence of his countrymen against the inconsiderate and unjust reproaches which had been heaped upon him." That night at his bivouac site, Johnston reminisced with Thomas Jordan about his California days and how disturbed he had been to find out that some people doubted his sincerity or integrity in transferring his department to a new commander and siding with the South. Obviously the views of others mattered to Johnston, but probably his foremost hope was vindicating Jefferson Davis's continued confidence in him.[31]

All the while, the Confederate army rested in line of battle, with a privileged few enjoying mail call while on line. Yet all knew what was coming the next day. Staff officers worked throughout the night to bring up supplies for the troops who had eaten their five days' rations in three; one Texan noted that it was "a well-known soldier's maxim that rations are carried easier in the stomach than on the back." One Louisianan reported that they could "see the twinkle of their fires, and hear indistinctly the hum of voices singing and shouting in careless security." Others reported hearing axes chopping wood and even dogs barking in the enemy camps. Preston Pond cautioning his tired Louisianans to "sleep near our guns, without undressing as we might be obliged to march during the night." Bradford Nichol, an artilleryman in Rutledge's Tennessee Battery, similarly remembered that his battery was "in harness since midnight." Perhaps William Preston Johnston, the son of the Confederate commander, best described the feeling years later: "[Many] familiar with the dangerous sports of their native South, must have felt as when hunting in the dense cane break, and, following the trail, they drew near the den of some great bear, hidden in the thicket, with whom momentarily they expected encounter and mortal struggle."[32]

Johnston felt the same tension, but he had to make this gamble— even if it cost him his own life. He thus spoke of rolling the "iron dice of battle," illustrating his idea that this attack was a major gamble. In the statement issued to the troops, he told them they were fighting "for all worth living or dying for." Johnston's son later related that his father had confided in him that he preferred a soldier's death. He likewise told his son's best friend, one of his brigade commanders, Randall Gibson, that he hoped Gibson would come through the battle safe, but then added significantly, "But we must win a victory." Most notably, Johnston remarked to Colonel John S. Marmaduke in the coming hours, "We must this day conquer or perish." Even if it took his own life, Johnston had to win this gamble, and the men in the ranks agreed. One of his Louisiana soldiers wrote before the battle that the idea of being conquered "nerve[s] us with disparate energy to do or die." Another wrote, "We *must* be victorious."[33]

5

"I Was Not Only Surprised, but Astounded"

The early hours of April 6, 1862, were like any others at Pittsburg Landing. The soldiers gathered around Shiloh were tasked to carry out their assigned duties in those predawn hours and minutes. One Ohioan in Sherman's division wrote that he was determined to rest that day: "I was worn out with the pressure of duties and felt that rest was absolutely necessary for me." Obviously no one knew that when day dawned, the war as well as the nation would be forever transformed.[1]

At Pittsburg Landing itself, the hive of all things relating to the Federal army, boats and wagons came and went in those predawn hours as supplies accumulated and new units arrived and camped temporarily before going into the field. One Federal marveled at the entertaining scenes at the landing, with "wagons upsetting or mules balking or barrels falling out & rolling down hill among the mules." On this busy morning, Illinoisan D. J. Benner was preparing to load 250 bales of hay and move it to his camp. On the river itself, the steamboat *Minnehaha* landed just before dawn, carrying the 15th Iowa. One of the soldiers remembered, "After we had maid way with our breakfast we brushed up our botts and slicked generally and when we had finished we was invited to go on shore." Also on board was Anne Dickey Wallace, wife of division commander W. H. L. Wallace. She was secretly on a trip to visit her recently sick husband, who would not have approved of her coming: "I knew he would not think it consistent with his duty to send for me, though I found it mine to go to him." Also in the army at Pittsburg Landing was her father, Colonel T. Lyle Dickey of the 4th Illinois Cavalry, as well as two brothers, two brothers-in-law, and numerous other, more distant kin.[2]

Inland from Pittsburg Landing, soldiers milled about, kept watch, patrolled, or slept as best they could, aided by the warming trend that had occurred over the last week. Some had duty, such as the men of Munch's Minnesota Battery, who were already "on the go to clean up the camp grounds." Lloyd Jones, on picket in front of the 16th Wisconsin, remembered nearly shooting several phantom Confederates but in reality hearing only "the occasional tinkle of a cow bell, or the movement of some wild animal through the underbrush." In the Chicago Light Artillery camp, several men had taken the unit's horses to a nearby creek and were "letting them nibble at the new grass on their way back to camp." Jonathan LeBrant in the 58th Illinois was working on a "rude coffin" for one of his unfortunate comrades, who had died of sickness. Others more happily prepared to visit friends in nearby camps, and Warren Olney of the 3rd Iowa was down in a ravine hunting flowers. Captain Daniel H. Brush of the 18th Illinois "arose early to enjoy a delightful Sabbath morning and commence the day by reading a good portion of the most interesting history of Joseph and his brethren, recorded in that best of books, the Holy Bible." Even a few women meandered around, most of them "laundresses" for the various regiments, although in the camp of the 18th Missouri one of the soldier's wives, Roxana Johnson, prepared breakfast. Officers went about their business just like their men. An ill Jesse Hildebrand moped around his headquarters tent just a few paces west of Shiloh Church.[3]

Farther out, Lew Wallace's troops began to awaken at Crump's Landing just downriver and a few miles inland, milling around camps and preparing for breakfast, sick call, and many other soldierly duties. At Savannah, just around the river's bend, Ulysses S. Grant and his staff began to stir early in preparation (not knowing Buell was already in Savannah) of riding out to meet him that day and then moving headquarters south to Pittsburg. The *Tigress* sat as silently as a steamboat could in the still waters of the river, its steam up and ready to move when ordered.[4]

Almost all of America went about their routines in that predawn darkness as well. As historian Edward Cunningham put it, "In a million homes across America, in the strange semi-light that prevailed in the dawn, there occurred the first gradual stirrings of Sunday morning. Housewives were up, making breakfast gruel or oatmeal, while teenage sons and daughters milked the cows or took care of other household chores in preparation for dressing and making the long trip to Sunday morning services." It was life as usual—nothing different from any other morning in America.[5]

Not all were merely going about their routine, however. A few miles to the southwest, Confederate officers were awake and watchful. Skirmishers to the front were carefully challenging anyone in the area; the password for Cleburne's troops was "Washington," whereupon they would be challenged by "who goes there," and the reply should be "Yorktown." Other officers to the rear were also stirring in the bleak darkness, waking their exhausted men for the coming attack. Patton Anderson wrote that around 4:00 A.M., "the men were aroused, without fife or drum, and silently but promptly resumed their arms, ready for the order to move forward." Some analyzed themselves in relation to what they knew was coming: an Alabamian wrote he was "trying to examine myself to see whether I was really in the faith or not." He also pondered whether he was "ready to take the life of my fellow man when the Scriptures of eternal truth positively declare 'Thou shalt not kill.'" He also thought of home and family, especially his little children. The later famed explorer Henry Morton Stanley ("Dr. Livingstone, I presume?") was in line in Shaver's brigade, and he and a friend decided to put violets in their caps: "Perhaps the Yanks won't shoot me if they see me wearing such flowers, for they are a sign of peace," his friend blurted, to the laughter of his company. Others were far too busy to ponder their future. Out on the far right, Samuel Lockett and a band of cavalry were making their way toward the Federal camps of David Stuart's brigade, descending the tall ridge south of Locust Grove Branch at several points only to find the Federal camps "silent as the grave." At one point, Lockett slipped by "a sleepy camp sentinel leaning against a tree." He watched cooks preparing breakfast, men cleaning their guns, and the normal reveille in another camp. Yet not all were uninformed. One Union surgeon and an orderly went out on "some night excursion" and were captured. They were "speechless with astonishment" as they were taken to the rear through lines and lines of Confederate infantry.[6]

Even a few local citizens were active on this morning. James Wood, at his small house and cotton gin on the Corinth Road, realized something dramatic was happening. He had seen the Confederate host gathering the day before and began moving his family and his priceless possessions southward, where they encountered the entire Confederate army. The Confederates let his family pass but pressed him into service as a guide. Lewis Seay had likewise moved his family several days ago, but he now returned to watch over his home. Wilse Wood lived at two cabins south of Shiloh Church, and he likewise moved his family across Lick Creek; unlike Seay, he did not come back. J. J. Fraley was also moving his family on the morning of April 6, having been told by a Confederate officer that they were "in much danger, as the soldiers were drawing in line nearby for battle." Nancy George buried a set of silver goblets before hurriedly leaving. Sixteen-year-old Alex McDaniel was hiding from the army that morning, "sitting on a log on the bank of Snake Creek fishing."[7]

The climactic moment was thus near; peace would be shattered at dawn. One Mississippian knew what was about to happen: "I thought of the hundreds, perhaps thousands that this day must pass into eternity. I thought of the many widows & of those that must this day be made." Realizing he could be one of the dead, he noted, "At this moment I trust I made a sincere, honest surrender of myself to God."[8]

The Federal army encamped at Pittsburg did not have this luxury. Grant and his army had no idea that the entire Confederate Army of the Mississippi was arrayed within a mile of their camps, poised to strike.

Fortunately for the Federals, several seemingly small events blunted the massive Confederate attack that was about to explode. Although almost everyone in the Federal camps had no idea that they were about to be attacked in force, some of the frontline commanders were active during the previous day and night, concerned that something was not right. Several colonels in one brigade, probably Hildebrand's, had a conference and agreed to strengthen the pickets. Wills De Hass of the 77th Ohio wrote that he worried security measures were thin and everything seemed "very strange." He took his concerns to Hildebrand, who "expressed himself in the same spirit, but remarked that he was powerless."[9]

Several patrols had also gone out from the forward camps during the preceding twenty-four hours. Even William T. Sherman, whom historians normally and falsely call totally negligent and unconcerned about security, sent out his share, including those that resulted in the skirmish on April 4. He also had civilian scouts out. In addition, Peter Sullivan, one of Sherman's colonels, adamantly insisted that Sherman had intended to send three regiments of infantry, five companies of cavalry, and a battery forward to scout on the morning of April 6. Similarly,

Prentiss sent out ten companies on Saturday evening, five each from the 21st and 25th Missouri. McClernand also sent out cavalry in the direction of Hamburg. Other lower-level commanders in Sherman's and Prentiss's frontline divisions likewise sent out patrols, including David Stuart and Everett Peabody; neither saw anything but a few slaves in a cotton field who stated that several Confederate horsemen had been around that day. Others ranged out from Peabody's brigade as well, including a small patrol from the 16th Wisconsin; likewise, Colonel David Moore of the 21st Missouri took three companies out Saturday evening for "a thorough reconnaissance over the extent of 3 miles [but] failed to discover the enemy." Unfortunately for the Federals, most of these major patrols or scouts moved due south or southeast and did not find the Confederate army to the southwest, although some saw Confederate cavalry.[10]

Others ran headlong into small numbers of Confederates. John B. Beach of the 77th Ohio of Sherman's division remembered a Confederate officer shooting at him on April 5; the bullet hit a tree above his head. Two officers in W. H. L. Wallace's division also ran into less than stealthy Confederates. Captain I. P. Rumsey and his brother rode forward of the lines on Saturday and saw Confederate cavalry to the front. "They are not ours," the Rumsey brothers surmised. Riding to Sherman's camps, the two encountered Sherman himself, who responded to their reports with confirmation that others had seen them too. "They have been up on the right three times," Sherman told them, "and fired on McDowell, but I have positive orders from Grant to do nothing that will have a tendency to bring on a general engagement until Buell arrives." According to their account, Sherman then examined his map and continually muttered under his breath that Buell should have been here "ten days ago." Rumsey also remembered that Sherman visited the isolated Stuart over near Lick Creek on Saturday, telling him to send a regiment out to scout the next morning as well.[11]

By late on April 5, the pickets were beginning to see ever-larger numbers of Confederates. Ed Gordon of the 57th Ohio reported his company fired nearly a hundred rounds at Confederates on April 5 while on picket duty. Yet these were not normal Confederates: "The horsemen appeared to be officers with field-glasses, reconnoitering our position, rather than cavalry trying to capture or kill our pickets." The men fired on the officers and "we saw many horses jump, and thought that several fellows were hit during the day."[12]

The observation of Confederates to the front did not translate into appreciation of the true situation, however. Sherman knew the enemy was before him; he just did not know in what strength and could not believe that they were in numbers larger than reconnoitering parties. He even had one soldier put under arrest for alleged false claims of a pending attack, but the man's captain refused to turn him over. Sherman desired no replay of his earlier skittishness that had led to charges of insanity. Down the line, Prentiss felt the same way; according to members of the 25th Missouri, Prentiss "hooted at the idea of Johnston attacking."[13]

One officer was not satisfied, though. During the night, Colonel Everett Peabody was unable to sleep and passed several hours in quiet conversation before deciding to send a small squad out to look around again. Major James E. Powell of the 25th Missouri, a former regular army officer, led a small reconnaissance forward and quickly returned, stating that he had uncovered the enemy pickets and he thought there was a strong force behind them. Peabody then decided to send out a much stronger patrol around 3:00 A.M. He had wrestled with the lack of action, especially after some of the Confederate local citizens Johnston had sent out were captured and confined. These talkative "spies," ostensibly looking for stray cattle, told of a vast army to the Federals' front. Other civilians told a similar tale, such as "a family of women and children" who came into the Federal camp on Saturday—pushed there, they said, by the arrival of the Confederate army. Peabody was hesitant to take on such responsibility when he was only the senior colonel commanding the brigade and not a general officer; he had just written, in fact, that it felt "funny to be called a General." Just the night before Prentiss had "hooted" at his nervousness. He acted forcefully this night, however, and sent out yet another patrol under Powell that would change the nature of the coming battle. Significantly, this hefty patrol—five companies of the 25th Missouri and 12th Michigan—was told to move partially across the front of Sherman's camps to the southwest instead of to the south or southeast. Colonel Francis Quinn of the 12th Michigan later reported their job was to "watch, and endeavor, if possible, to capture, a force of the enemy who were prowling near our camp." An Illinois soldier put it in more homespun terms: "A reconnaissance [went out] to catch some Rebs for breakfast."[14]

Powell's small patrol left its camps in a morbid mood. Peabody himself shook hands with several of the men, telling his officers, "I can not say anything more to General Prentiss, but he will soon see how near I was right. I must do this upon my own responsibility, but I will not live to receive censure or credit for doing so." The sleepy patrol meandered along a small farm road that initially went south but then turned westward as it neared the Corinth Road. Powell was a wise choice to lead the patrol, being "an old regular Army officer," one of the men noted, but he was less enthusiastic than normal because his young son was with him in camp. The boy was "the idol of the regiment," Oliver Newberry wrote. The rest of the Federals, likely not happy with their early duty either, encountered more difficulties as they proceeded in the darkness. Formed into three columns, one on the road and one on either side, they stumbled forward, at times getting confused and veering into each others' paths. It is a wonder that friendly fire did not claim some of the Federals in the predawn darkness and confusion. When the patrol approached the Federal picket line commanded by Captain A. W. Mc-Cormick of the 77th Ohio, they identified themselves as Missourians. One of the Ohioans related that his first thought was that "all Missourians were secesh," but Powell soon gave the password and reported he was "going out to catch some rebels for breakfast." Powell and his men then became even more watchful because they knew that nothing was between them and whatever lurked in the dark woods. The pickets had initially been as much as a mile out, but with the recent activity and the desire not to bring on an engagement, as Halleck and Grant had ordered, they were at places now no more than half a mile in front of the camps. Outside the picket line, Powell was on his own.[15]

Nearing the Corinth Road, on which they planned to advance, the patrol encountered three single shots in the darkness and heard the gallop of horses' hooves as the scouts of Brewer's Alabama Cavalry Battalion fled. Proceeding cautiously, they encountered a larger band of horsemen—Confederate Lieutenant F. W. Hammock's pickets. Seven of these Confederates fired at about ninety yards and ran to the rear. Powell cautiously continued but met another group of Confederate skirmishers under Lieutenant William McNulty. They too fired and withdrew. Although it was not unexpected or surprising to encounter roving Confederate horsemen or even skirmishers to the front, Powell wisely called a halt at the Corinth Road and formed his men into skirmish formation. He also decided to wait until dawn to proceed; he had had enough of this stumbling around in the dark, especially with at least a few of the enemy obviously to the front.[16]

As the first gray streaks of dawn began to appear behind them, however, Powell ordered the line forward, aligning on the Corinth Road. Most of the Federals moved through open timber, which afforded only meager sightlines, especially in the still-predominant darkness. The men on the right of his line, soldiers from the 25th Missouri, were better off and soon neared an open field, that of John C. Fraley's forty-acre cotton field. What these Missourians saw in the field startled them. Across the expanse knelt Major Aaron Hardcastle's 3rd Mississippi Infantry Battalion, skirmishers for Wood's brigade, Hindman's division, Hardee's Corps, Army of the Mississippi.[17]

Hardcastle's Mississippians were just as surprised to see the Federals. Although Shiloh would become known as a Confederate attack, here the Mississippians were the ones attacked by an advancing Union patrol. Whoever technically did the attacking was less relevant than the fact that both sides immediately took each other under fire, despite being armed with smoothbore muskets, with the distance between them far in excess of their range. These common Mississippi and Missouri farm boys were so green that they let loose massive volleys that had little chance of hitting anyone. Still, they fired, thus opening the horrendous Battle of Shiloh.[18]

Those unexpected shots portended the opening of the biggest battle America had ever seen. S. A. M. Wood was as startled as anyone and quickly sent word to Hardee, his corps commander. Bragg, Polk, and the rest of the Confederate leadership also heard the firing and knew what it meant. Back at Albert Sidney Johnston's headquarters near the rear of the army, Beauregard was again advising retreat. While the generals sipped coffee and ate a few biscuits "between dawn and sunrise," William Preston remembered, those shots rang out and Johnston asked that a staff officer note the time: 5:14 A.M. Other watches said 4:55 A.M. Bragg noted that "the enemy did not give us time to discuss the question of attack" as Johnston decisively alerted Beauregard: "The battle has opened gentlemen; it is too late to change our dispositions." Johnston mounted his horse, Fire Eater, and set out toward the front, leaving a flustered Beauregard behind in dismay. Johnston was confident: "Tonight, we will water our horses in the Tennessee River."[19]

The reaction was just as swift in the Federal army. Frontline regimental commanders such as Jesse Appler in the exposed 53rd Ohio in

Rhea Field heard the sounds and grew even more nervous. Sherman also heard the firing, as did Prentiss. Up and down the line, Union soldiers busy taking roll, eating breakfast, or tidying up camp turned an anxious ear to the sounds emanating from the woods to the front. Some thought it was just the same old skirmishing. Others thought it was firing by their own troops; one soldier in Leonard Ross' brigade remarked that his comrades thought it might be some patrol returning from the front and firing its weapons to unload them, as was common practice. Yet many had second thoughts. It was too early for a patrol to return to camp; why would they not take advantage of the dawn to see whatever it was they went out to scout? Then too, this firing seemed close—just beyond the line of pickets, if even that.[20]

The firing increased over the span of the next few minutes, causing more concern. Most of the previous days' firefights had quickly flamed out, but this one seemed to be growing and getting closer. In fact, the fighting in Fraley Field itself lasted about an hour as Powell advanced but was unable to push Hardcastle's Mississippians out of the way. The Confederate skirmish line did what it was supposed to: block and screen Powell from uncovering the bulk of the Confederate army. At such long ranges and with such green troops, however, little of the death and destruction Shiloh would later become known for occurred in this initial fighting. There were only a few wounded and dead on either side; it was, ironically, a tame beginning to a horrific battle. Meanwhile, the sun rose higher; Hardee described the morning as "bright and bracing." Staff officer Jacob Thompson similarly remembered that "the sky was without a cloud and the sun arose in cheering brilliancy."[21]

The situation changed once the Confederate command sent their troops forward. Powell initially detected some cavalry operating on his left flank, probably Clanton's Alabamians, and decided to fall back before he was cut off from his camps. Then Hardcastle's skirmishers retired into the woods in their rear. Powell, deciding to handle the cavalry and stick around to see what it all meant, posted his line and determined to see if the Confederates were indeed a small reconnaissance band sent out, perhaps, from Monterey or if they were screening a larger force. Powell soon got his answer as Hardee's corps suddenly burst from the woods in front, "animated," Beauregard wrote, "by a promising spirit." Although Powell could not see the length of Hardee's mile-wide line, he could see enough to satisfy him that the Confederates were there in force and that he must fall back. And he had no way of knowing that

Hardee was only the first line of an army submerged in the woods, with
Bragg, Polk, and Breckinridge all stacked up behind him.[22]

As the sun rose, it caused not a few soldiers versed in Napoleonic history to note it was the "sun of Austerlitz." Powell, however, was probably not paying much attention to the sun, although when he approached
Seay Field to the east he saw additional Federal troops coming to his
aid. The Union commanders to the rear, Peabody, Prentiss, and even
Sherman, were beginning to realize something significant was going on.
When wounded members of Powell's initial patrol began to flee, seeking any medical attention they could find, they emerged into Sherman's
camps and began to sound the alarm. The first regimental camp they
found was Appler's 53rd Ohio, which had already formed into line on
the sounds to the front. Appler sent word to Sherman that the Confederates were attacking, to which Sherman sent back, "You must be badly
scared over there." The courier gave Appler the message in a loud voice
so that the entire regiment could hear it. Laughter broke out, and the entire 53rd Ohio broke ranks and returned to camp without orders. It was
an unfortunate occurrence in the most advanced of all Union camps.[23]

Prentiss was initially no more convinced by the firing than was Sherman, but when a messenger from the front returned to warn him, Prentiss sent messengers scurrying to the rear to warn the other divisions.
Prentiss also rode to Peabody, with whom he had already argued. Once
he realized what the colonel had done, he scolded him for his action:
"You have brought on an attack for which I am unprepared, and I shall
hold you responsible," the general snarled. Peabody glared back and re-
torted, "General, you will soon see that I was not mistaken." Nevertheless, the men of the 25th Missouri were proud that they "had the honor
of opening the battle."[24]

By this time, Peabody had already sent out more of his brigade to aid
Powell's outnumbered command. Powell was retreating to his camps,
but arriving columns changed his mind—first those of the 16th Wisconsin pickets, who were now the front line, and then five companies
of the 21st Missouri, led in person by the regiment's colonel, David
Moore. Moore was not convinced it was a general attack, telling Powell
that it was only an enemy patrol and "we would finish them up in no
time." Captain Edward Saxe of the Wisconsin contingent was not so
sure about things either. His men were entirely green; they had just

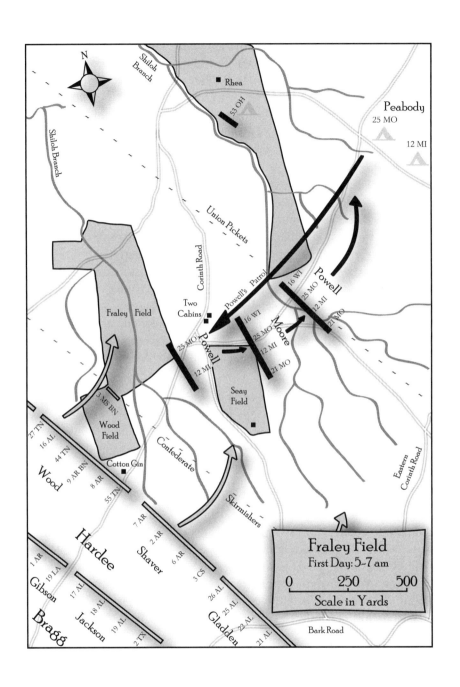

N

Shiloh Branch

Rhea

Peabody
25 MO

53 OH

12 MI

Shiloh Branch

Powell

Union Pickets

Corinth Road

Powell's Patrol

16 WI

Powell

Two Cabins

25 MO
12 MI

Fraley Field

16 WI

21 MO

25 MO

Powell

Moore

12 MI

12 MI

25 MO

21 MO

3 MS BN

Seay Field

Wood Field

Confederate

Cotton Gin

Eastern Corinth Road

27 TN
16 AL
44 TN
9 AR BN
8 AR
55 TN

Wood

Hardee

7 AR

Skirmishers

2 AR

Shaver

6 AR

Fraley Field
First Day: 5-7 am

1 AR
19 LA

3 CS

26 AL

0   250   500

Gibson

17 AL

25 AL

Bragg

Jackson

18 AL
19 AL
2 TX

Gladden

22 AL
21 AL

Scale in Yards

Bark Road

received ammunition for the first time the day before. When Moore ordered him to come along, Saxe asked where, and Moore responded that he could position his command to the left or right of the Missourians. Saxe took off his coat and threw it to the ground, barking, "Boys, we will fall in on the right; we will head them out." As ranking officer, Moore took charge and formed his motley band into a line in Seay Field, only to face another Confederate brigade, Robert Shaver's Arkansans. As Powell had retreated eastward, he had inadvertently moved across the front of Hardee's line, thus leaving Wood's position and taking the stand on Shaver's front. Caring not who was on his front, Moore could nevertheless see he had more on his hands than he could handle, and he sent word for the remainder of his regiment to move to the front as well. Lieutenant Colonel Humphrey Woodyard soon appeared with the other five companies of the 21st Missouri.[25]

Despite arriving Federal reinforcements, Shaver and Gladden, farther to the right, far outflanked Moore's short line but did not extend all the way to Lick Creek, which continually worried the Confederate high command. Bragg kept staff officers out to patrol the right flank of Hardee's and Gladden's brigades. Giles B. Cooke of Bragg's staff found from Gladden's right regimental commander, Daniel Adams, that his flank was still nearly a mile from Lick Creek. Bragg planned to use his reserve brigades to fill the gap, but just then, the main area of importance was still on Shaver's front. Here the fighting significantly expanded as Shaver's troops hit Moore's line. Greater casualties began to accrue as a result, despite the antiquated flintlocks of the 6th and 7th Arkansas. Soldiers went down all along the line, as did a few officers, such as Captain Saxe of the 16th Wisconsin. He fell on the north side of Seay Field, the first officer to die at Shiloh. The ranking officer was not doing much better; Moore himself was hit in the leg below the knee. It would eventually require amputation because the bone was completely shattered. Command of the small force fell to Woodyard.[26]

Fallen officers were not the greatest concern at this point, however. The main effort was to fall back to the support of the brigade, where a substantial line could be formed to halt what was evidently a major Confederate force. The forward elements of Peabody's brigade thus took successive stands as they gradually fell back under the increasing Confederate pressure, first on yet another small fork of Shiloh Branch and then farther back toward the brigade line. Fortunately, Peabody was at the same time posting his line on a ridge in front of the brigade camps, and the patrol and others who had joined them welcomed the sight of additional arms as they fell back. Peabody's presence also inspired the green troops, as this was not his first action. He had been wounded earlier in the war at the surrender at Lexington, Missouri. Now, the colonel rode the lines, encouraging, "Lexington, men, Lexington; remember Lexington!"[27]

Fortunately for Powell and Woodyard, the Confederate pursuit was anything but the "Alpine avalanche" that Beauregard later described, and the less than swift advance resulted in dwindling fire a little before 7:00 A.M. Such a lull illustrated the already-growing issues in the Confederate attack. The Confederate plan was already running late—perhaps fitting because the attack itself was as much as two days late. If the Confederate intention had been to surprise the enemy at daylight in their camps, the plan failed. Despite one Confederate officer describing his men as being "somewhat refreshed from the night's rest," the Confederate army was not up and formed before daylight. Granted, they would not have been able to get to the Union camps undetected anyway, but having the army ready before daylight and advancing forward would have added to what surprise they hoped to gain. Instead, when Powell's Union patrol encountered Hardcastle's pickets, Hardee's line was in the process of having breakfast and was not ready to move out. It took an hour or so for Hardee to get his men fed, in line, and ready to advance, thus allowing the preliminary fighting in Fraley Field to linger. It was only around 6:00 A.M., an hour after daylight, that Hardee's troops advanced to the attack.[28]

Once it started, the attack was anything but quick and overwhelming. The green troops found it difficult in the vast woods of Shiloh to keep alignment, on which all order and cohesion in Civil War tactics rested. "We marched in rank as much as possible," one Louisianan wrote, "but quite often the trees spread forth their branches so much and the terrain was so rugged that we had to break ranks and walk like serpents, making *zigzags*." He also noted that occasionally a tree limb would catch a musket just right and it would go off accidentally. Thus, the green officers frequently halted their equally green men to align the ranks before moving on, the most notable case being when Wood described "an interval" opening between him and Shaver. Shiloh was quickly demonstrating the vast difference between actual fighting and the level, open drill fields to which most of these men were accustomed. Thomas Jordan, who had talked Beauregard into letting him go into the fight because he had been held in the rear at Manassas, reported that he "repeatedly found [units] halted for want of orders." What would have been a quick movement against such small numbers later in the war turned out to be a fatal delay for the Confederates in those early hours at Shiloh.[29]

The Confederate line did advance slowly, however; Shaver met and drove back Woodyard in Seay Field and beyond. The rest of the army shuffled forward as well, with Bragg, Polk, and Breckinridge trying to keep the allotted distance between their lines and those to their front and wondering at the sounds: "That is Robinson's battery," several stated, "there goes Ketchum's." The rearward tension was evident: when it came his turn to advance, Breckinridge yelled at his men, "Fall in if you are going to fight, if you are not give your guns to someone else." At least one Kentuckian took exception, writing that it was "entirely uncalled for as we had not previously received orders from anyone to form." Along with the advancing hordes rumbled their ammunition trains and sundry other army implements such as ambulances. Most significantly, by this time Johnston was on the field, taking command and hurrying his troops forward. Parting with Beauregard near the latter's headquarters, Johnston initially followed the ever-important right (to turn the Federal left), following Gladden's and Shaver's brigades. A staff officer remembered, "Instantly he quickened to a gallop, with the staff and escort following, and right into the *melee* we plunged." When one of his staff recommended Johnston not expose himself so carelessly, the general only smiled and moved farther toward the front, cheered by the troops he passed. He instructed them, "Shoot low boys; it takes two to carry one off the field," and witnessed the minor fighting by Shaver's men in Seay Field, even helping to reform a portion of the brigade that evidently broke in this their first fight. To some of the Arkansas men, he shouted, "Men of Arkansas! They say you boast of your prowess with the bowie-knife. To-day you wield a nobler weapon—the bayonet. Employ it well." A Tennessean similarly remembered him telling them, "Forward! Every man do his duty and the day is ours!"[30]

Shiloh is often called a military surprise; P. G. T Beauregard described the coup as "one of the most surprising surprises ever achieved," and historian Wiley Sword has termed the battle the "Pearl Harbor of the

Civil War." The surprise at Shiloh is complicated, however, and in many
ways was not a surprise at all—depending on the definition. There is
also the thesis put forth by William J. Hardee and others that the Federals
actually attacked the Confederate army. "At early dawn," Hardee wrote,
"the enemy attacked the skirmishers in front of my line." Such an idea
is not widespread and bears little on the question of surprise at Shiloh.[31]

On the strategic (or operational) level, Shiloh was indeed a total surprise. One Indianan put it in succinct terms just one day after the battle
ended while writing to his mother: "Well the long looked for battle has
come and it came when no one was looking for it." Even higher-level
Federals admitted as much; Lieutenant Colonel Americus V. Rice, commanding the frontline 57th Ohio, wrote, "That we were sur-prised there
can be no doubt." In dealing with this larger context, despite skirmishing in the days before April 6, the Federal commanders from Grant on
down had no idea that the entire Confederate Army of the Mississippi
was confronting them. They did not believe that they would be attacked
in force and have to fight the biggest battle in American history to date.
In that sense, Shiloh was indeed similar to Pearl Harbor. Despite Grant
and Sherman taking the viewpoint to their graves that they were not
surprised, the accepted fact is that the Confederates slipped up on the
Federals and launched a massive attack that the Army of the Tennessee
was not expecting. Basil Duke later wrote that if these circumstances
do "not constitute a surprise, then there is no use for such a word in the
language." Others expressed a similar idea, with even the Confederates being surprised that their surprise worked so well. Colonel William
Preston on Johnston's staff marveled that the Federals "evidently did
not suspect that we were in force in the neighborhood." Beauregard had
been wrong all along; the Federals were not suspecting them, they were
not behind entrenchments, and Johnston's determination paid off.[32]

Many Federals did not even try to defend against accusations of surprise. Stephen Hurlbut later wrote, "It is certain that great principles of
war, which after all, are only applications of strong common sense, were
violated." He also reminded everyone that the reorganization on April
5 instituted "changes in command which are not made on the eve of
battle." A soldier in the 57th Ohio described how "we were unprepared
to meet them we were not expecting them and they came on us with
about forty thousand men and we had not a line formed yet and they
poured in on us like blackbirds into a cornfield." Interestingly, the visiting wife of the 11th Iowa's Colonel William Hall was asked if they were

surprised. "We were in our tent and not prepared to receive company," she responded, adding: "In fact, we were both en dishabille when a big cannon-shot tore through the tent. A caller at that early hour, considering its unexpectedness, and our condition, may possibly be regarded as a surprise." Even Prentiss himself later admitted, "I can only reply for myself that I had not the slightest idea that a general engagement was to be fought on that day." Major Benjamin Fearing of the 77th Ohio years later told a reporter that others may not have been surprised, but "so far as I was concerned I was not only surprised, but astounded."[33]

On the tactical level, however, the Federals were not as surprised as later newspapers described. The press ran stories leading readers to believe that the Confederates had sneaked up on the Union soldiers, reached their camps, and suddenly bayoneted the soldiers as they slept. That would have been a remarkable surprise indeed, but it did not happen that way. In the largest sense, the Federals knew the enemy was in their front; skirmishing across the front line had been frequent in previous days. More significantly, Peabody's patrol uncovered the Confederate army a mile out from the camps, so Johnston had to start his attack a mile from the Union camps. It took precious hours for the green Confederates, tramping through unknown terrain and woods and hampered by Federals taking stands and delaying the advance all along the way, to reach those Federal camps they were supposed to assault at daylight.[34]

In those intervening hours, Federal commanders from Sherman and Prentiss on down realized that they were indeed under attack in force and that they had to defend their positions. Thus, the Federals had several minutes in some cases and hours in others to sound the long roll, form their lines, and take positions to defend their encampment. One Federal in W. H. L. Wallace's division summed it up well: "We heard the cannon and soon after small arms, [and] preparation to fall in had been made by the boys and when an Orderly dashed with the word they were fighting in front it was not very much of a surprise." An Ohioan in Hildebrand's brigade similarly noted, "They were all in line of battle long before the rebels reached us." Iowan Samuel Byers noted correctly, "In most instances the Federal regiments fired first." Thus Everett Peabody, who received precious little credit after the battle, should actually have been lauded as a hero for putting in motion the events that sounded the alarm and allowed the Federals to meet the enemy formed and ready.[35]

In that intervening period between when Peabody's patrol found the Confederates at dawn and when the Confederates first began assaulting the Union camps after 7:00 A.M., the Union commanders all posted their regiments in appropriate lines. Sherman's division formed on the slopes of Shiloh Branch, with McDowell advancing from his camps southward on the right while still watching the Owl Creek bridge with two companies of the 6th Iowa and a howitzer from the 6th Indiana Battery. Ralph Buckland moved his men southward from their camps and formed his Ohio men on the lip of the ridge overlooking the slopes leading to Shiloh Branch west of Shiloh Church. Jesse Hildebrand also advanced his two Ohio units north of Shiloh Branch. Down the line, Prentiss formed his two brigades to the front of their camps, and David Stuart did likewise farther to the east overlooking Locust Grove Branch.[36]

Only the 53rd Ohio was outside the protective shield of Shiloh and Locust Grove branches, although Prentiss did not have the luxury of posting the majority of his men behind deep creek valleys either. His division primarily fronted the table land of the Shiloh divide, although a portion of Madison Miller's men on the left overlooked a growing valley as Locust Grove Branch flowed eastward. Still, the 53rd Ohio was on its own, and they would be the first to meet the enemy, exposed as they were. It did not help that their colonel was about to come unglued in the process. Yet even they formed a line of battle before the Confederates attacked their camp.[37]

Peabody had thus done yeoman work in allowing time for the remainder of the army to form their lines and take substantial positions. As a result, when the slow and plodding Confederate advance began to approach the Union camps around 7:00 A.M., they did not find sleeping and surprised Federals who offered little resistance. Rather, they found regiment after regiment with artillery batteries in line, ready and waiting to meet them.[38]

In that sense, Shiloh was no surprise, except perhaps to the Confederates who expected no such reception.

6

"This Valley of Death"

Patrick Ronayne Cleburne had come a long way—literally—to Shiloh that morning of April 6. Born in County Cork, Ireland, he later migrated to America, eventually settling in Helena, Arkansas. His connections with that state and its connection with the Confederacy brought him into the war and garnered for him one of the highest places in Southern memory. Yet Cleburne's choice to side with the Confederacy cost him dearly: his premature death at Franklin. April 6 was not a good day for him either, because it was his brigade that initially attacked the Union camps in the first phase of the battle.[1]

Cleburne's brigade of Arkansas, Mississippi, and Tennessee troops held Hardee's extreme left position. With the rest of the corps, the brigade advanced in line of battle around 6:30 A.M., the 15th Arkansas in front as skirmishers and the 2nd Tennessee still on the left en echelon guarding the flank. The regiments tried in vain to keep the correct alignments as regimental and brigade commanders found that the heavy timber played havoc on their neatly dressed lines. Cleburne was especially concerned with keeping a firm hold on Wood's brigade to his right; he purposefully remained on the right of his brigade to make sure it was done. Portions of Cleburne's troops moved through the northern extent of Fraley Field, with one eyewitness recalling, "Through this field General Cleburne's brigade moved in fine order, with loud and inspiring cheers." The terrain soon became more problematic as the men tramped slowly northeastward toward the Federal camps and began to cross offshoots of Shiloh Branch. One Tennessean wrote, "A worse place could not have been selected for men to go through, wading creeks, going through thick undergrowth & swamp land, sometimes in mud and water up to our waste." Moving over this undulating terrain, Cleburne's men soon began to meet isolated Federals, obviously pickets, some of whom they shot. Moving on, they suddenly topped the ridge that led down into the valley of Shiloh Branch. There they could see the white Sibley tents of Sherman's division on the other side: Buckland's brigade to the left of the road and Hildebrand's to the right. They could also see the Federal regiments formed up and in line—certainly odd for a surprise—and at places even moving forward. No wonder Cleburne quickly sent word back to Johnston that he had located "a heavy force."[2]

The reason Cleburne hit this solid Union line first was a result of the Confederate deployment. Hardee's corps had bivouacked in line of battle fronting northeast, not north in conformity with the general lay of the Federal camps that faced relatively south behind Shiloh and Locust Grove branches. The reason is less important than the result, but the misaligned deployment was mainly the consequence of deploying perpendicular to the Corinth Road at that position. Nine times out of ten (with Chickamauga being a notable exception), Civil War units deployed perpendicular to the axis of advance on which they moved. Where the Confederates first formed their line, the Corinth Road ran southwest to northeast, but the road took a sharp turn to the left just past the Confederate deployment area, between their first line and the Union camps. Thus the Federal camps, as was also custom, aligned perpendicular to the road, but at their position the road ran more north and south than at an angle. The result was that the initial Confederate attack struck the Federal camp line, and its attending infantry and artillery line, at an angle. Cleburne, on the extreme left, was consequently the first unit to hit the Federals, and it would take some time before the right of Hardee's Corps was able to swing around and attack as well. That Powell's augmented patrol was making stands in the intervening territory on that Confederate right flank made the swing into correct alignment even slower.[3]

Cleburne saw no reason to wait until all the frontline Confederate troops could make a coordinated attack, however. The brigades thus attacked piecemeal as they individually approached the Union line, with Cleburne leading the way. He deployed his artillery under Captain John T. Trigg and prepared to dive off into the valley and assault Sherman's camps. Cleburne ordered Trigg to "wake him up with a few shells," and the guns swung into action. These were the first artillery shots at Shiloh, around 7:10 A.M.[4]

Eleven or so miles to the north, Ulysses S. Grant was seated at breakfast when he heard the sound of those first artillery shots as they rumbled down the valley.

Cleburne did not know it yet, but the Federals were wide awake and did not need a wake-up call. In fact, they were not only awake, but were already in line, positioned to defend their camps. The Federals had their own problems, however—most notably Jesse Hildebrand at his headquarters tent just a few paces west of Shiloh Church. Hildebrand had felt so bad the night before that he had "retired" early, and he now requested Lieutenant Colonel Wills De Hass of the 77th Ohio to turn over command of that regiment to Major Benjamin Fearing and help him command the brigade. Similarly, in the 48th Ohio, Colonel Peter J. Sullivan and Lieutenant Colonel Job R. Parker were so at odds that they were not speaking to one another. Still, the line the Federals took partway down the gradual slope leading into Shiloh Branch assured them at least of a dominant position. Besides far outranging Cleburne's left flank, the Federals also had the advantage of terrain as the slope up the hill toward the Union line was gradual and cleared; the trees had been cut for firewood and part of the area burned. One Ohioan said it looked "as though some farmer had determined to clear a farm for himself and had abandoned the undertaking in disgust." The sight of the gradual slope easily fooled anyone who had not trudged up it. One of Cleburne's colonels, Benjamin Hill, was later convinced, writing that his troops were at the bottom of "a long hill, upon which the enemy were hidden." Moreover, the Union position on the military crest rather than the geographic crest assured the Federal regiments that the attacking enemy would have no blind spot to take cover in or use to reform lines. It also allowed the artillery of Sherman's division, Taylor's Illinois battery on Buckland's front and Waterhouse's Illinois battery of James rifles farther to the east on Hildebrand's front, to rake the enemy over the infantry's heads. The five remaining guns of Behr's Indiana Battery took a similar position in McDowell's line to the west, commanding, McDowell reported, "several openings to the front." It was a terribly strong position. One interested investigator noted, "each camp was a fortress in itself."[5]

Some of the Federal officers in command did not realize how strong it was. Wills De Hass stood at Shiloh Church, looking toward the loud noises already coming from the valley below, but could see little: "Scarcely a man was visible," he wrote. "But as the unclouded sun fell on their burnished arms the whole scene became lighted up, presenting a panorama most effective, and one which can never be forgotten." Similarly, Major Ezra Taylor, Sherman's chief of artillery, had been on the job less than a day. He arrived at his new division and duties on April 5, busily getting the new batteries situated in camp. He later reported that as a result of that difficult work on April 5, he had not had time to go out and scout his new front. Intending on doing so on April 6, Taylor called for "an early breakfast" so he could "make a thorough survey of the country in front of my position." He instead reported, "My horse was scarcely saddled when the approach of the enemy was discovered."[6]

Cleburne's troops soon found out how strong the enemy position was. In fact, Cleburne encountered major problems even before he tangled with the Union lines. Being the extreme left of the front line, he had nothing on his left flank and likewise found a growing gap on his right as Wood's brigade drifted to the east to keep connected with Shaver, the next brigade down the line. Even worse, as Cleburne's six regiments vaulted down into the creek valley, they discovered an extremely marshy bottom tangled with "green briers and grape-vines," according to Colonel Hill of the 5th Tennessee. Much of it was muddy and swampy where the creeks split into two separate branches. Cleburne described an "almost impassable morass" that limited movement on his right. To top it all off, the Federals were advancing on Cleburne at several points. The 57th Ohio had by this time moved all the way down into the valley under their lieutenant colonel, Americus Rice, commanding because Colonel William Mungen and Major Silas Walker were both sick, but they soon gave up their position for a more defensible location on the high ground nearer their camp. Sherman also ordered Buckland to send a regiment to the front. While riding back to his lines, Buckland chanced upon the feuding Sullivan and Parker of the 48th Ohio, who had actually managed to agree on something and requested that he allow them to do the duty. Parker thus marched the regiment down into the valley of Shiloh Branch to cross over to the other side. "Or regiment marched down the road to the Branch and was in the act of Crosing the Branch," Enos Brobson wrote, "when our lewtenant Col saw the rebels close by us." "For a short time our men wavered," Parker noted, but Brobson explained how they got out of it: "Our regiment Whealed around and marched up the hill." The Federal line soon stabilized and held firmly, but even then, the speed with which the Confederates advanced took Buckland's regiments by surprise. Brobson noted, "When our regiment fell in to ranks the rebels wasent more than 3 hundred yards of us." Another Ohioan elaborated, writing home that the enemy opened fire at twenty rods, "having crossed through a deep hollow with thick underbrush, which was the reason of their getting so close to us before we saw them."[7]

Other Federal commanders were just as confused, particularly Jesse Appler. Earlier that morning, Appler had grown more and more nervous as the minutes ticked away, and he could hear the sound of battle nearing. He could also look southward down the long length of Rhea Field and see Confederate columns of Wood's brigade sweeping past the opening. When Cleburne planted Trigg's Battery on the ridge opposite his camp, Appler began to panic. He sent more alerts to Sherman and struggled with what to do.[8]

Help was on the way, however. Allen Waterhouse, commanding the Illinois battery across the creek to the north, sent a section of guns under Lieutenant Abial R. Abbott that unlimbered on the knoll just north of the Ohio regiment's tents. There they took Trigg's artillery to task before being bested by numbers around 7:30 A.M. and retiring to the main body of the battery across Shiloh Branch. Also soon at hand was Sherman himself, who had by this time decided something was indeed happening. Sherman and his staff rode into Rhea Field, with a nervous Appler pointing in the direction of the enemy. Sherman rode to the high ground in the middle of the field and observed the Confederates crossing the southern end "as far as the eye could reach," he later wrote. There were others even nearer, though, unbeknownst to the general. An officer shouted, "Sherman, look to your right." Emerging from the creek bottom were Cleburne's skirmishers, the 15th Arkansas, and they let out a volley of buck and ball. One of the balls hit escort Thomas D. Holliday and killed him instantly. Sherman threw up a hand as if to shield himself, and one of the buckshot wounded him. That was all Sherman needed. He wheeled his horse around and sped away to command his division. As he galloped past, he yelled, "Appler, hold your position, I will support you." Probably thinking it was about time Sherman came around, Appler was on his own. Unfortunately for him, part of Cleburne's brigade was moving toward him at that very moment.[9]

Rather than move into the bog and get stuck there, Cleburne's brigade split and went around, with four regiments to the left and two to the right. Cleburne reported it "finally caused a wide opening in my line." It was so bad, Cleburne added, that "my own horse bogged down in it and threw me, and it was with great difficulty I got out." The regiments to the left crossed the creek and moved toward the Union line on the ridge, with William Bate's 2nd Tennessee refused on the left flank and the 24th and 5th Tennessee filling out the line to the right. The 15th Arkansas was also back in the main line from their skirmishing duty, as there was little skirmishers could do at this point: Cleburne was at close quarters with the enemy once he crossed the creek. He thus began his assault around 8:00 A.M.[10]

Cleburne met the quick volleys of Buckland's brigade as well as those of the 77th and 57th Ohio of Hildebrand's unit. Major Fearing in the 77th Ohio noted that the Confederate attack came "with a rush and a shout," and for a time it shook part of the 77th Ohio, which had a difficult enough time with their ponderous Belgian rifles. Indeed, one of the Ohioans commented that the regiment "was not in line of battle more than five minutes before the rebels opened fire on us." Still, they fought well. "We mowed them down by hundreds," Fearing wrote home, "and repelled their charge made up into our camp, and drove them back over the run they leaving many of their comrades behind." The Ohioans followed the retreating Confederates part of the way, retaking some of the ground they had earlier held, but the regiment soon returned "to our old position on the brow of the hill."[11]

The only real success Cleburne had was on the far left of his brigade, where the slightly detached 2nd Tennessee gained some ground by using a small hollow that fed southward into Shiloh Branch. The small valley ran between the 72nd and 48th Ohio on Buckland's right, and could have potentially given Buckland problems. He quickly ordered the 72nd Ohio to change front facing the ravine, with his left company at a right angle across the depression. There the regiment fended off several more attacks, but there were additional problems in the regiment, mainly brought about when Lieutenant Colonel Herman Canfield went down with a mortal wound. Because Major Leroy Crockett had been captured in the ruckus on April 4 and Buckland was commanding the brigade, the regiment now had no field officers as well as several captains out sick. Buckland quickly left the rest of the brigade in the hands of Colonel Joseph R. Cockerill of the 70th Ohio, who had bid his sixteen-year-old son a quick good-bye in the chaos, and Colonel Peter J. Sullivan of the 48th Ohio and remained on the right of the brigade, personally commanding his 72nd Ohio.[12]

Cleburne's troops made additional assaults up the hill, but they did not come close to breaking Sherman's line, isolated as they were and attacking without support from any other brigades. The heavy fire from the Federals cut down numerous Confederates, with one soldier of the

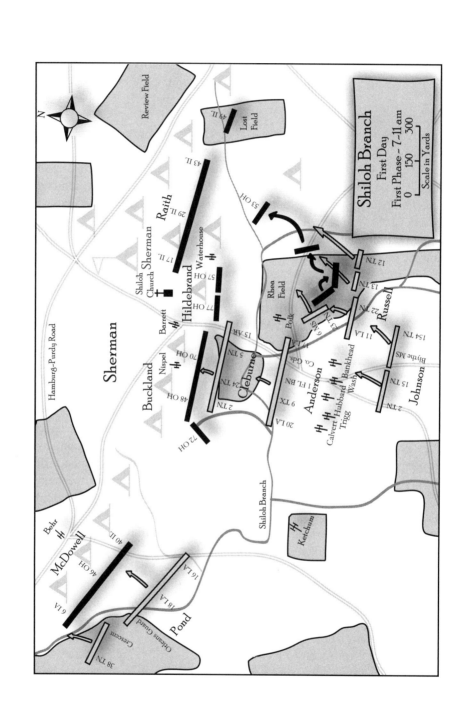

Shiloh Branch
First Day
First Phase ~ 7–11 am

0   150   300
Scale in Yards

Review Field

Lost Field

49 IL.

43 IL.

53 OH

Raith

29 IL.

Sherman

17 IL.

Shiloh Church

Waterhouse

57 OH

77 OH

Hildebrand

Rhea Field

Polk

6 MS.

12 TN.

13 TN.

22 TN.

Russell

154 TN.

Bankhead

Wash.

11 LA.

15 TN.

Johnson

2 TN.

Blythe MS

Barrett

Nispel

70 OH

Buckland

48 OH

72 OH

15 AR.

5 TN.

24 TN.

2 TN.

Cleburne

9 TX.

20 LA.

1 Fl. BN.

Co. Gds.

Anderson

Calvert Hubbard

Trigg

Sherman

Hamburg–Purdy Road

Shiloh Branch

Ketchum

Behr

40 IL.

McDowell

46 OH

6 IA.

16 IA.

18 LA.

Pond

Orleans Guard

Crescent

38 TN.

N

24th Tennessee writing that "the balls sung around my ears like bees." Trigg's artillery, which had by now been joined by Calvert's and Hubbard's batteries, all under corps artillery commander Francis Shoup, was not much help either. Cleburne noted, "So thick were the leaves, he could only see in one direction, while the enemy were playing on him from several." Beauregard had sent Thomas Jordan to the front to inspire the commanders to utilize their artillery "twelve guns at a point," but terrain like this mitigated the massing of artillery. Casualties thus began to mount, including Lieutenant Colonel J. T. Harris of the 15th Arkansas, who moved ahead of his line and fired his pistol at the enemy, only to be cut down quickly. Colonel Bate and Major William R. Doak of the 2nd Tennessee were also wounded, the latter hit nine times. Bate was hit by a ball through the leg as he led his regiment from the useless position on the left toward the center and an attack on the artillery firing so heavily on them. Before Bate went down, he yelled to his men, "My brave boys, the enemy must be driven back. I am going to charge them again!! How many of you will follow me?" The men moved on despite Bate's fall, letting out "a yell as Tennesseans only can give," one soldier remembered, but the attack again faltered. One member of the regiment remembered, "The mortification of a repulse in our first regular engagement was extreme; some wept, some cursed, and others lamented the death of some of our bravest officers and men." He added, "And not a few drifted to the rear." Despite his wound, Bate would go on to become a United States senator and sponsor the bill in the Senate to make this battlefield into a park. All that was years into the future, of course; now, Bate was more worried about the painful leg wound that ended his day early at Shiloh. Five other kinsmen would also be wounded or killed that day.[13]

The two Confederate regiments that went to the east of the morass had no better success. In fact, they were being cut up even more than their comrades to the west. The 6th Mississippi on the left and the 23rd Tennessee on the right scaled the ridge overlooking a tributary of Shiloh Branch and entered the northern portion of Rhea Field at an angle, only to find the air full of deadly projectiles. "Little clouds of smoke appeared, and we heard the cracking noise of timber being splintered by the bullets," one Mississippian wrote. Plus, they found the camp of Appler's 53rd Ohio, and the tents, ropes, and other campsite oddities quickly threw their lines into confusion.[14]

Despite the aid from the tents, Appler did not perform well. He had
already taken the regiment through several convoluted motions near
their camp before the men retired to the eastern edge of the field and
took position behind a few hay bales. Although the regiment fought
well, Appler was almost nonexistent even then, at one point (although
he later denied it) yelling to his men, "Retreat, boys, & save yourselves."
He then led the way. Once in the woods on a ridge to the rear, Appler
wanted to go farther, but several of his officers took a stand, with the
regiment's adjutant, Ephraim Dawes, telling him, "I was going to stay
. . . & he might do as he pleased." Again Appler shouted, "Fall back
and save yourselves." Some of the men did so and passed to the left of
the 49th Illinois. Appler would not be found until Monday night. Grant
later described his sort as "constitutional cowards, unfit for any military
position."[15]

Most of the Ohio regiment, with some leadership offered by Dawes,
nevertheless stood and fought east and then north of Rhea Field. The
Mississippians and Tennesseans of Cleburne's right flank found the
Ohioans in this first position and assaulted but could not drive them
back. The Tennesseans quickly broke and ran to the rear, to be reformed
later by Cleburne and Colonel Mat Martin, who was their former commander but "not then on duty." He would still be wounded with them
later in the day, sheepishly telling one Confederate who asked where he
was hit: "My son, I am wounded in the arm, in the leg, in the head, in
the body, and in another place which I have a delicacy in mentioning."
While the Tennesseans faltered, the Mississippians tried again, meeting
the same fate. Then they attacked a third time. Charging through the
53rd Ohio's camp and facing that regiment in front and Waterhouse's
battery on the ridge on their flank, which raked the line after some confusion as to whose troops they were, the Mississippians were cut to
pieces and had to fall back again.[16]

Ezra Taylor, commanding Sherman's artillery, reported that Waterhouse fought with "fine style and with excellent precision." Hundreds
of Mississippians and Tennesseans went down as a result. Lying down
in between assaults, one Mississippian told his friend, "I wish we could
get right-down in the earth." He had barely spoken the words when he
was killed. Most notable among the wounded Mississippians was their
colonel, John J. Thornton, who went down with a severe wound in the
thigh. He had taken the regimental colors after the bearer was hit, but
he was soon shot as well and put out of the war for good. As a member

of the Mississippi Secession Convention just over a year before, he had voted against secession and had purposefully been absent the day the document had been signed. Yet he was one of the first to join the Confederacy, being a militia officer before the war. Now he was wounded in defense of the action he could not bring himself to support. Major Robert Lowry was also wounded.[17]

Thornton was but one of many Mississippians and Tennesseans caught in the crossfire in Rhea Field that day. As an illustration of the extent of the damage, the Mississippians went into action with 425 men and had 300 of them killed or wounded in those three assaults. At 70 percent casualties, no wonder the regiment became known as the Bloody Sixth.[18]

Cleburne was thus having difficulty all along his line, unable to drive into Sherman's line at any point. Realizing the attack was spent on his right, Cleburne rode back around the morass to try to get better results on his left. That side was doing no better under Colonel Benjamin J. Hill, whom Beauregard had ordered to take command of Cleburne's four left regiments in his absence. In fact, Beauregard had sent staff officer Alexander R. Chisolm to the area to "see how things were going." Chisolm could not find Cleburne, but he found the brigade split apart. Isolated as they were from Wood, Shaver, and Gladden, Cleburne's regiments on the left responded that they needed support, which Chisolm reported to Beauregard.[19]

Support for Cleburne was fast approaching in the form of Braxton Bragg's corps in the second line of assault. Bragg correctly noted that the terrain had deformed Hardee's front line, with it "being weakened by extension and necessarily broken by the nature of the ground." Bragg's men were eager to participate. The general noted, "Such was the ardor of our troops that it was with great difficulty they could be restrained from closing up and mingling with the first line." Patton Anderson confirmed as much, writing that as the line moved forward, they suddenly realized they were no more than 200 or 300 yards behind Hardee instead of the prescribed 1,000 yards. They were also amazed at "rabbits, squirrels and other wild creatures of the forest scuttling by . . . driven frantic by the unwonted and terrific noises." Federal shots were also beginning to land among the men, causing one awkward scene involving an Arkansas captain in Gibson's brigade who had been pleading with his body servant slave to remain in the rear. The slave would not, but upon seeing a shell blow a tree apart and wound a man right in front of him, the slave declared, "Golly, Marster, I can't stand this." Similarly, on Ruggles's left, where a few Federals appeared, the general sent forward a gun and fired a few rounds, causing an inquiry from Hardee as to why his line was already firing. Despite the confusion, Bragg had five brigades to throw in, and two of those, on the far left, hurriedly came to Cleburne's support around the lowland of Shiloh Branch. Bragg followed them, moving forward in the rear of Ruggles's right, cautioning staff officers to bring forward ammunition trains to support the brigades.[20]

Some of the impetus for this move came from Albert Sidney Johnston, who had worked out the details by which he would go to the front and Beauregard would remain in rear, directing the overall operation. After participating in the advance on the right, Johnston rode back to the left near the two cabins that sat on the Corinth Road, watching Cleburne's brigade as it moved through Fraley Field toward Shiloh Church. Realizing the openness on Cleburne's left, Johnston called on Beauregard to provide aid, sending Jacob Thompson to find him. The staff officer remembered the scene: "The battle was then raging furiously. General Johnston was sitting on his horse where the bullets were flying like hail-stones. I galloped up to him amid the fire, and found him cool, collected, self-possessed, but still animated and in fine spirits." Johnston related he had just received a report that the enemy was "sending forward strong re-enforcements to our left," probably a reference to John McDowell. "Say to General Beauregard," Johnston yelled, "we are sweeping the field before us, and in less than half an hour we shall be in possession of their camps, and I think we shall press them to the river. Say, also, I have just learned from a scout, or messenger, that the enemy is moving up in force on our left, and that General [John] Breckinridge had better move to our left to meet him." As Thompson turned his horse, Johnston added: "Do not say to General Beauregard that this is an order, but he must act on what additional information he may receive. The reports to him are more to be relied on than to me."[21]

Beauregard was indeed in the rear, moving up with the army as it advanced. He soon took a position in the northern part of Fraley Field along the Plum Orchard Road, but events were already beginning to fool Beauregard even this early. Although the Creole had been in battle before at Manassas, he had been on the front lines there, where the other Johnston, Joseph E. Johnston, played the role in the rear that Beauregard now played at Shiloh. The sights of the rear of an army in combat were thus new to Beauregard, and would perhaps play a role in his command of the battle as the day progressed. Even this early, Beauregard had to utilize his large staff and escort to gather stragglers and reform them. He also sent them to bring up the ammunition wagons. Beauregard continued to operate in the flotsam of the army as he moved forward. In one instance, Jacob Thompson found a regiment without field officers. One of the captains stepped forward and told him "with great emotion, that they had no officers, and that he did not know what to do." Thompson informed Beauregard, who assigned staff officer Numa Augustin to take command of the regiment. Illustrating the chaos, by the time Thompson returned, the troops were gone.[22]

Lower-level officers were just as involved in deciding when to enter the fight, however. Bragg reported that his orders were "hardly necessary, for subordinate commanders, far beyond the reach of my voice and eye in the broken country occupied by us, had promptly acted on the necessity as it arose, and by the time the order could be conveyed the whole line was developed and actively engaged." Thus Bragg's troops began to enter the fight so that Breckinridge's units would not be needed on the critical left. Indeed, the threat soon proved to be false despite the entire reserve corps beginning to move in that direction. Still, some Confederate presence was needed to Cleburne's left, so Bragg sent forward Preston Pond and a few companies of cavalry under Captain T. F. Jenkins to fill the void. The plan, after all, was to plug the gap between Lick and Owl Creek, so Pond's Louisianans and Tennesseans filed off to the left and began to trudge through the branches that fed into either Shiloh Branch or Owl Creek. One Louisianan said that his major's "horse almost stayed there, having floundered up to its ears, and it was with much difficulty that we were able to extricate it from there." As Pond's soldiers battled the boggy creek bottoms, Pond and Chisolm of Beauregard's staff reconnoitered the front and found the enemy around a log house on the high ridge north of Shiloh Branch.[23]

Unfortunately for Bragg, he soon found that even he did not have enough numbers to fill the gap adequately. With his other regiments supporting Hardee's other brigades to the east, Pond was all he had to support Cleburne's left, and his brigade was not big enough. As a result, Pond had to split his brigade, sending the 38th Tennessee and the Crescent Regiment and a section of Ketchum's Battery to the left to take and hold the Owl Creek Bridge (one of the only avenues into the cul-de-sac besides the gap between Lick and Owl creeks). The other three regiments went in on Cleburne's left, traversing the valley of Shiloh Branch closer to Shiloh Church and there meeting McDowell's troops. With only three regiments, the 18th Louisiana, Orleans Guard, and 16th Louisiana, Pond became cautious—actually more than he needed to be, because McDowell was even more nervous. His line was greatly extended and contained large gaps, mostly due to the need to cover the Owl Creek bridge as well as send his left regiment, the 40th Illinois, across a small tributary of Shiloh Branch farther to the front and left to aid Buckland's flank. Neither Pond nor McDowell seemed to want to fight, despite some firing by the 6th Indiana Battery to clear out some Confederate skirmishers around a corn crib. Yet indications were that heavy fighting could start anytime, and the surgeons began to remove the sick from Union camps. One Ohio doctor commandeered two wagons and managed to get his sick as well as his papers out of the 46th Ohio campsite. Nevertheless, the action to Cleburne's left simmered down to minor skirmishing as Pond crept forward toward the camps. In the somewhat overly excited Orleans Guard, Major Leon Querouze cautioned his men, "My brave friends, this is the moment to show your mettle; be calm and do not hurry." They took him at his word.[24]

While Pond dawdled to the west, Bragg's more supportive contribution to Cleburne's effort was sending Patton Anderson's brigade forward, where it soon went into action immediately to the rear of Cleburne. In fact, Anderson's fresh regiments took over the assaults on Sherman's position, with Cleburne's men joining in. With the 5th Company of the famed Washington Artillery of New Orleans (the other four companies being in Virginia) "tearing through the woods like madmen," one observer noted, they unlimbered alongside Shoup's guns on the ridge south of Shiloh Branch and added to the firepower of some twenty-four guns. Under this fire, Anderson soon led his Florida, Louisiana, and Texas regiments forward over the ridge on which the artillery sat. The regiments first delivered a volley and then fell back below the brow to reload before surging into the valley around 9:00 A.M.[25]

Anderson found difficulty immediately. The enemy's skirmishers were causing him much delay, and he had not even reached the main line on the hill. Anderson chalked their success up to "features remarkably favorable for the operations of skillful skirmishers." Then there was the morass that had so defiled Cleburne. Anderson wrote that it was "thickly overgrown with various species of shrubs, saplings, and vines, so densely interwoven as to sometimes require the use of the knife to enable the footman to pass." Colonel August Reichard of the 20th Louisiana reported that the undergrowth was so thick he could not see "five paces ahead." The defile thus caused some separation between the regiments, especially the Confederate Guards and the 17th Louisiana. Then Anderson had to tangle with the enemy line, which he remarked had "all the advantages of presented by such shelter on the one side and obstacles on the other." Anderson nevertheless led his troops forward, covered by the "diversion" of the Washington Artillery to the rear. Unfortunately for them, some of Cleburne's retreating soldiers plagued Anderson's troops, throwing them into confusion. The right of the brigade, including the 17th Louisiana, the Confederate Guards, and the Florida battalion, despite losing their commander, Major T. A. Mc-Donell, made the most headway, but the brigade still had to fall back under the brow of the hill.[26]

Anderson's regiments were not stopping, however. Colonel W. A. Stanley, whose horse was shot from under him, and his 9th Texas made three separate assaults but could not make any headway. The 17th Louisiana made two attempts, but the regiment split in half during the advance and Lieutenant Colonel Charles Jones was thrown from his spooked horse. He succeeded in catching the horse and remounting, but all was chaos. He then received a minié ball in the left arm, had it dressed, and continued to command his regiment.[27]

A Louisianan in the Confederate Guards Response Battalion simply known as Private Harris showed similar bravery, if little tact. When the unit's flag went down, the private stepped forward and offered to carry it. "Take that flag, sir, and never yield as long as you can hold it," bellowed Major Franklin H. Clack. The Louisianan did so, even when Patton Anderson rode up and grabbed the banner. Having been turned back more than once, Anderson decided to lead his men personally and ordered Harris to give him the flag. The bearer refused, stating that his major had ordered him not to give it up under any circumstances. Anderson looked at the plucky color-bearer and remarked, "Then *you* will do, go ahead." Harris was later wounded severely, but it was all for nothing; Anderson could get no farther than Cleburne.[28]

More help was on the way as Polk's third corps began to enter the fight. A strong Federal line was blocking the way at Shiloh Branch, and Beauregard began to send the rearward units forward to help break through. Polk's four brigades moved forward, trudging through a thicket before deploying into line of battle. Despite the beauty of early morning, the soldiers knew what awaited them. Cannoneer John E. Magee wrote that "by the time the first streaks of early dawn tinged the eastern heavens, the roar of small arms was heard." As they passed down the Corinth Road, "occasionally halting at short intervals for the brigade in front to push forward," noted Lieutenant Colonel Robert H. Barrow of the 11th Louisiana, the left of each brigade spilled out into Fraley Field. Artillery rounds began to pepper their advance, killing and wounding a few soldiers of the 12th Tennessee of Russell's brigade and the 5th Tennessee of Stewart's; one shot cut off the flagpole of the latter. One Kentuckian described the enemy artillery as making "terrible havoc of horses, timber and every thing it could reach." Yet the carnage was just beginning as two of Polk's brigades eventually moved to the right and two went in on Cleburne's front at Shiloh Church. A watching Jesse Hildebrand was amazed that so many Confederates kept pouring out of the woods to his front. He wrote of the Confederates "presenting himself in columns of regiments at least four deep."[29]

Of most immediate help to Cleburne and Anderson was Bushrod Johnson's Mississippi and Tennessee regiments, which, after some convoluted marching to the left and then back to the right, met Ruggles's staff officer, L. D. Sandidge, who "begged" them to support Anderson's stalled advance. Johnson thus followed the same path as the others, directly up the Corinth Road. Johnson had literally walked out of captivity at Fort Donelson along with his aide, Captain John H. Anderson, who was beside his commander this morning. Now Johnson pushed off into the valley in support of Cleburne and Anderson, going in a little to the right of the other two. The morass that so hampered Cleburne and Anderson affected Johnson as well, with Blythe's Mississippi and the 154th Tennessee regiments (the latter retaining its old prewar militia number) moving to the right across one of the branches of Shiloh Branch and going through the northern limits of Rhea Field. Johnson was still with his left wing and reported that just crossing the stream "caused some delay in passing the artillery and the infantry of the left wing." Polk's Tennessee Battery managed to cross and unlimbered on the reverse slope of a ridge in Rhea Field. There it fired on Waterhouse around 9:00 A.M., but it paid a heavy price, losing several of its men and its commander, West Point–trained Captain Marshall Polk. Polk received a leg wound so severe that he could not be removed from the field. The battery fared little better; in just a few minutes, only one of the guns was serviceable. With the hope of doing something about the destructive fire from Waterhouse's Battery across Shiloh Branch, Bragg soon sent the two right regiments, Blythe's Mississippians and the 154th Tennessee, farther to the right to outflank the Union position.[30]

Johnson's infantry did no better on the left. That wing was shot to pieces in the valley of Shiloh Branch, much as Cleburne and Anderson had been before. In fact, Johnson admitted to "a momentary wavering of the ranks," which was remedied by the 15th Tennessee's commander, Lieutenant Colonel R. C. Tyler, who drew his pistol to enforce his order to reform. He would have three horses shot from under him during the debacle and would soon be wounded himself, forcing him to leave the field. Colonel Knox Walker's 2nd Tennessee also broke while moving up to support Polk's Battery. Johnson reformed them twice, only to see each time "the lines . . . broken from the unsteadiness of the men under fire." Portions of Anderson's brigade took up the assault alongside Johnson's troops, with the 9th Texas making two more fruitless assaults. All the while, casualties mounted in the stalled advance. To the right, Johnson's Mississippians lost both Colonel Blythe, "shot dead from his horse" according to Johnson, as well as the lieutenant colonel, D. L. Herron, mortally wounded ten minutes later. Also wounded was seventy-one-year-old John Thompson, who was fighting in the ranks beside his thirteen-year-old son. Yet the major casualty was Johnson himself, shot in the stomach. He fell as he was reforming Walker's 2nd Tennessee a third time. Command of the brigade fell to Colonel Preston Smith of the 154th Tennessee, and command of that regiment went to Lieutenant Colonel Marcus Wright, who was hit in the right knee but not disabled.[31]

An odd reunion of sorts took place as the wounded Johnson rode to the rear. He found his way to a hospital, where, as chance would have it, two of his former students were lying wounded, "awaiting our turn with the overworked surgeons." Johnson had taught at the University of Nashville, and two of his students had left at the beginning of the war and joined the 6th Mississippi. Wounded in Rhea Field, they were at the hospital when they saw Johnson ride up. Although wounded themselves, they helped Johnson off his horse and laid him on the ground. "He was glad to see us," Patrick Henry remembered, and "after inquiring as to our wounds, he asked us to look in the back pocket of his uniform coat and get a Yankee News paper, that some of his boys had picked up on the battlefield, that he wanted to read the News." The surgeons soon called the boys' turn, and "we left him there reading his paper."[32]

Even adding Polk's other brigade, Robert Russell's, to the melee did little to tip the scales at Shiloh Branch. Rather than send Russell's Louisiana and Tennessee brigade into the Corinth Road sector, Bragg motioned them in support of the Tennesseans and Mississippians of Cleburne's brigade in Rhea Field. Leaving Bankhead's Tennessee Battery at 9:00 A.M. to add to the growing weight of guns along the ridge south of the creek, Russell ranged out to the right, with the 11th Louisiana and 22nd Tennessee going into action in the general vicinity of the rest of the hodgepodge of regiments in the valley of the creek east of the morass. As they approached, one Tennessean described the terrain: "Double quick was the order and on we went through the woods, through thickets, through briars, through sloughs, through mud and water, over fences when it was possible to keep our lines dressed." When fugitives from the earlier attacks poured through his lines, Russell advanced even more quickly with the left, leaving the right wing a little behind. Fortunately, his division commander, Charles Clark, was there and told him to go on with the left and he would get the right moving. Clark sent the two right regiments farther to the east to find a flank that could be turned; obviously Sherman's line was not going to fall by frontal assault anytime soon. Polk wrote in understatement: "The resistance at this point was as stubborn as at any other on the field." Bragg told Colonel Alfred J. Vaughan and his 13th Tennessee that Waterhouse's battery was "a source of great annoyance to our troops, and that it must be taken at all hazards." The 13th Tennessee thus veered right, passing through the camps of the 53rd Ohio but eventually splitting apart, "a blunder by our major," one Tennessean recalled. Six companies went around the right while four moved directly toward the camps. The 12th Tennessee ranged even farther to the right toward a cavalry camp. There Colonel Tyree H. Bell and his 12th Tennessee apparently engaged what was left of the 53rd Ohio in the woods northeast of their camps. Bell had two horses shot from under him and was injured when thrown.[33]

At the same time, Russell's regiments on the left only participated in the growing chaos south of Shiloh Church. They were caught up in the same old attack-and-repulse sequence that had played out all morning. Division commander Clark was by this time back with the left, and with Captain John A. Buckner of his staff by his side, he first led the

11th Louisiana to attack Waterhouse's battery. They topped the ridge in Rhea Field and were immediately driven back by the storm of shot and shell, with the right of the regiment "embarrassed by the tents and picket ropes." Not all the regiment had even participated; instead, only a few companies had engaged the enemy as a result of the morass on the left and difficult terrain, what Robert Barrow described as "a creek, a dense thicket of undergrowth of briers and vines and a slough." As the Louisianans fell back (all except the color-bearer, who had to be ordered to the rear), Russell brought up the remainder of the regiment and the 22nd Tennessee. Then the attack was renewed amid the bloodshed. Even one of Bragg's staff officers, Captain W. O. Williams, joined in, with Clark reporting that he "was conspicuous for his courageous bearing, waving his sword in the front and being the first upon the hill in our second charge." Casualties again ran high in the unsuccessful assaults, including Colonel Samuel F. Marks of the 11th Louisiana. Another of the casualties was Lieutenant John Crowly of Company F, who had lost his right arm at Belmont. After returning from sick leave on April 2, he was now hit in the left arm by shrapnel, and it too would be amputated. One of his comrades noted, "He deserves to be 'retired' on full pay." Others went down too; Lieutenant William Yerger of Clark's staff was unhorsed in the chaos, but the most notable casualty was Clark. He had ridden back to the right wing and shouted that Marks's Louisianans had been repelled, yelling, "Can you take that battery yonder, which is annoying our troops so much?" Colonel Vaughan of the 13th Tennessee responded, "We can take it." Clark was soon hit in the right shoulder while exhibiting, as Russell described it, a "fearless bearing [that] was well calculated to inspire the men." The future governor of Mississippi nevertheless had to turn over command to Russell and leave the field with the help of Major Howell Hinds of his staff. He met Bragg in the rear, who listened to his report from the front and "kindly express[ed] his sympathy."[34]

In the rear, higher-level commanders such as Bragg were having problems too. With Clark's wounding, Polk compensated for his loss by "frequent exposure of himself to the hottest of the enemy's fire." Polk came out safe, but his nearby adjutant general, George Williamson, was wounded and had a horse shot under him. Bragg was also shaken by the death of his "noble and gallant charger." He described to his wife in vivid detail how about 10:00 A.M. his horse was hit by a minié ball in the forehead. It was, he wrote, "evidently intended for me and nothing but the head of the noble animal saved me." The horse held his head "aloft proudly surveying the field" for a moment, then fell on Bragg's leg. It was only with difficulty that he was able to get out. Bragg was not hurt but disturbed that he had to mount "an inferior animal" from his body-guard.[35]

For about two hours, then, between 8:00 and 10:00 A.M., four brigades made multiple assaults against Sherman's division and were never able to drive them away. If Pond's maneuvers to the left are included, a total of five brigades were never able to penetrate Sherman's line by frontal assault. Sherman noted, "Our men were so posted as to have a good fire at him as he crossed the valley and ascended the rising ground on our side." Manning Force described the terrain as "this valley of death." The terrain certainly benefited Sherman early at Shiloh.[36]

William T. Sherman was indeed fortunate early at Shiloh. Even if he would not admit that he had been surprised, there was indeed a strategic surprise, and his overcompensation even on the morning of April 6 had not helped matters. Sherman recovered quickly and well, however. Because he was given some forewarning by the fighting in front brought on by the advance patrol as well as Appler's awkwardly handled regi-ment, Sherman and his officers were able to form the division and meet the enemy prepared. And his officers mostly acted bravely. Although Buckland concentrated his efforts primarily on his old regiment, his line held, with plenty of tactical assistance from Sherman himself. The old and sick Hildebrand also rose to the occasion, moving up and down his line to encourage his men. He even ranged far to the left to the next position of the partial 53rd Ohio. Fortunately for Sherman, the terrain was to his advantage. Situated on the lip of the ridge north of Shiloh Branch, Sherman's line forced the Confederates to move through the vine-choked and swampy bottom to get to the point where they could assault his line. The uncoordinated use of Confederate brigades also allowed Sherman to deflect all the assaults against him, indicating that Beauregard's plan was not feasible and that the green troops and officers in the Confederate army were struggling to get a handle on their actions. All the while, Sherman held.[37]

While the infantry poured volley after volley into the oncoming Confederates, the division's artillery under Ezra Taylor also provided exceptional firepower. Taylor's own Chicago battery, now under Samuel

Barrett, cost many a Confederate his life or limb on the right, with Taylor reporting that Barrett's fire caused "both the yelling and the firing of
the enemy to cease for a time." Waterhouse's guns to the east also took
down several regiments, aided by long-range fire from Barrett's guns at
the church firing across the area of fallen timber.[38]

There were also others arriving in the area to reinforce Sherman as
the divisions camped in the rear began to realize that Sherman and Prentiss were fighting in their front. Hearing the firing, McClernand sent a
messenger to Sherman to see what was going on, and he returned with
a request for McClernand to send cavalry to the front to help him scout.
Sherman later admitted that it was not until about 8:00 A.M. that he "became satisfied for the first time that the enemy designed a determined
attack on our whole camp." McClernand grew more alarmed when fugitives began to move rearward and rode to the front and met Sherman.
By this time, Sherman had been to Rhea Field, had received a wound in
the hand, and was fully convinced he was under heavy attack. McClernand could hear that Prentiss's division was engaged as well, and he responded by sending a battery and a brigade to aid the assailed divisions.
The closest was Schwartz's artillery under George Nispel (Schwartz
was acting as McClernand's chief of staff and artillery commander and
would be severely wounded elsewhere), and Leonard Ross's infantry
camped at Review Field. The artillerymen were even then drilling, although Nispel was sick. When the ruckus began, he nevertheless led
the battery to Sherman's relief, going into position in Buckland's rear.
It was not so easy for the infantry brigade, however. Ross was away
on leave, leaving the ranking colonel, James S. Reardon of the 29th
Illinois, in command. Reardon was sick and sent word to Colonel Julius Raith of the 43rd Illinois to take command. As expected, Raith had
little experience in brigade command; he did not even have aides or
mounted orderlies. The long roll was nevertheless sounded throughout
the brigade's camps, and news of Raith's promotion arrived as he was
forming his own regiment. In the 17th Illinois, the long roll sounded,
and soldiers watched as several of the officers' wives scrambled out
of camp—all except Belle Reynolds ducking when a shell came close.
Mrs. Reynolds, one astonished onlooker wrote, "would turn her head
back and laugh." Despite the women in the camp, Raith quickly led
the brigade southward, taking a position with his right in rear of Hildebrand's small brigade farther up the ridge and his left extending diagonally to the east back toward his camps. In fact, the left of the brigade

hardly advanced past their camps. They had no time, because soon they saw the enemy advancing. Abram Vanauken of the 17th Illinois noted that "the rebels advanced in 5 heavy columns."[39]

Taking position between the church and Sherman's line, the men of the 17th Illinois peered forward and were disturbed to see Ohioans ahead of them, "doing badly that is not standing up and fighting like they ought." The sight of the Ohioans' commander, Jesse Hildebrand, encouraged them, though. "Their colonel [was] a fine looking old man," wrote Henry Hole of the 17th Illinois, and he "rode down our front and said 'Boys don't be afraid, you are on the right side.'" The Illinoisans rose en masse and cheered Hildebrand.[40]

While Sherman was appreciative of the help McClernand sent, Raith actually took the brigade to the wrong point. The most threatened position was not to the front, where Sherman seemed to be easily holding his own against five enemy brigades. The problem was to the left of his line, where a small gap lurked between him and Prentiss. As the clock ticked past 9:00 A.M., Sherman could hear a major ruckus to his left. He no doubt wondered how Prentiss was doing, and how that action would affect his line.[41]

He would soon find out.

7

"THE STRUGGLE FOR HIS ENCAMPMENTS"

If William T. Sherman had numerous advantages at his end of the initial camp line, Benjamin Prentiss, the next division to the east, had no such good fortune. Where Sherman benefited from hefty numbers, with more coming forward from McClernand's nearest camps, Prentiss was in the opposite situation. Sherman defended the right of the line with three brigades and still had one detached. Prentiss, conversely, had only two brigades, and one of those was not yet complete. Moreover, Prentiss's third brigade was not even organized on April 6 but was still gathering; some of the units had arrived at the landing the day before, and some arrived even on the morning of April 6. In addition, there were only two batteries of artillery then assigned to the division, and they were camped to the rear of the left brigade, offering Peabody's troops on the right little aid. Clearly, Prentiss's position was not manned nearly as thoroughly as was Sherman's. This situation only adds to the idea that Grant and Sherman did not expect an attack. Hurlbut later claimed that "one officer at least" (probably himself) recommended putting a more veteran division in front and organizing Prentiss's in the rear. Whoever this officer was, he obviously failed to sway the Union high command.[1]

Even worse, although Prentiss's two brigades were astride the Eastern Corinth Road, Peabody's brigade did not extend far enough to the right to firmly connect with Sherman's leftmost brigade under Jesse Hildebrand. As a result, there was a gap around a quarter of a mile between Peabody and Hildebrand. Fortunately for the Federals, however, the gap did not constitute an emergency. Camped in the expanse were two battalions of the 4th Illinois Cavalry under Colonel T. Lyle Dickey in what is today known as Lost Field; they presented an eight-company front. Additionally, the 53rd Ohio's later movements took the regiment into the small gap, helping to plug it in the face of the oncoming Confederates. This gap, concerning though it looked, was not fatal to Prentiss's position.[2]

The gap on the other end of Prentiss's line did prove fatal. His third brigade, not yet formed but with the regiments either present or nearing Pittsburg Landing on the morning of April 6, would have substantially covered the half-mile-wide gap between Miller's left and David Stuart's right. There were two battalions of the 11th Illinois Cavalry camped farther to the rear in the gap, but unlike the troopers of the 4th Illinois Cavalry in the smaller gap on Prentiss's right, they were too far to the rear to make any difference either tactically or psychologically. A wide gap thus yawned to Prentiss's left, providing the Confederates an opportunity they would not miss.

Then there were the command issues facing Prentiss, starting with his own failures. According to the 12th Michigan's chaplain, Prentiss was still not convinced that he was under full attack but thought the enemy was merely "a skirmishing party." Trouble also brewed in his command structure. His rapport with Madison Miller was fine, but Prentiss did not get along with Peabody at all. Little did Prentiss know then, but Peabody's patrol had actually benefited his troops, who would have been attacked whether or not the patrol went forward. Peabody gave the Federals a much-needed warning.[3]

Most disturbing of all, Prentiss did not have the terrain benefits that Sherman enjoyed. Prentiss's two brigades were camped astride the Eastern Corinth Road, which ran along the Shiloh divide on high ground traversing the battlefield. As a result, most of Prentiss's troops had no deep and boggy creek bottoms fronting their position. Madison Miller on the left had some beneficial terrain overlooking the headwaters of Locust Grove Branch, but those declivities were not nearly as substantial that far up the watershed as the valley was farther down at Stuart's position or as formidable as Shiloh Branch was at Sherman's location. The result was that Prentiss's troops, particularly Peabody's brigade, fronted primarily level ground that afforded the Federals little aid. The only advantage was that the area was more open, allowing the Federals to see farther ahead. Colonel Francis Quinn of the 12th Michigan reported: "I could see to the right and left. They [Confederates] were visible in line, and every hill-top in the rear was covered with them." Similarly, one of Miller's troops in the 18th Missouri wrote that the Confederates came at them "about four regiments deep." Perhaps at least on this small stage, Beauregard's intention to overawe the enemy in Napoleonic fashion had worked.[4]

Fortunately for Prentiss, the Confederates were slower in coming to his camps than to Sherman's, in part because of the resistance offered by Major Powell's patrol and Woodyard's reinforcements. The biggest factor delaying the Confederate attack on Prentiss's division, however, was the angle at which the Confederate front line hit the Union camps. Even with a slight bulge to the south in the camp line on Prentiss's front, the Confederates still needed time to swing the right brigades of Hardee's line around to hit the masses of Federals along the Eastern Corinth Road. Thus, as occurred at Shiloh Church, the Confederate brigades went in piecemeal as they arrived on the line, only slowly building to an all-out mass attack. The delay afforded Prentiss time to form his regiments, with the general personally turning out both brigades. Prentiss interrupted Miller's breakfast, but a soldier remembered they lost several men before ammunition was fully handed out. But form they did. "If you ever saw men in a hurry it was about then," one Missourian noted.[5]

S. A. M. Wood's Confederate brigade was the next unit to the right of Cleburne, and it should have hit the Union line as the corps struggled to swing its right around and orient itself east to west instead of southeast to northwest. In the swing, however, Wood managed to lose his connection with Cleburne as he went more east than north in the early minutes of the battle. The same trouble occurred between Wood and Shaver's brigade to his right. The regiments eventually began their move forward, however, with Shaver meeting the initial line of Peabody's brigade arrayed on a small ridge nearly a quarter of a mile in front of their camps. The Federal resistance in the form of the now-advanced 25th Missouri and 12th Michigan caught Shaver head on, the famed explorer Henry Morton Stanley of the 6th Arkansas describing in the enemy line "a row of little globes of pearly smoke streaked with crimson." Shaver agreed, writing, "The enemy's fire was terrific and told with terrible effect." Perhaps some of the Federals' determination came from the 12th Michigan's chaplain, Andrew J. Eldred, who rode behind his line and counseled that "all was at stake and if they would do their duty the God of heaven and their country would honor them." Eldred's entreaties lasted only so long as Shaver pressed on, inadvertently aided by Wood's detached brigade to the west. Wood's troops had crossed into the southern part of Rhea Field, with the 27th Tennessee on the left taking artillery fire from Waterhouse's Battery across the creek around 7:30 A.M. Wood swung to the east to the cover of the woods, enlarging the gap that was forming between him and Cleburne at Shiloh Church. The movement unintentionally put Wood directly on Peabody's right, and the Confederates quickly moved around the Union line's flank. The damage to Prentiss's first major line was done.[6]

The fighting around 8:00 A.M. was thus short. The Missourians and Michiganders of Peabody's brigade quickly fell back to their camp line and, according to one Confederate, "rallied for the struggle for his encampments." Amazingly, Wisconsin companies had time to take roll and begin breakfast, but soon the hail of bullets alarmed them again. One of the soldiers remembered, "The bullets commenced to come through the camp and the rebels were coming with them." A hasty line formed, and Prentiss again sent panicked messages to Hurlbut and Smith. On the mostly level ground, the division had no major terrain feature on which to form its line, and the Confederates were able to approach in easier fashion than elsewhere. Wood and Shaver thus drove in on Peabody's withdrawing soldiers around 8:30 A.M., with their artillery batteries, Harper's and Swett's Mississippi units, firing into the Union line from the right despite having a hard time keeping up with the infantry through the woods on what Captain W. L. Harper described as "weak and hungry horses." The Federals nevertheless made a stand, augmented by Colonel Benjamin Allen's 16th Wisconsin turning its line to the right to outflank Shaver. The Wisconsin regiment was in turn outflanked by the far right brigade of Hardee's line, Gladden's Alabama and Louisiana troops. As the Confederate line completed its swing to an east–west orientation, the Wisconsin troops fell back to their original position and a little farther back, but they paid for their movements with Lieutenant Colonel Cassius Fairchild being wounded in the leg and Colonel Allen having his horse shot from under him as well as a second horse as he was mounting. His troops had little sympathy for Allen; one soldier later wrote that the colonel was a glory hound and put them in every tight spot he could to get more attention. Conversely, others sent word of his bravery back to Wisconsin, writing that when the colors went down amid the fighting, Allen "marched deliberately up before and within a few rods of a rebel regiment, shouldered the colors, and marched as coolly back again." The shocked correspondent noted, "The rebels fired not a single bullet at him, but stood amazed at such a daring deed."[7]

The Federals were initially giving a good account of themselves, even without help from the terrain. Confusion in the green Confederate ranks helped, especially when a commotion erupted between Wood's and Shaver's brigades. Major Reuben T. Harvey of the 2nd Arkansas reported that a Tennessee regiment of Wood's brigade broke and "ran back, halooing 'Retreat, retreat.'" Harvey noted that his men thought those were orders and broke as well. S. A. M. Wood told a different story, saying that Shaver's units broke first and the panic spread to his brigade. Down the line, the Federals also made Swett's artillerymen pay, with Shaver writing, "It soon became apparent that unless something was done to relieve Captain Swett his battery would be rendered useless."[8]

A lagging Adley Gladden also found the advance rough on his sector, even more than Shaver. As Wood and Shaver swarmed slowly through the woods, Gladden proceeded forward to their right, with members of the 25th Alabama, according to Colonel J. Q. Loomis, in a "noble rivalry . . . as to who should do most." In crossing a creek, the 26th Alabama was inadvertently thrown out of line and could not retake its former position; the Alabamians quickly reformed on the right of the brigade and kept moving. The troops soon emerged onto open ground a little after 8:00 A.M.—one of the only terrain benefits Prentiss's Federal division had. Waiting on them was Miller's brigade, among which Prentiss had earlier arrived at a gallop and with a shout of "Colonel Miller, get out your brigade! They are fighting on the right." Similarly, a staff officer roared into the camp of the 61st Illinois, shouting, "This regiment not in line yet? They have been fighting on the right over an hour!" He wheeled his horse in the direction of the colonel's tent, and old colonel Jacob Fry soon had his men in line. He gave them a simple talk: "Gentlemen, remember your State, and do your duty today like brave men." One Illinoisan thought it was an odd speech: "That was all." He chalked up the state issue to the colonel's being a Democrat.[9]

Miller quickly formed his Illinois, Wisconsin, and Missouri regiments in line in the woods on the north side of Peter Spain's cotton field. One of Miller's subordinates joked with him that it seemed "cowardly" to hide, but Miller responded, "If it was to be done again, it would be done the same way." Prentiss then galloped up and ordered Miller to

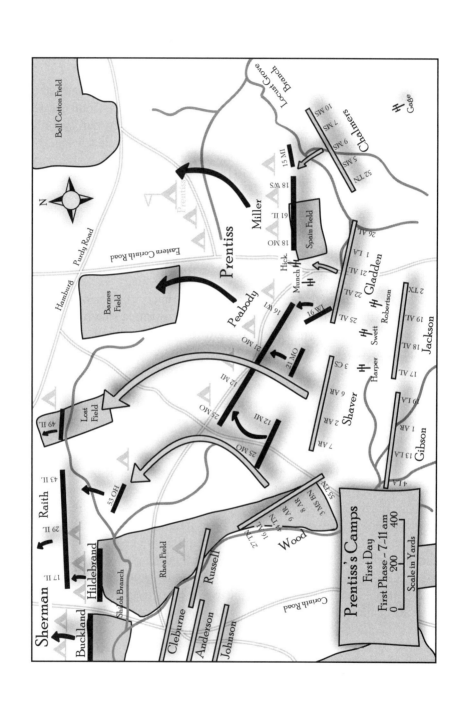

Sherman

Buckland

Shiloh Branch

17 Il.

Hildebrand

29 Il.

Raith

43 Il.

53 OH

49 Il.

Lost Field

25 MO

25 MO

12 MI

12 MI

21 MO

16 WI

21 MO

Peabody

Prentiss

Barnes Field

Eastern Corinth Road

Purdy Road

Hamburg

Bell Cotton Field

N

Miller

15 MI

18 WS

19 Il.

Spain Field

18 MO

Hick

Munch

22 AL

25 AL

16 WI

3 CS

6 AR

2 AR

7 AR

Shaver

Harper

Swett

Robertson

Gladden

26 AL

1 LA

21 AL

2 TX

17 AL

18 AL

19 AL

Jackson

1 AR

9 LA

13 LA

4 LA

Gibson

Goge

Chalmers

10 MS

7 MS

9 MS

5 MS

52 TN

Cleburne

Anderson

Johnson

Rhea Field

Russell

27 TN

16 AL

6 MS

9 AR

8 AR

3 MS BN

52 TN

Wood

Corinth Road

Prentiss's Camps

First Day

First Phase ~ 7-11 am

0   200   400

Scale in Yards

take a position on the south side of the field overlooking the headwaters of Locust Grove Branch. Miller did so, but, as he later wrote, "with great reluctance, I confess." After initial skirmishing with the Confederate advance, Prentiss thought otherwise as well and ordered Miller to retire again to the north side of the field. Prentiss decided he would rather have the benefits of an open field than a small valley. Gladden would thus have to assault across the field, a difficult task. Fortunately, the only two artillery units attached to Prentiss, Emil Munch's Minnesota and Andrew Hickenlooper's Ohio batteries, were on Miller's front and deployed astride the Eastern Corinth Road with the call "Action! Front!" getting their attention in their peaceful camps "situated in a beautiful cedar grove adjoining General Prentiss' headquarters." The artillerymen first realized something was going on when they heard firing and observed "a commotion at the headquarters," remembered Minnesotan Henry S. Hurter, "the general and his staff mounting and riding off in the direction whence the firing came." Soon the batteries were thundering southward as well: "Pounding guns and beating hoofs, every moment growing louder and louder, signaled to the waiting and impatient infantry the battery's advance." From their vantage point on line, the artillerymen aided Miller in his defense of the field, although it was a relatively small open area, and one artilleryman later complained that they had to fight the enemy "at short pistol range—and compelled to use nothing but canister and short-timed shells." Still, the guns, one of the Minnesota pieces labeled "old rake em down" by a cannoneer, did good work. They also provided slight cover for the left of Peabody's brigade, but because the woods were thick on most of his front, their service to him was less substantial.[10]

As Gladden's men tramped toward the field, they found just how well these green Federals could fight. A nervous Edgar Embly of the 61st Illinois wrote home that he "was looking as anxious for the Secesh as ever I did for a squirrel," adding, "but I did not look long before I seen their guns glittering in the brush." He later wrote how Prentiss himself told them "to fire low and when we shot be sure that we seen something to shoot at for every Secesh that we killed there would be one less to shoot at us." Prentiss's counsel made an impression on Embly: "I thought of that several times during the day."[11]

Miller's Federals opened up, and the fighting quickly grew heavy. One member of the 1st Louisiana wrote several days later, "We were in the hardest fighting all the time, whenever Genl Bragg found a hot place he would ride up & put us in himself." An Alabamian similarly described the action: "We ran up near enough to be certain that our balls would reach them." The Alabama troops let loose a destructive volley, but in doing so, they took heavy casualties. Colonel John G. Coltart of the 26th Alabama went down with a severe wound in the foot, but the most notable casualty was Gladden, who led the men in front of the brigade. He took a piece of shrapnel in the shoulder, which nearly tore off his left arm. One Confederate related that "half his men ran toward him," which caused enormous confusion in the ranks. An aide came to his support when he saw the general drop his reins, and Gladden confessed, "I am afraid it is a serious hurt." The staff officer described the arm as "crushed into a mass of bones and flesh, near the shoulder." The general moved to the rear and was put into an ambulance and taken to a hospital near army headquarters, where a doctor amputated the mangled arm. Gladden eventually went to Corinth, but he died days later. His nephew was also wounded in the fighting. Gladden's departure left the brigade in the hands of Colonel Daniel W. Adams of the 1st Louisiana, but Adams admitted that the fire was so hot that the brigade "began to falter and finally to fall back."[12]

During the confusion, Gladden's artillery in the form of Robertson's Alabama Battery moved up and supported his line. On orders from Gladden before he was wounded, the battery was standing idle in a creek valley, with Gladden urging Robertson to stay covered until he needed support. Even there, the bullets were thick overhead, flying "uncomfortably near," remembered Lieutenant Hubert Dent. It was here that the battery again came in contact with an impressively dressed Louisianan they had learned to respect and admire on the train trip northward from the coast. This time the man was less than impressive, as he was running from the fight and was evidently not wounded. Robertson concluded, "Appearances are deceiving." The battery soon charged forward at a gallop and unlimbered amid the retreating Confederates. Once deployed, Robertson found that his battery was within a hundred yards of the enemy, and cannoneers began to fall. Dent admitted, "The way the balls whistled past my head was not at all pleasant."[13]

Despite the stand made at Spain Field, the Federal line was far too overmatched to be able to hold much longer, especially with Confederate reinforcements coming to the front. As at Shiloh Church, Bragg's corps was not far behind, with Bragg now personally present on the right. He quickly sent units forward to aid in the attack on the initial

Union camp line. Pond's and Anderson's brigades thus advanced to Cleburne's aid at Shiloh Church, while the remainder of the corps moved forward to the east and aided in the attack on Prentiss. Randall Gibson's Louisiana and Arkansas regiments moved forward generally in the rear of Shaver's brigade but slightly to the right, breaking contact with its neighbor, Anderson's brigade to the west. They took a few casualties passing through Rhea Field, "the guns of the enemy at this point being served with little effect except upon the tree-tops around us," as Colonel B. L. Hodge of the 19th Louisiana remembered. Jones Withers's division of Bragg's corps on the right also moved up in support, although it took longer on that right flank to cover the distance required because of the angle at which the Confederate line struck the enemy camps. Withers recognized the problem and provided a solution as best he could: "It was soon perceptible that there was a gradual but steady inclination to the left, thus increasing the distance to and exposing our flank on Lick Creek." In response, Withers sent Clanton's Alabama cavalry to guard the right flank. Additionally, John K. Jackson's Alabama troops followed Shaver to the east, taking occasional casualties as they tried to maintain the correct distance from the first line. Chalmers's Mississippians and Tennesseans brought up the actual right flank of the line near Gladden's position at Spain Field.[14]

Although Wood and Shaver had less need for additional aid from Gibson and Jackson, Gladden was stopped at Spain Field and thus required aid. Bragg quickly sent Chalmers forward on the right of Gladden's bloody regiments, with the brigade trudging through a growing valley of Locust Grove Branch. Chalmers, whom one of his Mississippians described as "a very genteel clever looking fellow," had been sick but was recovering. Now he was tapped to hold the extreme Confederate right, as, in his words, "the space between Owl and Lick Creeks was about a half mile narrower where we first deployed our line of battle than it was in front of the enemy's line." Although he would never completely fill the gap, his brigade was nevertheless an insecure plug, especially when Chalmers formed the brigade into line of battle within sight of the enemy to the front. On orders from Withers, he advanced "by a gradual left wheel," trying desperately to find and then turn the all-important Union left flank.[15]

Ascending the steep hill out of Locust Grove Branch, Chalmers emerged in the general vicinity of the 18th Wisconsin's brand-new camp, where the regiment stood astonished at the developments. Another unit was also present to offer aid, the 15th Michigan. The regiment had been slated to join Prentiss but had only arrived at the landing on Saturday. In fact, Colonel John M. Oliver sent two companies with tents out that afternoon to their campsite and followed on Sunday morning with the other eight companies. Oliver wrote that he "found everything in confusion, and were immediately ordered into line of battle." He was under strength because some of his soldiers had been left behind to tend to the equipment. He also had no ammunition, but Prentiss hurriedly responded, "Our bayonets ought to be good for something." Thus did the ammunitionless regiment form into line in front of Chalmers' advance, with one Federal writing, "We stood at order arms and looked at them as they shot." Oliver wisely marched to the rear to find ammunition, and that left the 18th Wisconsin's left wide open while Chalmers's much larger brigade far outranged the small regiment to the east, allowing Chalmers to effectively flank Miller's line. Prentiss by this time was on hand and ordered Miller to fall back, but Miller was perhaps overwhelmed with the situation and later wrote, "I must have been a little excited, as he had to reiterate his order before I could comprehend." Miller caught on soon enough, however, spurred on by the disaster enveloping him, and he called his already-breaking line back. One of the Wisconsin soldiers wrote in his diary, "We passed our Encampment I saw Some breakfast cooked ready for Eating of course I did not sit down but ran up and took a pancake or Biscuit. . . . It served me for the day."[16]

Fortunately for Miller, Chalmers was having his own difficulty amid the ravines of Locust Grove Branch. He was with the 10th Mississippi on the extreme right of his brigade, and when he ordered the charge, only that regiment heard it. Colonel Robert A. Smith of the 10th Mississippi, a native Scot, had planned well, telling his men to fix bayonets and that within sixty yards of the enemy line, "I would order them to fire and then to charge with the bayonet." They went forward through heavy undergrowth and briars but received a volley, throwing them all out of order. The Mississippians "would not wait to form," Smith wrote, "but commenced firing and with a loud cheer rushed upon the foe." They struck the 18th Wisconsin, which could also see the tardy 9th and 7th Mississippi regiments coming at them as well. The 5th Mississippi and 52nd Tennessee never did get the order, although Colonel B. J. Lea of the Tennessee regiment had his horse shot from under him. These two regiments nevertheless followed in the wake of the successful attack.

One of the Tennesseans, describing his first taste of combat, noted: "My blood run cold and I felt my frame tremble to see the dead and hear the groans of the wounded, but in a few minutes they ran like wild turkeys and left their tents and baggage in our possession." Chalmers's Mississippians followed the retreating Federals on Miller's left across the valley north of their camps and onto the next hill, where orders from Johnston stopped their advance.[17]

At the same time, Adams, now in command of the injured Gladden's brigade, was again moving forward under Robertson's covering fire, putting additional pressure on the 18th Missouri and 61st Illinois in the field. The Louisianan took the colors of his regiment and led the brigade forward, sending them at the double-quick to attack Miller's right. "We rushed up to their tents with a great shout," an Alabamian remembered. As a result of the two brigades outnumbering the three small regiments, Miller's troops fully broke and fled through their camps around 9:00 A.M., leaving some seven stands of colors. "The enemy pouring in on our wright & left flank," wrote James Lawrence of the 61st Illinois, and "we was obliged to give way." In the chaos, Leander Stillwell reported seeing "a kind of flag I had never seen before. It was a gaudy sort of thing, with red bars. It flashed over me in a second that that thing was a rebel flag!" The two artillery batteries fared little better, with both Hickenlooper and a wounded Munch losing one gun each in an unwise movement ordered by Prentiss to change front to the right (another of Munch's guns had a broken trail and was sent to the rear). The brigade also left its wounded animals and men behind, with Hickenlooper leaving his favorite horse, Gray Eagle. The horse, Hickenlooper remembered sadly, "falls upon his knees, rises again, trembles for a moment, makes one or two ineffectual efforts to maintain an erect position, and then again plunges forward and rolls over upon his side, throwing me heavily to the ground." As sad as losing a horse was, the sadder aspect was the human toll. Thomas Crowder of the 52nd Tennessee wrote how "some of them with their branes shot out and two or three in a pile some had their limbs broken and begging to have their wounds dressed, others cursing the man that wounded him and some few was making peace with heaven." One Confederate talked to a wounded Federal, asking him why he "left his home and to come here to destroy people who had never harmed him." The Federal obviously could not argue and told the Confederate "he was sorry for it and if he was spared he would not do so any more." Prentiss's division also left behind its dead, one of whom was Prentiss's staff surgeon, Samuel W. Everett, who fell in the thickest of the fighting.[18]

There were numerous Confederate casualties as well. Captain John Thomas Wheat of the 1st Louisiana was killed in the fighting; he had served as the secretary of the Louisiana secession convention. In the 21st Alabama, Sergeant George Dixon was hit in the leg and was saved only by a gold piece he carried in his pocket. His sweetheart had given him the piece, and because it saved his life, he later had the bent coin inscribed: "Shiloh April 6, 1862 My Life Preserver G.E.D." The coin was found nearly a century and a half later on Dixon's body inside the recovered submarine CSS *Hunley*.[19]

Despite the casualties the Federals inflicted, the disaster soon spread. Everett Peabody was not doing any better west of the Eastern Corinth Road. With orders from Hindman to assault, Shaver and Wood moved forward and hit his four regiments with two large brigades, with two more stacked behind them. It was thus only a matter of time before Peabody's regiments broke as well, about the same time as Miller's, fleeing through their camps and heading for the rear. Peabody tried to reform a line and call back the stragglers, and his bravery cost him dearly. He was hit as many as four times—in the hand, thigh, neck, and torso—but was still on his horse barking commands and pleading for his men to stand firm. Then a fifth bullet slammed into his head just above the upper lip and crashed out the back, killing him instantly. He fell on the site of his headquarters, where he had made the momentous decision to send out the morning patrol. He had perhaps saved the army; at least he had given a warning and bought additional time for the army to prepare a defense. It cost him his life. "A braver or more noble man never lived," one of his mourning soldiers wrote in remembrance.[20]

Mass chaos reigned as both Miller's and Peabody's men fell back from their lines, withdrawing through the camps where the tents and other pieces of equipage broke up the retreat. Their cooked breakfasts were also calling them; the 16th Wisconsin passed directly through their camps without being able to eat anything. D. F. Vail of that regiment wrote, "We re-formed in our camp among the pots and skillets containing our uneaten breakfast which we had so recently turned our backs on." Vail ducked in to get his wife's picture but "left our camp amidst a rain of bullets; the air being filled with a continual whiz, whiz, whiz, until I was bewildered with the cross-firing I had gotten into." The Confederates were close on their heels, and their pursuit made the retreat even more chaotic. Soon Prentiss's entire division was streaming back in small groups and as individuals, passing through the Barnes Field area, seeking some type of support. Prentiss admitted, "My command [was] greatly reduced by reason of casualties and because of the falling back of many of the men to the river, they being panic-stricken—a majority of them having now for the first time been exposed to fire." Many did not stop until they reached the river or Snake Creek. A few did not even let those hindrances stop them but tried to swim or commandeer any vessel they could. One staff officer wrote that he asked one soldier, "What are you running for?" His reply was, "Because I can't fly." To another he asked, "What are you crying like a baby for?" The soldier responded, "I wish I was a baby, on mother's lap, and a girl baby at that." The net result was that Prentiss, who started the day with roughly 5,400 men in his division, could count no more than about 500 of those when he stopped along with Miller to piece together a new line over half a mile to the rear. Prentiss's collapse was total.[21]

Colonel Quinn of the 12th Michigan noted that the men fell back "very much scattered and broken." Captain Robert Brethschneider of Company K, 12th Michigan, had fought at First Bull Run in the 2nd Michigan, and the feeling must have been the same. Prentiss was still full of fight, however, even as he reined in the most stalwart of his troops to the rear. Quinn reported, "General Prentiss rode up and proposed heroically for us to fight our way back to our tents." A chaplain in the 12th Michigan reported he "modestly suggested that we would certainly be outflanked by them if it was undertaken," and a relieved Quinn added, "[He] finally gave this up and formed the line for defense where it was." Prentiss also finally "gave it up that it was a skirmishing party we had to deal with."[22]

Not everyone in Prentiss's division retreated. Hospital steward Samuel H. Eells of the 12th Michigan decided to stay in his camp and care for his wounded. "Everybody else was running off as fast as possible," he wrote, "but the surgeons resolved that they would not leave their wounded." They continued to work even though many of the hospital attendants ran as well. Even Eells became concerned when "the bullets began to come unpleasantly near and thick." One bullet came through the tent and broke a bottle of ammonia, with the liquid flying into Eells's face. Soon Confederates entered the tent, leveling their muskets. Eells was taken prisoner for his efforts, but Confederate general Thomas Hindman rode by and placed a guard to protect the steward from being bothered in his work. Two Confederate surgeons also arrived to provide aid for both sides.[23]

It could have been even worse for the Federals had the Confederates immediately followed up their success in front of Prentiss's camps. Hickenlooper's battery managed to alternate sections in a fighting retreat, no doubt slowing a pursuit. Amazingly, in the midst of the retreat, Hickenlooper was astonished to see the horse he had left at Spain Field trotting up to him despite bleeding freely from the neck. "With a look of recognition and a glad 'whinney' he halted at my side," a surprised Hickenlooper wrote.[24]

The Confederates flooding into the camps were amazed at the signs of unreadiness among the Federals. Some Federals were indeed surprised, and this no doubt inspired the accounts of soldiers (probably sick) being bayoneted in their tents. Bragg claimed that he saw some Federals "in costumes better fitted to the bedchamber than to the battle-field." Others agreed. One cannoneer wrote in his diary, "Everything in their camps indicated a complete surprise. All of their canteens and haversacks lay in wild confusion as though they had no time to get them." Sam Houston Jr. of the following 2nd Texas, described how the breakfasts were being cooked even as the Confederates reached the camps, indicating to him that "either no very heavy engagement was expected, or Prentiss' brigade was blessed with the most faithful cooks on record." Houston recounted how he "scalded my hand in fishing from a camp kettle, a piece of beef weighing some three pounds." Others found whiskey, but Houston said that his major "smashed the jug and offered the cheering assurance that the next galoot who brought whiskey into the ranks would be 'bodaciously' shot!" Food galore was available, but perhaps the Union soldiers' personal items most intrigued the Confederates; many a Southerner stopped to look at some Federal soldier's daguerreotype of his girlfriend or wife. Others consumed the love letters the Federals had been either writing or reading. Stopping to ponder the Confederate success, even William Preston marveled that "the surprise was complete. . . . The breakfasts of the men were on the table, the officers' baggage and apparel left in the tents, and every evidence remained of unexpected conflict and sudden rout."[25]

Yet the success had a cost. Hardee's advance was completely stopped as a result of all the chaos and temptation, as well as a few scattered shots from the enemy. Henry Morton Stanley admitted, "I had the momentary impression that, with the capture of the first camp, the battle was well-nigh over." But it was only the beginning, and the delay caused by the pause at the camps was critical. One Confederate described how "it was disgraceful to our Army to see men by hundreds plundering, while their brethren in arms were being struck down every minute." An Arkansan in Shaver's brigade wrote, "Such men are not worthy the name of soldier."[26]

Although the loss of officers such as Gladden compounded the Confederate problems, higher-level commanders were soon on the scene to make sure the attack continued. The most notable arrival was Albert Sidney Johnston. After watching the action on Cleburne's front at Shiloh Church around 8:00 A.M., Johnston rode back to the right—his special area of concern in his plan to hook around the enemy left. Illustrating his concern, he had earlier met Colonel George Maney and his five present companies of the 1st Tennessee Infantry and ordered him to move toward Lick Creek and guard the road toward Hamburg. "I have selected you for the post of honor to-day," Johnston told them, asking if each man had his requisite forty rounds of ammunition. "No, General, I 'ain't got but thirty-eight!" came the reply, whereupon a smiling Johnston told the soldier to see his orderly sergeant for two more rounds. The threat to the right flank was no laughing matter, however. Beauregard noted that a cavalry regiment, Forrest's Tennessee unit, and an artillery battery had been dispatched even before Maney to guard several fords on Lick Creek, including "Greer's, Tanner's, and Borland's." Beauregard evidently meant Greer's, Turner's, and Barnes's, the latter being the ford on the Hamburg-Purdy Road. Eventually, Wirt Adams's Mississippi Cavalry regiment and Isaac Avery's Georgia Dragoons were also sent to Greer's. Further illustrating Johnston's concern was his call for additional troops for the right, especially earlier on as he received reports of Gladden running into stiff resistance at Spain Field.[27]

In the process of moving back to the right, Johnston saw Polk near the two cabins and ordered him to send a brigade to the right. He requested Charles Clark, who was with Polk, to send Alexander P. Stewart's brigade in that same direction. Johnston decided to go too and led Stewart part of the way before galloping on. One of Johnston's escorts remembered, "Always at a gallop, we traversed a great part of the field. . . . He seemed cool and collected all the time." Johnston eventually reined up on the high ground around the now-captured camp of the 18th

Wisconsin, where he remained for several hours, from about 9:15 to 11:15 A.M. It was in this area that Johnston perceived the looting of the camps, spying a soldier emerging from a tent with arms full of plunder. Johnston scolded him, but then, thinking he had been too hard on the man, reached down and picked up a small tin cup. "Let this be my share of the spoils to-day," he said. Dudley Hayden told a similar story. A staff officer emerged with an arm full of Union coats and said, "Here, gentlemen, are overcoats for the entire staff." "None of that, sir," Johnston advised, "Remember, we do not come here to plunder."[28]

Johnston was able to get the Confederates back on task in short order. He first sent Gladden's brigade forward again, where it engaged in a long-range exchange of shots with the then-deploying units of W. H. L. Wallace's division. He countermanded the order when he learned of Gladden's fall. Hardee was also on scene, having left his line to the west in the hands of Thomas Hindman. The large staffs caught the enemy's eye. Artillery rounds began to fall nearby, and William Preston remembered, "General Johnston rode down the hill to escape the shells." Johnston was nevertheless in total command, and he had larger ideas in mind. In fact, he now put in motion one of the major command decisions at Shiloh—one that would have a profound effect on the rest of the battle. Johnston, who always intended to hook around the Union left flank and drive the enemy northwestward toward the Snake and Owl Creek swamps, evidently thought he had located the Union left and had turned it. Around 9:30 A.M., from his position atop the high ground near the 18th Wisconsin camp, Johnston put in motion the drive to the northwest.[29]

Some historians have postulated—and it is a reasonable argument—that Johnston personally heard the firing all down the line from Pond's brigade to Chalmers's, but he heard nothing farther to the east and reasoned that he had turned the enemy left flank. Moreover, spying a second line of camps in the distance to the northwest probably only solidified Johnston's belief that the bulk of the Federal army lay in that direction. He thus began to envelop the Federal camp line to drive the enemy into the swamps. He was unaware that he had found only the half-mile gap between Miller and Stuart, but the movement to the left was unmistakable. William Preston Johnston wrote, "With Hindman as a pivot, the turning movement began." Brigade commanders such as Shaver, Wood, and Jackson, as well as numerous regimental commanders, all reported receiving orders to pivot to the left. Shaver, for example, wrote, "After reforming my line I was ordered to make an oblique change of front to the left, with the view of making an attack upon an encampment to the left and rear of the camp just captured." The brigades who had fought Prentiss and their supports thus began to turn to the left. Wood passed through Lost Field, Shaver moved toward Review Field, and Jackson replaced Gladden's shot-up brigade, which stopped to refit and eventually formed a square, "thinking their cavalry was about to charge us," wrote one Alabamian. Chalmers also moved toward the northeast, but he quickly received orders to return to Jackson's right. Still in reserve, Stewart's brigade in Lost Field and Gibson's troops, which had moved up into Barnes Field, joined Adams's shot-up troops in a second line. Johnston now had four brigades in advance and three in reserve to push the enemy into the swamps while five more at Shiloh Branch held them in position.[30]

This movement had a major effect on Sherman's line to the west, with one Illinoisan in Raith's brigade describing "immense masses of the enemy's infantry pushing forward both from the front and left." The mass of Confederates, including a portion of Russell's and Johnson's brigades that had ranged far to the east and were caught up in the advance, threatened Raith's left flank by a little after 9:30 A.M. That Federal brigade began to crumble from left to right. The 49th Illinois was the first to break. F. A. Niles remembered that the order came to "about face and double-quick." Part of the problem could have been discord in the ranks, with one member of the regiment calling the unpopular Lieutenant Colonel Phineas Pease an "unprincipled dog who would stoop to anything if by so doing he thought he could succeed in placing himself at the head of the Regt." Or it could have had to do with a ball that struck Pease in the belt buckle, denting the shield. For whatever reason, the regiment broke after having formed its line late. The 43rd Illinois had moved farther southward near Waterhouse's battery, but it likewise became engulfed in both Sherman's and Prentiss's retreating soldiers, who, according to Adolph Engelman, ran "through our lines, and it was impossible to induce them to rally on us." Even worse, the Confederates were nearly in Engelman's rear, and he had to shift most of the regiment to the left to face the flank.[31]

The Federal withdrawal, including the 53rd Ohio in the gap, left Waterhouse's Battery alone, and the split 13th Tennessee soon began to threaten it. The artillerymen began to limber up and retire even as Waterhouse went down with a wound in the leg. Sherman's chief of artillery, Ezra Taylor, suddenly rode forward, however, fearing it was "the result of a too hasty retreat," and ordered Lieutenant Abial Abbott, now in command, to unlimber the guns again. This new position was about a hundred yards to the rear of the first, but the retreat had not been hasty. In fact, Vaughan's hard-charging and yelling Tennesseans as well as the wide-ranging 154th Tennessee of Johnson's brigade were nearing the battery, and Abbott quickly went down, shot in the shoulder. Lieutenant John Fitch took command and turned the guns almost to his rear to challenge the flanking enemy. Still, the Confederates soon engulfed the battery. Although Taylor later blamed the loss on the horses "not having sufficient drill," the battery's capture was actually more a result of Taylor's hasty order to redeploy in the face of numerous oncoming Confederates. Some of Raith's troops saw the capture and fired at the battery, hitting a Confederate who had raised their flag over the captured guns. A portion of the 43rd Illinois tried to haul off some of Waterhouse's guns before they too fell back, but they could not because of the "soft and ascending ground." Lieutenant Fitch managed to get two guns out, but he had to leave one of them behind during the retreat. Colonel Vaughan remembered the body of an officer near the guns, guarded by a "pointer dog" who would not let anyone come near his master's dead body.[32]

Even as Waterhouse's guns fell to the enemy, the mass weight of Wood and Shaver also bore down on Sherman's flank. Henry Morton Stanley wrote that the advance was so rapid that "we were no longer an army of soldiers, but so many school-boys racing, in which length of legs, wind, and condition tell." Sherman quickly began to realize that something was amiss on Prentiss's front. Although he did not know what it was, he knew he could not hold his lines fighting the enemy in front and on the flank and rear. Yet he tried. "Although our left was thus turned and the enemy was pressing on the whole line," Sherman wrote, "I deemed Shiloh [Church] so important that I remained by it, and renewed my orders to Colonels McDowell and Buckland to hold their ground."[33]

By 10:00 A.M., however, through no fault of his own, Sherman had to issue orders for his brigades to fall back. One member of the 57th Ohio later wrote that he could see "thousands of rebels" between them and the 53rd Ohio camp, and despite the regiment changing front to the east to confront the flanking Confederates, they soon broke. One flee-ing Ohioan remembered the Southerners yelling "Bull Run" and "Git you d——d Yankees." Major Fearing of the 77th Ohio similarly wrote home, "The left gave way and the devils took a battery and planted their flag directly on our left." He added, "They were . . . pouring in by thou-sands through the camp of the 53rd . . ., in this they were flanking us entirely." Down the line to the west, Colonel Joseph R. Cockerill of the 70th Ohio of Buckland's brigade reported, "The enemy was turning our left flank about one-half mile to the left of Shiloh Meeting-House, and was rapidly advancing at almost right angles with our line." Sherman wrote that "some change became absolutely necessary," and his with-drawal was a little more orderly than Prentiss's retreat, but it still took a toll. Hildebrand's unit was particularly hit hard; Sherman described it as being "knocked to pieces": "Hildebrand's brigade had substantially disappeared from the field, though he himself bravely remained." The 77th Ohio's major, Benjamin Fearing, was also impressed with Hilde-brand's effort: "He did good work . . . better than I supposed he would." Similarly flanked, Raith, Buckland, and McDowell all fell back to the road as well, with the 70th Ohio even taking an intermediate stand at its camps while Barrett's guns fell back to the Purdy Road. Also falling to the Confederates were Sherman's camps and headquarters. There an of-ficer in Cleburne's brigade managed to locate Sherman's personal order book, which he quickly gave to Cleburne.[34]

Although Johnston's turning movement had produced immediate ben-efits in ousting Sherman from his strong position, Johnston had never-theless made a massive miscalculation. The left of Miller's brigade was not the left of the Federal army, and thus the drive northwestward was premature. In fact, there were more Federals to the right in the form of David Stuart's brigade of Sherman's division, and there were also others from additional divisions already deploying farther to the north. Instead of turning the Federal left, Johnston was opening up his own right to a flank attack.

Johnston soon began to realize his mistake. When Jackson and Chalmers moved forward on the right of the sweep, they encountered additional Union camps and even traded long-range fire with more units arriving in the area, Hurlbut's division near the Peach Orchard. Definitive word came when Bragg's engineer, Samuel Lockett, returned from the early morning scout to find the Federal left. The engineer had watched as the Federals responded to firing to the west but noted, "It was evident that it was not understood." Sleepy officers "stir[red] out of their tents, evidently anxious to find out what it all meant." When the long roll sounded in the camps, however, Lockett decided he had better return and report, lest this large force take the Confederate army in the flank. He returned, finding Johnston, who asked who he was. Lockett explained, and Johnston spoke calmly: "Well, sir, tell me as briefly and quickly as possible what you have to say." Lockett then explained that an entire Federal division (probably only the small brigade under Stuart) was to the east. Johnston obviously had to take it into account; William Preston remembered Johnston "pondering [the situation] a little while." He soon took firm control and did what he had to do, however. Still intending to hook the Federal left, Johnston saw that it was too late to recall the troops he had sent to the northwest. He could only still get to the two far right brigades, Jackson's and Chalmers's. Johnston decided to take these units out of line, engaged at long range though they were, and send them under the division commander Jones Withers to the rear, behind Locust Grove Branch, and to the Bark Road. There, they could swiftly move and reach the River Road, on which he hoped the two brigades could really turn the enemy left. A somewhat confused Chalmers remembered, "We were about to engage them again, when we were ordered by General Johnston to fall back, which was done." With Chalmers in the lead and Jackson following, the two brigades sped away to the rear.[35]

Johnston now had an additional problem. Taking two brigades from his right and sending them even farther to the right created a two-brigade sized gap in his lines. No other recourse was left but to call forward his reserves. He sent word to Beauregard to send in Breckinridge, advising Lockett to guide the corps into position. The earlier threat on the left had been minimal, and Beauregard had not sent Breckinridge in that direction. Now, owing to a last-minute change that morning that put Bowen and Statham in reserve on the right and Trabue on the left, apparently anticipating the importance of the Confederate right in turning the Union left, Beauregard already had two of the three reserve brigades moving in that direction (staff officers Numa Augustin and George Brent had been on the Confederate right and reported their need in that sector). Augustin led Breckinridge forward, and Johnston soon also sent Preston and Captain Nathaniel Wickliffe to guide Bowen's and Statham's brigades into the gap on Gladden's right. One bewildered Mississippian wrote, "We were marched and countermarched around until we found ourselves in plain view of the Enemy."[36]

As they were moving into position, a couple of unfortunate incidents occurred in the ranks of the 15th Mississippi in Statham's brigade. A lieutenant shot himself in the hand with his pistol. More troubling, Adjutant James Binford was ahead of the line, leading the troops forward, when he received word his brother had been wounded. He immediately went to the rear at a run, passing through Company H, which was moving forward on the double-quick. "Looking in the direction of my brother and not at the men," Binford wrote, "I ran directly against the point of a bayonet which passed nearly through my left thigh, going between the bone and the main artery and stopped on the skin on the back side." Binford grabbed the musket and pushed the soldier back, but "everything turned perfectly dark." He was taken to a hospital at Shiloh Church, where surgeons dressed his "three-cornered" wound. As he lay there, he saw a surgeon drop amputated arms and legs out the window.[37]

Problems were thus emerging both individually and collectively. In the larger context, Johnston's premature actions had created the scenario in which two major concentrations of troops, one on each side of the battlefield, were pushing forward. By sending a huge portion of his army to the left in a wide sweep, Johnston committed much of his force to pushing the Federals to the northwest on the western third of the battlefield. Simultaneously, as Johnston unfolded a new right flank by sending Chalmers and Jackson to the right and replacing them in line with Bowen and Statham, he committed a large force that would later be augmented by others to the eastern third of the battlefield. Heavy fighting would rage on each flank as these units, well over two-thirds of the Confederate army, went into action. At the same time, a vacuum began to develop in the center.

8

"WE'VE GOT TO FIGHT AGAINST TIME NOW"

David Stuart grew more and more worried as the morning hours ticked away. Situated on the far left flank of the Union front line, he was the last of Sherman's and Prentiss's brigades to come under attack. Significantly, Johnston had to unfold his new right wing before Stuart would be confronted in force, and that took time. Yet time was not what Stuart wanted. He needed answers.

Stuart had reason to be confused. He had heard nothing from the right except a brief courier's report from Prentiss at about 7:30 A.M. saying that the enemy was in his front apparently in force. Stuart merely told the courier, "All right. Present my compliments to Gen. Prentiss." Privately, he was unconvinced. "Prentiss's men are d——d cowards," he told a surgeon. "They are scared and firing away their ammunition at an imaginary enemy among the trees and bushes." Nevertheless, there was still a tinge of nervousness as his small brigade contained only three regiments, the 54th and 71st Ohio and the 55th Illinois, and they were as green as any units in the army, although they made up for their greenness with their looks. The 54th Ohio was a Zouave regiment, with bright uniforms and French-style looks. Further, they were prepared, with the Ohioans intending to go out on another scout at 8:00 A.M. Adding to Stuart's uneasiness was his isolation on the River Road. The looming gap between him and Prentiss really began to worry him, and the nearest major body of infantry that could support him was Hurlbut's division camped more than half a mile north at Cloud Field. Stuart was stuck out on the flank, unsupported and perhaps not even remembered. Tied up at Shiloh Church and then in his own retreat from it, Sherman had little time to think of, much less issue orders to, his small brigade on the other side of the battlefield.[1]

Other issues disturbed Stuart as well. He had been named in the proceedings of a divorce case in Illinois, and his reputation was shattered, but he had to forget these problems now. He had only one lone courier and no artillery; Stone's Missouri Battery had packed up and left the brigade the day before as part of Grant's reorganization of artillery and cavalry. His own inexperience bothered him as well, especially in such a detached position. With little military education, and keenly aware of it, Stuart depended heavily on the lieutenant colonel in the 55th Illinois, Oscar Malmborg. A native of Sweden, where he had served in the army, Malmborg had been raised in a military family and had fought in the Mexican War after migrating to America. Stuart later reported, "Comprehending at a glance the purpose and object of every movement of the enemy, he [Malmborg] was able to advise me promptly and intelligently as to the disposition of my men. He was cool, observant, discreet, and brave, and of infinite service to me."[2]

From his headquarters at the Cantrell house in Larkin Bell Field, Stuart thus waited, watched, and listened as the sounds of battle erupted to the southwest early that morning. He could soon tell this was no normal skirmish, and he became even more sure when artillery opened up. On the other hand, his specific task was watching the ford where the River Road crossed Lick Creek to the southeast; his attention had to be focused in that direction although the fighting, obviously growing in sound by 9:00 A.M., was to the southwest. Stuart sent a portion of his command southeastward to guard the crossing, with four companies even crossing Locust Grove Branch and taking position just below the high bluffs on the other side. Still, he cast worried glances to the right, in the direction of Prentiss's position.[3]

Then Stuart found "a convenient position on the brow of the bank north of the creek [from which] with my glass I could observe all their movements." What he saw concerned him even more. There was apparently an avenue through which he could see some of Prentiss's camps, because he reported seeing "the Pelican flag [of the 1st Louisiana of Gladden's brigade] advancing in the rear of General Prentiss' headquarters."[4]

What Stuart could not see would have worried him even more. He did not know that Johnston had taken the precaution of sending multiple brigades against him. He also did not know that the entire Confederate

battle plan hinged on turning the Union left flank—which his small brigade held. But he did know he had to hold. He thus formed his brigade,
although some in the ranks thought they were still just turning out for
inspection. They would soon learn different.[5]

It took an hour or so for Johnston to rearrange his brigades, as Chalmers and Jackson had to pull out of line and march to the south of Locust Grove Branch. Some veterans indicated that they moved north of
the creek, but these were probably just skirmishers; the infantry and
artillery moved south of the creek. Chalmers had a long way to go, as
Johnston intended him to extend the right flank of the army over half a
mile. That meant he had to go all the way to the River Road and deploy
across it so that he would not only extend to the low ground around the
creek but also cut off any axis of retreat for the Federal army toward
Hamburg. Chalmers's task was to turn the Union left, and that meant
he had to move far enough to the right to make sure he found the real
enemy left flank this time.[6]

Chalmers obtained a local guide named Lafayette Veal, and the Mississippians made the march, around three-quarters of a mile, in less than
an hour. The course took the brigade south across the swampy Locust
Grove Branch to the high ground on which the Bark Road ran. There
they turned eastward and marched on the road until they reached the
valley of Lick Creek. It was by all accounts a harrowing march. Jones
Withers described the terrain as "rough, broken, and heavily timbered."
Another Confederate wrote, "We made a flank movement for about two
miles over the hills. This was a very fatiguing march." It took some additional time to rest the men and send out cavalry to make sure Withers
now flanked the enemy left. It also took time to get deployed into line
and to move across Locust Grove Branch and ascend the ridge on the
other side. As the infantry moved into position, Chalmers left his artillery unit, Gage's Alabama Battery, on the high ridge on the south side
of Locust Grove Branch. From that vantage point, they began to shell
Stuart's camps and infantry across the creek.[7]

Jackson's brigade was not far behind Chalmers's troops during the
march, and because they did not have as far to go, they actually engaged
the Federals before Chalmers did. Jones Withers described the brigade
as "descending rapidly the hill on which his brigade had rested"—a
perfect statement because there was no other way to descend the almost

vertical bluffs south of Locust Grove Branch. Jackson's front was farther up the watershed, but the valley was still steep, wide, and boggy,
with Jackson describing it as "a deep and almost impassable ravine."
Much like Chalmers, Jackson chose to leave his artillery, Girardey's
Georgia Battery, on the tall ridge south of the creek due to the difficult
terrain. It began to shell Stuart as well.[8]

In the meantime, Johnston's reserves arrived under Lockett's guidance. They had moved about the same distance as Chalmers and Jackson
but at the double-quick. Bowen in the lead moved down the Bark Road
to the Eastern Corinth Road, moving across some of the feeder branches
of Locust Grove Branch and then onto high ground on the south side
of the creek. Statham's troops were right behind and went into line en
echelon on Bowen's left, covered by the fire of Rutledge's well-drilled
Tennessee battery (the cannoneers had once "accomplished the marvel
of loading six times in a minute," one of them proudly noted). Preston
and Jordan placed the battery farther forward on the ridge near the 18th
Wisconsin camp. William Preston noted that the brigades went into line
at an angle, "en echelon of brigades" several hundred yards apart. Yet
even in this movement, the terrain caused some confusion, with the 1st
Missouri of Bowen's brigade becoming separated from the other regiments and winding up behind Withers's troops to the right. To scout the
front, Lockett and Breckinridge rode forward together until they took
a volley from Hurlbut's deploying Federals. Still, by 10:30 or 11:00
A.M., Johnston had his new right wing unfolding south of Locust Grove
Branch and was ready to continue the advance, which Withers was impatient to begin. He rode over to Bowen's men and pushed them forward
to the front lines.[9]

Johnston was in a cheerful mood, feeling confident about his latest
orders. In deploying Breckinridge's command, he moved from the camp
of the 18th Wisconsin, inadvertently forgetting to take with him his surgeon, D. W. Yandell, whom he had ordered to care for Union wounded:
"These men were our enemies a moment ago; they are our prisoners
now. Take care of them." Yandell did so, continuing a policy of compassion, which was not what the Federal prisoners expected. That said, there
was some Confederate cruelty to prisoners, with one Louisianan slitting
a wounded Federal's throat. Johnston obviously mandated compassion,
but he could only be at one place at one time. After leaving Yandell,
the general crossed Locust Grove Branch and ascended the ridge to the
high ground where he could see his brigades. Apparently he ranged all

the way to Jackson's right flank, well within sight of Chalmers eastern-most brigade. Colonel Joseph Wheeler reported that Johnston gave his 19th Alabama orders "with his own lips" to attack an Illinois camp, and Dudley Hayden recorded that he "ordered a Texas regiment to charge a camp." Similarly, an Alabamian in Jackson's brigade wrote of Johnston riding his lines shouting, "My noble boys we have achieved a grand victory, a very great victory." Other staff officers corroborated his presence south of Locust Grove Branch far on the Confederate right. Thus came the famous episode when a satisfied Johnston talked with Colonel Edward Munford, who remembered: "We sat on our horses, side by side, watching that brigade [Chalmers] as it swept over the ridge; and, as the colors dipped out of sight, the general said to me, 'That check-mates them.'" Munford went on to describe how he "told him I was glad to hear him announce 'checkmate,' but that 'he must excuse so poor a player for saying he could not see it.' Johnston laughed and said, 'Yes, sir, that mates them.'"[10]

Johnston may have put his forces into position to carry out his plan, but the troops still had to perform the hard fighting that would develop on the ridges bordering the Tennessee River. They did. All along the line, Johnston's brigades soon moved forward across the creek and drove away the enemy forces tasked with holding the camps on the northern slope. Admittedly, that consumed little effort by Bowen and Statham, who had nothing but an Illinois cavalry battalion's camp on Statham's front and the vacated 71st Ohio camp on Bowen's front. The Ohioans had departed earlier when Stuart's nervousness had grown, and he desired to have his brigade concentrated on one small line nearer to the ford he was tasked with holding. An artillery battery then arrived and deployed just east of the camp, providing some cover. Stuart had sent Hurlbut word asking for help, and within fifteen minutes, Mann's Missouri Battery of Hurlbut's division, under First Lieutenant Edward Brotzmann, arrived and deployed around 9:00 A.M. in the angle of the junction of the River and Hamburg-Purdy roads. It soon engaged Confederate artillery in Prentiss's camps. Also following Mann but not that far forward was Hurlbut's infantry, although still deploying to the rear. The cannoneers were soon outgunned and withdrew, however, leaving Stuart without any artillery support, as all the division artillery was back under Sherman's control at Shiloh Church, nearly two miles to the west. Stuart hurried to the 71st Ohio camp to order Mann's battery to the left, "where they would have had a splendid fire as well upon the enemy's battery as upon the advancing infantry." Indeed, Larkin Bell Field would have offered a fine killing zone almost all the way to the creek bottom, but the gunners were soon called back by Hurlbut, leaving Stuart without any artillery. Stuart also noted, "For above a quarter of a mile to my right no soldier could be seen, unless fugitives, making their way to the rear." Yet that was nothing compared to the view to the south. One of the 71st Ohio soldiers wrote home that the regiment "anxiously watched the movement of the rebels from a hill about a quarter of a mile distant, as regiment after regiment filed by and crossed the ravine and were fastly approaching us."[11]

While Chalmers and Jackson to the east met much firmer resistance, Bowen and Statham thus had an easier time moving forward across Locust Grove Branch, eventually taking the camps in their sector and aligning in the woods along and south of the Hamburg-Purdy Road. There, they waited for about an hour while the rest of the army caught up. It would have been folly to proceed alone, as so many Confederate brigades had been doing. Perhaps Johnston was learning the need to coordinate his attacks, and he thus held Statham and Bowen in position until Chalmers and Jackson could come up on their right and others could fill in the minor void to the left. Fortunately for Johnston, some of those units were already on the way; Beauregard had sent in Polk's last brigade, William Stephens's, now under Cheatham's direct command. The brigade eventually went on line in the center between Statham and Shaver. Gibson and Adams likewise remained in reserve in the area, although somewhat disconnected to the movement to the west.[12]

Intended as the major blow, Chalmers's and Jackson's brigades soon stepped forward and almost immediately met resistance from Stuart's skirmishers. Forming his men in the fields on the high ground south of the valley, Jackson was able to move down into the bottom and up the slope overlooking the creek fairly easily because there was pitifully little resistance on his front. "The command 'forward' was given," an Alabamian wrote, "and away we went; down the hill, over the swampy bottom, and up the steep ascent before us into the camp. Every moment we expected to receive a volley from the enemy." Only the 71st Ohio was in the area, however, having moved from their camps, leaving them uncovered and thus open to Bowen's units as they trudged through. The Ohioans' rotund colonel, Rodney Mason, was less worried about his

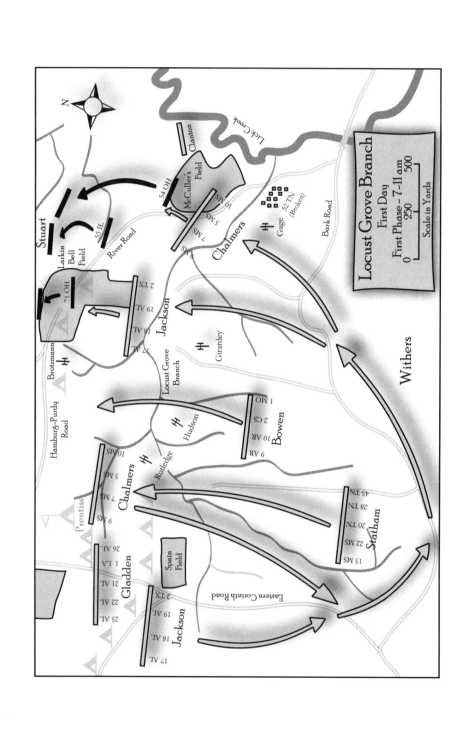

Locust Grove Branch

First Day

First Phase ~ 7–11 am

Scale in Yards

0   250   500

N

Lick Creek

Clanton

McCuller's Field

54 OH

10 MS

5 MS

7 MS

9 MS

Stuart

55 IL

Larkin Bell Field

River Road

71 OH

Brotzmann

Gage

52 TN (Broken)

Bark Road

Chalmers

Jackson

2 TX

19 AL

18 AL

17 AL

Girardey

Withers

Locust Grove Branch

Hamburg–Purdy Road

Hudson

Bowen

1 MO

2 CS

10 AR

9 AR

Prentiss

Chalmers

10 MS

5 MS

7 MS

9 MS

Rutledge

Gladden

26 AL

1 LA

21 AL

22 AL

25 AL

Spain Field

2 TX

19 AL

18 AL

17 AL

Jackson

Eastern Corinth Road

45 TN

28 TN

20 TN

22 MS

15 MS

Statham

camps than he was about his present position. His lone regiment, without artillery, confronted Jackson's entire brigade, and it was supported by artillery. A dispute about whose artillery was to the front caused more concern until "they easily decided it for us by a terrific discharge of shells," one of the Ohioans wrote home. Jackson was thus able to swiftly push Mason and his Ohioans back from the camps of the 54th Ohio and 55th Illinois in Larkin Bell Field, with the Alabamians taking the camps around 11:00 A.M. and the Ohioans falling back to the crest of the ridge to their rear.[13]

Those two regiments were not defending their own camps either. They were farther to the left, confronting Chalmers's advance. Stuart realized that his flank was extremely important because it was the army's flank as well. Even if Stuart did not know of Johnston's intention of turning that very flank, he knew that he did not want it turned, and the best way to do that was to keep a firm hold on the ravines leading into the river to the east. Stuart thus allocated two-thirds of his meager force to that flank, a mere 800 men, and he battled Chalmers as the Mississippians and Tennesseans advanced.[14]

The first contact came in the northern portion of McCuller's Field around 11:00 A.M., a little later than on Jackson's front, as Chalmers had farther to go than Jackson. Stuart had placed the 54th Ohio there to halt the Confederates, sending a few companies across the creek as scouts. These skirmishers did good work in scaring off at least a portion of Chalmers's brigade. The 52nd Tennessee broke when the skirmishers fired into them, and Chalmers reported that "repeated efforts to rally it" were not successful and labeled their conduct "shameful." Chalmers ordered the Tennesseans out of the ranks, and the only two companies that remained fought the rest of the day with the 5th Mississippi. Despite the chaos among the Tennesseans, Chalmers still far outnumbered Stuart, and the Federal skirmishers soon returned with word that large bodies of Confederates were on the way. A brisk firefight broke out as the Mississippians advanced somewhat eastward across Locust Grove Branch toward the Ohioans' lines in McCuller's Field, situated behind "a worm fence and thick underbrush," according to Jones Withers. Colonel T. Kilby Smith described his position as on "a kind of peninsula formed by a dense ravine on the one side and a creek on the other." Smith had his Ohioans lying down, their bright uniforms soon soiled by the mud; Smith himself remained atop his beloved horse. One of his soldiers described how he was continually "scratching his head, apparently as

much unconscious as though he was on dress parade." After a couple of
attempts, Chalmers soon had the Federals on the run as Stuart pulled the
Ohioans back, with the regiments reforming in "three oblique squares
in the woods." Obviously, Clanton's cavalry put at least some fear in
Stuart's troops, but the main concern was Chalmers, who continued up
the gradual slope.[15]

There he met the 55th Illinois, which likewise delayed the advance
for a short time but eventually withdrew as well. One Illinoisan complained that Malmborg "exhausted military skill in locating the regiment where it had the least possible defense," and he admitted that the
regiment "broke and ran in the most inextricable confusion." Stuart rode
among his beloved Illinoisans and soon had them rallied on a ridge to
the rear, but Malmborg again ordered, "Column by file; battalion, in-
verts face, forvarts march." The regiment quickly formed a square. One
Illinoisan related that Malborg "seemed to have the idea that the main
use of infantry was to repel the attacks of cavalry," and he had drilled
them extensively on the maneuver. But no cavalry came. The same Illinoisan wrote, "The disgusted lieutenant-colonel dissolved the square"
and posted his men in line. The Federals later learned the watching
Confederates were dumfounded at their antics, thinking it was "Yankee
tricks" to draw them into ambush. Nevertheless, both Union regiments
fell back to a tall ridge just north of a deep ravine, intending to hold the
Confederate assault there. In later maneuvering, Stuart had to send several of the Ohio companies farther to the left to hold that flank against
Chalmers's regiments, but they held for the moment. The 71st Ohio
similarly went into position on the right of Stuart's other two regiments,
immediately behind Stuart's own headquarters, although the two wings
were not connected and thus could not support each other. Stuart later
noted that he did not even know where the 71st Ohio was. Even so, the
54th Ohio remained steady alongside the 55th Illinois, with one Illinois
soldier writing, "God bless those Zouaves!"[16]

By 11:00 A.M., Chalmers and Jackson had thus taken the initial line
of encampments on their front, and it had been fairly easy. The Confederates on this far right flank had endured none of the trouble or casualties their comrades had on the far left flank. Yet it did not have to
be that way. Stuart's position overlooking Locust Grove Branch was
just as strong, or perhaps even more formidable, as Sherman's at Shiloh Church. The difference was that the Shiloh Church sector had been
much more heavily defended, with eventually four brigades and four

artillery batteries contesting the Confederate advance in that sector. The Union line grew weaker as it extended eastward, however, and Stuart's position was the weakest of all, with only three regiments and no artillery manning this all-important section of the line. Had four brigades and artillery been present to hold the line from the Tennessee River to Prentiss's camps, there is little doubt that they could have held the position as long or longer than Sherman did at Shiloh Church. It was not to be, and by 11:00 or 11:30 A.M., the Confederates had completed their capture of all six frontline Union brigade camps.[17]

Fortunately for the Federals, Ulysses S. Grant dove into this developing disaster. As he would do throughout the war, Grant met crisis and potential disaster with calmness and determination. The same thing had happened at Belmont and Fort Donelson, where Grant had also been away from the army and had also been surprised. In each case, he had taken firm control of the situation, stabilized his own forces, and then eventually counterattacked to win the battle.

First, however, Grant had to get to the battlefield. As at Fort Donelson, the Confederates struck while Grant was not with the army. At the earlier battle, Grant was admittedly conferring with naval officers on future actions, but his absence at Shiloh, although ostensibly to meet Buell on the morning of April 6, was nevertheless an example of his overconfidence. Grant did not let the initial stumble stop him, though. He had awoken early that morning to ride out to meet Buell, whom he did not know was already at Savannah. He took an earlier breakfast than usual. While waiting for his meal, he perused his mail and chatted with Brigadier General John Cook, who had arrived at Savannah from leave and reported for duty to Grant. His nonchalance changed in the middle of breakfast. As soon as a guard reported artillery fire from up the river and he heard the guns for himself, he knew something was amiss either at Crump's or Pittsburg. He left his breakfast and prepared to speed upriver. While preparations were being made and the *Tigress,* which already had steam up, was loaded with horses and staff, Grant sent several quick notes. One told Buell that he could not meet him that day but to send his arriving troops on up the river as quickly as possible. To Bull Nelson, whose division was already in Savannah, he sent a quick note telling him to march overland southward to Pittsburg Landing. If that was the point of attack, he would be desperately needed. If Wallace at Crump's Landing was the target, Nelson could fill in for divisions sent from Pittsburg to his aid. Grant also sent notes to Buell's rearward divisions commanded by Thomas J. Wood and George H. Thomas to hurry forward. Finally, Grant met Walter Gresham, who commanded the brigade and the post at Savannah. Gresham asked permission to go to the battlefield with his command, but Grant ordered him to stay put. "It seems like bad luck attends me," Gresham told his wife.[18]

Grant then stepped aboard the *Tigress,* Gresham following and begging a second time to be allowed to go. Grant denied him again and headed southward, the vessel rounding the large bend just south of Savannah. He later recounted that his first inclination had been that the attack had occurred at Crump's, but as the *Tigress* drew closer, Grant and his staff could see no smoke nor smell black powder. The noise, growing louder by the minute, was still farther south. Grant quickly realized that Crump's Landing was not the attack point; it was definitely Pittsburg.[19]

As the *Tigress* rounded the next bend and drew in to Crump's Landing, Grant saw Wallace aboard his own headquarters boat. Wallace had been back and forth from brigade to brigade that morning, obviously agitated: the general "rode past our regiment on his way to the landing very much excited," one 24th Indiana soldier wrote of Wallace's reaction when "Grant[']s boat whistled for our landing." The two boats were lashed together and Grant and Wallace spoke briefly, with Wallace informing him that firing had been heard since dawn. Not knowing what to expect at Pittsburg, Grant told Wallace to hold his division in readiness to march southward and to cover his western approaches. Wallace replied that he had already done both; the division was even then concentrating at Stoney Lonesome in the middle of the split encampment. Then Grant departed, telling Wallace only to await orders on what to do next.[20]

The *Tigress* steamed against the current toward Pittsburg, but when Grant arrived before 9:00 A.M.—more probably around 8:15 or 8:30 A.M.—he saw nothing that resembled a battle. The image of Grant arriving to panic-stricken mobs of soldiers fills histories of Shiloh, but in actuality, Grant arrived to a fairly calm scene. The landing was certainly busy with just-arriving regiments and batteries in addition to numerous wagons, sutlers, and other camp followers. No panic-stricken soldiers from that first break were there, however, as they could not conceivably have been at Pittsburg when Grant arrived between 8:00 and 9:00 A.M.[21]

If there was no panic at the landing, the noise still told Grant what was occurring, and he immediately set to work. He quickly met W. H. L. Wallace near the landing while he was in the process of moving his division to the front. From him Grant discovered the magnitude of the unfolding disaster. Grant immediately acted. He first began sending ammunition wagons to the front, having learned a major lesson at Fort Donelson. He also began to organize reinforcements by sending forward the various regiments that were stationary at the landing. He also took time to send a message to Lew Wallace, ordering his assistant adjutant general, John A. Rawlins, to send the army's quartermaster Captain A. S. Baxter to order Wallace to move to Pittsburg. Afraid he would "make some mistake," Baxter asked Rawlins to write out the orders. A befuddled Rawlins agreed to do so, but he had no paper or pencil. He went back onboard the *Tigress,* where he found ample writing material and wrote out the orders. Once Rawlins finished, Baxter set sail.[22]

The still-hobbling Grant then set out to the front on horseback, where he visited his division commanders. Staff officer W. S. Hillyer marveled at Grant being "cool and undismayed as ever" even though by the time he reached the front his divisions had already fallen back from the initial line of camps. Grant knew he had a big job ahead of him, but he took special care to encourage his commanders and men, steadying their nerves for what he hoped would be a drawn-out defense. In his mind, he was already realizing the key to survival—nightfall. If his army could fall back gradually during the day, eating up daylight, by nightfall or perhaps even earlier, he would have Lew Wallace there to add numbers to the defense. Nelson would, he hoped, also arrive soon, adding even more. During the night, Buell would be able to bring in even more of his divisions. Grant told his commanders as much; at one point he told an aide, "Delay counts everything with us. To-morrow we will attack with fresh troops and drive them." When another remarked that things were not looking so good, Grant replied, "Well, not so very bad. We've got to fight against time now. Wallace must be here very soon." Yet at the same time, Grant took no chances; he cautioned his own commanders to hold their lines as long as possible and sent various staff officers out to hurry forward the reinforcements.[23]

There was also a tinge of panic, as evidenced in some of Grant's messages. He obviously intended to hurry the various divisions on the way, but to Nelson he displayed perhaps momentary panic when he wrote that the Confederates were estimated at 100,000 strong and that Nelson's arrival might "possibly save the day to us." Those flashes of desperation were the exception, though, and Grant had the situation under control. Trading space for time could only benefit one side at Shiloh.[24]

Lew Wallace's division was not the only reinforcements on the way to the battlefield. Buell was soon on his way as well. Nevertheless, the attack caught even the Army of the Ohio by surprise. Bull Nelson's officer of the day remembered, "In a moment all the officers were standing in front of the tents in their underclothing with hand to the ear listening." A staff officer reported how "when the wind favored we could hear the volleys of musketry and the clamor of field pieces." Buell quickly went to the Cherry mansion but missed Grant. He also sent word for his divisions still on the road to hurry forward and for Nelson to march southward along the river to Pittsburg. Nelson's job was gargantuan, given the flooded terrain. While he looked for guides, Nelson sent staff officer Mills Kendrick and his cavalry to scout a route, and Kendrick reported that he made it through but "killed several horses and left behind a number of men in our haste." In the meantime, back at Savannah, all Nelson's men could do was wait. Jacob Ammen went to Grant's headquarters to see his old friend C. F. Smith, who, Ammen noted in his diary, "laughed at me for thinking that a great battle was raging; said it was only a skirmish of pickets, and that I was accustomed to small affairs." Nelson also visited Smith, who insisted again that "the rebels are all back in Corinth, and when our wagons and siege guns arrive, we shall have to go to Corinth and drag them out as we draw a badger out of his hole." It was only around 1:30 P.M. when Nelson finally found the necessary path and guide, "who professes to be a strong Union man and a desperate hater of rebels," according to Ammen.[25]

As the disaster continued to unfold throughout the day, Buell went on to Pittsburg with his chief of staff, Colonel James B. Fry. On the way, they saw the ever-increasing number of panicked stragglers seeking safety. "Groups of soldiers were seen upon the west bank," Buell wrote, "and it soon became evident that they were stragglers from the army that was engaged. The groups increased in size and frequency until, as we approached the Landing, they amounted to whole companies, and almost regiments, and at the Landing the banks swarmed with a confused mass of men of various regiments." Some even fled all the way to Crump's Landing, where officers left there gathered up as many as 800 to 1,000 men and sent them back to the battlefield.[26]

Buell soon met Grant on the *Tigress,* and their stormy relationship continued. After the war, Buell put the number of stragglers initially upon his landing at 4,000 to 5,000 but eventually growing as high as 12,000 to 15,000, "all striving to get as near as possible to the river." Grant admitted they were there, but he argued that there were no more than 4,000 to 5,000 at its worst hugging the bluffs. Hurlbut added that the mass was "swelled by camp followers and the floating trash that gathers round and impedes an army." Of course, the numbers played into the various arguments the generals later made, Buell that he saved Grant's obviously defeated army and Grant that he had the situation under control and Buell saved nothing.[27]

In reality, the truth of the numbers was probably somewhere in between. Many officers tried to get the frightened soldiers to return to the ranks, almost all without success. One officer on the *Choctaw,* Charles Scott, wrote of his attempts to talk to the "stone men. They were perfectly stolid." He tried a number of ways to get to them, even telling them to "come on Board as there were some Petticoats on Board that they could exchange for their Pantaloons." He "found Shame had no Effect." The only thing that worked was writing names and units down to publish in the newspapers. "This had some Effect," he wrote, "for they kept shy of me." He left so angry that he admitted, "If I had not been stopped I would have shot some of them." The coldhearted sailor even admitted that he had watched some men drown as they tried to swim the river: "I was willing to stand and look on without trying to render them Assistance."[28]

W ith Grant now on the field, the first phase of the first day's battle was over by 11:00 A.M. In that phase, Johnston's brigades had rolled over all six frontline Union brigade camps. The task had certainly not been easy, especially on the left, with Sherman making a determined stand at Shiloh Branch. Sherman had stalled five Confederate brigades for some three hours, and he was never driven from his position by their frontal assaults. Instead, it was Prentiss's retreat to the east that uncovered Sherman's left flank and allowed several Confederate units to turn his position. Sherman then wisely withdrew his division and Raith's brigade from the Shiloh Church line, but he had used up several hours of daylight at Shiloh Branch.

More Confederate success came in assaulting the Union center. Once the Southern commanders were able to get their brigades aligned the correct way, they easily overran Prentiss's two brigades, with the only major trouble spot on Gladden's front during its attack at Spain Field. The net result, however, was that Prentiss's division was shattered. Even with Johnston's miscalculation and a subsequent new right flank, the assaults at Locust Grove Branch were successful as well, to the point that Stuart had fallen back to a new line in rear of his camps, leaving them in Confederate hands. Thus was completed the fall of all six frontline Union brigade camps.

On paper, it seemed that the Confederates were doing well, sweeping the field of Union forces and driving them back all across the battlefield. In reality, the Confederate advance was not the quick steamroller action often thought of at Shiloh, and certainly not what Beauregard later described as "an Alpine avalanche." Once the belated Confederate assault began on the morning of April 6, the Confederates, for a number of reasons, including Peabody's patrol, growing Federal resistance, and their own greenness, did not even reach the point where they could assault the Union camps until 7:30 or 8:00 A.M. The Federal commanders used the time between the beginning of the battle at dawn and the Confederate attacks on the camps to form their lines and prepare for action. Those formed Federals then held for another several hours. In heavy combat across the board, the Confederates did not succeed in taking all the front line of camps until after 10:30 A.M., and closer to 11:00 A.M. on the far right. Thus, the Federal defense of the front line in this initial phase used up six hours.[29]

A deeper look into the action of the first phase reveals even more trouble for the Confederates than just piecemeal attacks and a slower progression than desired. Johnston had to use nearly all of his army to roll over the six frontline camps defended by seven Union brigades. By a little after 11:00 A.M., Johnston and Beauregard had deployed and had on line, facing the enemy, fourteen of their sixteen brigades. Only Gibson's Louisiana brigade was still idle in two ranks in Barnes Field, and Robert Trabue's Kentucky brigade was still in reserve. Gibson's unit had been deployed and followed up the Confederate advance; it just had not yet gone into action, although by this time it had taken friendly fire as well as long-range artillery. That meant that only the last brigade of Breckinridge's reserve was totally unengaged and could actually be classified as still in reserve, although it too had taken some casualties in following up the front line. Johnston had thus used seven-eighths of his army—nearly 88 percent—in attacking and taking the initial line of Federal camps. Moreover, it had taken that mass six hours to complete the job against a defender half its size. Obviously, terrain played a key role.[30]

Furthermore, even though these Confederate brigades were now aligned and ready to push on, they were terribly mixed up. The various corps that stretched all the way across the field were split apart, with the rearward corps moving forward and sending their own brigades in between the original frontline brigades. The problem ran deeper, however, with divisions and even brigades already beginning to break up and fight as separate components. The problem soon became so obvious that during the initial fighting, the Confederate corps commanders worked out among themselves a division of the line so that at least some command and control could be retained. When Bragg met Polk on the field around 10:30 A.M., Polk asked Bragg where to go. Polk was Bragg's senior, yet Polk asked Bragg what to do, thinking Bragg's position as chief of staff awarded him higher command authority. Bragg replied, "If you will take care of the center, I will go to the right." Bragg knew Hardee was already on the left; that officer had moved in that direction in response to "a heavy cannonade." Because Breckinridge's new wing eventually made his position the right, Bragg actually commanded the right center.[31]

That solution caused many other problems, however. The corps commanders had the trouble of now informing both their old and new commands of the change. Then there was the issue of personal connection. When Polk took charge of the Corinth Road sector, for instance, he retained command of Johnson's and Russell's brigades, which were his originally, but he also gained Patton Anderson's and Patrick Cleburne's. While Polk had been at Columbus, Kentucky, and then in northwestern Tennessee, Anderson had been in Florida with Bragg until recently, when they had all congregated at Corinth. Likewise, Cleburne had been with Hardee at Bowling Green. One wonders whether Polk knew Anderson or Cleburne and whether he could even recognize them by sight. Similarly, the division commanders' duties, with the possible exception of Jones Withers on the far right, were negated by the reorganization.[32]

More significantly, while fourteen of the sixteen Confederate brigades were deployed or in action, the Federal army, conversely, had only seven of its fifteen brigades fully engaged at the initial camp line by this point in the battle. While rearward Union divisions were making their way forward and even then taking a strong position across the lower half of the hourglass, most of McClernand's, W. H. L. Wallace's, and Hurlbut's divisions were not engaged except perhaps in extremely long-range exchanges.

The result was that by 10:30 A.M., Grant had only seven of his fifteen brigades, or approximately 46 percent of the army, not counting Lew Wallace or Buell, in heavy combat. Eight other brigades—a majority of the army—were behind the initial line of the morning, forming their own positions on which these battered defenders of the first phase could reform.

Taking the analysis one step farther, these eight brigades contained what veterans there were in the Union army. McClernand's and Wallace's divisions had been in action at Fort Donelson; they knew what to expect. Although most of Hurlbut's division had not been present, it had nevertheless been around longer than Sherman's or Prentiss's and thus should have had more coordination and power. A comparable set of Confederate veteran units was not available; most of those who had achieved at least some veteran status in the action on February 14 and 15 at Fort Donelson were now in Northern prison camps.

In short, while matters looked good for Johnston and Beauregard, a tiring and bloody Confederate army, having lost key leaders already, had taken six hours to dislodge the greenest half of the Union army from their camps. That same tired and bloody army was now coming up against a rested, fresh, veteran line of Federal divisions, augmented by the newly minted veterans of the first line who took their positions alongside them. The odds were trending more and more against the Confederates. They seemingly had spent much of their force in the initial action, with less now left to confront what by all accounts had to be a stronger line than the first one. Braxton Bragg was not wrong when he commented that the Federals caused "us to pay dearly for our successes." It happened in more ways than one.[33]

9

"Where the Fight Is
the Thickest"

John A. McClernand was perhaps more suited for the floor of the United States House of Representatives than he was for the battlefield, but he turned out to be well suited for combat too. The Republican Abraham Lincoln had appointed McClernand, a Democrat, to be a general so he could whip up public support for the war effort in his southern Illinois region—something Lincoln was especially worried about early in the war. There was discussion and fear in the North that southern Ohio, Indiana, and Illinois, whose economies were linked more to the Ohio River and slavery than the North's industry, might actually side with the South. Having a firm and popular supporter of the war like McClernand on his side would help keep southern Illinois on Lincoln's side, and there was no better way to keep McClernand's support for the war than to make him a general in it.[1]

Yet the political battles in Washington were nothing compared to what was unfolding at Shiloh this bright April morning. McClernand was in for the trial of his life. As this second phase of the first day's battle began at the famous sites that the general public has come to associate with Shiloh—places such as the Hornet's Nest, Peach Orchard, and Crossroads—the emergence and entrance of three more Federal divisions into the battle was a key factor. As the early fighting raged, word quickly reached McClernand, Hurlbut, and W. H. L. Wallace to form their divisions and move forward in support of the initial line. Some of the divisions had a long way to go, including some of Wallace's regiments who were camped nearly two and a half miles behind the front line. Accordingly, the three reinforcing divisions, with the exception of Raith's brigade of McClernand's division, did not move to the front line itself but chose to take strong positions to the rear where they met the withdrawing brigades from the front. Consequently, McClernand moved forward only to the Hamburg-Purdy Road area and posted his two remaining brigades there. Wallace took a position in a farm lane in the center, and Hurlbut moved into a large cotton field on the left. Each division commander, acting on his own, struggled to find the best position for his troops.[2]

They had to hurry; the Confederates were almost on them.

McClernand quickly moved forward with two brigades to aid Sherman, but it took time for his troops to get into position. Carroll Marsh was milling about camp that morning when he heard lively firing to the south. "This continuing without material interruption for some time," Marsh reported, he sent word to his regimental commanders to be ready to form up quickly. He had just sent those orders when McClernand told him to form the brigade and move to Sherman's assistance. Marsh did so, first taking a position to the right rear of Sherman's camps but then moving to the left, across the Corinth Road. There, Marsh placed the 45th, 48th, and 20th, as well as the Fort Donelson–decimated 11th Illinois, in a line extending from Woolf Field on the right to "a field used for reviews" (later aptly named Review Field) on the left. Behind them deployed Dresser's Battery under Captain James P. Timony, and in their center were Jerome Burrows's six Ohio guns. In this position, the Illinois infantry and artillery watched in awe as the Confederates soon emerged. Timony recounted that they crept up to less than a hundred yards, "deceiving us by their flags." Thomas Ransom of the 11th Illinois reported the enemy advanced in "four ranks and three columns steadily upon us."[3]

Abraham Hare, who commanded the first brigade in Richard Oglesby's absence, similarly formed his four regiments in front of their camps in Jones Field when he heard heavy firing to the south. "The roar of the battle in the distance was plainly heard," one Federal remembered, and soon "a great number of men were rushing through the camp to the rear, some wounded but most frightened and demoralized." As the 11th Iowa stood in line, a cannonball landed in the camp. The chaplain picked it up and "brought it out and showed it to us," remembered one of the Iowans. Hare soon received orders to march southward as well, going into a line with three regiments extending from Duncan Field on the left all the way to the northwestern corner of Review Field, with the 8th and 18th Illinois on the left and the 13th Iowa on the right. Hare's own huge 11th Iowa (750 men) took a position in reserve behind Marsh. Unfortunately for them, Hare's men found themselves under fire even before they reached their position, most likely from the advance skirmishers of Johnston's foremost brigade in that area, Shaver's. In the 8th Illinois, which was already devoid of field officers, Captain James M. Ashmore took command but was wounded immediately, and Captain William B. Harvey, now in command, was similarly hit and killed. The third ranking captain, Robert H. Sturgess, took command, and the regiment had not even engaged the enemy yet.[4]

With McClernand's solid line forming, Sherman and Raith fell back and posted their retreating units to their right along the Hamburg-Purdy Road, with Sherman ordering them to "adopt that road as their new line." To keep McClernand's brigades together, and because they were retreating on the left of Sherman, Raith's Illinois regiments obliquely retreated to the right and went into line west of Marsh, carrying the line across the all-important crossroads of the Hamburg-Purdy and Corinth roads. There, Sherman's brigades picked up the line, with Buckland's Ohio troops extending it westward and McDowell's troops going into position farther to the west. Buckland took position fairly easily, but McDowell took some time because of the "extended front of our line, at that time three-quarters of a mile in length, on and over a broken and wooded surface, and at the time when the only passable (the main) road was filled by the teams of the brigade." Pockets of Hildebrand's soldiers also formed among their comrades.[5]

In an interesting twist that illustrated the confusion of Shiloh, another Union brigade suddenly appeared on this line too. Sherman's message calling for aid had gone to both McClernand and Hurlbut, and the latter had dispatched his far right brigade under James Veatch. The brigade moved in ten minutes, despite one Federal indicating that when the firing was first heard, some had their muskets apart for cleaning and inspection and "everyone for a moment seemed as if riveted to the spot where he happened to be standing." Veatch marched toward Hurlbut's headquarters, where the remainder of the division was also forming, and then out the Corinth Road. There he formed a line in the rear of Marsh's brigade near the 11th Iowa, which, after moving positions under McClernand's watchful eye, was also in reserve near the Water Oaks Pond. Another reinforcing regiment came from the left as well, the 13th

Missouri of John McArthur's brigade of W. H. L. Wallace's division, which had earlier been sent to hold the Owl Creek Bridge. It took a similar position in reserve.[6]

This line was also studded with artillery, including five of Behr's Indiana guns moving to Sherman's position at the Crossroads, four of Schwartz's Illinois guns on the other side of the Crossroads, Burrows's six Ohio pieces in the center of Marsh's brigade, and Edward McAllister's six Illinois guns at the junction of Hare's and Marsh's brigades in Review Field. In addition, Barrett's Battery made a brief stand on this line but soon pulled back to Jones Field, and Timony's guns were behind the line. Trouble was brewing even amid the powerful artillery arm, however; when Sherman told Behr to move, the order came in English, and the former Prussian artillery officer had to have it translated into German.[7]

It was a good thing that so many Union troops, elements of seven Federal brigades—about half the army—answered the call to man the line on the right. The Confederates, because of Johnston's turning movement of 9:30 A.M., were massing upward of nine brigades on that flank, about two-thirds of their own army. Although it took the Confederates a few minutes to get the brigades aligned and moving to outflank the leftmost units of Sherman's original line at Shiloh Church, the Confederates faced no huge watersheds, so neither side held that much of a terrain advantage. Thus, the Confederates quickly got their bearings and were soon crashing through the woods, attacking toward the northwest. On top of the southern part of this hourglass, the semineutral terrain sparked a free-for-all that would make bloody Shiloh a reality.[8]

The Confederate assault did not disappoint. The gray waves moved forward, banners floating in the breeze, both sides equally awed by the sight. One Federal of the 15th Illinois remembered, "I never I think shall forget the feeling that came over me when I beheld it as the breeze unfurled it to our view, even though at the time bullets were flying like rain." Yet despite the pageantry, the Confederate ranks unwittingly slowed their progress and stifled their own striking potential. Significantly, Polk and Hardee found it difficult to get some of the more shot-up brigades moving forward from the Shiloh Church area. Cleburne's brigade, for example, was devastated and did not offer much

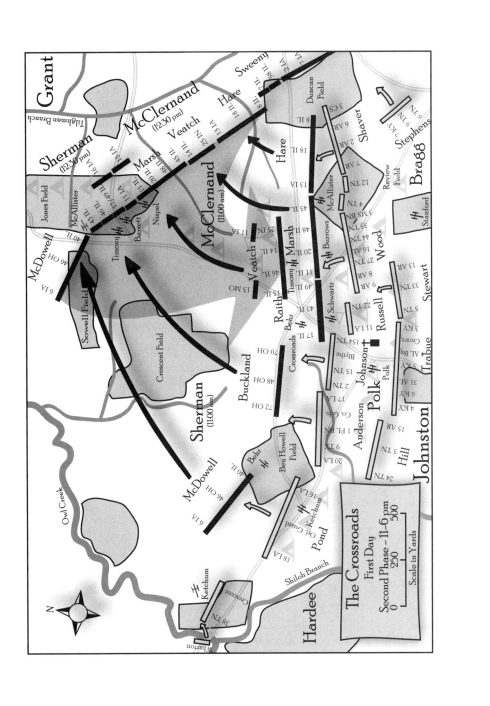

Grant

Tilghman Branch

Owl Creek

N

Sherman
(12:30 pm)

McClernand
(12:30 pm)

Jones Field

McDowell

Sowell Field

Crescent Field

Sherman
(11:00 am)

McDowell

Ben Howell
Field

Ketchum Pond

Shiloh Branch

Ketchum

Crescent
38 TN

Wharton

Hardee

Sweeny

Hare

McAllister

Marsh

Timony

Barrett

Nispel

Veatch

McClernand
(11:00 am)

Veatch

McClernand

Raith

Behr

Crossroads

Buckland

Behr

Odd Guard

16 LA

Ketchum

18 LA

20 LA

6 TX

1 FL BN

Co. Gds.

Anderson

Johnston

Polk

Polk

Blythe

Schwartz

9 AR

22 TN

13 LA

46 IL

15 IL

43 IL

13 MO

49 IL

11 IL

8 IL

Timony Marsh

20 IL

11 IL

Burrows

44 TN

16 TN

27 TN

4 TN

12 TN

3 MS BN

55 IL

McAllister

18 IL

13 IA

7 AR

2 AR

6 AR

3 CS

Shaver

Duncan
Field

Bragg

Stephens

9 TN

7 KY

Review
Field

Stanford

Wood

33 TN

9 AR

22 TN

11 IL

13 AR

3 TN

Stewart

154 TN

13 TN

2 TN

15 TN

31 AL

5 KY

4 KY

3 KY

AL Bn

Crews

Trabue

Russell

5 TN

15 AR

24 TN

5 TN

Hill

Johnston

70 OH

48 OH

72 OH

46 OH

9 IA

40 IL

18 IL

The Crossroads

First Day

Second Phase ~ 11-6 pm

0   250   500

Scale in Yards

support in the advance, with the 2nd Tennessee, 6th Mississippi, and 23rd Tennessee actually pulling out of line and becoming detached.[9]

Confusion in terms of splitting units also took a toll. The 12th and 13th Tennessee had separated from Robert Russell's other regiments in their wide flanking swing to the right, so they fought farther down their line, effectively breaking that brigade into pieces. Bushrod Johnson's brigade split apart as well when its commander went down. Probably the most notable problem concerned Alexander Stewart's brigade; the far right regiment did not get the order to advance and remained in its position. When Stewart halted his other regiments and returned to get the Tennesseans, he arrived back at his brigade to find that his three other regiments had already moved forward under the senior colonel, Alexander W. Campbell of the 33rd Tennessee. Braxton Bragg had sent them forward himself to plug the gap left by Gibson's angle to the right. That left Stewart with only one regiment, but it advanced as well in a different sector. In some cases, even regiments were shattered—the 11th Louisiana of Russell's brigade particularly. In reforming the troops after its first attack on Waterhouse's battery, Lieutenant Colonel Robert H. Barrow reported that "some of the companies composing it did not take their proper positions in line of battle, and many of the men were not even in their own companies or regiments."[10]

Many other problems developed as well, including a change in course for Shaver's brigade on the far right flank of this attacking mass. McAllister's Federal battery caught Confederate commanders' attention, and they ordered Shaver to dispense with his left oblique and move forward to flank the battery. The change brought trouble, however, as Shaver's right stumbled into W. H. L. Wallace's forming division in Duncan Field. Shaver found out quickly that more Federals were on this line than expected, but it only took him a moment to reform his startled units behind the brow of a hill.[11]

More concerning, the Confederates suffered a series of friendly fire incidents that occurred before and during this assault. The convergence of the Confederate units attacking northward at Shiloh Church and the brigades Johnston was sending to the northwest caused the Confederates to mistake one another as the enemy in a vortex around Lost Field. The 12th Tennessee of Russell's brigade, ranging far to the east, encountered Stewart's brigade and received fire from the 33rd Tennessee. Colonel Tyree H. Bell reported that it caused "great confusion among my men, and causing them to fall back about 50 yards." More ominously, the 4th Louisiana of Gibson's brigade fired at an officer dressed in blue, Aaron Vertner, who foolishly rode toward the rear with a captured Union flag tied around his waist and with a captured Union cap on his head. Someone yelled, "Here's your yankee," and the Louisianans fired at the Confederate officer, also hitting the 13th Arkansas and part of the 4th Tennessee of Stewart's brigade before their split. The Arkansans returned fire and then fell back. Gibson's horse was shot under him, and Colonel Henry W. Allen of the 4th Louisiana reported that "this was a terrible blow to the regiment; far more terrible than any inflicted by the enemy." One Louisianan reported that it would have gotten even more deadly had not "a woman in a sunbonnet . . . compelled us to restrain ourselves out of regard for her safety." Some friendly fire also took place as Wood's brigade raced toward the Federal line during the massive attack. Colonel W. K. Patterson of the 8th Arkansas wrote that he ordered his men to lie down behind "trees, stumps, and logs on the side of the enemy, preferring as we did, to fall by the shots of the enemy rather than to fall by our own guns." The captains of the 27th Tennessee wrote that many of their soldiers "met their death at the hands of those who should have come to their relief instead."[12]

Despite all the confusion, Confederate officers managed to get the mass of eight brigades, with Trabue and Gibson still in reserve right behind them, moving to the north and northwest. When they struck, it proved fatal to the Union line; it did not take the Confederates long to penetrate at multiple points. On the far left, Pond's brigade and portions of Cleburne's and Anderson's regiments succeeded in driving McDowell back and splitting the line between him and Buckland. McDowell could easily see Confederates between him and Buckland in Ben Howell Field and knew he was isolated. So did his men. Captain John Williams of the 6th Iowa wrote, "It now became evident that we must change our position or be entirely cut off from the rest of the army." McDowell posted the one present gun of Behr's Indiana Battery on his left and managed to hold the Confederates back long enough to make his escape due north instead of northeast toward the rest of the army. Even that turned out to be problematic, though, as the lieutenant colonel of the 6th Iowa, Markoe Cummins, suddenly about-faced his regiment and returned them to a fence. McDowell rode hard to the regiment and inquired, "What does all this mean?" A captain shot back, "It means, sir, that the Colonel is drunk." McDowell ordered the adjutant to relieve Cummins and put Captain Daniel Iseminger in command. (Cummins

was later cashiered, but he went east and raised a New York regiment.)
McDowell soon took a position at right angles to the rest of the army in
Crescent Field, facing east and fighting for his life. Although Iseminger
fell, mortally wounded, McDowell was eventually able to get his troops
to the rear, with the brigade and the 70th Ohio eventually crossing Crescent Field to Sowell Field.[13]

McDowell's retreat, although certainly not the disaster that other
units would later face, nevertheless was a crucial event. His withdrawal
left the Owl Creek Bridge uncovered. The Confederates of Pond's brigade soon took it, taking one of only three land avenues of advance or
retreat open to the Federals. (Chalmers had already closed another on
the River Road.) The 38th Tennessee and Crescent Regiment were detached from Pond's brigade to guard the bridge, where they met Wharton's Texas Rangers, who had moved northward west of the creek and
soon crossed over to the battlefield. Hardee, in command on that flank,
sent the cavalrymen forward after the retreating Federals with orders "to
pursue them and intercept their retreat."[14]

Pond's coup was not without mishap. William Ketchum was having
a hard time keeping up with his artillery; later he wrote that Pond advanced "through the woods, swamps, and old fields, without any regard
to roads." More problematic, Pond's Confederate regiments were also
victims of friendly fire. While driving the wedge between McDowell
and Buckland, a portion of the Confederate line to the right fired into
Pond's 18th Louisiana. Colonel Alfred Mouton reported it was "owing,
I presume, to the blue uniforms of a large number of my men." William
Preston Johnston later declared this to be the "penalty of doubtful colors," and described how similarly "over them waved flags and pennons
as various as their uniforms." Ahead of the other Confederates, Pond
stopped his attack and fell back a hundred yards or so. He only advanced again when the Confederates to the right moved forward.[15]

Buckland's Ohio regiments similarly broke apart and scattered. They
were hit not only by Anderson but also by some of Bushrod Johnson's
regiments now under Preston Smith, who was supported by the one
remaining gun of Polk's Battery. Portions of the 15th Arkansas and 5th
and 24th Tennessee of Cleburne's brigade also moved forward on Anderson's left. Buckland's Ohioans were also disrupted by the galloping
horses pulling the five cannon, limbers, and caissons of Behr's Indiana
battery (one gun was left to unsuccessfully cover the crossing of Owl
Creek). They received orders to move to the left and did so at a gallop,

throwing Buckland's line of battle, formed in the road, into chaos. Anderson and company struck at that exact same time, with the general motioning his troops forward with his hat because "the voice could not be heard." Buckland reported that "many of our men caught the infection and fled with the crowd," and "a large proportion of the men became panic stricken & fled to the River." The same occurred with the battery. Sherman rode over to meet the artillerymen and ordered them to deploy at the Crossroads, but Behr had no sooner given the order than he was hit and killed. Sherman reported, "The drivers and gunners fled in disorder, carrying off the caissons and abandoning five out of six guns without firing a shot."[16]

McClernand's brigades did no better on the left. Julius Raith's Illinois troops took the brunt of Robert Russell's and Alexander Stewart's partial Confederate brigades. Stewart was not present because he was leading another portion of his brigade farther down the line, but Alexander Campbell led the three regiments forward, only to find part of Russell's command ahead of them on the ground. Campbell tried to get them to charge, but the 11th Louisiana and 22nd Tennessee would not budge. Russell himself had been trying to get his brigade back together, recalling the wide-sweeping 12th and 13th Tennessee, but he soon found that Stewart's three regiments were between them and him. Campbell thus charged over Russell's troops, at which time they also took up the attack. Campbell was wounded in the attack, but he was able to remain on the field.[17]

Despite the problems on the Confederate side, Raith's Illinois regiments had to flee before Campbell's advance, leaving one of Schwartz's guns that they could not bring off because of the "softness of the soil." Losing Raith also affected stability; he fell from his horse with a nasty wound in the thigh that shattered the bone and would eventually take his life. McClernand later reported that Raith fell while leading a counterattack, and there is some evidence that the 17th Illinois advanced a little earlier to support Schwartz's Battery in its final position near the church and then again later to take advantage of the terrain. Likewise, some of Nispel's guns could have been momentarily retaken in the advance, later described by one foreign-born officer to Grant: "'Sheneral, Schwartz's battery is took.' 'Well, sir,' said Grant, 'you spiked the guns before they were taken?' 'Vat! schpike dem new guns? No, Sheneral, it would schpoil 'um.' 'Well, then, what did you do?' 'Do! Vy we went right in, and we took 'em back again.'" Four of Raith's men took him to the rear, although he soon ordered them to leave him and return to the ranks. Command of the brigade fell to a lieutenant colonel, Enos P. Wood of the 17th Illinois, but in reality the brigade's acting adjutant general, Lieutenant A. H. Ryan, commanded the regiments during much of the critical period of the Confederate attack.[18]

Farther down the line to the east, S. A. M. Wood's brigade made perhaps the critical assault of the mass attack. Ordered by Hindman to attack a battery to the front, with Hindman bringing Shaver's regiments to his support on the right, Wood confronted Marsh's brigade on what Hardee described as "a gentle acclivity." It was enough of a hill to allow Wood's Confederates some cover as they approached. Neals Olson of the 20th Illinois wrote that their fire had little "affect oing to their being protected by the Hill." Wood's troops nevertheless took mass canister from Burrows's guns, with one watching Illinoisan writing that the guns "opened huge gaps in the enemys ranks at every discharge and their dead lay in piles . . . yet still on they came." Despite the heavy fire, they soon made quick work of the battery and its horses, driving the Illinois regiments back and capturing Burrows's six guns, the 16th Alabama and 27th Tennessee flooding around the pieces. Numerous Federal regimental field officers went down in the chaos, including Lieutenant Colonel T. E. G. Ransom and Major Garrett Nevins of the 11th Illinois, Major Frederick A. Bartelson of the 20th Illinois, and Colonel Isham N. Haynie and Lieutenant Colonel William W. Sanford of the 48th Illinois. "The effect of losing so many field officers so suddenly was soon felt," Marsh admitted. The line simply melted away. Marsh attempted to restore order, but he later noted that they retreated "with a precipitancy as mortifying as it was unusual."[19]

The success also cost Wood dearly in terms of officer casualties. Colonel Christopher Williams of the 27th Tennessee was toppled from his horse, shot through the chest at the foot of the hill, and Lieutenant Colonel B. H. Brown also went down with a severe leg wound. Wood himself was not immune from damage; he was thrown from his wounded horse in the attack and friendly fire. The horse "became wholly unmanaeagable and threw me," Wood remembered, "dragging me along the tents and disabling me." He was knocked senseless, and it was hours before he recovered. While Wood was disabled, command of the brigade fell to Colonel W. K. Patterson of the 8th Arkansas, but he was delayed in taking command because his regiment and the 9th Arkansas Battalion had drifted away from the brigade to the left. Patterson noted, "We were left to our own judgment of what was proper to be done." Indeed, the brigade had broken into several parts and would fight the remainder of the day mostly separated.[20]

Hard fighting occurred down the line to the east as well. Bragg ordered Stewart to attack a battery, and the Tennessean asked his only present unit, Otho F. Strahl and his 4th Tennessee, "Can you take that battery?" "Show us where it is; we will try," Strahl answered. Supported by Stanford's Battery unlimbered in Lost Field as well as the 12th Tennessee of Russell's brigade on the right, led in person by Thomas Hindman, the 4th Tennessee stepped off to attack but soon met a storm of fire as they advanced across Review Field. McAllister's Illinois Battery easily outmatched Stanford's Mississippi gunners, mainly because Stanford's men had never fired a shot, or, as Polk wrote, "had never before heard the report of their own guns." "It was hot for a little while," one of the cannoneers wrote in his diary. Another described how several "bowlegged boys" were victims of "their knees knocking together." One of the newcomers to the battery wrote home that he had picked up a small New Testament in the enemy's camps and happened to open it to the passage where Jesus walked on the water and told Peter not to be afraid. It was a well-received lesson at that point. Another member of the battery admitted, "Oh, how I wish I was a dwarf" as rounds from McAllister's 24-pound howitzers began to fall. The Illinois artillery soon turned its focus on the charging Tennesseans, however, who lost 31 killed and 160 wounded in the attack despite wisely moving obliquely to the left into the cover of woods, from which they continued the advance. The regiment stopped within thirty paces of the Illinois guns and fired off one volley, then surged forward and took one of McAllister's guns. McAllister was wounded four times, but he managed to escape with the remainder of the battery, which galloped to the rear.[21]

McAllister's withdrawal doomed Hare's line, although the Confederate attack on the far right had the least success. Shaver's startled troops were not eager to go back into the trap at Duncan Field, despite being ordered to attack McAllister's battery by Hindman himself. Major James T. Martin reported to Hindman that his 7th Arkansas was almost out of ammunition, to which Hindman responded, "You have your bayonets." By this time, Stewart's 4th Tennessee was attacking the battery, so Shaver advanced across Review Field as well, driving Hare's left back a few hundred feet. Then Shaver's advance was stymied again by what Major Martin described as "the retreating Tennesseans [who] again completely ran over us, throwing our regiment into confusion. They were in such great haste to get behind us that they ran over and trampled in the mud our brave color-bearer." Panic nevertheless raced down the Union line to the 8th and 18th Illinois, who were themselves dealing with Shaver's attack. The change in command in the 8th Illinois, as well as Major Samuel Eaton of the 18th Illinois falling from a ball in the chest and senior captain Daniel H. Brush going down with wounds in the hand and thigh, were significant factors. Command of the 18th Illinois fell to Captain J. J. Anderson, although ironically a familiar face soon appeared in the Illinoisans' ranks: Captain William J. Dillon, who had been wounded at Fort Donelson. He chose this time to return to the regiment. Unfortunately, he was only on the ground a few minutes when he was instantly killed by a ball through the head. Because Shaver was having his own troubles, however, Hare's Illinoisans and Iowans were able to reform within a hundred yards of their first position behind a fence overlooking the northwestern portion of Duncan Field. In their new line, the Illinois regiments connected with the 7th Illinois of Wallace's deploying division, forming almost a right angle.[22]

With so much chaos and one Illinoisan describing how the "clouds of smoke rising all over the field made the day seem like night," the reserve Union units behind the main line were never able to put up much of a defense for fear of hitting their own men retreating right in front of them. William Camm of the 14th Illinois asked Veatch to "turn us loose with the bayonet," but Veatch replied, "No, no, you would lose every man." A well-respected and well-liked Colonel Cyrus Hall of the 14th Illinois reported that he ordered his prone men to rise and fire: "After a very few volleys had been delivered I saw a line of men dressed in blue uniforms in front." Hall ceased firing, but refugees from Marsh's command, as well as panicked horses from Burrows's battery, broke through Veatch's right. Captain Louis D. Kelley of the 15th Illinois described "horses without riders, who dashed through our ranks with great speed." In addition, several more key officers quickly went down, including Lieutenant Colonel E. F. W. Ellis, shot through the arm and then the heart, and Major William R. Goddard, shot through the heart, thus leaving the 15th Illinois without any field commanders and only two captains. The 25th Indiana on the far left of the brigade lost Colonel William H. Morgan to a leg wound. Colonel Hall admitted his men fell back "in rather bad order amid the confusion of the moment," and the rest of Veatch's brigade also broke, the right first. The regiments fled so quickly that the 46th Illinois left its colors; Colonel John A. Davis returned to retrieve them, but he was shot while doing so. Similarly, the 11th Iowa had to retreat, with its commander, William Hall, having a horse shot from under him and sustaining a wound in the ankle. Numerous guns also fell to the hard-charging Confederates, including Behr's five Indiana guns, two of Schwartz's, all six of Burrows's, and one of McAllister's—a total of fourteen pieces.[23]

Watching the disaster unfold before their eyes, Sherman and McClernand turned from encouraging their men to trying to form a new line. In the midst of the heavy fighting, Sherman came upon his young and impetuous staff officer, Taylor, who had wanted so badly to attack the enemy. Sherman remembered his impatience in the midst of the fight, remarking, "Well, my boy, didn't I promise you all the fighting you could do?" The young officer had already concluded that he had seen enough and told Sherman "I would relieve him from further obligations under that agreement." The same was not the case for Sherman's body servant, Bustamante, who considered himself one of the staff until the firing started. He then "rapidly made tracks to the river and never stopped until he reached Paducah."[24]

A few Federals managed to turn and make a stand, although most were astounded to find, as one Federal described it, "the rebels advancing almost parallel with us." A portion of the 11th Illinois took shelter behind some "oats in gunny sacks" in one of the camps. Dresser's battery and the 17th Illinois, its sick and horseless lieutenant colonel, Enos P. Wood, leading anyway, also turned to stand their ground. Unfortunately, Captain Timony, commanding Dresser's Battery, had been, in his own words, "struck by three shots, stunned by the explosion of a shell, and borne senseless to the rear" on the first line, leaving the artillerymen without their leader. Thus, the general withdrawal was so powerful that few chose to halt, and four of Timony's guns were soon overwhelmed, adding to the fourteen lost in the initial retreat. What defense there was, however, aided in stopping the Confederate surge on the north side of Woolf Field, where elements of Russell's, Anderson's, Stewart's, and Johnson's brigades and the independent 12th Tennessee took position. Several guns were also advanced, including the Washington Artillery and Cobb's and Bankhead's batteries as well as the one gun of Polk's unit. Captain Irving Hodgson of the Washington Artillery opened up on the Federal skirmishers still in front amid the camps, "creeping from their tents and making for the woods." The Confederates were not thinking of continuing the advance, however, as evidenced by Anderson telling a Bragg staff officer that he was sorry but he had somehow inadvertently "worked my way into the front line." The staffer returned a few minutes later with word from Bragg: "The general desires you to go wherever the fight is thickest."[25]

The lack of a major Confederate pursuit thus calmed the action on this flank. Although extremely successful, the attack nevertheless cost the Confederates dearly. Numerous officers were down, including Wood and regimental commanders Christopher Williams of the 27th Tennessee and Lieutenant Colonel A. D. Grayson of the 13th Arkansas, both mortally wounded. That unit was already without its colonel, J. C. Tappan, who was sick, and Grayson's loss left the command to Major James A. McNeely. He too was soon severely wounded. Casualties among lower-level Confederates were also high, and the various units, some of which had been fighting all morning, needed to be resupplied with ammunition. The captured guns and prisoners also had to be seen to. Then the obvious attraction of the foremost of the Federals' second line of camps drew many Confederates' attention. Some commanders, such as Tyree Bell of the 12th Tennessee, who was wounded while supporting Bankhead's Battery near McClernand's headquarters, took his men to the rear with canteens to get water from Shiloh Branch. In addition, action suddenly picked up in the center, drawing the attention of those nearest Duncan Field. The overall result was a stalled effort, with only several units and a few guns following to the north side of Woolf Field and stopping there.[26]

The mass Confederate attack had nevertheless driven away the entire Federal right. All was chaos as the Union brigades withdrew, leaving their dead and wounded and a number of cannon behind. The surgeons of the various regiments and brigades who had established field hospitals behind the lines were only one step ahead of the fleeing Union soldiers and managed to get a few patients out, but not all; bullets "whistled above and around us very freely," one surgeon wrote. Others were captured in the retreat, including McDowell's brigade surgeon and his wife, who was in camp for a visit. Similarly, Captain James H. Coats of the 11th Illinois and his young son had just returned to camp; both were wounded, with the son lying on the ground with "a large chunk out between the hip and knee."[27]

Individually and collectively, it was a disaster for the Federal army.

Amid the growing crisis, the lack of Confederate pursuit was a major blessing to the withdrawing Federals, and they did not waste it. As the Federal units fell back, many entered the large Jones Field due north from their position. Using this open space and the break given by the slow Confederates, Sherman and McClernand posted what was left of their artillery, five of McAllister's, two of Dresser's, two of Schwartz's, and all six of Barrett's guns, on the "upper end," or south side, of the field. Under the cover of the big guns, which fired down the road and along an open avenue that Marsh's brigade had recently cleared to provide a drill ground, the artillerymen effectively stopped any Confederate pursuit for nearly an hour and gave the Confederate gunners in Woolf Field all they could handle. One Illinoisan noted "a splendid artillery duel took place on the parade ground, at short range. . . . Balls were flying in every direction." The Confederates were very much in the fight, however, with one member of Barrett's Battery writing, "Their shell burst over and around us, killing and wounding many of our horses and some of our men."[28]

Meanwhile, Sherman and McClernand reorganized their divisions as best they could, although the units were badly jumbled. One Illinoisan admitted, "We had a perfect dread of fighting in other Regt.s, for if killed our friends would never know what had become of us." In addition, organization benefited cohesion. Working together in what Sherman termed "perfect concert," the two generals soon found that the disaster had not been as bad as they thought. Generally, the retreat was more chaotic the farther west the line ran. To the east, Hare's brigade of McClernand's division had only fallen back a few hundred feet and was still able to keep connected with Wallace's division to the left. Favorable terrain provided the Federals some help in the center, where a portion of Veatch's brigade, the 14th Illinois and 25th Indiana, took positions on the brow of a tall hill overlooking a creek and a spring. John W. Foster of the 25th Indiana "planted the colors and mounted a fallen tree," one Federal remembered, where he waved his hat and rallied the regiment. The other flank was a different story. Sherman's regiments had fallen back nearly a mile, and McDowell's entire brigade was cut off. Yet there had been some method in the madness. The retreat had been conducted much as a door swings on its hinges, with the hinges being Hare's hold on Wallace. The end of the door had swung far back, but it was still on the hinges, and the semblance of a line remained.[29]

Importantly, too, the various commanders were already reforming their lines. McDowell's full brigade went into line, and Carroll Marsh likewise had the majority of his brigade reformed along with half of Raith's and was already moving up to support the artillery in the south end of the field. That arm had been hit hard, however, and many of the cannoneers were scattered or wounded. The infantry thus came to their support; a portion of the 17th Illinois helped man Barrett's Battery. Other soldiers were joining any effective unit they could find. A portion of the 70th Ohio of Sherman's division joined in with the 11th Illinois and fought with them for the remainder of the day. The 46th Illinois also reformed, but they did so right in front of Barrett's guns. Officers and cannoneers shouted for the troops to get out of the way, which they quickly did.[30]

Amazingly, it soon became obvious that things were even better for the Federals than they thought. The Confederate push had inadvertently sent the Union right rearward, toward, not away from, Pittsburg Landing. Thus, Johnston's mistaken intention had not turned out the way he had hoped. Yet the main advantage the Federals had were the two aggressive commanders on this front, McClernand and Sherman. They talked as their units reorganized and considered their options. One was to fall back, which would potentially put the entire army in danger. Another option was to stay put and let the enemy come and attack them again, but that likewise seemed to provide no substantial long-term benefit. The only other option was to attack and, they hoped, surprise the Confederates. Although there is a fine line between audacity and stupidity, Sherman and McClernand decided to launch the attack, and their audacity worked. If there was a tactical surprise at Shiloh, it was not during the early morning Confederate initial attack on the Union camps, as is so commonly thought; rather, it was when Sherman and McClernand counterattacked around noon or 12:30 that afternoon, taking the Confederates on that flank completely by surprise.[31]

With McDowell's intact brigade as the core of the advance on Sherman's wing, the red-headed general moved to the south and quickly ate up large swaths of territory despite having to quickly reform his line because it struck the Confederates at a slanted angle. Still, Sherman drove the Confederates back all along the line. McClernand's and Veatch's reformed units advanced to the left, fighting behind trees and logs while the general rode behind the line yelling, "Forward." They captured some of the artillery that had been dueling with the Union guns in Jones Field, namely Cobb's Kentucky Battery and one gun of Polk's Battery, with the Kentucky guns falling to the 11th and 20th Illinois as well as the nearby 11th Iowa. There were of course casualties. One of the Illinoisans described "that peculiar chug when a bullet strikes a man." Still, once again, the door began to swing on the hinges, with Marsh's brigade to the right moving straight through all of his camps while some of Sherman's units on the right moved almost back to their positions along the Hamburg-Purdy Road. It was a slow and methodical advance, but McClernand's troops eventually retook his headquarters as well as the camps of Marsh's brigade. Around his own headquarters, McClernand already noticed that "the ground was almost literally covered with dead bodies, chiefly of the enemy." In all, the Union counterattack drove the Confederates back nearly half a mile on the far western side.[32]

A scramble in the surprised Confederate ranks soon stymied the advance, however, as Beauregard threw in his last reserves, Trabue's brigade. The brigade had followed at the rear of the army, with some of the troops reflecting on larger issues as the sound of battle bellowed from the front. John Crawford of the 6th Kentucky was particularly in a reflective mood, suddenly blurting out while the brigade rested behind the lines, "What does all this mean, anyhow . . . what's it all about?" Remembering why he had joined to fight this war, Crawford was man enough to admit, going in to battle, "I'm not half so angry as I was, I tell you!" When Breckinridge led Statham and Bowen to the right, he gave Trabue his final orders that day, telling him to incline to the left and operate under Polk's command. Trabue went straight in line of battle, with the 5th Kentucky opening ranks and passing around Shiloh Church, the Kentuckians singing "Cheer, boys, cheer; we'll march away to battle." Their jovial attitude soon changed as they began to see where "cannon balls had torn up ground and musketry barked trees." The piles of dead and wounded were also frightening. The brigade soon moved forward, perhaps even taking some part in the advance on the Crossroads in rear of Anderson, and on toward Crescent Field, taking some long-range and indirect fire that, fortunately for them, produced only a few casualties, including Confederate Kentucky governor George W. Johnson's horse, whereupon Johnson "shouldered a musket" and joined the ranks of the 4th Kentucky. Trabue soon met Hardee, telling him, "General, I have a Kentucky brigade here. What shall I do with it?" Hardee responded, "Put it in where the fight is the thickest, sir," and Trabue did.[33]

Turning to the right, Trabue found the enemy nearby, just across a hollow and in the camps of McAllister's and Burrows's batteries on a high ridge. He could also see them "in the woods across the field in front of his camps." Unbeknownst to him, they were the advance of Sherman and McClernand's counterattack, moving southward. Trabue thus moved to the left to confront them, changing front with only the 4th, 5th, and 6th Kentucky and an Alabama unit behind him. "Ignorant of the topography of the country," he thought twice about attacking so soon and thus settled into an hour and fifteen minute firefight.[34]

As the Federals continued to slowly advance, Trabue decided it was time to stem the tide. With other Confederate units coming up, he reported, "I gave order fix bayonets and move forward in double-quick time at a charge." A company of the 5th Kentucky led the way and almost came too close, with the entire Federal line firing on the advanced troops. "I do believe if we had not have fallen on our faces," remembered W. A. Coleman, "every one of our company would have been killed. I never heard bullets whistle round us so in my life. They come like hail." Trabue nevertheless ordered the attack to continue, and the Kentuckians quickly dove into the fight on the Confederate left between Anderson's and Russell's brigades, charging across the hollow and driving back Sherman's wing of the advance into an almost ninety-degree angle. Other Confederate brigades picked up the attack on Trabue's left, with portions of Cleburne's, Pond's, and Russell's brigades sweeping in an arc from north to east and driving back McDowell and a portion of Buckland's brigade to the tall ridge. Here, it was fresh brigade on fresh brigade as Trabue's regiments hit McDowell's unit, although the brigade's regiments soon separated with the 40th Illinois, their colonel, Stephen G. Hicks, wounded, fighting down the line at the angle from the other two regiments, the 6th Iowa and 46th Ohio. The 13th Missouri had somehow managed to slide in between the Illinoisans and Iowans. Nevertheless, with the line at a ninety-degree angle at the 40th Illinois's position, McDowell's units suffered a crossfire, and McDowell was thrown from his horse while riding across a hollow full of undergrowth. A veteran was kind in his description of McDowell: he was "a large man and somewhat corpulent," and "it was with difficulty that he arose to his feet and was conducted from the field."[35]

Over the course of the counterattack, which took up nearly two hours, the Union right caved in, and McClernand and Sherman saw that they again had to get the remainder of their troops out before they were cut off. Friendly fire from the artillery in the rear, particularly in the almost leaderless 15th Illinois, also proved fatal; the Illinoisans quickly showed their colors and the firing stopped. Many officers were also down in the renewed fighting, including individuals such as Lieutenant Colonel Evan Richards commanding the 20th Illinois and Lieutenant Colonel T. E. G. Ransom of the 11th Illinois, who, as McClernand described it, was "reeling in the saddle and streaming with blood" from his earlier head wound, yet "performed prodigies of valor." His horse was soon shot and he could not remain alert on foot, so he had to be taken to the rear.[36]

Despite such bravery, a second Federal withdrawal soon began, slower than the first and followed up again only timidly by the Confederates. The Union gate again swung on the hinge that was Hare's brigade connecting to Wallace's division. In the back-and-forth fighting around noon, Hare had fallen back another 200 yards or so, but he had kept his three regiments firmly in line near the 7th Illinois, Wallace's right flank regiment. They held there for several more hours, in fact being some of the last to leave McClernand's line.[37]

But leave they did, eventually. Sherman and McClernand reformed their lines facing both west and south in Jones Field, covered by the massed artillery and Marsh's out-of-ammunition brigade; Marsh reported that he had great difficulty doing so because of "officers [who] seemed little inclined to halt short of the river," particularly Colonel Crafts J. Wright of the 13th Missouri, who, according to Marsh, "refused to remain till threatened with arrest." Interestingly, the entire 46th Illinois marched back to its camp just across Tilghman Branch: "Finding myself within one-half mile of my regimental encampment, I marched my men to it and got dinner for them," Colonel John A. Davis reported. To his credit, he soon marched them back into the fight. Yet as more units fled from the Confederate countersurge, a crisis was again emerging on the Union right.[38]

Aid from the rear temporarily steadied this new line, including the quartermaster of the 43rd Illinois, who arrived in the field with a wagonload of "hard bread, bacon and ham, dried peaches and some whiskey," according to one Illinoisan. Also arriving were the 15th and 16th Iowa, which took a prominent position in the field itself, although the exact timing was later debated. Both regiments had been assigned to Prentiss, but the 16th had arrived the evening before and the 15th that morning. In fact, the 15th Iowa had drilled in front of Henry Halleck just five days previously in St. Louis. Once at Pittsburg, Colonel Hugh T. Reid left his men on their transports as he made his way out to find Prentiss and their campsite. Prentiss was obviously too engaged to discuss camping spots, which were by then in Confederate hands anyway, so Reid returned to the landing and ordered his men off the boats. They received ammunition and loaded their weapons, only to be first ordered to form a line at the landing to defend it as well as keep stragglers from going to the river. They went into position beside another just-arriving and unassigned unit, Edward Bouton's Illinois Battery. By then, the stragglers were beginning to surge upon them. Reid reported, "Most of them had the Bull Run story, that their regiments were all cut to pieces, and that they were the only survivors." The only way to keep them out of the landing, Reid said, was by "threatening to shoot them down."[39]

Grant then ordered the two units to support McClernand, but a comedy of errors soon developed. Cyrus Boyd explained that in the confusion, "Col Reid and Dewey galloped back and forth without seeming to know exactly what they were doing Col Dewey did a considerable amount of hard swearing and I had time to notice him wheel his horse around and take some consolation through the neck of a pint bottle." Reid then reported their guide at first became lost and took them "in a direction directly from the firing." Once on the right path, Colonel Alexander Chambers of the 16th Iowa reported that he met the rabble of the army falling back as his unit progressed forward: "Large numbers of men in squads were returning. Cavalry, infantry, and several batteries of artillery were met on the road without being disabled or having lost their horses or expended their ammunition." He also noted that he met more stragglers than were in the two regiments put together, although he proudly stated, "For the credit of the State of Iowa, not one of her quota did I meet." The Iowans braved the flooding tide and took a position in Jones Field, although they soon began to take casualties, including Colonel Chambers, who was hit in the "hip-joint" by a spent ball. It was, he reported, "very painful, and rendered me quite lame." Colonel Reid of the 15th Iowa also went down with a ball through his neck. It knocked him off his horse and paralyzed him for a few minutes. The plucky colonel soon regained use of his extremities and continued to command the regiment throughout the rest of the battle. Similarly, Lieutenant Colonel William Belknap, Grant's future secretary of war, was wounded in the shoulder and had his horse shot from under him. Others went down as well, with one Iowan noting, "We was in a vary hot place a little hotter than I want to bee." All he knew to do: "I asked God to take care of me."[40]

Perhaps the best reinforcement at this time, however, was that provided by Grant himself, who lifted morale and assured the troops that Wallace and Buell would soon be there. One Illinoisan wrote that Grant's presence "seemed to inspire all to greater service." In a second round of visits with his division commanders that afternoon, the army commander did not tarry at Jones Field, likely wanting little of McClernand and knowing Sherman viewed the situation the same way he did. Also, the Confederates were following only timidly at this point, with Cleburne's, Russell's, and Trabue's units all keeping a cautious distance, slowed by the undergrowth, deep ravines, and gullies that forced the men to carry ammunition boxes on their shoulders. A Confederate battery, probably Bankhead's back at Review Field, also fired from the right across their front. Also slowing the Confederate advance were Union prisoners. Trabue's brigade captured one feisty German. When they asked him why he came south to fight, he blurted out, "I vish I didn't," then explained, "Zey dell me to zay boo! at the Southern man unt he runs off." He added, "I zay boo! and shoots; but py tam! Southern man he runs the wrong vay!"[41]

Realizing they had to find a new, more stable line to the rear, Sherman and McClernand soon began sending their troops to the other side of the substantial Tilghman Branch. Sherman could see its defensive capabilities, and having seen what his men had done earlier that morning with Shiloh Branch, he planned to put the much more substantial Tilghman defile to good use. By 3:00 or 3:30 P.M., Sherman and McClernand had their troops falling back, but the cohesion of their units quickly faded as the substantial ravine created havoc in the Federal ranks. McClernand and Sherman were quick to rally and reorganize the units on the other side, though, and they soon had them going into a new line. On their far left, Hare's brigade did not fall back until around 4:30 P.M., careful to keep a hold on Wallace to his left. When Hare's troops broke, however, it was total. Robert Sturgess of the 8th Illinois reported, "The company officers lost control of their men from the promiscuous mingling together of the different regiments."[42]

Despite Federal confusion, the major fighting on the western side of the battlefield during this second phase had actually been a disaster for the Confederates. They had advanced en masse with two-thirds of their army and had bowled over the Union line, but with Sherman and McClernand counterattacking, the Confederate left wing was tied up for several more hours, effectively consuming daylight as Grant desired. The Union success was all due to the audacity of the Union commanders, who launched an attack in the middle of getting trounced. Moreover, the weight of the first Confederate attack and then the second drive, which thwarted the Federal counterattack, had sent the Union army back toward Pittsburg Landing, not away from it, as envisioned in Johnston's general plan. By early afternoon, the Confederate plan was in tatters, and the Battle of Shiloh was becoming a slugfest to see who would be standing at the end.

Unfortunately, it would only get more lethal as the afternoon wore on.

10

"I Shall Have to Put the Bayonet to Them"

Stephen A. Hurlbut was destined to play the same role McClernand and Sherman played at Shiloh, except on the opposite side of the battlefield. Unfortunately for him, he would not garner the same attention simply because he was not as flashy a general. He was not as noticeable as the excitable Sherman or the glory-seeking politician McClernand. Even though over half of each army was fighting on the western side of the battlefield, Hurlbut defended a more critical sector: the crucial left flank of the Union army. Hurlbut's task was simple in theory, and he would do it well, using up several hours before finally falling back to a new defensive area. While Sherman and McClernand did it in a flashy, dramatic manner, however, Hurlbut's defense was a determined, slow, and plodding withdrawal. Yet he devoured substantial amounts of daylight—just what Grant needed.[1]

Numerous soldiers left vivid recollections of that fateful morning in Hurlbut's division. Hurlbut himself rode through the camps ordering the long roll sounded. One member of the 3rd Iowa remembered, "There arose a noise throughout the camps which sounded more like the ghost of a battle than anything to which it can be likened. It was the men bursting caps to clear out the tubes of their guns." As the Iowans marched past the 32nd Illinois, they heard one of the officers telling the men that anyone who straggled would be "court-martialed for cowardice and shot." Both regiments raised a cheer. In William's brigade, one 32nd Illinois soldier described Colonel Isaac Pugh's warning given with his customary "remarkable squeak in his voice": "Boys! fill your canteens! Some of you'll be in hell before night and need water!"[2]

Although many of Hurlbut's units were up and marching in ten minutes, he had trouble getting all his force moving. Myers's Ohio Battery was, as he reported, "very slow in coming forward, and was brought up by repeated orders through my aides." The unit had just joined Hurlbut's division the previous Friday in the armywide reorganization of artillery and cavalry, and this certainly was not the first impression they needed to make. Despite the faulty beginning, Hurlbut formed his two brigades (Veatch's having gone to the right to support Sherman) in Wicker Field and began moving southward in line of battle, with refugees from Prentiss's line in what Hurlbut described as "broken masses" piercing his lines and yelling that they had been "cut to pieces." Passing through a skirt of woods and then into another large field containing a peach orchard, the brigades swept forward to the other side of a cotton field, where they engaged in long-range fighting with some of Chalmers's advance skirmishers. One Iowan remembered that after firing three or four rounds with their smoothbores at the enemy over 400 yards away, "the absurdity of firing at the enemy at that distance with our guns dawned upon us, and we stopped." Hurlbut placed Nelson Williams's brigade on the south side and Lauman's regiments on the western side, forming an almost ninety-degree angle before Hurlbut thought better of the idea thirty minutes later and called his troops back to a more uniform position facing south on the northern edge of the field, just south of the blooming peach orchard. Now the infantry could rake the field with fire, with Myers's Ohio and Ross's Michigan batteries adding to the firepower. Willard's Battery, the Chicago Light Artillery under twenty-seven-year-old Lieutenant Peter P. Wood from W. H. L. Wallace's division, also soon arrived.[3]

Yet Hurlbut was already having major problems even before he engaged the Confederates. In addition to sick staff officers and the rearward movement, Hurlbut also faced leadership problems. None of his three brigades was under its nominal leader, except Jacob Lauman, who had only commanded his brigade for a few hours. Colonel Thomas J. Turner was away from his brigade, leaving it under James Veatch. Isaac Pugh of the 41st Illinois had led the other brigade until Nelson Williams and the 3rd Iowa arrived, at which time Williams took command by virtue of rank. Pugh was not happy. "I think there was some unfair dealing in making the Brigade as it now stands," Pugh wrote his wife in confidence. "Genl Hurlbut is a drunkard & is drunk all the time when he can get anything to get drunk on." As for Williams, he wrote, "This Col Williams was tried by a Court Martial last fall for Drunkeness & cowardice"—on charges brought by his own men. Pugh determined that once in battle, if these "drunken cowardly dogs . . . shows the whole feather I shall assume the command of the brigade if it costs me my commission[.] I have taken about as much as I intend to." Obviously all was not well in the division as it went into battle on this Sunday morning.[4]

The issues with leadership soon became obvious. The Federals seemed to shoot at anything they saw, no matter how far off it was. When the 32nd Illinois let out a volley at no particular target while still on the south side of the field, Colonel John B. Logan (not to be confused with the more famous John A. Logan, who was recovering from a wound at Fort Donelson), scolded them and asked why. "They told me that they fired because the Twenty-eighth did," he wrote. Officers were also falling. A shell exploded directly above Lieutenant Colonel Benjamin H. Bristow of the 25th Kentucky, knocking him senseless and damaging his hearing and spinal column. Command of the regiment fell to Major William B. Wall, who then took several spent balls in the chest and leg but refused to turn over command. The most troubling command issue came when Nelson Williams went down from a cannonball exploding above him, killing his horse, knocking him senseless, and paralyzing him temporarily. Williams's wound put the brigade back in the hands of Isaac Pugh. One of Pugh's soldiers remembered, "The order had scarcely been given to us to fire by Col. Pugh, when General Hurlbut, who commands our division which is the 4th, rode up to him and informed him that Col. Williams, who commanded our Brigade, was wounded, and that he (Col. Pugh,) would have to take command." Pugh was with his regiment on the far left and had to rush to his proper position.[5]

The lack of leadership in Myers's Battery also became obvious. Having stopped "rather too far forward," as Hurlbut described it, the battery soon received a major shock while in the process of deploying. Robertson's Alabama Battery had moved forward after its Spain Field action and took advantage of several hay bales in the camps for a slight rampart. A long-range shot destroyed one of Myers's limbers, with Lieutenant Cuthbert Laing of the nearby 2nd Michigan Battery reporting that the caisson was "shivered to pieces." The entire command, captain and all, left their guns and fled. Hurlbut noted that "officers and men, with a common impulse of disgraceful cowardice, abandoned the entire battery, horses caissons, and guns, and fled, and I saw them no more until Tuesday." Hurlbut had some of the cannoneers of Laing's battery catch the horses and spike the guns. Isaac Pugh also sent some cavalrymen to do the job; several of the horses had to be cut out of their traces to free them. Myers was soon cashiered from the army, but the debacle had a larger effect than just in the cotton field. With Myers's retreat, Hurlbut thought that he needed more artillery on his front. He called for Brotzmann and Mann's Battery, then aiding Stuart's defense of the left. The artillery commander reported that he received orders to "cease firing and to bring the battery down to an open field, as Captain Myers' Battery was abandoned." Stuart would be on his own for the rest of the day.[6]

By far, the biggest problem Hurlbut had in forming his line was a quarter-mile gap that extended from his left on the Hamburg-Savannah Road to Stuart's position in the ravines to the east. To Hurlbut's delight, however, reinforcements soon came swinging up the River Road: a portion of John McArthur's brigade from W. H. L. Wallace's division. The brigade had stood in line for a while; "their flags were all unfurled," one musician wrote, "and they were really dancing impatiently to the music of the battle in front of them." Wounded soldiers and stragglers streamed by, and the brigade convinced some of them to join their regiments. McArthur and Augustus Chetlain had been unceremoniously reinstated from their arrest that morning and quickly had the men in motion. Like Hurlbut, who sent Veatch to the west, Wallace had also been called on for aid. He sent one of his brigades southward, taking position with the other two in the center. Thus, the Union defense was a fractured line that contained units under commanders with whom they had not originally served.[7]

Hurlbut was happy to receive the aid, no matter what division it came from. McArthur's entire brigade was not present, however; the 81st Ohio and 14th Missouri (later 66th Illinois) had been sent to guard the Snake Creek bridge, over which it was presumed Lew Wallace would arrive. Similarly, the 13th Missouri (later 22nd Ohio) went to support Sherman. Nevertheless, McArthur brought his 9th and 12th Illinois and Wood's Chicago Light Artillery on line about 10:30 A.M., placing them in the gap between Stuart and Hurlbut, with the 9th Illinois on the right overlapping the 41st Illinois of Hurlbut's division by two compa-

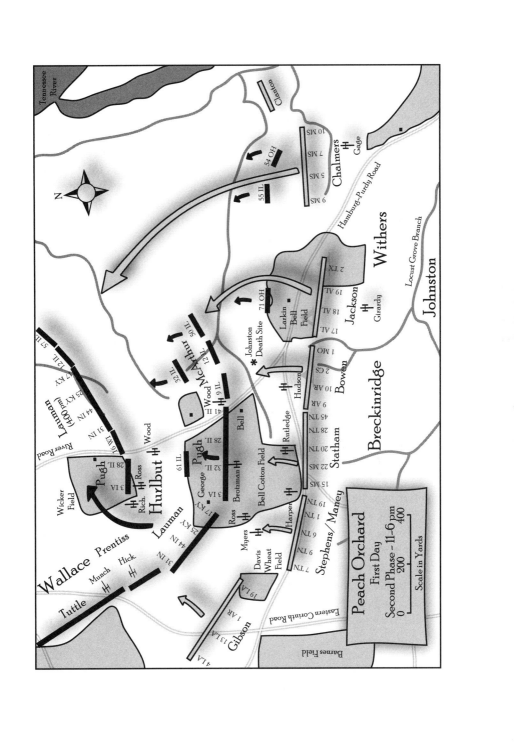

Tennessee River

N

54 OH

55 IL

10 MS
7 MS
5 MS
9 MS

Clanton

Gage

Chalmers

Hamburg-Purdy Road

Withers

Locust Grove Branch

Johnston

71 OH

2 TX

19 AL

18 AL

17 AL

Jackson

Girardy

Larkin
Bell
Field

Johnston
* Death Site

1 MO

2 CS

10 AR

9 AR

45 TN

28 TN

20 TN

22 MS

15 MS

Hudson

Bowen

Statham

Breckinridge

50 IL

11 IL

12 IL

McArthur

3 IL

41 II

9 IL

Wood

Bell

Rutledge

57 IL

12 IL

7 KY

25 KY

44 IN

31 IN

16 WI

River Road

Lauman
(400 pm)

Wood

Hurlbut

Pugh

Ross

Rich.

28 IL

3 IA

17 KY

George

32 II

3 IA

61 IL

28 IL

Pugh

Brotzman

Ross

H'harper

Bell Cotton Field

19 TN
1 TN
9 TN
6 TN
7 TN

Stephens / Maney

Eastern Corinth Road

Wicker
Field

Wallace   Prentiss

Lauman

Tuttle

Munch   Hick

44 IN

31 IN

Myers

Davis
Wheat
Field

19 LA

13 LA

1 AR

4 LA

Gibson

Barnes Field

Peach Orchard

First Day

Second Phase ~ 11-6 pm

0   200   400

Scale in Yards

nies. Soon more reinforcements arrived in the form of some of Thomas Sweeny's reserve regiments from the center. The 50th Illinois moved to the left and went into line east of the 12th Illinois, in view of Stuart's regiments fighting to the front. Later, around 2:00 P.M., Sweeny dispatched the 57th Illinois as well.[8]

Ulysses S. Grant arrived on Hurlbut's line as well, showing the troops that the commanding general was indeed on the field and encouraging his commanders and men alike. He had begun making his rounds with Sherman and McClernand on the far right and worked his way through the center, meeting with Wallace and Prentiss before finally making his way to the left and seeing Hurlbut. He later moved farther to the left and talked with Stuart's command. Grant spoke with Hurlbut, asking how long he could hold; Hurlbut replied "all day," if his flanks held. Grant assured him that Wallace was on the way and ordered him to hold out. With his staff officers, one soldier wrote, Grant "rode leisurely forward to the front line." He "wore an anxious look," he added, "yet bore no evidence of excitement or trepidation." Such was Ulysses S. Grant.[9]

The initial fighting of the second phase on this eastern side of the battlefield came on the extreme Union left as Chalmers renewed his advance to turn that flank. By this time, nearly 11:30 A.M., Stuart had his troops arrayed in a three-regiment front on a tall ridge extending out into two ravines that fed into the Tennessee River below. It was high ground but broken in nature, hindering movement for both sides. More importantly, Stuart had no artillery support. Additionally, Stuart's position was detached from the main line to the west, with a large ravine running behind Stuart's line but in front of McArthur and Hurlbut. Perhaps Stuart would have been better off if he had fallen back across the ravine and taken a position more in line with McArthur, but in the chaos, Stuart seemed to be the forgotten flank. Worse still, Gage's Alabama Battery had opened on his left, but Stuart noted that it had "little beyond threatening effect, the firing being too high." A more troubling development was the lack of ammunition his companies were soon reporting.[10]

Despite these problems, Stuart held for two hours. With Clanton guarding their right flank, Chalmers and Jackson advanced according to their orders to "wheel on a moveable pivot to the left." The attempt to turn the enemy flank thus met the 54th Ohio and 55th Illinois among the ravines south of their position. As he added additional pressure, Chalmers slowly moved forward. In his rear, Gage's Alabama Battery continued to bombard the Federals, but still the two Union regiments held, parrying Chalmers's continual efforts to turn the flank and drive the Federal line rearward. Chalmers's artillery was frequently delayed in moving forward; they had to cross "thickly wooded country over ravines and hills almost impassable to ordinary wagons." As they slowly progressed, waiting for their artillery, the Mississippians suffered several casualties, including Reverend M. L. Weller, the chaplain of the 9th Mississippi.[11]

Stuart's line was not holding as well farther to the west, where the 71st Ohio had taken a position on the right of the brigade with their big Belgian muskets. With Girardey's Georgia Battery having crossed Locust Grove Branch and now firing viciously over their heads, Jackson's Alabama brigade hit the right of Stuart's position at the double-quick and succeeded in driving it away from the cabins in Larkin Bell Field. One of the Ohioans told how "we saw a brigade of rebels marching right upon us in splendid style and trying to get around us." In the corresponding Confederate ranks, the chaplain of the 17th Alabama, I. T. Tichenor, reminded his boys that at that very hour, 11:30 A.M., "all their home folks were praying for them." By noon, the Ohioans had fallen back, led by their 300-pound colonel, Rodney Mason, who proved himself no leader of men. Some confusion concerning who was in front of them did not help, with McArthur sending word they were Union troops using a Confederate flag "as a decoy." Mason soon saw this was not true and ordered the regiment to fire. The Ohioans' lieutenant colonel, Barton S. Kyle, tried to reform the breaking masses but was killed in doing so. Mason admitted that his death "had a most disheartening effect upon the entire regiment, by whom he was greatly esteemed, the regiment having been recruited and organized by him." The Ohioans thus broke and fled down into the ravine behind them, allowing Jackson to move forward to the lip. It also allowed Jackson to put pressure on the flank of the still-resisting 55th Illinois to the east.[12]

By this time, Chalmers was also putting increasing pressure on the Illinois and Ohio troops holding the critical left flank. Even though the Federals were cut off from the rest of the army, Chalmers's Mississippians, later to be termed the "High Pressure Brigade," still found it difficult to move across the broken ground, especially farther east toward the river. Terrain and command thus allowed Stuart to hold on longer, but by 1:00 P.M. he was beginning to waver. Stuart consulted with Colonel T. Kilby Smith of the 54th Ohio and Malmborg of the 55th Illinois, and all decided they needed to fall back.[13]

Disaster soon struck, turning their orderly withdrawal into a rout. Chalmers's and Jackson's brigades followed up the Union retreat to the lip of the ravine. A Mississippi Confederate was amazed at what he saw: "We were right on top of you," he declared. "It was like shooting into a flock of sheep." Casualties were high as Stuart's soldiers tried to get down the ravine and then up the other side. Many were killed or wounded. One fortunate Illinoisan was hit in the head, only to stand up and declare, "Ain't I killed?" He was reassured by his lieutenant that he was still alive and ordered to once more retreat. Stuart's shaken troops took a brief stand on the other side, but Gage's gunners drove them away once more. The regiments fled rearward, toward the 5th Ohio Cavalry camp, where they reformed with a contingent of the 71st Ohio despite being out of ammunition. Colonel Smith remembered the critical shortage: "I never shall forget the despairing looks of some of the boys, who would come clustering around my horse and say, 'Colonel, what shall I do; my cartridges are all out?'" Realizing he could do nothing with empty guns, a wounded Stuart advised Hurlbut around 3:00 P.M. that he was retiring and that his flank would soon be turned.[14]

The withdrawal of the Union left was obviously a major blow to the Federals, but at least Stuart had used up several more hours of daylight. With only pockets of resistance now on his left, McArthur took no chances and eventually turned his line east of the River Road back in a crescent shape, corresponding to one of the deep ravines through which a branch of the larger ravine ran. His 9th Illinois faced generally south, but the 12th Illinois turned a little to the southeast while the 50th Illinois was farther to the northeast facing southeastward. There is evidence that part of the 71st Ohio also fought on this line. Having felt some pressure already from other Confederates and hearing the growing disaster to his east, McArthur now became the organized face of the Federal left. His refused flank would be able to hold at least for a while, he hoped.[15]

Fortunately for Hurlbut and McArthur, major activity soon moved to the high ground around the cotton field rather than remaining in the ravines bordering the Tennessee River. While Chalmers continued to operate in the area for a while, along with Clanton's Alabama cavalry regiment, which covered their right as well as brought up ammunition amid terrain where Chalmers's wagons could not venture, the fighting eventually gravitated to the left. Clanton was conspicuous in pushing both his cavalry and the infantry, sporting, one Alabamian noted, "a little battle flag upon the point of his saber." Still, the assaults and retreat among the ravines had taken the wind out of both sides on this flank. Indeed, Stuart would not play much of a role for the remainder of the day, and Chalmers, after advancing his regiments at the double-quick in pursuit "over several ravines and hills," commanded his brigade to halt while he rode over to Jackson's troops, which were idle at the moment, and requested that they take the advance for a while. Jackson reported that Chalmers "rode up to me and informed me that he had turned over that fight to my brigade and that his was resting." Chalmers would not be heavily engaged for a couple more hours.[16]

The other Confederate brigades on this eastern flank thus carried the load in the renewed fighting that began around noon and continued until after 2:00 P.M. Jackson, to Chalmers's left, had much better ground to traverse and thus was not nearly as worn out as the Mississippians to the right. Unlike Chalmers, Jackson's troops had not been involved in the firefight earlier at Spain Field. Yet if Jackson's Alabamians and Texans thought their brief and victorious tangle with the 71st Ohio was an indication of what was to come, they were wrong. They slowly crept forward, Girardey's Battery firing behind them, to the ravine that Stuart's brigade had found so troublesome. There they located McArthur's line, studded with the artillery of Mann's Battery, which had shifted from west of the River Road to the east and was deployed in the southern expanse of the small field across from the Peach Orchard. Urged on by Chalmers, Jackson's men found McArthur's Illinoisans firmly grounded on their side of the ravine.[17]

To Jackson's left, Bowen and Statham similarly advanced under Breckinridge, whom Thomas Jordan described that day as "the most impressive-looking man I ever had seen." A Texan described him as being "on horseback, with his right leg thrown around the pommel of the saddle, on which his elbow rested, and with his chin on his hand, was surveying the battle field as calmly as if there had been no bullets whizzing, or shells screaming, around him." Breckinridge had his moments of animation, though, when the 15th Mississippi reported they were out of ammunition in response to his order to take a battery. He thundered, "The 15th Mississippi doesn't need any cartridges. Take it with your

bayonets." Bowen and Statham found the path forward difficult, however. The open expanse of the Bell cotton field gave Hurlbut's Federals
ample warning, with the general remarking about the "glimmer of bayonets" that alerted him to the oncoming Confederates. A small mule lot,
"double staked with riders" one Tennessean remembered, also broke the
formations. One member of the 19th Tennessee thought it "seemed like
going into the very jaws of death," and sure enough, the brigade was
"saluted with a violent volley from the enemy" as soon as they topped
the ridge. A retreating Mississippian admitted five days later, "We did
not stand their fire but a few minutes in that charge."[18]

The Federal line, arrayed behind what Hurlbut described as "an old
fence, well overgrown by wild climbing vines and bushes," watched
the Confederate attack. "A brigade leaped the fence, line after line, and
formed on the opposite side of the field," recalled one 3rd Iowa soldier.
"It was a splendid sight, those men in the face of death closing and
dressing their ranks, hedges of bayonets gleaming above them, and their
proud banners waving in the breeze. Our guns, shotted with canister,
made great gaps in their ranks, which rapidly closed, not a man faltering
in his place. And now the field officers waved their hats. A shout arose,
and that column, splendidly aligned, took the double quick and moved
on magnificently. We could not repress exclamations of admiration."[19]

They also did not repress their fire, which turned Breckinridge's attack back in confusion. The calamity of the 15th Mississippi was illustrative of the chaos. When Breckinridge ordered the ammunitionless
Mississippians to take the battery, they tried, but they had reached only
part of the way when one of the captains, Lamkin S. Terry, ordered a
retreat. By this time, all the field officers were down, including future
Confederate general William F. Brantley. As the men began to stream
to the rear, Captain Michael Farrell took a position before the men and
declared "he would shoot the first man that ran." Unfortunately, Terry
confirmed his order to retreat, and the entire regiment bounded back.
Breckinridge was soon on their front, yelling, "What is the matter with
the 15th? Can't you take that battery?" A flabbergasted Captain Terry
"sprang up and thrusting his sword to the ground," rebounded, "General
Breckinridge, we can take hell if you will give us a leader." The men
immediately began yelling, "Farrell, Farrell." An embarrassed Terry offered the junior captain the command, but Farrell refused. Eventually
the 19th Tennessee drove the battery away, "and they never ceased after
that joking our men about it," one of the Mississippians remembered.[20]

The loudest action was an artillery duel between Harper's Mississippi Battery along the Hamburg-Purdy Road and Laing's Michigan guns. Harper had tried to keep up with Wood's brigade, but he finally found Cheatham and asked to be placed in his line. Cheatham put them in position looking out across Sarah Bell's field. Harper took stock of the odds: "As well as I could judge they had five guns; we four." Fortunately for Harper, terrain was on his side, with "the curve of the surface being near us, thereby causing their shot to ricochet over us, while ours might fall directly among them." "I attributed our miraculous escape," Harper added, "to this circumstance or the habitual high shooting of the enemy, for their missiles passed, with a perfect range, over us at from 5 to 20 feet high." Later, the Federals sent a cannon around the flank, but Harper countered by ordering "every gun at once to bear upon this one." With such help, the now wounded Harper soon drove the enemy away, and Cheatham complimented him by stating "it was the best handled battery he had seen."[21]

Several more infantry advances also took place amid the cannonade. The Federals described the fighting as continuing "unceasingly for about one hour and a half." Curiously, a herd of goats meandered between the lines right in the middle of the fighting. They were soon wiped out. A bewildered member of the 20th Tennessee wondered "why a soldier would shoot at a goat when so many of the enemy were present to shoot." Although some attacks on Hurlbut's right reached all the way "to within a few rods of our line," reported Hugh Reed of the 44th Indiana, the advances were uncoordinated, mainly as a result of the stiff Federal resistance and the open expanse the Confederates had to cover. A member of the nearby 3rd Iowa described one of the attacks: "When they had come within two hundred yards of our lines our men rose, and with cheers and yells poured volley after volley into the exposed ranks of the enemy, causing them to pause, and then fall back." Hurlbut and his brigade commanders were also wise in the use of their regiments. They took one out to refit and replaced it with a rested unit. Hurlbut also turned some of his right regiments—the Kentucky units of Lauman's brigade—partially to the left to flank the Confederates in the field. Still, the fighting was telling on the Union line as well. Laing's battery particularly suffered heavy casualties in both man and beast. The infantry also suffered; Lieutenant Colonel Ansel Tupper, commanding the 41st Illinois in Pugh's absence, was hit by a ball that entered and exited at his temples. Adding to the horror, the woods on the right caught fire.

Lauman described how the "dead and dying were soon enveloped in a general conflagration." A Confederate reported a particularly vivid scene: "The flesh had been burned from their set teeth, giving them a horrible grin."[22]

Through all the fighting, Hurlbut rode his lines, intent on keeping morale high and the regiments in place, parrying various threats such as when the enemy tried to use the valley on his left to force a wedge between Hurlbut and McArthur. One of his staff officers, L. D. Benner, wrote home, "I was along with the General the whole time, and we got into some very warm circumstances. The General was a little rash in his movements; for example, riding in front of our lines when the enemy was in plain sight, and pouring volley after volley into our ranks, but I thought if he was not afraid, I could go where he could." Later, Hurlbut sent Benner to deliver an order, which necessitated riding across the open field. A shot hit Benner's beloved horse, mortally wounding him. "I could have cried when I lost him," Benner noted. "He was not dead and sooner than see him suffer, I stepped around and put a pistol ball through his head. I was sorry to lose him as he was a splendid horse; and then I lost a fine saddle and bridle." Most of Hurlbut's men performed just as well, although one Illinoisan noted, "Some of the men it was thought would not fight did the best, and others who was thought to be invincible sneaked out of it."[23]

With little success occurring on this right flank, an impatient Albert Sidney Johnston decided he had to take charge of the stalled advance. From the high ground south of the Hamburg-Purdy Road, he watched his brigades struggle to push forward. Realizing that it was already 2:00 P.M., Johnston made a fatal decision. Despite the Confederates having several high-profile officers on this front, including vice president Breckinridge, division commander Jones Withers, and Tennessee governor Isham G. Harris, the troops seemed reluctant to proceed. Johnston had no more reserves to call forward, so he did the next best thing: he waded into his troops to inspire them to greater efforts. Beauregard later complained bitterly that Johnston as well as the corps commanders left their first duty and led brigades and even regiments. However, this was a critical point in the critical gamble. Johnston had to make a difference, and he had to do it himself. Just as key subordinates had continually let him down from Fort Donelson until now, he saw he had to risk his own life to personally do what needed to be done. He had to conquer or perish.[24]

Johnston rode forward to the rear of Bowen's brigade, coming under fire but taking refuge in the valley where the "mule lot" sat. Munford remembered Johnston sitting in "a depression about thirty yards behind our front line, where the bullets passed over our heads; but he could see more than half of his line, and, if an emergency arose, could meet it promptly." He also described how "the general passed his eye from the right of the line to his extreme point of vision in the direction of the left, and slowly back again." Taking in the situation, Johnston sent staff officers to position the brigades and rode up and down the line. Governor Harris remembered, "Here the firing was kept up with great energy by both armies for, perhaps, an hour, during the whole of which time the general remained upon the line, more exposed to the fire of the enemy than any soldier in the line." Harris added, "After the firing had been thus continued for near an hour, the general said to me: 'They are offering stubborn resistance here. I shall have to put the bayonet to them.'"[25]

Johnston ordered all the brigades to attack at once, but the response was not enthusiastic. Breckinridge rode to Johnston and told him he could not get his men to charge. "Oh, yes, general; I think you can," Johnston replied. Breckinridge further hesitated, but Johnston replied, "Then, I will help you. . . . We can get them to make the charge." In particular, Breckinridge had problems with some of his Tennesseans, mainly the 45th Tennessee, which George B. Hodge of Breckinridge's staff described as delivering "its fire at random and inefficiently, became disordered, and retired in confusion down the slope." The green Tennesseans also fired into the flank of the 20th Tennessee, causing Colonel Joel Battle to send a messenger over to have it stopped. Breckinridge even told Johnston that his Tennesseans "won't fight." A nearby Harris immediately barked, "Show me that regiment." Johnston eventually told Harris, "I will go to the front, order, and lead the charge." Harris also remembered, "Just as he was in the act of passing through the line to the front, he said to me, 'Go to the extreme right and lead the Tennessee regiment stationed there.'" The governor did so.[26]

Johnston thus used his considerable personal charisma, riding the line and whipping the men into a frenzy. He "told us a few more charges and the day was ours," a member of Bowen's brigade remembered while bullets flew past, one clipping Bowen's hair. Riding along the line of soldiers, Johnston tapped their bayonets with the little tin cup he had taken from the Wisconsin camp. "These must do the work," he shouted. "Men! They are stubborn; we must use the bayonet." One of Statham's Tennesseans remembered Johnston telling them that this position was the "key" to the landing and they should "unlock it" with their bayonets.[27]

With the line now "thrilling and trembling with that tremendous and irresistible ardor," one eyewitness wrote, Johnston wheeled Fire Eater around and yelled, "I will lead you!" The excited Confederates of Bowen's brigade immediately behind him burst forward, "as if drawn to him by some overmastering magnetic force," one of them remembered. The other brigades moved forward as well, with Jackson renewing his assault to the east while Statham picked up the advance to the west. One Tennessean described how Statham rode to the "front, [and] waved his sword and dashed forward." Harris led the shaky 45th Tennessee on foot, and Breckinridge and his staff, including his son, Cabell, were solidly among the troops. All across the board, the Confederates lurched forward in a wild attack. Johnston himself stopped to allow the wildly cheering Confederates to continue past him.[28]

The first Confederate success came on Jackson's front. The 9th Illinois unwisely became caught in the ravine to their rear and were cut to pieces by what Colonel August Mersy called "a most murderous crossfire poured into our ranks from the left." The regiment had used the reverse slope on the south side to shield the men as they loaded, then rose above the crest to fire. When the line broke, however, the position became a trap. Jackson's Alabamians and Texans were able to get on McArthur's left flank, and it showed when they were able to utilize the curving nature of the Union line to enfilade the Illinoisans. The 9th Illinois thus sustained the highest number of killed and wounded of any regiment at Shiloh. Although the rest of the line was not so open to enfilade fire, it still felt the effects. A sick Colonel Augustus L. Chetlain of the 12th Illinois, having risen from his sickbed that morning, held his position for a time, but his horse was soon shot down. It threw the colonel, bruising his hand and chest. He remained in command on foot, but he withdrew the troops to a more favorable position to the rear.[29]

The final section of McArthur's Federal line was destroyed with the devastation of the 50th Illinois, which was refused to the far left. The enemy came at them both from the front and from the left up the ravine they were facing. The right of Jackson's brigade was soon nearly in their rear, but the Federals were not at all convinced that the enemy was the enemy; one officer argued that the flag they saw was the stars and stripes. Colonel Moses M. Bane sent his lieutenant colonel, William M. Swarthout, and sergeant major to the front to find out. The sergeant major was shot dead when he tried to flee, and Swarthout was wounded in the leg after emptying his pistol while behind a tree. An Alabamian gave a perfect description of the affair from the Confederate side: because "they refused to surrender," one officer fell dead, but "the other stood behind a tree and called to his men on the hill to fire, but they either did not hear or refused to obey. We begged him to surrender as his escape was impossible, but the gallant fellow refused and fired upon us with his pistols." Swarthout then went down, yelling, "Don't kill me—I surrender." With Confederates on their flank and front and with Colonel Bane also down with a wound near the shoulder and chest, the regiment came apart and withdrew with the rest of McArthur's men, a wounded McArthur (right foot) worrying over a prized horse he had lent to a staff officer. When he learned that the horse had been killed, he bellowed, "Tell him to save the saddle."[30]

Peter Wood's Chicago Light Artillery was also caught up in the retreat. "We fought them inch by inch," wrote one cannoneer, "retreating in good order, and again and again going into battery and making our Bull Dogs bark at the most rapid rate that was practicable." He added proudly, "Not a premature discharge occurring all day." Still, the artillery had to retreat, taking a gun off with just one horse: "Our boys took hold of the tung and made a near-wheel horse of themselves, and by pushing, succeeded in bringing it off safely."[31]

The crisis on the left caused Hurlbut to send aid in the form of Mann's Battery, which fired obliquely to the southeast, and Colonel John Logan's 32nd Illinois, which was earlier pulled out of line south of the Peach Orchard and sent across the River Road to aid McArthur and cover Pugh's left. Led by a guide, Logan's regiment marched swiftly— so swiftly, in fact, that the front three companies outstripped the rest of the column and Logan had to send an officer back to hurry them forward. They took position before McArthur fell back, but refugees from McArthur's line to the front continually ran through his lines, although they held firm for the time being. Eventually, the 32nd Illinois also had to fall back when it ran out of ammunition and seemed determined to defend its position with fixed bayonets. Logan knew that would be suicidal, thinking his isolation came because "our situation had been overlooked or our brigade commander had fallen." He ordered the retreat,

Logan remaining with the rearmost files as the regiment withdrew. He was shot in the shoulder for his effort. The lieutenant colonel, John W. Ross, had gone down only moments before with a mortal wound, so the regiment's retreat soon turned into a leaderless rout.[32]

The renewed Confederate advance also lurched forward to Jackson's left. In addition to Statham and Bowen's advance, fresh troops also arrived. One officer described the results: many stragglers, "cheered by the arrival of even this small body of fresh troops, rallied." Along with Forrest's cavalry, George Maney had brought his companies of the 1st Tennessee to the field, along with the 19th Tennessee of Statham's brigade. Maney's orders from Johnston had been to make sure no enemy was coming from the Hamburg area, and when "perfectly satisfied" of the fact, he could return. He returned to the battlefield, leaving Forrest and Colonel David H. Cummings of the 19th Tennessee, who had no such discretionary orders but came anyway, to guard the ford. Maney thus retook command of his brigade as the ranking officer, and Cheatham described the terrain to Maney and told him of several unsuccessful attempts to dislodge Lauman's Federals to the front. Now he wanted to send Maney in as Breckinridge moved forward again on the right, allowing Maney to pick his assault column. The Tennessean chose his own troops as well as the fresh 19th Tennessee, along with the least shot-up unit of Stephens's men, the 9th Tennessee.[33]

The Federals' response was heavy. When the Confederates topped the hill from the small hollow, John Bowen reported, "We were received with a destructive volley, killing and wounding about 12 of my men. Simultaneously we returned their fire and charged ahead." The brigade nevertheless drove across the River Road at an angle and aided in pushing back McArthur and Hurlbut's left. The same was occurring on Statham's and Maney's fronts. The latter moved forward across the western edge of the cotton field, where the men of Lauman's brigade were still concentrated on some of the assaults to the west. Maney reported that his men were "so fortunate as to pass the field and gain the cover of the woods before the enemy's attention seemed fairly directed to me." Maney ordered his men to lie down, but as soon as the first volley poured over their heads, he had them up and charging again. It was apparently in this attack that Colonel David Cummings of the 19th Tennessee went down.[34]

Amazingly, the attack worked on almost the entire front, mostly because of Johnston's personal leadership. One of Breckinridge's Confederates noted in his diary that the enemy "stood two fires when they took to their heels in real Bull Run style." An artilleryman with Statham's brigade similarly wrote, "The yankee line on our front broke, and the Miss. Boys are all up and at them." Yet the tired Confederates "were unable to make but little speed," one Mississippian declared, thus allowing the enemy a little respite. Still, McArthur's regiments left the line first in the face of Bowen's and Jackson's charging Confederates a little after 2:00 P.M., and Hurlbut's troops withdrew about the same time, falling back through the Peach Orchard and forming a new line on the north side of the field. Beauregard, who was no fan of Johnston, accurately wrote that Johnston "gave resistless impulsion to his columns at critical moments."[35]

Johnston was jubilant, as were his commanders. Breckinridge rode among his troops, telling them after one volley, "This volley got half and another would get the other half." Johnston rode back behind the Confederate line to a small knoll to get a better view of his success and there determined, according to staff officers, that his work here was done and he needed to move over to the Confederate left. Harris found him there: "I had never, in my life, seen him looking more bright, joyous, and happy, than he looked at the moment that I approached him. The charge he had led was heroic. It had been successful, and his face expressed a soldier's joy and a patriot's hope." Johnston was also in a playful mood. Colonel Thomas M. Jack remembered him "slapping his thigh and smiling, upon a spent ball which had struck and stung him." Johnston also showed Governor Harris his boot, the flapping sole of which had been cut by enemy fire. He remarked, "Governor, they came very near putting me *hors de combat* in that charge." Harris asked if he was wounded, but Johnston said no. Unbeknownst to him, his life's blood was even then slipping away.[36]

Just because this particular Confederate assault was successful did not mean the battle was over or that the Confederates had won. In fact, the Federals immediately began to set up another defensive line, with an intermediate rear guard only about a hundred yards north of their original position, on the north side of the Peach Orchard. It also took a while for the Confederates, bloodied in the main attack, to reorganize and move on. Indeed, many a Confederate had fallen in the attack across the field, including Captain Francis Marion Aldridge of the 15th

Mississippi. He had been a member of the Mississippi secession convention, and figuratively signed his own death warrant when he signed
the ordinance of secession on January 15, 1861. Aldridge had a commission as lieutenant colonel of the 29th Mississippi, but he refused
to leave his regiment on the eve of the all-important Pittsburg Landing
offensive. It cost him his life; he was hit while leading his company
across Sarah Bell's cotton field. Similarly, Captain Alfred Hudson,
commanding Hudson's Mississippi Battery, also known as the Pettus
Flying Artillery, was killed on April 6, most likely in the fighting near
the Peach Orchard.[37]

Aldridge and Hudson were but two of many Confederates who fell
in the attack. The chief casualty was Albert Sidney Johnston. As Federal
artillery opened up from the new line, Governor Harris remembered
Johnston "paused in the middle of a sentence to say, 'Order Colonel
Statham to wheel his regiment to the left, charge, and take that battery.'" Harris delivered the order and returned to Johnston's side, but
was shocked at what he saw. "The General sank down in his saddle,
leaning over to the left," Harris remembered, adding that he did so "in
a manner that indicated he was falling from his horse." Harris held him
on the horse as best he could and worriedly inquired, "General, are you
wounded?" Harris described Johnston's "very deliberate and emphatic
tone," saying, "Yes, and I fear seriously."[38]

He was indeed wounded seriously, but a frantic Harris and the only
nearby staff officer, Captain W. L. Wickam, had no surgeon to deal with
the crisis; presumably, Yandell was still back at the 18th Wisconsin
camp treating the wounded, as Johnston had ordered him to do. All the
while, Johnston was obviously getting worse. Harris remembered, "The
general's hold upon his reigns relaxed, and it dropped from his hand."
Harris and Wickam took Johnston, still atop Fire Eater, into a ravine
behind them and "eased him to the ground as gently as I could," Harris
remembered. As Wickam galloped away to find Yandell or any other
doctor, Harris sent a nearby soldier to find any staff member he could.
With Johnston barely conscious, his head in Harris's lap, the governor
felt the entire world collapsing around him. "With eager anxiety I asked
many questions about his wounds," Harris remembered, "to which he
gave no answer, not even a look of intelligence."[39]

Staff officers soon began to arrive, including Johnston's brother-
in-law, William Preston, but they could do nothing but search for an
upper body wound. They found nothing. Later they found that he had

been hit as many as four times, mostly by shrapnel and spent balls. Only one bullet had penetrated the skin; Johnston had been hit behind the right knee, and the wound was bleeding freely. It had torn, not severed, the popliteal artery, and Johnston was dying from a loss of blood that Yandell might have been able to stop. Johnston had a tourniquet in his pocket, but it was of no use without the recognition that it was needed.[40]

George Baylor remembered Johnston's blood pouring out in a rivulet and pooling several feet away. Harris tried to pour brandy down Johnston's throat, "but he made no effort to swallow; it gurgled in his throat in his effort to breathe, and I turned his head so as to relieve him." Preston could only kneel beside him and cry, "Johnston, do you know me?" Harris reported the end: "In a few moments he ceased to breathe. He died calmly, and, to all appearances, free from pain—indeed so calmly, that the only evidence I had that he had passed from life was the fact that he ceased to breathe, and the heart ceased to throb. There was not the slightest struggle, nor the contortion of a muscle; his features were as calm and as natural as at any time in life and health." It was around 2:30 P.M., and the grown men could not help but cry. Preston sobbed, "Pardon me, Gentlemen; you all know how I loved him."[41]

The debate surrounding the effect of Johnston's death has been wide and deep, but in actuality his death at this point made little difference. The spinning wheels on the Confederate war machine had already wasted too much daylight. Some historians, taking their cue from remarks by Sherman and Hardee—both of whom, importantly, were on the other side of the field at the time—have argued that there was a lull caused by Johnston's death on the critical Union left. However, Civil War battles were full of lulls as attackers started, stopped, fell back, regrouped, and tried again. Braxton Bragg actually spoke of this phenomenon, describing "all parts of our line were not constantly engaged, but there was no time without heavy firing in some portion of it." Grant agreed, writing, "There was no hour during the day when there was not heavy firing and generally hard fighting at some point on the line, but seldom at all points at the same time." Any lull after Johnston's death was due more to the natural flow of battle than reaction to Johnston's demise.[42]

Still, Johnston was dead, the result of a need to make sure his gamble worked, or as one Confederate put it that night, "in order to make a sure thing of it." If his idea was to conquer or perish, he did the latter. All would have to wait and see if the conquer part might still happen.[43]

With news of Johnston's death quickly spreading to both sides, Hurlbut's Federal line fell back from its Peach Orchard defense to the north side of the field, taking an intermediate position consisting of a patchwork of troops including the 3rd Iowa and even the 61st Illinois of Prentiss's division. This line did not remain long. The Confederates almost immediately regrouped and pushed forward, with Johnston sending Harris to get Statham's brigade moving immediately on some artillery that had opened up near Wicker Field. While the initial line held temporarily, Hurlbut was able to piece together a more substantial force on the southern fringes of Wicker Field and in the woods to either side of it, including the 3rd Iowa and 28th Illinois of Pugh's brigade, the 12th Illinois of McArthur's, and even some of Stuart's regiments farther to the east. Adept at encouraging his men, Hurlbut spoke to each, telling the 3rd Iowa, for example, "I look to the 3d Iowa to retrieve the fortunes of this field." Yet with Stuart's eventual retreat to the east, Hurlbut made the dramatic decision to send Lauman's entire brigade of four regiments east of the River Road, hoping that it could shore up the left. Hurlbut sent word to Prentiss to try to extend his line to connect with Pugh's regiments, but the connection was never made, and Lauman's withdrawal caused Prentiss to begin thinking of refusing his line. Despite having his entire personal staff "disabled" and having to rely on Colonel Hugh B. Reed to send messages, Lauman led his regiments eastward across the River Road. Back on Pugh's front, Ross's and Wood's artillery added to the defense, as did Richardson's and Powell's guns from the center. In addition, the 57th Illinois, which was one of the reserve regiments of Sweeny's brigade, arrived and was sent to the far left to aid Lauman.[44]

This line was not very defensible either, however, with neither flank resting on anything substantial. The Confederates soon took advantage of this problem, with Bragg, now on the right, bellowing, "Bring up Chalmers' brigade." Chalmers quickly rode back to where he had left his regiments with orders to rest. He found the impressive brigade already on the move. The 31st Indiana on the left of Lauman's brigade, along with the 57th Illinois, took the brunt of Chalmers's attack, with one of the Federals remembering that they fought the "Mississippi Tigers." A twice-wounded (leg and shoulder) but still commanding Colonel Charles Cruft of the 31st Indiana reported, "Regiment after regiment marched up from a large ravine to the left, moving in echelon, in compact lines, with Confederate flags flying, in perfect order, as if on parade, and came steadily down upon our small front." A short counterattack by some of Lauman's plucky regiments did nothing to stall the Confederate advance, and Colonel Reed of the 44th Indiana reported that this engagement was "the most hotly-contested fight of the day."[45]

Because of the open left flank, this line collapsed around 4:00 P.M.—something strikingly similar to what was occurring on the opposite side of the field. The retreat was horrid at first. Colonel Amory K. Johnson of the 28th Illinois reported that he suffered a "murderous cross-fire" while withdrawing across Wicker Field, losing his lieutenant colonel, Thomas M. Killpatrick, in the process. Captain Matthew M. Trumbull, commanding the 3rd Iowa, reported that his unit "was then compelled in a great measure to cut its way out." Not all made it out unscathed, including Captain John Wesley Powell, who took a ball in his right arm. As he raised his hand as a signal to stand clear, "a musket ball struck my arm above the wrist which I scarcely noticed until I attempted to mount my horse." The arm was later amputated, but that did not stop him from making the first successful voyage through the Grand Canyon in 1869. As the Federals fled, Hurlbut sent a courier to Prentiss indicating he was withdrawing, but Hurlbut never saw the rider again, and he later learned that Prentiss never received his dispatch. Meanwhile, there was an attempt to form yet another line of defense in Cloud Field, with the 57th Illinois turning and firing off one volley while Richardson's, Welker's, and Wood's artillery formed in the southwestern corner and the 32nd Illinois made a short stand in their own camp. Nothing worked. The line soon disintegrated, and the soldiers fled through their own tents. One member of the 41st Illinois wrote, "It was now evident that our forces were to be driven in at all points, as every road was filled with the wounded and the cowards flying towards the river." Hurlbut's Federals did not stop again until they were within Grant's third, and last, major line of the day, north of Dill Branch.[46]

In the end, the fighting on this eastern third of the battlefield was exactly like that on the western third: both flanks gave in and retired to a third major line of defense behind the northern set of creeks. Hurlbut's defense of the left flank was not nearly as dramatic and awe-inspiring as McClernand's and Sherman's was on the right, but it performed the same critical service of using up daylight, especially on this critical left flank. In fact, while McClernand's and Sherman's divisions were falling back across Tilghman Branch as early as 3:00 or 3:30 P.M., Hurlbut held out until after 4:00 P.M. Hurlbut thus bought Grant five or six hours on this crucial left flank, certainly doing his part in what was turning out to be a bloodbath.

11

"At All Hazards"

Without the knowledge that his wife had just arrived at the landing a mere few hundred yards from him, W. H. L. Wallace sat down with his staff for breakfast that April 6 morning but was immediately interrupted. He detected volleys of musketry and boom of cannon shortly after 7:00 A.M. The officers rose from the table and began to organize their division, ultimately moving into position at the Hornet's Nest.[1]

Unbeknownst to Wallace, his line would form inside the vacuum left by the parting Confederate wings. Albert Sidney Johnston's earlier push to the left had positioned at least two thirds of his army on the western side of the battlefield, bypassing what would become known as the Hornet's Nest. When Johnston unfolded his new wing to the right, he likewise ultimately sent as much as a third of his army to the eastern side of the battlefield and the Hornet's Nest. The result was that the wings of the Confederate army, containing fourteen of the sixteen brigades, were fighting on either side of the center for most of the day. Rarely and only briefly did any of those units spill over into the center. Still, the Hornet's Nest has become the key to the battlefield in public memory.[2]

When the call came for help around 8:00 A.M., some of Wallace's soldiers were just washing dishes from the morning meal and joked that they hoped the attackers "would let us alone till we got the dishes dried." All joking soon ended when the men realized the army was indeed under full attack. While McClernand moved forward to support Sherman and Hurlbut advanced to support Prentiss and Stuart, Wallace had the most distance to travel and encountered a rising tide of stragglers and wounded from the front going the other way. Thus his units did not take their position in the newly forming line until after 9:00 A.M. One Iowan remembered, "We marched leisurely, making frequent halts, experiencing some difficulty in finding the remainder of our brigade among the moving troops." Even then, not everyone was in line. Several of the sick tried to go along. B. F. Thomas of the 14th Iowa noted one result: "John Gaston gave out after running more than a mile. The last I saw of him he was leaning over a stump vomiting." As a result of his continual movement, Wallace's lead brigade under Colonel James M. Tuttle beat the enemy to the Hornet's Nest by only a matter of minutes. Marching up the Eastern Corinth Road to the edge of Duncan Field filled with head-high weeds, Tuttle observed Confederates to the front. Wallace thus deployed the brigades in line of battle in the woods and advanced to a fence on the edge of Duncan Field. Tuttle rode his lines, yelling to his troops, "Boys remember that you are from Iowa."[3]

One observant Iowan noted, "It seemed we were put here to fill a gap." Indeed, to connect McClernand's division with Hurlbut, two regiments of Colonel Thomas W. Sweeny's brigade, the 7th and 58th Illinois, went in on the right in Duncan Field north of the Corinth Road. The troops took position behind a rail fence while Sweeny reconnoitered to the front near what he termed a "cotton-gin" and the Duncan cabins, which, unknown to him, contained a woman and five children. Sweeny deployed only those two regiments, keeping his other four in reserve and supporting the artillery. Powell's Missouri battery was also in this position for a short time a little later in the fighting, unlimbering farther forward in Duncan Field along the road but soon withdrawing, leaving one gun. "I was in a position where I was not only surprised but fully at the mercy of the enemy," Powell noted. To Sweeny's left was Tuttle's brigade of four Iowa regiments, the 2nd, 7th, and part of the 12th Iowa forming behind a fence and a farm road later termed the Sunken Road bordering Duncan Field. The rest of the 12th and the 14th Iowa straddled the Eastern Corinth Road and fronted a dense area of undergrowth from atop a small knoll. Many of Tuttle's Iowans laid down to wait for the enemy while Tuttle and Major J. S. Cavender, commanding the division's artillery, rode forward to scout.[4]

What was left of Prentiss's division moved northward and eventually continued the line to the east. One of Tuttle's Iowans remembered that Missourians of Prentiss's division "came through the bushes [and] they seemed to be much frightened. They were scattered like skirmishers and said the rebels were coming in heavy columns." A 12th Michigan captain admitted, "I could only find 13 of Company A." Another wrote home, "We got somewhat scattered on the first retreat and were not able to get together again." The 14th Iowa's colonel told them to lie down so his rifle-equipped regiment could fire into the bushes, but the Missourians would not stop. William Shaw then ordered the Iowans to lie down, and the fugitive Missourians went right over them. Only then did Shaw order his men up to fire, staggering the closest following Confederates. "We plunged into the bushes after them," noted B. F. Thomas of the 14th Iowa. The premature rush forward stopped any Confederate idea of a further advance at the time. Meanwhile, Prentiss's artillery took position as well, with the general himself locating Hickenlooper's remaining Ohio guns on a knoll on the right of his line. Munch's Minnesotans also took position, with the two sections acting independently and straddling the Eastern Corinth Road.[5]

Prentiss's troops soon rallied and took a position on Shaw's left, but their numbers were few after the thrashing they had endured earlier in their camps. Portions of the 18th, 21st, and 25th Missouri, 18th Wisconsin, and 12th Michigan were in the line, including Major James Powell, who had led the patrol that started the fighting in the first place. Unfortunately, as the Missourians later defended the 5th Ohio Battery, Powell was shot in the side and mortally wounded, leaving his young son alone in the army. Brigade commander Miller was there as well, still atop his horse, although most other officers had taken to foot for safety. Fortunately for Prentiss, the 23rd Missouri, which had arrived at the landing the night before and "lay on the river bank for the night," came forward to his support, first forming near Cloud Field. Colonel J. T. Tindall's Missourians almost doubled Prentiss's command to around 1,100, now mostly connecting Wallace with Hurlbut. Portions of six batteries also studded the line, with the remaining guns of Munch's and Hickenlooper's units from Prentiss's division up on the main line and Wallace's division artillery consisting of Stone's, Welker's, and Richardson's batteries as well as Powell's behind the line on a taller ridge, supported by Sweeny's reserve regiments and the detached 61st Illinois of Prentiss's division. As the troops waited for major action to begin, they could hear the fighting elsewhere: "To our right and left fighting is heavy," a 7th Iowa soldier wrote in his diary. To his immediate right, Lieutenant James B. Weaver, eventually to become the Populist Party nominee for president in 1892, thought little of politics. He took out a small testament his wife had given him and read a psalm. "It did me good," he later wrote her.[6]

Prentiss and Wallace quickly began to communicate, forging a bond that would be remembered in history. Yet this was not their first association; the two Federal commanders in the Hornet's Nest had once served in the same company in the Mexican War, Prentiss as captain and Wallace as a lieutenant. Such familiarity was helpful to the Federal cause this day.[7]

The initial major Confederate contact with the Hornet's Nest line came around 10:30 A.M., when the right of Shaver's Arkansas brigade spilled into Duncan Field as it moved on the extreme right flank of Johnston's mass attack. The right flank of the brigade, the 3rd Confederate Infantry, trudged out into the field, on the other side of which lay Wallace's brigades. A small break in the line separated McClernand and Wallace at this point, and Shaver was trying to take advantage of that opportunity to flank the 8th Illinois. Suddenly Wallace's men announced themselves with enfield volleys. The startled Confederates, thinking they were flanking the enemy, found themselves suddenly outflanked and ran back into the woods.[8]

The commotion and perhaps some quick staff work caught the attention of the Confederate commanders in the area. A surprised Shaver noted, "My right wing was very much exposed to the fire of their sharpshooters," adding, "The enemy appeared in considerable force." He notified Bragg, and the corps commander began to look for troops to throw against the enemy line. While Bragg searched, another brigade actually performed the duty. Beauregard had earlier sent Colonel William H. Stephens's small Tennessee brigade to fill the space between Gibson and Anderson, with orders to fight where they were most needed. Led by their division commander, Cheatham, Stephens moved to the right of Shaver's attack and began to prepare to assault. With Smith's Mississippi Battery providing cover, as well as long-range shots from Robertson's Battery down the Eastern Corinth Road, Stephens's troops stepped into the unknown area down the road about 11:00 A.M. It would be the first actual assault on the Hornet's Nest.[9]

Stephens faced numerous problems even before the attack. Johnston had sent the brigade's regular commander, Colonel George Maney, away to guard the bridge over Lick Creek, thus depriving it of its leadership. Stephens had taken charge as the ranking colonel, but he was ill and had only recently rejoined his men from his sickbed. He was still extremely weak, and a fall from his horse when it was shot immediately before the attack did nothing to calm his nerves or instill strength. His sickness, he later explained, "disabled me from rendering active assistance during the engagement," but he nevertheless went in with the 6th Tennessee.[10]

Stephens had fewer than a thousand men with which to make the attack. Such small numbers could do little against the massed infantry and artillery in the Hornet's Nest, but they tried anyway. Cheatham noted that the Union line was behind some log houses and a fence along "an abandoned road." Much of the small brigade went through the open Duncan Field. "So soon as the brigade entered the field the enemy opened upon us from his entire front a terrific fire of artillery and musketry, but failed altogether to check our movement until we reached the center of the field," Cheatham reported. A member of the 7th Kentucky related, "Somewhat near the center of the field the regiment halted and opened fire." There, crossfire from Sweeny's units to the left halted the advance, as the 2nd and 7th Iowa poured in their fire from the front. Several Confederates also fell in front of the 12th and 14th Iowa as the right of the brigade angled down the Eastern Corinth Road. The troops in the woods did little better, however, negotiating the slope as well as the mass vegetation. Cheatham watched as half of his division weathered the storm: "The enemy opened upon us from his entire front a terrific fire of artillery and musketry . . . when another part of the enemy's force concealed and protected by the fence and thicket on our left, opened a murderous cross-fire upon our lines." The small regiments ultimately fell back from the storm. One Kentuckian described how "the balls jumped me on each side and in great profusion during the charge and after we got into the timber they continue to pass us." Stephens claimed to have made a second attack, and contemporary evidence exists to support his claim.[11]

Whether Stephens made one or two attacks is less important than the confidence the Union forces gained from the ordeal. Stephens, and no doubt Cheatham, wanted no further part of the area and moved to the right to help fill the gap next to Statham's brigade. There Maney rejoined them and participated in the afternoon attacks. The Federals had the exact opposite reaction. Although they would later face much worse than Stephens's little brigade, they weathered the initial storm and built up confidence in their position. A visit by Grant in the late morning and then again around 4:30 P.M. further encouraged the troops. He spoke to Wallace and then Prentiss about their lines, their duties, and the need to

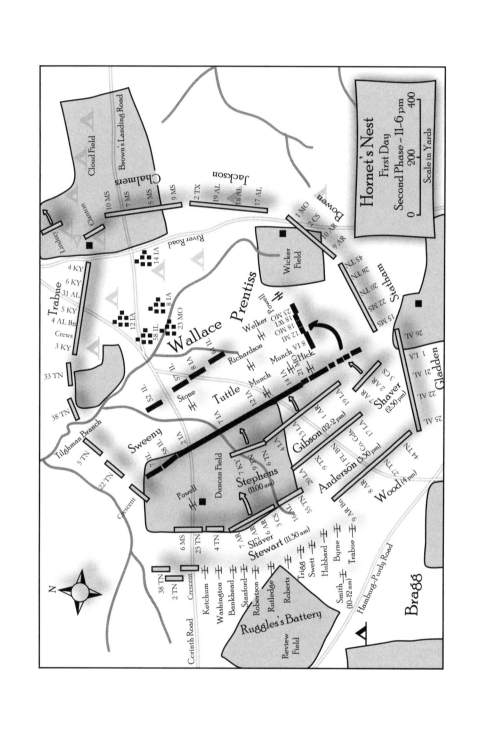

Hornet's Nest
First Day
Second Phase ~ 11-6 pm

0   200   400
Scale in Yards

hold until reinforcements could arrive. He told them that Buell and Wallace would be supporting them soon, to which one 7th Iowa soldier (and others) responded, "We doubted the report thinking it was circulated to keep up encouragement among us." Intending to use up as much time in holding this line as possible, Grant issued his customary orders to hold the position "at all hazards." Prentiss later wrote that he was "in constant communication with generals Hurlbut and Wallace during the day, and both of them were aware of the importance of holding our position until night." One Iowan, writing five days later, said that the troops were "determined to die rather than give back."[12]

By 11:30 A.M., Johnston's original turning movement to the west was having its effect. In that mass attack, the eight Confederate brigades had attacked Sherman's command, dislodged McClernand's division, and bent the Union right back at the junction of McClernand's and Wallace's divisions. The Union retreat, even with periodic halts, did not stop until it reached Jones Field, but the Confederates declined to follow all the way. A temporary stillness therefore settled over the western area of the battlefield. Stephens's sudden assault up the Eastern Corinth Road was noisy in comparison to the relative quietness that had emerged once McClernand and Sherman withdrew. Confederate commanders on the left thus temporarily turned some of their attention eastward toward the Hornet's Nest instead of following up the Union withdrawal to the north. Portions of several brigades banded together to head toward the sound of the guns.[13]

Pausing in the northward trek of the attack but still within easy sound of the "terrific firing" to the east, the ranking Confederate general in the area, Major General Thomas C. Hindman, began to gather units for a new assault, talking A. P. Stewart and his 4th Tennessee into joining him. Hindman was wounded just west of Duncan Field, however, his horse shot by a cannonball. One Tennessean declared that the shell "exploded inside the horse," and the shell and his horse's fall dulled Hindman's senses. Stewart thus became the ranking officer in the area (and Clark's division), although he commanded only one regiment from that division. He nevertheless took that regiment, the 4th Tennessee, and combined it with Shaver's troops to form the core of an assault line. He also gathered several more idle regiments, such as the beleaguered 6th Mississippi and 23rd Tennessee of Cleburne's brigade on the left and the separated 16th Alabama and 55th Tennessee of Wood's brigade on the far right. In all, Stewart amassed around 3,700 men and Swett's Mississippi Battery. This mishmash of four Confederate brigades stepped into Duncan Field around 11:30 A.M., their left across the Corinth Road and their right extending all the way into the woods where Stephens had attacked on the Eastern Corinth Road.[14]

Anticlimactically, there was no assault; Stewart reported that his mass of infantry only "engaged" the enemy when Shaver suddenly withdrew, explaining that he was out of ammunition. That critical issue should have been checked before an assault was attempted, but more likely the Confederates realized what crossing the open field would do; portions of Shaver's brigade had already been out in that field. Stewart had no choice but to pull everyone back, and the montage soon broke apart, with some soldiers leaving to refill cartridge boxes and others returning to the northern-facing orientation, where Sherman and Mc-Clernand were now counterattacking. Thus the largest number of men the Confederates would bring to bear in front of the Hornet's Nest that day did not even manage an assault.[15]

At least one Confederate commander was not about to let such a line of Federals block his path down the Eastern Corinth Road, and Braxton Bragg's name would become synonymous with the seemingly obsessive attacks in the center. Bragg's beloved horse had already perished before his eyes, and a second horse was also killed an hour later while he sought to push the Federals on the Confederate's left. When the corps commanders decided to divide up the front line, however, Bragg gained the sector with the least number of troops in it. There were nine brigades fighting to the west and only briefly spilling into the center, as well as five more brigades battling on the eastern third of the field. That left only two brigades (three if Shaver's resupplying command is counted) in the entire center third of the battlefield. Gladden's command, now under Colonel Zach Deas, had done little since the morning fight at Spain Field except form into a square, evidently in response to mounted Federals. That left only one fresh brigade for Bragg to use: Gibson's Louisiana and Arkansas troops.[16]

Bragg did what he could with such meager numbers. Unfairly, he has almost unanimously been faulted for using frontal bayonet attacks instead of turning the flanks of the Federal position. It must be remem-

bered, however, that the mass of the Confederate army was trying to
do just that. For much of the afternoon on April 6, there were no open
flanks to turn at the Hornet's Nest. There is also evidence that Bragg did
try a flanking movement. Staff officer David Urquhart later wrote that
Bragg "sent me to ask you [Thomas Jordan] to find and push forward
a strong force to flank those batteries on our right." Turning the Union
left flank was impossible, however, as long as Hurlbut's troops held that
sector—something Bragg soon discovered. The same situation existed
on Wallace's right. All that Bragg had at his disposal was a continual
and frustrating use of the frontal assault.[17]

Randall Gibson bore the brunt of Bragg's growing frustration, perhaps a carryover from Gibson unintentionally showing him up in front
of Johnston at Monterey. Gibson had even bigger problems, however:
he had no artillery. Bain's Mississippi Battery had been left at Corinth.
He also faced a massively thick area of undergrowth on rising ground—
so much so that one Louisianan wrote, "We were well drilled and were
constantly trying to reform our broken lines." Thus even getting to the
Federals was difficult.[18]

Yet the brigade was ably led; Gibson and two of his four colonels
would eventually rise to the rank of Confederate generals. Bragg quickly
sent them in, but Gibson then ran up against a solid Federal line that had
already repulsed or engaged several other Confederate columns, most
notably Stephens's direct attacks and Stewart's presumptive one. The
plucky Federals even advanced on occasion, with the 14th Iowa and
the left of the 12th Iowa counterattacking Stephens's troops as they fell
back. One member of the 12th Iowa described how "the left wing of our
regiment charged on them & they run out into an open field in front of
the right wing and they poured fire in to them." And the Federal line was
only getting stronger. Wallace sent the reserve 8th Iowa to fill in the only
weak point in the line, the area where Tuttle and Prentiss connected.
A Scotsman by way of the royal military, India, and Canada, Colonel
James Geddes of the 8th Iowa reported that he "immediately engaged a
battalion of the enemy."[19]

Moving up the Eastern Corinth Road, Gibson's regiments continued
to grapple with the terrain, moving through "an open [Davis wheat]
field under a heavy fire and half way up an elevation covered with an
almost impenetrable thicket, upon which the enemy was posted." They
also passed the Davis cabins on their right. Then they had to tangle with
the Federals. Colonel William T. Shaw of the 14th Iowa reported that his

prone men waited until Gibson's troops came within thirty paces before firing: "The enemy's first line was completely destroyed." Confederates told the same story. One Louisianan wrote that they pressed forward, unable to see anything, until a volley ripped through them: "Strange to say we all fell over backwards, but most of us got up next moment unhurt, and returned the fire." They could still see little to the front. Colonel B. L. Hodge of the 19th Louisiana described his surprised men "looking through the bushes, as if hunting an object for their aim." Captain E. M. Dubroca of the 13th Louisiana agreed: "We were first apprised of their proximity by a shower of musketry sweeping through our ranks." The Louisianans declared the bullets sounded like swarms of angry hornets, and the name stuck.[20]

The brigade was taking heavy casualties from an enemy they could not see, so several officers, including Colonel Hodge, ordered bayonets fixed. The men dove into the undergrowth but made it only "20 or 30 steps . . . it seeming impossible to make further progress." Officers ordered the men to fire again, but Gibson's regiments had to fall back and reform. Colonel Henry Allen and the other officers yelled, "Form on this line! Form on this line!" They soon advanced again, a now unhorsed Gibson leading the way on the left of his brigade, but were hurled back once more. Colonel Hodge reported, "It would, under the circumstances, have been madness to have kept my command there longer." One Confederate was catching on quickly, describing the enemy position "impregnable to infantry alone." A third attempt was no more successful, but the defending Federals still marveled at the Louisianans' and Arkansans' bravery: Colonel Joseph Woods of the 12th Iowa remembered, "Again and again repeatedly did he attack us, trying vainly to drive us from our position. He failed to move us one inch." Colonel Geddes, defending Hickenlooper's Battery on his front, wrote that the Confederates charged "most gallantly to the very muzzles of the guns." The battery was saved, but Geddes went down with a leg wound.[21]

There is some disagreement today whether Gibson's troops made three or four assaults into the Hornet's Nest. Gibson stated four, but his regimental commanders reported three. Contemporary soldier accounts give credence to Gibson's claim of four. It is entirely possible that the portion where Gibson stationed himself in the third charge, the 1st Arkansas on the right wing of the brigade, made an additional assault apart from the rest of the brigade. Still, the net result was the same: Gibson failed to break through the Federal line. Braxton Bragg was incredulous: "This result was due entirely to want of proper handling." He wrote his wife more explicitly, telling her "a want of confidence in their leader Gibson destroyed them."[22]

Bragg was not correct. Illustrating the unit's bravery during the attacks was a captain in the 4th Louisiana. As the regiment was moving forward, a cannonball took off half of a soldier's head. "He threw up his hands, walked two or three steps in advance of the charging ranks and pitched stiffly forward on his face," a horrified comrade wrote. A few feet from him was Captain H. M. Favrot. Much of the man's blood and brains splattered the captain in the face. "He drew his coat sleeve across his face," the Louisianan remembered, "wiping away the hideous defilement, and coolly crying, 'It's all right! Come on boys!' . . . as though nothing had happened." Such bravery kept the men moving forward, although the witness admitted, "A sickening shudder ran through the ranks."[23]

Bragg also entered the fray at times, ordering Colonel Henry W. Allen of the 4th Louisiana to "serve them as they had served me." Thus Bragg ordered the brigade forward in one of the many attacks, telling Samuel Lockett to take the colors of the 4th Louisiana and lead the way. Lockett did so, telling the color-bearer, "General Bragg says these colors must not go to the rear." In the open field, Allen soon emerged, bleeding from a wound in the cheek, and retook the flag, saying, "If any man but my color-bearer carries these colors, I am the man." He also barked the orders, "here boys, is as good a place as any on this battlefield to meet death!"[24]

Judging I would do nothing with this force," Bragg wrote, he ordered Gibson to hold his position in what Thomas Robertson called the "slaughter pen." Some of his officers derided him because he "retired to a ravine" when artillery opened up, but Bragg remained on the field and pondered his next move. Having used up Gibson's troops, he sent them to the rear, and many of the bewildered Louisianans discussed in amazement what had just happened. According to Louisianan Frank Richardson, a few actually "started a little game of poker." Staff officer Giles B. Cooke posted the 1st Arkansas and 19th Louisiana behind a fence, where they told him they "had retired three different times from the hornets nest." With few options, Bragg then turned to the only other feasible troops in the area: Shaver's Arkansas regiments, the members of which had been resupplying and resting since their 11:30 A.M. withdrawal from the line. Around 2:30 P.M., Bragg sent Shaver in along the same path that Gibson had taken.[25]

Shaver described the enemy as "posted in considerable force in a dense undergrowth in a heavy woods." "On the enemy's right was a battery of the presence of which (so completely was it concealed) I was not aware until it opened," Shaver added. The men moved forward over Gibson's and Stephens's dead and dying, only to meet "a terrific and murderous fire [that] was poured in upon me from their lines and battery. It was impossible to charge through the dense undergrowth." He also noted the enemy kept "close and quiet" until the line reached within fifty yards. On the other side, James Tuttle was by now counting the attacks and remembered, "Each time [the enemy was] baffled and completely routed." One observant 14th Iowa soldier also discovered what was going on and why he and the others in front of the woods were getting so much attention: "The rebels would not attempt to cross this field but deployed through the timber at the side of it." Still, Shaver could go no farther than Gibson had and retreated, with Major James T. Martin of the 7th Arkansas waiting until the enemy infantry "had delivered a volley and the artillery had fired" to do so. He was thus able to bring "off, though in a scattered condition, my entire command then living." On the field remained Lieutenant Colonel John M. Dean, commanding the 7th Arkansas, who was shot in the neck only a few steps from the Federal line. Colonel William T. Shaw of the 14th Iowa went out to find him and "placed a pocket handkerchief over his face and crossed his hands over his breast and we left him."[26]

Yet another brigade also made an attempt to get at the Hornet's Nest when Patton Anderson's troops, ordered to the right by Ruggles, renewed the assault. Anderson met a similarly wandering Marshall Smith of the Crescent Regiment, with Robert Looney's 38th Tennessee in tow, and they too decided to assault. Soon a large conglomeration of officers gathered to discuss the attack, including Anderson, Ruggles, cavalry commander Franklin Gardner, and even Polk. They worked out a plan by which Smith was to go in on the left along the Corinth Road while Anderson swung his regiments around to the right and attacked in Gibson's and Shaver's footsteps along the Eastern Corinth Road. Anderson faced the "thick underbrush" and also met the survivors of the 13th Louisiana of Gibson's Brigade, who told them they "could not get through the brush." Anderson went in anyway, at about 3:30 P.M., beginning what he described as an "ascent of the opposite slope, when a galling fire from infantry and canister from howitzers swept through my ranks with deadly affect." He continued: "The thicket was so dense that it was impossible for a company officer to be seen at platoon distance." His men fell back, "unable to make another charge by reason of the complete state of exhaustion they were in," Anderson reported.[27]

Marshall Smith was having no better time of it along the Corinth Road to the north. By this time, the 7th and 58th Illinois, as well as the right wing of the 2nd Iowa, had advanced to a position around Duncan's log cabin and a few cotton bales and turned their fronts to the left. The Illinois soldiers were able to hit the attacking Confederates in the exposed flank each time: "The enemy's ranks were visibly thinned by the steady and rapid firing which the men with the utmost coolness poured into them," remembered one Illinois officer in Duncan Field. Smith decided he had to be content with driving the Illinoisans back. The Federals retired to their original positions, but the line was still safe.[28]

At this time, around 3:30 P.M., Braxton Bragg still probably failed to realize that no more assaults would work. Yet he had received word that Johnston was dead. He thus left "a competent staff officer to direct them in my name" and hurried eastward to take charge of the situation there. As a result, he left Anderson's shot-up brigade on the line as well as four of Wood's regiments, although Wood was still recovering from his earlier fall. They would not assault but would try to hold the Federals in place.[29]

The remaining Confederate high command in the center was clearly changing tactics. Around 3:00 P.M., division commander Ruggles began to scour the area for artillery, hoping to blast the enemy out of the determined knot of defense. Others, such as Francis A. Shoup, also helped, and staff officers went far and wide gathering all or portions of eleven batteries—what Ruggles staff officer L. D. Sandidge described as "between fifty and sixty field guns." Ruggles placed them in two major groups on a line west of Duncan Field. A mighty roar emerged when the guns opened up, with many a joyous but ducking Confederate infantryman glad to have some added support. Sandidge summed it up: "No one who observed the effects of that firing could be but agreeably surprised at its result." Captain Smith P. Bankhead similarly wrote, "The effect of this tremendous concentrated fire was very evident." The Federals

responded well, however, with infantry and counterbattery fire; Lieutenant S. H. Dent of Robertson's Alabama Battery wrote home, "This
was the hottest place I ever got into."[30]

A controversy soon erupted over who actually gathered the artillery;
Ruggles eventually won when his name stuck. Regardless, the Confederate artillery had its effect, mainly on the line of Federal guns on the
ridge behind the infantry. The bombardment soon accomplished its task
of driving away Stone's, Welker's, and Richardson's batteries by 4:00
P.M. Grateful Confederate officers noted that it was not so much the
enemy's small arms that had repulsed their attacks on the Hornet's Nest,
but rather the well-served artillery. Gibson described his "regiments re-
coiling not so much from the infantry fire, heavy as that was, but from
the severe fire of a battery on a commanding point." With those guns
now gone, it was more of an even fight. The Union infantry line still
held, however, and some began to think they were doing something historic: "We held our position about six hours," one Federal remembered
in amazement. Another described the bed of the road on which they
aligned as "a carpet of paper from the cartridges we had bitten off."[31]

The position was nevertheless doomed by 4:30 P.M.—not because of
the weakness of the line, although the artillery's withdrawal took a lot of
punch out of the Union position, but mostly because of what was occurring on the rest of the field. Similar to what had happened to Sherman at
Shiloh Branch, this position was compromised not by its own weakness
but by a turning movement from someone else's weakened position. In
this case, unlike Sherman, it came from both sides. One Iowan defending the Hornet's Nest wrote insightfully, "Steadily the noise of battle
swung back on either side of us and still we held our ground."[32]

With Sherman and McClernand falling back behind Tilghman
Branch to the west, the mass of Confederate commands began to turn
eastward and move onto the flank of the Hornet's Nest. A mirror image
occurred on the Union left as Hurlbut's troops fell back about the same
time behind Dill Branch. On the Confederate left, portions of Trabue's,
Stewart's, and Russell's brigades dove in a circle on the Federal right.
On the Confederate right, John D. Martin reported that Breckinridge
ordered Bowen's brigade to "wheel to the left and march upon the enemy," although Colonel Lucius L. Rich, commanding the 1st Missouri,
"was shot off of his horse." Statham's, Jackson's, and Chalmers's troops
turned west as well, but the Federals continued to fight, killing and
wounding numerous flanking Confederates, including Bowen, who was

wounded when he was shot in the neck. Also wounded was Lieutenant Colonel Edward F. McGehee, lately a member of the Mississippi secession convention. Even Gladden's brigade, now under the wounded but still-commanding Zach Deas, moved forward and aided in the encirclement. Bragg ordered the advance, telling the Louisianans, "My old bodyguard I see your ranks are thinner but enough are yet left to carry your flag to victory—*Forward*." They nevertheless encountered stiff resistance. At one point, an Alabamian described how "we had to run for a hundred yards or more under a severe fire." By 5:15 P.M., however, the effects of the Confederate artillery and the converging Confederate wings were beginning to tell.[33]

Historians have often given the impetus for the surrounding maneuver to the understood tactic of moving to the sound of the guns, but Samuel Lockett related that the mastermind was Bragg. In the waning hours of the fighting, Lockett reported that Bragg sent him to the right and cavalry commander Franklin Gardner to the left to institute the move. Lockett remembered Bragg sent them to "inform the brigade and division commanders on either side that a combined movement would be made on the front and flanks of that position."[34]

With their flanks compromised, Prentiss and Wallace decided that they had defended their positions past the "at all hazards" point Grant had asked for. They certainly had—far beyond what Hurlbut, Sherman, and McClernand had done. It was too late, however. Gaps began to form in the line as Prentiss bent his left back to confront the Confederates moving from the east. Officers were also going down, among them Colonel Benjamin Allen of the 16th Wisconsin, Geddes of the 8th Iowa, and Colonel Tindall of the 23rd Missouri. Amid the confusion, Geddes reported shells from the gunboats "in their transit severing the limbs of trees [and] hurled them on my ranks." Even with all the maneuvering and confusion, the left flank remained partially covered, which was better than Sweeny on the right could do. Having sent his reserve regiments to other parts of the field, Sweeny had only the 7th and 58th Illinois with him in north Duncan Field.[35]

Sweeny did not refuse his flank, as Prentiss had done, and he was virtually on his own. One of Wallace's staff officers wrote that Wallace mainly stayed with the left of his division, near Prentiss and Tuttle and in almost constant communication with the latter. Wallace "had great confidence in General Sweeny and his brigade," one staff officer wrote, but naïveté in such a new position could also have led Wallace to depend on Prentiss and give greater than normal freedom to the swaggering Sweeny. Yet in one of the few instances of collaboration, Sweeny now rode over to consult with Wallace. As he did, the 7th Illinois was drawn into the retreat by the earlier withdrawal of McClernand's units, thus opening their flank. Staff officers from Wallace begged McClernand to return and cover the flank, but they could elicit no response. The 7th Illinois thus ran the gauntlet of converging Confederate wings. The 58th Illinois was not so fortunate despite the heroic efforts of its colonel, William F. Lynch. Rising in his stirrups, he commanded the regiment to "cut your way through them, Boys," and upon seeing a white flag emerge, Lynch rode to the carrier and struck the standard with his sword, bringing it down.[36]

Tuttle's Iowans were also thinking of getting out, but time was running out. The right of the brigade, the 2nd and 7th Iowa, made it out under Tuttle's guidance. He reported that they "retired through a severe fire from both flanks and reformed." One of his soldiers detailed the confusion in his diary: "When I began to despair fearing all was lost, the rebels begin to waver, and we rush through, everything in confusion." The 12th and 14th Iowa also formed a line facing the opposite direction from which they had fought all day—northeast—and began to cut their way through. They were subsequently bewildered when the retreating 23rd Missouri, having lost its colonel, ran wildly to the northwest across their front. More troubling were the Confederates right behind them. "It is strange what a fatal effect a cross fire has," concluded in understatement one 14th Iowa soldier trying to get away. Moving toward what Colonel Joseph Woods of the 12th Iowa described as "the high ground between our position and General Hurlbut's headquarters," the Iowans nevertheless opened on the Confederates to the north and drove them back.[37]

The Iowans knew what would happen if they stopped, however, as the Confederates were following up their withdrawal with Anderson's, Wood's, and Shaver's brigades as well as detached units such as the Crescent Regiment. A last-ditch effort was thus made to run the gauntlet. Wallace led the way, continually turning and directing his troops. As he encountered a line of Confederate skirmishers ahead, with more following in the rear, he paused to decide what to do. Rising in his stirrups to get a better view, he was hit in the head and tumbled from his horse.

Staff officer William McMichael later informed Anne Wallace that he "uttered a brief exclamation of pain, and then fell apparently lifeless to the ground." Other staff officers repositioning the division's artillery near the landing knew something was amiss when they saw Wallace's riderless horse: "I saw poor Prince, the General's horse, coming on a lope without a rider," staff officer I. P. Rumsey wrote. He added that it "was the saddest moment in my life." Although they tried to carry Wallace's body to the rear a short distance, the four bearers became so endangered by the following Confederates that they left Wallace along the road and fled to safety. One of Wallace's staff, later captured, returned to Wallace's mangled body and laid him near some ammunition boxes to keep him from being run over. He remained with him until forced to the rear under guard. Apparently Leonidas Polk was nearby and asked someone to find out who the brave officer was who fell in his sight. Papers on Wallace's body identified him. Believing Wallace was dead, the Confederates applied a blanket.[38]

The chances of Wallace getting out even if he had not been hit were by this time small, as the wings of the Confederate army were even then clamping shut. Most of the brigades that had battled Sherman and McClernand all day were sweeping to the right and eventually emerged along the Corinth Road; a few of the extreme left brigades, such as Pond's and Cleburne's, trailed off and fought the new Federal lines being established to the west, but most made the encirclement effective. The same thing occurred to the east, where Chalmers, Jackson, and Bowen were plunging in circular fashion to the left. They too emerged near the Corinth Road, crossing Cloud Field diagonally and running into stiff resistance as numerous Federal regiments tried to run the gauntlet and reach the safety of the landing. Soldiers of Gladden's, Bowen's, Jackson's, and Chalmers's brigades all reported meeting stiff resistance; most had to fall back several yards and rally before forming a junction with those brigades sweeping in from the west. Jackson's Alabamians, for example, crossed a torn-down fence on the edge of Cloud Field and took severe fire in the open area. One soldier yelled at the color-bearer of the 17th Alabama, "They are firing at the flag, lower it, so that it may not be a mark for them." "Never," yelled the bearer, "I'll die before this flag shall be lowered." A watching Alabamian cheered the bravery, but noted, "He held it aloft steadily while it was swept by the leaden shower as though a hurricane passed by." The bearer himself was ultimately shot. The brigade was also running out of ammunition, prompting many to beg their officers, "We are out of cartridges . . . give us ammunition." The units were quickly resupplied and moved forward again, effecting the junction to the rear of the Hornet's Nest.[39]

Thus surrounded, the retreating Federals reacted in various ways. Some gave up; others were filled with rage, including Wallace staff officer Rumsey, who was angry at Tom Sweeny for falling back. Rumsey later proclaimed that Sweeny's conduct "caused the calamity of our division and the loss of our dear general's life." Others just wanted to escape. One Confederate wrote home, "They threw down their guns and scampered off like cowardly dogs." A Union colonel rode up to Jackson's brigade and shouted, "Stop firing, you are killing your friends." Colonel John C. Moore of the 2nd Texas reported his men, "not being deceived," fired at him and killed the officer. Another Federal officer tried to run the gauntlet in a buggy, but when shot, he "sprang to his feet and fell backward." Some of the regiments managed to run the gauntlet in the valley of a small creek later termed Hell's Hollow, but they could not get past the camps of Williams's brigade of Hurlbut's division. The fleeing Iowa regiments were turned back by Jackson's and Chalmers's troops from the far right, with Chalmers galloping forward to catch up with his men, who had moved forward without him. Jackson's regiments marched through a "burning wood" to get there, but they helped close the gap nevertheless. About the same time, Trabue's regiments from the far left closed the gap at the junction of the Hamburg-Savannah and Corinth roads.[40]

The awful truth soon dawned on the trapped Federals. Soldiers of the 18th Missouri asked their colonel what to do. He first advised fighting on, but he soon saw they were surrounded and "said we had better lay down our arms." One Missourian remembered, "The rebels then come out of the brush in great numbers yelling and hooping for Jeff Davis which made our hearts shudder." Confederates soon formed them in a line so they could be counted. Brigade commander Madison Miller similarly decided to give up, with the colonel trying in vain to surrender his sword to first Polk and then Breckinridge, both of whom refused to receive it; he succeeded in giving it to a lower-ranking officer. Colonel William T. Shaw of the 14th Iowa, hit with a branch and temporarily stunned, saw a Confederate battle line immediately in front and admitted, "I think I was for the first time that day a little surprised." An Alabamian calmly stated, "Colonel, I think you will have to surrender, as you are entirely surrounded and the rest of your troops have already surrendered." Shaw responded, "Well, Major, it looks that way." He compared times with the Confederate officer, noting it was 5:45 P.M. Similarly, C. P. Searle of the 8th Iowa was in no good mood as he surrendered. A spent ball had hit him in the arm, and then a lively round hit his canteen. The wet combination caused him to think "it was my life blood," but he was relieved when he found it was only water. Then a Confederate told him, "You d——d Yankee, give me your sword." Searle thought, "Oh how I did want to give it to him point first."[41]

As the Confederate wings clamped shut, some 2,200 Federals eventually surrendered, including Prentiss and brigade commander Madison Miller. The troops closest to the Hornet's Nest and Prentiss generally surrendered first around 5:30 P.M. Prentiss realized that "further resistance must result in the slaughter of every man in the command." One Louisianan standing within fifteen feet of him remembered Prentiss told them they had "whipped the flower of the United States Army" and bellowed, "Cheer boys, cheer as much & as loud as you see fit for you have done well." The Louisianan remembered, "We did not cheer tho out of respect to the fallen chief." Prentiss also admitted, "I can't understand how you have surrounded us in this moment." The 12th and 14th Iowa made it a little farther toward the landing, surrendering on the high ground a few minutes later, with Colonel Shaw of the 14th Iowa and Colonel Isaac V. Pratt of the 18th Missouri surrendering to Chalmers's men. Others captured high-ranking officers as well. Colonel Marshall Smith received the sword of Lieutenant Colonel Quin Morton, now commanding the 23rd Missouri. The prisoners soon stacked their arms, and several Confederates marched them southward about five miles that evening. Prentiss was brought to the north end of Duncan Field, where Ruggles and his staff met him.[42]

Polk and Cheatham quickly sent their cavalry northward to chase those who had escaped. Both generals claimed to have ordered Colonel A. J. Lindsay of the 1st Mississippi Cavalry to gather all the mounted forces in the area and give chase, which was strikingly similar to the Napoleonic use of cavalry as shock troops after the infantry and artillery put the enemy on the run. Perhaps with visions of Murat in his head, Lindsay sent his lieutenant colonel, John H. Miller, ahead with the regiment and began organizing others to add to the chase. The cavalrymen moved down the line of the Shiloh divide and soon spied Ross's 2nd Michigan Battery. The troopers "suddenly came in view of the battery, about 300 yards distant," Miller reported. The Michiganders were trying to retreat down a "deep cut," one Confederate remembered, obviously speaking of the upper end of Dill Branch Ravine, with their guns limbered up and horses hitched but trying to deploy the battery to fight. Miller immediately charged and captured all but one of the fleeing guns and limbers. Colonel Lindsay, having failed to round up any more cavalry, arrived at the end of the capture and noticed another battery nearby, across the ravine. Lindsay took chase and almost captured Mann's Battery as well. Finding "myself in the presence of several brigades of the enemy's infantry drawn up in line," however, Lindsay settled for only one caisson.[43]

The cannoneers became the last of the organized Federals to surrender in the vicinity of Hell's Hollow. The defenders of the Hornet's Nest had done their duty and would eventually be regarded as the heroes of the battle, but at 5:30 or 6:00 P.M. that afternoon on April 6, most probably only thought about the Confederate prison camps that awaited them.

12

"THEY CAN NEVER CARRY THIS LINE IN THE WORLD"

P. G. T. Beauregard had methodically moved forward in the rear of the Confederate army, making his headquarters at various places, first at a position on Plum Orchard Road in Fraley Field and then at the Rhea House nearer to Shiloh Church. In the afternoon, he moved forward again, this time to the Crossroads about 2:30 P.M., where the 38th Tennessee and the Crescent Regiment, recently guarding the Owl Creek Bridge, passed and cheered him. One Louisianan declared Beauregard was "standing amid his staff on a stump"; even that far in the rear, the bullets still fell thick. When Governor Harris and others arrived and told him the bad news of Johnston's death, Beauregard maintained his composure. Later, he confided that he was more worried about taking command: "At the time I was greatly prostrated and suffering from a prolonged sickness with which I had been afflicted since early in February." He admitted that he would rather have avoided the command, but it was his; at the height of the battle on the afternoon of April 6, Beauregard had to continue the fight and could not afford to waste time on sentimental thoughts. He asked Harris about the fighting on the right and continued on, sending the news out to his corps commanders with orders to keep it as best they could from the troops. Harris also kept calm, opting to remain with Beauregard: "I came here as a volunteer aide to General Johnston," Harris told Beauregard. "As he has fallen, I no longer have any duties to perform. I intend to remain until the battle is over, and would like to be useful, if there are duties that you can assign me to."[1]

In as secretive a manner as possible, William Preston and the remainder of the staff took Johnston's body first to Shiloh Church and then to

his April 5 bivouac site, where they left it with Johnston's friend Throckmorton and Captain Wickham. The staff then returned to serve Beauregard that afternoon; they had a wealth of knowledge about the battle,
after all. However, their hearts were still with Johnston, and so was the
entire army's. Word began to spread, reaching the corps commanders
and the rank and file soon thereafter. A tenderhearted Beauregard allowed Johnston's staff to leave the army and carry Johnston's remains
back to Corinth the next morning, leaving around 6:00 A.M. Preston
thankfully wrote that Beauregard had given him *"carte blanche."* On
the way back, the morbid party saw a wounded Thomas Hindman in a
hospital and passed the Hornet's Nest prisoners. Once at Corinth, they
telegraphed the news to Jefferson Davis and Johnston's son, then prepared to take him south for burial.[2]

Despite the loss, Beauregard knew he had to press his command forward, and his officers were already doing so. Hardee and his brigades
as well as Polk's command followed Sherman and McClernand into the
defiles of Tilghman Branch and beyond, not really knowing what they
would find but pressing forward nonetheless. They regularly reported
their progress, with Hardee sending word through Alexander Chisolm,
"We are getting along very well, but they are putting it to us very severely." On the right, Breckinridge was following Hurlbut's withdrawal
toward Dill Branch, taking a position beneath a huge oak tree in which
a Federal shell exploded, raining down debris on general and staff alike.
In the center and then on the right, Bragg was following with the troops
he could gather. The Confederates had to hurry onward, however; the
hours were slipping by, and nightfall was approaching. Storm clouds
began to gather on the far western horizon as well. Beauregard's staff
officer, B. B. Waddell, remembered that "heavy, broken clouds were
passing in the west." Either rain or darkness could prevent a complete
Confederate victory.[3]
    Historiographical storm clouds were even then forming as well.
Much debate occurred, then and later among historians, about the large
surrender and its effects on the remainder of the first day at Shiloh.
Some have argued that the Confederates would have been much better
served to bypass the Hornet's Nest, leaving a holding force to keep it
occupied and to continue onward with the majority of the army. Although this island-hopping strategy, used so famously in the Pacific the-

ater in World War II, would have potentially worked, it was not feasible that day, mainly because it would have required an overall grasp of the battle and an ability to coordinate such a movement. Although Beauregard's good staff work kept him well informed about the developments throughout the day—much better than Johnston farther forward— coordinating the kind of cohesion necessary to hold a force in place while sending the rest of the army forward was beyond the Confederate army's capabilities because of confusion, inexperience, and difficult terrain. Napoleonic strategy called for neutralizing any threat to the rear before moving on, and the emphasis on capturing the enemy—and most notably his standards—was immense. Thus it was neither surprising nor fault-worthy that the Confederates concentrated at the end of the day on the mass of Federals still holding out in the center.[4]

A more heavily debated issue regarding the Hornet's Nest concentrated on its role in the battle. Veterans of the position, particularly the Iowans, forever claimed that they held long enough for Grant to establish a third major line and thus won the battle for the Federals. The Iowans definitely had something to point out—five of the fifteen brigade commanders in Grant's army were from the state. Yet their claim, while heartfelt, was not accurate for several reasons. First, it was not a given that Grant had won, even when he held that third line and nightfall came. Second, Prentiss's claims to the contrary, he and Wallace apparently did not make the decision to specifically sacrifice themselves. Prentiss later wrote an extremely self-centered report in which he argued that he and Wallace "consulted and agreed to hold our positions at all hazards, believing that we could thus save the army from destruction." He added that they had been told the other divisions had fallen back to the river, making the case that they purposefully held when everyone else had retreated and did so knowing they would be sacrificed. Such is post-battle fabrication; no other evidence is needed than the fact that both Prentiss and Wallace were either mortally wounded or captured in the act of falling back. The main factor in determining whether they won the day, however, was the fact that Grant was already building his new line farther back by 2:30 P.M. By 5:00 P.M., when all the other divisions were back in that line as well as the artillery from the center, the new line was already strong and would have held as easily then as it did later, especially had Wallace and Prentiss withdrawn to that line. Grant did not need Wallace and Prentiss to hold on and sacrifice themselves; he had a third major line already formed to save the day.[5]

In addition, veterans of the Hornet's Nest were by no means the only Federals to claim that they had saved the Federal army that day. One Kentuckian in Lauman's brigade wrote in his diary on April 7, "I firmly believe that General Hurlbut's division saved the day on yesterday and gained it today." Hurlbut wrote that his division held "the key point of the left of the army." A 52nd Illinois soldier similarly touted the action on the Union right: "Of the hundred and one things at Pittsburg Landing which went to save the Battle no one of them was so important as this." Moreover, none other than Henry Halleck wrote the secretary of war, Edwin M. Stanton, on April 13, "It is the unanimous opinion here that Brig. Genl W. T. Sherman saved the fortune of the day on the 6th and contributed largely to the glorious victory of the 7th." He asked that Sherman be made a major general. For his part, Sherman later cited a late afternoon event on the right as the one that "saved the day." Additionally, in his usual manner of bravado, McClernand, just days after the battle, wrote Abraham Lincoln: "My division, as usual, has borne or shared in bearing the brunt." McClernand also said in his official report, which Grant passed on with a "faulty" endorsement, that his defense of the last line "probably saved our army, transports, and all, from capture." Then there was Buell; he also claimed to have saved Grant's army. Although all these assertions are debatable, the sum of the whole attests to the fact that there was no common agreement then that the Hornet's Nest had saved the day.[6]

Grant never took the position that the Hornet's Nest saved his army on the first day at Shiloh either. In his articles and memoirs, he did not emphasize Wallace and Prentiss over the others. In fact, Grant seemingly faulted them in the larger context of the battle, writing, "In one of the backward moves, on the 6th, the division commanded by General Prentiss did not fall back with the others." Grant also went on record in the same publications that the harshest fighting at Shiloh took place on McClernand's and Sherman's front. Obviously there was important and heavy fighting at the Hornet's Nest, but in the larger context, it was no more important than events occurring elsewhere, especially on that ever-strengthening last line.[7]

That final Federal defense line was powerful indeed. Grant put his chief of staff, Colonel Joseph D. Webster, an artilleryman by trade, to work forming the line, and Webster naturally used artillery as the centerpiece of the position. Realizing that Pittsburg Landing was the key to receiving Buell's reinforcements, Webster put the majority of his artillery in that area, willing if necessary to allow the right of the line near the Snake Creek Bridge to fall back before the left did near the landing. Obviously this would hamper Lew Wallace's ability to move his troops into line, but Buell far outnumbered Wallace, so the landing was the key point.[8]

Webster first located the siege guns of Madison's Illinois Battery, which were still on a steamboat in the early afternoon, waiting to be used in the advance on Corinth, Mississippi. With a battle raging around him, Webster saw no Corinth siege in sight, and he also saw no need to let the guns sit idle. Whether they would provide that much use tactically against charging assault lines was debatable because they were more useful in long-range bombardment, but they were nevertheless big guns. Their psychological impact would be immense—both to the Federals who took position in their rear and to the Confederates who had to attack them. Thus the big 24-pound siege guns, with affectionate names such as Old Abe, Dick Yates, Sec. Hatch, and Jesse K. DuBois, along with an eight-inch siege howitzer, were hauled to the high ground just inland from the landing and placed in such positions that they could command both the upper reaches of Dill Branch ravine and the level table land—the neck of the hourglass—through which the Corinth and River roads ran. Webster and Grant probably thought that if the Confederates were going to attack, it would be on the even surface rather than through the monstrous valleys of Dill or Tilghman branches. Grant described Dill as a "deep and impassable ravine for artillery or cavalry, and very difficult for infantry."[9]

Webster also placed many other units in this line to support the siege guns. He positioned three other idle artillery batteries that had just arrived at the landing the day before, including the 8th Ohio Light Artillery down the small spur of the ridge from Pittsburg Landing. He likewise sent Edward Bouton's Illinois battery to the right of the line to cover the Tilghman Branch crossings and to guard the Snake Creek Bridge for Lew Wallace. Bouton reported his "horses never had been harnessed," so his men had to drag the guns up the hill from the landing, "our horses not being sufficiently trained to assist us." Similarly, former Swedish officer Axel Silversparre's Illinois unit did not even have horses yet and had never fired their cannons. In the middle of the battle, Webster drilled the Illinois artillerymen and set up a small earthwork of corn sacks to steady their nerves. Probably the 11th Iowa, by Grant's personal order, going into line to their right and the 54th Ohio and 55th Illinois of Stuart's brigade taking position to their left steadied their nerves more than anything else.[10]

By 3:00 P.M., Webster was building an artillery line that was formidable, but it became especially so when the batteries that had been engaged on the battlefield all day began to take position in the line. Receiving shells from the ammunition boat *Rocket,* these batteries added even more firepower to the last line. When the wounded Munch's Minnesota battery arrived from the Hornet's Nest, Webster sent its five guns (with an additional serviceable gun made out of two damaged ones) down the ridge spur to join the Ohioans. Powell's Battery took position to Silversparre's left, nearer the landing and in their camp of the night before. To fill in the line between Silversparre and the siege guns, Webster placed parts of Stone's, Dresser's, and Mann's batteries, all covering slight valleys that led to Dill Branch, which the Confederates could conceivably use as cover to approach the line.[11]

Other batteries went into line west of the siege guns. Richardson's, Schwartz's, and Welker's batteries deployed to cover the Corinth Road. Farther to the right, Hickenlooper's remaining Ohio guns, fresh from the Hornet's Nest, took position in what would become the angle of the last line. In all, Webster collected about fifty guns and placed them in a half-mile expanse inland from the landing, with additional artillery spaced out farther to the west. One Ohioan remembered him riding down the line "hat in hand, his golden hair sprinkled with gray," yelling, "Boys, hold your ground; we have a mile and a half of artillery on the line and Nelson and Buell are on the other side of the River." He further noted, "The cheers that went up from the boys started more than one mule for the river." Another remembered Webster telling them, "Stand firm, boys; they can never carry this line in the world."[12]

Then there were also the biggest guns of all, anchoring the extreme left flank just south of Pittsburg Landing. The USS *Cairo* had departed earlier in the week, but the *Lexington* and *Tyler* were available and took a position off of Dill Branch ravine. Their big naval guns would do wonders in holding the line—as well as scaring the wits out of the enemy.[13]

Artillery did not hold the line by itself, however. By a little after 4:00 P.M., thousands of infantrymen began to flood into line as well, buoyed by the sight of the guns. A despondent Federal in the 7th Iowa rallied when he reached the guns: "When we came to this our last line, and seeing a line of 20 or 25 cannon to support us I had more hope." Hurlbut staff officer Benner remembered, "Behold, here stood two 32 pounders mounted. A new courage was inspired, and our men commenced rallying to support this battery." Grant issued general orders for the division commanders to take charge of any units on their fronts, regardless of the order of battle, and form them for the defense. Thus on the right, Sherman and McClernand contested the Confederate pursuit in several successive lines north of Tilghman Branch. McClernand did more than Sherman, who admitted that he took a position behind a 200-yard-wide field and "contented myself with keeping the enemy's infantry at that distance during the rest of the day." Hurlbut and the wounded Stuart and McArthur fell back from the left and took a position in the line amid the artillery. Stuart's 54th Ohio and 55th Illinois again held the extreme left supporting Powell and Silversparre. Hurlbut tried to animate the men, riding up to the 41st Illinois as they fell back, yelling, "What regiment is that?" The men told him their identity, to which he responded, "I am glad to see that brave regiment is here to cover this retreat." On another occasion on the last line, Hurlbut rode in front of the 28th Illinois and called Colonel Amory K. Johnson to the front. Hurlbut then told the regiment: "I would rather risk my life and honor with the remnant of the 28th than any other Regt on the field." Others began to collect as well, including Wallace's fugitives. Hurlbut remembered that "broken regiments and disordered battalions came into line gradually upon my division."[14]

Most fortuitously, terrain was again on Grant's side as this third phase of battle began. Over and above the defiles of Dill and Tilghman branches, the width of the triangle continually narrowed toward its apex, which meant Grant would have more men per allotted space than when the fighting raged to the south, where the battlefield was much wider. Grant's line kept getting stronger.

The Confederate advance toward this Union last line of defense was not easy. When he arrived on the right, Braxton Bragg found chaos amid the success. "Here I found a strong force," he wrote, "consisting of three parts [Breckinridge, Jones, and Cheatham], without a common head." Thus even before any Confederate units engaged the Federals again, there was a massive attempt to distribute ammunition and get the army reorganized and aligned for the advance, which, according to

Samuel Lockett, took time that was "inestimably valuable." Benjamin Cheatham similarly reported, "A halt was made for the purpose of some concentration of our forces of all commands for a concerted attack upon the enemy." Lockett related that many Confederates fell out of ranks to go see the captured enemy, who were stacking arms. Even getting all the units pointed in the right direction was difficult, as some had finished the capture of the Hornet's Nest actually facing southward. The brigades also had to fan out, redeploying in a much longer line covering the entire expanse from the river to Owl Creek. Bragg and the others thus pushed their men to advance even as they watched the "descending sun warning us to press our advantage and finish the work before night should compel us to desist." Bragg noted that the command was "Forward! Let every order be forward," and Lockett remembered Bragg riding around yelling, "One more charge, my men, and we shall capture them all." All the while, Grant happily watched the sun sink lower and lower in the west.[15]

There were, of course, other units in the Confederate army that were not involved in surrounding the Hornet's Nest or that were diverted while in that process, and they were able to test the last line more quickly than the others. With Sherman and McClernand falling back north of Tilghman Branch, most of the Confederate units turned eastward and helped reduce Wallace's division. A few, however, most notably Pond's and Cleburne's brigades on the extreme left, veered off the turning arc as various Federals caught their attention. Wharton's unattached Texas Rangers actually made the first contact as they followed up the Union retreat near Cavalry Field. Crossing Tilghman Branch, they met the 29th Illinois and 13th Iowa, along with the remaining guns of McAllister's Battery, in a temporary position waiting to fall back to the main line. The Federals made a stand, buoyed by the color-bearer of the 13th Iowa, who was told to "stand there until I fell dead." "That is my intention," he told the officer. Also emerging was the 52nd Illinois, which had been sent over from Sweeny's brigade in the center. "The enemy could be heard in their movements but could not be seen on account of trees and underbrush," remembered Captain Edwin A. Bowen, but as soon as the head of the single-file column emerged, they ambushed the cavalrymen. McClernand also watched: "Waiting till they approached within some 30 paces of our line, I ordered a fire, which was delivered with great coolness and destructive effect. First halting, then wavering, they turned and fled in confusion, leaving behind a number of riders and horses dead on the field." Brewer's Battalion of Mississippi and Alabama cavalry were similarly probing to the west, as was John Hunt Morgan's cavalry, which got into a small fight at Glover Field with the 14th Missouri guarding the Snake Creek Bridge. The Missourians and attached Illinoisans, complete with hunting rifles and squirrel tails attached to their caps, did good service despite their desire to be in the thick of the fight; Henry P. Andrews wrote home, "Our regiment escaped very lucky for we had a Col that was such an infernal coward he would not take us where he thought there was any danger."[16]

Unfortunately for them, the Iowans at Cavalry Field were not allowed to move on. The regiment, apparently turned around, was endeavoring to move to the left; it did so after the small firefight with Wharton. Yet moving left took them directly into the sweeping left wing of the Confederate army, where they encountered a portion of Cleburne's brigade, now up and active after its disastrous morning at Shiloh Church. While portions of the brigade such as the 6th Mississippi fought elsewhere and the 2nd Tennessee apparently did not fight at all because of its heavy casualties, the 23rd Tennessee had by this time rejoined its parent unit, and they, along with Hill's 5th Tennessee and the 24th Tennessee, encountered the Iowans as they moved southeastward. Both were startled, but Cleburne attacked around 4:30 P.M., sending the Iowans on their way.[17]

By far the heaviest fighting on this wing, outside the Hornet's Nest area, occurred as the only major brigade-sized unit not involved in the concentration in the center moved across Tilghman Branch around the same time. Although some of Preston Pond's regiments were elsewhere, with the 38th Tennessee and Crescent Regiment taking part in capturing some of the Federals in the center, Pond led the 16th and 18th Louisiana and the Orleans Guard forward and caught another group of Federals falling back. Preferring to wait until his artillery was up and could support him, Pond "crawled on my hands and knees" to a point where he could see the enemy line with his "glasses," and he "found the Federals there in large force"; he "could easily distinguish a number of flags, and I think more than two Batteries." Peremptory orders from staff officer S. W. Ferguson, "speaking as for General Hardee," told Pond to attack, however. The Louisianan demurred, and Ferguson rode to Hardee, who repeated the order. Pond thus obeyed, but not happily: "Very well Sir," he responded, "I will obey the order but do so under protest." Fortunately for his men, Pond was able to use the ground as cover and actually slipped up on the Federals. Tilghman Branch had a large fork that

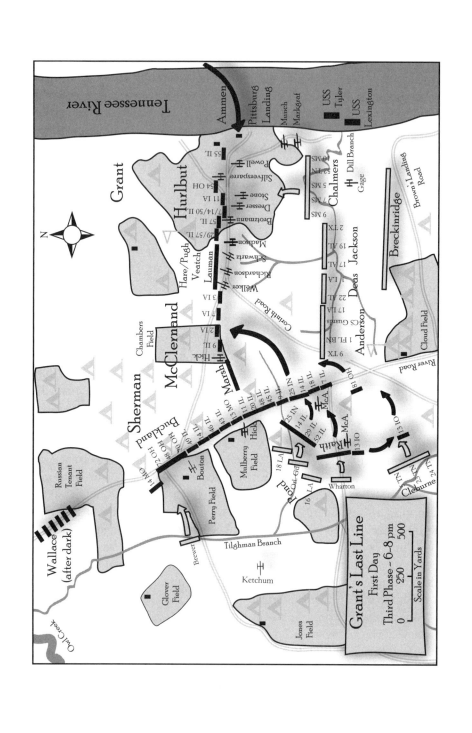

Grant's Last Line
First Day
Third Phase ~ 6–8 pm

Scale in Yards
0   250   500

moved off to the east and ran toward Grant's final line. Pond sent his Louisiana troops up this deep valley, covered as they went, until it was time to climb the steep sides and attack the Federals falling back on the main road across Tilghman Branch.[18]

To Pond's front and right as he poured out of the ravine was a small temporary line consisting of the 14th Illinois and 25th Indiana of Veatch's brigade, the 29th Illinois of Raith's brigade, and the 52nd Illinois of Sweeny's brigade, forming what McClernand called one leg of an "obtuse angle with the center, opposing a double front to the enemy's approach." James Veatch held tactical command of the spur, although several accounts also placed Sweeny on the ground. He apparently received his left arm wound there. Veatch and his staff took refuge in a patch of woods to the rear—something Lieutenant Colonel William Camm and Major John W. Foster, commanding the 14th Illinois and 25th Indiana, respectively, discussed doing as well. Both paced behind their regiments and met up on each flank. "Your men are begging you to take shelter and so are mine," Foster told Camm. "Would there be any impropriety in our doing so?" Camm told him not if they could do it "without losing sight of the ground in our front." Both took to the trees immediately behind their line, with Camm taking a ball in his sword as well as one that hit the tree he had just reached, "throwing bark in my face."[19]

Behind this temporary line, which was endeavoring to get away itself, an even more stable Federal line was forming back at the River Road with a conglomeration of units that mostly had fallen back during the day. The far left of the extension was the 81st Ohio, which had been guarding the Snake Creek bridge all day and had only recently moved to the front upon Grant's personal order. A portion of the regiment crossed a particularly often-swept part of the road; one Ohioan declared that he did so with a "hop, step and jump." He singularly remembered a mule kicking at his dead partner, still in its traces, bullets rattling against the broadside of the wagon to which the mule was unfortunately tethered. Along the road, too, stood the 7th and 18th Illinois supporting the three remaining guns of McAllister's Illinois Battery, with members of the latter regiment helping to work the guns. Farther to the right, around the curve of the crescent-shaped line, stood the 9th Illinois and Carroll Marsh's entire brigade supporting Hickenlooper's three Ohio guns, with Marsh and company forming the other leg of the obtuse angle Pond was unwittingly entering.[20]

Despite his reluctance, Pond's use of terrain was admirable. Yet it did not work out as he had planned. Unfortunately for him and his Louisianans, they came out of the ravine at exactly the wrong spot; their new position was right in the middle of the crescent-shaped formation of Federals. Even worse, Pond sent his regiments over the top en echelon, staggered to the right rear, but eventually all had a taste of the deadly converging fire. The 18th Louisiana took the brunt of the initial fire; the Orleans Guard stood dumfounded as they watched their sister regiment withdrawing "mutilated, cut to pieces, leaving behind it a path of blood." Then it was the guard's turn. It received the same rough treatment. In the attack, four color-bearers went down, with the fifth nervously handling the banner as the regiment swept forward. Major Leon Querouze went down with a wound in the knee, and an attending major who had followed along "as a friend" took command and ordered the retreat. The 16th Louisiana was handled less roughly because of its rearward position, although mysterious fire from friendly troops to Pond's right rear did not help matters. Major Daniel Gober of the 16th Louisiana summed it up well: "The position and strength of . . . [the enemy] were evidently unknown or gravely misapprehended."[21]

Alfred Roman was especially upset. He later wrote, "Up the uncovered hill we rushed, with crossed bayonets, the Confederate yell ringing its well known sound of victory." His thought of victory soon turned sour: "So scorching was the fire from the right, from the center, from the left." The Federals had the high ground and a distinct numerical advantage; the Confederates were attacking piecemeal. It was disastrous, and Roman was still ill about it decades later. He blamed Pond, whom he accused of not being on the line, and other generals, including the division commander, Ruggles, whom he described as almost nonexistent: "Only once did I chance to see our Division Commander, as he passed near us, in the early part of the first day, apparently not knowing where he was, and what troops he had before him."[22]

The Federals continued their withdrawal to a more stable line despite turning Pond back. The wounding of key officers such as Abraham Hare, who was hit in the hand and arm and had to be carried to the rear, took its toll; Hare yielded his brigade to Colonel Marcellus Crocker of the 13th Iowa. Major H. B. Stark of the 52nd Illinois was also slightly wounded, although one of his captains later decried that he could not command the regiment the next day "on account of alleged injuries." There were also so many other Federals stampeding to the rear to try to escape Trabue's and Russell's Confederate brigades to the south that Veatch's more permanent line eventually had to fall back into a more parallel position with McClernand. He reported that the enemy was "driving back the whole left wing of our army and advancing close to our rear, near General Hurlbut's headquarters. A dense mass of baggage wagons and artillery crowded upon our ranks, while we were exposed to a heavy fire of the enemy both in front and rear." William Camm reported he fell back "sidewise, fearing a shot in the back." Marsh's brigade thus bent itself back and became the angle point, the sides of which ran to the landing to the east and Snake Creek bridge to the west. Marsh's new line fronted Tilghman Branch on its western face and the upper reaches of the deep ravine that Pond had used for cover on its southern edge. Thus any Confederate who stepped into the area was daring death.[23]

The major attempt to break Grant's last line came ironically at its strongest point along the river, illustrating the lack of understanding of the terrain on the Confederate side as well as its continuing intent to deal with the Union left. By the time the Confederate commanders sorted out the mess in the center and ushered everyone into the correct positions, the day was fast dwindling and a hasty attack had to be made if anything was to happen at all. Thus only a few Confederate brigades were able to get moving toward the river, and it was mostly those brigades that had been on the Confederate right all day and had wound up on the eastern and northern sides of the encirclement. As they fanned out down the Brown's Landing Road toward the river, Chalmers's Mississippians again became the extreme right, with Jackson next on their left. Two regiments of Gladden's brigade, now under Deas, formed up on Jackson's left, and all of Anderson's brigade except the 20th Louisiana went in next, with both Gladden's and Anderson's troops so far up the ravine that they actually had to cross two major ravines because the creek split into two channels. Trabue's Kentucky brigade and the rest of Breckinridge's corps advanced to the support of Chalmers's Mississippians, taking a position near the Indian mounds on the bank of the river. One Tennessean in Statham's brigade denounced the lack of farther forward movement, however, wondering why "for some unaccountable reason to us, we stood there and watched them rally and re-form their lines." Such was the confusion in the vacuum of the Hornet's Nest.[24]

All these brigades except Breckinridge's crossed the water-filled Dill Branch ravine, which Withers described as "deep and precipitous." After crossing, they quickly saw trouble ahead on the high ground. Anderson's units made it to the north wall of the second ravine but remained only about fifteen minutes before retiring to a safer position. The 22nd Alabama and 1st Louisiana under Deas crossed but hugged the ground as well, not engaging the masses of enemy artillery to their front. "The shell fell all amongst us," noted one of the Alabamians, "and we had to file down under the hollow to avoid the fire." Jackson's Alabamians and Texans were more determined, with their skirmishers engaging the enemy ahead, but the troops were mostly out of ammunition. They had had no time to replenish it in the chaos of capturing the Hornet's Nest. Bragg told them to attack with the bayonet, but they politely declined and remained in their position, sheltered behind the lip of the ravine. Although Colonel John C. Moore of the 2nd Texas reported that the artillery "balls generally passed over our heads and across the ravine," Jackson reported that the men "could not be urged farther without support." Moore added that his men "made a rapid retreat from our unpleasant position and proceeded back to the camp last taken."[25]

That left only one brigade that actually made an attempt to storm Grant's last line. Chalmers's Mississippians were almost dead on their feet; they had been operating for about thirteen hours, much of it in ravines just like this one. They had marched nearly six miles throughout the day and had participated in fighting at Spain Field, Locust Grove Branch, Hurlbut's left, and the Hornet's Nest, and they were now attempting to break the Federals' last line. Other additional factors also worked against Chalmers's troops, including the terrain and the fifty pieces of artillery that could conceivably play on the brigade—not to mention the gunboats *Tyler* and *Lexington* in the river, which took advantage of the curving nature of Dill Branch to fire into Chalmers's flank and rear. Similarly, the two batteries specifically deployed on the spur of the ridge south of Pittsburg Landing, Munch's and Maragraff's, enfiladed the Confederates on their flank. John C. Moore of Jackson's brigade described how the Federals "changed the position of some of their guns, placing them so as to bring on us a raking fire up the ravine from our right." By all accounts it was a hot place for Chalmers and his Mississippians as well as the other brigades forming on the north side of the creek. With so much Federal firepower, Chalmers later wrote that the firing on the evening of April 6 was "the heaviest fire that occurred during the whole engagement."[26]

Yet the biggest problem for the Confederates was the terrain itself. Dill Branch was an enormous declivity, with almost vertical sides reaching up nearly a hundred feet. The bottom itself was boggy and muddy, tangled with vines and briars. The closer to the river it came, near where Chalmers advanced, backwater stood as much as knee deep. Just getting across the ravine was hard enough with the field batteries on the spur and the gunboats shelling the advance. Once across and advancing above the lip of the ravine, the entire Federal line took the Mississippians under fire. Despite other batteries, including Stanford's Mississippi and Ketchum's Alabama units making their way to the river and unlimbering their guns, all Chalmers had to aid him was Gage's Alabama Battery, which had miraculously followed the brigade along its entire trek throughout the day. One of the Alabama artillerymen wrote that "we used our horses completely up the first day, and the men too, as we were fighting amongst the highest kind of hills; it was down one hill and up the other and at the bottom of the hills were the ravines, and they were so boggy that a man could hardly cross them, and in some cases, we had to build bridges so as to enable our battery to cross." Now the exhausted cannoneers were deployed on the southern lip of the ravine, but they quickly garnered the attention of nearly every Union gunner on the field. Chalmers reported that they "suffered so severely that it was soon compelled to retire." The unit lost one gun in the ravine itself, and Chalmers was on his own.[27]

With all the confusion, it is difficult now to determine exactly the extent of the fighting on Chalmers's front as dusk approached. Chalmers described "charge after charge," but it was probably not that dramatic. In fact, the Mississippians hardly made any assault beyond their skirmishers advancing toward the Federal line, which was a den of artillery and small arms fire. Colonel Robert A. Smith of the 10th Mississippi wrote in his unpublished report that after returning fire, "several ineffectual attempts were made to induce a charge but the exhaustion of the troops was so great that . . . our weakened line could not attempt it and a retreat to the ravine back out of range was ordered." Chalmers wrote that his men were "attempting to mount the last ridge" when they were "met by a fire from the whole line of batteries protected by infantry and assisted by shells from the gunboats." Soon Chalmers had the same idea that Deas, Anderson, and Jackson had to his left: there was no body of men on earth that could break that line with all that artillery. Polk remarked, "Here the impression arose that our forces were waging an unequal contest." At that point, they were.[28]

About the same time—around dark—Beauregard sent word by staff officer Numa Augustin from his headquarters two miles back to cease the attack and rest. Beauregard had decided he could mop up the defeated Federals the next day. For all the wrong reasons, Beauregard made the right decision. Admittedly Beauregard was not in a position to make such a decision; a staff officer wrote that he was actually "in conversation with Genl. Prentiss . . . beside the rivulet which flowed at the base of the hill in rear of Shiloh Chapel." However, he did have staff officers who were reporting to him, and the same feeling also evidently pervaded much of the army. In actuality, the on-the-ground brigade commanders were already falling back on their own. As John K. Jackson wrote, "Finding an advance without support impracticable, remaining there under fire useless, and believing any forward movement should be made simultaneously along our whole line, I proceeded to obtain orders from General Withers." Similarly, Chalmers later declared that he never received Beauregard's order to fall back but eventually did so on his own.[29]

The contemporary evidence shows that few officers disputed Beauregard's order at the time. Most thought it was too late in the day and took the idea of a Confederate writing home the next day: "Had Beauregard possessed the power of Joshua to command the sun to stand still in the heavens for the space of an hour our victory would have been as complete as that of the great Hebrew warrior." Beauregard's staff officers declared that Bragg and the rest of the commanders were elated at the victory, with Bragg telling the general, "We have carried everything before us to the Tennessee River. I have ridden from Owl to Lick Creek, and there is none of the enemy to be seen." More believably, David Urquhart of Bragg's staff later admitted that nothing could have been done: "At the time the order was given, the plain truth must be told, that our troops at the front were a thin line of exhausted men, who were making no further headway, and were glad to receive orders to fall back." He added that Beauregard's recall was "most timely." Most telling is the account of Dr. J. C. Nott, Bragg's medical inspector and staff officer. He wrote that he spent almost the entire day with Bragg, including the fighting at Dill Branch, and testified that he thought the withdrawal order actually came from Bragg. He went so far as to write,

"My impression was (this was also the conclusion of General Bragg), that our troops had done all that they would do and had better be withdrawn." He also related, "If he [Bragg] had received and disproved such an order, it is probable that something would have been said about it." Clifton Smith of Beauregard's staff related that once he delivered similar orders to Bragg and Ruggles, who was with the corps commander, Bragg sent the order on to Withers and rode back to Beauregard's headquarters with no apparent ill will. It is also highly significant that Bragg laid no blame on Beauregard for stopping the advance in his April 9 letter to his wife. Rather, he told her the troops were "disorganized, demoralized, and exhausted," and he went on to describe the lack of food and ammunition.[30]

However, many Confederates later blamed Beauregard for calling off the attack right at the moment of Johnston's victory. For his part, Bragg later decided the idea was not so good and related, perhaps relying on hindsight, that he asked the staff officer who gave him the order if he had given out the order to the brigades. When an affirmative answer came back, Bragg related that he said, "If you had not I would not obey it. *The battle is lost.*" He also claimed he questioned whether the victory was actually "sufficiently complete," as Beauregard stated in the order, asking, "Was a victory ever sufficiently complete?" At least one Confederate claimed Bragg was so indignant at the order that he broke his sword over his leg. Some, including Albert Sidney Johnston's son, went so far as to blame Beauregard for throwing away Johnston's victory, arguing that there was up until Johnston's death "the predominance of intelligent design; a master mind, keeping in clear view its purpose." Indeed, some historians have argued that if Johnston had lived, he could possibly have inspired the men to do almost superhuman things, much like he did at the Peach Orchard. In reality, given the nature of the ground, the strength of the Federal line, the status of the troops, and the disorganization in the Confederate army, it mattered little who was then in command of the Confederate army: Beauregard, Johnston, or even Napoleon. Still, a few of Polk's cavalrymen actually made it to the river and watered their horses. Johnston's prophecy had at least partially come true.[31]

One additional factor played into the defense of the Union's last line as well, although it had little bearing on actual tactical action. By 6:30 P.M., Nelson had arrived at last, sending a party of signal corps officers across first to get orders from Buell while he waited on the east bank. A few companies under Jacob Ammen cut the opposite bank down to get to the steamers and were then ferried over into Grant's already almost impregnable line. The first troops had been surprised at the sight across the river, with one wondering to himself why they were needed when Grant had several brigades in reserve. Only in crossing the river did he understand these were not brigades but rabble. Moreover, the gunboats opened up, and he thought "it must be close work if they were employed." Evidently some Confederate artillery began firing from the riverbank upstream as the troops began crossing. Several eyewitnesses, including Anne Wallace on her steamboat, described "the shells [that] bursted all around the boat as we crossed." Wisely, the ammunition boat *Rocket* was quickly sent out of range. Nearing the west bank, Nelson marveled at the mass of skulkers on the banks, haranguing them: "Get out of the way, you d——d cowards! . . . If you won't fight yourselves, let these men off that will." Buell quickly met Nelson and Ammen and rushed them into line. "Don't stop to form, colonel, don't stop to form," urged a staff officer to Jacob Ammen.[32]

Although Buell and his soldiers would later claim that they saved Grant's army that day, they actually only sent in parts of three regiments before the fighting ended at dark. Jacob Ammen's brigade had led Nelson's division through the swamps east of the river, and although all three regiments crossed, the 24th Ohio moved a half mile inland, leaving only twelve companies of the 6th Ohio and 36th Indiana to engage on Grant's last line. But they were there, supporting Stone's Battery, likely supplying more of a morale boost to Grant's troops than any actual tactical advantage. Still, Colonel William Grose of the 36th Indiana gave his men a speech: "Keep cool, not get excited or disgrace ourselves, but to remember our flag and country."[33]

One Federal described the effect on Grant's army as "dark objects were seen" across the river, and all wondered what it was. Soon the word spread: "It is the advance guard of Buell." Many in Grant's army unashamedly admitted their dependence on the reinforcements. One Iowan wrote in his diary that after asking what unit the arriving troops were and being told Nelson's, "We are no longer in doubt now Buel is here, and we may yet win the battle if not the day." A chaplain in the 12th Michigan wrote his local newspaper nine days after the battle, "There can be no doubt the Confederate army completely whipped us the first day of the fight and had it not been for the arrival of Gen.

Buell, all would have been lost." A 41st Illinois soldier wrote three days after the battle, "But for Buell's forces I believe we would all have been whipped and killed, or taken prisoners." A member of the 3rd Iowa similarly admitted, "To General Buell's timely arrival Sunday night we are indebted for our salvation." On and on the declarations went, but perhaps a surgeon in the 72nd Ohio summed it up best: "God Bless Gen. Buel for saving us."[34]

Nelson's arrival lifted Grant's spirits too, as, fortunately for him, the day ended. "The sun looked like a ball of fire as it went out of sight," rejoiced one of his officers. Yet Grant had played his hand perfectly. A Cincinnati *Gazette* reporter remarked how "for the first time since sunrise you fail to catch the angry rattle of musketry or the heavy booming of the field guns." Another reported the firing ended "almost instantly," at which time "a very oppressive silence" loomed and only ended when a band struck up "Hail Columbia."[35]

With the lull, Grant knew he had survived. Still, the critical question was what to do next.

13

"LICK 'EM TO-MORROW, THOUGH"

Ulysses S. Grant was at a crossroads—concerning the battle of Shiloh, but in the larger context as well. He had just endured the bloodiest day's fighting in American history. Three days later, he was still marveling at "the most continuous firing of musketry and artillery ever heard on this continent." He wanted all that fighting and bloodshed to mean something positive, and he knew that the decisions he made as night fell would go on to affect not only the battle but also the campaign, the conquest of the Mississippi Valley, and likely the war itself. Who knew how else these decisions would affect the future?[1]

Grant was fortunate in having several factors available to him in making those decisions. His army had indeed survived the day, surprised even if he would not admit it, and was now encased behind a strong defensive line that would certainly hold during the night, giving him time to think. Grant was also receiving reinforcements by the thousands even as he hunkered down in his last line and the sun set behind the dense trees on the western horizon. Reinforcements were almost never a bad thing, and they certainly eased Grant's thoughts this night.[2]

The most important factor for the Union that night, however, was Ulysses S. Grant. He would make a reputation in the present war of never giving up or in. Much of that reputation was built at Shiloh.

Reinforcements began to file into Grant's line—from two directions, no less—making his decisions easier. Yet as close as Buell and Lew Wallace had been at dawn that morning, neither had made it to the battlefield that first day in time to make any appreciable difference in the

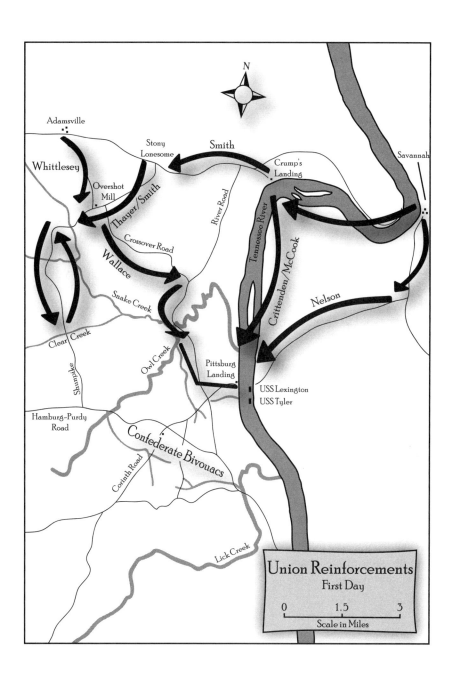

N

Adamsville

Whittlesey

Stony
Lonesome

Smith

Crump's
Landing

Savannah

Overshot
Mill

Thayer/Smith

River Road

Crossover Road

Wallace

Tennessee River

Crittenden/McCook

Snake Creek

Nelson

Clear Creek

Turnpike

Owl Creek

Pittsburg
Landing

USS Lexington
USS Tyler

Hamburg–Purdy
Road

Corinth Road

Confederate Bivouacs

Lick Creek

Union Reinforcements
First Day

0   1.5   3

Scale in Miles

fighting. Most of Buell's army did not arrive until during the night and the next day. Similarly, Wallace's arrival should have been fairly simple, but it turned out to be anything but. As a result, Grant had had to fight the first day basically on his own—but he had survived.

Grant's staff, effectively a public relations machine, would eventually label Wallace lost on April 6 and timid and frightened on April 7. In reality, Wallace was anything but lost or timid. After concentrating his brigades at Stoney Lonesome, Wallace awaited official orders from Grant, but the hours passed: "Ten o'clock, and still the air laden with noises of the struggle going on . . . 10:30—Yet no order." At 11:30 A.M., Baxter finally arrived, but their conversation "did not exceed three minutes," according to the quartermaster. What was said and what the orders stated cuts to the heart of the controversy, but all this information was lost. Wallace remembered that his orders told him to move to the right of the army, which he interpreted as Sherman's division, so the Shunpike was the route he chose. Grant, on the other hand, claimed that the order said to move along the River Road to Pittsburg Landing. Grant never saw the order, however, and later admitted that he was "not competent to say just what order the general actually received." The original order had been through Grant to Rawlins to Baxter to Wallace; it could have said anything. It is certain, though, that Wallace allowed his men thirty minutes to eat lunch and then acted according to the plan worked out before the battle, in which he viewed the Shunpike as "the nearest and most practicable road to the scene of battle."[3]

Wallace began marching at noon, joined at Overshot Mill by Whittlesey's brigade from Adamsville, which had to corral its transportation, received three days earlier, including "about forty wild mules, many of which had never been under harness." Two regiments and one piece of artillery, as well as the division's baggage, were left to guard the western approach, the 68th Ohio of Thayer's brigade at Stony Lonesome and the 56th Ohio of Whittlesey's unit apparently at or near Adamsville for a time before moving to Crump's Landing. Many of the troops left behind were not happy: "Our being left to guard this point caused dissatisfaction among many of the officers and men, and some attempted to go to the battlefield on their own motion," one Ohioan remembered. Yet not all were disappointed. Another Ohioan wrote home, "Some of our boys are dissatisfied because we were not allowed to be in the fight and share the glory if any but I am very well contented without any such glory."[4]

Along the march, Wallace received several couriers from Grant, including cavalrymen sent to hurry him up. The entire situation changed, however, when Grant's aide-de-camp, Captain W. R. Rowley, arrived as the division awaited a crossing of Clear Creek. Rowley, arriving at the head of the column, asked where Wallace was going. The general replied that he was heading for the right of the army. Wallace remembered Rowley "turned quite pale" and, touching him on the arm, whispered, "Ride to one side with me." There he explained: "Don't you know Sherman has been driven back. Why, the whole army is within half a mile of the river, and it's a question if we are not all going to be driven into it."[5]

Wallace admitted "myself more than shocked by this intelligence, heightened in effect, as it was, by Captain Rowley's energetic style of expression." He also admitted being temporarily "struck . . . dumb—too dumb for question." He soon recovered, however, and decided on the only conceivable choice left him: to go back and find a crossing to the River Road. In a decision that has been roundly criticized, Wallace then countermarched his division, with his first (and favorite—his old unit) brigade marching the entire length of the division so it would again be first in line. Guided by a local citizen named Dick Pickens, Wallace used a narrow crossover road and eventually entered the River Road, continually spurred on by additional staff officers sent by Grant: James B. McPherson and John Rawlins. Wallace found McPherson "sensible" but got into a shouting match with Rawlins, who demanded he toss the guns to the side and march on. "Damn the guns," Rawlins shouted, but Wallace shot back, "My order was bring the whole division and I would do it." At the Snake Creek crossing, local citizens told them the enemy held the bridge, and tension mounted as the troops guessed they would have to fight their way through. Charles Kroff wrote in his diary that his regiment formed a V, and Colonel George McGinnis told them, "Boys remember you are from Indiana." They met the pickets of the 14th Missouri and detachments of the 2nd and 4th US Cavalry regiments, however, and a relieved Alvin Hovey reported, "We were received with cheers instead of bullets."[6]

Ever since, Grant and countless historians have faulted Wallace. Even some of his own men did likewise: William F. Rhoads of the 11th Indiana summed it up when he wrote his sister nine days later, "We started about noon and took to wrong road and got in behind the secesh and had to go back and take another road." Wallace of course defended himself, writing, "I made an honest effort to get to the field the first day." Even though he had not arrived as planned, his mere presence in the area still gave Grant the psychological aid of telling his men help was on the way, and Grant believed it himself. At one point in the day, upon spying a column marching from the west, Grant exclaimed to a staff officer, "Now we are all right, all right—there's Wallace." It proved not to be, but they were there now. One Indianan wrote home that they played the part of Blucher to Wellington on this day. One wonders whether Grant saw it that way, and Wallace would spend the rest of his life trying to explain his actions and gain Grant's approval. Some have even speculated that Wallace's famous *Ben-Hur* was inspired by the real-life drama of Shiloh. At least for now, though, Grant was no doubt grateful, if a little agitated.[7]

Ironically, Buell and Nelson received no such criticism for making no better time, and Buell is remembered in history as playing more the role of Blucher than Wallace. In actuality, Nelson's troops left Savannah later than Wallace left Stoney Lonesome. Still, by late evening, Nelson's regiments had endured the route: "The doctor had not exaggerated the difficulty of the path; if horse or man got off the path he would sink in the mud of the swamp. We had five miles of this infernal path." Although Buell had clearly not saved Grant's army (Colonel William Grose reported losing only two men killed and one wounded that evening), the biggest boost to Grant's troops was the morale effect as word spread that Buell had arrived and that several more divisions were on the way.[8]

The night of April 6 and 7 was thus a critical time. Grant had work to do, not the least of which was positioning all these new reinforcements, which eventually totaled upward of 24,000 fresh troops. Because Wallace appeared on the right flank, he took over that sector, allowing Sherman and McClernand to squeeze in toward the landing, making that entire portion of the line stronger. Wallace placed his brigades on line in the order they marched in, with Smith's troops forming up in Perry Field alongside Sherman's, Thayer's men to their right, and Whittlesey's regiments farther to the right at the Russian Tenant Field. One company of the 20th Ohio took station in a log cabin. Wallace's artillery studded the line, including Thompson's Indiana Battery in Perry Field and Thurber's Missouri guns on Whittlesey's front. It took a while, but Wallace had his troops completely deployed by 1:00 A.M.[9]

The major infusion came from Buell's troops. Nelson continued to feed his brigades into line, with the 24th Ohio joining the others of Ammen's brigade already engaged as the new extreme left flank of the army. Nelson's deployment was not easy, mainly because of the horde of stragglers at the landing by nightfall. Estimating them as 7,000 to 10,000 in number, Nelson later recalled how they met his troops with cries of "We are whipped; cut to pieces." Nelson added, "They were insensible to shame or sarcasm—for I tried both on them—and, indignant at such poltroonery, I asked permission to open fire upon the knaves." Despite the chaos, Nelson had his entire division over the river by 9:00 P.M. that night. Sanders Bruce's all-Kentucky brigade went into position on Ammen's right with William Hazen's Indiana, Kentucky, and Ohio regiments on their right. The division unfortunately had some conflict, mainly between Bruce and Nelson. Staff officer Horace Fisher later wrote that Bruce was "repeatedly in arrest and the brigade was practically in command of Colonel [Thomas D.] Sedgewick." The division had also left its artillery at Savannah, but they nevertheless moved through Hurlbut's exhausted troops and claimed the front line, sending out skirmishers and patrols to keep from being surprised—again.[10]

More infantry made up for the lack of artillery. At Savannah, Buell's assistant quartermaster, Captain A. C. Gillem, organized the waterborne effort to get the other divisions to the battlefield. The lead elements of Thomas L. Crittenden's division thus arrived at Pittsburg around 9:00 P.M. that night, with the rest filtering in after midnight in a massive rainstorm. They unloaded quickly to allow the boats to return and ferry McCook down. What Crittenden found at the landing was appalling; he estimated 6,000 to 10,000 "demoralized soldiery." "I was so disgusted, that I asked General Buell to permit me to land a regiment and drive them away. I did not wish my troops to come in contact with them." Crittenden's division landed nevertheless, "forcing our way through this mob," Crittenden wrote. They bivouacked in column in the rear of Nelson's division with only two brigades of Kentucky and Ohio troops, William Sooy Smith's and Jeremiah Boyle's. One Ohioan of Boyle's brigade wrote how "it was dark and it rained and the only relief we had was to pull off our knapsacks and sit on them for a change. I remember that the rain ran down the back of my neck into my shoes." Unlike Nelson, Crittenden was able to bring his artillery along—Bartlett's Ohio battery and Mendenhall's US regular artillery. Others went along as well, including medical personnel with only "their instruments and

hospital knapsacks and such dressings and stimulants as could be carried on horseback." Also arriving was one of Gresham's regiments, David Wood's 14th Wisconsin.[11]

All the while, McCook's division was still on the way. It was twelve
miles out of Savannah on the morning of April 6 when McCook heard
from Buell to hurry forward. One Federal in the 34th Illinois remembered, "We got orders to trough down everything that we could possibly do without and start for Savana. We could hear the cannons all
day long." McCook's leading brigade commander, Lovell Rousseau,
reported that he had to "take the fields and woods adjacent to the high-
way, from the narrowness of the latter and its being filled with wagon
trains and artillery." One Federal declared the march was "very trying
on the muscles." Once in town, McCook's men marveled at the amount
of wounded already being brought to Savannah, with one Federal describing how the wounded were "occupying nearly every store room,
and dwelling house." Conversely, McCook found nothing "whatever to
convey my division to this battle-field." He soon had his staff "compel-
ling the captains to get out of their beds and prepare their boats for my
use." As a result, the leading elements of the division, Lovell Rousseau's
command, did not arrive at Pittsburg until around 5:00 A.M., and Kirk's
and Gibson's brigades were still on their way as dawn approached. Fortunately, McCook also brought a US regular battery under William R.
Terrill. Still approaching Savannah were Thomas J. Wood's and George
H. Thomas's divisions, with one Indianan writing, "We marched like
thunder we had to wade creeks and branches we were doing our best to
get to the fight we were all anxious to get there."[12]

Elements of three of Buell's divisions were thus at Pittsburg by dawn,
and the placement of so many of the Army of the Ohio brigades on
the left allowed Grant to squeeze his army's line even more—much as
he had done on the right at Wallace's arrival. It was fortunate because
the Army of the Tennessee was in shambles, particularly Prentiss's and
W. H. L. Wallace's divisions. Others were gun-shy, with George Nispel
writing that his cannoneers built a small parapet of dirt in front of their
guns during the night, "thinking the enemy during the darkness of the
night might make an attempt to charge and capture our guns."[13]

The night was thus long and miserable for all involved. The Army of
the Tennessee had lost the majority of four out of five division camps.
Lew Wallace's troops had none of their tents or equipment, and Buell's
forces likewise had left theirs at Savannah. Upon informing Colonel

John A. Davis of the 46th Illinois that his men had no food, a captain was told to tell his men to "sit down and suck your thumbs." One fortunate Illinoisan in Hurlbut's division noted, "We were furnished with some crackers and raw meat which was eaten without cooking, as we dare not make a fire." Sleep was also hard to come by, with Lieutenant Colonel William Camm of the 14th Illinois lying down to keep warm with the wounded Colonel Veatch, who "moaned and moved so that I could not rest." The rainstorm that developed and rolled through the area on the night of April 6 only made it worse. Carroll Marsh related that his men "gladly seized this opportunity for a little rest, but a drenching rain soon setting in prevented much sleep." Adding to the misery were the gunboats in the river, which, under application from the former naval officer Nelson, who thought it was a bright idea at the time, fired salvos throughout the night at ten- or fifteen-minute intervals, intending to harass and keep awake the Confederates but having the same effect on their own troops. Numerous other maladies also affected individual soldiers that night, with one exhausted artilleryman who had worked his rammer all day describing "the regular old school-boy leg ache, such as I used to lay awake nights and yell with when I was a little shaver, after a hard day's play." Yet the men made the best of their situation, with some even taking the time to sing hymns. Illinoisan George Smith remembered one soldier struck up "Jesus Lover of My Soul," and others joined in until four verses had been sung in the darkness of night.[14]

Ulysses S. Grant could personally attest to the misery that night. Between his throbbing ankle and the pounding his army had taken during the day, he was in little mood for misery. But misery was his lot. He had seen horrors that day that made him almost sick, vastly overshadowing what he had seen in Mexico or earlier in this war. Not the least sickening sight was the decapitation of one of his scouts, Captain Irving Carson, by a Confederate cannonball right next to him. One watching Indianan described how "a six pound ball struck an oak tree close by and glancing took off the head of General Grant's adecamp Capt. Carson. And passing through our comp. ranks took off the legs of poor George White." Despite being covered with blood and brains, Grant, with Buell tagging along, still managed to travel his line in the evening. He also encouraged the troops, telling them, "Boys, remember the watchword is Donaldson."[15]

Other less-than-enjoyable experiences had also occurred during the day as Grant "continuously rode along the line of battle, through the hottest of their fire, for the whole distance of about five miles," wrote one of his escorts five days later. Grant was nearly wounded in an event that he later said occurred on the second day, but which most historians believe actually occurred on the first. A canister shot hit his sword scabbard and bent it. Who knows what it would have done to his leg if it had been an inch or two in either direction? In addition, one of his own officers upbraided Grant. While awaiting Nelson's troops, Grant unwittingly wandered into the line of sight of several signal officers, hard at work communicating across the river. Lieutenant Joseph Hinson, who was already angered at trying to keep Grant's men out of the way, barked at Grant, "Git out of the way there! Ain't you got no sense?" A calm Grant simply apologized and rode away. The signal detachment was repaid during the night, however. One officer, unaccustomed to the name or seeing the crossed flags insignia, took them as Confederate spies and had them put under guard.[16]

Yet Grant and his troops had survived and were getting stronger, despite the carnage all around them in the hospital tents and steamboats in the river. One boat nearly swamped, and a surgeon feared it might sink; the captain backed into the river so no more could come aboard. At another location, so many men gathered around a huge bonfire that one soldier remembered "a solid wall of men not less than thirty feet thick." Amid the chaos, as he suddenly had some calm moments to sit and think, Grant began to look for a place to make his headquarters. He first gathered himself beneath a large oak tree just atop the high ground at the landing. With the rain coming in, he decided after midnight to walk over to the small cabin that he had used earlier. By this time, any structure whatsoever was being used as a hospital for the wounded, and a weak-stomached Grant could take no more than a few seconds amid the terror and screams of the wounded in the cabin. Despite his swollen and aching ankle and the torrents of precipitation, he decided to return to what he called his "tree in the rain." It was there that Grant, collar pulled up and hat close down on his face, made some of the most significant decisions of the war.[17]

Grant stuck to the big decisions, not having directed the battle in much of any way besides encouraging the troops with visits. He had continually moved reinforcements to the front and directed the beginning of a final line, but that was about it. Hurlbut even wrote, "It was rather a series of independent conflicts, on our side, controlled, as best they might be, by the division or detachment upon which the attack fell, but with no unity of movement nor possibility of combined action, extending over the whole, or any considerable part of the field." Buell also found fault for "the want of cohesion and concert in the Union ranks" and "the absence of a common head." "It was little more than a fearful *melee* at best," recalled one veteran, but it worked. Colonel William T. Shaw of the 14th Iowa later explained the phenomenon: "They outgeneraled us, but we outcolonelled them." Still, that lower-level grit put Grant in a position to come out on top. Grant's army was not that bad off for the wear, and although he had won nothing yet, as is often portrayed when historians write about Shiloh, Grant had nevertheless put himself in a position to win. Trading space for time had worked to perfection. He explained his thinking to Sherman by using his victory at Fort Donelson as an illustration. Grant told Sherman around 4:00 P.M., the latter remembered, "that at a certain period of the [earlier] battle he saw that either side was ready to give way if the other showed a bold front, and he was determined to do that very thing." Moreover, with Wallace's arrival, his losses were basically replaced even without Buell, with Grant later claiming, perhaps incorrectly, that "victory was assured when Wallace arrived."[18]

It all could be thrown away, however, and fairly easily. History is replete with examples of military commanders who retreated when they did not have to after a disastrous but not fatal day of fighting. As with George McClellan on the Virginia Peninsula or Joseph Hooker at Chancellorsville, both of whom still possessed a vast advantage in terms of numbers of troops, a lesser commander than Grant could have retreated during the night. Doing so would have no doubt given the Confederates a major victory on the scale of a Chancellorsville, blunting the enthusiasm for the continual Union advance toward Corinth and buying time for Van Dorn and new levies to arrive. Moreover, before the idea of a possible withdrawal is dismissed as what-if history, it must be noted that the idea was actually on many minds that night. John Rawlins later stated that Buell came to Grant while he was at the landing in between his rides out on the battlefield and asked what preparations he had made for withdrawing. Grant replied, "I have not yet despaired of whipping them, general." Although Buell later denied such an event, the mentality fits each of the actors. More believable were the accounts of Grant's own officers. McPherson asked Grant, "Shall I make preparations for a retreat?" Grant responded, "Retreat? No! I propose to attack at daylight, and whip them." In particular, William T. Sherman was man enough to admit he was thinking in terms of retreat. He came to Grant under his tree in the rain with the idea of broaching the subject, thinking "the only thing just then possible, as it seemed to me, was to put the river between us and the enemy and recuperate." At the last minute he became embarrassed and blurted out, "Well, Grant, we've had the devil's own day, haven't we?" A determined Grant, his mind already made up, responded, "Yes, lick 'em to-morrow, though."[19]

Ironically, the decision to stay created another choice for Grant: what to do next? With retreat out of the question, the choices left to him were to hold his line on the defensive or attack. Once again, a lesser commander than Grant may have held his line and let the Confederates waste themselves away in futile attacks, never going on the offensive to win a major victory. Although this strategy would have garnered a technical victory, it would not have produced the clear victory that Shiloh became. There are many historic examples of this strategy—generals such as William Rosecrans and Buell at battles such as Corinth, Stones River, and Perryville. Although all are considered Union victories, they are not in the realm of a clear-cut win such as Shiloh, and in fact are sometimes referred to as draws, especially on the tactical side. In each case, the defending general, having been driven back, was content with holding a defensive line and not counterattacking. History records those battles as lesser-scale wins.[20]

Grant was not of the defensive mind-set, of course, especially with so many reinforcements available to him. Thus he made the decision to counterattack in the midst of having been beaten back all day long— certainly a courageous decision. Just three days later, he wrote of his "feeling that a great moral advantage would be gained by becoming the attacking party." Sherman elaborated on the decision less than three years later, writing, "We agreed that the enemy had expended the furor of his attack, and we estimated our loss and approximated our then strength, including Lew Wallace's fresh division, expected each minute." He also noted that Grant thought that with Lew Wallace's division and those of his own five divisions who had "recovered their equilibrium," he would "be justified in dropping the defensive and assuming the offensive in the morning." The idea was probably premature because Buell was evidently needed to go on the offensive. One maritime officer noted as much in wondering whether Buell would arrive in time: "We will not make as good use of our victory as we could if he was here." Grant nevertheless made his decision. Sherman remembered, "He then ordered me to get all things ready at daylight the next day to assume the offensive." Similar orders also went out to the other division commanders and also to Buell's generals.[21]

There would thus be a second day at Shiloh, with the Union on the offensive "as soon as the day dawned," Grant planned. To make sure the troops were ready, he had ammunition wagons moving throughout the night. One Federal wrote that "6 of our teams were ordered to haul ammunition all night to the battle field for Buell," whose army had no transportation. Many of Grant's soldiers had a hunch that this would happen; one of Lew Wallace's newly infused troops wrote, "No one talked of tomorrow. We knew we had to fight a victorious enemy who was expecting an easy ending to the battle, nothing less than an unconditional surrender, but we knew in our hearts that we were going to lick them." And this second day's fighting—never before examined in detail or regarded as very important among historians—would be a major factor in the battle. If the first day put Grant in a position to win the battle, the second day's fighting would determine the extent of that victory.[22]

There was one additional factor in the equation leading up to the second day's fighting. This was the remarkable lack of preparation in the Confederate army during the night, especially compared to what was occurring behind the Union lines. One Tennessean summed it up well when he wrote, "While we were quiet the enemy was busy." Bragg disgustedly wrote his wife of the lack of preparation, telling her, "Tho millions of cartridges were around them, not one officer in ten supplied his men, relying on the enemy's retreat." In an almost complete reversal of what was occurring with Grant, Beauregard posted his headquarters at Shiloh Church, where almost all his commanders came and congratulated him. Despite the arrival and congratulations from his senior commanders, Beauregard took little if any action to reorganize or prepare his army, only ordering his commanders to fall back and bivouac as far as necessary to get out of reach of the Federals, particularly the gunboats. He did think to send word to Corinth for the commanding officer to form any stragglers into companies and regiments and forward them to the battlefield. He even ordered cavalry to the front to prevent surprise by the enemy. These meager preparations were about it, however.[23]

In addition to illness and exhaustion, much of Beauregard's lack of preparation was the result of overconfidence, which was fueled by a dispatch received during the day indicating that Buell was in north Alabama or was being delayed. The overconfidence trickled down to the rank and file as well, most of whom looked to their own comfort during the night. Many individual Confederates nevertheless took the opportunity to exchange their guns or equipment for better versions found in the camps and on the battlefield. Isadore Girardey, commanding the battery attached to Jackson's brigade, replaced a broken-down limber in his battery and restocked his ammunition from the Federal camps. "The Yankee ammunition is in capital order," he wrote, "especially the friction tubes, which are superior to ours." The troops particularly welcomed the food they found in the Federal camps. Otho F. Strahl reported that his men spent the night in a Union camp "and took supper and breakfast at their expense." Many Confederates related the fine assortment of food they found, including ham, eggs, butter, and coffee. In addition to food, they found love letters, photographs, and other trinkets. George Dawson of the 1st Missouri wrote that he found "everything a soldier could want to which we helped ourselves. We ate their grub, and slept in their cots as quietly as if we had no enemy in 100 miles."[24]

Contrary to Dawson's account, most Confederates did not sleep well. Augustus Mecklin of the 15th Mississippi wrote, "I attempted it myself but the balls would whistle & the musketry would roar around my ears." One Tennessean remembered, "Many of us could not sleep that night for talking over the happenings and incidents of the day, a goodly number of our friends had been killed or wounded and we were busy till a late hour loading up and hunting for our missing comrades and friends who had fallen. Many sad rehearsals of where this and that one had fallen." The gunboats kept almost everyone awake as well, with Colonel Frank Schaller of the 22nd Mississippi reporting that he had to move camps a couple of times because of the fire. The rain did not help; nor did the sights of the mangled bodies on the battlefield. Mississippian Alfred Smith wrote, "When any of us walked about we had to have a light to keep from falling over the dead that lay around." Only later in the night, when lightening flashed, was there enough light to fully reveal the ghastly scene: "Then the veil of night was rent & the curtain of darkness was lifted it was that sickening sights fell before my eyes. Near me at one time lay a dead man, his clothes ghastly, bloody face turned up to the pattering rain drops that fell upon that brow cold in death." One Tennessee artilleryman described sleeping, only to find the next morning that "I had slept in the tent with two dead yankees." Although the famous Bloody Pond has received an inordinate amount of attention after the war and even today, numerous soldiers also discussed the staggering amount of blood on the battlefield. One Louisianan wrote, "The Yankee camps, that we took were beautifully located with fine springs running down in branches, but on Monday morning I saw those branches having their waters all colored with blood." A Federal officer noted he went to the spring his regiment had used but "found a rebel soldier, one of the 18th La. laid full length, spread out and arms downward in the water." Sam Houston Jr. gave an eerie account of the phenomenon: "In the darkness I had filled my canteen, and drinking from it with a comrade, we decided that we had found a brackish spring; but the next morning in replenishing my stock of water, I emptied the canteen to find its contents strongly tinctured with blood."[25]

The bloodshed and carnage made many a Confederate think in religious terms. Several left accounts of praying, offering thanksgiving for safety, and asking for protection the next day. Some sang hymns. "Knelt down and tried to return thanksgiving and prayer to God," Tennessean Alfred Fielder wrote. Another described soldiers gathered around "a minister, who in most eloquent patriotic words was praying to God. Many were there on their knees around him and his loud voice alone was heard in that part of the battlefield."[26]

Yet there were warning signs that the next day would not be so easy and that Beauregard may not get to keep all his captured plunder. Alexander R. Chisolm of Beauregard's staff admitted, "Despite the excitement of our apparently complete victory, there was room left in our minds for some most unpleasant sensations, especially when the top of some lofty tree, cut off by a shell, would come toppling down among the men." Despite being separated from his young son and fearing him dead, Nathan Bedford Forrest provided good intelligence as his cavalry regiment fielded skirmishers along the brink of Dill Branch ravine. He watched as Buell crossed and sent Confederates in Union uniforms into Federal lines. Yet Forrest could find no one who would listen to his report. He explained the situation to Hardee twice, but then he was only a lowly colonel amid many generals. Others reported the same thing. Robert Trabue wrote that after getting his men settled in McDowell's camps, he "rode till 11 P.M. to find a general officer to whom to report for orders." He found none. He then sent out a staff officer with an escort who "rode all night without success." Confident of the morrow, Beauregard and Bragg spent the night in Sherman's camp, Hardee and Withers with Bowen's brigade in Peabody's camps, and Polk and Cheatham moving all the way back to Cheatham's camps at his April 5 bivouac site. The various brigades camped haphazardly as well, with Chalmers's men and a couple of Jackson's regiments bedding down in Stuart's camps while Breckinridge's two brigades bivouacked east of Shiloh Church with portions of Russell's troops closer to the church and some of Cleburne's brigade in Prentiss's camps. A portion of Anderson's men camped near Rhea Spring. Wood's brigade occupied McClernand's camps, and some of Russell's regiments occupied Marsh's tents.[27]

A more surprising warning came from Benjamin Prentiss. While his troops were being marched off the battlefield toward Corinth, Prentiss moved to Shiloh Church under guard of Alexander Chisolm of Beauregard's staff. Beauregard interrogated him, asking whether Grant was on the field, where Buell was, and if C. F. Smith was fighting. Prentiss spent the night near Beauregard and Bragg in Sherman's tent, sandwiched between Thomas Jordan and Jacob Thompson, with Clifton Smith nearby. There he told them the vital intelligence that Buell was arriving: "You gentlemen have had your way to-day, but it will be very different to-morrow," he crowed. "You'll see! Buell will effect a junction with Grant to-night, and we'll turn the tables on you in the morning." Jordan showed Prentiss the telegram stating that Buell had been seen in Alabama, but Prentiss was not convinced. It is hard to perceive which was more astonishing—that they did not believe him, or that he told them to begin with—although staff officer Smith related that he thought Prentiss was being agreeable to "propitiate them and thus make good terms for himself."[28]

The only major Confederate units to remain on the front line during the night were Pond's brigade and his artillery, Ketchum's Battery. Having been outside major Confederate operational control since midafternoon, when the Louisianans did not partake in the concentration at the Hornet's Nest but rather attacked straight ahead on their own, they did not get the withdrawal order and remained in line of battle overlooking Tilghman Branch. Pond was almost overwhelmed with the responsibility he felt for the left flank. Braxton Bragg had personally reinforced the notion of its importance to him on the evening of April 5. Pond even sent skirmishers across Owl Creek during the night. Thus he was the only Confederate brigade in a position to immediately confront the massive Federal surge the next morning.[29]

Adding to the misery were the gunboats; the resting Confederates never knew where the next round would fall. Some took it personally. Patrick Cleburne, who Francis Shoup described as "sitting on a stump drinking coffee out of a bucket, and was as utterly in the dark as I was," burned red with hate: "History records few instances of more reckless inhumanity than this." Some were more curious, especially about the unexploded ordinance; a Tennessean saw some "artillery boys carrying one of them, which they had found, and they were showing the monster as a curiosity." Many tried to use whatever cover they could, spending the night in captured Federal tents, but many of those were full of bullet holes and could not keep out the drenching rain, much less the naval ordnance. The same Tennessean described where a gunboat shell landed in a Sibley tent: "It did not leave a rag." One miserable Confederate wrote home describing his habitation: "I write in Capt. Fulton's tent, Quartermaster of the 53rd Ohio regiment." He added, "the enemy is still throwing shells from his gunboats and some of them fall uncomfortably near our tent."[30]

The night of April 6 thus passed slowly and miserably for all involved. Fortunately, the thunderstorms ended before dawn and the weather cleared, but there was still plenty of misery to go around, especially for the thousands of wounded who lay on the field or were subjected to crude Civil War medicine.

And as the dawn of April 7 approached, it was only about to get worse.

14

"ON MONDAY MORNING THE THING CHANGED"

Lew Wallace had marched almost all day on April 6 while Grant's army fought for its life at Shiloh. He was there now, though, and ready to enter the action on the second day. Yet there were still issues that concerned him as he prepared to advance in the predawn hours of April 7. In addition to concern over how his late arrival would be perceived at headquarters, the pelting rain and the gunboats kept everyone awake. Wallace also had to consider the terrain and the Confederate resistance. The best he could do under the circumstances was to gather as much information as he could from those who had seen the ground on the opposite side of Tilghman Branch.

Wallace—as well as Buell, for that matter—certainly talked to Sherman and McClernand and anyone else he could find to gather as much information as possible. Ironically, the one officer Wallace did not talk to was perhaps the most important: Grant himself. Grant did not see fit to ride down the line all the way to the far right, where Wallace was deployed; he merely sent a staff officer to inform him of the next day's plan. Wallace might well have associated the coolness in relation to his controversial march, although all the trouble with the Grant staff, which would eventually cast a proverbial cloud over his entire life, was in the future. All Wallace knew now was that he was expected to advance the next morning despite having little information and no communication with the army commander.[1]

As fate would have it, Wallace would make the first contact on April 7.

For decades after the Battle of Shiloh, veterans of the Army of the Tennessee and the Army of the Ohio argued over which army had led the attack in the first phase on April 7. Grant's Army of the Tennessee should get the distinction of first engaging the Confederates. Buell moved across Dill Branch about the same time as Wallace, but Grant's forces engaged the Confederates first simply because Preston Pond's brigade and Ketchum's Battery had not fallen back with the rest of the Confederate army during the night. They were still on line in the 8th Illinois camp at dawn the next morning and disputed the Union advance on the right.[2]

Pond certainly let his presence be known as dawn came that damp morning, with one observer noting, "The heavens were still hung with murky clouds, and the air was cold." If anything, the white coats of the 18th Louisiana and Orleans Guard showed their position. The men had turned their blue blouses inside out, choosing to take their chances as conspicuous targets rather than being mistaken as the enemy, as they had been the day before. One writer noted that the Louisianans gave "the appearance of going to a masquerade ball." Yet in actuality, it was Ketchum rather than Pond who alerted the enemy of their position. Ketchum's gunners on Pond's right took Wallace's and Sherman's troops under fire at dawn, unlimbering despite "our men [being] chilled through by the cold rain, sleeping without tents or much covering," one observer noted. Indeed, the infantry did little except get out of the way. Colonel Robert F. Looney of the 38th Tennessee reported that at first they were caught in front of the guns, with Ketchum firing over their heads. The infantry was thus "exposed to the shells of friends and foes," and it quickly moved behind Ketchum's gunners. Joseph Thompson wrote home that most threw down anything they had, but he "had my Yankee knap-sack buckled so tight that I could not get rid of it. . . . In trying to get it off, I fell into a creek but my trinkets . . . went flying."[3]

The Union cannoneers took up the fight as soon as it was light enough to see across the valley to the southwest. Posted on the knoll of the ridge in front of the junction of Smith's and Thayer's brigades, Thompson's Indianans, under the command of First Lieutenant George R. Brown, began firing around 5:30 A.M. Wallace realized that more firepower was needed to drive the enemy battery away and thus called for Thurber's five guns in front of Whittlesey's brigade to open up farther north, providing a crossfire on Ketchum's position and the infantry that to Wallace seemed to be "lining the whole length of the bluff."[4]

The "duello," as Ketchum described it, continued for an hour or more, despite Ketchum being outgunned and actually changing positions. During this time, Grant rode over to see Wallace and gave him his orders to advance. By that time it was daylight and Wallace could get a more substantial view of what he faced: the Confederate artillery, supported by a full brigade across the creek, told everyone that the Confederates were going to contest any advance. Wallace wrote that if defended against, "it was apparent that crossing the hollow would be at heavy loss." Although Pond's troops were the only ones contesting anything at this point, they nevertheless had an effect on Wallace and the other officers on the right. They deemed a slow and careful advance the best option.[5]

Despite the terrain of the Tilghman Branch ravine, Wallace's three brigades advanced en echelon at 6:30 A.M., with skirmishers of the 14th Missouri of Grant's army out front. Others, such as Lieutenant Colonel Manning Force, had crossed with skirmishers earlier around dawn, providing priceless intelligence about the terrain. That terrain immediately took a toll in the crossing, even without much Confederate resistance nearer to Owl Creek. The rains during the night had caused the bottoms to become even more boggy, the hillsides ever more slippery, and the creeks deeper than normal. Just the tramp through the bottom was difficult enough. One Indianan wrote, "Some of the boys got in the mud up to their waists, but I was more lucky—merely got in the mud a little over the shoe mouth deep." Just as Buell found it difficult to cross his brigades over Dill Branch on the left, a careful Wallace took over two hours to get his men across Tilghman Branch. Wallace perhaps thought the entire Confederate army was opposing his movement, or perhaps he was overly cautious in light of his perceived failure the day before. Either way, he made a timid advance to start the day, which was already developing into a duplicate of the first day's fighting when the Confederates had mired down in Shiloh and Locust Grove branches. This time, however, it was in reverse, with Buell facing the daunting Dill Branch ravine and Wallace confronting the deep and foreboding ravine of Tilghman Branch.[6]

The division nevertheless moved on, Smith down the old road that led across the creek to Jones Field and Thayer and Whittlesey stacking up to his right and rear, moving through Glover Field where Brown deployed his guns. Wallace took the westernmost route because he could easily see that Pond's brigade did not stretch all the way to Owl Creek and that his flank, covered only by cavalry, could be easily turned. By 8:00 A.M., Wallace had all three brigades across Tilghman Branch and then turned the division to the left and began to ascend the high ground that led upward to the wide-open spaces of Jones Field and Pond's left. He moved forward and took a dominating position, "almost without opposition," he noted, on the high ground in the northeast corner of the field by 9:00 A.M., planting Thompson's and Thurber's batteries in front of the infantry.[7]

Fortunately for Wallace, Pond was just as frightened of him as he was of the Confederates. He watched Wallace advance from a prominent knoll southwest of Tilghman Branch, increasingly worrying about his isolated position. Pond eventually decided to fall back to the rest of the army. With a slow advance on Wallace's part and continual fire from Ketchum's guns and skirmishing by Wharton's rangers, however, Pond was able to maintain his position until around 9:00 A.M., when he finally marched away to the south. He fully credited Ketchum's gunners for the lengthy defense, writing that he "would no doubt have been cut off or cut to pieces but for the cool, intrepid, and gallant conduct of Captain Ketchum." In fact, once Wallace crossed Tilghman Branch, Ketchum continued to fight, and Pond increasingly depended on him to hold the line. While his infantry withdrew, Ketchum remained, exposed and almost alone. Pond had determined that because "the whole was in great peril, I thought it better to sacrifice the pieces than the regiment, if anything had to be lost." However, Ketchum was so skilled that he was successful in bringing his guns off, covered only by Wharton's Texas cavalry. A grateful Pond could only write, "In fact, the safety of my command is due to him."[8]

Despite his slowness, Wallace crossed the most important terrain feature to his front, and with relative ease. With a firm footing on the high ground by 9:00 A.M., Grant now could advance over the more level tableland of the lower half of the hourglass. It was here that the majority of the battle had raged the day before, and it was shaping up to be a repeat. Yet what Wallace found on the south side of Tilghman Branch disturbed him greatly. The large, open field that he would have to cross and the damaged and ransacked camps of Hare's brigade no doubt gained his attention, but the main thing that upset Wallace was that he was south of Tilghman Branch alone. When he advanced at 6:30

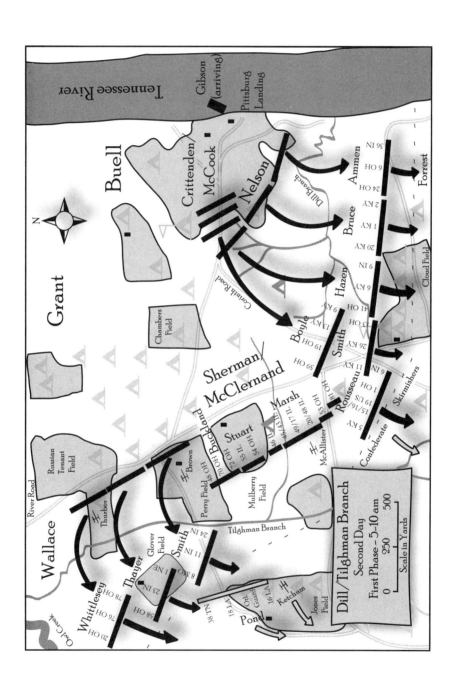

Tennessee River

Gibson (arriving)

Pittsburg Landing

Buell

Crittenden/McCook

Nelson

N

Grant

Dill Branch

Ammen

36 IN

9 OH

24 OH

Bruce

2 KY

1 KY

20 KY

Forrest

Cloud Field

6 IN

Hazen

6 KY

9 KY

41 OH

13 OH

26 KY

Smith

11 IN

Rousseau

1 OH

9 IN

15/16

19 US

Skirmishers

5 KY

Confederate

Boyle

19 OH

59 OH

Corinth Road

Chambers Field

Sherman/McClernand

Marsh

53 OH

11 IL

48 IL

20/17 IL

11 IA

13/43 IA

46 IL

McAllister

Stuart

54 OH

55 IL

72 OH

70 OH

Buckland

48 OH

Brown

Perry Field

River Road

Russian Tenant Field

Wallace

Thurber

Glover Field

Thayer

Smith

24 IN

11 IN

1 NE

8 MO

23 IN

Whittlesey

78 OH

76 OH

58 OH

20 OH

Mulberry Field

Tilghman Branch

38 TN

18 LA

16 LA

Ohio Guard

Ketchum

Jones Field

Pond

Owl Creek

Dill/Tilghman Branch
Second Day
First Phase ~ 5–10 am

0   250   500
Scale in Yards

A.M., it was with the understanding that the rest of the army was advancing as well—certainly Sherman, McClernand, and the rest of the Army of the Tennessee to his left. Wallace's crossing of Tilghman Branch did not break any speed records, allowing the others plenty of time to move forward, especially because they had no one to contest their advance as Pond had contested his. But it was not to be. While Buell was moving south of Dill Branch on the extreme left, the rest of the Army of the Tennessee was lagging far behind between the two wings. Around 9:00 A.M., a nervous Wallace called a halt in Jones Field to await the rest of the army's advance, later writing somewhat derisively, "As General Sherman's division, next on my left, had not made its appearance to support my advance, a halt was ordered for it to come up."[9]

To secure his position while he waited, ultimately for some two hours while the Confederates began to respond again with artillery, Wallace took a position on the dominant ridge in the northern extremity of Jones Field with Whittlesey, Thayer, and Smith in line from right to left. Whittlesey's men covered the right flank by keeping a tight hold on Owl Creek amid several smaller but still imposing ravines than ran off to the west. Wallace had his men lie down to keep them covered, and one Federal reported several of the men actually fell asleep on this line, "although there were shells exploding around us almost every moment." Alvin Hovey wrote his wife soon thereafter, "The rebel batteries began to rain their showers of shell and ball amongst our men." A 24th Indiana soldier declared "the enemies cannon balls bounded among us lively." He also described how one shell killed a mounted man in Thompson's Battery by nearly cutting him in two, with the mangled corpse falling to the ground "in a pile." He continued, "The Sargent wiped the blood and stuff off the saddle and put one of the powder boys up in the saddle." An 11th Indiana soldier wrote home, "You have heard of men dodging a canon Ball and so have I well I had a chance to try it and am shure a man can do it." To oppose the Confederate artillery, Wallace opened with Thompson's six guns and Thurber's five pieces. Wallace thus bided his time, keeping his right flank well covered by what he deemed the "absolute protection" of Owl Creek. Yet when he looked to his left, he saw nothing.[10]

Sherman, McClernand, Hurlbut, and the rest of the Army of the Tennessee were out there, but just not as far forward as Wallace. The hodgepodge of units thrown together in the last line the night before was not advancing quickly at all. It was not because of any Confederate resistance; rather it was because of the gun-shy commanders and the effect of the day before. Such temerity certainly could be expected, and many units of Grant's army were not even prepared come daylight. Carroll Marsh reported that "at daylight Monday morning the men in line were supplied with some provisions." Sherman reported he did not get orders to "advance and recapture our original camps" until daylight, and only then did he send staffers to bring up the men and reorganize the division, mainly finding and bringing Stuart's detached brigade to the right. Likewise, it took Hurlbut in reserve until midmorning to get his brigades in line and to the front. It is no surprise that while thus reorganizing, the tardy Army of the Tennessee heard firing both to their left and right.[11]

Sherman, McClernand, and Hurlbut—all that were left of the division commanders—formed a makeshift line that stretched between Wallace and Buell. Sherman, though wounded twice already and with numerous horses shot under him, earlier formed the core of his division on Wallace's left, with the two present units of David Stuart's brigade on his right and Buckland's brigade on the left. Hildebrand's troops were missing, although he would reform them as best he could and remain in the rear, where McDowell's regiments were also found. To Sherman's left eventually came a portion of Hurlbut's division in the form of Lauman's brigade. McClernand formed all but two regiments of Marsh's and Raith's brigades supported by the guns of McAllister's battery, with Pugh's and Veatch's brigades of Hurlbut's division extending southeastward toward Buell's forces. Interspersed in between was a collection of other regiments, including the 81st Ohio, 13th Missouri, and 7th Illinois of W. H. L. Wallace's division, the 28th and 46th Illinois of Hurlbut's, and even the 53rd Ohio of Sherman's division. It certainly was not a perfect rendition of the army, but it was better than the alternative they had faced the day before.[12]

By 8:00 A.M., a very late Sherman, McClernand, and Hurlbut began to move forward through the damage of Veatch's camps to a line on the northeast side of Tilghman Branch, fronting Cavalry Field with the infantry and McAllister's guns. Little official explanation was given for the slow advance and quick delay, although one Ohioan wrote that the line marched two miles, "occasionally halting & allowing our Bttery to play on 'em, feeling the woods." McClernand reported he "ordered a halt, and adjusted my line in a wood" while McAllister fired on an enemy battery across the creek. Later he stopped to readjust again.

Sherman noted he stopped, "patiently waiting for the sound of General Buell's advance." Some of the troops became so disengaged that they read newspapers; one officer reported, "finding a rebel paper I was soon absorbed in it after dismounting and getting a seat on a log in front of the regiment." The advance nevertheless continued, with the troops slowly crossing the creek and pushing up the steep and slippery banks. One Illinoisan wrote, "We had to ascend a very steep hill and to reach the top we had to crawl on our hands and knees." The men also had to aid the artillery: "It was too steep for them there so we had to pull the cannon up with ropes." All this took time, with Sherman and company being careful and the terrain causing significant delay. Thus it was only around 10:00 A.M. that Sherman, McClernand, and Hurlbut finally reached the high ground southwest of Tilghman Branch, where they connected with a relieved Wallace to the right. They also encountered something else. Finally, large numbers of Confederates loomed ahead. It seemed Beauregard had finally established a line of resistance on this northwestern flank, and at least two enemy artillery batteries engaged Willard's and McAllister's guns, which had been slowly dragged up the hill. Shiloh's second day was about to get heated.[13]

The first shots on the Union right that morning awoke Prentiss, who was sleeping between his two guards, Jordan and Thompson, near Shiloh Church. The Federal general erroneously exclaimed, "Ah! Didn't I tell you so! There is Buell!" It was actually Wallace, but the sentiment was correct. Buell was on the field and already on the move as well. The effect was not lost on the common soldiers. One Confederate wrote home, "On Monday morning the thing changed." A Federal added, "This time the attack came from our side and rather surprised the Greybacks."[14]

If the Army of the Tennessee could claim the first action on the morning of April 7, it was not because Buell's Army of the Ohio was lagging behind. In fact, they were up just as early and actually moving forward earlier than Wallace, who had delayed his advance until around 6:30 A.M. because of the artillery resistance on his front. The ball of energy that was Bull Nelson, "as aggressive as he was obnoxious," in the words of Buell's biographer, had his division up by 4:00 A.M., soon afterward notifying Buell of his readiness. Jacob Ammen later remembered that Nelson came to his headquarters early that morning and told him to "put the Tenth Brigade in motion, as soon as you can see to move, at dawn; find the enemy and whip him." Ammen chuckled at "that energetic and wide-awake officer" and noted that "he went towards the Nineteenth Brigade." With all of Nelson's brigades thus roused, along with the other divisions, Buell sent Grant word that he was ready to attack, then did so, placing the time of his advance at "soon after 5 o'clock." The significant fact that there was no Confederate resistance on Buell's front made his advance much easier and quieter.[15]

Just because Buell's troops did not have a force to confront them did not mean that the Army of the Ohio had an easy time in their advance. In fact, the Federal left faced a myriad of problems that did not even begin to include the enemy. It was a testimony to the army's organization and leadership that it was even there and able to fight. In the just-dawning light, they looked magnificent to the jaded veterans of Grant's army. An Iowan wrote in his diary, "It was a grand sight to see Regiment after Regiment marching to our front with colors flying—as they advance they spread in order to extend the line." Many in Buell's army did not feel good, however; few had slept over the past twenty-four hours, and they were exhausted by the wearisome marches. Brigade commander William Hazen wrote, "I passed the night by the side of an oak-tree, holding my horse, and tormented by the disgusting smells of old camps moistened by the rains."[16]

Parts of Buell's army were actually still arriving as the sun began to peek over the Tennessee River floodplain. Buell posted Crittenden's two brigades in line on Nelson's right, then turned his attention to Mc-Cook's arriving troops. Elements of Rousseau's brigade had arrived in the last few hours. United States regulars remained aboard their boats, believing it was better to stay comfortable for the time being. The boat captains wanted to get out of harm's way, but there was little they could do. As dawn neared, Rousseau's brigade, accompanied by McCook and representing his entire division at that point, moved inland led by the Madison Brass Band playing "Yankee Doodle." Others played "Benny Havens, Oh!" One Federal shouted for the band to stop as it would "draw the fire of the enemy." Major Stephen D. Carpenter told the band to continue on, grumbling, "That's exactly what we are here for." Another remembered someone asking who they were, and when they replied "the Regulars," the unimpressed straggler replied, "Go on you'll get regular h——ll." McCook urged the men on, particularly his old regiment, the 1st Ohio, telling the men that if any of them ran he would "blow his brains out." Rousseau also got into the speech making, which one Federal admitted "cheered us up amazingly." Rousseau eventually took his position on Crittenden's right, and the other brigades moved up and supported Rousseau as they arrived, with Kirk's next in line and Gibson's bringing up the rear later in the morning.[17]

The immediate problem for Buell's troops was getting across the Dill Branch ravine, with Jacob Ammen describing the "bayou . . . the steep, high bank," reporting that "the march was made slowly and with caution, the skirmishers examining the ground with great care and to my entire satisfaction." On the division's right, the ravine broke into two separate obstacles, causing even more trouble for Hazen. The previous night's heavy rains only made trudging across the ravine more difficult, with the freshly trampled and shot up dirt from the action the night before now even slicker and muddier. The unfortunate soldiers who had to cross were thus only moderately prepared to slide down the sides in their opening movement southward. Then they had to climb, and perhaps slide back down two or three times, before they could scramble out of the obstacle by grabbing any sort of tree or bush growing on the slopes. Trying to do that with equipment on and musket in hand was especially daunting, and trying to maintain any order while doing it all was nearly impossible. The terrain was also heavily wooded in places, causing the flags to get entangled with the limbs. Staff officer Horace Fisher recommended to Nelson that the flags be put in their cases and carried covered, and so the division fought that day with their flags encased. Despite Nelson bragging that his division moved "in perfect order, as if on drill," the lines of troops were necessarily broken, winded, and wet as Nelson's division emerged from the declivity that was Dill Branch around 7:00 A.M. Ammen reported that the men "advanced in good order, considering the nature of the ground." It was only mere fortune that the Confederates had not resisted.[18]

Like Wallace, Nelson took nearly two hours to cross Dill Branch, two waves covering each other as they progressed. However, he did so more quickly than the divisions to his right, which caused Buell to order Nelson to halt and allow Crittenden and McCook to catch up. Nelson did so in Cloud Field, where Hurlbut had tried to make a stand the day before and where so many of the defenders of the Hornet's Nest had fallen captive. Nelson's troops moved into the relatively unscathed camps of Jacob Lauman's brigade and could see Hurlbut's headquarters in the center of the field aside the River Road. It was here that Nelson

first encountered Confederate skirmishers from Forrest's cavalry about
7:00 A.M., although the Confederates offered little resistance and no
battle line was deployed. Nelson nevertheless exercised a great deal of
caution.[19]

Despite the delay in advancing, Nelson's division moved ahead of
the others, leaving his right uncovered for a moment. Ironically, Crittenden's division had much easier terrain to traverse but was still delayed. The division was able to traverse at worst the upper reaches of the
ravine, where the relief was not as daunting, and at best the high table
land where the Corinth and River roads ran through the neck of the
hourglass between the headwaters of Dill and Tilghman branches. Having only joined the brigade "a day or two previous," brigade commander
Sooy Smith was understandably nervous but moved forward immediately on Nelson's right, eventually positioning his line of battle amid
Nelson William's brigade camps where so many of Wallace's troops had
surrendered twelve hours ago. There he met a heavy Confederate skirmish line, which attacked his position and actually threw the right of the
brigade back temporarily. To his right en echelon was Boyle's troops,
nearer to the Corinth Road, with Buell at times following along and
issuing orders directly to brigade commanders.[20]

Crittenden was moving slowly, but he had to deal with issues other
than terrain. He had to deploy his division before he moved out. In addition, Nelson had advanced onto the ridges overlooking Dill Branch the
night before, giving his division a head start over Crittenden. McCook
likewise could not be faulted for his tardy arrival on Crittenden's right,
as he proceeded to the front as quickly as possible after landing with
only one brigade. The location and care of the previous day's wounded
also slowed the advance; it was around this time that Buell's troops
found a wet and cold W. H. L. Wallace on the battlefield, in terrible
shape but still alive. The wounded general was quickly taken to the rear,
where his wife, Anne, soon received the joyous news that her husband
was not dead after all. "Oh! Joy," she wrote when she finally reached his
side, "he was breathing."[21]

The danger to Nelson's open right flank, therefore, existed for only
a few minutes, because Crittenden soon arrived to secure the line. By
this time, around 8:00 A.M., Crittenden's right was also covered by the
just-arriving units of McCook's division. They marched forward over
the flat tableland, although the staggered arrival of the brigades proved
more of a hindrance than the terrain. Nevertheless, by 8:00 A.M. Rous-

seau's brigade was able to take a position in line to the right of Boyle's troops. Rousseau's regiments deployed squarely in the middle of the rising ground of Stacy Field north of the Corinth Road, in front of the 3rd Iowa campsite, and threw out two companies of each regiment as skirmishers. While there, Buell, who was on the right of his line, was erroneously told this was where Prentiss had been killed the day before. By this time, Kirk's brigade had also arrived and quickly moved forward, deploying in line behind Rousseau's troops, back near and north of the crossing of the Corinth and River roads.[22]

Thus, Buell had two full and a portion of a third division on the field and in line, with the remainder of McCook's troops hurrying forward. Although the majority of the batteries lining the ridge west of Pittsburg Landing inexplicably remained in place throughout the day, a portion of the Army of the Tennessee followed behind. They were not needed now, however; Buell, like Wallace, had already traversed the most problematical portion of his sector, Dill Branch ravine, and he did so with hardly a shot being fired at him. The lack of Confederate reorganization and planning was telling on the eastern side of the field just as it was on the western side. Had the Confederates offered even a semblance of resistance, it could have served to delay Buell's advance much as Pond slowed Wallace and the others to the right. An all-out defense could potentially have stopped Buell's advance completely, much like Grant's defense of the ravine the evening before. At least it could have delayed Buell significantly, as Sherman had done the day before at Shiloh Branch. Yet the Confederates had no major force anywhere near Dill Branch, much less in place to defend it.[23]

Still, it had taken upwards of two hours for Buell to advance to the high ground south of Dill Branch and reorganize for the all-out attack. But even getting his army organized and in position to advance was not enough, as the flanks were still a concern. Buell's line stretched for a mile and half from the river on the left to north of the Corinth Road, where Rousseau was to link up with the Army of the Tennessee. Although the left flank was seemingly secure against the Tennessee River, Buell still needed support on his right, and that had to come from the Army of the Tennessee. Once again, like Wallace, Buell had nothing on his right, prompting McCook to keep his second brigade in reserve in the rear to handle any threat to the flank. Sherman, McClernand, and Hurlbut had been delayed in the region between Wallace and Buell, not even crossing Tilghman Branch until later in the morning, and that delay forced both Wallace and Buell to halt while the center caught up and provided cover for the flanks in a continuous line across the triangle. Fortunately, Sherman and company crossed Tilghman Branch by 10:00 A.M. All Federal troops could again prepare to move forward.[24]

Once supported on the right, Buell's forces moved southward as the sun rose higher in the sky to their left. Nelson led the way as Ammen on the far left passed to the east of Cloud Field and into the upper reaches of some of the same smaller ravines that Chalmers had dealt with the day before. Hazen and Bruce to the right had a much easier time of it, moving through the deserted camps of Hurlbut's division east of the River Road. Crittenden and McCook likewise moved forward to Nelson's right, although Rousseau and McCook continually remained north of the Corinth Road and Nelson kept at first east of and then later astride the River Road. Because the two roads gradually ran away from each other at an angle, the two wings thus separated, leaving Crittenden in the center to fill the void. He quickly brought Boyle's brigade up from its reserve position and put it on Smith's right, with both brigades advancing between the two major roads. Thus did the Army of the Ohio, now in the formation in which it would meet the enemy, trudge onward, skirmishing lightly with the few Confederates in the front but anticipating they would soon meet even more.[25]

As Buell's brigades moved onward through the small spit of woods separating Cloud and Wicker fields along the River Road and Cloud and Duncan fields along the Corinth Road, the troops began to develop a new feeling. The farther out the men marched on the lower half of the hourglass, the more they saw the carnage of the day before. "Empty and broken packages which had contained 'canister' and 'grape' shot were in evidence, dead and wounded men were more numerous, [and] signs of the fight were coming to view more and more," one Ohioan related. It grew more pronounced the farther south they trudged until it became almost overwhelming. Unfortunately, that carnage would only increase on this second day as Buell's troops began encountering stiffer resistance as well. Buell's men met Forrest's Confederate skirmishers as close as Cloud Field, but they did not heavily resist the forward Union movement. Still, it was enough to alert all on the Federal side that the Confederates were still there.[26]

By 9:00 A.M., Buell had his divisions safely covering the roughly mile and a half expanse from the river to the Army of the Tennessee north of the Corinth Road, and he was in contact with the enemy. He also had elements of Grant's army as a reserve, with Tuttle's division now deploying in line behind Buell, Colonel Thomas Morton of the 81st Ohio commanding one brigade and Silas Baldwin of the 57th Illinois the other. Few of Buell's troops thought much of the veterans of Shiloh's first day, however. Buell alternatingly described "parts of about two regiments—perhaps 1,000 men," "similar fragment[s]," and "other straggling troops of General Grant's force." Obviously, Buell would be primarily on his own here on the left as Confederate resistance grew, first through long-range artillery and then in the form of heavier small arms fire. The Federals soon realized for certain that the enemy had not marched away but was still on the field. Federal officers strained their eyes through binoculars to see across the open spaces to the front of each division. There they saw increased indications of Confederate activity and realized that the battle was again about to get heated. The Confederates had finally awoken and were preparing a defense.[27]

P. G. T. Beauregard was confused when so many Federals began to come from every direction on the morning of April 7, and so were his men. Brigade commander Robert Russell, behind the lines, noted, "It was almost impossible to determine when and where the main attack commenced, on account of the constant firing of our troops in every direction." He added that it "contributed greatly to the confusion which afterward ensued." Other units, such as Cleburne's brigade, firing off their wet guns in the rear did not help. Obviously, this was not how the mopping-up operation was supposed to begin.[28]

Their confusion was nothing compared to Preston Pond's fears. Logically thinking he was in line with the rest of the army, daylight proved him wrong. "I discovered that our main line had fallen back and that my brigade was alone in the presence of the enemy," Pond wrote. He realized that instead of being with the rest of the army, he was alone, with only Ketchum's guns and a few cavalry units to support him. "I regarded the position as perilous," Pond admitted. He sent a hurried message to Daniel Ruggles, his division commander, and determined to hold on.[29]

The lack of certainty in Pond's sector was only a small part of the confusion and chaos taking place on the Confederate side. In the commotion, Beauregard let slip away perhaps his best opportunity to retrieve any semblance of victory from the deteriorating situation. Had Beauregard thought that there would be a major contest on the second

day and that he would be on the defensive, and had he been able to
get his units organized and deployed in the critical areas, he would no
doubt have been able to contest and perhaps even stop Grant and Buell's
advances across Tilghman and Dill branches. Even if he had not been
able to stop them completely—and it is important to remember that
Sherman and Prentiss had not been able to do so at Shiloh and Locust
Grove branches the day before—Beauregard could have possibly delayed the initial Union advance significantly, causing major casualties
and perhaps forcing Grant to rethink his options. It was not to be, and
the blame must lay on Beauregard. Although many Confederates and
some historians since Shiloh have castigated him for calling off the last
assaults of April 6, he should not receive the blame for that. Fewer Confederates and historians faulted Beauregard for the lack of preparation
during the night, but that is exactly where blame should lie.[30]

Beauregard did have many obstacles to reorganization during the
night. The army was completely exhausted after fighting thirteen hours
and marching for three days before that. The troops ended the day in
haphazard form, with corps, divisions, brigades, and sometimes even
regiments scattered. The gunboats were firing rapidly into the Confederate lines. The Confederates faced many legitimate woes during the evening and night, but Beauregard had done absolutely nothing to remedy
the situation. Only a few Confederates seemed to recognize it, among
them Forrest. James Chalmers later wrote how Forrest had found him
during the night and exclaimed, "If the enemy attack us in the morning
they will whip us like hell!"[31]

In their defense, few Confederates were thinking in terms of being
assailed. Rather, they were thinking of finishing off their own attack. An
Arkansan remembered, "We were preparing our breakfast and discussing what would be done with the prisoners and other matters concerning
the forthcoming surrender, as we supposed, when a courier came and
ordered our Colonel to move his men forward." A Tennessean wrote
their offensive orders were to "stand their ground but not shoot until
they were ordered to charge the enemy." Even if Beauregard expected
to finish Grant off the next day, however, some attempt at reorganization
ought to have taken place during the night. Thus, much like the day of
fighting on April 6, time was on Grant's side. A delayed Confederate
attack on the second day only allowed Grant time to strengthen his lines
and bring in more troops. Even when not expecting an attack—as evidently Beauregard was not—military protocol dictated that a defensive

line be formed for security. Yet nothing was done, with one Louisianan writing, "You should have seen us, not expecting a battle that day we loaded ourselves with every thing that we could lay our hands on." It was only after daylight, according to Samuel Lockett, that he and other staff officers were tasked with "getting them into some sort of manageable organization."[32]

The Confederate disorganization became obvious as the minutes ticked away and Pond alone faced the Union advance. Yet that early morning action on the Confederate left had a stark effect on Beauregard at his headquarters near the church. He was still intent on finishing off Grant, with Johnston's staff officer, George Baylor, writing that Beauregard told him that "the enemy were making a stand at only one point, and he expected to capture them that morning." However, it did not take long for the Confederates to discover what was happening. Hearing the heavy firing to the front left, Beauregard quickly began to react, sending his corps commanders (once he found them) to various sectors, with Hardee to the right, Bragg to the left, and Breckinridge to the center. Polk was missing, and the thought crossed Beauregard's mind that he might have been captured. Beauregard also started isolated groups of Confederates over in the direction of the firing and stretched out cavalry and staff officers Brent and Chisholm in the rear to stop and gather up stragglers. Yet the similar sound of movement of Buell's forces over on the Confederate right soon told the same story there. The effect was not lost on Beauregard. There was also "a scattering fire in every direction," one Tennessean wrote, as the troops fired off their guns to see whether the powder was dry. It must have all been very confusing for the ill and exhausted Beauregard, who was consumed with renewing the attack, not receiving one. One observer described the scene: "There came to him every minute the most conflicting accounts of the enemy's movements. First, it was reported the enemy was flanking our right. The General quickly gave an order to send a brigade in that direction. The order had hardly issued before another courier contradicted this report, and stated that no enemy was visible in that direction. The General, smiling, remarked to one of his aids: 'This is one of Morph's blind games. I wish I had him here to help me play it out.'" Thus even as messengers began to arrive stating what he already could hear, Beauregard was growing more concerned. He wrote four days later that the opening action in Jones Field "assured me of the junction of his forces," adding, "Soon the battle raged with a fury which satisfied me I was attacked by a largely superior force." Beauregard quickly mounted and wondered what the pulse of a commander going into battle was. He had his surgeon, Dr. R. L. Brodie, take his and his staff's pulse. He later wrote, "It varied from 90 to 130." Obviously all were anxious.[33]

The initial heavy firing on the left made it the most critical sector in many Confederate officers' minds, and most started out in that direction, with one Confederate griping, "We were not permitted to take our breakfast before they attacked our lines." The first units to move forward were the other brigades of Ruggles's division, with Bragg sending staff officer Giles B. Cooke to tell Ruggles "to move instantly to the left." Pond had sent him a note telling of his engagement, and the growing noise from Jones Field illustrated the fact. Ruggles quickly gathered his other two brigades under Gibson and Anderson, the call "fall in to face the enemy again" ringing out. Unfortunately, the brigades encountered trouble even before they moved toward the Union line. Thomas Jordan wandered along and countermanded the order momentarily, and Anderson's unit was split in half by "permitting others troops to cut them out on the march and in falling into line." Even when on line, first farther to the left and then more in the center, Anderson described the confusion of the "arrival of troops in fragments of brigades, regiments, and companies." Randall Gibson similarly described how his men moved through a ravine that fed into Tilghman Branch: "An abrupt descent of 50 or 60 feet, perhaps more, from a ridge to a swamp, added very much to the fatigue of the men and disturbed very decidedly the regularity and rapidity of this movement." In addition, all units were well below strength as a result of attrition and straggling. One Mississippian wrote, "It was truly humiliating to the line officers to go into it with but a handful of men, as they had to do."[34]

Fortunately, Ruggles was not on his own. Many other brigades were also beginning to move to the left in response to the initial firing, Beauregard's orders, or both. Robert Russell noted, "At the discharge of the first guns I formed my brigade in line of battle." Three of his regiments were with him at Review Field, although casualties from the day before caused Russell to admit that "the force was small." The 11th Louisiana of his brigade had split up, partly fighting on the extreme right and a larger portion attaching itself to Anderson's brigade, but Russell led the other three Tennessee regiments to the left and took position by 10:00 A.M. on the western side of Jones Field. With only portions of brigades similarly coming onto the line as the minutes passed, including a couple of regiments of Gladden's brigade under Zach Deas and some of Maney's units while the bulk of both were fighting on the right, Russell had the most intact brigade on the Confederate left early in the fight. Thus fell to him the initial duty of holding that critical flank.[35]

Russell received more help as the morning minutes passed, although various Confederate units slowly moved forward, the fire having left the men. A wounded Major Aaron B. Hardcastle, whose troops had begun the battle about twenty-four hours ago, reported that he led his men forward but they were "much exhausted and worn-out. They marched very slowly." Most significantly for the defense on the left, Frank Cheatham led a portion of his division into line a little later; the division commander thus took over from Russell the command of the left flank. Cheatham's presence was probably more significant than the troops he brought. He had advanced from his April 5 bivouac site along with Polk, who had gone during the night to find him, with only portions of the 154th, 6th, 9th, 15th, and 2nd Tennessee regiments (a few others had been sent on ahead to rejoin their parent brigades). Temporarily delayed by a "stampede" that Marcus Wight explained resulted from a rumor that the Federals were in the army's rear and attempting to cut them off, Polk soon ordered Cheatham to go into line at the church, but Cheatham then received orders to support Breckinridge in the center. Arriving on the scene, Breckinridge told him he was fine if Cheatham could hold the left. Cheatham thus began moving in that direction, but the right of the line was cut off by heavy woods—probably the undergrowth in front of the Hornet's Nest. Thus Colonel Preston Smith and most of the troops wound up on the right with Hardee. Cheatham arrived on the far left with only a fraction of his command, the 6th Tennessee and six companies of the 9th Tennessee, which was only a fraction of what he started with, which itself was only a fraction of his original division. He was nevertheless the ranking officer on the left and took over, adding his troops to the left of Robert Russell's regiments and others trying to hold the left flank secure. Yet the marching wasted much time, and it was midmorning before he arrived in force on line. Still, Cheatham was ready to enter the fight—something he routinely did, as evidenced by the mortality among his staff. In particular, he had two "boys" on his staff, A. L. Robertson and John Campbell. The latter was killed, "his entire head having been carried away by a cannon shot." Also on his staff was future Tennessee governor and state legislator James D. Porter.[36]

In the same general area, Bragg was soon also hard at work forming a line. On his regimental gathering trip, staff officer Chisolm pushed Anderson's brigade forward north of Breckinridge, but later ran up on Bragg, to whose corps Anderson belonged. Chisolm informed Bragg of what he had done, adding that if it did not meet his approval, "I had time to countermand the order." Bragg replied that he approved, stating that the "word is *forward.*" He also told Chisolm, "I will throw my command in here on the left." Bragg thus took overall command of the Confederate left.[37]

Similarly, although Hardee was on the far right flank, his entire corps was massing together in a makeshift line extending southeastward along the developing line on the Confederate left. Joining this line between Russell and Cheatham near Owl Creek and Gibson and Anderson farther south were portions of Wood's and Shaver's brigades fronting Jones Field as well as part of Cleburne's in the woods south of the field. Wood's brigade took a position on the left of the corps. It had been formed earlier by the senior colonel, W. K. Patterson of the 8th Arkansas, because Wood was still reeling from his injury the day before. The tired and sleep-deprived soldiers of this brigade nevertheless soon came on line with Wood back in command on the western side of the field. Shaver's Arkansans appeared on Wood's right, although likewise in a dilapidated state because of being moved before "the wearied and almost famished men had procured anything to eat," noted Major James T. Martin of the 7th Arkansas. Cleburne's regiments took a position on Shaver's right in the woods south of the field, but their numbers had sorely dwindled as well. Cleburne reported, "I blush to add, hundreds of others had run off early in the fight of the day before—some through cowardice and some loaded with plunder from the Yankee encampments." The hearty souls were there, however, and interspersed between the brigades were other regiments lost from their parent units. One contemporary writer, perhaps with some overstatement, described the Confederate line as resembling "a shuffled pack of cards, in which none adjoins its next in suit except by chance." The Confederate situation was clearly not good.[38]

The Confederate response on the right was even more mediocre than it was on the left. Pond demonstrated a semblance of resistance on the western side of the field, delaying Wallace's advance across Tilghman Branch for two or three hours as the cautious Federals slowly moved into Jones Field. The lack of any Confederate showing on the eastern side for at least a half mile and no major resistance for over a mile allowed Buell to move much farther out in the same time period. An unsupported and engaged Wallace was able to make less than a half mile by 9:00 A.M., while Buell advanced well over a mile from the landing by that time. Like Wallace, he then met a formed Confederate resistance and also slowed to a crawl as both sides felt each other out.

It took time for this Confederate front to be organized, and many officers on the right worked hard to see to it, including Withers, Chalmers, and the ranking corps commander in this sector, Hardee. The presence of a large number of officers and the ostensible leadership they provided did not make the entire reorganization run completely smooth, however. A major problem developed when Withers took his division through a convoluted series of orders that saw them almost leave the field in order to form up far to the left, obviously in response to the initial fighting to the west. By now realizing that the Federal advance was also heavy on the right, Beauregard sent staff officer Chisolm to "inquire why Genl Hardee had ordered troops to form and wait on the Bark road." Hardee by this time had also detected the enemy movement and quickly sent Withers back to the front on the right. Even as they were forming the main line, the troops exhibited weariness that concerned the officers; at one point when observing the 2nd Texas going into line, Hardee remarked to staff officer William Clare, "Those men don't move as if they would fight."[39]

Nevertheless, officers seemed to be everywhere, especially Hardee. Artilleryman Irving Hodgson wrote, "He seemed to be the master spirit, giving orders and seeing that they were properly executed." Because of his and others' efforts, the Confederate line became more formidable as the minutes passed. While Bragg amassed his defense on the left of the line, Hardee over on the Confederate right began to piece together a line near where Chalmers's regiments had spent the night. The core of the Confederate right was Jones Withers's division, mostly Chalmers's and Jackson brigades, although Jackson was not present; his infantry was under the command of John C. Moore of the 2nd Texas. There were also three regiments of Gladden's brigade in line, as well as portions of others such as Maney's, Bushrod Johnson's, and Alexander P. Stewart's. Withers and Hardee formed these brigades along the Hamburg-Purdy Road on the south side of Sarah Bell's cotton field, near where many of these brigades had fought so desperately the day before.[40]

At about the same time, in the center, Confederate officers also began to piece together a line, studded primarily by the three brigades of John C. Breckinridge's corps. Taking a position in front of Crittenden and McCook in what the day before was the Hornet's Nest, Breckinridge's corps was the only one that, although somewhat by accident, had all its units together with their original corps commander. Statham's troops, with Bowen's brigade now under John D. Martin to their right, held the Hornet's Nest area, with Trabue's Kentuckians eventually extending the line to the left through Duncan Field and toward Ruggles's line then forming on the left. Although all three of Breckinridge's brigades were there, they had all come, somewhat surprisingly, from different locations that morning, and Breckinridge seemed to have more control over Martin and Statham than he did Trabue, who often melded to Bragg's orders farther to the left.[41]

Although Confederate forces were constantly coming on line, causing the Federals to think they were being reinforced, chaos was still rampant. Some brigades such as Robert Shaver's reported they were in line and ready to march for "some considerable time" before orders arrived. Because of the lack of effort the night before and the confusion even after daylight, Beauregard had lost perhaps his best chance of stopping the Federal onslaught when he did not defend the Tilghman and Dill branch line, utilizing the natural terrain's defensive attributes at a point where the field of battle was most constricted. Having not done so, Beauregard now had to set up a defense on increasingly widening and relatively level terrain, which meant his line was increasingly longer and his defensive aids were correspondingly fewer.[42]

The personal sadness among the gathering Confederates rivaled the tactical issues they faced on this early morning. As the various Confederate brigades moved forward and the wounded moved to the rear, many heartrending events took place as soldiers left wounded and dead friends and family in the various campsites and hospitals to go to the front. None is more touching than the case of a Kentucky officer, John Caldwell. He wrote in his diary, "But before I go I must look upon the faces of my noble dead." He later added,

> I have seen them again. The flaxen hair of little Tom Caldwell is matted over his once sunny face. Poor Lan's face is so blackened by wound in forehead that I would not have known him but for wound and dress. Chestnutt is calm as if sleeping. George Small's face is dark and lower-

ing. The light of battle has faded from his face. My noble friend Casey appears to have been in great pain when he died. How I pity his family. Smith seems to have died easy. Johnson appeared calm. Tom Lyles suffered greatly, shot through the bowels. Walker suffered a good deal but endured it like a man. Kennerly was in great misery, shot in bowel. John Pillow died last night. What a message I have for his family, "Tell my mother I died like a soldier."[43]

The result was a shocked and bewildered Confederate line that was thrown together hurriedly and haphazardly. Colonel Alexander W. Campbell of the 33rd Tennessee illustrated the confusion, stating that his orders were to "prepare for action immediately and form into brigades as they most conveniently could." Indeed, at times Beauregard put staff members such as his aide Samuel Ferguson and engineer Samuel Lockett in command of unorganized units gathered quickly and sent to the front. When asked if he could command a battalion, Lockett replied, "If ordered to do so, I think I can." Beauregard then introduced Lockett to the gathering as Colonel Lockett. Lockett managed to form together men of numerous regiments, many of them from the 7th Kentucky and 7th and 9th Arkansas, and declared it to be the Beauregard Regiment. Other staffers aided as well; Alexander Chisolm reported that he rode along the lines and "started forward every regiment I could find." Beauregard also put officers as high as brigadier generals in charge of recently formed bodies of troops, including John K. Jackson and Alexander Stewart, the latter's brigade admittedly split up with all four regiments fighting apart from the others on this second day. Thus even amid the chaos, Beauregard fashioned a line that extended from Larkin Bell's field on the eastern side of the battlefield along the Hamburg-Purdy Road to Sarah Bell's cotton field, and thence along the line of the Federal defense of the day before in the Hornet's Nest and Jones Field. The line was much closer to the Federal advance on the left than the right, with the entire line facing in somewhat of a northeasterly direction. Yet in this line Beauregard estimated he could put no more than 20,000 troops, and the original leadership was decimated: the army commander was killed, three of five division commanders wounded, and five of sixteen brigade commanders incapacitated.[44]

The battle lines were nevertheless drawn by 10:00 A.M., and the first phase of this second day's action came to a close. It had not been a very destructive phase, with only minor skirmishing all across the field, the exception being Pond's defense in Jones Field. Still, Beauregard had managed to form a line across the battlefield and was already providing stiffer resistance. Federal skirmishers soon became overmatched and the infantry and artillery had to take up the fight. To no one's surprise, the fighting quickly grew to as fevered a pitch as anything the day before.[45]

Shiloh Church gave its name to the battle but did not survive the war. No contemporary photos of the church exist, but drawings and paintings such as this view hint at its appearance. Courtesy Shiloh National Military Park.

One of only three known contemporary views of the Shiloh battlefield, this image shows steamers lined up at Pittsburg Landing immediately after the battle. Courtesy Shiloh National Military Park.

The siege guns of Madison's Illinois battery show Grant's last line immediately after the battle. Courtesy Shiloh National Military Park.

Major General Henry W. Halleck commanded the Union Department of the Mississippi in St. Louis and oversaw the operations along the Tennessee River. Courtesy Library of Congress.

Major General Charles F. Smith initially commanded the Union expedition up the Tennessee River, although he later turned over the command to a reinstated U. S. Grant. At the time of Shiloh, Smith was suffering from a leg injury that eventually took his life. Courtesy Library of Congress.

Major General Ulysses S. Grant commanded the Union armies at Shiloh. Blame for the enemy surprise, massive casualties, and unfounded rumors of his being drunk during the battle fell heavily on him. Courtesy Library of Congress.

Major General John A. McClernand's division saw some of the hardest
fighting at Shiloh. The career politician was a nuisance to Grant but fought
well at Shiloh and in subsequent battles. Courtesy Library of Congress.

Brigadier General W. H. L. Wallace was new to brigade command but provided stellar service in defending the Union center on the first day at Shiloh. He paid for his dedication with his life. Courtesy Library of Congress.

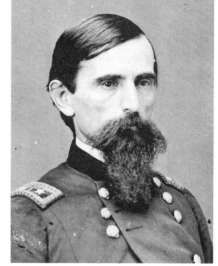

Major General Lew Wallace's division camped away from the battlefield. His roundabout march on the first day and his small number of casualties on the second have been unjustly criticized by historians. Courtesy Library of Congress.

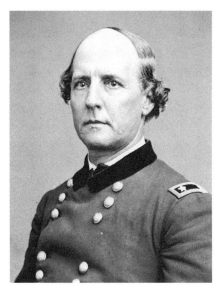

Brigadier General Stephen A. Hurlbut's division provided the critical defense of the Union left flank on the first day and was also engaged on the second. Hurlbut, often dismissed for his drinking and unscrupulous political actions, nevertheless fought well at Shiloh. Courtesy Library of Congress.

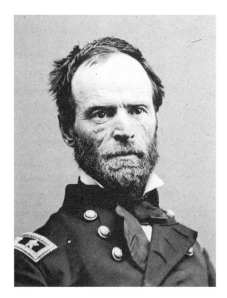

Brigadier General William T. Sherman held the front line of the Army of the Tennessee at Shiloh and as a result took major blame for being surprised. He quickly recovered and fought well the rest of the battle. Courtesy Library of Congress.

Brigadier General Benjamin M.
Prentiss held the Federal center on
the first day, going down in history
as the defender of the Hornet's Nest
despite most of the troops belonging
to W. H. L. Wallace's division.
Prentiss was captured and spent
six months in captivity. Courtesy
Library of Congress.

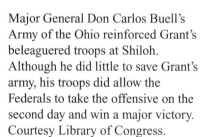

Major General Don Carlos Buell's
Army of the Ohio reinforced Grant's
beleaguered troops at Shiloh.
Although he did little to save Grant's
army, his troops did allow the
Federals to take the offensive on the
second day and win a major victory.
Courtesy Library of Congress.

Brigadier General William "Bull" Nelson's division arrived at Pittsburg Landing at the end of the first day and led the counterattack on the Union left on the second day. Courtesy Library of Congress.

Brigadier General Thomas L. Crittenden pushed his division of Buell's army
forward on the second day and became engulfed in the massive fighting in
the center of the battlefield around the Hornet's Nest. Courtesy Library of
Congress.

Brigadier General Alexander M. McCook led his division into major fighting near the Crossroads on the second day of battle. Courtesy Library of Congress.

Brigadier General Thomas J. Wood's division arrived on the afternoon of April 7, too late to take part in the battle proper, although a few casualties did occur. Courtesy Library of Congress.

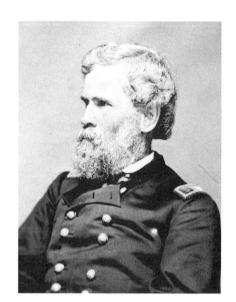

Colonel Joseph D. Webster served as Grant's chief of staff and set up the last line of defense at Pittsburg Landing at the end of the first day of fighting. Courtesy Library of Congress.

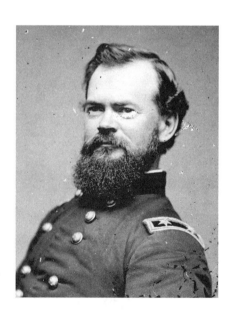

Lieutenant Colonel James B. McPherson was a staff engineer at Shiloh but would rise to army command later in the war. Courtesy Library of Congress.

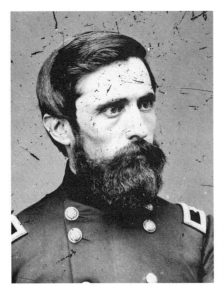

Captain John A. Rawlins served on Grant's staff and would become something of a caretaker for the general throughout the war. Sent to hurry Lew Wallace on the first day, Rawlins and Wallace got into a shouting match over the speed of the march. Courtesy Library of Congress.

General Albert Sidney Johnston led his Confederate Army of the Mississippi in a do-or-die gamble at Shiloh. He died, and the army was defeated, ending the best chance the Confederacy had to recoup its losses in the west. Courtesy Library of Congress.

Major General Braxton Bragg served as chief of staff of the army as well as a corps commander. He has often been wrongly condemned for his failed attempts to break the Union center on the first day. Courtesy Library of Congress.

General P. G. T. Beauregard served as Johnston's second in command, although he led most of the planning for the battle. Although he desired to retreat before launching the attack, Beauregard took over for Johnston and fought well on the second day at Shiloh. Courtesy National Archives.

Major General William J. Hardee led the advance Confederate corps in the attack at Shiloh. As a result of the chaos, he served capably if not stellarly in the rest of the battle, particularly on the second day. Courtesy Library of Congress.

Major General Leonidas Polk led his corps into battle but soon saw it broken and divided. His corps would become the most fractured during the battle. Courtesy Library of Congress.

Brigadier General John C. Breckinridge, former United States vice president, led the Confederate reserve corps at Shiloh and managed to keep his three brigades organized throughout both days, leading Beauregard to depend on him heavily on the second day. Courtesy Library of Congress.

Governor Isham G. Harris of Tennessee traveled with the Confederate army once his capital at Nashville fell. He was a volunteer aide to Johnston at Shiloh, and the Confederate commander died in his arms during the battle. Courtesy Library of Congress.

Colonel Jacob Thompson was a Mississippi politician who had formerly served as secretary of the interior. He volunteered on Beauregard's staff at Shiloh. Courtesy Library of Congress.

Federal Colonel Julius Raith was mortally wounded while commanding a brigade in McClernand's division. His body was taken home to Belleville, Illinois, where this funeral procession took place. Courtesy David Raith.

This 1884 image shows Benjamin Prentiss, mounted at far left, at the spot where W. H. L. Wallace was mortally wounded. Others in the photo include J. S. Cavender, who commanded Wallace's artillery battalion, standing second from left; T. Lyle Dickey, Wallace's father-in-law and colonel of the 4th Illinois Cavalry, mounted fourth from left; James M. Tuttle, one of Wallace's brigade commanders, standing fifth from left; and Cuthbert W. Laing, who commanded a battery in Hurlbut's division, standing sixth from left. Courtesy Keith Brady.

15

"Very Hotly Engaged at an Early Hour"

P. G. T. Beauregard cost himself severely in not being in any position to dispute the enemy crossings of Dill and Tilghman branches. Once he began to get his bearings and realized what was happening, however, Beauregard fashioned a respectable battle line along the entire length of the Confederate army. The Creole marveled at how his tardy yet firm troops took the line: "From the outset our troops, notwithstanding their fatigue and loses from the battle of the day before, exhibited the most cheering, veteran-like steadiness." It was a good thing, given what was coming at them. The Confederate army would need all the steadiness it could muster.[1]

Many factors were out of his hands, though. Once again, the terrain at Shiloh dictated how and where the second day's major action would take place. The fighting raged through three broad phases on the first day, with the first tied to the southern set of creeks, the second and most vicious to the high ground between the southern and northern creeks, and the third to the northern creeks. This second day's action would be exactly the same, except in reverse. The Federals were now on the offensive, with the first phase taking place as they began to negotiate and cross the northern creeks. The difference here was that with the exception of Pond's limited defense, the Confederates did not dispute those crossings, as Sherman and Prentiss had done at Shiloh and Locust Grove branches the day before. Thus, all elements of both Federal armies were able to easily, if slowly, cross Dill and Tilghman branches, reaching the high ground on the southernmost half of the hourglass at an earlier hour.

The second phase of the second day, however, matched the second phase of the first day in every detail. Both took place roughly during the same part of the day, both raged all across the battlefield, and both involved all armies being fully committed. And once again, the heaviest and most vicious fighting raged on the high ground between the southern and northern creeks, the lower half of the hourglass. This was where the battle had slowed down the day before, with the entire Federal army making stands at the famous sites such as the Peach Orchard, Hornet's Nest, and Crossroads. On this second day, the fighting would again slow to a crawl as the armies battled in the same areas. In addition, just as it had been the day before when McClernand and Sherman had utilized counterattacks as major defensive tools, the second day's fighting would see the same tactics.

And in a morbid sense of injustice, one of the hardest-fighting Confederate brigades from the day before ushered in the major fighting on the second day.

James Chalmers was a jack-of-all-trades. He was a prewar lawyer in Mississippi, but like many others who made their fortunes in law, he was also a planter. He owned more than forty slaves on his DeSoto County plantation. In addition, he was a politician, having served as a delegate to the Mississippi secession convention in 1861. He was also a self-taught military man, serving as an officer in the prewar militia and then as colonel of the 9th Mississippi before taking brigade command. The ability of this self-taught tactician was evident in his hard fighting the day before, but Chalmers and his brigade served yet another role on the morning of April 7. He was the Confederate right's guinea pig.[2]

Most of the Confederate officers and men were still dawdling behind the lines; for example, Withers was putting his men through a convoluted series of marches that took him to the rear with the intention of moving to the left, where Pond and Ketchum were in action and making an awful noise. All the while, Chalmers and his Mississippians on the far right of the Confederate army served the same basic role that Pond played on the left. Having been left there by Withers, Chalmers was the foremost Confederate unit on the eastern side of the field. Withers called him the "rear guard until this otherwise fragmentary command could be worked into some shape." Even as the farthest unit to the front, however, Chalmers was still not in direct contact with the Federals, as

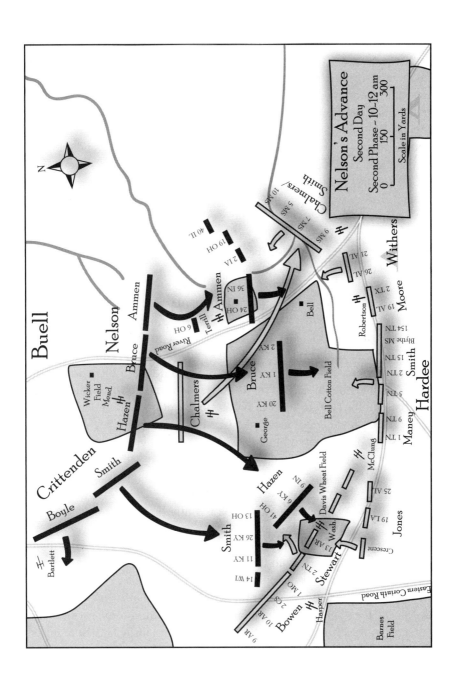

Buell

N

Nelson

Ammen

Bruce

River Road

Wicker Field Mead.

Hazen

Chalmers

Crittenden

Smith

Boyle

Bartlett

Smith

Hazen

13 OH

41 OH

6 KY

9 IN

Davis Wheat Field

26 KY

11 KY

14 WI

Stewart

13 AR Wash.

2 TN

Bowen

Harper

1 MO

2 GS

10 AR

9 AR

Eastern Corinth Road

Barnes Field

6 OH

Terrill

Ammen

24 OH

36 IN

40 IL

19 OH

21 IA

Chalmers / Smith

10 MS

7 MS

5 MS

9 MS

Withers

21 AL

26 AL

2 TX

Robertson

19 AL

Moore

154 TN

Blythe MS

15 TN

13 TN

2 TN

5 TN

9 TN

1 TN

Maney

Smith

Hardee

Bell

Bruce

2 KY

1 KY

20 KY

George

Bell Cotton Field

McClung

25 AL

19 LA

Crescent

Jones

Nelson's Advance
Second Day
Second Phase ~ 10–12 am

Scale in Yards
0   150   300

Pond had been at dawn; Beauregard's orders to fall back had been delivered to Chalmers but had not reached Pond. Thus Chalmers was not on the front at dawn, allowing Buell's troops to pass through Dill Branch ravine and reach the high ground without any opposition. They soon ran into Chalmers, however, first hitting Forrest's skirmishers at Cloud Field and then the brigade itself a little farther to the south. Chalmers reported that he planned to follow Withers to the left, "but before we could get away the enemy came charging rapidly upon us, and the fight of the second day commenced."[3]

Chalmers met the overpowering elements of Buell's three divisions around 9:00 A.M. and began to battle their advance. Most notably, the Mississippian placed a line in the woods just south of Wicker Field, hoping to delay Nelson in his effort to push the Union left forward. He sent word to Withers of his plight, whereupon the latter canceled his rearward movement just as it was completed, marching back to the initial bivouac positions to form a line. A grateful Chalmers later noted that Withers "was always found at the right place, at the right time, guiding and supporting whatever portion of his division needed assistance."[4]

Just organizing the division was a tall task for Withers. Chalmers's troops were well in hand, but Jackson's and Gladden's needed reorganization. In fact, Jackson was not even on site, although a portion of the brigade consisting mostly of the 19th Alabama and 2nd Texas took a position along the road in front of Sarah Bell's cotton field under the command of the Texans' colonel, John C. Moore. Joseph Wheeler reported that his troops were tired but animated by the firing to the front, calling it "such music as they loved." Adding weight to Moore's line on the right was a contingent of Gladden's brigade, although neither Gladden nor Adams, who had likewise been wounded the day before, were there. Zach Deas was also missing. He was fighting on the left with Russell, but the 21st and 26th Alabama took their posts on Moore's right, near where they had camped the night before. Eventually, the Alabamians connected with Chalmers to the east when the Mississippians later fell back, although their commanding officer, Lieutenant Colonel William D. Chadick, reported they went in "with very little efficiency, owing to the physical exhaustion of the men and the condition of our arms." The latter issue was most problematic for the Alabamians; Chadick reported that the powder in their loaded weapons had gotten wet in the night, and "I had not a ball-screw in the regiment and could not extract them." He reported that his men were "exceedingly dispirited" but still went on line and fought through two engagements as well as fire from the rear before Chadick reported his situation to Withers, who told him to go to the rear and take care of the problem. Chadick led the men backward and, still not having a ball puller, had his men unbreech and clean the barrels. Ironically, there was another regiment of Gladden's brigade only a quarter of a mile down the road to the west, the 25th Alabama, but the parts were never assembled in all the confusion. Nevertheless, Withers soon had elements of all his brigades in line and resisting the Union advance.[5]

Additional aid came to Withers's support as Chalmers delayed Nelson's advance and the minutes passed. William Hardee was on this right front, having spent the night to the rear in Prentiss's camps, and although he did not have any of his original corps with him, he soon took command of the sector. Other troops likewise arrived to bolster the line. Frank Cheatham's wayward division, which had marched all the way back to its bivouac site of April 5, had arrived on the field and was split, with Cheatham and a few units going on to the left but the bulk remaining on the right. Preston Smith, who had taken over for the wounded Bushrod Johnson the day before, went in on Moore's left in front of the cotton field and the mule lot with the 154th Tennessee, part of Blythe's Mississippians, and a small contingent of the 2nd Tennessee. To Smith's left was the other brigade of Cheatham's division. Maney's command consisted of the 1st and 9th Tennessee along with the 15th Tennessee of Smith's brigade and a small part of Blythe's Mississippi regiment, which asked to be attached. Maney had gotten his troops in line when the firing commenced, with the intention of finding Cheatham. Jones Withers found him first, however, and ordered Maney to gather any troops he could and support Chalmers on the far right. Maney wrote, "This order was accompanied with the information to me of a fierce attack by the enemy on General Withers and a pressing need of re-enforcement, and was not to be disregarded." An unhappy Cheatham later complained that he was deprived of Smith's men "through the orders on him of an officer ranking him." Also added to the line as the minutes ticked away were isolated regiments such as Gladden's Alabamians on Maney's left, A. P. Stewart's 5th Tennessee between Smith and Maney, and the 19th Louisiana of Gibson's brigade nearer to the Davis wheat field. Hardee also managed to place McClung's Tennessee Battery between the wheat field and cotton field and Robertson's Alabama guns on Moore's right. Federal reports mentioned more artillery than just Robertson's around

Chalmers's position, however, and some evidence indicates that Bankhead's Battery was on the right as well. In addition, one of the cannoneers in Swett's Mississippi Battery wrote in his diary that they engaged with Chalmers's troops on this second day. Whatever was there, by 10:00 A.M., it was a formidable line.[6]

It needed to be, because Buell was surging ahead, intent on breaking through whatever lay to his front. In fact, George Maney seemed to be over his unwanted change of command when he arrived on the front, stating he indeed found Withers "much in need of re-enforcement." Much like the initial Confederate attack of Hardee's corps the day before, however, Nelson's division was not properly aligned with the Confederate defense, which curved along the path of the Hamburg-Purdy Road, thus placing the Confederate right farther advanced than the rest of the line, with Chalmers's brigade even farther forward by itself at Wicker Field. Buell noted that "the obliquity of our line, the left being thrown forward, brought Nelson's division first into action, and it became very hotly engaged at an early hour." Indeed, the division approached the first major Confederate resistance not long after moving out of Cloud Field toward Wicker Field. With skirmishers out ahead, Nelson's three brigades moved in a southwesterly direction, bringing the right of Bruce's brigade and the left of Hazen's regiments to the edge of the field. There, they encountered Chalmers's Mississippians, supported by artillery, and had to alter the alignment somewhat as they were then nearly perpendicular to the enemy artillery.[7]

The first major contact came as Buell's divisions entered the Wicker Field area, with Nelson's three brigades moving obliquely to their right to stay on the high ground of the hourglass. In shifting up on the high ground, Ammen still had some of the upper reaches of the ravines to deal with, but his troops were no longer crossing the widest and deepest portions. The shift also sent Bruce and Hazen farther to the right, crossing over the River Road. By the time Nelson reached Wicker Field, Ammen was still completely east of the road, but Bruce had moved westward enough to straddle it and Hazen was completely west of the route, with his left at Wicker Field and his right extending into the woods toward Crittenden's troops. By 10:00 A.M., Nelson was thus in position near Wicker Field, steadily advancing but doing so cautiously. Even as the soldiers advanced, bullets began to pepper the area. One

Ohioan recalled that it sounded like a woodpecker pecking on trees. He later laughed at himself for "several involuntary dodgings made by my head to avoid the bullets which had already whistled past me." In what steadily grew almost to battle proportions, Nelson's skirmishers, particularly those of the 9th Indiana in Wicker Field under famed writer Ambrose Bierce, encountered more than they could handle on the south side. Bierce described how "we had expected to find, at most, a line of skirmishers similar to our own." He went on, "What we had found was a line of battle, coolly holding its fire till it could count our teeth." They had found Chalmers's Mississippians, far out ahead of Hardee's and Withers's developing line to the rear at the Hamburg-Purdy Road, but ready nevertheless. Chalmers reported that he "waited quietly until the enemy advanced within easy range, when we opened fire upon him and he fled." The nervous line of Federals hastily withdrew across the field. Bierce described the mud flying as bullets hit the ground around them. He also chuckled at one of the breathless officers of the skirmish line, who ran back and reported to his colonel, "The enemy is in force just beyond this field, sir."[8]

The result was heated skirmishing in Wicker Field. There were many more Federals than Confederates, but the stiff defense that Chalmers's Mississippians initially put up indicated the pluck that the Federals would run into as the day progressed. Chalmers also had some artillery with him, probably guns of Robertson's Alabama Battery or perhaps another unit nearby, even Swett's or Bankhead's, which Nelson's skirmishers claimed to have captured for a brief moment amid the fighting. Artillery fire from the main line to the rear also checked Nelson, who admitted, "My division began to give ground slowly." Yet the fighting cost Chalmers as well. Most notably, he lost Major F. E. Whitfield of the 9th Mississippi to a wound in the hip. Chalmers ominously reported to Beauregard's staff officer, Alexander Chisolm, then on a fact-finding mission concerning why Withers had moved, that he would be "obliged to fall back before a largely superior force" if not immediately supported.[9]

Nelson was ultimately able to push Chalmers away from Wicker Field when Chalmers's regiments exhausted their ammunition and retired all the way across the Bell cotton field to take a position on Moore's right rear around 11:00 A.M. There, taking a breather in the rear in Stuart's camps, the brigade found "an abundant supply [of ammunition] of the appropriate caliber." Chalmers's withdrawal allowed the Federals to proceed cautiously, however, with the whole confrontation around Wicker Field consuming considerable time. It also brought about a new factor in this second day's battle: the Confederate artillery. As Nelson's brigades tramped southward from Wicker Field, they came under heavy fire from the guns deployed on the Hamburg-Purdy Road, namely Robertson's Alabama and McClung's Tennessee batteries. Nelson immediately halted to figure out what to do. Lieutenant Dent of the Alabama battery provided a different perspective: "I could see the enemy running up following our men at about the second or third discharge I could see them turn and run the other way."[10]

Nelson's quandary came because he had no artillery of his own to combat the Confederate gunners. Because of the haste with which Nelson had moved to Pittsburg Landing and the route overland that he had taken the afternoon before, he had left all three of his artillery batteries in Savannah, to be brought down later. Nelson thus fired off a message to Buell asking for artillery support, and Buell was quick to respond. Crittenden and McCook had been able to bring along some of their artillery on the steamboats, and Buell sent Nelson two of the army's three batteries on the field, one each from McCook and Crittenden. Captain John Mendenhall's four guns of the combined Batteries H and M of the 4th United States Artillery of Crittenden's nearby division had first begun to move with their parent division, but Buell diverted them to the left. Mendenhall deployed his sections in separate areas but then gathered them together squarely in the middle of Wicker Field around 10:00 A.M., where he was quickly supported by Hazen's brigade in the field itself, the 41st Ohio and 6th Kentucky on the right and 9th Indiana on the left. Bruce's nearby brigade also supported the guns. Nelson told Bruce, the latter remembered, "This was one of the best batteries in the service and he would look to my Brigade to protect it." The battery opened on the Confederate guns across the field, although Mendenhall could only fire at "the smoke of his pieces" because the timber hid the enemy. Still, Nelson noted that their fire gave his division "most refreshing relief." Over the next few hours, Mendenhall dueled with several batteries, which often ceased firing and changed position, only to reopen fire. Mendenhall retained his position, although he did disperse his guns over a wider area to keep the incoming damage minimal. He also had to keep from firing into his own advancing columns.[11]

Also coming to Nelson's support was Captain William R. Terrill's Battery H of the 5th United States Artillery. It had farther to travel;

the battery was assigned to McCook's brigades farther to the right but had only landed at Pittsburg minutes before. When it deployed, however, it took a toll. Nelson described the battery as "a host in itself." Terrill quickly moved to the south and deployed one section to the right and two sections astride the River Road just northeast of a small pond around 10:00 A.M., where he found Nelson's division, in Terrill's words, "sorely pressed by the enemy." Covered by the 6th Ohio, it took on Robertson's Alabamians a little over a quarter mile to the south while the regiments of Sanders Bruce's brigade deployed in support astride the road. Bruce placed the 1st, 2nd, and 20th Kentucky in line facing southwest, watching the growing artillery duel, and Nelson rode up to the 6th Ohio of Ammen's brigade: "Colonel Anderson, I have conferred upon your regiment the honor of defending this battery, the best in the service. It must not be taken!" Nelson described the effect: "It was handled superbly. Wherever Captain Terrill turned his battery silence followed on the part of the enemy." Grateful for the assistance, Nelson rode to the 6th Ohio and in his customary short blurts (one Ohioan admitted, "He is no speech-maker") told them he was proud of them. Both Terrill and Nelson later sent handwritten thanks for the 6th Ohio's assistance. Unfortunately, one of the regiment's casualties was Heinrich Nortman, a member of one of the companies left at Savannah to guard the baggage. Nortman had made such a fuss that he was allowed to go with the regiment, and he was killed while acting as a skirmisher.[12]

Despite the action near the artillery, Nelson's far left brigade, Jacob Ammen's, soon became the focal point of the fighting. The 6th and 24th Ohio and 36th Indiana deployed east of the River Road in the woods, with the 6th Ohio in reserve with the guns and the other two on the front line, where they held the far left flank of the Union army. Their line, especially the left, faced a growing hollow that eventually turned into a ravine that fed into the river. Despite throwing out a strong body of skirmishers to the left, Buell was still concerned about the flank: "Though somewhat protected by rough ground, it was supposed the enemy might attempt to turn [it]." William Grose wrote home that the brigade actually changed front to the east in order to protect the flank, but upon encountering more of the enemy to the south, it changed front yet again to battle Confederates east of the River Road. Given what Chalmers had learned the day before about turning flanks in this area, Ammen was correct to be on alert.[13]

Despite the growing resistance, Nelson's division continued its south-westward movement, with Hazen's regiments filing out the southwest corner of Wicker Field and advancing across the left of the Hornet's Nest area toward the Davis wheat field. Bruce trudged forward toward the Peach Orchard, with Ammen on the left advancing east of the road. Approaching the northern edge of the Peach Orchard and cotton field that had seen so much action the day before as Hurlbut struggled to hold that left flank, Nelson pushed on ahead, sending his skirmishers forward to locate the enemy and annoy or even capture the artillery that was firing on the division. The heavy line of skirmishers, particularly from the 1st Kentucky of Bruce's brigade and the 9th Indiana of Hazen's, advanced toward the cotton field under orders to "annoy the cannon-eers" but wound up driving away the artillerymen and taking one of the guns before the Confederates could get back to their main line. Just as quickly, however, they had to give it up when the "largely-superior force of the enemy," according to Bruce, began to move forward.[14]

Nelson had stumbled into what strategy the Confederates could muster this early on the second day of battle. In what was developing as a Confederate plan, Beauregard had determined to continue attacking and still perhaps finish off what Johnston had started the day before. Thus, Beauregard ordered Breckinridge to be the chief attacker in the center, with Hardee to support the advance en echelon on the right. Beauregard ordered Hardee and Withers to advance with Breckinridge's attack, but Withers had trouble understanding the larger concept: Breckinridge "was neither then nor subsequently in that portion of the field," he sadly noted. Still, they advanced with the idea of connecting with Breckinridge: "We were then informed," one Alabamian wrote home, "that Genl Breckinridge was driving the enemy before him & up the river & we were with some other regiments, to attack them in the flank."[15]

Hardee thus issued orders for his Confederate lines to advance and counterattack Nelson's troops across the cotton field and beyond, including in the woods to the west around the wheat field and Mendenhall's guns. It would be the first day all over again, with the Confederates trying to drive the enemy back from the ridge in the midst of the field. Hurlbut had found it to be a good defensive position the day before as the Confederates of Breckinridge's corps launched attack after attack without success. Only with the personal leadership of Albert Sidney

Johnston had they been successful, but alas, there was no Johnston on the field today. It was William Hardee.[16]

Unfortunately, Hardee was no Johnston—at least not on this second day of Shiloh. He nevertheless sent his mixture of troops forward in what became successive assaults; some counted as many as three different advances. In the end, Bruce's Kentuckians held firm in the cotton field and Ammen's regiments held their own for a while to the east. Still, the Confederate offensive gained Buell's attention, with the general reporting that Nelson's division was "very heavily pressed by the greater numbers of the enemy."[17]

Much of the faltering of the Confederate assaults was primarily due to a growing series of issues, including the mounting hunger and exhaustion of the troops. Bragg remarked that the men "fought bravely, but with the want of that animation and spirit which characterized them the preceding day." Falling numbers also took a toll, with Bragg estimating that the entire army on line on this second day was but "half our force." He added, "Many instances of daring and desperate valor, deserving of better success, failed for want of numbers."[18]

There was also major confusion about who was who. The lingering smoke on this breezeless morning after the rain added to the confusion. John C. Moore reported that an officer rode up and "inquired for General Withers," whereupon Moore asked "from whom I received this order." The answer came back: "General Hardee." After issuing orders and then changing his mind, Hardee gave orders to Moore to advance across the field but not to fire, as Breckinridge would be to his front. As Moore advanced, with the regiments of Gladden's brigade still on the right, he was continually cautioned by Hardee's staff officers not to fire on Breckinridge's men. Even when Moore's troops developed Bruce's and Ammen's brigades to the front—and they certainly looked like Federals—he received orders not to fire. The disastrous episode resulted in Moore's regiments taking an almost point-blank volley from Nelson's troops, which staggered the command and halted any advance. A member of the 21st Alabama wrote, "We also understood that we were in the 2nd line of battle, but we soon found that we were in the first." Moore called it a "truly sad mistake" and reported that "so sudden was the shock and so unexpected was the character of our supposed friends, that the whole line soon gave way from right to left in utter confusion. The regiments became so scattered and mixed that all efforts to reform

them became fruitless." Sam Houston Jr., who was wounded in the upper thigh or groin on this second day, also explained the surprise: "The
fence before us became transformed into a wall of flame." A sudden
volley of musketry from the rear did not help matters on the right where
Gladden's Alabamians were. Charles Stewart of the 21st Alabama related, "I hear that the Col was making a Speech & his men were excited
& understood him to say fire[.] this done our Regiment a great deal of
harm—it was bad enough to be killed by our enemies." It was such a
crisis that Chalmers had to bring up his brigade under Robert A. Smith
from a quick rest to support the new line. Yet even Chalmers's stalwart
Mississippians were taken in by the chaos and had to fall back to the
original line along the high ground around the Hamburg-Purdy Road,
some 400 yards from the Union position.[19]

Unfortunately for the Confederates, Hardee was still misinformed
and not happy about the break in his line. He blamed it on the 2nd Texas,
which already had many command problems. Moore was commanding
the rest of Jackson's brigade, and the regiment fought under Lieutenant
Colonel William P. Rogers, who had just arrived the day before. It took
him a while to get back into the swing of command. He initially could
not even find his unit and spent the first few hours on Breckinridge's
staff until he ran across his Texans, who "greeted me with a shout,"
Rogers wrote. On this second day of battle, he was now in command in
the chaos around Sarah Bell's cotton field.[20]

Making the situation worse, Hardee acted as the antithesis of Johnston's leadership the day before. Instead of buoying his men's morale
and spirits, he took aim at them instead of the enemy. When the Texans
recoiled, Hardee declared them to be a "pack of cowards" and sent his
staff officer, Captain William Clare, to reform them. Clare was wounded
in the attempt, and the episode landed Moore under arrest after the battle and caused Hardee many problems as well, especially when Texas
senator Louis Wigfall came to Moore's defense and Mississippi senator
James Phelan also became involved. Moore was miffed about several
things, including Hardee giving orders directly to the regiments instead
of "through myself as commander of the brigade." Even worse, one of
Hardee's staff officers upbraided one of the Texans who had dared to
fire at the perceived friends ahead. Moore reported that the staff officer
"rode up and drew his pistol, threatening to blow off the man's head if
he fired again." The biggest issue, though, was the coward remark. The
story got out, through a mistaken Senator Phelan, that the Texans had

fired on Hardee; unfortunately, Phelan had interwoven two episodes. Apparently Hardee reprimanded another regiment that day as well, and, intent on taking no such tongue-lashing, the soldiers about-faced and fired a single volley over the heads of Hardee and his staff before turning back around and continuing the fight. Hardee later told Phelan, "I expected to be riddled." When Phelan mixed up that episode with the 2nd Texas incident, a vast misunderstanding developed.[21]

Moore's men were not the only ones who had advanced in the debacle, however. The just-arriving Preston Smith reported that Chalmers, now acting as a larger unit commander and leaving his brigade under Robert A. Smith of the 10th Mississippi, met him and "led my command in person to the point where he most needed support." Chalmers gave him precious little time to get acclimated; Smith advanced immediately upon taking position and drove the front-ranging Federals back, although "at a considerable loss in killed and wounded on our side." Similarly, Maney's regiments advanced as soon as they came on line: "I immediately ordered my whole line to the charge," he wrote, "and it was made with spirit." Neither could go farther, however, probably only driving skirmishers back, then falling back as a result of exhaustion and Federal fire. The troops went into line at the Hamburg-Purdy Road, where Withers rode by and shouted at Maney "to remain at and hold it at all hazards." Bloody Shiloh was becoming a tactical stalemate.[22]

Although Hardee's attacks were stalled on the cotton field front, Chalmers's reorganized Mississippians to the right did have some success, mainly because they were able to take advantage of the open Union left flank. Chalmers, who was back with his men by now, noted, "Believing that one bold charge might change the fortunes of the day, I called upon my brigade to make one more effort, but they seemed too much exhausted to make the attempt, and no appeal seemed to arouse them." Then Chalmers took the 9th Mississippi's flag in hand and called on his men to follow, which they did with "a wild shout." In the same advance, Colonel Joseph Wheeler took the colors of the 19th Alabama and led his regiment forward on foot.[23]

The advance was successful because Ammen's brigade on the far Union left was not as tucked into the folds of the ravines bordering the river as David Stuart and John McArthur had been the day before, and Chalmers's Mississippians, who had been eventually successful even against those odds the day before, knew an opportunity when they saw one. The Mississippians thus began to hit Ammen's left flank, with Scottish colonel Robert Smith's "clarion voice," Chalmers remembered, being heard "above the din of battle cheering on his men." He hoped once again to turn the line and force the Federals back; Colonel William Grose of the 36th Indiana remarked on the "continuous efforts to turn our left." In this attack, Lieutenant Colonel William A. Rankin, commanding the 9th Mississippi, went down with a mortal wound.[24]

As a result, Ammen had to halt his advance and even withdraw toward Wicker Field. Buell noted that Ammen was "checked for some time by his endeavor to turn our left flank." Even Terrill's artillerymen had to withdraw for a short time under the Confederate threat, leaving a caisson on the field. He had sent his four left guns to the skirmish line, but they soon found it too hot, with Terrill reporting that the firing was "most galling." The gunners fell back, alternatingly doing so by section with "fixed prolonge," whereby the guns were pulled rearward by rope while still being worked on the move. Nevertheless, Chalmers reported that he actually retook his original position of the morning. The crisis soon ended, however, as reinforcements came up on Ammen's left, some from the much-reviled Army of the Tennessee. W. H. L. Wallace's division had been so decimated the day before that it was held in reserve on this day, most of it, inexplicably including the artillery, not taking part in the army's advance on the Union right. Buell nevertheless called up what regiments did advance to form on Ammen's left, including the 2nd Iowa of Tuttle's brigade, which had helped hold the Hornet's Nest line in Duncan Field the day before, and the 40th Illinois of McDowell's unit. Several veterans of Ammen's brigade stated that the 15th Illinois was also on the line. Later, support from the 19th Ohio of Boyle's brigade of Crittenden's division also helped. The Iowans and others dove into the ravine-infested area east of Ammen's position and quickly secured the flank from Chalmers's charging Mississippians. It was fortunate that so many reserves were available; Terrill reported, "We checked their advance three times." Ammen thus held. The bombastic Nelson uncharacteristically wrote that his stellar defense "gave me a profitable lesson in the science of battle."[25]

Amazingly, Ammen attempted to advance in the midst of it all. Despite facing an unidentified Confederate battery and Chalmers's Mississippians east of the road, the 36th Indiana and 24th Ohio pushed back across the small field east of the River Road and the Peach Orchard, utilizing the fences on each side for cover. The 24th Ohio unfortunately found the distance too great for their muskets to take effect. Lieutenant Colonel Frederick C. Jones reported, "We found the range too great for our muskets, many of the balls striking the ground in front of the enemy, while theirs, fired from the best rifles, flew past us like hail." William Grose of the 36th Indiana was not pleased with the delay, however, ordering a "fat Captain," lying behind a fence, to attack. The Ohio officer refused. Grose called one of his own companies to take the buildings, and the regiments made a dash across the field, some seventy-five yards, with the cover of a few small buildings aiding their advance. In the process they captured some prisoners and a few flags the enemy had captured the day before. In the advanced position, the Ohioans' muskets took effect, but the 36th Indiana soon exhausted their ammunition and had to fall back. Ammen ordered the Ohioans, now "some distance in the advance of the main line of our army," rearward to the south side of the field as well. Casualties were high, including the 24th Ohio's major A. S. Hall, and the entire back-and-forth fighting consumed a couple of hours. The wounded Colonel Grose won the admiration of many men, however. One Ohioan wrote, "He placed himself in front of his regiment, and in the thickest of the fight, between the two fires, and urged on his men, until his horse was shot and himself wounded." The soldier continued, "Even then he could not be prevailed upon to drop to the rear, but sword in hand, still encouraged his men by his presence."[26]

At the same time, Nelson also pushed his other brigades forward, and the center of the division soon met the reformed Confederate line south of the cotton field. The attack mainly fell to Bruce's Kentuckians, but they were, not surprisingly, checked in the open expanse. Colonel Thomas D. Sedgewick of the 2nd Kentucky nevertheless rallied his troops and pressed forward, driving toward the small skirt of woods and the mule lot that Bowen's Confederates had used as cover the day before. "Gaining the edge of the thicket," Sedgewick wrote, "the fight became almost hand to hand. Here the slaughter on both sides was terrible." The Kentuckians advanced so far as to momentarily take the guns of Robertson's battery, but a vicious Confederate counterattack by portions of Jackson's and Gladden's brigades turned the Federals back and retook the guns. Sedgewick described how the Confederates "made a desperate effort to obtain possession of our colors." He also reported how his regiment fought its way back out to the right, emerging with only about a third of the men in formation, "but with our colors safe, although riddled with grape and musket-balls." The regiment eventually reformed in the rear.[27]

Jacob Smith, a captain in the 2nd Kentucky, gave a vivid description of the fighting and his wounding. While advancing toward the battery, he was hit in the hip by a ball. "The shock of a musket ball striking one in the hip has about the same feeling as if a person is struck with a blunt instrument or club, and produces a paralyzing sensation," he wrote. He at first thought someone had hit him with a musket, "and for an instant was rather angry at an imaginary assailant, but remembering that I had called out to a man in gray uniform who was pointing his gun toward me to drop his piece, as well as feeling warm blood running down my leg, soon convinced me that the Confederate soldier had not obeyed my order as promptly as I know my own men would have done." Smith later wrote, "My only fear for myself was that I would bleed to death, but by the use of a silk handkerchief I stopped the outside flow of blood by pushing the soft silk cloth into the entrance and exit of the bullet."[28]

The same story occurred in Bruce's other regiments. In the 1st Kentucky, David Jones wrote that Buell urged them forward. "Just as the regt got to the brow of the hill," he continued, "a terrible fire of grape, canister, and musketry was opened upon us, which staggered our line, and committed dreadful havoc among us." The regiment lost sixty men in the attack; like the others, it had to withdraw "after a half hours hard fighting."[29]

The fighting was thus extremely heavy. S. H. Dent of Robertson's Battery back on the Hamburg-Purdy Road illustrated the number of close calls among his men. He had a splinter scratch his nose but came close to much worse damage. "I had on a yankee hat with a feather in it and it (the feather) was cut off and Robertson says it must have been done by a ball—for he said he looked at me and saw the feather and a moment after it was gone and bullets were flying round thick—I knew nothing of it myself until some time after—I do not think there are ten men in the company who did not have some such narrow escape."[30]

Nelson's unsuccessful advance into Bell's cotton field opened up an additional issue for his division. As Bruce's brigade fell back to a line north of the cotton field, the lay of the land provided cover from frontal fire. A Kentuckian wrote home that they were "in an orchard in range of the enemies battery but protected by a slight elevation from their fire." However, the position also allowed Confederate artillery in the Davis wheat field to rake the line from the west. The Hamburg-Purdy Road took a sharp bend to the northwest just west of the cotton field, and so did the Confederate line. Hazen's troops to the west thus encountered Hardee's and even the right of Breckinridge's line father north than did the rest of the division, causing them to pull up shorter than Bruce and Ammen, who advanced until the same level of resistance stopped them farther south. Hazen had to wheel his brigade to the right—"a half change to front to the right," in his words—to align with the Confederates position. Thus the Washington Artillery, deployed in the wheat field, was able to fire almost due eastward down the line of Bruce's regiments in the cotton field. Buell reported the battery was "flanking the fields in front of Nelson," and casualties began to mount as Nelson decided what to do.[31]

As time ticked away toward noon, the battle on the far Confederate right had ground down, with both immovable sides watching one another and with little territory changing hands. The reinforcements and artillery support had secured Ammen's left, and both Ammen and Bruce were secure in their position along the northern border of the cotton field and in the woods to the east. Stragglers were beginning to leave the ranks, however, forcing Bruce to ride to the hospital in the rear and drive them back to the main line. Others were busy in the rear as well. Lieutenant Charles C. Horton, Nelson's ordinance officer, was bringing up additional ammunition to fill the men's cartridge boxes. Yet that did not mean they had the strength to oust the Confederates, who were almost just as secure in their Hamburg-Purdy Road line. They too had artillery support and a clear field of fire to discourage any Union advance. Despite several bloody assaults from both sides, the fighting in this sector lessened because neither side saw any reason for futile charges.[32]

Lessons were abundant as the two armies ground to a stalemate on the eastern side of the battlefield. The Confederates learned quickly that they were not facing the same old battered Army of the Tennessee alone. The sheer numbers that Grant was able to throw at them that morning, "pouring them continually upon us," Hardee noted, took them by surprise, and they were not privy to the information that even more Union brigades were on the way.[33]

The Federals learned lessons as well. If there was any thought that the Confederates might be unable to continue, the notion was quickly quashed as Hardee put up a major line of battle that effectively halted the Union advance in its tracks. Buell's forces had proceeded easily for a mile, but there was little Confederate resistance in the area at the time. When they ran up on the first major Confederate defensive line along the Hamburg-Purdy Road, however, all stopped. Hardee recognized this semimiracle as well, writing that "the battle reanimated our men, and the strong columns of the enemy were repulsed again and again by our tired and disordered, but brave and steadfast, troops."[34]

And not only were the Confederates putting up a strong defense, they were also counterattacking. The numerous assaults across the Bell cotton field hearkened to the attacks of the previous day, and Chalmers's flanking attempts, though ultimately unsuccessful, likewise illustrated the Confederates' offensive potential. The Confederates were certainly not giving in to such massive Union numbers. At worst, they were holding their own; at best, they were showing amazing offensive capability, considering their current state after the long day of battle the day before. One Tennessean noted, "We could drive the enemy before us as easily as on Sunday, but when a successful charge was made on those in front we would find ourselves threatened on the flank and rear by hosts of the enemy and were compelled to fall back to keep from being surrounded by them."[35]

The result was a stalemate on the eastern side. It would only be canceled when an outside factor produced changes to the dynamic of the battle. And although it was too early to tell whether it would be that change in dynamic, even heavier action to the west of the cotton field was now emerging. The right of Nelson's division, Hazen's brigade, and Crittenden's division had found a hornet's nest themselves around the Davis wheat field.[36]

16

"UP TO THE MOUTHS OF THE GUNS"

John C. Breckinridge had traveled a long way from the halls of Congress to the muddy fields of Shiloh. As a senator from Kentucky and vice president of the United States just a few years earlier, Breckinridge was a national figure who had come in second in the 1860 presidential race, losing to Abraham Lincoln. The war that the election then sparked called Breckinridge to service in the military, and he rose through the ranks to command the Confederate reserve at Shiloh. He had helped break the Federal left the day before, but now Breckinridge, along with his consolidated corps of three brigades, was tapped to play the starring role on this second day.[1]

Beauregard had always planned on renewing the battle on April 7, although many factors changed the dynamics by dawn—namely that Grant had received fresh troops. Yet Beauregard was still in an offensive mind-set, and despite a slow, stuttered start to the morning's operations, he was ready to make his major attack. He hoped this assault would blunt whatever these new circumstances threw at him, with the continual hope of still driving Grant to destruction or surrender.[2]

Breckinridge would be his hammer. Little is known of Beauregard's reasoning, but it could have been that Breckinridge's command was the most organized of his four corps, with all three brigades in line next to one another with their original commander. Although that was indeed the case, control of the corps was still questionable in that Breckinridge's left brigade, under Robert Trabue, was still somewhat detached, mostly north of the Corinth Road. Trabue reported taking orders from Bragg and Polk more than he did from Breckinridge, his own corps commander. Part of Beauregard's planning might also have been the result of terrain awareness. Having no doubt heard from his commanders, especially Bragg and Hardee, about the major ravines on the left and right of his line, Beauregard perhaps opted to make his attack in the center where the Shiloh divide offered ample level ground over which he could advance. As Breckinridge's troops occupied that ground, it made sense to use his most organized corps on the most favorable terrain.[3]

Thus orders went out, particularly to Hardee on the right, to advance but to watch for Breckinridge's major attack that would roll forward in the center. Hardee was then to continue the attack, indicating Beauregard's continued wish to push Grant back into the river; it was simply a continuation of his plan from the day before. Matters became confused with Buell's advance, however, forcing Hardee to engage much more quickly than planned while Breckinridge took some time to work out the details of his attack. The confusion of who was who in the Peach Orchard area thus led to friendly fire as well as surprise, as the soldiers of the 2nd Texas discovered.[4]

Still, the fighting on Breckinridge's front began nearly as early as elsewhere, with specific orders from Beauregard to advance and attack in conjunction with the remainder of the army. Beauregard staff officer Alexander Chisolm took orders to Breckinridge to advance and attack along with Hardee to the right, but to "communicate with Genl Hardee so that there might be no accident from firing into our friends." Hardee had received the same orders, but the attacks were not coordinated. Breckinridge balked at the order and protested that, in Chisolm's words, "he should obey your [Beauregard's] order, but he thought that he was leaving his left and rear exposed to a large force of the enemy." Chisolm rode to Beauregard for clarification, and the general sent additional troops to Breckinridge's left. Breckinridge also corralled any troops he could, such as Cleburne's arriving brigade, and ordered him to attack with him on his left. The delay in the attack resulted in Breckinridge advancing a little later and with much less force than Hardee did on the right. The simultaneous advance of Hazen's and Smith's brigades into the wheat field also completely upset the plan; it succeeded in disconnecting any cooperation between Hardee and Breckinridge. Heavy fighting thus raged as Breckinridge's troops moved forward, with the right brigade under John D. Martin advancing and becoming involved in the fighting on Hardee's left just east of the Eastern Corinth Road.[5]

Today, William B. Hazen is one of the more recognizable names of the Civil War—not so much for what he did but because he was in the right place at the right time. Hazen certainly saw his share of military action; he graduated from West Point and fought Indians on the frontier before the war. During the Civil War, he is most noted for commanding the brigade that defended the Round Forest during the heavy fighting at Stones River in December 1862. He saw additional action throughout the western theater, including the bloodbath at Chickamauga and the more finessed campaigns on Atlanta and to the sea.[6]

Nevertheless, Hazen's defense of the Round Forest near Murfreesboro led to his name being inscribed in the memory of the nation. After the battle, in 1863, members of his brigade garrisoned the area and built a monument to their dead on the ground they had defended. Today, millions of Civil War buffs and tourists have visited the Hazen Brigade monument, which holds the distinction of being the oldest in-place Civil War monument in the nation. But Stones River was not Hazen's baptism of fire in the Civil War. He and his Ohio troops faced that rite of passage nearly a year earlier, when they met John Breckinridge and William Hardee in Shiloh's wheat field.[7]

Thus far, Hazen's brigade had not been engaged in Nelson's fighting to the left. Ammen and Bruce had been the recipients of Confederate fire along the southern side of the Bell cotton field, and they were stalled. Moreover, Chalmers's Mississippians were threatening their left flank, which quashed many of the offensive notions Nelson may have had; he could not advance and drive the enemy when they were threatening to turn his own flank and drive him back. Matters soon settled into long-range firefights and artillery duels on the Union left. Meanwhile, Crittenden's two brigades had moved into line on Nelson's right, taking position on the tall ridge immediately behind the Hornet's Nest. Smith and Boyle were moving toward a line on the ridge overlooking Duncan Field, where the Federal artillery of Wallace's division had covered the infantry the day before until being driven off by Ruggles's massed guns. It was also here that the defenders of the Hornet's Nest had formed a line of battle in the opposite direction, trying to fight their way out of the encircling mass of Confederates.[8]

Unfortunately for them, Hazen's troops, as well as Crittenden's coming up on his right, did not have the luxury of such a relatively straight and stable line as did the rest of Nelson's brigades. With the 9th Indiana on the left and the 6th Kentucky on the right, and with nine companies of the 41st Ohio in reserve (one company had been left in Savannah to guard the trains), Hazen's movement diagonally to the southwest originally took him into and west of Wicker Field. The continued movement brought the brigade west of the Peach Orchard, with only the 9th Indiana breaking into the clearing around the William Manse George cabin in the extreme northwest corner of the large clearing that included the orchard and the old cotton field. There the Indianans were subjected to a heavy fire while out in the open. Enemy artillery rounds hit the cabin, splintering and moving logs amid the Federals. The Indianans quickly continued forward diagonally and sought the cover of the timber west of the field, with Nelson riding among them and thanking them for their gallantry. The 41st Ohio and 6th Kentucky had no such problems as they advanced through the woods to the west, although the scene itself was enough to give them pause. Here in the heavy underbrush near the left of the Hornet's Nest, heavy fighting had raged the day before and fires had broken out, burning the wounded and dead alike.[9]

While advancing west of Bruce and Ammen, however, Hazen soon found an anomaly that would play large in the fighting. The Confederate line followed the Hamburg-Purdy Road on the Confederate right all the way westward past the cotton field, but there it began to veer to the northwest, leaving the road and taking a line in the Hornet's Nest and onward to Jones Field. The early resistance by Pond's brigade had allowed the Confederate defense to take a more forward position on the left than it had on the right. Because the Confederate line bent near the Davis wheat field, the left of Nelson's division was able to proceed farther southward than Hazen and Crittenden, thus causing the Union line to draw back toward the northwest. Hazen was the angle of the line; Bruce and Ammen faced southward, but Hazen could not proceed without hitting a major Confederate force. Hazen thus stopped to change his front, an effort that was complicated when the 6th Kentucky had trouble getting all its companies into a coordinated effort. Hazen, along with one of Buell's staff officers, rode to the problem spot and led the wayward four companies to their correct positions. Once aligned, Hazen led his brigade forward through the thick underbrush, which soon began to take a toll on orderliness. "All semblance of organization was lost in the grand rush," one private recorded; "a change of direction took place early in the advance which tended to complicate matters still more and complete the disorder in the ranks." Thus Hazen halted again to align his front at a rearward angle with the rest of the division, which allowed the Confederate battery in the wheat field to rake Nelson's brigades to the east in the flank. Such a development helped stop the Federal advance in the cotton field, with Nelson describing the "battery which so distressed us." In an effort to gain some relief as well as present a solid front to support Hazen, Bruce soon turned the 1st Kentucky to the right in the western portion of the cotton field, which it did amid heavy fire, and sent the reserve 20th Kentucky forward to support the right as well.[10]

Hazen knew better than to plunge ahead without any support, however, especially because he had only three regiments, and one of them, the 9th Indiana, had taken casualties both in Wicker Field and in the opening near the George cabin. The regiment had been the hinge; it still faced southward while the Ohioans and Kentuckians to their right had bent their line back to conform to the enemy's line. The famed Emerson Opdycke wrote his wife that the backward move nevertheless took care of the problem momentarily: Hazen "most effectually baffled them by changing front skillfully and opportunely." Still, Hazen had little artillery support as Mendenhall's four guns remained in the rear in Wicker Field before later moving forward to Hazen's right to support Crittenden's division. Hazen, it seemed, was caught in a vortex.[11]

Fortunately for him, Hazen did have support. The line to the east containing Bruce and Ammen was stable, if not able to move forward, and Crittenden was moving up on Hazen's right, securing that flank as well. William "Sooy" Smith's brigade trailed along Hazen's right and rear, facing west, with the 13th Ohio on the left, the 26th Kentucky on the right, and the 11th Kentucky in reserve. Adding to Smith's strength was an element of Grant's army, the 14th Wisconsin. This regiment had arrived at the landing during the night and had taken a position near Smith's troops' bivouac. With no orders the next morning, the regiment advanced with Buell's forces and fought with them all day. The Wisconsin infantry went in on Smith's right, next to the Kentuckians. Crittenden's other brigade, Boyle's, moved forward as well to Smith's right rear, nearer to McCook's troops.[12]

It was fortunate that Hazen had such support, because he fronted not only part of the thicket south of the Hornet's Nest that had given so much trouble to the Confederates the day before, but also the angle of the Confederate line, where, bent as it was around him, he could conceivably take fire from three directions. Such a position seemed ill-suited to attack, but the Confederate battery raking Nelson's line to the east was not letting up and the brigades down the line had to have some relief.[13]

Moreover, Breckinridge had finally gotten his brigades moving forward, and that meant Martin's Confederate line was moving on Hazen and Smith diagonally from a position near the Eastern Corinth Road. Martin's initial advance gained ground; Marshall Smith of the Crescent Regiment described how the Federal skirmishers on his front withdrew upon the Confederate advance. Martin pursued the enemy "entirely across an old field." Federal commanders were also adamant that the Confederate line was advancing. Ambrose Bierce wrote, "A great gray cloud seemed to spring out of the forest into the faces of the waiting battalions." Hazen similarly wrote, "The enemy was now heard to be advancing upon our new front," and Colonel Walter C. Whitaker described the "boldly advancing rebels." Numerous officers, including Hazen, Lieutenant Colonel George S. Mygatt of the 41st Ohio, and Colonel Gideon Moody of the 9th Indiana, all reported Martin's diagonal attack threatening their right flank, which was open as a result of Smith's brigade still being to the right rear. Even worse, Confederate artillery in the form of the Washington gunners was following up the Confederate advance and, despite an unfortunate friendly fire incident from the rear, fired heavily into the Union lines.[14]

Emerson Opdycke of the 41st Ohio perceptively wrote, "This would not do long." The Federal line was prone but quickly leaped to its feet to meet the enemy advance, with cries of "Rise up 41st . . . Fire, Fire" ringing among the Ohioans. Yet simply holding was not all Hazen envisioned. Faced with such issues, he decided to meet the assault with an advance of his own, and soon the words "Charge bayonets 41st" rang out. Hazen thus began to assault toward the wheat field. The result would be some of the most vicious fighting at Shiloh; veteran and historian David W. Reed described it as the "most stubborn" fighting of the second day.[15]

The Confederate line facing Hazen was actually two lines. The first consisted of Martin's brigade of Breckinridge's corps forming the front as it advanced ahead of Hardee's left. It angled off toward the northwest with the rest of the corps. The second line south of the wheat field was technically under Hardee's command, although the corps commander remained closer to the right of his line near the cotton field. This formidable second line west of McClung's Battery included a hodgepodge of units, such as the 25th Alabama and 19th Louisiana of Gladden's and Gibson's brigades, respectively, on the right. The Louisianans were yet another regiment claimed unilaterally by Withers and initially sent to the right. Chalmers had placed the Louisianans' colonel, B. L. Hodge, in charge of his own regiment as well as the nearby Crescent Regiment and the 25th Alabama. Although a part of Pond's brigade, the Crescent Regiment likewise had been detached and was not with the brigade on the far left at dawn. It received specific orders from Beauregard to move to the right. On the left of the line under A. P. Stewart sat Bate's 2nd Tennessee and the 13th Arkansas from Cleburne's and Stewart's brigades, with Harper's Mississippi Battery deployed at the crossing of the Eastern Corinth and Hamburg-Purdy roads. Captain Smith P. Bankhead also arrived with two pieces of artillery to support Stewart. In the center was the main firepower, however, consisting of the Washington Artillery. The New Orleans artillerymen, as well as McClung's guns to the east, were the ones raking Nelson's line to their right. This entire line formed as a second reserve force in the field behind the main line of Breckinridge's advancing corps.[16]

If Hazen had any thought that this Confederate force might be tired and melt before his attack, he should have looked to his right and left. Nelson had met a determined Confederate line near the cotton field that was not showing any signs of breaking and was actually counterattacking. To his right, Crittenden's troops were beginning to confront a powerful line in that area as well, and indeed Breckinridge's Confederates there would soon be on the attack. Hazen had perhaps the most troublesome position, however: he was where the Confederate line bent, allowing a converging crossfire to rake his regiments. Further, the Confederates were determined; they "greeted us with perfect showers of canister and cries of 'Bulls Run,'" remembered one Federal.[17]

Hazen was still determined to attack as well, and he soon did. By 11:00 A.M., his skirmishers had uncovered the approaching Confederate line, but skirmishers could only do so much. Hazen soon ordered his regiments into the breach, assaulting the Confederate line to drive it back and perhaps even capture or at least drive away the Washington Artillery that was causing so much havoc. Led by capable officers, including Captain J. M. Wright of Buell's staff, who led one of Hazen's regiments, the blue line of Hazen's brigade began to surge forward. One amazed Ohioan wrote, "The distinctive feature of this engagement was that neither force was in position, but advancing, when the firing began."[18]

Fortunately for Hazen's men, Smith's brigade next in line also advanced, although it took some time to turn obliquely to the left from its westward-facing orientation and get properly aligned for the heavy fighting in the wheat field. William Sooy Smith's three regiments nevertheless soon advanced with the 13th Ohio and 26th Kentucky in the front line and 11th Kentucky in reserve, and all saw there would be rough fighting ahead. Buell happened by and ordered the 13th Ohio's adjutant to scout ahead, where he found "their line of skirmishers creeping slowly through the grass in an open field before us." He reported the advance and the brigade readied to fight, at which time a young Ohioan tried to give an officer his money to be sent home in the event of his death. Frank Jones refused, replying, "I could offer no especial security against loss, for I was just as liable as he to be shot." Jones recommended giving it to the surgeon. The man did so, and he was hit in the forehead and killed instantly only minutes later.[19]

Despite the oblique turn, Smith soon led his regiments forward into the thicket extending south from the Hornet's Nest, leaving a gap in the line to the right to be filled by Boyle's reserve brigade. Yet Smith had farther to go and did not advance as quickly or as far as Hazen. Still, Smith's brigade plunged in on the right of Hazen's troops, actually crowding the 26th Kentucky out of line. It wound up behind the 13th Ohio of Smith's unit and the 6th Kentucky of Hazen's. Indeed, all three regiments began to intermingle in the chaos of the attack. Lieutenant Colonel Cicero Maxwell of the 26th Kentucky noted, "Such was the density of the thicket through which we passed, the rapidity of the charge, and the enthusiasm of the soldiers, that the regiments became mixed together."[20]

Hazen's regiments were up to the task, however, and remained better organized, especially his left, where the 41st Ohio drove against the Louisiana guns. They lost four color-bearers while advancing toward Martin's Confederate line, which they soon drove back toward the Confederate guns. At one point, Captain Emerson Opdycke grabbed the flag and carried it forward until another captain who ranked him made him give the honor to the senior officer. Yet the Ohioans were taking massive fire; Opdycke told his wife, "It seemed to me that a thousand bullets passed within an inch of my head every moment." Opdycke soon came upon the very captain who had taken the flag from him; he was down with a leg wound. Opdycke wound a handkerchief around the leg to stop the bleeding, but not without "the blood spurting over me plentifully." In the second Confederate line, the confused command situation on this part of the field showed as single regiments of at least five brigades— Gladden's, Gibson's, Pond's, Stewart's, and Cleburne's—held the wheat field, with batteries of two other brigades also in the line, the Washington Artillery of Anderson's and Harper's of Wood's brigade. It was a hodgepodge of units, but with Martin's retreat, they were now the front line. They nevertheless put up an effective and devastating fire. One Federal remembered the Confederate "line of battle, in front of a row of tents. Officers were riding up and down the line, waving swords and shouting."[21]

Despite the growing success, Hazen took heavy casualties in the effort, most coming from two sources. One was the well-served Confederate artillery. Irving Hodgson's cannoneers in the field tore great swaths in Hazen's line, and Harper's Mississippians tore at the flank from their position near the crossing of the two roads to the west. McClung's Battery on Hazen's left also hit the Federals hard. The other source of disaster for Hazen's troops was the angle of the Confederate line. When his troops went in, they approached the curve of the Confederate line, allowing units on both ends to rake them in the flank. Most of the time, a commander would gladly maneuver to be able to position his troops on the enemy's flank, but the lay of the land and the Confederate line created the situation that Hazen walked into. Nelson agreed, noting, "The woodland in front of us at times [was] a sheet of flame."[22]

The miraculous part was that Hazen, despite taking artillery fire and being outflanked on his right as well as on his left, although at a much greater distance, was able to drive forward to the guns of the Washington Artillery. While the Kentuckians on the right were taking heavy fire, the Indianans and Ohioans to the east were steadily advancing, with the 41st Ohio actually approaching the muzzles of the guns soon after beginning their advance. The weakness of the Confederate line, with only three regiments in the area as well as the lack of command and control among so many recently assembled units, allowed the Federals to advance quickly, but the cost was great. One Ohioan wrote, "The movement quickly went beyond control in a headlong pursuit; all formation was lost."[23]

Hazen's three regiments would lose more men at Shiloh than any other of Buell's or Lew Wallace's reinforcing brigades: 406 in total. One Ohioan wrote, "The ranks are stripped almost before they realize that they are in battle. The colors go down once, twice, half a dozen times, but always there is a new hand to raise the flag undismayed." Although the 9th Indiana sustained more casualties than any other regiment in the division—the result also of its action in Wicker Field and the George cabin—the 6th Kentucky and 41st Ohio also sustained well over a hundred casualties each. In fact, the 41st Ohio and 9th Indiana were the two hardest-hit regiments of the second-day troops under Buell and Wallace, with the 6th Kentucky standing as fifth. Hazen was in a hot spot.[24]

The 41st Ohio was in the front and center of the chaos, with Captain Opdyke leading the regiment, colors in hand. Hazen was also at the front, riding about rallying the weary and spurring his brigade on. Captain Aquila Wiley remembered Hazen carrying "a little switch [rattan] in his hand, that I think did more to inspire his command with coolness and firmness than the most imposing weapon would have done." Wiley admitted, "It was my first engagement, and I didn't feel any too solid myself, and I remember distinctly that the sight of that switch steadied me."[25]

Despite the casualties, Hazen's troops drove on, with the unformed Federals pushing aside the Confederate infantry covering the artillery and engaging the battery. The Louisiana gunners gave as good as they got, however. One Kentuckian wrote, "The cannon balls cut off trees 3 feet through. It was a awful thing." Yet the gunners also took casualties. Captain Irving Hodgson, commanding the guns, later declared that the "badly-torn wheels and carriages of my battery from Minie balls will convince any one of the close proximity to the enemy in which we were." Hazen reported, "We pushed directly up to the mouths of the guns, which were manned till the cannoneers were cut down by my men." The center of the brigade actually fronted the New Orleans gunners, and the 41st Ohio, despite losing four color-bearers, shot down the cannoneers and took the battery around 11:00 A.M., although members of Smith's brigade who had crowded in on the right, notably part of the 13th Ohio, also claimed to take the guns. Other regiments were also jumbled in the fray, with the 6th Kentucky's colonel, Walter C. Whitaker, striking down a cannoneer with a "bowie-knife he had taken from a Texan he had captured." Hazen saved the life of a Confederate captain; one of his soldiers was "in the act of running him through with his bayonet," but Hazen stopped him and sent the Confederate to the rear. As all moved on the same point, it is possible that the two Union brigades so commingled that elements of both were present in the wheat field and made it to the guns. Nevertheless, the result was that the Confederate line momentarily broke as Hazen's bloodied brigade was on the verge of providing the first major success of the day for Grant or Buell.[26]

Unfortunately for Hazen, his success was only short-lived. After taking so many casualties, most of them in the attack on the guns, the brigade was tiring and thinned. They had been advancing in fits and starts for about six hours now. Worse, the Confederate response was already taking a toll, with artillery fire from the left, from McClung's Battery, raking Hazen's lines. Then from the south and west came what Buell described as "a heavy force of infantry" that was thrown toward Hazen's flank. Crittenden described Hazen's men driving out of the thicket "at once four or five times their number, who came charging and shouting upon our lines."[27]

The perpetrators were initially Stewart's small command, consisting of the 2nd Tennessee and 13th Arkansas. Stewart related that his two regiments "went gallantly into action and assisted in driving the enemy to the woods beyond an open field." The major numbers, however, came from Martin's reformed troops. Hardee, now out of his jurisdiction, nevertheless rode over to Martin and ordered the brigade to again advance diagonally across the field, hitting the right flank of Hazen's brigade. Martin reported that Hardee "now rode forward, ordered a charge, and most gallantly led, amid a shower of bullets and cannon." Hardee would later return to Corinth with a slight bullet wound on the arm and his coat tattered with holes. Also leading the way was Major Thomas H. Mangum, now in command of the 2nd Confederate Infantry. Martin had his second horse shot from under him, but the brigade drove the Federals "before us as sheep," remembered one of Martin's Confederates.[28]

The Crescent Regiment also began to counterattack from the south. One of the Louisianans wrote that after being driven back a few yards and the battery being in danger, "this got us mad, and we made a terrible charge firing as we did so." The Louisianans raced forward along with the other regiments nearby, including the 19th Louisiana under Colonel Hodge, but he was thrown from his horse and was "stunned and bruised," rendering him unable to command. The Louisianans quickly drove the 41st Ohio away from the guns and back toward Wicker Field, with Captain Hodgson later applauding the regiment who "gallantly came to our rescue, charging the enemy at the point of the bayonet, putting them to flight, and saving our three extreme right pieces, which would have been captured but for them." Because of dead horses, the Federals were not able to remove the guns, but they took time to ram mud down the tubes to render them unusable. Hazen then reported, "The command went back as fast as it could go, and without the semblance of formation." Hazen and his staff rode among the broken masses trying to rally the men, but he admitted in disgust, "As fast as one group was left, while attention was given to others the first would move to the rear, and so everything went back in utter disorder." Many of the Federals chose to retreat along the edges of the field for cover, causing even more confusion.[29]

Thus driven back, the Ohioans nevertheless reformed with the help of Bruce's aide, Lieutenant Wickliffe Cooper. The 9th Indiana on the left was sent reeling backward as well, but the 6th Kentucky on the right, which Hazen personally conducted forward, was continually dealing with being flanked by the elements of Stewart's and Martin's brigades and Harper's Battery. Thus the entire brigade fell back, continually taking casualties as they retreated in disorder to the north. It did not stop with just Hazen, however. The right of Bruce's brigade also fell back in the chaos, with the 1st Kentucky reforming in the woods north of the cotton field. As they retreated, a friendly fire incident almost erupted as some of the other Kentuckians also changed positions toward Ammen's troops farther to the east. With their flags still in the cases, Bruce's men were nearly fired upon until one of Nelson's aides recognized an officer on "a certain dapple grey horse" and realized it was Bruce's brigade. There was no time to send out word not to fire, so staff officer Horace Fisher galloped in front of Ammen's brigade and shook hands with the officer, thus showing Ammen's troops that they were friendly. Despite the near catastrophe, Bruce's men had done some heavy fighting. One of Buell's men wrote home, "We did not fall back very far, nor until we had slaughtered a fair proportion of the Secesh."[30]

Back at the main area of confrontation in the Davis wheat field, there was continual give-and-take even as Hazen's regiments retreated. One Louisianan wrote that in the middle of the Crescent Regiment's attack, a company of cavalry "rode through us at a full run," causing the Louisianans to fall back temporarily. Colonel Marshall Smith seized the moment to take his colors and rally his troops, telling them, "Rally around your colors boys & follow your colonel." The men did so, again driving Hazen's troops with the bayonet. One observer described how "the Washington Artillery, which was always getting into dangerous places, and often too near the cover of the enemy's sharp shooters, who seemed to take a special grudge against our gallant boys, was saved by a timely charge of the Crescents, who, pouring a heavy volley into the enemy, enabled the artillerists to limber up and haul off their pieces to the rear." As the charge petered out, some of Breckinridge's troops in Martin's brigade took up the slack and pushed farther forward.[31]

Making the chaos in the Federal ranks even greater, Hazen was missing. As the brigade fell back in confusion, Hazen was nowhere to be seen, worrying even Nelson. When Nelson asked Colonel Whitaker of the 6th Kentucky about Hazen (he had advanced with that regiment), Whitaker replied, "We fear he is killed or wounded; none of us have seen him since the charge." Nelson offered a $50 reward to anyone who would recover his body. Several men of the 6th Kentucky volunteered but did not find him. Only later did Hazen emerge, "unharmed and in his usual robust health."[32]

Hazen later reported that as he was crossing the wheat field in retreat, he feared his horse could not jump the fence and thus took to the edges of the field, like many of his soldiers. Along with Emerson Opdyke, Hazen rode to the west and tried to circle back to his command by heading east. In the deep woods and underbrush, he quickly became disoriented and moved instead to the west, finally emerging along the line of Lovell Rousseau's brigade, particularly the section of line held by the US Regulars. Fearing he would again get confused, Hazen went back to the landing, from which he could follow his earlier path back to his brigade. By the time all that had occurred, the day was ended.[33]

Back at the wheat field, the Federals were soon able to turn the tables on the attacking Confederates despite the chaos; Marshall Smith, commanding the Crescent Regiment, called it an "ambush." The Confederates had outflanked Hazen, but now the 2nd Tennessee and 13th Arkansas under Stewart and even portions of Martin's troops on the left were similarly treated. To Hazen's left, Bruce turned his flank to the west and fired into the following Confederates, but the major ambush came farther to the west on Hazen's right. There the attacking Confederates drove forward into the waiting fire of Sooy Smith's brigade of Crittenden's division. These Federals had changed their front to the south in response to the heavy fighting in the wheat field. Chaos emerged as they did so, with Lieutenant Colonel Cicero Maxwell of the 26th Kentucky describing how "the position of the brigade was then somewhat changed." Several regiments found themselves partially blocked, but the whole nevertheless soon surged forward.[34]

Engulfed in the greater carnage of the wheat field, the 26th Kentucky, which had lost its major, John L. Davidson, came apart, only to be reorganized behind Boyle's brigade and eventually assigned to cover artillery in the rear. The 13th Ohio was also caught up in the heavy fighting, claiming to have aided in capturing the Washington Artillery. The right of Smith's brigade, the 11th Kentucky and the attached Wisconsin troops, were still in line, however, and in a perfect position to hit the counterattacking Confederate left flank. Just as the Confederate line had earlier curved in a concave nature, forcing Hazen into a vortex of fire, so too did the Federal line curve where Hazen and Smith linked together. Smith's right thus poured a horrendous fire on the counterattacking Confederates, with Hardee's charging left sweeping into a similar concave that Hazen had endured. The result was that Smith's brigade, led by division commander Crittenden, now outflanked the Confederate line that had outflanked Hazen. Stewart's small command bore the brunt of the counterattack, but Marshall Smith of the Crescent Regiment also reported that he had to fall back "in order to prevent being flanked." Still, Sooy Smith's troops also took heavy fire. As one of Crittenden's staff officers described the fighting to a friend, "The bullets flew about as thick as the shot did when we were hunting quails above Davenport. I thought every gun was bearing on me."[35]

Smith's counterattack could last only so long, however, because the stable regiments on the right were caught up in the momentary panic as it ran through the entire brigade. Colonel Pierce B. Hawkins of the 11th Kentucky near the far right noted, "From some cause or other we were compelled to fall back to the original line of battle." The main cause he spoke of was a timely volley from the 1st Missouri on the right of Martin's brigade. That created confusion, and Marshall Smith's Louisianans followed it up with yet another counterattack, forcing some units such as the 13th Ohio to fall back over 400 yards. Still, Smith's Federals remained near the front and made a brief advance once more, although they ultimately had to fall back to a line with Hazen's reforming brigade. Their presence on the Confederate flank nevertheless stunned the enemy advance, halting it until the Union line could reform. Moreover, Buell was on site aiding his troops; one of Buell's Federals wrote home, "General Buell was with our division during the entire day and I never admired a man more."[36]

The fighting was thus long and horrific, with both sides demonstrating major attempts to advance, only to be routed and driven back. One of the 14th Wisconsin soldiers wrote, "All that I remember . . . was that I loaded as fast as possible and wherever I saw a Secesh I shot at him." Yet in the end, Hazen's troops fell back from the wheat field nearly all the way to Wicker Field, where they began to reform and think about moving forward again. And there was destruction even amid the retreat. Parts of the fleeing mass diagonally crossed the western portion of the Bell cotton field, where McClung's guns and Maney's infantry once again tore into them across the expanse of several hundred yards. Similarly, Smith's troops as well as the 13th Kentucky of Boyle's brigade, sent over to support Smith, fell back as a result of the "breaking" of the 14th Wisconsin of Grant army. One Wisconsin soldier evidently agreed, writing, "We charged one battery 3 times." All nevertheless soon reformed and held their ground west of Wicker Field, capturing several prisoners in the effort and repulsing the advancing Confederates. Crittenden later reported that he "did not deem it right to advance my lines without an order from General Buell, lest I might expose the right of General Nelson." It is equally probable, however, that Crittenden did not want to tangle again with the vortex of Confederates in the thicket.[37]

One of the more permanent results of the fighting in this area, on Smith's right, was the death of young J. D. Putnam of the 14th Wisconsin. One of Putnam's fellow soldiers "avenged poor Putnam," remembered James K. Newton, by killing the Confederate who killed Putnam "before he could take his gun from his face." Putnam's comrades buried him at the foot of a tree and carved his name and unit in the base. Such care not only assured Putnam's identity (he is one of the minority of known burials in the Shiloh National Cemetery today), but it also fixed beyond any doubt the exact location of the regiment. A granite version of the stump that stood on the site as late as 1900 now stands on that spot in the Shiloh National Military Park.[38]

Thus the fighting roared back and forth. One Wisconsin soldier wrote, "We drove the rebels & they drove us & then we would drive them again." Then, mercifully, the fighting began to simmer down. Each side watched the other, which was exactly the same thing that was happening to the east with Hardee and Nelson. In both sectors, the artillery began to take over, with Buell sending Mendenhall's four guns to a position between Hazen and Smith. Both sides realized that they had a formidable opponent before them and were thus loath to order any additional attacks.[39]

The result was unmistakable. Despite increased numbers of relatively fresh troops swarming forward onto a mishmash of a Southern line, the Confederates were not giving way. Despite the scare in the wheat field when the line temporarily collapsed, the Confederate defense was holding, and the units were fighting nearly as well as they had the day before. The Confederate army, worn out and disorganized as it was, was even able to launch several major counterattacks. They did not have the power to drive away the Federals, but they did manage to show the Northern commanders that the Confederate army was not quitting. Speaking volumes, Thomas Crittenden later stated that the action in the wheat field was the heaviest fighting he saw in the war.[40]

Yet it soon became so quiet around the wheat field that George Maney was able to send a portion of his command to find Cheatham on the left, where the fighting was growing to a furious pitch. He also sent Colonel Charles Wickliffe of the 7th Kentucky, earlier separated from his regiment. Wickliffe found his unit under the command of Samuel Lockett and took over, only to be mortally wounded in the head while leading the regiment forward in Breckinridge's advance. Hardee's ability to hold his position and even send troops away to reinforce other parts of the field was an amazing feat, given what he faced. All in all, the Confederates under Hardee were more than holding their own on the right.[41]

17

"WE DROVE BACK THE LEGIONS OF THE ENEMY"

Alexander McCook's troops had never seen anything like it. Although some of the men had been in action in small battles in Kentucky, most notably Mill Springs in January, Shiloh far outdid anything they had ever seen. The enormity of the battle and the hard fighting they were encountering as they advanced on this April 7 morning was different from anything they had experienced. Yet their training—even what little some of them had—took over and allowed them to work as a unit, rigid and machinelike even amid the chaos.[1]

Before these troops even entered the massive combat that raged on this second day, however, they faced what probably took a larger toll on them as humans. While moving forward toward the Confederate lines, they had to tramp across yesterday's battlefield with all its horrors. The site of thousands of wounded and stragglers nearer the landing affected the troops. They saw even worse sights as they advanced onto the real battlefield on the lower half of the hourglass. Lovell Rousseau described the carnage: "Within a quarter of a mile of the Landing, and directly on the way to our position on the field, lay hundreds of dead men, mostly our own, whose mangled bodies and distorted features presented a horrible sight. Numerous dead horses and our partially sacked camps gave evidence of the havoc, and, which was far worse, of the reverses and disasters of the day before." Rousseau added that the result gave his men the impression "that they must fight the battle for themselves," adding that it was "rendered apparent . . . that the work before us was by no means easy."[2]

Most hauntingly, as the number of wounded and the dead of both sides increased, their presence affected organization because few wanted to step on a body itself, whether living or dead. Humanity and respect kept many from doing so, but a tangible reason also surfaced in the inability to step soundly on an unstable body, whether dead or alive. Soldiers could easily lose their footing while stepping on an arm, leg, or torso, which might slide out from under them, especially if covered with blood or other internal bodily matter. These relatively green soldiers thus found it easier to step aside, even if it meant a breakup in organization on the company level.

The brigades under Thomas Crittenden and Alexander McCook moved through one of the most terrifying zones on the battlefield. Although perhaps not as horrible as the eastern portion where Johnston's Confederates had attacked time and again across that open cotton field, and certainly not nearly as obliterated as the western side where half the Union army had grappled with two-thirds of the Confederate force the day before, the center of the line nevertheless contained its own horrors. The Hornet's Nest had seen its share of heavy fighting because of the repeated Confederate assaults throughout the previous day and the huge artillery bombardment in the late afternoon, but there was also the horrible fire that had broken out on the left of the Hornet's Nest, burning alive the wounded and mangling the dead. The center of the battlefield was a horrific place already, but the regiments under Crittenden and McCook were about to enter the area under heavy Confederate fire. Colonel James P. Fyffe summed it up well: his regiment "moved forward, and soon began to participate actively in what appearances seemed to indicate would be a severe contest with the rebel army."[3]

Leading the way was Thomas Crittenden, who was an anomaly in himself. He hailed from Kentucky, where his father was a United States senator. The elder Crittenden had inherited the mantle of Henry Clay and had tried his best to forestall war with compromise. Perhaps his work was as much on behalf of his family as it was for his nation because of the sectional splits among his sons. In a vivid illustration of this brother-against-brother war, Thomas had sided with the North when his father's peace efforts failed, while his brother George went South. The Crittenden brothers would have faced each other at Shiloh had George not been relieved for drunkenness just a few days earlier. His old command, under Breckinridge, now lay in the Hornet's Nest awaiting Thomas Crittenden's advance.[4]

Crittenden's leading brigade had already encountered heavy fighting when it shifted to the left and became absorbed into the struggle around the wheat field. When the Confederates advanced and flanked Hazen's line, retaking the guns of the Washington Artillery, Smith's brigade in turn took the Confederates in the flank and drove them back. The heavy fighting alerted Crittenden to the need to call up his other brigade under Jeremiah Boyle because Breckinridge's brigades farther to the west were advancing at the same time. Boyle's Kentucky and Ohio regiments had been marching on Smith's right rear, between him and Rousseau's brigade of McCook's division, but they soon moved forward and relieved Smith's troops, who were out of ammunition and stunned by the ferocity of the Confederate resistance and counterattack. The 13th Kentucky especially provided good work in stabilizing the line in what Colonel Edward H. Hobson described as the "chaparral."[5]

The fire there was extremely heavy, and Elijah Tucker of the 13th Kentucky took a ball in the forehead. "My life was only saved by my enameled leather cap-brim, which caused the ball to glance off," a thankful Tucker wrote. The blow still knocked him to his knees, and he admitted he was "addled considerably for a few minutes." Amazingly, after the ball glanced off Tucker, it hit another man under the eye, killing him instantly.[6]

Despite the growing carnage, Smith's shaken troops soon filled their cartridge boxes and returned to the line, allowing Boyle to shift to the right and deploy on the tall ridge overlooking Duncan Field, in the same position where W. H. L. Wallace's artillery had fought the day before in support of the infantry in the Hornet's Nest. Crittenden had his two brigades deployed side by side, and even better, he had the most artillery support of anyone in the army. By this time, Mendenhall had brought his guns westward and deployed them on the high ground west of Wicker Field, where he would take several different positions over the next few hours. In addition, the last battery Buell had available also deployed on Boyle's line. Bartlett's Ohio battery took a position on the high ridge just east of Duncan Field, placed by Colonel James Fry, Buell's chief of staff. One Ohioan marveled at the battery: "It seemed that the horses and the wheels of the gun carriages scarcely touched the ground as they flew to the rising piece of ground where they engaged the rebel battery and gave them shot for shot."[7]

Better yet for the Federals, Crittenden was not alone. McCook had elements of his division to Crittenden's right—one brigade at first, but

the division was growing with the continual arrival of the rest of Mc-
Cook's brigades. At this point, Lovell Rousseau's brigade was the only
one on line, but Kirk's troops were trailing along in reserve, watching
the ever-important flank, and Gibson's brigade was even then nearing
the landing and would soon march out the Corinth Road and join their
division. The entire brigade had crammed aboard the *John J. Roe,* along
with two artillery batteries, and only landed at Pittsburg after 11:00
A.M.[8]

Having just now loaded their guns, Rousseau's troops advanced
alone, crossing the upper reaches of Tilghman Branch. They fought
off a couple of determined advances from Confederate skirmishers
and drove the others back to Duncan Field. One regular described the
massive volleys sent out toward what was evidently a Confederate skirmish line north of Tilghman Branch: "As the last skirmisher reached
the lines, the ball opened on our side by the command to 'fire at will,'
and for an hour or more the whistle of the bullets about our heads was
supplemented by the ear-splitting roar of our own musketry." As the
whistling bullets became less thick over the next few minutes, all knew
the enemy was falling back. The brigade thus moved on and soon entered the northeastern extremity of Duncan Field north of the Corinth
Road; the enemy held the "gentle ridge beyond." Rousseau was at a dis-
advantage there, however, because the lowest portion of the field was on
this end and he would either have to hold on and wait for a general advance or strike out on his own to obtain any semblance of good ground.
Fortunately for Rousseau, Kirk's brigade was following behind and at
times during the advance even took a position on Rousseau's right rear
to cover the flank McCook was so worried about. McCook also ordered
the 77th Pennsylvania of Kirk's brigade to remain in the rear as a general reserve and eventually utilized the 32nd Indiana in the same fashion. The Army of the Tennessee units to their right had also by this time
overcome their extensive caution and moved across Tilghman Branch
to cover their right. Rousseau's brigade extended into the woods north
of Duncan Field, where it almost connected with elements of Hurlbut's
division in the form of Veatch's and Williams's brigades.[9]

After sending the Madison Band, playing "Yankee Doodle," to the
rear, Rousseau advanced into Duncan Field. There he stopped on the
rising ground, covering his troops but allowing a view to the front to
gather information on the Confederate line. A watching soldier from
Boyle's brigade thought the sight of the regulars marvelous: "They

formed as though they were on parade." Rousseau had the 6th Indiana, 1st Ohio, and US infantry contingents from the 15th, 16th, and 19th regiments in line in the field and extending into the woods to the right, while the 5th Kentucky remained in reserve. In addition, the 15th Michigan of Grant's army, the same troops under Colonel Oliver who had marched out to Prentiss's line the day before without ammunition, had attached itself to Rousseau during the morning, much as the Wisconsin troops had done to Smith's brigade. The Michiganders advanced along the Corinth Road, on Rousseau's left. Others in support, consisting of many of Grant's troops, formed a reserve. One of Prentiss's soldiers wrote home, "We were drawn up in the rear of the center of the line of Battle as a reserve to support the center keeping about eighty rods in the rear of our line." It was clear, however, that Crittenden and McCook were center stage.[10]

The units Crittenden and McCook faced were perhaps the best-organized component of the Confederate army. Breckinridge's corps was small, with only three brigades, but he was better able to control their movements than, for example, Bragg, with his six large brigades. Breckinridge was thus the only one of the four major components of the army to have all its brigades present together, most of the regiments in their respective brigades, and their commanding officer commanding the whole. This was a testament to Breckinridge, who had organized his troops early that morning.[11]

Statham and Bowen had ended the day on the Confederate right after their fighting near the Peach Orchard and quickly took a position in the center. Trabue's regiments had fought all day on the left and camped along the Hamburg-Purdy Road in McDowell's camps; his arrival was thus a little more complicated. He had been one of the most prepared officers during the night, unsuccessfully looking through the darkness for superiors. By daylight, he had his troops fire off their muskets and clean them, and he was soon in line of battle, awaiting orders in the rear. Watching others such as Ruggles's brigades move forward, Trabue still awaited orders, which came when his aide returned with word from Beauregard to "move forward to whatever point the firing seemed heaviest." A chagrined Trabue moved toward Shiloh Church, deploying east of the church itself. Then on Bragg's orders he moved forward to the Duncan Field area. There he came upon the rest of Breckinridge's command, although he may not have even known his close proximity to them at the time. Trabue positioned his artillery, Byrnes's Battery, on the left, just in the woods overlooking Duncan Field on the high ground north of the Corinth Road while the infantry lay down on what one officer described as the "wet cold ground." Byrnes scouted to the front and found that the enemy was approaching. He asked for a detail from the nearby 6th Kentucky to help man his guns. One of the Kentuckians stepped forward and yelled, "No detail—ask for volunteers and we are there."[12]

In Duncan Field, Trabue observed several things. He probably realized he was on Breckinridge's left, putting the corps together, but he also saw Rousseau's troops filing along the north side of the road and into the other side of the field, covered by the tall ridge in the center. Fortunately for him, Trabue had his entire complement of infantry and the battery with him, and he had help; continuing the line to Trabue's right along the western side of Duncan Field was Statham's brigade, also with its full complement of infantry, although Rutledge's Battery was no longer with them. The brigade did have the services of Stanford's Mississippi Battery, deployed near its position of the day before when it took part in Ruggles's concentration. Some evidence states that Hudson's Mississippi Battery was in this line as well despite Hudson's death the day before. Finishing out Breckinridge's line was Bowen's brigade under Martin on the far right, which, as a result of the heavy fighting at the wheat field, now connected with Hardee's line near the crossing of the Eastern Corinth and Hamburg-Purdy roads. At the junction was Harper's Mississippi Battery, providing cover on the brigade's right.[13]

It did not take long for Beauregard to utilize this powerful force in the general advance, although Breckinridge debated with him the merits of the attack. Breckinridge nevertheless went forward, Statham's brigade in Breckinridge's center advancing toward Boyle's troops around Duncan Field. Future Confederate general Thomas B. Smith, now a captain commanding a company in the 20th Tennessee, was part of this command. Around the same time Martin's regiments tangled with Hazen's attack and Trabue on the left began to feel pressure from McCook. Although tardy, Breckinridge would hopefully provide the hammer blow Beauregard desired.[14]

Confederate artillery opened the fighting by firing into Boyle's lines and bringing great limbs down on the Federals, one of whom admitted

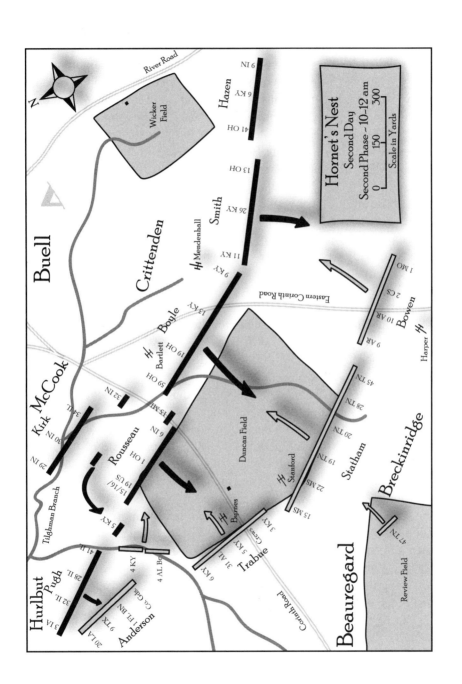

Hornet's Nest
Second Day
Second Phase ~ 10–12 am

Scale in Yards
0   150   300

the fright: "The shot and shells were over us, some in the tree tops tore off great branches and they came crashing down and gave us a scare." The soldiers soon learned, however, that these limbs "were not hard to dodge." Worse, Crittenden's division was divided and fighting in seemingly two different directions. Smith's attention remained focused on aligning with Hazen's troops to the left and keeping his right on the Eastern Corinth Road. That deployment led him to attack along with Hazen almost due south. Thus Smith ran into the far reaches of Hardee's left and Harper's Battery, but it also put his forces in a perfect position to repel the Confederate counterattack that drove Hazen back.[15]

As a result, the westward-facing Boyle had to fight Statham almost alone. First taking Smith's position and restoring order from his attack that supported Hazen, then taking a position on their right when Smith reformed his lines and resupplied his ammunition, Boyle's troops were arrayed with the 9th and 13th Kentucky alongside the 19th Ohio in the front line and the 59th Ohio in rear. The cannoneers of Bartlett's Battery, six guns in total, were in position on the right center near the 19th Ohio. The Ohioans, as skirmishers for the brigade, advanced and for a short time tangled with the Confederates in Duncan Field before falling back up the ridge. The 59th Ohio later took a frontline position when Buell took the 19th Ohio out of line and sent it to the east to support Nelson's tested division, with Nelson leading the regiment into line. From the high ground for about an hour, Bartlett's gunners shelled the Duncan house area, driving back Confederate skirmishers and dueling with Stanford's Mississippi Battery on the opposite side of the field. Colonel James P. Fyffe of the 59th Ohio reported, "A spirited duel was progressing between the supported and opposing batteries."[16]

Thomas Jefferson Stanford, positioned at the same place he had held the day before, watched as a battery fired "all the morning." Stanford admitted, "Up to this time I had supposed [it] to be one of our own," but then it opened on Stanford's guns. He scouted to the front to make sure it was an enemy battery, which it was, and the Mississippians were soon returning the fire. "I opened on them with solid shot and spherical case at a range of 500 yards," Stanford reported.[17]

During the artillery duel, Crittenden and Boyle preempted Breckinridge's delayed assault by resuming their advance; the regiments swung westward toward the Confederate line around a little after 11:00 A.M. Boyle led his regiments down the steep slope of the ravine that ran just north of the old farm road that Tuttle's brigade had manned the day before. They crossed the road, and the right of the brigade swept into Duncan Field, keeping their right aligned on the Corinth Road. In the open field, according to Colonel Samuel Beatty, the Ohioans captured "a citizen prisoner . . . under suspicious circumstances" and sent him to the rear. They also met the murderous fire of Statham's brigade. To the Mississippians and Tennesseans in the ranks of Statham's regiments situated behind a fence, it probably seemed like joyous justice to now be on the defensive against the enemy crossing the open field—something they had been forced to try numerous times the day before. The result was predictably the same: Boyle's regiments slowed, then stopped altogether under the withering fire from Statham's regiments at the edge of the woods. Stanford's Mississippi cannoneers added to the destruction from their position just west of the field, making the open spaces dangerous for anyone who attempted to cross.[18]

The exact distance the Federals advanced is in question, with some claiming to have captured or driven away temporarily a few Confederate pieces of artillery. Confederate reports bear this out; staff officer Chisolm wrote that he and Lockett led stragglers forward, both having their horses shot, in an attempt to assist Breckinridge in holding his line. Chisolm wrote that with their help, "Genl Breckinridge was able again to possess himself of his artillery'[s] former position."[19]

Despite the temporary success, Boyle and Crittenden quickly realized that they would not be able to drive the Confederates back so easily, especially with Statham soon on the offensive. One Ohioan wrote that as they were "going down to edge of Duncan field . . . at the same instant the Confederates moved into the field opposite us in front of their Battery." Boyle's troops remained for a while, watching as Statham's regiments "came about one third of the way across the field with a flag or two in the lead." They soon halted the advance, though; one Mississippian wrote home, "We made a charge on a battery and five or six regiments was firing at us from nearly every direction." Augustus Mecklin of the 15th Mississippi remembered they then "halted for the cannon to play a while." The Confederates were thus stopped for now, but it was enough of a show of force to cause Boyle to retire across the field and up the incline to the high ridge on which the battery and the 59th Ohio held firm. There Crittenden took stock of his options while Bartlett and Mendenhall covered the division with their artillery. The batteries were having problems of their own, however, losing men and horses at such a rate that a lieutenant yelled, "Unhitch the traces and save the horses."

Mendenhall countered the order quickly: "We lose all or none." The cannoneers thus returned to their posts—and it was a good thing they did, because in the back-and-forth cycle that the second day of Shiloh was becoming, the Confederates were now following up their repulse of Boyle's attack with another advance of their own: toward the Hornet's Nest.[20]

The Hornet's Nest area had proven to be just as defensible for the Confederates as for the Federals, with the open space of Duncan Field providing most of the leverage for defense. Having learned little from the day before, however, the Confederates made one more assault on the Hornet's Nest. After driving Boyle back, the men of Breckinridge's corps, Statham's and Martin's regiments, restarted their advance before noon, moving through the thicket to the east of the Eastern Corinth Road and Duncan Field. Bartlett's Battery, especially the two left guns facing that direction, took up the challenge, with several gunners showing particular courage. Bartlett described David W. Camp at the Number 5 position on the left gun as "a mere boy, only fourteen years old." Bartlett wrote that he worked the gun "with the skill and bravery of an old soldier during the entire engagement. I did not for a moment see him flinch."[21]

In defending the Hornet's Nest once again against Statham's and Martin's attack, Crittenden and Buell faced the crisis of the day in the center. Both flew into action. Crittenden placed the 9th Kentucky in the forefront and ordered the commander, "Remain here, Colonel, and I will send the 59th to support you." Illustrating the crisis, at that moment Buell rode up, "erect, and with his whole manner indicating the greatest urgency," as one Kentuckian described him. Buell countered Crittenden's order "with much earnestness": "No, Colonel, go in at once—and quickly." Crittenden eventually got both regiments into position; one of his Ohioans wrote, "We were advancing through the thick underbrush where the hard fighting of Sunday had been done. We were firing our muskets until they were hot to handle." With Colonel Samuel Beatty's 19th Ohio having moved to the left to aid Nelson, Buell placed the straggling Wisconsin troops and the reformed 26th Kentucky of Smith's brigade in line to cover Bartlett's guns.[22]

Colonel James Fyffe of the 59th Ohio and Colonel Benjamin Grider of the 9th Kentucky led their regiments into what was variously described as a "jungle" and "chaparral." One Kentuckian wrote his father in an attempt to adequately describe the conditions: "The place where our Reg fought was as thick with undergrowth as any place between our house & the schoolhouse." Adding to the confusion, Mendenhall's battery was also firing into the area, but officers were sent to stop them. Once that was done, Boyle's regiments took up the advance again, only to find the small hollow of Briar Branch covered in water and mud "over shoe-top deep," Grider reported. Even worse, after crossing the soggy bottom, the two regiments trudged through the thick undergrowth and ran right up on Martin's advancing brigade fewer than ten paces away. A heavy volley riddled the regiments, with Fyffe reporting, "At this point occurred the heaviest loss to the regiment." Martin also reported the heavy fighting, stating, "Twice again we drove back the legions of the enemy. . . . I think they concluded we had 5,000 instead of 1,000 men." Confederate artillery in the area helped as well, with some of the Federal companies bolting under the withering fire but then rallying. A Kentuckian wrote, "If the 59th Ohio had Supported us we could have taken the battery from them but they did not come to us & we could not hold our position." He added, "they did not show their spunk." Eventually, however, the tide turned in the Kentuckians' favor, and the deadly fighting raged as the Confederates slowly fell back, having only gotten to within sixty yards of Bartlett's left section. "They retired slowly and sullenly," Grider wrote, "fighting over and disputing well every inch of ground, taking advantage of every tree, thicket, log, or other protection." After penetrating through the undergrowth and viewing a field ahead with artillery and infantry, as well as cavalry on their flanks, the Federal regiments wisely fell back to the edge of the undergrowth. Boyle, not knowing where they were and who was around, wisely halted his regiments until support arrived.[23]

In similar fashion, Statham's troops to the north were repulsed in front of Boyle's right regiments on the ridge. After moving out into the field and halting for a while, Statham's Confederates restarted their advance. They received little return fire for a while, perhaps because Crittenden's and Buell's attention was focused to the left on Martin. Yet when the Federals did open up, it was with a fury, and many of Statham's Mississippians were caught out in the open. Some declared they were firing on friends because so little fire initially came back. Once the Mississippians ceased firing, the Federals opened up and "we saw their blue coats & knew too well that they were foes," Augustus Mecklin wrote. The Mississippians hit the ground and took cover, but Mecklin noted, "The balls came swarming like bees." A few soldiers began to peel off here and there, and it quickly became a deluge: "Soon it became evident that we could not long stand such heavy fire." Colonel Frank Schaller of the 22nd Mississippi admitted, "My men cut and retreated." He was hit in the left foot by a canister shot when he took the regiment's colors and tried to rally the men; he only succeeded in attracting Federal battery commander Bartlett's attention. Adding to the chaos was the smoke of the enemy guns and patches of dense underbrush. "Human nature could stand no more," recalled one Tennessean, and the brigade retreated. It soon turned into a rout as Stanford was able to provide little assistance because his long-range ammunition had played out. "We went off about a half a mile," one Mississippian remembered. "And was badly scattered."[24]

Even worse for the Confederates, the Federals were advancing again. Statham's infantry was not interested in reforming the line at its original position, leaving Stanford's Mississippi guns to provide any stability at the edge of the field. After Breckinridge's men were "met with a check," Stanford brought his canister up "and prepared to give them a warm reception." He did so "as soon as their front was unmasked, and for thirty minutes we held them in check, their ranks broken and wavering in many places." At the same time, Stanford pleaded with the infantry to rally and support his guns. Although one cannoneer reported that the infantry was "deaf to the call of duty and honor," the line was eventually reformed to the rear.[25]

Helping stabilize the situation on Breckinridge's front were the only Confederate reinforcements arriving on the second day. In addition to small portions of regiments left behind at Corinth who were sent forward during the night, the 47th Tennessee under Colonel Munson R. Hill arrived early on the morning of April 7. They had left an instruction camp at Trenton, Tennessee, on April 5, and arrived on the battlefield after hard marching through the awful weather. They quickly exchanged their shotguns for better weapons, and Alexander Chisolm led them forward to join Breckinridge's command in the center. Chisolm reported, "I observed Col Hill's Tennessee regiment (recruits from Trenton) drawn up ready to move. I ordered the Col to go to the assistance of Genl Breckinridge which he did promptly." The result, as one member of the regiment described it, was quick and certain: "While we were lying down & the cannon balls & bomb shells were flying over our heads I was trying [praying] that God might protect me." By entering the fight at a critical time and place, the regiment helped solidify the center. For now, Breckinridge's line was holding, but just barely. It seemed neither side could make any headway.[26]

North of the Corinth Road, McCook's lone brigade was having no better success in breaking through Breckinridge's line. In advancing like the others, Rousseau had to halt several times to maintain his line and make sure he was not getting into anything he could not handle. He also went through a convoluted change of front for a time, at one point forming almost a right angle with Crittenden's men. Moreover, his right flank continually worried him—that flank being the location of the tenuous link with the Army of the Tennessee. Fortunately, McCook was on site directing the larger movements, including the continually arriving reserve regiments. He swiftly issued orders through his staff, which included his brother, Dan. At one particularly hot point, McCook gave his brother an order to carry to a hazardous portion of the field and said only, "Good-bye Dan." Fortunately, Dan survived.[27]

By that time, Trabue's brigade had arrived to take their position blocking any advance on the Corinth Road. These Kentuckians, supported by Byrnes's Battery, held the line in the field, and long-range fighting developed for quite a while. In the process, Rousseau advanced the brigade, netting almost 200 yards in the field, although they were soon stopped. Artillery fire from the enemy was also heavy, forcing the 6th Indiana, under the sick Thomas T. Crittenden, to change to a more covered position. Artillery fire from their own side almost did as much damage; Bartlett's battery threw a few shells into the Federal ranks before Colonel Crittenden sent an officer to have it stopped. At another point, the Indianans also changed front to the left to secure the flank that was beginning to become a problem as a result of the growing distance between Crittenden's and McCook's divisions. The main impediment was Trabue's infantry, however, and McCook soon pressed forward to engage the enemy. Rousseau remembered, "The advance was admirably made, and with alacrity the brigade steadily, briskly, and in excellent order, moved forward." He also reported how "the fire of musketry was the heaviest I ever heard." Yet neither side could obtain an advantage; Rousseau wrote, "My line when fired on halted of itself and went to work."[28]

Ultimately, and probably in concert with Breckinridge's general movement to the right, Trabue advanced to break the Federal line. Union counterbattery fire from Bartlett's guns had been getting uncomfortably close; one 6th Kentucky officer wrote, "At least ½ of the shells thrown burst directly over the Regt, killing and wounding a Considerable number. Here this Regt. suffered more than at any other one place." Trabue thus went on the offensive and attacked even as the enemy advanced, which was becoming a pattern on this second day. Rousseau later put the Confederate attack in the context of their offensive action during the entire day, relating that he was holding the main road to Pittsburg and the Confederates were "evidently pressing for that point." The attack was fierce. McCook told Rousseau to hold his position "at every hazard" and that he would support him with the rest of the division when he could. That proved unnecessary, and Rousseau succeeded in throwing Trabue's attack back after severe combat that lasted about forty minutes. "Twice the rebel flag went down," Colonel Crittenden wrote, "and twice the enemy withdrew the regiments opposed to us and brought fresh regiments to replace them." The attack ultimately failed, however, and Trabue's brigade fell back to the wood line of Duncan Field.[29]

During the fighting, an amusing incident occurred in the ranks of the Confederate 6th Kentucky. John Philpot was a quiet and stout soldier, but he was deathly afraid of bees. When a bullet grazed his head, he threw down his gun and, a watching Kentuckian related, "began striking and scratching furiously about his head with both hands, jerking his hat off—in the manner of a man fighting bees and apparently pretty badly stung." Just as quickly, Philpot "regained his senses, and seemed to realize that he had been making a spectacle of himself." His friends kidded him about not knowing the difference between a bullet and a "honey-bee."[30]

At the same time, heavy fighting erupted north of the field between Bragg and elements of the Army of the Tennessee. The Federal response illustrated the concern Buell felt for McCook's flank and the corresponding left flank of Grant's army. With Anderson's brigade now on Trabue's left, he was the ranking general in the isolated area, and was bent on breaking the enemy line. Whether Anderson knew this was the area of linkage between Buell and Grant is unknown, but he evidently saw something that looked assailable. Anderson rode up to Major Thomas B. Monroe of the 4th Kentucky, who told him that Trabue was in command here. Anderson soon met Trabue, and the two decided to attack an enemy battery to the front, with Trabue agreeing to give Anderson two regiments to accomplish the task. Then, in a moment, Trabue thought better of the plan: "Upon reflection I think I had better not let those regiments leave their present position," Trabue told Anderson, "since I am directed to support this battery if attacked." Anderson was crestfallen and could only hold his position for now.[31]

Fortunately for Anderson, Braxton Bragg came along and ordered two of Trabue's regiments, the 4th Alabama Battalion and 4th Kentucky, to move to the left, north of the field where the junction actually was. Trabue later complained that two of his units were thus detached, saying it was done "without my knowledge." These units nevertheless attacked Rousseau's right and the link between Grant and Buell, using the growing valley of a small creek that fed into Tilghman Branch for cover. Making it worse for the Federals, the two lone regiments of Trabue's brigade soon received the promised support from Anderson's brigade. These Confederates turned their full attention to McClernand and Rousseau, engaging in bitter combat that raged back and forth across the wooded terrain north and northwest of Duncan Field. The forcefulness of the attack stunned the Federals; one remembered there was "no lack of gallantry on the part of the Confederates whom we encountered that day."[32]

McCook described the enemy attack as "continuous and severe." For a moment it looked like the Confederates might actually turn McCook's right, thus splitting the two Union armies. McCook therefore acted quickly to shore up the front, sending his reserve 5th Kentucky, the so-called Louisville Legion, into the breach and directing Kirk's brigade in the rear to move to that flank and lend support. He also brought up the just-arriving lead regiment of Gibson's brigade, August Willich's 32nd Indiana, and held them in reserve. The Kentuckians and the US Regular Army troops thus fought hard in the woods; Captain Peter T. Swaine of the 15th US Infantry wrote that they "poured such a deadly fire of rifle bullets into the ranks of the enemy that what bid fair at first to be a defeat was turned to a most glorious success." McClernand's troops on the other side of the breach fought just as well, buoyed by the regulars: "Their perfect discipline and regular movements lifted a load from our breasts, and filled us with a confidence we had well-nigh lost the day before." Unknown to the Army of the Tennessee troops, the regulars were just as raw as anyone else on the battlefield, but the name carried with it a certain grandeur, and it helped on this occasion.[33]

Trabue's and Anderson's regiments had moved through such blind terrain that the Federals hid until they were upon them. One regular in

Rousseau's brigade wrote home, "Our battalion laid flat on the ground, and quietly waited the order to fire . . . when on our right two rebel regiments came rushing down upon us, their flags were flying and they seemed determined to break our ranks." The volley from the massed Federal troops at close range threw Trabue's regiments back, but even worse happened when the Federals began to advance. The two regiments fell back on Anderson's brigade to the west, and together they somehow stopped the enemy advance, driving them back once more. Trabue reported, "Thus forward and backward was the ground crossed and recrossed four times." The lieutenant colonel of the 5th Kentucky, Robert A. Johnston, was wounded in the fighting but remained at his post.[34]

In the fighting, Major Thomas B. Monroe, commanding the 4th Kentucky, also fell, shot through the shoulder. Soldiers took him to a hospital, but he died two hours later and was buried under a tree at Shiloh Church. The men carved his name in the tree; it was still readable decades later. Another of the casualties in the fight was Kentucky's Confederate governor, George W. Johnson. He had his horse shot the day before and then entered the ranks of the 4th Kentucky as a common soldier, taking the oath as a private. He was shot through the body and left for dead, but the Federals took him to a steamboat, where he died a couple of days later.[35]

The fighting in the northern part of Duncan Field illustrated the brother-against-brother nature of the war. Here Kentucky units of Trabue's brigade fought against the 5th Kentucky of Rousseau's brigade. Most states did not experience such fraternal divisions, but the border states like Missouri and Kentucky had to endure the horror of fighting their own fellow Missourians and Kentuckians. In addition to the complicated politics and social structures of the border states, now they were fighting each other on the battlefield.[36]

By 11:30 A.M. on April 7, the entire Army of the Ohio that was on the field was totally engaged. Additional units, particularly in McCook's and Wood's divisions, were still arriving and heading out to the front, but the present portion of the army was almost entirely locked in major combat. Nelson, Crittenden, and McCook had all run into stiff resistance after their easy crossing of the most defensible terrain on the battlefield. Indeed, once the unorganized Confederates under Hardee and

Breckinridge formed a line, they gave a good account of themselves and stopped Buell's advance despite the less defensible ground and wider battlefield. All three of Buell's divisions were stalled at the point of their first major contact with the main Confederate line of defense. Even more distressing, those Confederates had not only managed an impressive defense given their exhaustion and casualties from the day before, but they were also counterattacking across the board, driving back the Federals at several points and causing major confusion and casualties at others. Although the Confederate attacks were not necessarily successful, they still forced Buell to rush artillery and additional infantry to the threatened points.

The comparatively fresh Army of the Ohio was not overwhelming the enemy, and much of the problem seemed to be on the command level. Nelson was stopped, with major issues of command and control in his division causing many of the problems. He evidently spent most of his time on the far left with his favorite brigade commander, Ammen, which made sense because the critical left was nearly turned several times. He also evidently oversaw Bruce, with whom he did not get along. That left Hazen's brigade, the division's right, without higher command—even more so after Hazen became lost. Similarly, Crittenden seemed to become confused in the thick woods of the Hornet's Nest and provided little direction as his regiments became clogged together and made little progress. In fact, both Hazen's and Smith's brigades seemed to be exhausted after their vicious fighting in the wheat field. McCook was doing no better. He kept much of his division in reserve behind a single frontline brigade doing most of the fighting. It seemed that Buell's army, admittedly green, was having a hard time with command and control, and the results were mediocre. The only energy it seemed to demonstrate came wherever Buell was, and he could not be at all places at all times. Indeed, regimental commanders frequently mentioned such lack of command in their reports. One wrote that he had to send his lieutenant colonel to "report to any general he might find the condition of affairs." This was not a formula for success.[37]

Conversely, and perhaps because of the less than stellar showing from Buell's troops, Beauregard's Confederates were performing much better than could be expected. If anyone thought the Confederates would be intimidated by the arrival of thousands of relatively fresh troops, it was not happening. One astonished Indianan wrote a few days later, "They fought like mad dogs. They would fall back a little and rally again, and fight desperately. I just thought that they would fight us till they were all killed. They would come up in such good order. We would flank them and we sometimes would nearly have them surrounded, but they would fight their way out." By late morning, Beauregard was holding firm on the right and in the center, and Buell was at a standstill. Something dramatic was needed to break the stalemate that was developing on Buell's front on this second day of Shiloh.[38]

18

"The Tables Are Turning"

Lew Wallace is one of the enigmas of Shiloh. Despite his postwar fame as a politician, diplomat, and most notably the writer of *Ben-Hur* and numerous other novels, he is still perhaps best known, certainly among Civil War buffs, as the man who became lost on the way to Shiloh. Although the story is untrue, it stuck, largely because Wallace became a victim of Ulysses S. Grant's staff, whose reports virtually ended his major war career shortly thereafter. Wallace never got over the accusation that he was lost or had disobeyed orders, despite all his successes. Wallace biographer, Gail Stephens, rightly calls this phenomenon the "Shadow of Shiloh," which loomed over Wallace the rest of his life.[1]

There is also another aspect of Shiloh that more serious students often complain about in regard to Wallace. Many look at him as timid and lethargic once he finally did enter the battle. They note his limited casualties as proof that he did more sitting than fighting on this second day, and it is true that Wallace's three brigades lost far fewer men than any of the three main engaged divisions in Buell's army. In fact, at 296 total casualties, Wallace's division lost fewer men in the entire battle than some individual regiments. Numerous units such as the 8th and 12th Iowa and the 23rd Missouri lost nearly 500 men each, most of them captured, but the 9th Illinois lost 366 killed and wounded. On the Confederate side, the 6th Mississippi lost over 300, mostly wounded.[2]

Casualty figures alone do not always demonstrate the amount of fighting a unit saw, and even more importantly, they do not always indicate the effectiveness of any certain unit in battle. In this case, Wallace mostly kept his grateful men prone. Harry Watts of the 24th Indiana remembered, "The boys did not need the Order twice for the grape and canister were whistling over our heads too close to be pleasant." Another Indianan wrote, "I was soon tired of this kind of fighting—laying

down in front of a lot of cannon while the batteries practiced marks-
manship over our bodies." More importantly, small casualty totals do
not always show the major impact maneuvering divisions could have in
battle. None other than Beauregard, perhaps not knowing all the divi-
sion-level details, summed up Wallace's effect when he reported that his
right and center held firm, but the left proved to be the trouble spot. That
was Wallace's sector.[3]

The Confederate line facing Wallace and the rest of the Army of the
Tennessee was indeed as strong on the left as it was on the right and
center, where Hardee and Breckinridge had blunted Buell's advance and
even managed to counterattack. As on the right and center, the left was a
hodgepodge of units that came together over time. One Illinois Federal
summed it up by writing his wife, "The next morning (Monday) with
tremendous energy on both sides the fight again commenced and for
some hours it seemed as if neither side gained." Part of the reason was
that by 10:00 A.M., when the major fighting began, there was more Confederate organization than a cursory examination showed.[4]

On that Confederate left, two major sectors developed, one under
Polk and the other under Bragg. In the no-man's-land between Marsh's
camps and Tilghman Branch, which the remnants of the Army of the
Tennessee were even then approaching, Daniel Ruggles had the majority of his division (including his cavalry) of Bragg's corps on line with
Anderson on the right with the 20th Louisiana, 9th Texas, 1st Florida
Battalion, and the Confederate Guards Response Battalion. The only
regiment missing was Charles Jones's 17th Louisiana, but he formed
a command of his own men and others from different regiments and
fought elsewhere on the field. Attached to Anderson was also the 11th
Louisiana of Russell's brigade. To Anderson's left was Gibson's brigade
containing the 4th and 13th Louisiana and the 1st Arkansas. The 19th
Louisiana had been separated and was fighting with the Crescent Regiment under Hardee near the Davis wheat field. The other brigade in
the division was Pond's, and after its frontline fighting during the early
morning, he had withdrawn and eventually went back into line on Anderson's right, near Trabue's position, before being taken out of line
again and sent to the right. He eventually received conflicting orders
from Ruggles, then Beauregard, then Polk, then Beauregard again, and
then finally Ruggles. No wonder Colonel Alfred Mouton of the 18th

Louisiana described their day as "constantly marching and counter-marching." Illustrating the chaos, at one point when orders countering his own came for Pond, staff officer Giles B. Cooke exasperatingly rode to Bragg and asked if he had sent additional orders to turn Pond back. Bragg replied that he had not, but counseled, "But as they are turned back, let them go." Fortunately, Pond's men stumbled upon half a barrel of wet hardtack in one of the camps, which they consumed. Nevertheless, for a brief time at the beginning of Pond's chaos, all three brigades of Ruggles's division were at one time fighting alongside each other, much as Withers's brigades were doing on the far right. Bragg's two divisions were not together, but there was at least a semblance of organization on the division level.[5]

On the high ground overlooking Jones Field and a major ravine leading into Tilghman Branch, Hardee's entire corps similarly formed a solid line. Most of Cleburne's regiments were represented on the right in the ravine itself, although only about 800 men were present for duty. Cleburne had brought them to the field earlier in the morning after hearing the firing and concluding that "Buell had arrived and we had a fresh army to fight." Cleburne nevertheless had them fire "off my wet guns." Hill's 5th Tennessee as well as the 23rd and 24th Tennessee were in line, as was the 15th Arkansas. The only missing units were the shot-up 6th Mississippi and Bate's 2nd Tennessee, who were on Hardee's front down the line. The general had them lie down to await the Federal onslaught, which they could see. The approaching Union line stretched, Cleburne reported, "as far as the eye could see."[6]

To Cleburne's left was more of Hardee's corps, Shaver's brigade containing the 2nd, 6th, and 7th Arkansas. The 3rd Confederate regiment was missing, but the majority of the brigade was there. Once getting orders to move onto Cheatham's right, Shaver had finally led his brigade to the Jones Field sector, where all but the 7th Arkansas, which was sent back to cover a battery, went on line facing northeast at the extreme southern end of the field. To Shaver's left came Wood's brigade with the 8th, 9th, and 16th Alabama and 27th and 44th Tennessee. The 3rd Mississippi Infantry Battalion and 55th Tennessee were not represented, and the 16th Alabama actually went in with Cheatham nearby, with Lieutenant Colonel John W. Harris reporting that one of Cheatham's aides ordered him to join his general and that "he urged the necessity of the case in such strong terms that I obeyed his order." Still, all three of Hardee's brigades were on line with all but five of the seventeen regiments in the corps represented. Unfortunately for the corps, Hardee himself was over on the far right.[7]

Other units eventually took a position along this portion of the line as they wandered in, including Venable's 5th Tennessee of Stewart's shattered brigade on Cleburne's left as well as Smith's Mississippi Battery between Shaver and Wood and Girardey's Georgia artillery between the 5th Tennessee and Cleburne. Both batteries dueled with the Federal artillery in Jones Field despite some of the caissons being to the rear, unable to cross the ravines. The lack of any of Hardee's original artillery on this line illustrated the mix-up in the long arm; Girardey hailed from Jackson's brigade of Bragg's corps, while Smith was detached from Stephens's brigade of Polk's corps.[8]

While Hardee's troops confronted the Federals in Jones Field, the Confederate line extended on westward toward the Owl Creek bottom, which needed to be reached with the main line to prevent a flank attack such as that which had so doomed the Federal left the day before. It was there that a seeming mixture of all sorts of commands made the line relatively weaker. On Wood's left was the majority of Russell's brigade, the 12th, 13th, and 22nd Tennessee; only the 11th Louisiana was missing. Next came another isolated regiment of Stewart's brigade, the 33rd Tennessee. Two regiments of Maney's brigade took a position on the Tennesseans's left despite the rest of their brigade and commander fighting under Hardee to the east. Nevertheless, the 6th and 9th Tennessee manned the Confederate line near Sowell Field, while the last two regiments on line, the 22nd Alabama and 1st Louisiana of Gladden's brigade, now under Colonel Zach Deas of the 22nd Alabama, carried the line to a small ravine that fed into Owl Creek. Bragg commanded in this sector, although the troops of Russell's and Stephens's commands came from Polk's corps. Bragg seemed especially concerned with his left, sending staff officer Cooke to "let me know when my left is broken by the enemy."[9]

In the midst of this line were additional troops that cannot be documented, either because they were conglomerations of various units or because reports are too vague to be able to pinpoint any position. The Confederate ranks were nevertheless aided by these wandering and almost leaderless bands. Similarly, all Confederate artillery batteries cannot be accounted for in this initial Confederate line, but it is certain that several were there. One example was Ketchum's Alabama Battery,

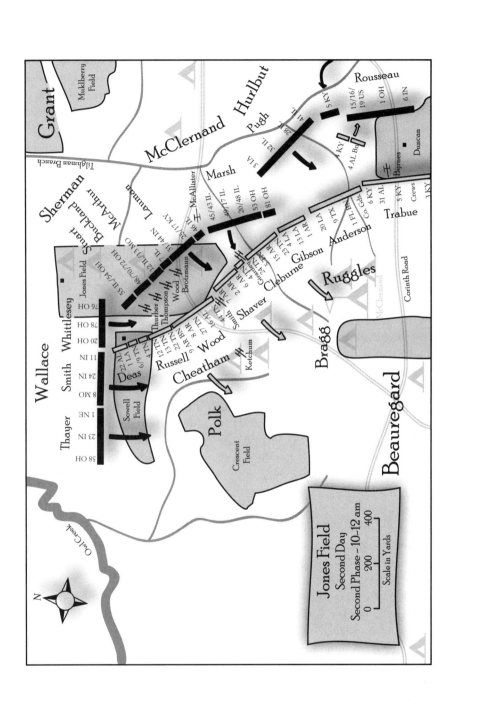

Grant

Muhlberry
Field

Tilghman Branch

McClernand

Hurlbut

Rousseau

Pugh

Marsh

82 IL

41 IL

5 KY

15/16/
19 US

1 OH

6 IN

Duncan

32 IL

31 IL

4 KY

4 AL Bn

Byrnes

McAllister

45/43 IL

17 IL

20/48 IL

53 OH

18 OH

13 LA

20 LA

9 TX

1 FL

Co. Gds

Crews

5 KY

6 KY

31 AL

3 KY

Trabue

Sherman

Buckland

McArthur

Lauman

Stuart

24/17 KY

31/44 IN

12 IL/14/13 MO

48/70/72 OH

55 IL/54 OH

Jones Field

Brotzmann

Wood

5 AR

15 AR
Crescent

23 AR

13 AR

Gibson

Anderson

Cleburne

Ruggles

76 OH

78 OH

20 OH

Thurber

Thompson

9 AR
2 AR

4 TN
24 TN

2 AR
7 AR

19 LA

6 MS

1 TN

Smith

Shaver

Bragg

Beauregard

Wallace

Smith

Whittlesey

11 IN

24 IN

8 MO

1 NE

23 IN

58 OH

Deas

22 AL
1 LA

6/9 TN

12 TN
13 TN
22 TN

8 AR

Russell

Wood

Cheatham

Ketchum

Polk

Corinth Road

McClernand

Thayer

Sowell
Field

Crescent
Field

Owl Creek

N

which is not accounted for after its dawn fight in Jones Field. However, fight it did, as exemplified by one cannoneer who told the story
of Bragg arriving at the battery's position. Having heard Ketchum was
wounded—which was true, but only by a spent ball that still "came very
near unseating him from his horse"—Bragg came to see for himself. He
met Ketchum, shook his hand, and told him he was "glad to see that he
was not hurt, and that he could not spare him, that we were doing good
service, and were his main dependence." The artillerymen gave three
cheers on two occasions for Bragg, whom they referred to as Warhorse.
On another occasion, one of Bragg's staff officers ordered Ketchum to
move forward in line with another battery to the right. The staff officer
found Ketchum packed up and ready to move—he presumed to the rear.
When told to move forward, Ketchum replied, "Captain, we are only
getting out of the line of fire, they have gotten our exact position." The
staff officer remembered, "I was of course aware of that as I was there
myself," and repeated the order to move forward. He then "got out of the
woods as fast as possible."[10]

The Confederate line on the left was thus as strong and organized
as the center and right. When taken as a whole, the entire Confederate
line was not as cobbled together as commonly thought. In fact, Hardee's
and Breckinridge's corps fought together as units, and both Ruggles and
Withers's three-brigade divisions, each the same size as Hardee's and
Breckinridge's corps, fought together as units though not as a corps.
Only Polk's corps seemed to be less organized, but even then, much
of Cheatham's division fought together on the right under Hardee, although without their commander. Clark's division was the most shattered, probably as a result of his wounding early in the first day, with
Russell fighting independently on the left. The other brigade, Stewart's,
seemed to be the most devastated brigade in the army. Although all its
regiments engaged, none fought together on this second day. Similarly,
the artillery was completely disorganized, with few batteries fighting
alongside their parent brigades.[11]

Thus Confederate officers retained much of their organization
during the second day's fighting, certainly at the brigade and division
levels. Only Stewart's brigade was hopelessly shattered, and that had
occurred during the first day, not during the night or on this second day.
Most other brigades were missing only one or perhaps two regiments.
Beauregard thus retained much more organization and control than often thought, and he thus fought better than often realized. One Union

artilleryman declared on this second day, illustrating the power of the Confederate legions, "It was worse than the day before."[12]

Although the units were amazingly coherent, the glaring problem was corps command structure. The first day got off to a horrible start as a result of Beauregard's stacking of the corps; the various commanders could not oversee their entire commands when fractured by brigades of other corps splitting their organization. It is consequently remarkable that the Confederate army managed to fight together as brigades and divisions to the degree they did on this second day, which was actually better than they had done on the first day. Neither Hardee's nor Breckinridge's corps fought together on the first day; nor did Withers's and Ruggles's divisions. Yet the corps commanders never remedied their disorganization; they were placed on opposite ends of the field from their commands on the second day. Polk, for instance, commanded a few troops of his corps, but not enough to constitute his entire organization. Bragg commanded the far left while his divisions fought on the right and left center. In the most glaring case, Hardee commanded the right while his entire corps fought together on the left. Only Breckinridge commanded his original troops.

By late morning, Beauregard and his corps commanders likely wished they had done a better job of organizing the army during the night. Yet the army had come together well and was holding its own against the Federal frontal assaults on the right and center. Indeed, one of Hurlbut's Illinois soldiers marveled at the Confederate defense: "The enemy, however, fought with a zeal worthy of a better cause." The left was just as strong. In fact, if there was any difference in the strength of the Confederate left and right, it was in the focus of the commanding general. Although Beauregard initially looked toward the left with Pond's resistance, he soon seemed to be completely fixated on his right and center, pushing Breckinridge's attack that would, he hoped, end the Union thrusts and reap the long-awaited victory deprived him the night before. Thus all attention seemed to be paid to the right while, unfortunately, Beauregard's biggest threat—and indeed his undoing—came from the left.[13]

The fighting on the Confederate left initially took the same form as that all across the battlefield, with the strong Confederate line stopping Sherman's, McClernand's, and Hurlbut's advance in its tracks. The

Army of the Tennessee, running up against this formidable Confederate line, did no better than their Ohio counterparts in the morning's fighting; in fact, they had to take cover because of the volume of enemy musketry and artillery fire, especially in the Jones Field sector. The Confederates were in line in thick underbrush at the southwestern edge of the field, and the Federals in one regiment could not see over the brush because every one of the field officers in the regiment had lost his horse the day before. One Illinoisan leaped atop a stump in the field, which offered a better view. "He turned and called to the Colonel that the Rebels were behind the brush," an observing Federal wrote. "The Colonel shouted but that same moment the Rebels gave us a volley." Because of the heavy fire, Wallace and Sherman moved forward to take advantage of the ground so their men would be protected while the generals decided on their plan. As a result, the Union line surged forward across what Alvin Hovey of the 24th Indiana described as a "slight depression" that fed into Tilghman Branch to the east. There, on the reverse slope of the hill, the infantry units were able to cover themselves while the artillery of Wallace's division and the three guns of the Chicago Light Artillery positioned their guns so that only the muzzles poked over the ridge and only the upper torsos of the cannoneers were vulnerable. The Chicago artillerymen appreciated the favor, but they were nevertheless chagrined at even being in the action again; they declared that Ezra Taylor kept his prized battery back at the landing all day. They were certain Taylor had it out for them, but all they could do was fight.[14]

The earlier lackluster advance of Sherman's and McClernand's men also pointed to additional problems. One was the lack of overall command. Unlike the day before, and unlike Buell on his front, Grant chose to remain at Pittsburg Landing much of the day, forwarding the arriving troops to the front. It would only be later in the day that Grant rode to the front lines, thereby leaving his own army and Wallace's infused division on their own. Another problem was the growing fatigue of the originally engaged Army of the Tennessee. If Grant had entertained any notion of defeating Beauregard without any help from Buell, the lackadaisical advance on the morning of April 7 of the portion of the Army of the Tennessee engaged on April 6 foreshadowed what effect it would have had. Moreover, the slow advance allowed the Confederates to build up strength. By around 10:00 A.M., when Cheatham and Polk finally took position in line, the Confederate force in the woods was substantial enough to stop the Federal advance. Thus the result was much the same as Buell had encountered to the east. Sherman and McClernand ran up against a firm Confederate line that they could not budge, especially with their tired and weakened veterans. Heavy skirmishers went to the front, but everyone could see it would take the entire Union line to do any good.[15]

The Confederates were not content to merely defend their positions either. As elsewhere that second day, the Confederate officers in command at Jones Field, including Bragg and Cheatham (who would have three horses shot under him in the course of the battle), decided to launch a counterattack and drive the enemy away. All elements of Hardee's corps, especially Wood's and Shaver's brigades fronting the field itself, moved forward to blunt the enemy advance. Skirmishers were sent ahead, including Henry Morton Stanley of the 6th Arkansas, and they soon ran into their counterparts: "We met our opponents in the same formation as ourselves, and advancing most resolutely." Stanley was unfortunately captured in a clearing before the rest of the brigade could come up. The main brigades to the rear soon surged forward as well, sweeping through the southern end of the field at an angle toward the northeast, driving back the enemy skirmishers. Perhaps looking for any success that could be used to solidify morale, a nearby Beauregard described it as "one of the most brilliant charges of infantry made on either day of the battle," and an observer noted that Beauregard "clapped his hands with joy, and declared that it was the grandest charge he had ever witnessed." The already tired Confederate brigades soon saw it was not in their best interest to be caught out in the open expanses of Jones Field, however. Shaver's regiments recoiled under the "terrific and murderous fire," with Shaver reporting that as they fell back, "considerable disorder and confusion prevailed, the commands becoming mixed up." Adding to the chaos, a shell exploded near Shaver as he tried to rally his men: "I was stricken down and rendered senseless by the explosion." Shaver was apparently unconscious for a while; he reported that when he woke up, he "was alone, neither friend nor foe being in sight." Colonel Alexander T. Hawthorn of the 6th Arkansas was also slightly wounded by a cannon shot on Monday.[16]

Wood's brigade to the northwest did no better, hindered by the heavy fire of Thompson's Battery. As Wood and Shaver moved diagonally into Jones Field, the battery was able to rake down their lines, sitting as it was on the left front flank. Wood described how the enemy artillerymen "waited until nearly two-thirds of the entire line was in the open ground. They then opened." Wood had nearly made it across the field but was forced to return to the woods when other portions of the line to the left fell back. The left of the brigade under Colonel C. A. McDaniel of the 44th Tennessee had not proceed as far as the right, the result of Russell falling back on McDaniel's own left. Colonel W. K. Patterson of the 8th Arkansas similarly reported that his regiment soon gave in to "disorder," but he noted it was fortunate because it allowed a more dispersed target for Thompson's gunners. Out in front as skirmishers, Major John H. Kelly's 9th Arkansas Battalion declined to recross the field but took to a ravine to the right, coming out on Cleburne's front down the line and only then returning to their brigade.[17]

The Federals, realizing the chaos in the enemy ranks, tried to press forward in return, with Sherman's command trudging up and over the hill toward the enemy line on the western side of Jones Field. Attached to it was the late-arriving brigade under Jacob Lauman of Hurlbut's division, which had been kept in the rear to cover the line of artillery near the landing. Jesse Connelly of the 31st Indiana admitted, "We were in hopes we should not be called on to go out again," but their hopes were dashed and they soon joined Sherman in Jones Field. Heavy fighting erupted as the infantry swept forward and Thompson's and Thurber's artillery shelled Shaver's and Wood's line. The now-reorganized Confederates presented a solid wall of fire themselves, however, throwing back the Union line farther to the east amid McClernand's troops while Sherman's men, supported by Lauman's brigade, managed only to maintain their position in the middle of Jones Field. Casualties quickly mounted; Major Fred Arn of the 31st Indiana fell mortally wounded in Lauman's brigade. The 25th Kentucky was so devoid of officers, with Major William B. Wall's wounds from spent balls causing him to leave the field, that Colonel John H. McHenry of the 17th Kentucky had to take command of the 25th Kentucky as well.[18]

Worse results occurred in the southeast corner of the field, where two guns of McAllister's battery deployed amid McClernand's troops. McClernand told McAllister, "Captain, your guns are all I have left; do your best today." McAllister covered the infantry advance diagonally across the southeastern portion of the open ground toward Shaver's shaken regiments, and the Arkansans' flintlocks provided no additional morale. Shaver later reported in their defense, "It is with great difficulty that men can be made to stand their ground when they are suffering from the fire of their adversaries and are in possession of the knowledge that from the inefficiency of their pieces they are doing no execution in return." Yet they managed to hold. Major R. T. Harvey, now commanding the 2nd Arkansas after the loss of both colonel and lieutenant colonel, reported that the "officers and men [were] becoming disgusted, [and] determined to rally." Although McClernand's units retook Hare's camps, they were driven back by the Confederate line in the woods. Captain William T. Frohock of the 45th Illinois termed this the "severest contest of the day." In a unique event, Charles Wright of the 81st Ohio remembered seeing a black man run forward with a cartridge box and begin to fire at the Confederates from behind a tree. The scene was so uncommon that it startled the Ohioan, and he long remembered that the man "would glance along the line of the 81st, and a smile of intense satisfaction would light up his dark face."[19]

The satisfaction did not last long. Another Ohioan described firing only "some 8 or 10 volleys" before disaster struck. McClernand noted with disgust that the 53rd Ohio of Sherman's division broke, Marsh adding "without any apparent cause" and "in a manner that can only be stigmatized as disgraceful and cowardly." Although the regiment's lieutenant colonel, Robert A. Fulton, reported that a Union battery fired into it and one of Sherman's staff officers ordered it to retire twice (members also blamed the 81st Ohio for breaking first), Marsh reported that they fled with a speed "even [John] Floyd might envy." The Ohioans were not the only unit that fell back, however. A member of the hard-fighting 45th Illinois noted that the "53rd and 71st Ohio came very near getting us gobbled up by their cowardice, and did cause us to retreat, for some distance." Marsh had to order his own troops rearward to change front with the rest of the line, and McClernand admitted that his "right staggered for a moment" before recovering, although Lieutenant Colonel Adolph Engelman of the 43rd Illinois told a different story: "The line fell back in great confusion"—all the way into Tilghman Branch ravine. The advance was therefore slow and plodding, with the Federals unable to make any headway across the field. It also produced casualties, including Colonel John A. Davis of the 46th Illinois, who was severely wounded.[20]

During the heavy fighting, one member of the 81st Ohio described just how little thinking some comrades did. Hugh Carlisle remembered one of his friends approaching him and asking for his ramrod, as he had shot his away. Carlisle told him, "I've got use for my ramrod." He also told him to throw his gun away and pick up one that had a ramrod, whereupon the friend exclaimed, "I believe I will. I never thought of that." Carlisle concluded, "After a battle it was nothing unusual to find a ramrod sticking in a tree where it had been shot by some excited fellow."[21]

With the repulse of the Federal advance, a cheer rose up from the Confederate lines on the left; one 46th Illinois soldier admitted in his diary, "The rebel yells will never be forgotten." Yet all was not well on the Confederate line. The men in the Confederate line, as exhausted as their counterparts, were showing signs of strain. Lieutenant Colonel O. F. Strahl of the 4th Tennessee, which was detached from its brigade commander, Alexander Stewart, and which was fighting in the southwest portion of Jones Field, reported how numerous stragglers attached themselves to his regiment. "The stragglers demonstrated very clearly this morning that they had strayed from their own regiments because they did not want to fight," Strahl noted. "And that they still would not fight." He added that the effect on his own men was not good: "My men fought gallantly until the stragglers ran and left them and began firing from the rear over their heads." The 4th Tennessee broke, but Strahl soon had them reformed. Time was beginning to catch up with the exhausted Confederate army.[22]

Matters were even worse for both sides in the heavy woods south of Jones Field, with some of McClernand's and Hurlbut's brigades breaking at times under the Confederate defense and counterattack. Hurlbut later wrote that the Confederates "were very dashing in attack but not singularly patient in defense." In the heavy woods between Marsh's camps and Tilghman Branch that had seen so much back-and-forth action the day before, part of Pugh's just-arrived brigade as well as Veatch's in reserve behind them were, despite artillery support from Mann's Battery under Edward Brotzmann, stunned by Confederates of Anderson's brigade and his attached Louisianans. The Confederates took advantage of a slight breastwork of logs from trees cut by Marsh's brigade before the battle to clear a parade ground. Some of Veatch's regiments were so badly depleted that they were of little use to begin with, especially in the officer corps. Having lost all of its field officers, the 15th Illinois had sergeants commanding companies. Veatch put Lieutenant Colonel William Camm in charge of the regiment even though he was a member of the neighboring 14th Illinois. Another illustrative example was the 3rd Iowa of Pugh's brigade. It went into action on this second day commanded by First Lieutenant G. W. Crosley. Anderson's brigade thus had a limited force in front of it, and regiments of Gibson's brigade were also present, as were the remnants of Cleburne's brigade, now down to a mere 800 effectives. This patchwork line under Ruggles and Polk was as a result able to stop Hurlbut's advance, even when portions of McClernand's command to the right returned to this part of the front from their retreat into Tilghman Branch. The combat was still close; one Federal wrote that the "colors of the Forty-sixth [Illinois] and the rebels [were] planted within 30 yards of each other." Another described hand-to-hand fighting. With reinforcements, the Confederates were even able to throw Hurlbut back a few hundred yards; Gibson claimed to have temporarily "captured a field battery from the enemy under a galling fire." One of his Louisianans wrote of the confusion in the action, declaring that the brigade crossed one ravine to attack the battery, but Ruggles "countermanded the order six times." Each time they went forward to the lip of the ravine, they were called back. Out of ammunition and jaded by the terrain, they could not endure such confusion. Yet morale was soon bolstered as one of the Louisianans, a former musician in Mexico, picked up a fife and let loose "Dixie" "with great enthusiasm," one soldier remembered.[23]

Still, bitter fighting took place in the woods east of Marsh's camps, with both sides taking heavy casualties. Cleburne's brigade, which formed a line across a ravine that fed into Tilghman Branch, was not excited about charging the enemy lines of Hurlbut's and McClernand's divisions, but it did so after peremptory orders arrived. Cleburne, spying enemy troops on his left toward Jones Field, first received orders from Breckinridge to advance with his brigades to the right, but Cleburne declined, saying he was isolated and his flank was open on the left. He told the courier he would "be destroyed if I advanced." Bragg happened to come along at that time, however, and told Cleburne the order was "positive, and I must immediately advance." Fortunately for Cleburne, he had not advanced far when one of Breckinridge's batteries to the right, probably Byrne's, started firing diagonally across his path, "obliging me to halt," a relieved Cleburne wrote. Other batteries soon joined in. Cleburne moved into the ravine to allow Girardey's Battery behind him to fire over their heads. This duel continued for a while; Cleburne called it "the fiercest I saw during the day." He was satisfied being "merely spectators of the fight," although falling tree limbs killed some of his men.[24]

The artillery duel eventually ended, and when the attack was renewed it was disastrous for Cleburne. The brigade entered thick undergrowth and woods from which they could not see, although the enemy could still fire on them. Many men and officers went down, including Lieutenant Colonel James F. Neill, commanding the 23rd Tennessee. By taking such casualties, the brigade "was repulsed and almost completely routed in this unfortunate attack," Cleburne reported, noting that only the 15th Arkansas rallied to form a line again, despite their commander, Lieutenant Colonel Archibald K. Patton, being killed.[25]

Anderson, to Cleburne's right, had his own problems. He had entirely raw troops, but Bragg reported Anderson's "personal gallantry and soldierly bearing supplied the place of instruction and discipline." He participated in the initial attack on the Federal lines, but it took him several assaults before the men proved successful by advancing "with a volley and a shout." In this particular area, Anderson fought the Federals over the fallen logs from the parade ground, with the sharpshooters of each side using this timber to advantage to take down artillerymen and officers.[26]

The crisis spot came closer to the Union left, where the link between the Army of the Tennessee and the Army of the Ohio was not secure amid the small valley that fed into Tilghman Branch. Apparently little lateral communication occurred between the two armies and their officers. As a result, a portion of the Confederate line, the 4th Alabama Battalion and 4th Kentucky of Trabue's brigade and Anderson's brigade after its shift to the right, were able to get between the two wings and, while threatening Rousseau's right, also pestered Hurlbut's left flank, stopping his advance and even throwing it back momentarily. McClernand reported he had to shift troops to the left, causing what he described as "one of the severest conflicts . . . that occurred during the two days." McClernand wrote that it was so critical at this point that "repulse seemed inevitable." Hurlbut was calmer, writing that McClernand was brave but "impetuous and very avaricious of glory, and occasionally these qualities developed rashness."[27]

Hurlbut's troops had watched the massive artillery duel to their right, with one confused soldier blurting out a question as to which side a certain battery was on. He was quickly answered from the rear by "It is ours of course." Turning around, the men saw Hurlbut atop his horse, calmly smoking. The calm soon ended as Hurlbut and McClernand realized the issue on their left flank. In one of the few cross-army communications, McClernand asked Lovell Rousseau, the extreme right brigade of Buell's army, to aid the threatened Army of the Tennessee line. Hurlbut also rode over and talked to Rousseau and even McCook. Rousseau sent his reserve, the 5th Kentucky, into the breach, and McClernand bragged on the Louisville Legion in his report. "Extending and strengthening my line," the general wrote, "this gallant body poured into the enemy's ranks one of the most terrible fires I ever witnessed." Hurlbut also sent a portion of Pugh's men, the brigade having inadvertently split, to the crisis area. "Suddenly we confronted the enemy," wrote one member of the 3rd Iowa, "standing in compact line of battle, as if just dressed to begin an advance." Heavy fighting broke out, but quick-thinking reinforcements took care of the enemy threat and the Confederates fell back to their original line. McClernand proudly thanked Rousseau and the Kentuckians for their "generous response . . . to my request for succor."[28]

With such concern about holding their own lines, the original portion (not including Wallace's "fresh" division) of the Army of the Tennessee's advance from Jones Field southward thus netted no greater advantages than Buell's fighting on the left, and it even produced the same Confederate defense and counterattacks. The Federal advance was stymied all along the line; one mystified staff officer wrote, "The roaring was incessant—one peal after another. Our men charged bayonets on them again and again. They would rally and come down on us with a determination that seemed invincible." One Illinoisan, Richard Gapen, illustrated the idea that the Confederates fought well on this second day, declaring to his sister at home that "they also got reinforcements of some thirty thousand under Gen. Bragg and were brought in about noon which gave new life to the enemy and made the fight desperate for a while." Although the statement was not true, it indicates the ferocity with which the beleaguered Confederates were fighting.[29]

With the Federal effort stalled all across the battlefield, Grant and Buell needed some type of catalyst to change the dynamic of the unfolding second day. Lew Wallace, who has been described as lethargic at Shiloh, provided the maneuver that turned the tide against this initial Confederate line. None of the other divisions had been able to drive the enemy by frontal assaults, and there was little reason to believe Wallace would be able to do so either. Whether out of a need to keep his troops out of pointless combat, out of a recognition that maneuver can sometimes attain with fewer casualties what major assaults could not attain, or perhaps out of timidity, as has often been asserted, Wallace chose not to advance directly against the Confederate line, "much to the disappointment of our men," George McGinnis remembered. In fact, he kept his men prone whenever he could. Lieutenant Colonel William D. McCord of the 1st Nebraska wrote about one firefight, "The regiment was ordered to lie down, or we could not possibly have escaped as well as we did." Although Wallace had not yet seen much action—only the easily repulsed Confederate cavalry charge under John Wharton—an opportunity for new thinking now presented itself. The Confederate "flank was now exposed," Wallace wrote, adding, "I resolved to attempt to re-turn it." He chose to flank the Confederate line, netting, he hoped, the same result with less fighting and fewer casualties.[30]

The changing terrain on the battlefield made such a maneuver possible. Unlike the previous day, the battlefield was now expanding rather than constricting in width. The constriction on the first day played into Grant's strategy, allowing the Federals to hold a progressively shorter line when they were on the defensive. Conversely, the widening battlefield on the second day allowed the Federals to outflank the smaller numbers of Confederates, who could not construct a completely solid line. The terrain, as in so many cases at Shiloh, seemed to be set up to aid the Federal army.[31]

Although Nelson on the far left had his hands full and was not thinking in terms of turning Withers's right (indeed, he was enduring his own flank being turned), Wallace on the far right had no such worries and soon began to put his plan into operation. He took advantage of the open Confederate left, which by this time sat a little inland from the ravines bordering Owl Creek. In an effort to use the terrain as effectively as possible, the Confederate left rested on a smaller ravine that ran inland from Owl Creek, but the hollow was far too small to provide the kind of secure terrain feature on which to secure a flank. Lieutenant Colonel Manning F. Force remembered, "This valley was evidently regarded as impracticable and as a sufficient defense," but Wallace nevertheless turned it as he advanced to the front and right, wheeling the division to the left "to change front by a left half-wheel of the whole division." Smith's and Thayer's troops performed the operation admirably, but

Whittlesey on the right was crowded out of position as a result of the swamps of Owl Creek, and he had to find a suitable place to rejoin the division. He went to Wallace's far left, which provided the added bonus of securing Sherman's connection with him. Thus Smith in the center with the 11th and 24th Indiana and 8th Missouri and Thayer on the right with the 1st Nebraska, 23rd Indiana, and 58th Ohio advanced westward into Sowell Field, which sat on a long and prominent ridge jutting into the Owl Creek bottomland. They took a position in the field facing due south, which placed them at an angle to the Confederate left, which faced northeastward.[32]

Meanwhile, Whittlesey's brigade also moved forward, finding an opening on Smith's left next to Stuart's command of Sherman's division. Yet Wallace was more concerned about his right and throwing more weight into the effort to outflank the Confederates. He thus pulled the 20th and 78th Ohio out of Whittlesey's line and sent them back to the right of the division, leaving only the 76th Ohio on the left. On the far right, the two regiments soon faced a section of Confederate guns, probably Ketchum's.[33]

Despite the confusion in Whittlesey's ranks, the effect of the move was almost instantaneous. "We advanced yelling like we were wild," one Indianan related. "The whole Rebel Army broke and ran for their lives," he continued, adding, "A soldier knows when he is flanked and wont stand for it." Zach Deas on the far Confederate left sounded the first note of alarm, "perceiving the enemy's skirmishers on our left and rear." Robert Russell, commanding the "division" that included Deas's men, described how he was preparing to advance when he "perceived the enemy was forming a line perpendicular to ours and in the rear of our left flank, and also planting a battery on our left flank." He added, "This rendered a change of front necessary and caused us to retire." Casualties took a further toll. Alfred Fielder of the 12th Tennessee wrote that as "we were ordered to fall back in double quick some of our men became panic stricken and it was with difficulty that they could be prevailed on to rally." In the confusion, Major R. P. Campbell of the 12th Tennessee, who had taken over from Colonel Tyree Bell because of his wounds, and Colonel A. J. Vaughan of the 13th Tennessee had their horses shot from under them. Vaughan temporarily turned over command to his lieutenant colonel until he could remount and retake command. One of Ruggles's staff officers also fell captive to the 20th Ohio.[34]

Beauregard soon realized what was happening on the left and quickly determined that this was now the critical front. He went himself to rally the men and prevail on them to hold and perhaps even counterattack to continue the previous day's victory. One of Russell's Tennesseans wrote that after they rallied, "Gen Beauregard rode up and made a short speech."[35]

Although Beauregard quickly shifted troops to that critical left, both sides' artillery soon took over. Thompson's artillery kept the Confederates from forming any heavier resistance on the left, and a "fine duel" took place for a few minutes. Thompson's gunners fired so fast that they soon depleted their ammunition, and Wallace ordered Thurber forward to take their position. "Thurber obeyed with such alacrity that there was scarcely an intermission in the fire," Wallace proudly reported. Yet the Confederate artillery took a toll as well. Alvin Hovey remembered "the shell and shot of our battery and the battery of the enemy rained thick and fast above and around us." Frank Cheatham, astonished that the enemy "seemed to have thrown his whole disposable force against our left flank," reported he was "greatly annoyed by the want of artillery" but soon received some aid from Smith's Battery, working one of the guns himself.[36]

Under the cover of the guns, the Confederate line, outflanked as it was, attempted to advance again under Beauregard's urging and solidify the flank, but it was soon driven back by Wallace's infantry and began to peel away from left to right. Because of the retreat on the left, Polk to the south likewise had to pull back to a new line, which in turn uncovered Breckinridge's troops, who were fighting hard in the Hornet's Nest area. They also began to withdraw before noon to a new line along the Hamburg-Purdy Road, one Illinoisan in Hurlbut's division emphasizing how the enemy "run, run, run." They did not run far, however; Beauregard soon began patching together a new line on the left and center. Hardee was able to maintain his hold on the road farther east, providing a secure line for Breckinridge to form on.[37]

Despite hurling what Alvin Hovey of the 24th Indiana called "every missile known in modern war" at the Federals, the initial Confederate line had broken. Confederate commanders scrambled to reposition the line along the Hamburg-Purdy Road, but they soon realized that the retreat was not the disaster it could have been. No great damage had been done besides falling back to a new line; at no place had the line been punctured, and it had not even fallen back on the right. The effect was the line swinging back on hinges located on Hardee's front. The line now ran from Hardee's position south of the cotton field along the road beside the wheat field to the crossing of the Hamburg-Purdy and Eastern Corinth roads. The line then continued a little northwestward along Breckinridge's front south of Review Field and on to the Crossroads that had seen so much fighting the day before. Although the road took a sharp turn to the west toward the crossing of Owl Creek, the Confederate line—elements of Anderson's, Gibson's, Cheatham's, and Russell's units—continued straight northwestward toward Crescent Field, again attempting but failing to reach the Owl Creek swamps and a secure left flank. Thus in several hours, despite heavy fighting that one Kentuckian in Grant's army wrote "was tremendous, I believe equal to yesterday," the lines had not moved much.[38]

Still, by noon, Wallace had been able to do what none of the other Federal commanders had achieved: he broke the initial Confederate line of resistance. Buell and most of the elements of Grant's own army had battered themselves against the solid Confederate line, enduring heavy casualties and failing to advance much past the initial point of major contact. For whatever reason modern tacticians want to provide for him, the fact remains that Wallace utilized maneuver rather than frontal assaults, and the results were spectacular. "Our advance was slow, but steady and certain," explained Colonel George F. McGinnis of the 11th Indiana. Not only did Wallace save major casualties in his own command, but he likely did so in other commands as well; they would probably have continued the frontal assaults of the morning. By a simple act of maneuver, allowed by the features of the terrain on the western side of the battlefield, Wallace was able to start the process of driving the entire Confederate army rearward anywhere from a half mile on his front on the far Confederate left to a quarter of a mile in the center to a continually decreasing space nearer to the Confederate left, where the line maintained its former position.[39]

The Confederate high command did not miss the significance of Wallace's advance. Beauregard noted, "On the right and center the enemy was repulsed in every attempt he made," but not on the left. Jacob Thompson, the former secretary of the interior, now serving on Beauregard's staff, was equally in wonder of Wallace's move. He wrote, "About 11.30 o'clock it was apparent that the enemy's main attack was on our left, and our forces began to yield to the vigor of his attack." Wallace's coup also had a large effect on his own side; one Michigan artilleryman wrote of the change: "A brighter day began to dawn, the dark cloud which hung over us began to wear away, and thoughts of victory began to cheer us." An Illinoisan similarly stated, "The tables are turning."[40]

And Wallace was not finished. It was only noon.

19

"Making Them Pay Dearly for Their Purchase"

P. G. T. Beauregard could be justifiably pleased with his army's work on the morning of April 7, especially considering its lack of reorganization and rest during the night. Much of that was his own fault, but the army came together remarkably and solidly, putting up actually a more organized front than it had the day before in terms of high-level unit cohesion. Unfortunately, it had taken three or four hours of the morning to do it, and the Confederate officers were thus only able to place their line far back from the Federal jumping-off point, allowing Grant and Buell nearly a mile of undisputed territory to reclaim during that time.

Still, Beauregard's troops, although tired and haggard, had put up a strong fight, turning back almost all Federal advances on the right and center and frequently counterattacking and driving the enemy back. The only problem was on the far left, where Wallace had managed to outflank the line, causing it to fall back. The divisions were going into a second line about noon, however—one that would, they hoped, prove to be just as formidable as the first one. Thus as the afternoon began, Beauregard's troops were somewhat holding their own, although the hope of driving back Buell's and Grant's fresh legions, some of them still landing at Pittsburg, was no longer realistic.[1]

Fighting soon began again as the Union divisions met the reestablished Confederate line. On the Federal left, Nelson and Crittenden reconstituted their drives southward, although the going was difficult and they were turned away once more. Nelson's brigades attacked through the Peach Orchard in the early afternoon, but they continued to run into stiff resistance from Withers's Confederates, who repelled the first assault by Bruce's brigade. The fall of Colonel Thomas D. Sedgewick from a spent ball did not help matters.[2]

There was an additional problem emerging on the Union left. Nelson's diagonal path southwestward had increasingly brought his division west of the River Road, with both Hazen and Bruce west and only Ammen east of the path during the heavy fighting of the late morning. In the massive turn of attention to the right around Hazen's attack, a gap had also resulted between Ammen and Bruce, forcing Bruce to look to defending his flank as the Confederates tried unsuccessfully to split the brigades and turn the flank of Bruce's left regiment, the 2nd Kentucky.[3]

As the division continually advanced into the field and onward, however, Ammen too moved across the road, leaving the entire area east of the road defenseless except for the 2nd Iowa and the 19th Ohio, which Buell had sent over from Boyle's brigade. At one point, the 20th Kentucky, the reserve of Bruce's brigade, also helped defend the flank. Still, because of Nelson's southwestward movement combined with the continually expanding width of the battlefield the farther southward the fighting raged, Nelson's left was growing more open by the minute. Had the Confederates collected enough manpower, they could easily have tested, if not attacked, this open Federal flank once more. By this time, however, the Confederate line had all it could do to repulse the frontal assaults.[4]

In addition, more Federal troops shuttled into the line, allowing the divisions to contract and form a heavier mass in each sector. The Confederates had no corresponding reinforcements and a wider field to defend. The result was a thinned line and a much weaker defense. Ammunition was also running low in many commands. A wounded but still fighting Marcus Wright of the 154th Tennessee, for example, reported his ammunition was exhausted, and Preston Smith actually retired his men out of the line. On reporting his action to Chalmers, Smith noted, "I received a shot through the right shoulder with a Minie ball, inflicting a painful wound and disabling my sword arm." Most of the line remained, though, and Smith's troops later rejoined Withers, with Smith still fighting despite his wound. They were able to keep delaying Nelson with another repulse of his now-timid division around 1:00 P.M.[5]

On Crittenden's front farther to the west, both Smith and Boyle turned their attention southward. Smith's troops reconstituted their attack over the ground they had fought over earlier near Davis's wheat field, but this time Boyle's troops followed on Smith's right. The division basically moved southward astride the Eastern Corinth Road in correlation with the angle of the new Confederate line. They moved through the almost impenetrable undergrowth that the Confederates had found so daunting the day before, only in reverse. The difficult terrain once again played havoc with their alignment, as did Harper's Mississippi Battery from its position near the crossing of the Eastern Corinth and Hamburg-Purdy roads. The supporting Confederate infantry likewise held out into the afternoon, although one joyous Kentuckian in Crittenden's division summed up the gladness felt at the little bit of ground gained: he told his father the Confederates had run over "Grant's men all day Sunday and hallowed Bull Run at our boys but on Monday they raised their yells & whoop & hallowed but there was too many Ky boys for them."[6]

The fighting on Crittenden's front raged furiously, with each side advancing and being repulsed in what developed into a series of assaults by the Federal brigades. Like farther east, the Confederates were again able to hold off the Federal advance, although Alexander Stewart described the problems he faced on this portion of the line. His men soon ran out of ammunition, and he took them to the rear when a section of Bankhead's Battery appeared. He had trouble finding ammunition and noted, "The men being worn out and imperfectly supplied with ammunition, it was extremely difficult to get them forward." He managed to do so, but they ran out of ammunition again and left the line once more. Even the return of Colonel J. C. Tappan of the 13th Arkansas, who had been away on sick leave, did not inspire the men to hold their ground. He nevertheless took command from Major James A. McNeely, who had been wounded by "a bomb" in the counterattack at the wheat field.[7]

The increasing Federal numbers started to tell as the afternoon began, and no better place illustrated this than the center of the line where McCook's troops drove hard to the west. McCook was now handling his brigades better than earlier in the day, but he had two different issues, in addition to the obvious problem of Confederate resistance, to contend with as he followed up the Confederate retreat. A small fight broke out just west of Duncan Field, where Rousseau captured a Confederate battery and McClernand's headquarters. Perhaps more threateningly, because both brigades of Crittenden's division were now driving due south along the Eastern Corinth Road and McCook advanced due west along the main Corinth Road, a wide gap, or what Buell described as "a considerable widening of the space," developed between McCook and Crittenden. It grew wider the farther the divisions advanced along their parent roads. The opposite effect occurred on his other flank to the right, however, where he linked with Grant's Army of the Tennessee. Because of McCook's westward movement and Grant's southwestward advance, the two ran into each other, causing some confusion. The problem of too many troops on McCook's right was much better than too few on his left, and his brigades eventually moved in front of Grant's, prompting James R. Hugunin of the 12th Illinois to remark, "We could do but little else than to watch those brave fellows, occasionally putting in a shot or two, but always at long distance." McCook would have been better off moving southwestward between Crittenden and McClernand, but he chose to continue westward along his axis of advance, which was the Corinth Road.[8]

The Army of the Tennessee command most affected by McCook's surge was McClernand's division, but he soon stabilized his lines and even advanced to the left front, following the Federals toward Woolf Field where he personally reconnoitered at the edge and oversaw the placement of Edward Bouton's guns. McCook's brigades took over the advance and soon far overlapped McClernand's, however, with Buell ordering several of Grant's regiments to the rear so that his troops could take the lead. Although the glory-hungry McClernand may have been chagrined at being shunted to the rear, others were glad to see the Army of the Ohio. Moving toward the new Confederate line from the north, Sherman noted that it was here that "I saw for the first time the well-ordered and compact columns of General Buell's Kentucky forces, whose soldierly movements at once gave confidence to our newer and less-disciplined forces."[9]

McCook proceeded westward until Rousseau's troops reached Woolf Field and the "thicket" around Water Oaks Pond, where heavy fighting had occurred the day before. Hurlbut described the area as "the dreaded point of woods known as the 'Green Point,'" and the Federals would indeed soon learn to dread the area. Although his men were running out of ammunition, Rousseau nevertheless advanced, but not until making sure Kirk's brigade was immediately to his rear. Rousseau rode back to talk to Kirk, requesting him to stay close. Kirk responded that his men would do so and that they were "ready for anything."[10]

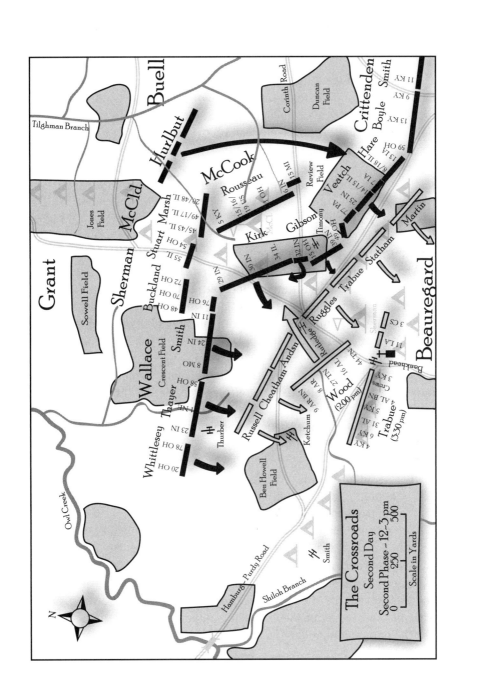

The Crossroads
Second Day
Second Phase ~ 12–3 pm

Scale in Yards
0   250   500

Grant
Buell
Sherman
McCld.
Hurlbut
McCook
Crittenden
Beauregard

Tilghman Branch
Jones Field
Sowell Field
Corinth Road
Duncan Field
Review Field
Smith
Boyle
Hare
Veatch
Gibson
Kirk
Martin
Statham
Trabue
Ruggles
Rutledge
Anderson
Cheatham
Russell
Wood (2:00 pm)
Trabue (3:30 pm)
Bankhead
Crews
Ben Howell Field
Ketchum
Thurber
Buckland
Stuart
Marsh
Smith
Wallace
Crescent Field
Thayer
Whittlesey
Owl Creek
Hamburg–Purdy Road
Shiloh Branch
Smith

11 KY
9 KY
13 KY
59 OH
13 IL
18 IL
7 IA
14 IL
15 IL
25 IN
Vd. L
6 IN
15 MI
5 OH
16/ 15
15/ 16/
19 OH
5 KY
20/ 48 IL
49/17 IL
45/43 IL
54 OH
55 OH
72 OH
70 OH
48 OH
76 OH
11 IN
24 IN
8 MO
58 OH
1 NE
23 IN
78 OH
20 OH
29 IN
30 IN
34 IL
32 IN
15 OH
49 OH
Timony
27 OH
44 TN
16 AL
8 AR
9 AR Bn
27 TN
11 LA
3 CS
Sherman
3 KY
4 AL Bn
3 IL
31 AL
6 KY
4 KY
N

Rousseau's regiments quickly found the enemy on the other side of Woolf Field, taking refuge in some of McClernand's camps. The brigade actually entered the field, but was turned back by the heavy Confederate line on the other side. Because of Rousseau's heavy fighting in Duncan Field and the resulting empty cartridge boxes, Rousseau again met Kirk, who "at once gallantly and eagerly offered to take my position in front, and did so." Rousseau promised to support him if needed "by the bayonet." A seemingly less than involved McCook oversaw the movement, with Kirk's regiments going in a little to the right of Rousseau's center and the right of the brigade moving through Kirk's left. "All was done without the least confusion or even excitement," Rousseau recalled. Before departing for the rear, Rousseau again told Kirk that if needed before resupplying his ammunition, he would support Kirk's brigade with the bayonet.[11]

McCook thus positioned Kirk's reserve brigade at the edge of the field, the 29th and 30th Indiana and 34th Illinois in line with the just-arrived guns of Bouton's battery unlimbering in their midst for support. Confederate fire immediately took its toll, though, with one Illinoisan writing, "The swish of canister and the droning of musket balls began to give us a new experience. . . . We began to realize that we were earning our thirteen dollars a month." Betraying his nervousness for the growing expanse on his left, McCook also posted the lead regiment of Gibson's brigade, the volatile and noisy Prussian Marxist August Willich's 32nd Indiana, on Kirk's left while oddly sending the reserve regiment of Kirk's brigade even farther to the left. The 77th Pennsylvania, the only eastern regiment on the field, moved into action due south toward Review Field, prompting one Pennsylvanian to admit: "Thinks to myself now pretty soon we will know what war is." The trade was good for the Pennsylvanians, as Willich ran into the heavier resistance by far. Willich's "regiment of dutch," as one of the Illinoisans in their division described them, had been the first of Gibson's regiments to land and had on Grant's orders immediately moved forward without the brigade. The regiment had made a name for itself at Green River earlier in the war and was considered "invincible," according to one Illinoisan. Thus they were allowed to operate independently of their brigade. Willich reported that the regiment marched "as fast as possible" but received "no special direction," whereupon Willich marched to the sound of the fighting. The Indianans amazingly arrived on McCook's line, taking a position behind the lines as a reserve, but Willich was not satisfied and as he told it, "I asked General McCook for permission to pass with the regiment to the front and make a bayonet charge." McCook agreed, and the regiment marched to the front in column formation, "with flags flying and drums beating," one of Rousseau's regulars wrote. They moved around the left of Rousseau's and Kirk's men and marched out into the open expanse of Woolf Field. The Dutchmen, who were sitting ducks, were immediately struck by the unbelieving Confederate line and recoiled under what McCook described as "a most withering fire of shell, canister, and musketry, which for a moment staggered it." Their opponents were Breckinridge's brigade, augmented by Russell's command, which had marched from the extreme left. Anderson's troops were also in this line.[12]

Willich's setback occurred right in front of the 34th Illinois. The Illinoisans had to cease their fire and then endure the Indianan's retreat through their line. "A part of them broke and run directly through our lines," wrote an aggravated Will Robinson of the 34th Illinois, "and which created some confusion, and I must say almost a panic." The retreat thus spread to the Illinoisans, which withdrew a few yards before they reformed again. The watching Confederates took advantage of the Federal confusion and followed up the retreat, only to be stopped once more by the Illinoisans' heated fire.[13]

One of the Federals in Kirk's brigade, Bergun H. Brown of the 29th Indiana, described the heated contest. "For a time things seemed to be on a quiver," he wrote home, but he assured his folks that he had not been unnerved: "I was quite well prepared for the occasion by hearing the cannons one whole day and then passing through Savanna where the wounded had been conveyed, but still more so by passing over the battlefield where the dead, dying and wounded lay." Prepared or not, Brown still moved on "under a most telling fire[.] I must acknowledge that my hair stuck up some but not so much so but that I got them down and commenced firing like fun." He and the others took advantage of the ground cover and laid down, although he still managed to "bunt," with his head, he noted, "one of their nearly spent balls off the track."[14]

Matters were little better in the reformed 34th Illinois, which was already deprived of its colonel, Kirk, now commanding the brigade. Lower-level problems emerged as well. One of the company captains had been left in Savannah sick; he had made it that far only by riding in an ambulance. Then the first lieutenant was put "hors du combat" by a shell that flew past his head. "He fell fainting to the ground," one of the Illinoisans wrote, and was carried off the field. Fortunately the second lieutenant was a man of great courage, and he took command of the company.[15]

Despite the problems on his front, McCook was growing more concerned about the expanse to the left and hurried to bring up the rest of Gibson's brigade. It had just landed at Pittsburg after a slow boat ride against the current (it "gave us plenty of time for sober reflection," one Ohioan remembered). The brigade was not in the best fighting trim, however, because its normal commander, Brigadier General R. W. Johnson, had been left at Columbia as a result of severe sickness. Thus Gibson, the senior colonel, was "accidentally in command," he dryly noted, but there was a luminary among the staff: Captain Henry Clay, grandson of the famous statesman. With the 32nd Indiana back in line on Kirk's left, Gibson took a position to the rear of Rousseau, but McCook quickly brought them forward and placed the 39th Indiana and the 15th and 49th Ohio in line on Willich's left, extending the line from Woolf Field down to the southwestern corner of Review Field where the 77th Pennsylvania was engaged. Thus McCook had two of his brigades in line by a little after noon while Rousseau's brigade filled its cartridge boxes from three wagons brought from the landing by McCook's ordinance officer, Lieutenant J. A. Campbell. McCook had ordered him to go to the rear three hours earlier to search for ammunition, and he returned at a critical moment.[16]

McCook, supposedly on the offensive, could do little but position his brigades to plug gaps because the Confederates to the south and west continually pushed forward in attacks and demonstrations. William Preston Johnston later termed McCook's division "the point of a wedge," and it was an apt description. Gibson noted that immediately after taking their positions, the Confederates "opened a terrific fire on our whole line simultaneously," with no fewer than three batteries shelling the brigade at the same time. McCook thus found himself on the defensive: "The enemy seemed to increase in the vigor and the rapidity of his attack," he marveled. He also added that he believed 10,000 Confederates attacked his two brigades, and that "the fires from the contending ranks were two continuous sheets of flame." The Confederates had some success by driving away Bouton's Battery, which temporarily left two guns because, as Bouton reported, the horses had not "been drilled sufficiently to stand fire." Colonel

Thomas Crittenden of the resupplying 6th Indiana of Rousseau's brigade reported that the recaptured guns of Bouton's battery "soon left the field, under the steady advance of the enemy's infantry and a severe fire from the artillery."[17]

Despite their only battery under Terrill fighting to the left, McCook nevertheless stabilized the situation and even counterattacked. "Our volleys were delivered with rapidity, regularity, and effect," Gibson proudly noted. Despite some effort to turn Gibson's left flank, he assaulted along with the rest of McCook's troops. Gibson's brigade advanced diagonally toward the Crossroads, perpendicular to the line McClernand had held the day before on the same ground. The reinstituted Confederate line would not budge, however, and Gibson suffered heavy casualties. Major William Wallace, the only field officer in the 15th Ohio, had a close call, with his horse shot from under him. Unable to break the Confederate line, the brigade fell back 150 yards to its original position "in good order, keeping up a constant fire," noted Colonel Thomas J. Harrison of the 39th Indiana.[18]

Kirk's brigade to the right suffered the most in the attack. As the three regiments of the brigade advanced across Woolf Field, they met the firm resistance of Wood's Confederate brigade supported by Rutledge's Tennessee Battery in line west of the field. Wood had been withdrawn from his Jones Field line earlier and placed in reserve, throwing down the still-standing tents in the area of the Crossroads so they could see any Federal advance. His men watched as Beauregard and Governor Harris rode the lines and reformed broken regiments on this second line. Harris, a consummate politician, could not constrain himself and "made them a speech." Talk quickly turned to volleys, however, and the fighting was extremely heavy, with one of Grant's men watching from the rear writing that "both armies [were] as hotly engaged as it is possible for men to be." The casualty figures illustrated the ferocity of the engagement, with both the 34th Illinois, which charged right through Water Oaks Pond, and the 30th Indiana to their right, both in the open field, taking much heavier casualties than the other two regiments. One of the Illinoisans wrote, "We had to cross a field about 40 rods wide and through a perfect storm of bullets, shot, and shell. Our men fell thick." Another noted proudly, "We were cut up but we never faltered." The 29th Indiana suffered far fewer casualties in its position in the woods north of Woolf Field, and the Pennsylvanians barely suffered at all in their advance near Review Field. But the fighting was heavy in Woolf

Field, with Kirk experiencing heavy casualties—second only to Hazen in Buell's army. Kirk's official losses were only about sixty fewer than Hazen's.[19]

The most prominent casualties in the brigade were officers, which greatly affected their men. Colonel Sion S. Bass fell with two wounds while leading the 30th Indiana in the field itself, leaving the command to Lieutenant Colonel Joseph B. Dodge. Major Charles N. Levanway, commanding the 34th Illinois in Kirk's absence, was killed when a shell burst nearby and a fragment tore into his neck. His death shook the regiment, as his head was turned as he fell to the ground "so that his face was reversed, the back of his head being between his shoulders." Kirk realized the need for leadership among his Illinoisans and rode into the fray. He took the regiment's standard and succeeded in rallying the troops, only to himself fall with a nasty wound "at the point of the right shoulder." As Kirk was being removed to the rear, McCook told him he would soon wear a brigadier's star. Lieutenant Colonel Joseph B. Dodge of the 30th Indiana took command of the brigade.[20]

A familiar story thus developed in this fighting. Kirk assaulted across the field and pond but was driven back. One Illinoisan described the action: "After firing each man lay on his back & loaded like skirmishers, then rose to his feet and fired again, all taking advantages of any natural shelter as trees logs &c, but always preserving a good line." Gibson likewise could make no headway against the Confederate line and had to fall back to his original position. The Confederates could, it seemed, hold all day long against frontal assaults.[21]

This truth apparently dawned on McCook, who was soon content to hold what he had. Part of McCook's wariness to order another assault no doubt lay in his concern for his left flank. With Crittenden's right brigade, Boyle, nearly a half mile to the east, something had to be done to fill the gap, but no other troops of Buell's army were available until Wood's division arrived. That division did not arrive at the landing until noon, however, and would not arrive on the front line until nearly 2:00 P.M. The fighting in the gap thus threatened the 49th Ohio, which had to change front twice to make sure they covered the left of the brigade. Lieutenant Colonel Albert M. Blackman wrote that the Confederates "advanced up a ravine and opened his fire, quartering on my left and rear." Throughout its maneuvers, the Ohioans were also under artillery fire, although Blackman noted that most of it did no damage, "their range being too high." Fortunately for the Federals, Grant still had some reserves consisting of the least-damaged portions of his own army, and he now sent them forward to plug the gap created when Crittenden and McCook marched away from each other along the major roads. Had the Confederates then massed enough power to counterattack, a major blow could have potentially been delivered to the Federal attack, but as a result of the growing confusion in the Confederate army and the growing exhaustion of men and officers alike, little of significance occurred besides two cavalry assaults and the capture of the wounded Colonel Joel A. Battle of the 20th Tennessee. Sadly, the colonel had already lost two sons at Shiloh, one the day before around the Peach Orchard and the other earlier this day in the fighting at Duncan Field. The latter son, Joel A. Battle Jr., had been found and buried by classmates he had left in 1861 at Miami University in Ohio; when Colonel Battle heard that his captors had been his son's classmates, he "sat down and wept like a child."[22]

Two separate units sent forward from Grant's army soon plugged the gap and secured the Ohioans' flank. McClernand and McCook were by this time working in tandem, and a portion of Hurlbut's division, the 14th and 15th Illinois and 25th Indiana under Veatch that had been crowded out of line by McCook's westward advance, sidestepped across McCook's rear to his left. McClernand had sent Hurlbut to the rear to bring up reserves, and the latter did so directly across Review Field, across which Colonel William Camm reported his men advanced at the double-quick, with the field being "used before the battle as our review or parade ground." Camm also described the effects of his horse stumbling onto a dead Confederate: the horse "fell with one knee in the upturned skull, covering the leg with brains." Camm had to dismount and clean away the gore. Veatch's troops nevertheless went into line on the left of the Pennsylvanians constituting McCook's left, with McCook waving his sword and shouting to the 15th Illinois, "Now give them a touch of Illinois! Forward! Charge!" A conglomeration of units from W. H. L. Wallace's division, now under Tuttle, also advanced into the breach on Veatch's left. Tuttle had advanced behind Crittenden's division all day, acting as his reserve. It was from this reserve that Buell had sent the 2nd Iowa to shore up Nelson's left flank earlier in the morning. Now the 7th Iowa and 9th Illinois of Tuttle's division and the 8th and 18th Illinois and 13th Iowa of Hare's attached brigade manned the gap, connecting Veatch and Crittenden. The April 6 veterans of Grant's army were again showing some spunk.[23]

The portions of the Army of the Tennessee not crowded out of line were also fighting hard west of the Army of the Ohio. Like Buell's army, McClernand and Sherman moved forward around noon, following the Confederate withdrawal until they reached the new line. Here Sherman with Buckland's and Stuart's brigades, the latter now under Colonel T. Kilby Smith of the 54th Ohio, fought the left wing of the Confederate army. Stuart was so weak from his wound of the day before that he could only lead his men onto the field in "an effort to excite the enthusiasm of the men" before turning back to a hospital. Others wounded the day before were back, however. Colonel Peter J. Sullivan of the 48th Ohio remained with his regiment all day until a shot broke his right arm. A portion of Buckland's brigade took a position in the fighting on the same high ground it had defended the day before amid the retreat and counterattack on the Federal right. The 70th Ohio, which had gone into line facing west the day before, now formed on the left of the brigade that occupied the same position, although it now faced due south. No doubt the wounded and dead still lying where they had previously fallen had a sobering effect. Sherman would not let any of his regiments retire, however, even when out of ammunition. Knowing any rearward movement would have a negative effect, he kept all on line whether they could shoot or not. He later commended his men for "thus holding their ground under a heavy fire, although their cartridge boxes were empty." Fortunately for them, Grant had ammunition trains moving forward from the landing all during the day.[24]

Although McClernand would be shunted out of line by McCook's deployment of his brigades north of and astride the Corinth Road, Sherman still advanced forward, although he had little offensive punch left; he had to depend more on what happened with the fresher divisions on each flank. Still, he led his men southward toward the thicket around the pond, which he described as "this dreaded woods." McCook was doing his part on Sherman's left, facing heavy fighting and enduring equally heavy casualties, but it once again fell to Lew Wallace to provide the Confederates reason to retreat on this more stubborn left flank.[25]

The renewed fighting on the extreme Confederate left took the same form as it had all across the battlefield. The still offensive-minded Confederates hit Wallace's division as it plunged into Crescent Field, with Smith on the left, Thayer in the center, and Whittlesey on the right, although the wayward 76th Ohio of Whittlesey's brigade was still on the division's left flank, connecting and sometimes supporting Stuart's brigade of Sherman's division. The division had returned to its generally southward-facing orientation from its flanking position, but it met increasing resistance. The fighting grew extremely heavy as they advanced across the hills and valleys in the field. Thayer reported how they advanced, "halting as we ascended the brow of each hill . . . and giving them another volley and then moving forward again." Once again, the main Confederate force included Deas's two regiments on the far left, the brigade of three Tennessee regiments under Russell, and others under Cheatham with part of Anderson's brigade to the right, supported by Ketchum's guns. The Confederates advanced at times but lost several men in the fighting, including S. L. Ross, "a citizen of Henderson County," and Colonel T. J. Freeman of the 22nd Tennessee, both wounded. In desperate fighting, during which Russell and Deas both made several advances only to fall back again, Wallace's division soon neared the southern end of the field, there meeting Cheatham's battle line. Thayer wrote how the "battle now raged with unabated fury for nearly two hours," with a Confederate artillery battery especially causing concern as it "was exceedingly well served, it having obtained excellent range." As Wallace described it, Crescent Field contained "frequent swells, that afforded protection to the advancing lines." He added, "And [that] was the secret of my small loss."[26]

Wallace waxed poetic when describing the action in Crescent Field in his later report. He vividly described his troops advancing, "their banners gaily decking the scene." He described his men holding the "hillocks" and how "suddenly a sheet of musketry blazed from the woods." The feeling on the ground was not as lyrical; the Confederates delayed Wallace's advance over an extended period of time. Moreover, Sherman's timid advance again left Wallace's left open, causing some concern from Wallace and the left regiment, the 11th Indiana. Colonel George F. McGinnis reported the Confederates fighting Kirk in Woolf Field were "nearly in rear of our left flank." He was determined not to retreat, however, although Wallace told him to do so "if it got too hot for us." McGinnis explained, "The reputation of our regiment was at stake, and knowing that no portion of our division had been compelled to fall back during the day, we determined to hold the position to the last." McGinnis simply turned his left companies to the east to present another front, and the Confederates were never able to take advantage of the momentary opportunity. Yet Union casualties were frequent, even

covered as the Federals were by the hillocks. Alvin Hovey, colonel of
the 24th Indiana and destined to become a high-ranking general, had
his cap "knocked off by a cannon ball." His men were lying down, but
he remained on his horse; his lieutenant colonel, John Gerber, waved
his cap and "gave three cheers for my escape." The regiment, which
saw the entire thing, heartily responded, but a moment later, Gerber was
killed. One of his soldiers wrote, "He fell from his horse in a pile on the
ground, a cannon ball struck him in his breast."[27]

Desperate action also took place west of Crescent Field, where Whittlesey's regiments were stationed in the woods facing McDowell's former camps. Even Confederate cavalry, probably Wharton's Texas Rangers, made an appearance, trying unsuccessfully to get around Wallace's
right flank. The main problem was a Confederate section of artillery
that first held a forward position but then retired to the camp of the 46th
Ohio. From there, the Confederate gunners of Smith's Battery rained
down shells on Whittlesey's troops. Manning Force of the 20th Ohio described the bombardment as a "severe and exceedingly well-aimed fire."
He added, "Muskets and bayonets at all exposed were bent and snapped
off; my sword was struck, but the men were so well sheltered that but 1
was killed and 10 were wounded." Fortunately Whittlesey was able to
bring up his own artillery support, which then evened the odds.[28]

Despite the heroic stands against the Confederate counterattacks,
Wallace had not moved forward any more easily than the other divisions to his left. John Thayer illustrated some of the problems, such as
ammunition trains being delayed as a result of the rugged terrain on the
Union right. However, the major issue was the stiff Confederate resistance. Thayer described the Confederates "contesting the ground rod by
rod with a courage and determination that would have honored a better
cause."[29]

By around 1:00 P.M., the cautious Wallace decided to utilize the same
tactics that had worked so well earlier in the morning and try to outflank
the Confederate line. Rather than assault Beauregard's left, he held the
line in position with his left brigades supported by Thurber's Battery.
Wallace carefully interchanged reserve for frontline regiments that
were out of ammunition; the 76th Ohio replaced the 1st Nebraska "with
perfect order," Thayer wrote. At the same time, he worked around the
Confederate flank with portions of Thayer's brigade and two regiments
of Whittlesey's, the 20th and 78th Ohio. The movement garnered the desired result once more, and the Confederate line began to fall back again

to yet a third line south of the Hamburg-Purdy Road. Robert Russell described how Wallace "forced a line across our left flank," and that was all Russell's men could stand. Major R. P. Caldwell, who reported that the loss of their colonel had already depressed the men, described his troops as "exhausted and unable to fight." At the same time, McCook also ordered an advance across his entire front, which likewise drove the left center of the Confederate line back to its third position nearer the church. Wallace had done it again.[30]

The effect of Wallace's turning movement, combined with increasing pressure on this second major Confederate line, had a stark effect, causing Beauregard to withdraw all his forces from the Hamburg-Purdy Road line southward to a third major position in the area of Prentiss's camps and Shiloh Church. With his former line untenable and with a widening field that left his flanks continually open to being turned, just as Wallace had now done twice, Beauregard opted to constrict his next line, making it shorter and therefore more powerful. All across the board, Confederate brigades and individual regiments began to fall back to a shorter line the generals had already located, leaving a few regiments and Wharton's Texas Rangers as a rear guard for the former line before being removed themselves. This shorter line still covered the two major avenues of escape if needed, the main Corinth and Eastern Corinth roads. Officers barked orders to fall in. One Confederate described how "here an officer on horseback would exhort and appeal like a preacher at a revival, and here a fierce Commander would draw his sword and threaten to kill a straggler if he didn't go back to the line." Some good-natured ribbing also took place as various units moved up to solidify a weak spot in the line. One such example was a Louisiana regiment falling back, only to meet the Confederate Guards Response Battalion coming up: "Let us get up there; we will show you how to stand," they cajoled. One Louisianan was quick to state, "Pretty soon they came tumbling back, just as we did."[31]

In this third line, Bragg's and Polk's troops went into a solid position along the same line that Hardee and Breckinridge would soon fall back to on the right near Prentiss's camps. Most of Ruggles's brigades were drawn out of line and sent to help cover the right, with Pond's brigade still marching back and forth several times across the rear of the Confederate army before taking a firm position near the church. Also on the left with Pond was Trabue's brigade. Their line ran through the church cemetery and near Sherman's old headquarters. Bankhead's Battery un- limbered at the cemetery, and brave color-bearers marked the position of the new line. One Louisianan described his unit's color-bearer, who "firmly believed he was not born to be shot." The bearer, he wrote, stood "there with a perfectly composed look until we came up."[32]

A renewed Federal effort all across the field followed the Confed- erate retreat. Nelson's brigades finally succeeded in gaining the south side of the Bell cotton field and the Hamburg-Purdy Road by 2:00 P.M., an hour after their earlier repulse. The Federals of Ammen's brigade retook the farthest camps to the south on this section of the line, Stu- art's. Bruce's brigade moved across the cotton field in similarly minor fighting, capturing a battery and turning the guns on the fleeing Confed- erates, and Hazen's troops retook the area they had fought over earlier in the morning around the wheat field. The Confederate Washington Artillery was gone by this time, but the Federal brigade took the po- sition for good. The Confederates of Withers's division and Hardee's larger conglomeration of units retired to the southwest to form a new line near Prentiss's camps. Nelson described the territory "which the enemy with much promptitude abandoned to our use." Withers agreed, writing that "the command slowly and in good order retired through two of the enemy's camps, not a gun being fired, and formed line of battle as ordered." Some of the lack of fighting could have been the result of an absent Nelson; the former naval officer, intent on providing aid with the gunboats, went to direct their fire, leaving Ammen in command of the division.[33]

This new Confederate line on the right was covered with ample ar- tillery, with the Napoleons of Robertson's Battery again barking in de- fiance. Lieutenant S. H. Dent noted that he "took the same position we had on Sunday morning after driving the enemy from their camp." Hardee ordered the battery to hold "at all hazards," and the men fought well in another heated exchange that eventually erupted. Some of the men described the fighting as "the hottest place they were ever into." Lieutenant Dent, covering a road with one of the guns, noted, "One said it was the only time he felt like running—In fact he did run a little way—but I called him back to his post."[34]

In the center, the left of Hardee's line and the right of Breckinridge's corps also fell back, as much under Beauregard's orders as from the combined pressure of both of Crittenden's brigades and Mendenhall's guns. Bartlett's Ohio battery ceased firing while he took his caissons to the landing in search of more ammunition. In advancing on the attack, the 14th Wisconsin of Grant's army assaulted Harper's Mississippi artillery and succeeded in capturing one of the guns and driving the rest off, although it took them two attempts to do it. The first resulted in being counterattacked in Barnes Field. Lieutenant Putnam Darden, who had taken over for the wounded Harper, reported that his infantry support was gone, his limbers were empty of canister, and his men "began to fall of exhaustion at their posts." The battery had no choice but to limber up and move away, leaving the single gun. The 13th Kentucky of Boyle's brigade and 11th Kentucky of Smith's unit worked together to assault another section of Confederate artillery, perhaps Bankhead's, but the gunners abandoned it before the Kentuckians arrived. To their left, the 9th Kentucky and 59th Ohio similarly worked together to assault, and after being driven away by the as yet uncaptured section to the right as well as their own artillery fire from the rear, they eventually took an additional section of guns.[35]

One of the Confederate batteries lost on this line was Captain Thomas J. Stanford's from Black Hawk, Mississippi. He had dueled with Bartlett and Mendenhall all day at Duncan Field and had fallen back to the second major line with Breckinridge's brigades. When Crittenden's troops advanced to within fifty yards, he was unable to withdraw four of his six pieces as the Confederate infantry "ran in wild confusion right past the battery," as one of the cannoneers noted in his diary. Breckinridge rode up and told Stanford to remove his guns, but it was too late. Still, Stanford made the Federals pay: "Large gaps were made by every gun at each discharge," he wrote. He saw several regimental flags and ordered his men to fire at those. Two went down, only to come back up again. Still, the Federals were nearing the guns, and Stanford had to decide what to do. An alarming loss of horses told him that he probably could not get out anyway, so he determined to stand and "if need be, to sacrifice my battery" to allow the infantry of Breckinridge's corps to form another line. He did so, losing four guns, but firing to the last and "making them pay dearly for their purchase." One of his cannoneers, John Magee, described how "most all of our horses were killed, and those living were so badly tangled up, it was impossible to get them under the heavy fire of minie balls raining around us." An attempt to recover the guns under covering fire from Bankhead's Battery was successful, but no horses were available to draw the guns off.[36]

Crittenden's two brigades thus took the Hamburg-Purdy Road, holding a line just south of the road and still astride the Eastern Corinth Road. To aid their new position and to cover a new attack if one came about, Terrill's regular battery unlimbered on a small rise of ground in the southeastern corner of the crossing, firing on the withdrawing Confederate infantry and engaging Confederate artillery that in turn had opened up from their new line at Prentiss's camps. An artillery duel thus developed down the length of Barnes Field. Terrill also shelled the Confederate line to the west, enfilading the enemy in front of McCook's division. Terrill wrote, "Our fire must have told fearfully, for very soon General McCook's whole line rapidly advanced and drove the enemy before them." Because of casualties, Terrill helped work one of the guns with only two others before a company from the 6th Ohio moved forward to take the place of the wounded cannoneers.[37]

The Army of the Tennessee contingent also got in on the chase. The 8th and 18th Illinois attacked and captured two Confederate guns of an unidentified battery, perhaps Cobb's Kentucky battery, with the color-bearer of each regiment placing the flags on each gun. Soon thereafter, one of the 18th Illinois's captains, Charles Reed, began working one of the guns by himself before others joined him, turning both cannon on the enemy before hauling them away to their camp as prizes. One Illinoisan proudly wrote, "None of us Ever Fired A Canon Before but Every one Remarked that we must be old Artillery men from the way we Handled our Gun and from the Sharp Shooting we Done." The two guns of McAllister's battery also unlimbered near the Crossroads and shelled Confederate rear guard batteries to the front while portions of Veatch's brigade advanced all the way toward Lost Field, near the 4th Illinois Cavalry camp.[38]

On the far Union right, Wallace's division likewise followed up the Confederate withdrawal, carefully probing for a new line, which they found around Shiloh Church. Wallace began to think of again turning it, later telling his wife, "Slowly, step by step, I drove them before us, turning their left flank." Before that could happen, however, Beauregard took the offensive again, letting the Federals know that this battle was not over.[39]

Just because the Confederate army was falling back did not mean that their offensive force was spent. In probably the most vicious and famous counterattack of the day, on Bragg's order S. A. M. Wood led his brigade forward from his position near Shiloh Church around 1:00 P.M., driving toward the Federal line where the Army of the Ohio and Army of the Tennessee connected. Although he had no way of knowing that this was the best place to strike, Wood nevertheless found a weak spot in the enemy line.[40]

Wood struck right where the two linked, hitting the left of Sherman's division and the right of McCook's. Although he had no more than about 650 men because some stragglers on the left "declined the charge," he drove toward Water Oaks Pond. Wood later wrote, "The charge was made across a swampy ground in part, at the right was a pond of water & mud." "The charge was most gallantly made," he continued, "crossing a pond of water in some places waist-deep, and then entering an open field." Major John H. Kelly of the 9th Arkansas Battalion led part of the line. Wood wrote that after "dashing through the pond, [he] sat on horseback in the open ground and rallied his men in line as they advanced." Not as fortunate was Colonel Coleman A. McDaniel of the 44th Tennessee, who took a "grape ball" in the arm, necessitating his removal from the field as a result of loss of blood. Major Samuel T. Love of the 27th Tennessee also fell and had to be left in the hands of the enemy. Upon his wounding, his Tennesseans fell apart, not to be reorganized on the field.[41]

The bulk of Wood's troops advanced several hundred yards. Major Kelly reported, "The firing of the enemy was quite spirited and the resistance so obstinate that we found it impossible to dislodge him completely." Still, the Confederates managed to drive a wedge between Grant's and Buell's armies. The 11th Indiana began to turn and pour a crossfire into Wood's open left flank so that Wood had no choice but to fall back to the edge of the field, unable to sustain his success or even permanently drive the Federals back. Rutledge's Tennessee Battery provided artillery cover, so the brigade managed to hang on for a while until units to the left broke under Lew Wallace's relentless volleys. The Confederates had to return through or around the pond, and Beauregard continually shifted troops to support Wood. The Confederates gradually fell back, however, taking increasing fire on the flank from Wallace's advance. Eventually, the brigade retook its position in the Confederate line—the third major one of the day.[42]

Wood had once again shown that the Confederate army was not the shell that it is so often described as. It was a powerful force that could severely punish the Federals should they make any mistakes. As a result, the Union divisions only cautiously crept forward, not knowing what might lie ahead at the next major Confederate line.

20

"Get Away with What We Have"

By 2:00 P.M. P. G. T. Beauregard at Shiloh Church was beginning to wonder about the wisdom of further resistance. Despite the initial success of Wood's attack, his army was being overpowered by continually arriving Federal divisions who were turning his unstable flanks. One Louisianan described it in simple terms: "They appeared to me like ants in their nest, for the more we fired upon them the more they swarmed about; one would have said that they sprouted from the ground like mushrooms."[1]

Yet another Union division had come forward in midafternoon. Thomas J. Wood's two brigades made the anxious trip to Savannah and then to Pittsburg by river. William Bradford wrote in his diary an almost minute-by-minute account: "We are now on the boat crossing the river." The division landed after noon: "We could scarcely hear anything but the roar of cannon and firearms." They quickened their steps as they made their way to the front, arriving around 2:00 P.M. The trip had not been without incident, however. A 40th Indiana soldier told his diary of the river trip from Savannah: "The national colors of the regiment were knocked overboard and lost." Later a shirker in the 57th Indiana said he was sick upon nearing the fighting and declared he would stop; his captain told him "if he did I would kill him." The man kept going and fought well.[2]

The first brigade, consisting of the 15th, 40th, and 57th Indiana and the 24th Kentucky under Colonel George D. Wagner, went in by order of Grant and took the position of Tuttle and Veatch in the gap between McCook and Crittenden. Before doing so, the 15th Indiana met up with one of their comrades, William McKinney, who had had an interesting journey to the field. McKinney had been sick when the regiment left Nashville; he later went down the Ohio and up the Tennessee, arriving at Savannah before his brigade. McKinney reported to Grant when the battle started but was told to wait for his regiment. Now united, the Indianans rushed forward with the rest of their brigade.[3]

Unlike Gibson earlier, Wagner held his entire unit together before moving forward at a run. At the front, the brigade gave "three cheers for the Union," but they got off only a few volleys and were not heavily engaged. One disappointed Indianan noted, "We got but a glimpse of the foe before they were gone from our sight in the forest." Only the 24th Kentucky endured casualties—four men wounded—but they did manage to capture some prisoners and recapture some of Grant's men. A little later, the division commander arrived with the other available brigade of Wood's division, led by future president James A. Garfield. The men were dirty from the forced march. Garfield rode along their line, telling them, "Boys, wash up and clean up. We will give you some fun pretty soon." Most of the division's third brigade under Milo Hascall were traveling on a roundabout way through Lawrenceburg and did not arrive until later. They marched to the clear sound of cannon even during the night and received constant rumors of victory and then defeat. George H. Thomas's division was also making its way toward the landing.[4]

Beauregard could not know which Union divisions were on the way and which ones had arrived, but their effect was nevertheless apparent as the afternoon wore on. All anyone on the Confederate line could tell was that fresh troops were continually coming forward, so the Federal lines were getting thicker by the hour. In such a "position most perilous," as Bragg described it, Beauregard began to constrict the Confederate flanks as almost all units moved toward the center. One observant Federal remarked how the battle "narrowed to a front of not over half a mile wide." Beauregard's third major line at Prentiss's camps and Shiloh Church was clearly narrower than the earlier ones, making it stronger but at the same time opening the flanks to being turned. Even with the offensive potential the Confederates retained, as demonstrated by Wood's attack, Beauregard weighed the possibility of fighting a reinforced army against the chance of success.[5]

The status of his soldiers told Beauregard all he needed to know. The Confederate army had shown surprising resilience during the fighting that morning and even in the early afternoon, but the limit of their endurance was evident by 2:00 P.M. Jacob Thompson, on Beauregard's staff, later noted that "stragglers in great numbers came in, and, although great and unremitting efforts were made to rally them, yet the complaint of exhaustion was such that it was impossible to rally them only to a limited extent. The fire and animation had left our troops." John K. Jackson found it was "very difficult to make men reform after they have lost their pride sufficiently to obtain their consent to flee." Only small numbers were thus left: Gladden's original brigade was reduced to 224 men, and Cleburne could count only fifty-eight of his troops. Officers were continually going down as well, including Colonel Alfred Mouton, with a ball in the face. The "educated, refined, and wealthy" Creole major, Anatole P. Avegno, commanding the 13th Louisiana, also went down with a leg wound that would soon take his life.[6]

This reality led Beauregard to expose himself to enemy fire. On two different occasions earlier that afternoon, the general took colors in hand and, while sending his staff under the cover of a hill, led his troops forward in a number of counterattacks. On one occasion, Beauregard saw his beloved Orleans Guard and took their flag, yelling, "Allons mes braves Louisianois en avant." Albert Sidney Johnston had done the same thing the day before; now Beauregard saw the same need at this crisis stage. One of Beauregard's staff officers censured him for exposing himself, to which he replied, "The order must now be 'follow,' not 'go!'"[7]

At this stage in the battle, Beauregard sat at his headquarters on a knoll just east of Shiloh Church, watching as his tiring army began to falter. He sent messengers rearward in the vain hope they might encounter Earl Van Dorn's army approaching the battlefield. Word soon arrived from Corinth that he had yet to even arrive there. (Two regiments of Van Dorn's command did arrive in Memphis on April 7.) Consequently, Beauregard began to think about breaking off the fight and retreating. His staff agreed. Governor Harris asked a staff officer if it was not wise to get away while they could. Thomas Jordan confronted Beauregard: "General, do you not think our troops are very much in the condition of a lump of sugar thoroughly soaked with water, but yet preserving its original shape, though ready to dissolve? Would it not be judicious to get away with what we have?" Beauregard responded quietly, "I intend to withdraw in a few moments." Beauregard later explained his thinking in his report of the battle, writing that his army "opposed . . . an enemy constantly re-enforced, our ranks were perceptibly thinned under the unceasing, withering fire of the enemy, and by 12 m.[,] eighteen hours of hard fighting had sensibly exhausted a large number." As Beauregard sat with his staff near the church around 2:30 P.M., he made the decision to retreat. He sent out staff officers to order the various commands to the rear in a "deliberate, orderly withdrawal from the field," with one staff officer writing it was "to commence on the right."[8]

To cover the retreat, Colonel Robert F. Looney of the 38th Tennessee and several other officers amassed a conglomeration of a thousand or so men and led the last major counterattack of the day around 4:00 P.M. Beauregard ordered Looney to charge the "infernal scoundrels and drive them back." The 38th Tennessee responded, "We will; we will." The assault moved past Sherman's headquarters and hit Kirk's and Gibson's brigades, but it failed to drive them back. Still, this attack provided Beauregard with time to withdraw. Despite wounded soldiers who "begged piteously to be taken to the rear," Looney withdrew behind Breckinridge's corps, stationed as a rear guard on the "favorable ridge commanding the ground of Shiloh Church." Beauregard told Breckinridge, "This retreat must not be a rout, sir." Hardee also positioned portions of six or eight batteries under Francis Shoup there. One artilleryman in Swett's Mississippi Battery wrote that Hardee ordered them to fire "with an elevated trajectory." He added, "After firing six shells and failing to develop anything, the Gen'l rode away, we following." One Federal admitted that the "Jonnies were like the old woman, they got in the last word."[9]

The final act of Shiloh was a reversal of the terrain's effect on the first day of battle; Breckinridge now used the same creek that had first shielded the Federal army as his own last line of defense. For Beauregard, Shiloh Branch was this afternoon what Dill and Tilghman branches had been for Grant the day before. The Confederate army soon filed by the strong position, Bragg remaining near with his favored artillery. He only left after sending a staff officer to confirm the retreat order. Ruggles also tarried, sending staff officer L. D. Sandidge to tell Breckinridge that his entire division would remain if needed. "Sandidge," Breckinridge told the staff officer, "go tell your Louisianans God Bless them! If they hear not our guns at dawn of the morning, send back a flag that we may have honorable burial, for we are enough to die!"[10]

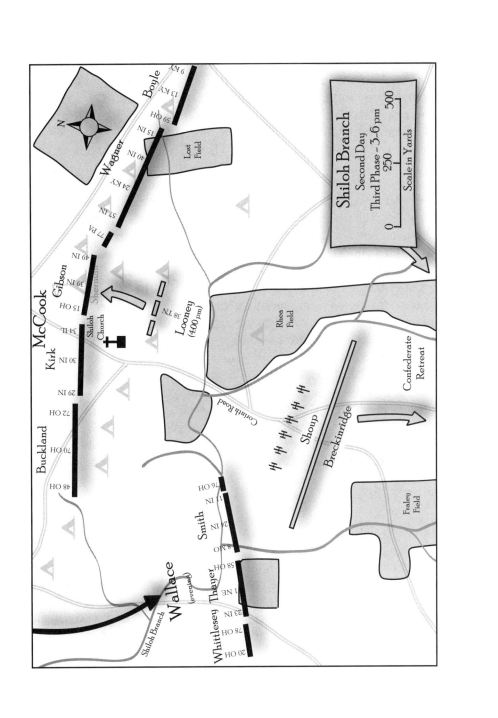

Shiloh Branch
Second Day
Third Phase ~ 3–6 pm

Scale in Yards

0   250   500

Although Beauregard claimed in his report that "never did troops leave a battle-field in better order," the remarkable cohesion the Confederate army had shown on April 7 was no longer evident by 4:00 P.M. The weary and famished soldiers dragged themselves along the route of retreat, burning camps and equipment as they went. Some had lost all they had and suffered more than others. Some artillery units had no ammunition and, even worse, no horses; they were ordered to spike the guns and leave them on the field. The retreat was miserable for all. One Confederate wrote, "Our troubles had now just begun." Another wrote his wife, "The trip back to Corinth used me up worse than the battle as we were gone five days and slept about ten hours during the time. We ate nothing almost, traveled very hard, and it rained on us every night."[11]

The retreat became worse as night set in. Shoup barely got his guns out after taking a wrong road: "In a few minutes I found myself back where I had started from," he later wrote and admitted, "I nearly jumped out of my boots with joy when we came up with the infantry." Breckinridge likewise fell back later in the evening to an intermediate line at the April 5 deployment area and then back to Mickey's the next day, leaving only cavalry out front. His corps remained there, caring for the wounded, burying the dead, and coordinating with Chalmers's Mississippians at Monterey. Making matters worse, another major rainstorm moved through, providing heavy rain on the night of April 7 and making the roads even more impassable. One Confederate described lifting "wagons out of the mud several times"; a mule "mired down half way up his back, and I do not think he ever got out."[12]

Back on the battlefield on the afternoon of April 7, one excited Illinoisan remembered, "Our courage was wonderfully stimulated by seeing the finest display of gray backs as they climbed the hills and disappeared from our view." Along the all-important Corinth Road, McCook's division advanced to and a little past Shiloh Church toward the lowlands of Shiloh Branch, but they stopped there. Lovell Rousseau badgered the 1st Ohio for progressing too far until it was learned that a mud-covered Grant, with a mud-covered Sherman not far behind, had issued the orders. August Willich became so enraged at the 32nd Indiana for firing at extreme distances that he halted the regiment "and practiced them in the manual of arms, which they executed as if on the parade ground, and then reopened deliberate and effective fire." Crittenden and Nelson to the left also moved cautiously, but the Confederate "attacks . . . [were] feeble and easily repulsed." Crittenden's troops approached the Confederate defense of Prentiss's camps and captured several isolated sections of artillery as the Confederates withdrew. Nelson's troops advanced to a point where they could cover the River Road and then went into bivouac. Buell later rode over the area with Nelson's staff officer, Horace Fisher, who recounted: "We went up and down—through ravines, bushes, sloughs—in a perfect maze—with constant reminders from Gen. Buell to remember those particular points. I can honestly say that I could not have found my way back through them to save my life, for it was very nearly dark when we did this."[13]

Lew Wallace proceeded farther south than the rest of the Federals, moving through the burned camps of Sherman's division and crossing Shiloh Branch but then returning to go into bivouac north of the creek. According to Grant's staff, Wallace sent a note of panic to Grant, who accepted it "very much out of humor." Grant sent Sherman to talk to Wallace, and Sherman joked that he would "see that Wallace did not get hurt." The chiding continued afterward when Grant insinuated that his staff officers could not find Wallace at his headquarters, adding bitingly, "Captain R. found every other Division Commander without difficulty."[14]

Emotions ranged all over the spectrum as a feeling of victory came over the Federals. As his men took their final positions, William Camm, now commanding the 15th Illinois, had just finished "scolding the men for dodging like a lot of geese, when you shy a stick over them." Just then a shot passed close to his head, and he instinctively ducked. Some of the men shouted, "Don't dodge." Others were more serious. One particularly poignant episode occurred when McCook's troops moved to Shiloh Church. One of McCook's staff members, Ephraim Otis, struck up a conversation with an obviously mortally wounded Confederate. The Southerner said he was from the 5th Kentucky and asked if Thomas Crittenden was around. He said he had played with Crittenden as a boy while living on the same street in Frankfort. The staff officer took the message to Crittenden, who rushed to the church, but he was too late. The Kentuckian had already died.[15]

Federal cavalry verified the Confederate retreat, but there was no Union pursuit that day. Although one Confederate explained that "the enemy having had enough of us did not attack our new position," Grant admitted that "my force was too much fatigued from two days' hard fighting and exposure in the open air to a drenching rain during the intervening night to pursue immediately." Later, he added more reasons in his memoirs: he "had not the heart" to order the famished and bone-weary men forward; he also added that he "did not feel disposed positively to order Buell, or any part of his command, to pursue." Perhaps the biggest reason was that Grant had received instructions during the battle on April 7 not to pursue to Corinth. As for Buell, he noted, "I was without cavalry, and the different corps had become a good deal scattered in a pursuit over a country which screened the movements of the enemy, and the roads of which I knew practically nothing." Perhaps Sherman summed it up best years later when he told a historian, "I assure you, my dear fellow, that we had quite enough of their society for two whole days, and were only too glad to be rid of them on any terms."[16]

After being held in reserve during most of the battle, the Federal cavalry was apparently gathered to follow that afternoon, but it was not ordered into action. One chagrined Illinois trooper admitted that "the cavalry was not of much service here on account of the heavy timber[.] they could not work but we could stand in a line of battle and let them shoot us down." The Federal infantrymen were not impressed with the cavalry's lack of action, either, whether it was their fault or not. One foot soldier said, "I would give as much, for the services of blind men on Sow horses, and that seems to be the prevailing opinion." Yet had Grant sent his cavalry after the retreating Confederate army, it is likely he would have reaped vast benefits. An older and more mature Grant of 1863 or 1864 would likely have done so, but this was the evolving Grant of 1862, and he let a splendid chance slip through his grasp. Indeed, the Federal cavalry could have done wonders at this point. "Our condition is horrible," Bragg wrote Beauregard, with "troops utterly disorganized and demoralized." He later added, "If we are pursued by a vigorous force we will lose all in the rear." Breckinridge, commanding that rear guard, agreed: "My troops are worn-out, and I don't think can be relied on after the first volley."[17]

The Federal troops were not interested in more fighting; they preferred to return to their camps and rest or locate items from their previous camps. What they found devastated them. Ralph Buckland reported, "Officers and men lost nearly everything, except what they had on their persons when the fight commenced." Most of the standing tents were riddled, with one soldier in Stuart's brigade finding sixty bullet holes in his tent; a member of the 20th Illinois counted 128 in his. George Carrington of the 11th Illinois found his "sheet iron cook stove" was "bored full of holes by bullets." He had to fill the holes with mud to be able to cook again. Out in the 53rd Ohio camp, a disheartened Ephraim Dawes wrote home that his camp was trashed and he had lost almost everything: "My Commission I found in the mud next morning." Sherman inspected his headquarters and found his extra horses all killed, still tied to the rope line. He also found papers obviously left by the Confederate headquarters contingent. More hauntingly, others found dead soldiers in their tents; George Smith of the 17th Illinois wrote, "I found a Confederate soldier of the 5th Mississippi dead in my bed." Alexander Downing of the 11th Iowa found a dead Confederate in his tent: "We carried the body out to the parade ground and then got a shovel to clean away the blood from the place where the body had lain in the tent." As bad as it was in Grant's camps, it was worse for Buell's and Wallace's troops; they did not receive their equipment until about April 15, when their baggage finally arrived and they chose campsites. One Missourian began sleeping on wet hay; he wrote his wife, "My Savior had such a bed in Bethlehem."[18]

Perhaps even worse, rumors of another attack continually circulated, and the skittish Federals were not about to be caught by surprise again. Some commanders had their men up and in line of battle before dawn for weeks after the battle, and Sherman ordered an abatis across his front (Colonel Worthington's 46th Ohio building actual earthworks). Sherman cautioned his division that "all false alarms must be avoided" and warned them against "all discharge of muskets at the moon or tops of trees."[19]

Despite winning a major victory, Ulysses S. Grant was in a ticklish position. He had been under strict orders from Halleck not to bring on an engagement, but he had fought the largest battle in American history. Pursuit might bring more fighting, more casualties, and more wrath from Halleck, but Grant had to follow up, if for no other reason than to see that Beauregard was actually retreating and to secure his front. Grant thus reported to Halleck on April 8, "Our cavalry, supported by infantry, are now pursuing him, with instructions to pursue to the swampy grounds near Pea Ridge." He thus sent Wood's division of

Buell's army (Buell now making it plain that he was following Grant's directions) and Sherman's tired division southward on April 8. Sherman reported how "one after another . . . the abandoned camps of the enemy lined the road, with hospital flags for their protection." At the fork that led to Monterey and Mickey's, Sherman sent out cavalry, which soon uncovered the enemy. He asked Wood to take the left road toward Atkins's Ford and Monterey while he took the right fork toward Mickey's. Wood saw few Confederates, mostly cavalry that provoked him to form his brigades in hollow squares, but he certainly viewed the effects of the battle and withdrawal: "The line of retreat was marked by abandoned and destroyed stores and munitions of war and arms. Various field hospitals filled with wounded were discovered on both sides of the road by which he had retreated."[20]

Sherman was not so fortunate on the other road. Federal cavalry quickly began to meet Confederates to the front on the Ridge Road, with the Confederate rear guard made up of contingents of Adams's, Wharton's, and Forrest's cavalry regiments (several later claimed John Hunt Morgan was there as well). These were drawn up over a mile and a half in front of Breckinridge's position at Mickey's near a field of fallen timber that would forever lend its name to the skirmish that resulted there. Sherman quickly ordered Hildebrand to send out the 77th Ohio with skirmishers to the front.[21]

Major Thomas Harrison of the Texas Rangers watched as the Federals cautiously advanced, declining to attack and calling such an action "extremely hazardous." He soon consulted with Forrest, who was the ranking officer on the field, and the two (mostly Forrest) decided to attack, with Forrest leading the way. Major Benjamin Fearing of the 77th Ohio wrote home, "The cavalry came down upon us like an avalanche. It lasted but a moment, and they run over and through us slashing and cutting down and our best men ridden over and shot." The Confederate cavalry so surprised the 77th Ohio skirmishers that they fled back to the main brigade, breaking through a portion of the 4th Illinois Cavalry arrayed to pursue the enemy. Next came the line of battle of the 77th Ohio, with Sherman there as well. Texas cavalry commander Harrison reported that the cavalry drove through the skirmishers as well as the cavalry, where a classic hand-to-hand fight erupted even though the Texans had no sabers. Harrison nevertheless attested to his men's "superior skill in the use and management of pistol and horse." Hildebrand could only admit, "The rebel cavalry literally rode down the infantry."[22]

Mississippian Alfred Smith gave a vivid account of the close fighting in a letter to his mother. When ordered to charge, he wrote, "We got in among them," and "the enemy run like dogs." He continued, "I shot men with my rifle and pistol until my heart was sick at the slaughter." He related that he shot several when "I put my gun within two feet of their breasts." The Federals nevertheless fought back. Smith remembered, "I saw a fellow drive a bayonet into a Texas Ranger and shove him clear off his horse." He also described how another "made a pass at me with his bayonet and only missed me about six inches as I spurred my horse past and in an instant I wheeled and shot him through the breast and he tumbled over like a beef." Smith then took a prisoner and "drove him off in double quick time" as the cavalry realized more Federals were on the way. "We had to leave very hastily," he added.[23]

In the chaos occurred one of the most famous incidents of the war. Forrest had outridden his troops and found himself alone amid the enemy infantrymen. He had no other recourse but to fight his way out and was horribly wounded in the back in the process. Sherman was nearby and later acknowledged, "I am sure that had he not emptied his pistols as he passed the skirmish line, my career would have ended right there." Rarely did two eventual icons of the war come so close in combat as they did at Fallen Timbers.[24]

The wounded Forrest and the remainder of the cavalry soon dispersed into the woods when fronted by the bulk of Hildebrand's brigade. However, they had provided all the delay needed to keep Grant from a full-fledged pursuit to Pea Ridge. The stunned Federals, having lost around sixty casualties, including nineteen killed and thirty wounded in Hildebrand's brigade, wanted no more, and it was a good thing. Had they proceeded, they would have met Breckinridge's entire corps drawn up near Mickey's just a mile or so to the front. One of the Mississippians in line certainly thought they were about to engage again: "The anxiety and excitement of the first day's battle were [again] felt this evening as we lay in wait behind that fence." Yet Sherman merely destroyed the nearby Confederate camp, collected anything he could from the field, and saw to the dead and wounded before making his way back to Shiloh, confident in the security of the Union forces there.[25]

With the rear covered, most of the Confederate army took days to get back to Corinth, although some moved more directly, with Beauregard arriving late on Monday night. The rest of the army filtered in throughout the night and the next day. Once there, the troops reoccupied their still-standing tents around the railroad town. One Louisianan wrote, "The dreary place seemed like paradise; our tents were palaces, and old friends whom we rejoined hugged like brothers." They also found the sick who had been left and the wounded who had already made their way back. They also found some soldiers who had apparently taken little part in the battle. The 23rd Tennessee found one man who had "left his company and regiment early on Sunday and did not get with them any more, but returned to camp with his ammunition and a good supply of Yankee goods." Most of the veterans of Shiloh were "all very tired and worn out, most of us sick." One Louisianan responded to an inquiry about what he managed to attain: "Nothing but hard knocks."[26]

By the evening of April 8 and certainly the next day, much of the Confederate army was thus back in Corinth, with only small groups walking in over the next few days. Beauregard later issued orders for all stragglers and civilians with military arms to be arrested. Only Breckinridge remained at the front, and he too soon arrived with his three brigades without having any contact with the enemy.[27]

As the smoke cleared on the battlefield, the survivors of Shiloh began to try to make sense of what had happened. One Tennessean wrote his wife, "I am confused and can't write as I ought to do[.] it is impossible for me to give you all the particulars." Even Braxton Bragg had trouble making sense of it all. He wrote to his wife on April 9, "How to begin a letter confounds me. So much has been crowded in a small space of time that the mind becomes confused." Emotions grew even rawer for those on the battlefield who had to endure the sights; dead bodies, horribly mangled by war, were made worse by the ravaging hogs that fed on them during the nights. "The stench [is] almost unbearable," one Indianan told his diary. A later-arriving Federal wrote home, "I did not go to the battlefield, the scent was enough for me; it was very disagreeable." One Ohioan described the scene near a fallen tree: "At or near the root was a dead sow. About thirty or thirty-five feet along the log lay a dead hound. And up near the top of the tree was a dead Confederate."[28]

The mass of wounded was obviously the first priority. Most of the care for these men fell to the surgeons, who began their duties during the battle. With no organized system of retrieval as the war would later see, both sides depended on musicians and chaplains to help gather the wounded. Regimental and assistant surgeons provided what care they could on or near the front lines, some of them paying with wounds or death themselves, while brigade and division surgeons in the rear set up actual hospitals. The majority of the Federals were compassionate even to the enemy wounded, although Indianan Eli Clampitt wrote home that "the rebels raised the black flag and when I saw it old Eli made good use of the beyonet as I passed the wounded Enemy[.] . . . Cap said I used my beyonet a little too much on the wounded." Later, he noted, "We will have to kill some of the CS over for I see them wiggle and I think they are coming to life." Yet most were more humane. One Federal surgeon wrote, "We made no distinction as to regiment, Union men or Rebels in our attendance." Another wrote, "Severe as the labor was on me I continued at it all night and till the afternoon of Monday. I did not even sit down ten minutes." Federal surgeons were also aided by various entities in the North such as the United States Christian Commission and the United States Sanitary Commission. Civilians such as Mary Ann Bickerdyke also cared for the wounded and the ever-growing number of sick. One Illinoisan, writing to his wife and children, said of her, "She is the best woman in the world (except wives and Mothers)—she is so kind to the Boys that are sick." One of the nurses described her situation, including their "black dresses with large white aprons." Some of the nurses who flocked to Pittsburg Landing after the battle died of disease themselves and were buried on the battlefield.[29]

Despite the care provided by the mostly dedicated surgeons, chaplains, and nurses, the medical facilities at Shiloh were quickly overwhelmed, and it took time to get the wounded northward to hospitals along the rivers. Doctors lacked stores, ambulances, dressings, and tents, and with thousands of patients to see, it took days to care for all the wounded. Unfortunately, many of the wounded died during that period; some were brought in days after the battle, with additional wounded being produced even later. As members of the 3rd Iowa sat around a large campfire amid the miserable rain on the morning of April 9, a nearby cannonball overheated and exploded, wounding several men. A similar disaster occurred in the 29th Indiana by "one of our curious boys touching off a bomb shell for fun." It mangled his leg and wounded several others.[30]

The Confederate wounded had an added degree of difficulty. One Mississippian related how he would not have made it without the help of his comrades: "I would have been left on the wayside for the Yankees or buzzards." Many of the Confederates were taken in at local houses;

one Indianan declared, "There was not a house within ten miles round but was full of wounded." Others did the best they could; one Mississippian wrote, "In our return we found the poor fellows lying in fence corners in the woods and every where they could find a dry or high place to rest." Those who made the trip back to Corinth were especially tortured. One Tennessean wrote, "The groans of our wounded could be distinctly heard as our ambulances were crossing over the rough roads." With the care provided at Corinth and elsewhere, however, many wounded and sick Confederates were later able to stand trips farther south, and towns all along the railroads running west and south of Corinth such as Okolona, Oxford, Grenada, Winona, and Brandon soon had wounded and sick soldiers to care for. Many cemeteries along the rail lines to this day contain small plots of Confederate soldiers brought there from the horrible fields of Shiloh.[31]

The dead left on the battlefield were a different matter altogether. It was in the interest of all involved to bury them as quickly as possible. Much care was taken to bury the Union dead. One Iowan noted in his diary, "Muffled drums are continually heard as Regiments or Companies bury their dead." An Illinois soldier related, "As I write volley and volley of musketry is being fired over the graves of our men. . . . We dig long holes in the ground, lay them side by side without any coffin, fire a salute over the grave, and then cover their cold bodies with the Tennessee clay." Many regiments buried their own dead in regimental plots, taking care to identify all who were identifiable. Headboards went up, although they could not be expected to last long. Other, more permanent ways of identification also emerged, such as placing identification papers on the body and even in one case placing the papers in a bottle that was placed on the body. Most, however, would soon be forever unknown.[32]

Less care was taken for the Confederates. One Federal reported that he dreaded his detail to bury them: "They are all swollen and smell awful bad and so terrible many of them. I do not see how I can stand it." The Federals noticed all sorts of details about their enemies. One Illinoisan wrote home that their "underclothing is most all maid of cotton flannel." Many rumors also swirled that the Federals found whiskey and powder in their canteens, which made them fight better while alive and turn dark when dead. The Confederate dead were buried near where they fell, with one Federal writing, "At close intervals for some 2 miles in width you will meet with little mounds of freshly thrown up Earth beneath which rest the remains of some rebel soldier or some slain Horse or mule." Many of the dead were placed in mass graves across the field, nine or ten of them altogether, although many smaller trenches were dug that contained only a few bodies. "They dig long holes and pile them in like dead cattle and have teams to draw them together like picking up pumpkins," wrote one Illinoisan. He added, "It smells bad." The largest trench was east of the Peach Orchard, but most were dug on the western part of the field, illustrating the heavy fighting that took place in that area on both days. One Federal wrote of 150 Confederates in one mass grave, "and 20 more laying there to be put in and they was still digging it longer[.] they was layed in 4 deep." It was obviously an emotional task; one Illinoisan later wrote, "Months passed before I recovered from the effects of it."[33]

Beauregard made an attempt, at the behest of civilian Confederates, to send a group to gather his dead from Shiloh. In a letter to Grant on April 8, he could not help but explain his reasons for withdrawal: "It being apparent that you had received and were still receiving re-enforcements." Still, he soon came to the point and asked permission "to send a mounted party to the battle-field of Shiloh for the purpose of giving decent interment to my dead." With the process already moving along, Grant responded, "Owing to the warmth of the weather I deemed it advisable to have all the dead of both parties buried immediately. Heavy details were made for this purpose, and now it is accomplished. There cannot, therefore, be any necessity of admitting within our lines the parties you desire to send on the grounds asked." Although the Federals were still burying the dead on April 9 when Grant wrote back and even afterward (one Missourian wrote on April 13 that "We are finding them every day"), the decision remained the same.[34]

Although initial estimates were far wide of the mark—one Confederate wrote his family that "there must have been at least one hundred thousand men killed and wounded on both sides"—each army ultimately produced official casualty figures. The Federals reported 1,754 killed, 8,408 wounded, and 2,885 missing for a total of 13,047. Out of an estimated total of 67,167 present for duty, the Federal casualty rate was just under 20 percent. Totals in individual units were equally astounding; the 9th Illinois lost 366 killed and wounded out of 578. When Colonel August Mersy viewed his thin line the day after the battle, he was reported to have muttered, "Vel, vel; dis is all dat is left of my little Nint!" The Confederate tally was even worse, 10,699 casualties

(1,728 killed, 8,012 wounded, and 959 missing) out of an official total of 44,699 engaged, just under 24 percent.[35]

Although recent research has shown the Federal numbers to be pretty accurate, it has also revealed that reported Confederate brigade numbers were on average a third lower than actual losses. The Federals agreed; Grant reported that Sherman and McClernand buried more Confederate dead than Beauregard reported for his entire army. If the Confederate numbers are booted up a third, such a tally would reach 14,265—a casualty rate near 32 percent. Historians have often said Shiloh produced more casualties than in all of American history before that time. Although this is not true, the three armies nevertheless endured two horrific days of battle on the banks of the Tennessee River in April 1862. To that date, no battle had been fought in North America that matched it.[36]

Yet time marched on. One week later, a Federal soldier wrote, "The sun is shining brightly, the birds are singing so sweetly, & all the world seems as bright & joyous again as ever."[37]

21

"FINISH THE JOB WHILE WE ARE AT IT"

Once events returned to some normality, emotions ran the gamut for the soldiers who had just been through the ordeal that was Shiloh. Many men openly wept, including the colonel of the 24th Tennessee, whose clothes had been riddled by balls but was himself unhurt. One of his soldiers wrote how "the first time he met me after the battle he threw his arms around my neck and wept like a child. He says Providence protected him." Others displayed similar emotion: "I can hardly write. My heart is full—and when I try to tell . . . my eyes fill with tears." Many had the sights of the battle "indelibly fixed in my memory." Others used humor to cope, such as a Louisianan who described a minor wound of a friend, Tom Butler: "He run butting against a Minnie ball." He quipped that he must have thought his head was stronger: "Fortunately, Tom was right for once—though I don't think his head hurt the ball much. Tom is as proud of his wound as a young couple of their first baby."[1]

The size of the battle was almost unfathomable to the soldiers. They compared it to the only things they knew, including Waterloo and battles closer to home. One Tennessean wrote, "Beauregard says Manassas was a baby to it." A Federal similarly wrote, "It seemed to me it was 'Bull Run' quadrupled." More closely related was Fort Donelson; Lew Wallace said the former was "child's play" in comparison. One soldier even compared the effect of the fighting at Shiloh to McClellan's army, which he noted was kept back by "old pine logs painted black, mounted behind breastworks. Out West, we have had to fight against genuine iron and steel guns that were manned by just as good gunners as we had ourselves." One Federal simply wrote, "We do not know the name historians will give to this awful battle but it aught to have a big name." Later in the war, many soldiers routinely went back to Shiloh for comparisons with other battles.[2]

Many soldiers reacted with thankfulness to God for preserving them. Bishop Leonidas Polk wrote his wife, "All glory and honor be unto His holy Name for my protection and defense, for it was he who did it." Polk had much to be thankful for in addition to his own safety; two of his sons were safe as well, one on his staff and one in Bankhead's Battery. Others also chimed in with thanksgiving; Alfred T. Fielder wrote in his diary, "My soul appeared to be almost melted within me in thankfulness to God for his preserving care."[3]

Although today Shiloh is regarded almost unanimously as a major Union victory, some participants struggled with deciding on the victor and the loser. Most Federals asserted victory. One Illinoisan was "satisfied that we won and saved our skins and our lives," but added, "we would have been lost had not General Buel . . . come to our aid as soon as possible." Others were more sure. Charles W. Beal wrote, "We whip them so bad that [they] are ashamed of it." Others recounted the rumor that Beauregard said he would water his horse in the Tennessee River or hell, which was in itself inaccurate. One soldier added, "But I don't think he done neather one." The Confederates were somewhat more ambivalent, with few basing their assumptions on Beauregard's declaration of victory. Some admitted that they did not know where they stood, yet one Confederate with a clear view wrote that the South "cant stand miny more cuch losses."[4]

Although the Battle of Shiloh had tremendous political, strategic, and military ramifications, the effect of the battle on the local inhabitants was just as stark. The lives of the few citizens who lived on what became the Shiloh battlefield were turned upside down by the fighting, and the change was not temporary. Because of the sound of musketry that one local described as "a heavy shower of rain falling" and cannon that "roared like a heavy thunder," the inhabitants of Shiloh would never be the same.[5]

Most of the locals had realized what was happening and had left before the battle. "On all the farms in this vicinity there is not the sign of an inhabitant and when they were here they just barely lived," wrote one Federal. "Everything is in a dilapidated State & the Army has burnt every rail in the whole country." A few families remained until it was too late. A few of the Wickers later told of the "sounds and smells" of the fighting as they hunkered in their tiny cabin in Wicker Field, a scene of heavy fighting on the afternoon of the first day and the morning of the second. They described the agony of bullets flying around and through their cabin. Another local woman took her daughter and two grandchildren and lived under the bluff of the river without food until Tuesday, when they finally came out. Some of the Duncan clan caught in the cabin in Duncan Field on the first day were rescued by family members during the night between the two days of battle—and it was a good thing because the house was partially destroyed during Monday's fight. Miraculously, only one civilian death is recorded, that of George Washington Sowell, who lived at the field that now bears his name near Owl Creek. His wife, with her husband sick in bed and dying already, refused to leave and remained with their six children amid the fighting. He apparently died when a shell went through the house.[6]

More than just the immediate population was affected. Many letters and diaries of civilians describe the anguish of listening to the battle raging around Pittsburg Landing. For miles around, local Tennesseans listened intently, some from as far as Jackson, Tennessee, fifty miles away. Those closer to the fighting who had observed the initial Confederate marches were confused as to the delay, with one writing, "Expected today but as we have heard no cannonading it is still delayed." Once it started, though, the sound let all know that it was continuing. "The fight is still going on. We know by the reports of the cannon," wrote one listener. Another described "the hours of anxious suspense, through which we passed, as we distinctly heard the sound of musketry, the beating of drums, falling artillery creating havoc and death, and with bated breath we awaited news from the battle, which loved ones were engaged in that fierce conflict." One Southerner realized the implications of what they heard: "The fight is raging, the cannon can be distinctly heard at this distance and at every sound we know some valiant son of the South has fallen in defense of Southern soil, women and children. We await the result of this day's work with an all-absorbing interest. Upon it may depend our future fate, whether we be slaves or freemen."[7]

Nowhere was the sound more listened to than at Corinth, where many of the civilians, convalescents, and military personnel left behind awaited news of the fighting. "Saturday, April 5, 1862, dragged its weary length along in much expectancy," wrote Mrs. F. A. Inge.

"No engagement took place." Then the sound of firing came the next morning. One soldier wrote, "We were aroused by the muttering thunder tones of distant battle. Everyone stood aghast; scarcely a word was spoken for hours together." "It seemed that the ground was vibrating with the shock," Inge continued, "the agony of that day can never be written." Susan Gaston similarly wrote, "The sound of the guns first reached us on Sunday morning; we hurried from the breakfast table to the yard and listened to the continued roar. It was like far away sea waves when they strike the shore." A soldier who had been left behind in Corinth likewise wrote, "Heavy cannonading commenced in that direction this morning at 8 o'clock and kept up several hours." Rumors soon began to fly: "The news is coming in from the field," John Gates wrote his wife; "it is said we are driving the enemy back down the river." He added more to his letter that afternoon: "The news is coming in from the field very favorably but nothing authentic." One soldier even reported the rumor that "our forces have crossed the river and are in full pursuit of the enemy," but he noted, "I believe little I hear." Eventually the wounded started to pour into Corinth, as did prisoners. The sick had already been sent southward to "clear the Hospital for the wounded," one observer noted, but those preparations would still prove to be inadequate.[8]

Nearer to the battlefield, the agony can be discerned in the account of a nine-year-old girl who admitted, "When I heard the canons roar and the guns popping and the horses screaming it seemed as if everything was lost." Yet she remembered the resilience of her mother, who dealt with the enemy, the wounded, and the locals alike. At one point she described a terrible scene:

> As I went back into the house I saw a woman screaming and wringing her hands and mother was trying to quiet her. She said that she [had] two sons in the battle,—one on each side fighting against each other. Mother told her that she would have to bear up that she also had two sons and one son-in-law and that her daughter was down there in the middle of that fighting with her five little children and we can not help her so you see we will have to help each other over this great sorrow and pray to God to help us all.[9]

After the battle, the civilians who could get past the Union sentries soon found their homes devastated. Almost everything was gone, including James Wood's cotton gin, along with the cotton. Wilse Wood's two cabins, site of Johnston's early headquarters, were gone. J. J. Fraley could only find one of his cows and a horse, both of which he had left running wild the morning of the battle. It dawned on him that the mare's survival was because no one could "bridle her in the open." In most cases, artillery fire had destroyed the buildings, either tearing them apart or sparking fires that soon engulfed them. Orchards, cemeteries, and sundry other man-made entities were likewise damaged or destroyed. Animals were also affected; one soldier noted that "*Horses, Cows, Calves,* and even *Rabbits* were killed." Only a few structures remained, mostly to the rear of Grant's last line, where less fighting had occurred. The destruction was almost complete on the bottom half of the hourglass, however, where the fighting had raged most heavily on both days.[10]

Shiloh Church, which eventually lent its name to the battle, survived. Yet it too was destroyed within a few weeks; accounts differ in regard to its final demise. Most sources indicate that the Federals tore it down for firewood, bridges, and even souvenirs. A perhaps fictitious story described one Federal spying a musket propped in a corner. He pulled the musket out and the whole church fell, injuring him and those with him. The church cemetery was also heavily damaged.[11]

Although the armies eventually moved on, a few Federals, the 7th Missouri and the 14th Wisconsin, remained in the area as garrison over the next summer. Even with the continued Federal presence, residents soon began to return and rebuild. Nancy George only found one of the silver goblets she had buried before leaving, but her husband, Manse, was more concerned about a place to live. Their cabin, which sat near the Peach Orchard, had been destroyed, so George bought a surviving cabin from a less-fought-over area of the field and moved it to his home place.[12]

In addition to the physical devastation, the inhabitants also returned to a devastated economy. As meager farmers, they had few hopes for a crop that season. The Federal army remained through the planting season, and even if they could get to work, they soon realized that their already meager farmland now contained a vast assortment of lead bullets, cannonballs, and equipment. Trees were either shattered or filled with bullets, making lumber useless. Prices obviously went up in such an area of need; one farmer bought a barrel of salt for $30 in gold, only to have it confiscated by soldiers.[13]

In addition, the battlefield was now a vast burial ground, making the land even less suitable for farming. More than 3,000 men had died at Shiloh, and although some were removed to burial plots at their homes, most of the dead of both sides were buried on the battlefield itself. The hundreds of dead horses and mules only added to the problem. These graves often washed open and adversely affected the area's water supply—occurrences that continually reminded the locals of their situation.[14]

The Federals could also be the downfall of the locals. Sometimes they played tricks on the civilians; one cavalryman who entered Lawrenceburg on Buell's march to Shiloh described how "we went in to Laurenceburgh on a charge with our sabers drawn, and it was fun to see the rebbles, running in every direction and hallowing as loud as they could yell, that the d——d Yankees were coming and they would kill them all." More ominously for the locals around Pittsburg Landing, Grant ordered several of them held as captives after the battle, and a few were held on his steamer *Tigress*. "General Grant treats us politely but says he must detain us," wrote one local. They remained in custody until Halleck arrived and released them on April 15.[15]

The Shiloh battlefield was thus a place of horror and misery, but it was home for these Tennesseans. About all they could do was return and try to make a new life. As long as soldiers were there, trading with them was an option, although civilians often came out on the short end. Many civilians came to the battlefield to gather souvenirs; one wrote that there were "a great many ladies and citizens" going over the field. The Union soldiers soon learned they could take advantage of the situation. One described shooting a limb from a tree and selling it as a cane from the battlefield. Another described finding a rusty musicians' sword, which they told a buyer came from a Confederate officer. The Federals also sent their own souvenirs home; one soldier sent flowers from the battlefield to his girlfriend. The situation improved as time passed, however. One Ohioan who visited six months after the battle described the locals "enjoying themselves in gathering and eating peaches found in abundance." He reflected on the peace and quiet: "How changed from that Sunday six months ago."[16]

Most, if not all, of Shiloh's soldiers left the battlefield changed people. The wounded would never be the same, and hearts were heavy over the dead. A saddened Isham G. Harris no doubt saw his hopes of retaking Tennessee drift away, but he was personally distraught as well; in addition to Johnston, Shiloh took the life of his brother, a major in the army, as well as a nephew. Most notably, the effect of Johnston's death was not lost on anyone. His brokenhearted staff, all except Brewster, Wickliffe, and Harris, took Johnston's body back to Corinth, where Mrs. Inge and other ladies cleaned the body and uniform so that Corinth citizens could pay their respects. Inge found one of the sandwiches and some of the cake still in Johnston's pocket. She could only lament: "Three days before he had left this room in all the vigor of mature manhood; now he was asleep in the same room, a martyr to his country's cause." From Corinth, Johnston was taken to New Orleans and buried in a tomb in St. Louis Cemetery. Federal forces captured New Orleans in late April, so Johnston's body rested in an occupied city for the remainder of the war before being moved to Austin, Texas, in 1867.[17]

Jefferson Davis was devastated at the loss of his friend. When word reached Richmond that Johnston had fallen, it was tempered with news that he was winning the battle when he died. That thought prevailed for a time, although the terrible realization soon emerged that the Confederacy had lost Johnston in a losing effort. One of his brigade commanders Randall Gibson later wrote, "The West perished with Albert Sidney Johnston, and the Southern country followed." Jefferson Davis lamented, "We had no other hand to take up his work in the West."[18]

Another group that would endure the effects of Shiloh for months, sometimes even years, were the prisoners. Far fewer Confederates than Federals were captured, but they were placed in a "corral" at the landing before being routinely sent northward to prison camps. Henry Morton Stanley was one of them, and he confessed that "we were a sad lot of men." They could also be trouble. One Federal described at least some of them as "very saucy and boasted that it would be impossible to whip them, and that Beauregard was not whipped only overpowered." The major feat at Shiloh, however, was the Confederate capture of a bulk of Union prisoners at the Hornet's Nest on the first day. Some 2,200 Union prisoners had to be dealt with, which was no small task when the Confederate army at the time could not manage to coordinate and feed its own army, much less thousands of additional prisoners.[19]

Confederate authorities did the best they could. They first sent the lot southward on the evening of the first day, where they camped in a cornfield. The next day, the exhausted prisoners moved on to Corinth;

one described how they "laid down in the Streets." They could not stay in Corinth, but there were not enough railcars to ship them all. Most soon managed transportation to Memphis in "old leaky freight cars," one Federal wrote. "Got wet had to stand up or lay or sit in the mud and Water all night," he added. From Memphis, where they were housed for a few hours in a large building, they moved southward to Grenada, Jackson, and Meridian, Mississippi, and eventually to Mobile, Alabama. All along their trip, Confederate civilians came out to see them. "Had about 1500 men women and children to see us Yankees," one of the prisoners remembered at Grenada. One Southerner described Prentiss as "a nice looking man," although "he looked as wild as a buck[,] his eyes appeared ready to pop out of his head." Prentiss was especially sought out everywhere. One Confederate in Meridian wrote, "They were a fine looking body of men, Gen. Prentiss, of course, being the most observed. Aside from his rank, he would have, perhaps, attracted notice in any crowd." Another noted, "They appeared lively and jovial[.] They were well dressed and behaved with Respect."[20]

The prisoners moved to various camps in Alabama and Georgia, but the viewing continued. One Federal wrote that they stopped at every little town "so the rebels that lived ther could get a peap at us." As they began to settle down in camps, however, the novelty wore off. Quality of life differed at the various prisons, with some prisoners complaining of treatment while others noted good handling. "This is a healthy place and our comfort is well provided for," wrote one Federal from a prison camp at Selma, Alabama. Almost all the prisoners were eventually exchanged, including Prentiss. Most were free by October or November 1862, ready to go back into the ranks, which many did. Benjamin Prentiss went on a speaking tour touting his activities. Unfortunately, there was also a sizable number of men who perished as prisoners.[21]

As bad as conditions were at Corinth, the Federals still on the battlefield were even worse off. Although the Confederate retreat was grueling, their camps were safe in Corinth. Not so with the Federal camps, and many units had to rebuild completely. They began to rummage through the battlefield to locate equipment, finding all types of oddities, including diaries on Confederate bodies. A Federal found a line of knapsacks left by some Confederate regiment in its deployment area. Thomas Wood's troops captured a field desk with Johnston's battle plan and address to his troops inside. He wrote that it showed "how grand and well organized was the attacking force, . . . as well as proves how momentous was the conflict through which our troops have so fortunately and honorably passed."[22]

The destruction of the Army of the Tennessee camps, coupled with the lack of transportation for the Army of the Ohio units, caused mass suffering and sickness in the days after the battle. Added to that were major rainstorms. The result was sickness and low morale in the Union army. "We never saw our tents for 8 days, & it rained 7 nights out of 8 & we had nothing in the world to shelter us," wrote one of Buell's men. One Illinoisan wrote home that the men "have been camping out in the woods in huts built of brush and poles as our tents and teams were left behind and have not come up." Another elaborated that the troops built "little coops and dens out of bark and leaves to sleep under at night to protect ourselves from the rain storms." The muddy roads and clogged landing inundated with wounded caused additional logistical problems, and the army had to go on half rations. One Indianan wrote, "I have not had a meal since Saturday night. Have lived on excitement and coffee."[23]

Tension eased when wagons started moving again, but the arrival of more Federals also helped. Numerous Union regiments arrived in the days and weeks after the battle, including John Pope's entire Army of the Mississippi from its recent Island No. 10 victory on April 7. Most came up the Tennessee River, although there was a continual problem with Confederates taking potshots at them as they passed on transports. All sorts of regiments arrived from siege batteries to engineers, all intent on operations against Corinth.[24]

To a man, those who arrived after the battle were aghast at the sights and smells of the battlefield. One Iowan looked over the field and admitted, "I returned, sickened, depressed, and disgusted with all things." One arriving Federal wrote home that he "saw the Battle ground and smelled it too." Another described how it was a "horrible sight to witness on a emty stomache." Many marveled that the brush "was most all shot off smothe between 4 and 6 feet from the ground. Some trees was full of balls from the ground up twenty feet." Sanitation in such an area was impossible, and many died of sickness. Chaplains performed funerals regularly.[25]

Luminaries arrived in fewer numbers than additional soldiers, but they provided a disproportionate surge in morale. Most notable among these were state governors, who came ostensibly to care for their troops but probably came to see and be seen by a voting population. Governor Richard Yates of Illinois arrived on April 14 to cheers from the Illinois soldiers. These cheers, one Federal wrote, "frightened his horse so that he threw the Goviner off but no danger done the Goviner." Wisconsin's governor Louis P. Harvey also arrived, but he suffered a much crueler fate than being thrown from his horse. While transferring from one boat to another, he fell off the steamboat *Demleith* and drowned in late April. His body was recovered far down the Tennessee River. Governor Oliver P. Morton of Indiana also arrived, although his visit was evidently much less eventful.[26]

By far, the most famous arrival at Pittsburg Landing was the commanding general himself, Henry W. Halleck. He landed on April 11 to pomp and circumstance, complete with artillery salutes from field batteries as well as the gunboats. The troops were glad to see him; one Iowan wrote his sister, "he is a go-a head man," adding that everyone had confidence in him. Halleck quickly went to work, even camping out at the landing with the men. Normally he would stay in a house, but in this instance, he thought camping was the better option. He admitted to his wife that living in a tent was "not very comfortable," but he went on to say, "It always agrees with my health, and I rather like it notwithstanding the inconvenience. Moreover, it will have a good effect upon the soldiers to camp out with them." Yet in camping out with the army, he immediately saw problems, telling his wife, "This army is undisciplined and very much disorganized, the officers being utterly incapable of maintaining order." He was intent on cleaning up the mess.[27]

Halleck immediately began professional activities, such as having engineers map the field—something the Confederates also did. Cartographers such as Leon Fremaux and Jeremy Gilmer on the Confederate side and George Thom and Nathaniel Michler on the Union side produced detailed but somewhat inaccurate maps of the fighting. Halleck's chief goal, however, was to instill professionalization into the army leadership, particularly the Army of the Tennessee.[28]

Like before, Halleck's chief target was Grant, and Grant came out of Shiloh with few accolades from anyone. Numerous soldier letters and diaries disparaged him; one Federal wrote, "General U. S. Grant is about played out with the troops." Another wrote, "The men express their feelings in regard to the Battle and censure Grant severely for not being better prepared for the surprise. A gloom is cast over the entire

Army. And Grant's laurels won at Donaldson are forgotten in our late disaster here at Pittsburgh Landing or as the Rebels call 'Shilow.'" In addition to the accusations of surprise, Grant was also accused of being drunk at the battle. He had to be helped on his horse because of his sore ankle, which did not help appearances. Despite the rumors, there is no evidence that Grant was drunk, and he later had his defenders, such as Mrs. Cherry herself, who wrote that he always acted gentlemanly and never drank anything alcoholic.[29]

Others also caught the ire of the American people for their actions at Shiloh, although one Federal took up for them, writing, "I wish some of our patraotick citizens could have been hear men who stay at home and find fault with our Generals." William T. Sherman suffered, literally: "My right hand is temporarily disabled by inflammation from a wound," he wrote his senator brother, and it was still causing major problems as late as April 22. Yet the surprise cost him more dearly. One soldier wrote, "He is either a traitor or a fool. I don't know which but it is charitable to suppose the latter." Sherman ultimately landed on his feet, however, mainly because he had something Grant did not have: the full support of Henry Halleck. Many Ohio troops were also castigated, particularly the 53rd and 71st Ohio, although there were many in both regiments that served bravely and proudly. Benjamin Fearing wrote of Ephraim C. Dawes of the 53rd Ohio, who had done so much to rally the regiment after Appler's antics doomed them: "I pity poor Dawes. He did good work, and is now broken hearted at the disgrace of his command."[30]

Despite the controversies, the armies began to rebuild, especially the shattered Army of the Tennessee. John McArthur took command of the devastated Second Division, although he had to take a medical leave himself as a result of his wound. Eventually Thomas A. Davies took over, and Thomas J. McKean took command of what was left of the Sixth Division. In the weeks after the battle, numerous promotions, discharges, and reorganizations also took place, aided by many wounded or missing returning to their commands. In the especially hard-hit artillery, battery personnel counted cannon and distributed guns. Sherman later admitted he had lost seven guns and recaptured seven—"not the identical guns we had lost, but enough in numbers to balance the account." Fortunately for the Federals, one Illinoisan noted that Union artillerymen routinely took off a wheel before they left a gun, and the Confederates "had no time to hunt up wheels." Others policed the battlefield and gathered thousands of weapons, pieces of equipment, and ammunition.[31]

Some were less than thrilled about the reorganization, however. W. H. L. Wallace's Second Division was especially bothersome, with Smith and Wallace both unfit for action, the former dying later in the month at the Cherry Mansion from his leg infection. Command fell to Colonel Tuttle, but he soon returned home sick, leaving the command to Colonel James Baker of the 2nd Iowa. He had his own problems, and because the other regiments had their field officers captured or absent, for a time in late April one of the brigades fell to the ranking officer in the unit, Lieutenant Colonel James C. Parrott of the 7th Iowa. Parrott wrote his wife, "You can see that the 2nd and 7th stand high when they place the brigade in command of a Lt Col." Not knowing what to do with the remnants of the regiments who had surrendered in the Hornet's Nest, the idea emerged to create a small Union Brigade of the uncaptured parts of the 8th, 12th, and 14th Iowa and the 58th Illinois. This did not set well with those who valued individual regimental pride. One Iowan reported the 58th Illinois's reluctance, saying they "had considerable trouble to make them consent" and that they were once "called out to put down a fuss between the 58th Ill & 8th Iowa." The 58th Illinois also had trouble with other units: "Col. Baldwin of the 57th is trying to have a consolidation effected with his Reg't," wrote one of the regiment's soldiers; "God forbid that such a thing should take place."[32]

Like the Confederates, Federal commanders soon began to try to make sense of what had happened and wrote reports—although that in itself quickly led to disagreements. John McClernand wrote to Abraham Lincoln, stating, "My division, as usual, has borne or shared in bearing the brunt." Grant warned Washington not to trust McClernand's and Lew Wallace's reports, and members of individual units such as the 14th Wisconsin also argued against commander's reports, in this case Sooy Smith's. Even Grant and Buell traded shots over who won the battle. Yet there was plenty on which to agree, and commander after commander wrote glowing congratulations to their troops. Grant wrote, "In numbers engaged, no such contest ever took place on this continent; in importance of results, but few have taken place in the history of the world." Many a Federal soldier recited his words in letters home about this being the largest battle ever upon the continent. The congratulations even extended to the secretary of war, Edwin Stanton, who ordered a

100-gun salute in Washington, DC. The reverberations of Shiloh quite literally reached all the way to the Potomac River.[33]

The armies thus began to make sense of what had happened, and those in Richmond and Washington slowly realized the magnitude of Shiloh. In addition, word began to spread all over the world, and reaction began to come in from leading observers in Europe. In Washington, Lincoln was pleased, especially when coupled with Island No. 10 and a few weeks later with the capture of New Orleans.[34]

Newspaper accounts such as those of the famed Whitelaw Reid—although sometimes wildly inaccurate—quickly spread the news to the waiting populace. Reid's account of surprised soldiers being bayoneted in their tents haunted Grant and Sherman for the rest of their lives. Soldiers writing home to inform loved ones and friends of their own well-being or the loss of comrades also carried the horror of Shiloh to the states and abroad. The tension among family members at home who awaited these letters was evident as they corresponded with each other about any bit of news heard from the battlefield. Families were especially brokenhearted when a soldier wrote his own last farewell, such as when Noah Gebbart wrote his wife and children: "I am now on a sick bed and this may be the last communication from your husband and father."[35]

Many of the soldiers expressed concern for the feelings of those at home. One Northerner described "an old father and mother—loving brothers and sisters—all—bowed to the very dust with unspeakable grief." James Butterfield of Illinois wrote home the next Sunday: "How often I have thought of the tears that are wept by mothers sisters and wives in the North yes many a heart will go to church this day wrapped in the deepest sorrow and gloom." Details only made it worse. A son reported the death of his brother to his mother: "When Orvil was raising to get another fire at them, a ball struck in the head. He died instantly. It, the bullet, going in one ear and coming out the other." He added, "It is a lonesome time for me now." Yet the homesick soldiers expressed thanksgiving at being spared themselves: "The Next Sunday after the Battle here," one Union soldier wrote home, "we had a prayer of thanks to the Lord by our chaplain for the great victory which was won here." McClernand was also quick in "offering grateful acknowledgements to a kind Providence for the eminent success which had crowned our labors in the cause of liberty and constitutional government."[36]

The agony only increased when the bodies began to arrive home. Although most dead soldiers were interred immediately in the days after the battle, a few were later exhumed and shipped home. One Confederate in Meridian, Mississippi, described a heartrending sight: "One old gentleman, from Scott County, had a coffin, containing the body of his son, who fell in the fight of Sunday." The process often produced gory problems. One Federal recalled how a soldier buried for two weeks "did not hardly hold together to be put in the case." Mostly those of high rank were sent home. The 15th Illinois buried their lieutenant colonel, major, and a captain all in one box, then later disinterred them and sent them home. Everett Peabody was first interred in a gun box in his camp, his headboard reading, "A braver man ne'er died upon the field; A warmer heart never to death did yield." After his brother came west to find out about his death, with an introductory letter from the governor of Massachusetts, Peabody's body was taken to Boston in a "metallic casket," where the governor oversaw those giving their respects. In like vein, Julius Raith was returned to Belleville, Illinois, where a former lieutenant governor spoke at his funeral; sadly, his wife had died several years before, and now Raith left seven- and nine-year-old orphan boys. Similarly, Anne Wallace nursed her husband, the mortally wounded W. H. L. Wallace, in the parlor of the Cherry Mansion. Walter Gresham wrote home, "Genl Wallace of Illinois is now in my room mortally wounded." He seemed to rebound when his wife was with him, continually running his fingers over her hand in search of her wedding band. Wallace ultimately perished, however, and Anne took him home to Ottawa, where he was buried in the family plot behind their home.[37]

Other funerary efforts turned out better. Colonel James Tuttle's brother suddenly showed up at camp one day, saying his family had received word the colonel was dead; he had come to retrieve the body. Tuttle informed his brother in person that "he guest he couldant take it yett awhile."[38]

It took only a few weeks for the Federal mass to begin its move on Corinth, which was, after all, the goal of the operation. Yet even that small delay afforded Beauregard enough time to solidify his position, entrench even further, and assemble a reinforced army larger than that which he had taken to Shiloh. "The Army is again well organized," Beauregard staff officer Chisolm wrote as early as April 22. Halleck thus let Beauregard recoup much of what he had lost as a result of Shiloh. The delay was inevitable, however, given the problems the Federals faced after the battle. Indeed, the affects of Shiloh hung with the troops for weeks. One Federal wrote that he could still hear the "music of bullets and for days after the battle we could hear this particular sound in our ears." Another admitted, "The noise of explosions was in my ears for days."[39]

Emotions were mixed as to fighting again, but all knew it had to be done. "I am anxious to push forward and finish the job while we are at it," wrote one Federal. Opinions on how difficult it would be varied among soldiers. Grant himself marveled at the Confederates' ability to keep fighting, arguing that Fort Donelson should have been the knockout blow. They counterattacked hard at Shiloh, however, and although he later wrote in his memoirs that "I gave up all idea of saving the Union except by complete conquest," his contemporary correspondence indicated he still expected a swift end to the rebellion. Others were also confident. "The Rebels made a death struggle here such as they will never be able to make again," noted Thomas Harrison. Another mused that they "will soon have to fight the bugars again but I do not think we will have as hard fighting to do." Iowan Francis Harmon wrote his brother, "I think the rebbles will crawl in a hole pretty soon and pull the hole in after them or clime a tree and pull the tree up after them." As for the Confederates, they too looked for the climactic battle, but given what they learned at Shiloh, they seemed to think their chances were even better now than before: "I am satisfied that they will outnumber us but when we have them out of reach of their Gun Boats we will whip them worse than at Shiloh."[40]

The Corinth campaign soon began, all the Union armies moving by early May. The war was shifting back to focus on the railroads that crossed at Corinth, with Halleck nevertheless sending operations against the flanks at Bear Creek. At one point a bridge was set afire and floated, burning, all the way past Pittsburg Landing. Still, the main effort was toward Corinth, and Halleck moved swiftly through the first week of May toward the town, encountering forward Confederate brigades left behind after Shiloh at Monterey and Farmington. By May 8, a quick-moving Halleck was within three or four miles of the town.[41]

Then the Confederates struck, first on May 9 at Farmington and then in an abandoned effort later in May. Halleck became extremely cautious as a result. He began to implement true siege proceedings, digging his way the last couple of miles to Corinth. He was there by May 28, and Beauregard had little option but to fight or evacuate. He chose the latter, desiring to save his army instead of losing it while trying to hold a defenseless position. So almost without a fight, and with much less bloodshed than at Shiloh, Beauregard left Corinth and the railroads to the Federals. Thus the real battle for Corinth and her railroads had taken place at Shiloh. Indeed, Shiloh would rank as the biggest battle of the Tennessee River campaign, and it was likewise the largest battle in the campaign to defend or open the Mississippi Valley.[42]

In the largest strategic context, the battle also marked the best opportunity the Confederacy would have to win back its lost territory in that Mississippi Valley. No better opportunity presented itself later on in the war, and no less than John McClernand argued that a major defeat at Shiloh would have seen the war "rolled back over Tennessee, Kentucky, and Missouri." In addition, Shiloh was also the best opportunity for the Confederacy to reach parity in the west; nowhere later would they have similar numbers with such potential benefits. It was certainly a gamble at the time; Johnston felt he had to do or die. He died, and the argument can also be made that his Confederacy took a major step toward extinction on April 6–7, 1862.[43]

Shiloh only grew in status even as other larger battles came and went. It was the first big battle for many of the men engaged and thus was seared into their memory like no other. Numerous soldiers' diaries reflected the one-year anniversary of the battle. Others produced poems or songs to commemorate the fight; the pastor at the Baptist church in Ottawa, Illinois, preached a sermon on W. H. L. Wallace the Sunday after the battle. Others looked at the results more concretely. William T. Sherman saw strictly the military benefits of Shiloh: "It was not then a question of military skill and strategy, but of courage and pluck, and I am convinced that every life lost to us that day was necessary, for otherwise at Corinth, at Memphis, at Vicksburg, we would have found harder resistance, had we not shown our enemies that, rude and untutored as we then were, we could fight as well as they."[44]

Others were more philosophical. William Camm, writing of the possibilities for fewer Shilohs in the future, noted, "What a pity it is that men do not use reason instead of rifles, and common sense instead of cannon." Others simply wanted to commemorate. Buell's division commander, Thomas J. Wood, wrote the day after the battle that the fighting should "render the site of the battle a classic spot in the annals of our country." Colonel Hugh T. Reid of the 15th Iowa similarly wrote, "While we mourn our comrades in arms the gallant dead whose lives were sacrificed on the altar of their country, we are solaced with the belief that a grateful people will in after times pay a proper tribute to their memory."[45]

Reid's desire was actually already coming to fruition and would, unknown to all of the participants at the time, grow beyond anything they ever dreamed. Many Federal regiments had already fashioned "a neat fence of wicker work" around their burial plots, but one regiment took the ornamentation even further. In the 11th Illinois campground, George Carrington told of the effort to commemorate its dead on April 8: "Tommy Newport made a monument of oak five or six feet high, this was set up and the names cut thereon, Co and Regt, letters painted black, the monument painted white. We built a fence with poles around the grave." It soon became known, and is still marked to this day, as the White Post burial place.[46]

It was the first monument erected at the Shiloh battlefield.

EPILOGUE

A split nation had collectively held its breath as Americans fought one another at Shiloh in April 1862. Tensions ran high at such elevated stakes. Brother fought against brother, including the example of the Sheldon family of Perryville, Tennessee, who had four siblings in the battle—two on each side. Even in 1884, their mother related, "It seems impossible for them to agree on anything." Yet over time, the wounds began to heal, both literally and figuratively. Amid controversies among generals and observations as to who had done what, definite memories of Shiloh began to emerge, often taking a form unlike the original events. William T. Sherman weighed in on the phenomenon, writing, "I begin to doubt whether I was at the battle of Pittsburg Landing of modern description."[1]

Changes were also taking place on the field itself, often fostering that healing and the developing memory. Even as the meager burial sites on the battlefield often washed open, the Federal government saw fit to lay the Union dead to rest in the eventual Shiloh National Cemetery in 1866. The Confederate dead were left on the field itself. Others similarly began to mark significant sites associated with the battle, including the Cantrell family, who planted a cedar tree in 1865 where legend held that Johnston had fallen. Disputes emerged even then over the actual site, and they continue today. Veterans also began to return to the field to remember, and those who could not visit reminisced. Francis Shoup remarked years later about beautiful dogwoods in bloom and how "I never see them now that I do not think of Shiloh."[2]

The evolution of Shiloh's memory in the public mind took a major leap in 1894, when Congress established the Shiloh National Military Park. One veteran had exemplified the thinking: "Instead of squandering means over idle parades, . . . it is respectfully and earnestly suggested that Congress adopt some measure for the preservation of the remains at Shiloh. . . . also, that the church at Shiloh be rebuilt as a national memorial." A commission of veterans, including such luminaries as generals Basil Duke and Don Carlos Buell, oversaw the park, where monuments and artillery pieces began to dot the battlefield, commemorating what had happened there and the men who had fought at Shiloh.[3]

Attending the rise of the battlefield as a park was a corresponding body of literature that emphasized particular aspects of the battle. Veterans and amateur historians such as Joseph Rich, Otto Eisenschiml, and DeLong Rice wrote books about the battle, but no writer became more important to the growing literature than David W. Reed. As a member of the 12th Iowa and then as the first historian and later commission chairman at the Shiloh National Military Park, Reed literally wrote much of the history of the battle. It is not surprising that he emphasized the area where he had fought, the Hornet's Nest. In his regimental history of the 12th Iowa, he wrote, "The Thermopylae of modern times, was the 'Hornet's Nest' at Shiloh" and "for some hours it was the turning point in the battle, and beyond doubt saved what was finally saved of the first day's wreck at Shiloh." Contemporary articles in *Century* and other magazines and several panoramas and paintings such as Thure de Thulstrup's 1888 L. Prang and Company lithograph, along with the park's later long-running introductory film *Shiloh: Portrait of a Battle,* only carried the Hornet's Nest thesis to wider public attention over the decades.[4]

Although the larger impact of the Hornets' Nest is debatable, the entire battle of Shiloh should definitely have such a special place in America's collective memory. The battle was incredibly important to the larger Civil War; it was definitely do or die for both sides. When Johnston stated that he had to conquer or perish, he was right. Unfortunately for him, Grant figuratively conquered and Johnston perished. The best opportunity for the South to turn its fortunes may have died with Sidney Johnston at Shiloh.[5]

It is thus fitting that special commemorations recently took place on the 150th anniversary of the battle. Yet more than intended was perhaps said in those commemorations. The Shiloh National Military Park staff provided a commemorative illumination of the battlefield for the sesquicentennial, placing 23,746 candles on site, each one representing an official casualty at Shiloh. The journey through the dimly lit battlefield was impressive as candles lit monuments, artillery pieces, and other objects in an eerie glow. One candle perhaps told more than any, however. In front of the tablet in the bottom of the ravine where Albert Sidney Johnston died, a lone flame pierced the darkness, obviously in commemoration of the general who had died there trying to win the victory. But perhaps the single candle commemorated more than just Johnston's death. It could also be construed as embodying the Confederacy's partial death on the field where Sidney Johnston had declared, "We must this day conquer or perish." He, and perhaps the Confederacy itself, perished on the plains of Shiloh.[6]

APPENDIX

Shiloh Order of Battle,
April 6–7, 1862

ARMY OF THE TENNESSEE
Maj. Gen. U. S. Grant

FIRST DIVISION
Maj. Gen. John A. McClernand

First Brigade
Col. Abraham M. Hare (w)
Col. Marcellus Crocker
  8th Illinois
  18th Illinois
  11th Iowa
  13th Iowa

Third Brigade
Col. Julius Raith (mw)
Lieut. Col. Enos P. Wood
  17th Illinois
  29th Illinois
  43d Illinois
  49th Illinois

Second Brigade
Col. C. Carroll Marsh
  11th Illinois
  20th Illinois
  45th Illinois
  48th Illinois

Unattached
Dresser's Battery (D),
  2d Illinois Light Artillery
McAllister's Battery (D),
  1st Illinois Light Artillery
Schwartz's Battery (E),
  2d Illinois Light Artillery
Burrows's Battery,
  14th Ohio Light Artillery
1st Battalion, 4th Illinois Cavalry
Stewart's and Carmichael's Companies
  Illinois Cavalry

Second Division
Brig. Gen. William H. L. Wallace (mw)
Col. James M. Tuttle

First Brigade
Col. James M. Tuttle
  2d Iowa
  7th Iowa
  12th Iowa
  14th Iowa

Third Brigade
Col. Thomas W. Sweeny (w)
Col. Silas D. Baldwin
  8th Iowa
  7th Illinois
  50th Illinois
  52d Illinois
  57th Illinois
  58th Illinois

Cavalry
Company A, 2d Illinois Cavalry
Company B, 2d Illinois Cavalry
Company C, 2d United States Cavalry
Company I, 4th United States Cavalry

Second Brigade
Brig. Gen. John McArthur (w)
Col. Thomas Morton
  9th Illinois
  12th Illinois
  13th Missouri
  14th Missouri
  81st Ohio

Artillery
Willard's Battery (A),
  1st Illinois Light Artillery
Maj. J. S. Cavender's Battalion
  Missouri Artillery:
Richardson's Battery (D),
  1st Missouri Light Artillery
Welker's Battery (H),
  1st Missouri Light Artillery
Stone's Battery (K),
  1st Missouri Light Artillery

Third Division
Maj. Gen. Lew Wallace

First Brigade
Col. Morgan L. Smith
  11th Indiana
  24th Indiana
  8th Missouri

Third Brigade
Col. Charles Whittlesey
  20th Ohio
  56th Ohio
  76th Ohio
  78th Ohio

Second Brigade
Col. John M. Thayer
  23d Indiana
  1st Nebraska
  58th Ohio
  68th Ohio

Artillery
Thompson's Battery,
  9th Indiana Light Artillery
Buel's Battery (I),
  1st Missouri Light Artillery

Cavalry
3d Battalion, 11th Illinois Cavalry
3d Battalion, 5th Ohio Cavalry

FOURTH DIVISION
Brig. Gen. Stephen A. Hurlbut

First Brigade
Col. Nelson G. Williams (w)
Col. Isaac C. Pugh
  28th Illinois
  32d Illinois
  41st Illinois
  3d Iowa

Third Brigade
Brig. Gen. Jacob G. Lauman
  31st Indiana
  44th Indiana
  17th Kentucky
  25th Kentucky

Second Brigade
Col. James C. Veatch (w)
  14th Illinois
  15th Illinois
  46th Illinois
  25th Indiana

Artillery
Ross's Battery,
  2d Michigan Light Artillery
Mann's Battery (C),
  1st Missouri Light Artillery
Myers's Battery,
  13th Ohio Light Artillery

Cavalry
1st and 2d Battalions, 5th Ohio Cavalry

FIFTH DIVISION
Brig. Gen. William T. Sherman (w)

First Brigade
Col. John A. McDowell (w)
  40th Illinois
  6th Iowa
  46th Ohio

Third Brigade
Col. Jesse Hildebrand
  53d Ohio
  57th Ohio
  77th Ohio

Second Brigade
Col. David Stuart (w)
Col. T. Kilby Smith
  55th Illinois
  54th Ohio
  71st Ohio

Fourth Brigade
Col. Ralph P. Buckland
  48th Ohio
  70th Ohio
  72nd Ohio

APPENDIX

Artillery
Maj. Ezra Taylor
Taylor's Battery (B),
    1st Illinois Light Artillery
Waterhouse's Battery (E),
    1st Illinois Light Artillery
Morton Battery,
    6th Indiana Light Artillery

Cavalry
2d and 3d Battalions,
    4th Illinois Cavalry
Thielemann's two companies
    Illinois Cavalry

Sixth Division
Brig. Gen. Benjamin M. Prentiss (c)

First Brigade
Col. Everett Peabody (k)
    12th Michigan
    21st Missouri
    25th Missouri
    16th Wisconsin

Not Brigaded
16th Iowa
15th Iowa
23d Missouri

Cavalry
1st and 2d Battalions,
    11th Illinois Cavalry

Second Brigade
Col. Madison Miller (c)
    61st Illinois
    18th Missouri
    18th Wisconsin

Artillery
Hickenlooper's Battery,
    5th Ohio Light Artillery
Munch's Battery,
    1st Minnesota Light Artillery

Unassigned Troops
15th Michigan
14th Wisconsin
Battery H, 1st Illinois Light Artillery
Battery I, 1st Illinois Light Artillery
Battery B, 2d Illinois Artillery
    (siege guns)
Battery F, 2d Illinois Light Artillery
8th Battery, Ohio Light Artillery

ARMY OF THE OHIO
Maj. Gen. Don Carlos Buell

SECOND DIVISION
Brig. Gen. Alexander McD. McCook

Fourth Brigade
Brig. Gen. Lovell H. Rousseau
    6th Indiana
    5th Kentucky
    1st Ohio
    1st Battalion, 15th United States
    1st Battalion, 16th United States
    1st Battalion, 19th United States

Sixth Brigade
Col. William H. Gibson
    32d Indiana
    39th Indiana
    15th Ohio
    49th Ohio

Fifth Brigade
Col. Edward N. Kirk (w)
    34th Illinois
    29th Indiana
    30th Indiana
    77th Pennsylvania

Artillery
Terrill's Battery (H),
    5th United States Artillery

FOURTH DIVISION
Brig. Gen. William Nelson

Tenth Brigade
Col. Jacob Ammen
    36th Indiana
    6th Ohio
    24th Ohio

Twenty-second Brigade
Col. Sanders D. Bruce
    1st Kentucky
    2d Kentucky
    20th Kentucky

Nineteenth Brigade
Col. William B. Hazen
    9th Indiana
    6th Kentucky
    41st Ohio

Fifth Division
Brig. Gen. Thomas L. Crittenden

Eleventh Brigade
Brig. Gen. Jeremiah T. Boyle
   9th Kentucky
   13th Kentucky
   19th Ohio
   59th Ohio

Fourteenth Brigade
Col. William Sooy Smith
   11th Kentucky
   26th Kentucky
   13th Ohio

Artillery
Bartlett's Battery (G),
   1st Ohio Light Artillery
Mendenhall's batteries (H and M),
   4th United States Artillery

Sixth Division
Brig. Gen. Thomas J. Wood

Twentieth Brigade
Brig. Gen. James A. Garfield
   13th Michigan
   64th Ohio
   65th Ohio

Twenty-first Brigade
Col. George D. Wagner
   15th Indiana
   40th Indiana
   57th Indiana
   24th Kentucky

ARMY OF THE MISSISSIPPI
Gen. Albert Sidney Johnston (k)
Gen. P. G. T. Beauregard

First Army Corps
Maj. Gen. Leonidas Polk

First Division
Brig. Gen. Charles Clark (w)
Brig. Gen. Alexander P. Stewart

First Brigade
Col. Robert M. Russell
  11th Louisiana
  12th Tennessee
  13th Tennessee
  22d Tennessee
  Bankhead's Tennessee Battery

Second Brigade
Brig. Gen. Alexander P. Stewart
  13th Arkansas
  4th Tennessee
  5th Tennessee
  33d Tennessee
  Stanford's Mississippi Battery

SECOND DIVISION
Maj. Gen. Benjamin F. Cheatham (w)

First Brigade
Brig. Gen. Bushrod R. Johnson (w)
Col. Preston Smith
  Blythe's Mississippi Regiment
  2d Tennessee
  15th Tennessee
  154th Tennessee
  Polk's Tennessee Battery

Second Brigade
Col. William H. Stephens
Col. George Maney
  7th Kentucky
  1st Tennessee (Battalion)
  6th Tennessee
  9th Tennessee
  Smith's Mississippi Battery

Cavalry
1st Mississippi
Mississippi and Alabama Battalion

UNATTACHED
47th Tennessee

SECOND ARMY CORPS
Maj. Gen. Braxton Bragg

FIRST DIVISION
Brig. Gen. Daniel Ruggles

First Brigade
Col. Randall L. Gibson
  1st Arkansas
  4th Louisiana
  13th Louisiana
  19th Louisiana

Second Brigade
Brig. Gen. Patton Anderson
  1st Florida Battalion
  17th Louisiana
  20th Louisiana
  Confederate Guards Response
    Battalion
  9th Texas
  Washington (Louisiana) Artillery,
    Fifth Company

Third Brigade   *Cavalry*
Col. Preston Pond, Jr.   Alabama Battalion
   16th Louisiana
   18th Louisiana
   Crescent (Louisiana) Regiment
   Orleans Guard (Louisiana) Battalion
   38th Tennessee
   Ketchum's Alabama Battery

SECOND DIVISION
Brig. Gen. Jones M. Withers

First Brigade   *Second Brigade*
Brig. Gen. Adley H. Gladden (mw)   Brig. Gen. James R. Chalmers
Col. Daniel W. Adams (w)   5th Mississippi
Col. Zach C. Deas (w)   7th Mississippi
   21st Alabama   9th Mississippi
   22d Alabama   10th Mississippi
   25th Alabama   52d Tennessee
   26th Alabama   Gage's Alabama Battery
   1st Louisiana
   Robertson's Alabama Battery   *Cavalry*
                                     Clanton's Alabama Regiment
Third Brigade
Brig. Gen. John K. Jackson
   17th Alabama
   18th Alabama
   19th Alabama
   2d Texas
   Girardey's Georgia Battery

THIRD ARMY CORPS
Maj. Gen. William J. Hardee (w)

First Brigade
Brig. Gen. Thomas C. Hindman (w)
Col. Robert G. Shaver (w)
Col. Daniel C. Govan
  2d Arkansas
  6th Arkansas
  7th Arkansas
  3d Confederate
  Warren (Swett's) Light Artillery
  Pillow's (Miller's Tennessee) Flying
    Artillery

Third Brigade
Brig. Gen. Sterling A. M. Wood (w)
Col. William K. Patterson
  16th Alabama
  8th Arkansas
  9th (14th) Arkansas (battalion)
  3d Mississippi Battalion
  27th Tennessee
  44th Tennessee
  55th Tennessee
  Harper's (Jefferson Mississippi)
    Battery
  Georgia Dragoons

Second Brigade
Brig. Gen. Patrick R. Cleburne
  15th Arkansas
  6th Mississippi
  2d Tennessee
  5th (35th) Tennessee
  23d Tennessee
  24th Tennessee
  Shoup's Battalion
  Trigg's (Austin) Arkansas Battery
  Calvert's (Helena) Arkansas Battery
  Hubbard's Arkansas Battery

RESERVE CORPS
Brig. Gen. John C. Breckinridge

First Brigade
Col. Robert P. Trabue
  (Clifton's) 4th Alabama Battalion
  31st Alabama
  3d Kentucky
  4th Kentucky
  5th Kentucky
  6th Kentucky
  Crew's Tennessee Battalion
  Lyon's (Cobb's) Kentucky Battery
  Byrne's Mississippi Battery
  Morgan's Squadron, Kentucky
    Cavalry

Second Brigade
Brig. Gen. John S. Bowen (w)
Col. John D. Martin
  9th Arkansas
  10th Arkansas
  2d Confederate
  1st Missouri
  Pettus (Hudson's) Flying Artillery
  Watson's Louisiana Battery
  Thompson's Company Kentucky
    Cavalry

Third Brigade
Col. Winfield S. Statham
  15th Mississippi
  22d Mississippi
  19th Tennessee
  20th Tennessee
  28th Tennessee
  45th Tennessee
  Rutledge's Tennessee Battery
  Forrest's Tennessee Cavalry

UNATTACHED

Wharton's Texas Regiment Cavalry
Wirt Adams's Mississippi Regiment
  Cavalry
McClung's Tennessee Battery
Roberts's Arkansas Battery

NOTES

MCM	McLean County Museum
MDAH	Mississippi Department of Archives and History
MHS	Missouri Historical Society
MIAU	Miami University
MSCPL	Memphis Shelby County Public Library
MSU	Mississippi State University
MU	Murray State University
NARA	National Archives and Records Administration
NC	Navarro College
ND	University of Notre Dame
NL	Newberry Library
NYHS	New York Historical Society
OHS	Ohio Historical Society
OR	*War of the Rebellion: A Compilation of the Official Records of the Union and Confederate Armies* (Washington, DC: US Government Printing Office, 1880–1901)
ORN	*The Official Records of the Union and Confederate Navies in the War of the Rebellion,* 30 vols. (Washington DC: Government Printing Office, 1894–1922)
RBHPC	Rutherford B. Hayes Presidential Center
SHSI	State Historical Society of Iowa
SIU	Southern Illinois University
SNMP	Shiloh National Military Park
SNMPAF	Shiloh National Military Park Administrative Files
SNMPRF	Shiloh National Military Park Regimental Files
SNMPVF	Shiloh National Military Park Vertical Files
SOR	*Supplement to the Official Records of the Union and Confederate Armies,* 100 vols. (Wilmington, NC: Broadfoot Publishing Company, 1994)
STRI	Stones River National Battlefield
TSLA	Tennessee State Library and Archives
TU	Tulane University
UA	University of Alabama
UAR	University of Arkansas
UI	University of Iowa
UM	University of Mississippi
UMB	University of Michigan—Bentley Library
UMCL	University of Michigan—Clements Library
UMEM	University of Memphis
UNC	University of North Carolina
UO	University of Oklahoma
USAMHI	United States Army Military History Institute

USM University of Southern Mississippi
UT University of Tennessee
UVA University of Virginia
UWS University of Washington
VCPL Vigo County Public Library
VHS Virginia Historical Society
WHS Wisconsin Historical Society
WRHS Western Reserve Historical Society
WS Wiley Sword Collection
WSU Wright State University

PREFACE

1. Examples of differing kinds of treatment include Grimsley and Woodworth, *Shiloh;* Woodworth, ed., *The Shiloh Campaign;* Luvaas, Bowman, and Fullenkamp, *Guide to the Battle of Shiloh;* Gudmens, *Staff Ride Handbook;* Frank and Reaves, *Seeing the Elephant;* Isbell, *Shiloh and Corinth;* Groom, *Shiloh, 1862.*

2. Force, *From Fort Henry to Corinth;* 124; Hosea, "Second Day at Shiloh," 6:195.

3. SOR 1, 1:643.

4. Payson Shumway to wife, April 13, 1862, Payson Z. Shumway Papers, ALPL.

PROLOGUE

1. Welch, *Archeology,* 1, 255, 266; Harbert, *Early History,* 42–43.

2. For various land grants, see the chains of title for landowners, Series 1, Boxes 20–22, SNMPAF.

3. "Pittsburg Landing Name Explained," *Memphis Commercial Appeal,* May 3, 1952; Fullwood, *Shiloh,* 13, 19, 22–23; Brazelton, *History of Hardin County,* 35; Mary E. Stricklin, "Shiloh Church," Shiloh Church, SNMPVF; "Shiloh School Property Deed," Shiloh Church, SNMPVF; "How Bloody Shiloh Got its Name," *Memphis Press Scimitar* clipping, undated, Shiloh Church, SNMPVF.

4. Reed, *Battle of Shiloh,* 8; Shedd, *History of Shiloh National Military Park,* 8; Smith, *This Great Battlefield,* 4.

5. US Bureau of the Census, Federal Manuscript Census, Population Schedule, 1860, Hardin County, Tennessee, NARA; John Paul Howell to Ronnie Brewington, September 26, 1990, Rhea and Howell Family, SNMPVF.

6. US Bureau of the Census, Federal Manuscript Census, Population Schedule, 1860, Hardin County, Tennessee, NARA; "Thomas Walker," Land Owners
at the Battle of Shiloh, SNMPVF; Pitts Tucker to James J. Fraley, December
17, 1860, WS; James J. Fraley to Pitts Tucker, December 19, 1860, WS.

7. Charles Marshall, "Miscellaneous Incidents of the Civil War," Historical Reports: Research Reports on Army Units in the Army of the Tennessee,
SNMPVF, 1–2; "Bill of Sale," Rhea and Howell Family, SNMPVF; US Bureau of the Census, Federal Manuscript Census, Slave Schedule, 1860, Hardin County, Tennessee, NARA; US Bureau of the Census, Federal Manuscript
Census, Agricultural and Manufacturing Schedule, 1860, Hardin County, Tennessee, NARA; US Bureau of the Census, Federal Manuscript Census, Popula-
tions Schedule, 1860, Hardin County, Tennessee, NARA.

8. *Story of the Fifty-fifth,* 68; US Bureau of the Census, Federal Manuscript
Census, Agricultural and Manufacturing Schedule, 1860, Hardin County, Ten-
nessee, NARA; "List of Houses on Shiloh Battlefield Mentioned in Reports,"
undated, Series 1, Box 39, Folder 631, SNMPAF; Brazelton, *History of Hardin
County,* 67; US Bureau of the Census, Federal Manuscript Census, Population
Schedule, 1860, Hardin County, Tennessee, NARA; Edith Tillman to James
Sasser, February 10, 1992, Tillman Cemetery, SNMPVF.

9. Smith, *This Great Battlefield,* 5.

10. Smith, "Gallant and Invaluable Service."

CHAPTER 1: "A GRAND DESIGN"

1. OR 1, 7:684.

2. OR 1, 10 (2): 340; *Journal of the State Convention and Ordinances,* 24–
25; *Official Journal of the Proceedings of the Convention of the State of Louisiana,* 235; "Joint Resolutions on the State of the Union," February 2, 1861, and
unknown to John J. Pettus, February 2, 1861, in Mississippi Governor, John J.
Pettus, Correspondence and Papers, 1859–1863, Series 757, MDAH; OR 1, 31
(3): 459.

3. McPherson, *Battle Cry,* 333–335.

4. For the western theater, see Hess, *Civil War in the West;* Woodworth, *Decision in the Heartland.*

5. Connelly, *Army of the Heartland,* 39–40; Jefferson Davis to Leonidas
Polk, 1862, Leonidas Polk Papers, LC; Charles Bivens Autobiography, undated, Charles Bivens Papers, CWTI, USAMHI, 1; Presley Judson Edwards
Autobiography, 1898, CHS; Johnston, *Life of Gen. Albert Sidney Johnston,*
291; Albert Sidney Johnston to Leroy Pope Walker, September 11, 1861, Albert Sidney Johnston Papers, LC; A. M. Clayton et al. to Jefferson Davis, September 3, 1861, Civil War Collection, TSLA.

6. OR 1, 7:131, 683; Jason Hurd to Marie, January 8, 1862, Jason Hurd Papers, CWD, USAMHI. For Belmont, see Hughes, *Battle of Belmont.*

7. Roland, *Albert Sidney Johnston,* 299.

8. Marszalek, *Commander of All Lincoln's Armies,* 109.

9. OR 1, 7:436, 440, 683; OR 1, 10 (2): 311; Woodworth, *Jefferson Davis,* 57; W. J. Stubblefield Diary, January 1862, MU, 2; Sherman, *Memoirs,* 1:220; Cooling, *Forts Henry and Donelson,* 65; Connelly, *Army of the Heartland,* 17.

10. For Grant, see Simpson, *Ulysses S. Grant.*

11. OR 1, 7:72–74; Force, *From Fort Henry to Corinth,* 92; Grant, *Personal Memoirs,* 1:169–170; Hess, *Civil War in the West,* 57.

12. OR 1, 7:420; Simpson, *Ulysses S. Grant,* 118.

13. OR 1, 7:131, 259, 418, 423, 425–426, 861; Reed, *Battle of Shiloh,* 7; J. B. Lindsley Diary, February 16, 1862, Lindsley Family Papers, TSLA; Henry M. Erisman to brother, March 12, 1862, Henry M. Erisman Papers, HCWRT, USAMHI; D. Thompson to father, March 15, 1862, Timothy Brookes Collection, USAMHI; John Spencer to D. D. Spencer, March 13, 1862, Spencer Family Papers, CWD, USAMHI.

14. OR 1, 10 (2): 3–7, 13–15, 17, 21, 24, 42, 56; Marszalek, *Commander of All Lincoln's Armies,* 120–122; Grant, "Battle of Shiloh," 1:466.

15. Schenker, "Grant–Halleck–Smith Affair"; Marszalek, *Commander of All Lincoln's Armies,* 119; John A. McClernand et al. to Ulysses S. Grant, March 9, 1862, Ulysses S. Grant Papers, NARA; OR 1, 10 (2): 3–5, 21; Lorenzo Thomas to Henry Halleck, March 10, 1862, Ulysses S. Grant Papers, NARA.

16. OR 1, 7:124–125, 130, 136–144, 159, 166–167; Grant, *Personal Memoirs,* 1:173; Bradford Nichol Memoir, February 14, 1862, TSLA; Ulysses S. Grant to J. C. Kelton, January 31, 1862, Lew Wallace Papers, NARA; Henry N. Peters to family, April 23, 1862, Peters Family Papers, UAR.

17. OR 1, 10 (2): 10–11, 16, 20, 22–24, 28; James H. Hall to family, April 1, 1862, James H. Hall Papers, UMB; Woodworth, *Nothing but Victory,* 142; N. D. Starr to Henrietta, June 13, 1862, AC, USAMHI; Edwin A. Bowen Diary, March 20, 1862, Edwin A. Bowen Papers, HL. For more on Buell and Halleck, see Engle, "Don Carlos Buell"; Rafuse, "McClellan and Halleck."

18. OR 1, 7:125; OR 1, 10 (2): 10–11, 16, 20, 22–24, 28; James H. Hall to family, April 1, 1862, James H. Hall Papers, UMB; Woodworth, *Nothing but Victory,* 142; N. D. Starr to Henrietta, June 13, 1862, AC, USAMHI.

19. OR 1, 7:131, 153–157; ORN 1, 22:570–574; unsigned, undated memoir in USS *Tyler* File, SNMPRF.

20. OR 1, 7:421; Hedley, *Marching through Georgia,* 37; ORN 1, 22:643–645, 783.

21. OR 1, 7:435; ORN 1, 22:643–646, 783; Daniel Clark to brother, March 17, 1862, Woods Family Papers, NL; Hedley, *Marching through Georgia,* 38–40; Reed, *Battle of Shiloh,* 8–9; Christian Zook to Father, March 24, 1862, 46th

Ohio Infantry File, SNMPRF; Daniel Ruggles to P. G. T. Beauregard, March 2, 1862, HC; P. G. T. Beauregard to Daniel Ruggles, March 6, 1862, G. T. Beauregard Papers, NC.

22. OR 1, 7:422, 888; OR 1, 10 (2): 38, 42.

23. George Carrington Diary, March 3, 8–9, 11, 1862, CHS; Charles Lutz to brother, March 4, 1862, Charles Lutz Papers, CWD, USAMHI; Edward Larkin to Mary, March 27, 1862, 7th Illinois File, SNMPRF; William Skinner to Sister and Brother, March 27, 1862, 71st Ohio File, SNMPRF; Charles Kroff Diary, March 11, 1862, Sheery Marie Cress Collection, UO; Christian Zook to Father, March 9, 1862, 46th Ohio Infantry File, SNMPRF; OR 1, 10 (2): 34; Connelly, "Hoosier at Shiloh," 78; Cluett, *History of the 57th,* 16; OR 1, 10 (1): 16–17; A. N. Currier to Br. Stoddard, March 26, 1862, 8th Iowa File, SNMPRF.

24. James Balfour to Willy, April 4, 1862, 45th Illinois File, SNMPRF; John Ruckman to John Kinsel, March 19, 1862, 57th Ohio File, SNMPRF; Foster, *War Stories,* 55; Morton, "Opening of the Battle of Shiloh," 7–8; Edward Larkin to Mary, March 27, 1862, 7th Illinois File, SNMPRF; Fletcher, *History of Company "A,"* 45–46; Jessee, *Civil War Diaries,* 1–8; Kiper, *Major General John Alexander McClernand,* 96; Daniel Clark to brother, March 22, 1862, Woods Family Papers, NL. For a view from the river pilot perspective, see Sobieski Jolly, "Reminiscences of My Life as a Master and Pilot on the Ohio and Mississippi Rivers," undated, Sobieski Jolly Papers, CIN.

25. Joseph Blackburn to wife, March 12, 1862, 70th Ohio File, SNMPRF; Gibson and Gibson, *Assault and Logistics,* 78–79; OR 1, 10 (1): 8–9; OR 1, 10 (2): 39, 43; Hurst, "Great Battle of Shiloh," 180.

26. OR 1, 10 (1): 12, 15, 22, 26; OR 1, 10 (2): 28, 39; Wallace, *Life and Letters,* 175–176; S. W. Fairfield to wife, March 17, 1862, Sylvester Wellington Fairfield Civil War Letters, IHS.

27. Thomas Stuart Birch Diary, March 17, 1862, EU; OR 1, 10 (1): 12, 15, 22, 26; OR 1, 10 (2): 28, 39; William Parkinson to family, March 25, 1862, William M. Parkinson Letters, EU; S. W. Fairfield to wife, March 17, 1862, Sylvester Wellington Fairfield Civil War Letters, IHS; Charles Cowell Diary, March 11, 1862, Charles Cowell Papers, USAMHI; Foster, *War Stories,* 55; John Steele to brother, March 18, 1862, Steele–Boyd Family Papers, USAMHI; Wallace, *Life and Letters,* 175–176; I. P. Rumsey Memoir, undated, I. P. Rumsey File, SNMPRF, 5; Worthington, *Brief History,* 7.

28. J. M. Thurston Journal, March 16–17, 1862, MAHS; David McKee Claggett Diary, March 13, 1862, ALPL; Adolph Engelmann to Mina, March 21, 1862, Engelmann–Kircher Family Papers, ALPL.

29. OR 1, 10 (1): 8; Charles Cowell Diary, March 12, 1862, Charles Cowell Papers, USAMHI.

30. James Balfour to Willy, April 4, 1862, 45th Illinois File, SNMPRF; OR 1, 10 (1): 9; OR 1, 10 (2): 29, 57; Reed, *Battle of Shiloh,* 10; Sherman, *Mem-*

oirs, 1:227; John E. Thompson to friend, March 17, 1862, John E. Thompson Letter, UT.

31. OR 1, 10 (1): 9–16; George Sawin to Wife, March 15, 1862, George Sawin Letters, CHS; Charles Kroff Diary, March 14 and 16, 1862, Sheery Marie Cress Collection, UO; Moore, "Study of Early Crump, Tennessee," 32; William M. McCarty Diary, March 17, 1862, William M. McCarty Papers, CWD, USAMHI; B. J. Gaston to family, March 16, 1862, Benjamin J. Gaston Letters, UA; Ephraim Dawes to Kate, March 16, 1862, Ephraim C. Dawes Papers, NL; Charles G. Field to Adley Gladden, March 12, 1862, WS; Alvin P. Hovey Autobiography, undated, Alvin P. Hovey Papers, IU, 23–24; Todd Oliphant Diary, March 18, 1862, LC.

32. OR 1, 10 (1): 12; OR 1, 10 (2): 12, 15, 21, 24, 34, 65. For Sherman, see Marszalek, *Sherman*.

33. Sherman, *Memoirs*, 1:226; Daniel, *Shiloh*, 75; Dawes, "Battle of Shiloh—Part I," 7:109. For Worthington, see Brewer, *Tom Worthington's Civil War*. For Worthington's rebuttal, see Worthington, *Brief History* and *Shiloh*.

34. OR 1, 10 (1): 12, 22; OR 1, 10 (2): 12, 15, 21, 24, 34, 65; Connelly, *History of the Seventieth*, 16–18; Taylor, "Reminiscences," 6; unsigned, undated memoir in USS *Tyler* File, SNMPRF; Reed, *Battle of Shiloh*, 8; Avery, *History of the Fourth Illinois Cavalry Regiment*, 60.

35. OR 1, 10 (1): 22–23, 28; Hart, *History of the Fortieth*, 80; Flemming, "Battle of Shiloh as a Private Saw It," 6:133; J. L. Bieler to "President and Comrades," undated, 6th Indiana Battery File, SNMPRF.

36. Manning F. Force Order, March 15, 1862, Manning F. Force Papers, UWS (copy in LC); Wood, *History of the 20th OVVI Regiment*, 16; Christian Zook to Father, March 23, 1862, 46th Ohio File, SNMPRF; OR 1, 10 (1): 22–23, 29; Sherman, *Memoirs*, 1:228.

37. OR 1, 10 (1): 22–23.

38. Ibid., 25; Hobart, *Truth about Shiloh*, 1:228; Hedley, *Marching through Georgia*, 40; Smith, *History of the Thirty-first*, 20; Connelly, "Hoosier at Shiloh," 79; Thompson, *Recollections*, 200–203; Simeon McCord to sister, March 25, 1862, Simeon McCord Papers, Earl Hess Collection, USAMHI; Edward H. Reynolds Diary, March 20, 1862, CWTI, USAMHI; Levi Losier to Lydia, March 16, 1862, CWD, USAMHI; Stephen A. Hurlbut to John C. Fremont, September 9, 1861, Stephen A. Hurlbut Papers, NARA; Hobart, *Semi-history*, 7; Olney, *Shiloh as Seen by a Private Soldier*, 6–7; Jacob Lauman to wife, March 19 and April 4, 1862, Jacob Lauman Papers, CHS.

39. Connelly, "Hoosier at Shiloh," 78; Ambrose, *History of the Seventh*, 47; OR 1, 10 (1): 27; SOR 1, 1:643; R. W. Surby, "Fighting Them Over," *National Tribune*, March 29, 1883; Ephraim Dawes to Kate, March 16, 1862, Ephraim C. Dawes Papers, NL; Sherman, *Memoirs*, 1:232; Stacy D. Allen Memo, September 8, 1996, Significance of the Upper Landing on the Tennessee River, SN-

MPVF; Christian Zook to Father, March 24, 1862, 46th Ohio File, SNMPRF; George Lemon Childress Diary, March 19 and 21, 1862, ALPL; Henry H. Baltzell Memoir and Diary, ALPL, 9.

40. Johnston, *Life of Gen. Albert Sidney Johnston,* 530–531; James Drish to wife, March 29, 1862, James F. Drish Papers, ALPL.

41. OR 1, 10 (2): 32–33, 36, 41–43; S. W. Fairfield to wife, March 17, 1862, Sylvester Wellington Fairfield Civil War Letters, IHS; Buell, "Shiloh Reviewed," 1:490; Horace Palmer to sister, March 13, 1862, Horace Palmer Papers, AU.

CHAPTER 2: "TIME IS PRECIOUS AND MUCH NEEDED"

1. Moore, *Rebellion Record,* 5:156; Cunningham, *Shiloh and the Western Campaign,* 395.

2. Freeman Williams to father, December 6, 1861, HC; OR 1, 4:404; V. M. Elmore to sister, May 9, 1862, V. M. Elmore Letters, UA; David W. Ogden Reminiscences, undated, William S. Ray Papers, UAR, 29–30; Roland Oliver to wife, February 23, 1862, Roland Oliver Papers, Louisiana Tech University; Special Order 409, March 17, 1862, Charles C. Jacobs Papers, DSU; A. R. Belser to sister, June 5, 1861, HC; Jesse R. Kirkland to wife, June 19 and 22, 1861, Jesse R. Kirkland Papers, MDAH; B. J. Gaston to family, March 30 and 31, 1862, Benjamin J. Gaston Letters, UA; W. L. Culberson to sisters, February 28, 1862, 19th Louisiana File, CWIC; Alexander Livaudais Diary, March 30, 1862, 18th Louisiana File, CWIC; Rufus W. Daniel Diary, March 23, 1862, Arkansas History Center; OR 1, 10 (1): 544.

3. OR 1, 7:661, 672, 674; OR 1, 8:629, 634, 673; OR 1, 10 (1): 566.

4. OR 1, 7:436; Beauregard, "Campaign of Shiloh," 1:569; J. B. Lindsley Diary, February 17, 1862, Lindsley Family Papers, TSLA; Theodore P. Lockwood, "My War Record," 1909, Lockwood Collection, UM.

5. OR 1, 7:436–438; OR 1, 10 (2): 297; SOR 1, 1:658; Roman, *Military Operations of General Beauregard,* 1:326; John P. McCown to Leonidas Polk, March 14, 1862, Leonidas Polk Papers, NARA; Jordan, "Recollections of General Beauregard's Service," 404; Woodworth, "When Merit Was Not Enough," 20; "Partial Account of G. T. Beauregard's Actions after Battle of Manassas," undated, Samuel Richey Confederate Collection, MIAU; Jobe Foxworth Diary, March 23, 1862, MDAH.

6. Johnston, "Albert Sidney Johnston at Shiloh," 1:550.

7. OR 1, 7:259, 427, 911; OR 1, 10 (2): 297, 310, 326–327, 338, 341, 349, 361, 378; Eugene F. Falconnet Diary, April 6, 1862, Eugene Frederic Falconnet Papers, TSLA; "Sketches of the Confederate War, Giving an Account of His Connection with the Confederate Service, 1861–1865," undated, Thomas

Smith Manuscript, MDAH; Daniel, *Cannoneers in Gray,* 22; Albert Sidney Johnston to Isham G. Harris, December 28, 1861, Isham G. Harris Papers, LC; Braxton Bragg to wife, March 29, 1862, Braxton Bragg Papers, LC; B. J. Gaston to family, March 16, 1862, Benjamin J. Gaston Letters, UA; Bushrod Johnson Diary, March 23, 1862, Bushrod Johnson Papers, NARA.

8. Henry Marshall to Greene C. Furman, March 13, 1862, Greene Chandler Furman Papers, LC; Williams, *From that Terrible Field,* 52; OR 1, 7:261; OR 1, 10 (2): 310, 314, 353, 365; Roland, *Albert Sidney Johnston,* 326; Dillard, "Beauregard–Johnston–Shiloh," 99; Johnston, *Life of Gen. Albert Sidney Johnston,* 496, 716; Johnston, "Albert Sidney Johnston at Shiloh," 550; David Urquhart to Thomas Jordan, August 25, 1880, David Urquhart Letter Book, UNC. For more on Johnston, see Daniel, "Assaults of the Demagogues."

9. OR 1, 7:259, 427; OR 1, 10 (1): 385, 405; OR 1, 10 (2): 302; T. Harry Williams, *P. G. T. Beauregard,* 124; Johnston, "Albert Sidney Johnston at Shiloh," 549; Beauregard, "Campaign of Shiloh," 574.

10. OR 1, 7:259, 427; OR 1, 10 (1): 385, 405; OR 1, 10 (2): 302; B. F. Batchelor to Julia, March 29, 1862, HC; Worsham, *Old Nineteenth,* 35; Elliott, *Soldier of Tennessee,* 35; Dawson, "One Year at War," 192; Williams, *P. G. T. Beauregard,* 124; W. J. Stubblefield Diary, March 18, 1862, MU, 2; Black, *Railroads of the Confederacy,* 142; Johnston, "Albert Sidney Johnston at Shiloh," 549; B. J. Gaston to family, March 16, 1862, Benjamin J. Gaston Letters, UA; John C. Breckinridge to unknown, March 27, 1862, and John C. Breckinridge to John S. Bowen, March 29, 1862, Letters, Telegrams Received and Sent by General Breckinridge's Command, December 1861–January 1863, NARA; Beauregard, "Campaign of Shiloh," 574; François Palms to Henrietta Lauzin, April 4, 1862, Gras–Lauzin Family Papers, LSU; John A. Cato to wife, March 20, 1862, John A. Cato Papers, MDAH.

11. OR 1, 6:823.

12. Ibid., 819, 824, 828, 836, 875–876, 894; OR 1, 7:915; Johnston, *Life of Gen. Albert Sidney Johnston,* 552; Rowland and Howell, *Military History of Mississippi,* 267; Thomas Webber to parents, March 12, 1862, Thomas Webber Papers, CWTI, USAMHI; Scott Peters Diary, April 13, 1862, Peters Family Papers, UNC.

13. OR 1, 6:825, 827, 832, 842, 847; OR 1, 7:863, 890; J. H. Miller to Mr. McKissick, April 3, 1862, HC; Daniel Ruggles to P. G. T. Beauregard, May 2, 1887, Archie K. Davis Papers, UNC.

14. OR 1, 10 (2): 297, 354, 371; Moore, *Life for the Confederacy,* 22, 26; Roman, *Military Operations of General Beauregard,* 1:316; Alexander Livaudais Diary, March 30, 1862, 18th Louisiana File, CWIC; Johnston, *Life of Gen. Albert Sidney Johnston,* 543; Braxton Bragg to wife, March 29, 1862, Braxton Bragg Papers, LC.

15. OR 1, 10 (1): 11–12; OR 1, 10 (2): 197, 328, 330, 332; W. W. Mackall to James R. Chalmers, undated, James R. Chalmers Papers, NARA; Beauregard, "Campaign of Shiloh," 576; Johnston, *Life of Gen. Albert Sidney Johnston,* 541–542; A. H. Gladden to Daniel Ruggles, March 15, 1862, A. H. Gladden Papers, USC; James R. Chalmers to Daniel Ruggles, March 16, 1862, WS; Daniel Ruggles to James Chalmers, March 13, 1862, HC.

16. OR 1, 10 (1): 12, 385; OR 1, 10 (2): 298, 339; Maury, *Recollections,* 167; Roman, *Military Operations of General Beauregard,* 1:265; Francis Palms to Henrietta Lauzin, April 4, 1862, Gras–Lauzin Family Papers, LSU; Memo, April 24, 1862, Army of Tennessee Papers, TU; Williams, *From that Terrible Field,* 52.

17. OR 1, 10 (1): 29–31; Sword, "General G. T. Beauregard's Role," 3:44; OR 1, 10 (2): 300–301, 330–332, 342–343, 357, 360; OR 1, 7:883; Davis, *Rise and Fall of the Confederate Government,* 1:476 and 2:55; Daniel, *Soldiering in the Army of Tennessee,* 43; B. J. Gaston to family, March 16, 1862, Benjamin J. Gaston Letters, UA.

18. Richardson, "War as I Saw It," 97–98; Williams, *From that Terrible Field,* 52; Thomas Richardson to wife, March 26, 1862, Thomas Richardson Letter, LSU; William S. Dillon Diary, April 5, 1862, UM (copy in 4th Tennessee File, SNMPRF); OR 1, 10 (1): 12; OR 1, 10 (2): 300, 318, 341; Roman, *Military Operations of General Beauregard,* 1:267–268; General Order 13, March 25, 1862, Orders and Circulars of the Army of the Mississippi, 1861–1865, NARA.

19. Richardson, "War as I Saw It," 98; P. G. T. Beauregard to William J. Hardee, April 3, 1862, P. G. T. Beauregard Papers, LC; McKnight, "Brig. Gen. James Morrison Hawes," 131–137; OR 1, 7:904; Daniel, *Cannoneers in Gray,* 24; W. H. Haynes to "General," March 10, 1862, Charles C. Jacobs Papers, DSU; OR 1, 10 (1): 12; OR 1, 10 (2): 300, 318, 341; Roman, *Military Operations of General Beauregard,* 1:267–268.

20. OR 1, 10 (2): 311, 394; Oliver, "Your Affectionate Husband," 11; McBride and McLaurin, *Randall Lee Gibson,* 74; George W. Randolph to Braxton Bragg, April 2, 1862, Frederick M. Dearborn Collection, HU; Braxton Bragg to Daniel Ruggles, March 31, 1862, HC; Patton Anderson Autobiography, undated, James Patton Anderson Papers, University of Florida, 16 (copy in Sketch of General Anderson's Life, Florida State University).

21. Shoup, "How We Went to Shiloh," 137; Johnston, "Albert Sidney Johnston at Shiloh," 550; Beauregard, "Campaign of Shiloh," 578; Roman, *Military Operations of General Beauregard,* 1:266; Johnston, *Life of Gen. Albert Sidney Johnston,* 550–551; P. G. T. Beauregard to William Preston Johnston, March 9, 1877, P. G. T. Beauregard Papers, MDAH.

22. OR 1, 10 (1): 385; OR 1, 10 (2): 371, 373; Cunningham, *Shiloh and the Western Campaign,* 119–120; Johnston, *Life of Gen. Albert Sidney Johnston,* 589; A. R. Chisolm Report, April 14, 1862, SNMPRF.

23. Prichard, "Glory Denied," 2:12; OR 1, 10 (1): 385; OR 1, 10 (2): 298, 340, 342, 379; OR 1, 52 (2): 296; Davis, *Breckinridge,* 302; George G. Garner to Daniel Ruggles, March 9, 1862, Garner/Ruggles Message, USM; Braxton Bragg to wife, March 23 and 29, 1862, Braxton Bragg Papers, LC.

24. Thompson and Thompson, *Seventeenth Alabama Infantry,* 43–45; Horatio Wiley to Josie, April 4, 1862, Shiloh Subject File, ADAH.

25. Cunningham, *Shiloh and the Western Campaign,* 101–103.

26. A. K. Blythe to Charles Clark, March 21, 1862, Charles C. Jacobs Papers, DSU; C. J. Johnson to wife, April 1, 1862, Charles James Johnson Papers, LSU; G. W. Baylor to Daniel Ruggles, April 2, 1862, WS; Gleeson, *Illinois Rebels.*

27. T. C. Buck to sister, April 12, 1862, Stanford's Battery File, SNMPRF; Johnston, *Life of Gen. Albert Sidney Johnston,* 548; OR 1, 10 (2): 325–326, 338; B. J. Gaston to family, March 31, 1862, Benjamin J. Gaston Letters, UA.

28. William Parkinson to family, March 25, 1862, William M. Parkinson Letters, EU; B. J. Gaston to family, March 16, 1862, Benjamin J. Gaston Letters, UA; Bushrod Johnson Diary, March 24, 1862, Bushrod Johnson Papers, NARA; Francis Marion Aldridge to wife, March 24, 1862, Francis Marion Aldridge Papers, MDAH; I. P. Rumsey to father, March 9, 1862, I. P. Rumsey Papers, NL; Lew Wallace to S. C. Wilson, April 2, 1862, Lewis Wallace Collection, CHS; George Carrington Diary, March 21, 1862, CHS; Daniel Clark to brother, March 17, 1862, Woods Family Papers, NL; Thomas Jordan to Lexington commanding officer, March 28, 1862, P. G. T. Beauregard Papers, LC; OR 1, 10 (2): 305, 340; Thomas Jordan to L. D. McKissick, March 31, 1862, HC.

29. OR 1, 10 (1): 463, 560; OR 1, 10 (2): 350, 362; Thomas Richardson to wife, March 26, 1862, Thomas Richardson Letter, LSU; B. J. Gaston to family, March 31 and April 3, 1862, Benjamin J. Gaston Letters, UA; John H. Gates to Eliza, April 6, 1862, John Hooper Gates Papers, TSLA; Liberty Independence Nixon Diary, March 31, 1862, AU; W. M. Young to James R. Chalmers, March 21, 1862, James R. Chalmers Papers, NARA; "Record of Bells," undated, P. G. T. Beauregard Papers, NARA; P. G. T. Beauregard to Planters, March 8, 1862, Orders and Circulars of the Army of the Mississippi, 1861–1865, NARA.

30. C. J. Johnson to wife, April 1, 1862, Charles James Johnson Papers, LSU; Eddins, "Four Years in the Confederate Infantry," 21 (copy in Richard F. Eddins Papers, CWTI, USAMHI); Thomas Richardson to wife, March 26, 1862, Thomas Richardson Letter, LSU; Walter A. Overton Diary, March 18, 1862, MDAH.

31. Thomas Richardson to wife, March 26, 1862, Thomas Richardson Letter, LSU; Special Orders 468 and 469, both March 28, 1862, William Yerger Papers, MDAH; S. S. Calhoon to P. G. T. Beauregard, August 3, 1876, P G. T. Beauregard Papers, MDAH; "History of Old Tishomingo County," 31–32, Alcorn County Chancery Clerk Archives, Corinth, Mississippi; Inge, "Corinth,

Miss., in Early War Days," 443; Hawes, *Reminiscences;* Allardice, *Confederate Colonels,* 210; Paxton, "Dear Rebecca," 184; Jesse P. Bates to wife, March 27, 1862, Jesse P. Bates Letters, Civil War Collection, TSLA (copy in 9th Texas File, STRI); John Tyler Jr. to William L. Yancey, October 15, 1862, John Tyler Jr. Letter, University of Missouri, Columbia; Frank Batchelor to Julia, March 29, 1862, HC; John D. Thomas Diary, April 1862, UM; OR 1, 10 (1): 775; OR 1, 10 (2): 305; Beauregard, "Campaign of Shiloh," 577; Richardson, "War as I Saw It," 98; John A. Cato to wife, March 27, 1862, John A. Cato Papers, MDAH.

32. List of Steamers in Federal Use, undated, P. G. T. Beauregard Papers, NARA; John C. Breckinridge to H. P. Brewster, March 25, 1862, John C. Breckinridge Dispatch, USM; W. A. Howard to wife, March 19, 1862, W. A. Howard Manuscripts, IU; OR 1, 10 (1): 385; OR 1, 10 (2): 312, 316–319, 329, 368, 375–376, 378; C. J. Johnson to wife, April 1, 1862, Charles James Johnson Papers, LSU; U. S. Grant to Brigadier General Stone, March 30, 1862, Ulysses S. Grant Letters, ALPL; Woodworth, *Jefferson Davis,* 95–96; Kendall, "Recollections of a Confederate Officer," 1,058.

33. Williams, *From that Terrible Field,* 52; OR 1, 10 (2): 381; Special Order 5, April 1, 1862, and "Countersigns to Commence April 2," undated, both in Orders and Circulars of the Army of the Mississippi, 1861–1865, NARA.

CHAPTER 3: "THE PLAINS OF SHILOH"

1. OR 1, 10 (2): 43, 70, 80–84, 88; Badeau, *Military History of Ulysses S. Grant,* 1:70; Grant, "Battle of Shiloh," 1:466; OR 1, 10 (1): 184.

2. Walter Q. Gresham to wife, March 20 and 29, 1862, Walter Q. Gresham Papers, LC.

3. OR 1, 10 (2): 50, 53, 62–63, 73–74, 80, 359; Amos Sanford to wife, March 30, 1862, Amos Sanford Papers, SIU; John N. Ferguson Diary, March 20, 1862, LC; Elsie Caroline Duncan Hurt Diary, undated, MSCPL, 29–30; William Parkinson to family, March 25 and 26, 1862, William M. Parkinson Letters, EU; William R. Stimson to wife, 1862, William R. Stimson Papers, LC; Connelly, *History of the Seventieth,* 19; Smith, *Life and Letters,* 192–193 (original Smith letters in Thomas Kilby Smith Papers, HL); David H. Thomas to parents, April 3, 1862, David Harrison Thomas Papers, OHS.

4. S. W. Fairfield to wife, March 17, 1862, Sylvester Wellington Fairfield Civil War Letters, IHS; Taylor, "Reminiscences," 6; OR 1, 10 (2): 45; Christian Zook to Father, March 23, 1862, 46th Ohio File, SNMPRF; Thompson, *Recollections,* 196; OR 1, 10 (1): 83, 85; SOR 1, 1:643; James Drish to wife, March 29, 1862, James F. Drish Papers, ALPL.

5. Taylor, "Reminiscences," 6.

6. Mason, "Shiloh," 1:95; Johnston, *Life of Gen. Albert Sidney Johnston,* 531–532; "The Battle of Shiloh: The First Day's Fight," *Southern Watchman,* April 23, 1862 (copy in E. Merton Coulter Collection, University of Georgia). For detail on terrain at Shiloh, see Smith, *Rethinking Shiloh,* 1–25.

7. Reed Map, First Day, 1900, Series 6, Box 1, SNMPAF; Edwin C. Bearss, "Historical Base Map: Shiloh National Military Park, April 6–7, 1862," SNMPVF.

8. Beauregard, "Campaign of Shiloh," 1:577; Reed Map, First Day, 1900, Series 6, Box 1, SNMPAF; Buell, "Shiloh Reviewed," 1:495; Gentsch, "Geographic Analysis," 100; Johnston, "Albert Sidney Johnston at Shiloh," 1:551–552; OR 1, 10 (1): 577; Grant, "Battle of Shiloh," 472; Johnston, *Life of Gen. Albert Sidney Johnston,* 569.

9. Gentsch, "Geographic Analysis," 26; Buell, "Shiloh Reviewed," 495; Reed Map, First Day, 1900, Series 6, Box 1, SNMPAF; Force, *From Fort Henry to Corinth,* 100.

10. OR 1, 10 (1): 567; Grant, "Battle of Shiloh," 469, 472; Buell, "Shiloh Reviewed," 495–496; Gentsch, "Geographic Analysis," 26; Beauregard, "Campaign of Shiloh," 585.

11. Grant, "Battle of Shiloh," 469. Buell, "Shiloh Reviewed," 495–496; Gentsch, "Geographic Analysis," 26.

12. Grant, "Battle of Shiloh," 472; Reed, *Battle of Shiloh,* 9; Gentsch, "Geographic Analysis," 29–31.

13. Gentsch, "Geographic Analysis," 84, 105; Reed Map, First Day, 1900, Series 6, Box 1, SNMPAF.

14. Reed Map, First Day, 1900, Series 6, Box 1, SNMPAF; Buell, "Shiloh Reviewed," 495.

15. Reed Map, First Day, 1900, Series 6, Box 1, SNMPAF.

16. Ibid.

17. Smith, "Forgotten Inhabitants"; Leroy Guthrie to M. Crowder and Family, April 4, 1862, 18th Missouri File, SNMPRF; Helweg, *Lone Survivor,* 44; Daniel Clark to brother, March 17, 1862, Woods Family Papers, NL.

18. John D. St. John to father, April 14, 1862, Bela T. St. John Papers, LC; E. C. Sackett to family, March 21, 1862, Sackett Family Letters, ALPL; Edward Larkin to Mary, March 27, 1862, 7th Illinois File, SNMPRF; Isaac Pugh to wife, March 22, 1862, 41st Illinois File, SNMPRF; unknown to Mattie, April 1, 1862, 31st Indiana File, SNMPRF; McEathron, *Letters and Memoirs,* 5 (copy in 15th Illinois File, SNMPRF).

19. SNMP Tablet G, Mon 10; OR 1, 10 (1): 25, 28; Reed, *Battle of Shiloh,* 53, 55; Lash, *Politician Turned General,* 92–94; Connelly, "Hoosier at Shiloh," 79; Thompson, *Recollections,* 200–203; Simeon McCord to sister, March 25, 1862, Simeon McCord Papers, Earl Hess Collection, USAMHI; Edward H. Reynolds Diary, March 20, 1862, CWTI, USAMHI; Levi Losier to Lydia,

March 16, 1862, CWD, USAMHI; Stephen A. Hurlbut to John C. Fremont, September 9, 1861, Stephen A. Hurlbut Papers, NARA; Hobart, *Semi-history,* 7; Olney, *Shiloh as Seen by a Private Soldier,* 6–7; Jacob Lauman to wife, March 19 and April 4, 1862, Jacob Lauman Papers, CHS.

20. OR 1, 10 (1): 24–28; Hobart, *Truth about Shiloh,* 102; Hart, *History of the Fortieth,* 81; Dawes, "Battle of Shiloh—Part I," 7:123; Jorgensen, "Scouting for Ulysses S. Grant."

21. Barber, *Army Memoirs,* 48; Cockerill, "Boy at Shiloh," 6:15; SNMP Tablet H and Monument 12 and 13; Hart, *History of the Fortieth,* 81; Flemming, "Battle of Shiloh as a Private Saw It," 6:134; Reed, *Battle of Shiloh,* 55; OR 1, 10 (1): 25; OR 1, 10 (2): 53–54; *Report of the Proceedings of the Society of the Army of the Tennessee,* 74–75; Medrick, "Skirmishing in Sherman's Front," 1:537; Dawes, "Battle of Shiloh—Part I," 124; Lawrence, "Stuart's Brigade at Shiloh," 489.

22. OR 1, 10 (1): 26, 28; SNMP Tablet E and Mon 6, 7, and 8; Reed, *Battle of Shiloh,* 48; Morrison, *History of the Ninth,* 29; Charles Cowell Diary, April 3, 1862, Charles Cowell Papers, USAMHI; James C. Parrott to wife, March 17 and April 3, 1862, James C. Parrott Papers, SHSI; Jacob Lauman to wife, April 4, 1862, Jacob Lauman Papers, CHS; John N. Ferguson Diary, April 3, 1862, LC; Wright, *Corporal's Story,* 33; Cluett, *History of the 57th,* 16; OR 1, 10 (2): 53–54, 91; SOR 1, 1:635; Edwin A. Bowen to D. W. Reed, undated, 52nd Illinois File, SNMPRF; George Lemon Childress Diary, March 23–25, 1862, ALPL.

23. William F. Hinkle Diary, undated, IHS; Adolph Engelmann to Mina, March 31, 1862, Engelmann–Kircher Family Papers, ALPL; OR 1, 10 (2): 43, 70, 80–84, 88; Badeau, *Military History of Ulysses S. Grant,* 1:70; Force, *From Fort Henry to Corinth,* 104; John A. McClernand to Ulysses S. Grant, March 27, 1862, John A. McClernand Papers, NARA; untitled article, *Warren Independent,* April 22, 1862, Luther Howard Cowan Papers, TSLA; Grant, "Battle of Shiloh," 466; OR 1, 10 (1): 184; William Parkinson to family, March 29, 1862, William M. Parkinson Letters, EU.

24. James Balfour to Louisa, March 26, 1862, 45th Illinois File, SNMPRF; SNMP Tablet D and Mon 3 and 4; Reed, *Battle of Shiloh,* 45; Downing, *Downing's Civil War Diary,* 39; Wallace, *Life and Letters,* 180; OR 1, 10 (2): 52; OR 1, 10 (1): 135, 230; SOR 1, 1:631; Adolph Engelmann to Mina, March 31, 1862, Engelmann–Kircher Family Papers, ALPL; James A. Black Diary, March 22, 1862, ALPL.

25. Benjamin Prentiss to Henry Halleck, February 19, 1862, Benjamin Prentiss Papers, NARA; T. W. Holman, "The Story of Shiloh," *National Tribune,* September 14, 1899; SNMP Tablet I and Monument 18; Reed, *Battle of Shiloh,* 58–61; OR 1, 10 (2): 57, 66, 67, 93; Charles Bacon to father, March 22, 1862, Charles Bacon Papers, Civil War Soldiers' Letters Collection, USAMHI;

Morton, "Opening of the Battle of Shiloh," 10; *Report of the Proceedings of the Society of the Army of the Tennessee,* 63; Morton, "Boy at Shiloh," 56; Peter Bagley Diary, April 4, 1862, 23rd Missouri File, SNMPRF; Levi Minkler Diary, April 6, 1862, 18th Wisconsin File, SNMPRF; Willard W. Felton Diary, April 5, 1862, WHS; unknown to family, April 20, 1862, 18th Wisconsin File, SNMPRF; G. H. Hash to family, March 26, 1862, George H. Hash Papers, NC. For Prentiss, see Bates, "Without Doubt."

26. James A. Black Diary, April 5, 1862, ALPL; Ephraim Dawes to unknown, March 21, 1862, Ephraim C. Dawes Papers, CHS; Foster, *War Stories,* 59; Connelly, "Hoosier at Shiloh," 79; unknown to Mattie, April 1, 1862, 31st Indiana File, SNMPRF; OR 1, 10 (1): 27; OR 1, 10 (2): 50; Dawes, "Battle of Shiloh—Part I," 113; Griffin A. Stanton Journal, March 30, 1862, UMEM; Ephraim Dawes to unknown, March 21, 1862, Ephraim C. Dawes Papers, NL; Force, *From Fort Henry to Corinth,* 102–103; F. S. Gates to family, April 1, 1862, 72nd Ohio File, SNMPRF.

27. OR 1, 10 (1): 84, 133, 233, 276; OR 1, 10 (2): 35, 46–47, 62, 87–88, 91–93; OR 1, 52 (1): 34; SOR 1, 1:642; Wardner, "Reminiscences of a Surgeon," 3:184; Grant, "Battle of Shiloh," 473; W. H. L. Wallace to John A. McClernand, April 3, 1862, and unknown to John A. McClernand, April 5, 1862, John A. McClernand Papers, ALPL; Jacob Lauman to wife, April 4, 1862, Jacob Lauman Papers, CHS; Hirman Scofield Diary, March 27 and April 4–5, 1862, NL; John N. Ferguson Diary, April 3, 1862, LC; Stephen A. Hurlbut General Order, April 1862, Jacob Lauman Papers, NARA; McEathron, *Letters and Memoirs,* 5; Walter Weener to P. Den Bleyker, May 2, 1862, Walter Weener Papers, UMB; Plummer, *Lincoln's Rail-Splitter,* 74; Douglas Hapeman Diary, April 4–5, 1862, ALPL; Enoch Colby to father, April 4, 1862, Francelia Colby Reminiscences, CHS; W. H. L. Wallace to Ann, April 3, 1862, and W. H. L. Wallace to John A. Rawlins, April 4, 1862, Wallace Dickey Papers, ALPL; "Journal Belongs to Hugh T. Carlisle of Fremont Sandusky County Ohio," undated, Hugh T. Carlisle Papers, CWD, USAMHI, 64; Special Order 13, April 3, 1862, John A. McClernand Papers, ALPL; Grant, *Papers,* 5:8; Wallace, *Life and Letters,* 180, 182; Anders, *Twenty-first Missouri,* 60, 63; I. P. Rumsey Memoir, undated, I. P. Rumsey File, SNMPRF, 6; James Lawrence to aunt, March 30, 1862, James Lawrence Papers, CHS; William Parkinson to family, March 25, 1862, William M. Parkinson Letters, EU; Thomas Stuart Birch Diary, March 27, 1862, EU; Cunningham, *Shiloh and the Western Campaign,* 109–110; Morton, "Opening of the Battle of Shiloh," 9; Jones, "Battle of Shiloh," 4:52–54.

28. OR 1, 10 (1): 84, 133, 233, 276; OR 1, 10 (2): 62, 87–88, 91–93; OR 1, 52 (1): 34; SOR 1, 1:642; Wardner, "Reminiscences of a Surgeon," 3:184; Grant, "Battle of Shiloh," 473; unknown to John A. McClernand, April 5, 1862, John A. McClernand Papers, ALPL; Jacob Lauman to wife, April 4, 1862, Ja-

cob Lauman Papers, CHS; John N. Ferguson Diary, April 3, 1862, LC; Stephen A. Hurlbut General Order, April 1862, Jacob Lauman Papers, NARA; McEathron, *Letters and Memoirs,* 5; Walter Weener to P. Den Bleyker, May 2, 1862, Walter Weener Papers, UMB; Douglas Hapeman Diary, April 5, 1862, ALPL; Enoch Colby to father, April 4, 1862, Francelia Colby Reminiscences, CHS. For an example of German ethnicity, see the correspondence in the Joseph Maas Papers, FHS.

29. OR 1, 10 (2): 21, 50–51; OR 1, 10 (1): 84; SOR 1, 1:659; Force, *From Fort Henry to Corinth,* 101; Grant, "Battle of Shiloh," 481; Sherman, *Memoirs,* 1:229; I. P. Rumsey Memoir, undated, I. P. Rumsey File, SNMPRF, 6; "The Shiloh Campaign," *National Tribune,* March 27, 1884; James Balfour to Willy, April 4, 1862, 45th Illinois File, SNMPRF; Philip Shaw Diary, April 2, 1862, 32nd Illinois File, SNMPRF; Bushrod Johnson Diary, March 30, 1862, Bushrod Johnson Papers, NARA; Louis Elseffer to unknown, February 13, 1885, Harry S. Elseffer Papers, LC; Schenker, "Who Failed to Fortify Pittsburg Landing."

30. OR 1, 10 (1): 84, 133, 233, 276; OR 1, 10 (2): 62, 87–88, 91–93; OR 1, 52 (1): 34; SOR 1, 1:642; Grant, "Battle of Shiloh," 473; unknown to John A. McClernand, April 5, 1862, John A. McClernand Papers, ALPL; McEathron, *Letters and Memoirs,* 5; Douglas Hapeman Diary, April 5, 1862, ALPL; Enoch Colby to father, April 4, 1862, Francelia Colby Reminiscences, CHS; George Sawin to Wife, March 23, 1862, George Sawin Letters, CHS; Hart, *History of the Fortieth,* 82; Jacob Lauman to son, March 24 and 26, 1862, Jacob Lauman Papers, CHS; Isaac Park to wife, March 24 and 25, 1862, Parks Family Correspondence, ND.

31. "Civil War Reminiscence of Major John Dance," undated, John Dance Papers, Northwest Corner Civil War Roundtable Collection, USAMHI; unknown to Mr. Moore, 1867, United States Sanitary Commission Records, 1861–1867, NYHS; Ulysses S. Grant to Julia, March 29, 1862, Ulysses S. Grant Collection, SIU; Isaac Parks to wife, March 30, 1862, Isaac Parks Letter, SIU; Isaac Parks to wife, March 24, 1862, Parks Family Correspondence, ND; James Drish to wife, March 29, 1862, James F. Drish Papers, ALPL; George Lemon Childress Diary, March 24, 1862, ALPL; John L. Harris to parents, March 21, 1862, John L. Harris Correspondence, ALPL; James R. Zearing to wife, March 21, 1862, James R. Zearing Papers, CHS; George Carrington Diary, March 27, 1862, CHS.

32. OR 1, 10 (1): 27–28, 78–79, 83–86, 257; Camm, "Col. William Camm War Diary," 842–843; R. W. Surby, "Fighting Them Over," *National Tribune,* March 29, 1883; Henry H. Wright, "An Iowa Soldier's Story of Shiloh," *National Tribune,* May 3, 1883; Downing, *Downing's Civil War Diary,* 39; Wright, *History of the Sixth,* 62; Williams, *Historical Sketch,* 15; Reed, *Battle of Shiloh,* 26; OR 1, 10 (2): 52, 61, 63–64, 70, 82, 87, 90, 375; Bushrod John-

son Diary, March 24, 1862, Bushrod Johnson Papers, NARA; George Sawin to Wife, March 23, 1862, George Sawin Letters, CHS; L. H. Cowan to "Dear Ones," March 30, 1862, Luther Howard Cowan Papers, TSLA; J. W. Parker to cousins, March 29, 1862, WS; Lew Wallace to W. H. L. Wallace, April 5, 1862, Lew Wallace Collection, IHS; Lew Wallace to S. C. Wilson, April 2, 1862, Lewis Wallace Collection, CHS; Todd Oliphant Diary, April 1, 1862, LC; Connelly, *History of the Seventieth,* 19–20; R. P. Buckland to L. G. Rawson, June 6, 1862, Rawson Family Papers, RBHPC.

33. I. P. Rumsey Memoir, undated, I. P. Rumsey File, SNMPRF, 5; Felix H. Robertson to S. H. Dent, April 25, 1909, Stouton Hubert Dent Papers, ADAH; John Ruckman to John Kinsel, March 19, 1862, 57th Ohio File, SNMPRF; L. H. Cowan to "Dear Ones," March 30, 1862, Luther Howard Cowan Papers, TSLA; OR 1, 10 (1): 27–28, 89; OR 1, 10 (2): 62, 80; Williams, *Historical Sketch,* 15; Grant, "Battle of Shiloh," 472; E. C. Sackett to family, March 21, 1862, Sackett Family Letters, ALPL; Alpheus S. Bloomfield to sister, April 21, 1862, Alpheus S. Bloomfield Papers, LC; Henry Burrell to brother, March 1862, Henry Burrell Papers, USAMHI; Camm, "Col. William Camm War Diary," 842; Wallace, *Life and Letters,* 179, 181; William Parkinson to family, March 25, 1862, William M. Parkinson Letters, EU; Neh. C. Thomas to Susannah, April 20, 1862, 58th Ohio File, SNMPRF; A. N. Currier to Br. Stoddard, March 26, 1862, 8th Iowa File, SNMPRF; Fleecy to Lowry Hinch, March 18, 1862, Lowry Hinch Papers, USAMHI; Samuel Latta to Mary, April 10, 1862, Samuel Rankin Latta Papers, TU (copies in TSLA and 13th Tennessee File, SNMPRF); I. P. Rumsey Memoir, undated, I. P. Rumsey File, SNMPRF, 5; Henry H. Wright, "An Iowa Soldier's Story of Shiloh," *National Tribune,* May 3, 1883; Adolph Engelmann to Mina, March 31, 1862, Engelmann–Kircher Family Papers, ALPL; James A. Black Diary, March 31, 1862, ALPL; Martin V. Miller Letter, April 5, 1862, WS.

34. OR 1, 10 (2): 25, 34, 39, 43–44, 46–47, 51, 58, 70, 79; OR 1, 10 (1): 291; Maurice J. Williams Diary, April 4, 1862, 36th Indiana File, SNMPRF; Nathan Crawford to Rachel, May 26, 1862, Nathan Crawford Letter, UT; Clark, "Buell's Advance"; Grose, *Story of the Marches, Battles, and Incidents,* 99; Hight and Stormont, *History of the Fifty-eighth,* 50; Villard, *Memoirs,* 1:240; Buell, "Shiloh Reviewed," 491; Robert C. Lane Diary, March 1862, ALPL; Aurelius M. Willoughby Diary, March 23, 1862, ISL.

35. OR 1, 10 (1): 330; Force, *From Fort Henry to Corinth,* 105; Horace N. Fisher, "A Memory of Shiloh," undated, Horace N. Fisher File, SNMPRF; A. W. Ellis, "Shiloh," *National Tribune,* October 12, 1882; Nelson endorsement to Ammen letter, undated, Jacob Ammen Papers, ALPL.

36. Hight and Stormont, *History of the Fifty-eighth,* 51; OR 1, 10 (2): 70–71, 85, 89, 91–93, 330–331; George J. Reed to wife, April 2, 1862, Reed Family Papers, LC; Maurice J. Williams Diary, April 4 and 5, 1862, 36th Indiana

File, SNMPRF; Aurelius M. Willoughby Diary, March 31 and April 1 and 3, 1862, ISL; George to wife, April 9, 1862, 58th Illinois File, SNMPRF; Isaac Longnecker to unknown, March 25, 1862, Fulton-Lenz Collection, CWTI, USAMHI; William Stahl Diary, April 2, 1862, MC, USAMHI; Joshua Taylor Bradford Diary, April 2 and 5, 1862, LC; Almon F. Rockwell Diary, April 5, 1862, LC.

37. OR 1, 10 (2): 94.

38. Ibid., 91–94; Robert C. Lane Diary, April 1862, ALPL.

CHAPTER 4: "I WOULD FIGHT THEM IF THEY WERE A MILLION"

1. OR 1, 10 (1): 385, 400; OR 1, 10 (2): 310, 366, 367; Daniel, *Shiloh,* 117; Horatio Wiley to Josie, April 4, 1862, Shiloh Subject File, ADAH; P. G. T. Beauregard to Leonidas Polk, March 27, 1862, P. G. T. Beauregard Papers, LC; Bushrod Johnson Diary, March 28, 1862, Bushrod Johnson Papers, NARA; Beauregard, "Campaign of Shiloh," 1:579; Presley Judson Edwards Autobiography, 1898, CHS; Liberty Independence Nixon Diary, March 26, 1862, AU; Johnston, *Life of Gen. Albert Sidney Johnston,* 582; C. J. Johnson to wife, April 4, 1862, Charles James Johnson Papers, LSU.

2. OR 1, 10 (1): 385; OR 1, 10 (2): 383–384; Beauregard, "Campaign of Shiloh," 579; Chisolm, "Shiloh Battle-Order," 1:606; Jordan, "Notes of a Confederate Staff-Officer," 1:594–595; Roman, *Military Operations of General Beauregard,* 1:270, 275; Johnston, *Life of Gen. Albert Sidney Johnston,* 551; E. S. Drake to sister, April 13, 1862, E. Steel Drake Papers, HCWRT, USAMHI.

3. OR 1, 10 (1): 385, 596; OR 1, 10 (2): 387; P. G. T. Beauregard to W. P. Johnston, March 9, 1877, P. G. T. Beauregard Papers, MDAH; A. H. Gladden to Daniel Ruggles, March 15, 1862, A. H. Gladden Papers, USC; Beauregard, "Campaign of Shiloh," 581; Johnston Vandiver to wife, April 15, 1862, Johnston Vandiver Papers, CWD, USAMHI; Roman, *Military Operations of General Beauregard,* 1:270–271; Daniel to Miss Honnoll, April 4, 1862, Robert W. Honnell Papers, DU; Alfred Roman Memoir, August 20, 1878, Alfred Roman Memoirs, University of Louisiana, Lafayette (original in Civil War Collection, TSLA); Duncan, *Recollections,* 42; McDonough, *Shiloh,* 69; Daniel to Miss Honnoll, April 4, 1862, Robert W. Honnell Papers, DU; Thomas Richardson to wife, March 26, 1862, Thomas Richardson Letter, LSU.

4. Horatio Wiley to Josie, April 4, 1862, Shiloh Subject File, ADAH; H. W. H. to parents, April 10, 1862, Shiloh Subject File, ADAH.

5. Johnston, "Albert Sidney Johnston at Shiloh," 1:550, 553; Beauregard, "Campaign of Shiloh," 578; Roman, *Military Operations of General Beauregard,* 1:266; Johnston, *Life of Gen. Albert Sidney Johnston,* 550–551; David Urquhart to Thomas Jordan, August 25, 1880, David Urquhart Letter Book, UNC.

6. OR 1, 10 (1): 397; OR 1, 10 (2): 387; Johnston, "Albert Sidney Johnston at Shiloh," 554; Roman, *Military Operations of General Beauregard,* 1:329; Davis, *Rise and Fall of the Confederate Government,* 2:57; Albert Sidney Johnston to Jefferson Davis, April 3, 1862, Alfred Roman Papers, LC.

7. Johnston, "Albert Sidney Johnston at Shiloh," 553; Jordan, "Notes of a Confederate Staff-Officer," 595; Chisolm, "Shiloh Battle-Order," 606. For an original copy of Special Order 8, see the copy in Albert Sidney Johnston Special Order 8, ALPL.

8. OR 1, 10 (1): 392–395; Beauregard, "Campaign of Shiloh," 581.

9. B. J. Gaston to family, April 3, 1862, Benjamin J. Gaston Letters, UA; OR 1, 52 (2): 296–297; William Stephen Ray Memoir, 1915, UAR, 12; William Preston to children, April 3, 1862, Albert Sidney Johnston Papers, FHS.

10. Horn, *Army of Tennessee,* 124; Thompson, *History of the First Kentucky Brigade,* 87; Sword, *Shiloh,* 102; Allen, "Shiloh! The Campaign and First Day's Battle," 18; Williams, "Beauregard at Shiloh," 1:29; Williams, *P. G. T. Beauregard,* 129; A. R. Chisolm to "Aunty," April 22, 1862, Alexander Robert Chisolm Papers, NYHS; Jacob Thompson to wife, April 3, 1862, Civil War Letters and Documents Collection, UMCL; C. J. Johnson to wife, April 4, 1862, Charles James Johnson Papers, LSU.

11. OR 1, 10 (2): 388, 394; Beauregard, "Campaign of Shiloh," 582; Jordan, "Notes of a Confederate Staff-Officer," 596; Roman, *Military Operations of General Beauregard,* 1:275; P. G. T. Beauregard to Daniel Ruggles, April 25, 1887, P. G. T. Beauregard Letter, HNOC; Daniel Ruggles to P. G. T. Beauregard, May 2, 1887, Archie K. Davis Papers, UNC; Williams, *P. G. T. Beauregard,* 129; C. J. Johnson to wife, April 4, 1862, Charles James Johnson Papers, LSU; Daniel, *Cannoneers in Gray,* 25; Edwin C. Bearss, "Artillery Study—Shiloh NMP," February 1964, SNMPVF, 34; Berrien, *Military Annals of Tennessee,* 350, 435, 499; Joseph O. Freeman to wife, April 3, 1862, 51st Tennessee File, STRI; Dempsey Neal Diary, April 6, 1862, NC; James Pope Diary, April 3, 1862, Pope–Carter Family Papers, DU.

12. OR 1, 10 (1): 394, 520; C. J. Johnson to wife, April 4, 1862, Charles James Johnson Papers, LSU; Polk, "Facts Connected," 457; Daniel, *Shiloh,* 123; Livaudais, *Shiloh Diary,* 24; "Journal of the Orleans Guard," April 4, 1862, HNOC; Inge, "Corinth, Miss., in Early War Days," 443; Inge, "Corinth, Miss., in War Times"; Johnston, "Albert Sidney Johnston at Shiloh," 555; Johnston, *Life of Gen. Albert Sidney Johnston,* 604.

13. OR 1, 10 (1): 400, 415; OR 1, 10 (2): 392; Livaudais, *Shiloh Diary,* 23–24; Daniel, *Shiloh,* 123; Baylor, "With Gen. A. S. Johnston at Shiloh," 609; Inge, "Corinth, Miss., in Early War Days," 443; Bassham, "Through a Mist of Powder and Excitement"; Johnston, *Life of Gen. Albert Sidney Johnston,* 553, 562; C. J. Johnson to wife, April 4, 1862, Charles James Johnson Papers, LSU.

14. Symonds, *Stonewall of the West,* 66; Johnston, "Albert Sidney Johnston at Shiloh," 555; Polk, "Concentration before Shiloh—Reply to General Ruggles," 180; Roman, *Military Operations of General Beauregard,* 1:329, 530; Alfred Tyler Fielder Diary, April 4, 1862, TSLA; Braxton Bragg to William J. Hardee, April 3, 1862, Correspondence of the Western Department and the Army of the Mississippi, 1861–1862, NARA; OR 1, 10 (1): 400, 406, 414, 420, 427, 461; John A. Buckner to Jefferson Davis, August 25, 1862, Rosemonde E. and Emile Kuntz Collection, TU; Bushrod Johnson Diary, April 3, 1862, Bushrod Johnson Papers, NARA; Reed, *Battle of Shiloh,* 12; Force, *From Fort Henry to Corinth,* 119; Charles Kroff Diary, April 5, 1862, Sheery Marie Cress Collection, UO; Smith, *Confederate Diary,* 4; R. H. Wood to Mary, April 9, 1862, R. H. Wood Letter, UVA; Robert D. Smith Diary, April 4, 1862, 2nd Tennessee File, SNMPRF; W. J. Stubblefield Diary, April 4, 1862, MU, 3.

15. "Journal of the Orleans Guard," April 6, 1862, HNOC; Joseph D. Thompson to Mary, April 9, 1862, Joseph D. Thompson Papers, TSLA; OR 1, 10 (1): 464, 494, 521, 533, 547; OR 1, 10 (2): 388–392; Polk, "Facts Connected," 461–463; W. A. Caruthers Diary, April 15, 1862, TSLA; Marcus J. Wright Diary, April 5, 1862, Civil War Collection, TSLA; Livaudais, *Shiloh Diary,* 22–23; Liberty Independence Nixon Diary, April 3, 1862, AU; Clark, "New Orleans German Colony," 1,002; Clarke, *Diary of the War for Separation,* 119; McBride and McLaurin, *Randall Lee Gibson,* 75; unknown to editors, April 11, 1862, Shiloh Subject File, ADAH; Terry, "Record of the Alabama State Artillery," 315–316; Johnston, *Life of Gen. Albert Sidney Johnston,* 564–565; Symonds, *Stonewall of the West,* 66; William Preston Diary, April 4, 1862, NARA; Robert D. Smith Diary, April 5, 1862, 2nd Tennessee File, SNMPRF; Liberty Independence Nixon Diary, April 5, 1862, AU; Dudley Hayden Diary, May 3, 1862, *Richmond Dispatch,* WS.

16. P. N. Newman to John C. Breckinridge, April 3, 1862, John C. Breckinridge Papers, CHS; Albert Sidney Johnston to John C. Breckinridge, April 3, 1862, Albert Sidney Johnston Papers, CHS; Francis Marion Aldridge to wife, March 27, 1862, Francis Marion Aldridge Papers, MDAH; John S. Jackman Diary, April 3–4, 1862, LC; John W. Taylor to parents, April 11, 1862, Clyde Hughes Collection, UNC; OR 1, 10 (1): 554, 614; OR 1, 10 (2): 390–391; Rufus Parkes Diary, April 3, 1862, Civil War Collection, TSLA; W. E. Coleman to parents, May 5, 1862, Civil War Collection, TSLA; Augustus Hervey Mecklin Diary, April 4, 1862, MDAH.

17. John W. Taylor to parents, April 11, 1862, Clyde Hughes Collection, UNC; OR 1, 10 (1): 406, 414, 420; William Preston Diary, April 4, 1862, NARA; Dudley Hayden Diary, May 3, 1862, *Richmond Dispatch,* WS; unknown to editors, April 11, 1862, Shiloh Subject File, ADAH.

18. OR 1, 10 (1): 406, 414, 420; Kerwan, *Johnny Green of the Orphan Brigade,* 19 (original diary in FHS); William Preston Diary, April 4, 1862, NARA.

19. Samuel Latta to Mary, April 10, 1862, Samuel Rankin Latta Papers, TU; Joseph D. Alison Diary, April 5, 1862, Holloway's Cavalry Company File, SNMPRF; Alfred Tyler Fielder Diary, April 5, 1862, TSLA; Baylor, "With Gen. A. S. Johnston at Shiloh," 610; Benjamin D. Wall to mother, April 18, 1862, WS; OR 1, 10 (1): 400, 406, 567, 614; George W. Jones Diary, April 4, 1862, Stanford's Battery File, SNMPRF; SOR 1, 1:651; P. G. T. Beauregard to Daniel Ruggles, April 25, 1887, P. G. T. Beauregard Letter, HNOC; Johnston, *Life of Gen. Albert Sidney Johnston,* 563, 566; Ruggles, "Concentration before Shiloh—Reply to Captain Polk," 51; Taylor Beatty Diary, April 5, 1862, UNC.

20. Jones Withers to Clement Clay, February 13, 1862, Clement Clay Papers, DU; OR 1, 6:820; OR 1, 10 (1): 386, 454, 459, 540, 545, 573, 580, 584–586, 590–591, 596; Robert Shaver Report, April 12, 1862, Thomas C. Hindman Papers, NARA; Thomas O. Crockett to cousin, February 1, 1862, Thomas O. Crockett Papers, CWD, USAMHI; Thomas Richardson to wife, March 26, 1862, Thomas Richardson Letter, LSU; Robert D. Smith Diary, April 4, 1862, 2nd Tennessee File, SNMPRF; C. S. Stewart to Julia, April 12, 1862, 21st Alabama File, SNMPRF; Reed, *Battle of Shiloh,* 12; Jordan, "Notes of a Confederate Staff-Officer," 599.

21. OR 1, 10 (1): 386, 454, 459, 540, 545, 573, 580, 584–586, 590–591, 596; Thomas Richardson to wife, March 26, 1862, Thomas Richardson Letter, LSU; Robert D. Smith Diary, April 4, 1862, 2nd Tennessee File, SNMPRF; W. B. Bate to Julia, September 21, 1861, William B. Bate Papers, University of Tennessee at Martin; "Charges and Specifications against Col. S. S. Heard, 17th Regiment Louisiana Volunteers," March 17, 1862, HC; William Stephen Ray Memoir, 1915, UAR, 18; Braxton Bragg to S. A. M. Wood, April 3, 1862, HC; C. S. Stewart to Julia, April 12, 1862, 21st Alabama File, SNMPRF; Reed, *Battle of Shiloh,* 12; Jordan, "Notes of a Confederate Staff-Officer," 599.

22. OR 1, 10 (1): 86–93; OR 1, 10 (2): 90, 299, 387–388; Wright, *History of the Sixth,* 67; untitled article, *Warren Independent,* April 22, 1862, Luther Howard Cowan Papers, TSLA; Robert Major to unknown, April 5, 1862, Hathaway Family Papers, USAMHI; Jones, "About the Battle of Shiloh"; Medrick, "Skirmishing in Sherman's Front," 1:537; Shoup, "How We Went to Shiloh," 137; Beauregard, "Campaign of Shiloh," 582; William to Julia, April 10, 1862, HC.

23. Ed A. Gordon, "A Graphic Picture of the Battle of Shiloh," *National Tribune,* April 26, 1883; *Report of the Proceedings of the Society of the Army of the Tennessee,* 78; Jesse Connelley Diary, April 9, 1862, ISL; Connelly, "Hoosier at Shiloh," 80; SOR 1, 1:631; OR 1, 10 (1): 89, 400, 464; OR 1, 10 (2): 92; Young, *Around the World,* 471; Grant, "Battle of Shiloh," 466–467; Wallace, *Life and Letters,* 181; Williams, *From that Terrible Field,* 54; Jordan, "Notes of a Confederate Staff-Officer," 596–597; Downing, *Downing's Civil War Diary,* 40; George Carrington Diary, April 4, 1862, CHS; Leroy Crockett to Nellie,

March 27, 1862, Leroy Crockett Papers, CWD, USAMHI; Livaudais, *Shiloh Diary,* 23; SOR 1, 1:631; untitled article, *Warren Independent,* April 22, 1862, Luther Howard Cowan Papers, TSLA; Philip Shaw Diary, April 4, 1862, 32nd Illinois File, SNMPRF; M. Harvey Diary, April 6, 1862, 57th Illinois File, SNMPRF.

24. Medrick, "Skirmishing in Sherman's Front," 537; Wright, *History of the Sixth,* 69; OR 1, 10 (1): 248, 612; Force, *From Fort Henry to Corinth,* 118; Dawes, "Battle of Shiloh—Part I," 7:117; Ephraim Dawes to Kate, March 19, 1862, Ephraim C. Dawes Papers, NL.

25. OR 1, 10 (1): 89; OR 1, 10 (2): 94; Force, *From Fort Henry to Corinth,* 118; R. W. Surby, "Fighting Them Over," *National Tribune,* March 29, 1883.

26. OR 1, 10 (1): 386, 397, 400, 403, 405–407, 464, 495, 532, 536, 547, 567, 587, 591, 614; OR 1, 10 (2): 375, 384; Beauregard, "Campaign of Shiloh," 584; Rufus Daniel Diary, April 5, 1862, CWD, USAMHI; Boynton, *Sherman's Historical Raid,* 35; Sandidge, "Battle of Shiloh," 173; unknown to editors, April 11, 1862, Shiloh Subject File, ADAH; Rufus W. Daniel Diary, April 4, 1862, Arkansas History Center; SOR 1, 1:651; Alfred Tyler Fielder Diary, April 4, 1862, TSLA.

27. OR 1, 10 (1): 386, 397, 400, 420, 567; OR 1, 10 (2): 393; SOR 1, 1:652; William S. Dillon Diary, April 5, 1862, UM; Henry George, "Seventh Kentucky at Shiloh," 7th Kentucky File, SNMPRF; Joseph D. Thompson Diary, April 5, 1862, TSLA; James R. Binford, "Recollections of the Fifteenth Regiment of Mississippi Infantry, CSA," undated, Patrick Henry Papers, MDAH, 25; John E. Magee Diary, April 5, 1862, DU; Richardson, "War as I Saw It," 99; "Extra," April 4, 1862, *New Orleans Picayune.* For an original copy of Johnston's proclamation, see the Allyn K. Ford Collection, Minnesota Historical Society.

28. Johnston, "Albert Sidney Johnston at Shiloh," 555; Beauregard, "Campaign of Shiloh," 582–583; Jordan, "Notes of a Confederate Staff-Officer," 597; OR 1, 10 (1): 407; Lockett, "Surprise and Withdrawal," 1:604.

29. OR 1, 10 (1): 400, 527, 603, 612; Joseph D. Alison Diary, April 5, 1862, Holloway's Cavalry Company File, SNMPRF; Dudley Hayden Diary, May 3, 1862, *Richmond Dispatch,* WS; "Journal of the Orleans Guard," April 5, 1862, HNOC; Baylor, "With Gen. A. S. Johnston at Shiloh," 609; Beauregard, "Campaign of Shiloh," 587; Presley Judson Edwards Autobiography, 1898, CHS; Thomas J. Crowder Memoir, undated, TSLA, 1; unknown to Jose, April 9, 1862, Henry D. Mandeville and Family Papers, LSU; Roman, *Military Operations of General Beauregard,* 1:277–278, 282, 347–348; Johnston, *Life of Gen. Albert Sidney Johnston,* 562, 568–570; William Preston Diary, April 5, 1862, NARA.

30. OR 1, 10 (1): 403, 407, 567; Beauregard, "Campaign of Shiloh," 583; Roman, *Military Operations of General Beauregard,* 1:278; Johnston, *Life of Gen. Albert Sidney Johnston,* 568–571; Johnston, "Albert Sidney Johnston at

Shiloh," 555; Roland, *Albert Sidney Johnston,* 324; unknown to uncle, April 10, 1862, William Massie Papers, DU.

31. Sandidge, "Battle of Shiloh," 174; Lockett, "Surprise and Withdrawal," 604; Daniel, *Shiloh,* 128; OR 1, 10 (1): 409; Jordan, "Notes of a Confederate Staff-Officer," 599.

32. Smith, *Reminiscences of the Civil War,* 2; Bradford Nichol Memoir, April 6, 1862, TSLA; Livaudais, *Shiloh Diary,* 24–25; Kendall, "Recollections of a Confederate Officer," 1058–1059; Thomas J. Crowder Memoir, undated, TSLA, 1; "Battle of Shiloh," *St. Louis Republic,* April 26, 1862; Dudley Hayden Diary, *Richmond Dispatch,* May 3, 1862, WS; Johnston, *Life of Gen. Albert Sidney Johnston,* 560.

33. Johnston, *Life of Gen. Albert Sidney Johnston,* 569, 583–584, 613; OR 1, 10 (1): 396; Allen, "Shiloh! The Campaign and First Day's Battle," 39; Engle, "Thank God, He Has Rescued His Character"; Paxton, "Dear Rebecca," 183; Confederate Letter, April 12, 1862, Wilson S. Beckley Papers, UMCL.

CHAPTER 5: "I WAS NOT ONLY SURPRISED, BUT ASTOUNDED"

1. Jordan, "Battle of Shiloh," 205; Thomas McFadden to unknown, undated, 46th Ohio File, SNMPRF.

2. Thomas Stuart Birch Diary, March 26, 1862, EU; William Nicholls to friend, April 18, 1862, 15th Iowa File, SNMPRF; D. W. Burwell to Mrs. Gregory, March 18, 1862, Rufus Bates Papers, CWD, USAMHI; David Helmick to Buck Family, March 25, 1862, David Helmick Papers, CWD, USAMHI; Skaptason, "Chicago Light Artillery," 89; D. J. Benner to uncle, April 9, 1862, Luther Howard Cowan Papers, TSLA; Henry C. McArthur Diary, April 6, 1862, SHSI (copy in 15th Iowa File, SNMPRF); Wallace, *Life and Letters,* 183, 185.

3. August Schilling Diary, April 6, 1862, BCHS; Kimbell, *History of Battery "A,"* 40; Olney, *Shiloh as Seen by a Private Soldier,* 13; Jones, "Battle of Shiloh," 4:54; Jonathan B. LaBrant Diary, April 6, 1862, CWD, USAMHI (copy in 5th Illinois File, SNMPRF); Daniel Harmon Brush Diary, April 6, 1862, ALPL; Grant, "Battle of Shiloh," 1:467; Fletcher, *History of Company "A,"* 49; Anders, *Eighteenth Missouri,* 49; *Annals of the War,* 682; Wallace, *Life and Letters,* 183, 185.

4. Grant, "Battle of Shiloh," 467.

5. Jacob Miller to brother, April 6, 1862, Jacob Miller Papers, USAMHI.

6. Robert D. Smith Diary, April 6, 1862, 2nd Tennessee File, SNMPRF; Nixon, "Alabamian at Shiloh," 152; OR 1, 10 (1): 495; Stanley, *Autobiography,* 187; Lockett, "Surprise and Withdrawal," 1:604; Williamson, *Third Battalion,* 31; Roman, *Military Operations of General Beauregard,* 1:282. For Stanley, see Hughes, *Sir Henry Morton Stanley.*

7. Charles Marshall, "Miscellaneous Incidents of the Civil War," Research Reports on Army Units in the Army of Tennessee, SNMPVF, 1–2; "Personal Interview with Mr. Aleck McDaniel," July 22, 1938, Milligan, *Seeing Shiloh;* Smith, "Forgotten Inhabitants," 36–45.

8. Augustus Hervey Mecklin Diary, April 6, 1862, MDAH.

9. Buell, "Shiloh Reviewed," 1:499–500; *Annals of the War,* 680, 682; Thomas McFadden to unknown, undated, 46th Ohio File, SNMPRF.

10. OR 1, 10 (1): 257, 277–278, 282, 285; Ballard and Cockrell, *Chickasaw,* 2, 27, 72; Force, *From Fort Henry to Corinth,* 120; Johnston, *Life of Gen. Albert Sidney Johnston,* 579; Peter Sullivan to O. M. Poe, June 18, 1878, Peter John Sullivan Letters, LSU; Neal, *Illustrated History,* 130; Dawes, "Battle of Shiloh—Part I," 7:119; John A. McClernand to William T. Sherman, April 5, 1862, John A. McClernand Papers, ALPL.

11. Downing, *Downing's Civil War Diary,* 40; John B. Beach Memoir, 1915, ALPL, 2; Wallace, *Life and Letters,* 191; I. P. Rumsey Memoir, undated, I. P. Rumsey File, SNMPRF, 15; Avery, *History of the Fourth Illinois Cavalry Regiment,* 61.

12. Ed A. Gordon, "A Graphic Picture of the Battle of Shiloh," *National Tribune,* April 26, 1883.

13. Dawes, "Battle of Shiloh—Part I," 117; Flemming, "Battle of Shiloh as a Private Saw It," 6:137.

14. "Battle of Shiloh," *St. Louis Republic,* April 26, 1862; Wiley Sword, "Shiloh: The Untold Story—New Information about the Battle" (unpublished essay, 2012), WS, 4; Christian Zook to family, April 5, 1862, Christian Zook Papers, CWD, USAMHI; Morton, "Opening of the Battle of Shiloh," 11; OR 1, 10 (1): 280, 284; witness to editor, April 15, 1862, 12th Michigan File, SNMPRF; *Harvard Memorial Biographies,* 1:163; Neal, *Illustrated History,* 124–127; M. Harvey Diary, April 6, 1862, 57th Illinois File, SNMPRF.

15. Oliver Newberry to mother, April 13, 1862, Oliver Perry Newberry Papers, NL; Reed, *Battle of Shiloh,* 11; Dawes, "Battle of Shiloh—Part I," 138; Neal, *Illustrated History,* 127; Gordon, "Graphic Picture."

16. OR 1, 10 (1): 603; Williamson, *Third Battalion,* 31. For Hardcastle, see Charles Van Adder, "Colonel Aaron B. Hardcastle, 45th Mississippi Infantry," 3rd Mississippi Battalion File, SNMPRF.

17. OR 1, 10 (1): 603. The 3rd Mississippi Battalion became the 45th Mississippi; see the 45th Mississippi Infantry Papers, MDAH.

18. OR 1, 10 (1): 603.

19. Ibid., 403, 464; Johnston, *Life of Gen. Albert Sidney Johnston,* 582, 585; Johnston, "Albert Sidney Johnston at Shiloh," 1:558; Roman, *Military Operations of General Beauregard,* 1:349; P. G. T. Beauregard to Isham G. Harris, March 9, 1880, Pierre Gustave Toutant Beauregard Papers, DU.

20. OR 1, 10 (1): 248; Johnston, "Albert Sidney Johnston at Shiloh," 557.

21. OR 1, 10 (1): 401, 568, 602–603.

22. Ibid., 386.

23. Ibid., 403; Johnston, "Albert Sidney Johnston at Shiloh," 556; Dawes, "Battle of Shiloh—Part I," 138.

24. OR 1, 10 (1): 278, 280, 282; *Harvard Memorial Biographies,* 1:164; Morton, "Opening of the Battle of Shiloh," 15; Stone, "Battle of Shiloh," 7:59; Morton, "Boy at Shiloh," 59; Oliver Newberry to mother, April 13, 1862, Oliver Perry Newberry Papers, NL.

25. OR 1, 10 (1): 282–283; Neal, *Illustrated History,* 125; Jones, "Battle of Shiloh," 56–57; Starr and Holman, *21st Missouri,* 9–12.

26. Giles B. Cooke Report, undated, Giles B. Cooke Papers, VHS; OR 1, 10 (1): 282, 285, 575; Morton, "Opening of the Battle of Shiloh," 17.

27. OR 1, 10 (1): 282, 285, 575; Morton, "Opening of the Battle of Shiloh," 17.

28. OR 1, 10 (1): 386, 420.

29. Ibid., 591; Livaudais, *Shiloh Diary,* 25; Clark, "New Orleans German Colony," 1,003; Jordan, "Notes of a Confederate Staff-Officer," 1:599.

30. OR 1, 10 (1): 401, 403; Ulmer, "Glimpse of Albert Sidney Johnston"; Johnston, *Life of Gen. Albert Sidney Johnston,* 584, 589; Roman, *Military Operations of General Beauregard,* 1:284–285, 524, 529; T. J. Walker, "Reminiscences of the Civil War," undated, UT, 4; Isaac Ulmer Memoir, undated, Isaac Barton Ulmer Papers, UNC; Clarke, *Diary of the War for Separation,* 122; John C. Caldwell Diary, April 6, 1862, CWTI Collection, USAMHI (copy in 9th Kentucky File, SNMPRF); Bevens, *Reminiscences,* 22.

31. OR 1, 10 (1): 464, 568; Reed, *Battle of Shiloh,* 23; Beauregard, "Campaign of Shiloh," 586; "Surprise at Shiloh," *National Tribune,* April 5, 1883; James C. Veatch, "The Battle of Shiloh," *National Tribune,* March 15, 1883; W. A. Howard to family, April 10, 1862, W. A. Howard Manuscripts, IU (copy in 33rd Tennessee File, SNMPRF).

32. Alex Oliphant to mother, April 8, 1862, 24th Indiana File, SNMPRF; Americus V. Rice to William Gribben, April 13, 1862, Ohio Memory Community Collection, OHS; OR 1, 10 (1): 403; Duke, *Personal Recollections of Shiloh,* 8; J. F. Ferguson, "The Army Surprised or the Commanders Careless," *National Tribune,* May 10, 1883; "The Surprise at Shiloh," *Chicago Tribune,* April 18, 1881.

33. Charles H. Floyd to friend, July 6, 1862, Charles H. Floyd Letters, ALPL; OR 1, 10 (1): 240–241; J. L. Bieler to "President and Comrades," undated, 6th Indiana Battery File, SNMPRF; Stephen A. Hurlbut, "Pittsburg Landing and Shiloh," undated, WS, 9, 11; John Ruckman to John Kinsel, April 12, 1862, 57th Ohio File, SNMPRF; Henry Reinoch, "Surprised at Company Inspection," *National Tribune,* April 19, 1883; A. J. Eldred to Sir, April 16, 1862, 12th Michigan File, SNMPRF; Wilkie, *Pen and Powder,* 161; Hickenlooper, "Battle of Shiloh—Part II," 5:472; John E. Smith to Elihu Washburne, May 16, 1862,

Elihu Washburne Papers, LC; "Shiloh—Was It a Surprise," 1884, Ephraim C. Dawes Papers, NL.

34. Henry H. Wright, "An Iowa Soldier's Story of Shiloh," *National Tribune,* May 3, 1883; R. M. Kelly, "Not Surprised, but Unprepared," *National Tribune,* April 19, 1883.

35. Gordon, "Graphic Picture"; G. S. Smith, "One Brigade That Was Not Surprised," *National Tribune,* April 19, 1883; Byers, *Iowa in War Times,* 126; M. Harvey Diary, April 6, 1862, 57th Illinois File, SNMPRF.

36. OR 1, 10 (1): 254.

37. Ibid., 264.

38. Frank E. Peabody to D. W. Reed, April 24, 1908, Series 1, Box 11, Folder 95, SNMPAF.

CHAPTER 6: "THIS VALLEY OF DEATH"

1. Symonds, *Stonewall of the West,* 9–63.

2. Robert D. Smith Diary, April 6, 1862, 2nd Tennessee File, SNMPRF; Gordon, "Graphic Picture"; OR 1, 10 (1): 403, 568, 580; William Preston Diary, April 6, 1862, NARA.

3. Allen, "Shiloh! The Campaign and First Day's Battle," 49.

4. OR 1, 10 (1): 401, 513, 580; Roman, *Military Operations of General Beauregard,* 1:524, 527; William Preston Diary, April 6, 1862, NARA.

5. Benjamin D. Fearing to sister, April 13, 1862, Ephraim C. Dawes Papers, NL; F. M. Posegate, "The Sunday Battle at Shiloh," undated, Stephen E. Williams Collection; Cockerill, "Boy at Shiloh," 6:17; OR 1, 10 (1): 255, 581, 587; Johnston, "Albert Sidney Johnston at Shiloh," 1:552; De Hass, "Battle of Shiloh," 682–685; A. C. Waterhouse to Cornelius Cadle, June 23, 1895, Series 1, Box 15, Folder 196, SNMPAF.

6. *Annals of the War,* 685; OR 1, 52 (1): 23.

7. OR 1, 10 (1): 270, 581, 587; 19–20; Americus V. Rice to William Gribben, April 13, 1862, Ohio Memory Community Collection, OHS; John Ruckman to John Kinsel, April 12, 1862, 57th Ohio File, SNMPRF; Bering and Montgomery, *History of the Forty-eighth,* 19–20; *Report of the Proceedings of the Society of the Army of the Tennessee,* 79; Enos P. Brobson to friends, April 20, 1862, Enos P. Brobson Letter, TSLA; Virgil Moats to Eliza, April 9, 1862, Virgil Henry Moats Papers, UMCL.

8. Dawes, "My First Day Under Fire at Shiloh"; Ephraim Dawes to Kate, March 16, 1862, Ephraim C. Dawes Papers, NL.

9. OR 1, 10 (1): 264, 273; Sherman, *Memoirs,* 1:230; Skaptason, "Chicago Light Artillery," 86; Dawes, "Battle of Shiloh—Part I," 7:141; Ephraim Dawes to Marshal, April 21, 1862, Ephraim C. Dawes Papers, NL.

10. OR 1, 10 (1): 581; Peebles, "From Participant in Battle of Shiloh."

11. "The Shiloh Campaign," *National Tribune,* July 24, 1884; Flemming, "Battle of Shiloh as a Private Saw It," 6:132, 140; Benjamin D. Fearing to sister, April 13, 1862, Ephraim C. Dawes Papers, NL.

12. OR 1, 10 (1): 266–267, 568; Cockerill, "Boy at Shiloh," 6:15; *Report of the Proceedings of the Society of the Army of the Tennessee,* 80–82.

13. J. W. Cullom to Mary, April 10, 1862, 24th Tennessee File, SNMPRF; OR 1, 10 (1): 581, 585; Beauregard, "Campaign of Shiloh," 1:586; Cunningham, *Shiloh and the Western Campaign,* 172; Johnston, *Life of Gen. Albert Sidney Johnston,* 594; Robert D. Smith Diary, April 6, 1862, 2nd Tennessee File, SNMPRF.

14. OR 1, 10 (1): 581; Howell, *Going to Meet the Yankees,* 84.

15. OR 1, 10 (1): 264–265, 568, 581; Grant, "Battle of Shiloh," 1:473; Dawes, "Battle of Shiloh—Part II," 7:143; Ephraim Dawes to Kate, April 13, 1862, and Ephraim Dawes to Marshal, April 21, 1862, Ephraim C. Dawes Papers, NL. For more insight, see Bjorn Skaptason, "Retreat and Save Yourselves: A Study in Union Leadership Failure at Shiloh" (MA thesis, Loyola University, Chicago, 2010).

16. OR 1, 10 (1): 273, 581; Cox, "Sixth Mississippi Regiment at Shiloh"; Watkins, *"Co. Aytch,"* 33; Kelsey, "Battle of Shiloh," 72.

17. OR 1, 10 (1): 273; Theodore P. Lockwood, "My War Record," 1909, Lockwood Collection, UM; Howell, *Going to Meet the Yankees,* 86; John J. Thornton Compiled Service Record, 6th Mississippi Infantry, NARA; "The Sixth Mississippi at Shiloh," undated, 6th Mississippi Infantry Papers, MDAH; Smith, *Mississippi in the Civil War,* 19; OR 1, 10 (1): 581; Howell, *Going to Meet the Yankees,* 86–87.

18. OR 1, 10 (1): 568, 581.

19. Ibid., 581, 587; A. R. Chisolm Report, April 14, 1862, SNMPRF (copy also in Samuel Richey Collection, MIAU).

20. OR 1, 10 (1): 465, 495; Giles B. Cooke Report, undated, Giles B. Cooke Papers, VHS; Sandidge, "Battle of Shiloh," 174; Kendall, "Recollections of a Confederate Officer," 1,059; Bevens, *Reminiscences,* 67.

21. OR 1, 10 (1): 401, 403; Johnston, *Life of Gen. Albert Sidney Johnston,* 594, 598; Beauregard, "Campaign of Shiloh," 586.

22. OR 1, 10 (1): 401–402; Beauregard, "Campaign of Shiloh," 587.

23. OR 1, 10 (1): 401, 465, 471; Roman, *Military Operations of General Beauregard,* 1:286, 525; Livaudais, *Shiloh Diary,* 26–27.

24. OR 1, 10 (1): 255, 516, 471; J. L. Bieler to "President and Comrades," undated, 6th Indiana Battery File, SNMPRF; Hart, *History of the Fortieth,* 86; Thomas McFadden to unknown, undated, 46th Ohio File, SNMPRF; Livaudais, *Shiloh Diary,* 27; Felix Ross Diary, April 6, 1862, ALPL.

25. OR 1, 10 (1): 471; J. K. Street to Ninnie, April 12, 1862, John Kennedy Street Papers, UNC; Reed, *Battle of Shiloh,* 14; Daniel, *Cannoneers in Gray,*

26; Clarke, *Diary of the War for Separation,* 125. For more on Anderson, see his "Autobiography of Gen. Patton Anderson."

26. OR 1, 10 (1): 471, 496–497, 502–504, 507, 510, 513; Reed, *Battle of Shiloh,* 77.

27. OR 1, 10 (1): 505, 508–509; J. K. Street to Ninnie, April 12, 1862, John Kennedy Street Papers, UNC; Thomas Richardson to wife, March 26, 1862, Thomas Richardson Letter, LSU; Reed, *Battle of Shiloh,* 43.

28. "A Brave Standard Bearer," undated, Arthur W. Hyatt Papers, LSU.

29. OR 1, 10 (1): 262, 407, 414, 420, 423, 427, 433; SOR 1, 1:652; Alfred Tyler Fielder Diary, April 6, 1862, TSLA; John E. Magee Diary, April 6, 1862, DU; Beauregard, "Campaign of Shiloh," 586; W. J. Stubblefield Diary, April 6, 1862, MU, 3.

30. OR 1, 10 (1): 440, 443–445; Wiley Sword, "Shiloh: The Untold Story—New Information about the Battle" (unpublished essay, 2012), WS, 8; Sandidge, "Battle of Shiloh," 175.

31. OR 1, 10 (1): 440, 444–445, 508; Lee, "Maj. John C. Thompson"; Marcus J. Wright Diary, April 6, 1862, Civil War Collection, TSLA.

32. "Reminiscences of the Battle of Shiloh, as Recalled by Major Pat Henry, a Participant," undated, Patrick Henry Papers, MDAH.

33. OR 1, 10 (1): 408, 413, 416, 423, 425; Reed, *Battle of Shiloh,* 80; Samuel Latta to Mary, April 10, 1862, Samuel Rankin Latta Papers, TU (copy also in MSU). For more on Vaughan, see Peterson, *Confederate Combat Commander.*

34. OR 1, 10 (1): 415, 419–420; C. J. Johnson to wife, April 11, 1862, Charles James Johnson Papers, LSU; Vaughan, *Personal Record,* 16; A. P. Stewart to William H. McCardle, April 30, 1878, William H. McCardle Papers, MDAH. For more on Clark's division, see the orders and returns in the William Yerger Papers, MDAH.

35. OR 1, 10 (1): 412, 419; Braxton Bragg to wife, April 9, 1862, Braxton Bragg Papers, MHS.

36. OR 1, 10 (1): 249; Force, *From Fort Henry to Corinth,* 129.

37. Ephraim Dawes to Kate, April 13, 1862, Ephraim C. Dawes Papers, NL.

38. OR 1, 10 (1): 116, 273.

39. Ibid., 115–116, 122, 139, 141, 143, 146, 248–249; B. Smith, "What Another Soldier Thinks About It," *National Tribune,* March 29, 1883; Special Order 354, April 4, 1862, John A. McClernand Papers, ALPL; Abram J. Vanauken Diary, April 6, 1862, ALPL.

40. Henry Hole to sister, April 22, 1862, Henry F. Hole Papers, ALPL.

41. OR 1, 10 (1): 249.

CHAPTER 7: "THE STRUGGLE FOR HIS ENCAMPMENTS"

1. Stephen A. Hurlbut, "Pittsburg Landing and Shiloh," undated, WS, 11.

2. OR 1, 10 (1): 249; T. Lyle Dickey to Ann, May 17, 1862, 4th Illinois Cavalry File, SNMPRF.

3. Cunningham, *Shiloh and the Western Campaign,* 153–154; A. J. Eldred to Sir, April 16, 1862, 12th Michigan File, SNMPRF; witness to editor, April 15, 1862, 12th Michigan File, SNMPRF.

4. OR 1, 10 (1): 280; "The Life of Elias Perry," undated, Civil War Collection, MHS.

5. Cudworth, "Memories of Fifty Years Ago," 232–233; James Lawrence to family, April 8, 1862, James Lawrence Papers, CHS; S. F. Martin to brother, April 11, 1862, Civil War Collection, MHS.

6. A. J. Eldred to Sir, April 16, 1862, 12th Michigan File, SNMPRF; Stanley, *Autobiography,* 189; "From the 12th Regiment," *Niles Republican,* April 26, 1862; OR 1, 10 (1): 278, 573; Reed, *Battle of Shiloh,* 68.

7. OR 1, 10 (1): 278, 280, 285–286, 386, 609; V. F. Vail, "Company 'K,' of the 16th Wisconsin, at the Battle of Shiloh," 16th Wisconsin File, SNMPRF, 6; Charles Swett to D. W. Reed, September 6, 1909, Series 1, Box 14, Folder 186, SNMPAF (copy in Swett's Battery File, SNMPRF); "Colonel Allen's Bravery," E. B. Quiner Scrapbooks, WHS, 5:230; Jones, "Battle of Shiloh," 4:56.

8. OR 1, 10 (1): 574, 577, 591; Alex Boyd to sister, April 25, 1862, Alex Boyd Letters, CWD, USAMHI (copy in 9th Arkansas File, SNMPRF).

9. OR 1, 10 (1): 537, 544–545; Stillwell, *Personal Recollections,* 10.

10. OR 1, 10 (1): 537, 544–545; *Report of the Proceedings of the Society of the Army of the Tennessee,* 63; Anders, *Eighteenth Missouri,* 9; James H. Hall to family, April 1, 1862, James H. Hall Papers, UMB; Hickenlooper, "Battle of Shiloh—Part I," 5:412–413; Hurter, "Narrative of the First Battery," 640; August Schilling Diary, April 6, 1862, BCHS; Fred L. Haywood to sister, April 6, 1863, Fred L. Haywood Letter, Kansas Historical Society; T. D. Christie to sister, October 28, Christie Family Letters, Minnesota Historical Society; William J. Christie to brother, May 16, 1862, William J. Christie Letters, LSU.

11. Ed Embly to family, April 28, 1862, HCWRT, USAMHI.

12. James Cooper to Farley, April 22, 1862, James Cooper Papers, NC; "The Death of Gen. Gladden," Shiloh Subject File, ADAH; Nixon, "Alabamian at Shiloh," 152–153; OR 1, 10 (1): 536, 568; Dinkins, "Battle of Shiloh," 306; A Touching Incident," undated, Adley Gladden Papers, CWTI, USAMHI.

13. S. H. Dent to wife, April 9, 1862, Stouton Hubert Dent Papers, ADAH; Felix H. Robertson to S. H. Dent, April 25, 1909, Stouton Hubert Dent Papers, ADAH.

14. OR 1, 10 (1): 465, 480, 487, 492, 532, 554; Reed, *Battle of Shiloh,* 16, 72, 76.

15. Clarke, *Diary of the War for Separation,* 118; OR 1, 10 (1): 548; John A. Cato to wife, March 27, 1862, John A. Cato Papers, MDAH (Cato Papers also in USAMHI).

16. OR 1, 10 (1): 548; Anders, *Eighteenth Missouri,* 55; "The Fifteenth Regiment at the Battle of Pittsburg Landing," *Monroe (MI) Commercial,* April 17,

1862; Sword, *Shiloh,* 161; Levi Minkler Diary, April 6, 1862, 18th Wisconsin File, SNMPRF; Willard W. Felton Diary, April 6, 1862, WHS.

17. OR 1, 10 (1): 548; Robert A. Smith Report, April 9, 1862, Robert A. Smith Papers, MDAH; Thomas Jefferson Crowder Memoir, undated, TSLA, 2; John F. Sharp, History of Company F, undated, 5th Mississippi Infantry Papers, MDAH.

18. OR 1, 10 (1): 280, 536–537, 548; Stillwell, *Personal Recollections,* 11; Hurter, "Narrative of the First Battery," 640–641; Thomas Jefferson Crowder Memoir, undated, TSLA, 2; August Schilling Diary, April 6, 1862, BCHS; Nixon, "Alabamian at Shiloh," 152–153; Hickenlooper, "Battle of Shiloh—Part I," 414–416; James Lawrence to family, April 8, 1862, James Lawrence Papers, CHS; Elizabeth Boyle Everett Diaries, April 14, 24, and 26, 1862, MAHS; S. H. Dent to wife, April 9, 1862, Stouton Hubert Dent Papers, ADAH.

19. Finding Aid, 2007, John Thomas Wheat Papers, UNC; Williams, *From that Terrible Field,* 55; Hicks and Kropf, *Raising the "Hunley,"* 62–63.

20. *Harvard Memorial Biographies,* 1:165; Oliver Newberry to mother, April 13, 1862, Oliver Perry Newberry Papers, NL.

21. OR 1, 10 (1): 278, 283, 574; V. F. Vail, "Company 'K,' of the 16th Wisconsin, at the Battle of Shiloh," May 8, 1897, 16th Wisconsin File, SNMPRF, 2; Smith, *History of the Seventh,* 44.

22. OR 1, 10 (1): 280–281; A. J. Eldred to Sir, April 16, 1862, 12th Michigan File, SNMPRF.

23. S. H. Eells to friends, April 13, 1862, Samuel Henry Eells Papers, LC.

24. Hickenlooper, "Battle of Shiloh—Part I," 416–417.

25. OR 1, 10 (1): 403, 598; SOR 1, 1:652; John E. Magee Diary, April 6, 1862, DU; Johnston, "Albert Sidney Johnston at Shiloh," 1:558; Houston, "Shiloh Shadows" (original in Samuel Houston Jr. Papers, University of Texas); Richardson, "War as I Saw It," 103; Hardee, "Biographical Sketch of Major-General Patrick R. Cleburne," 153; Spenser B. Talley Memoir, 1918, TSLA, 8; Alfred Tyler Fielder Diary, April 6, 1862, TSLA.

26. Houston, "Shiloh Shadows," 330; unknown diary, April 6, 1862, 6th Arkansas File, SNMPRF; Stanley, *Autobiography,* 191; Samuel Latta to Mary, April 10, 1862, Samuel Rankin Latta Papers, TU; SOR 1, 1:654; Roman, *Military Operations of General Beauregard,* 1:527; John E. Magee Diary, April 5, 1862, DU.

27. OR 1, 10 (1): 386, 401, 454, 612; Horsely, "Reminiscences of Shiloh."

28. OR 1, 10 (1): 407, 414–415, 427; Reed, *Battle of Shiloh,* 73, 81; Wingfield, *General A. P. Stewart,* 55; Ulmer, "Glimpse of Albert Sidney Johnston"; Johnston, *Life of Gen. Albert Sidney Johnston,* 612; Dudley Hayden Diary, May 3, 1862, *Richmond Dispatch,* WS.

29. OR 1, 10 (1): 404, 569; Johnston, *Life of Gen. Albert Sidney Johnston,* 595, 597, 608; Charles S. Stewart to Julia, April 6, 1862, 21st Alabama File, SNMPRF.

30. OR 1, 10 (1): 427, 532, 537, 554, 574, 598, 601; Johnston, "Albert Sidney Johnston at Shiloh," 559; Johnston, *Life of Gen. Albert Sidney Johnston,* 597; McDonough, *Shiloh,* 106; H. W. H. to parents, April 10, 1862, Shiloh Subject File, ADAH.

31. J. S. to friend, April 17, 1862, Rombauer–Becker Family Papers, HUS; OR 1, 10 (1): 115, 139–141, 144, 249, 273, 277, 446, 450, 591; OR 1, 52 (1): 24; F. A. Niles, "Several Surprises at Shiloh," *National Tribune,* March 29, 1883; T. W. Morgan to William, April 4, 1862, 49th Illinois File, SNMPRF; J. G. Burggraf to Eliza, April 14, 1862, John G. Burggraf Letters, Willamette University; Vaughan, *Personal Record,* 16.

32. OR 1, 10 (1): 115, 139–141, 144, 249, 273, 277, 446, 450, 591; OR 1, 52 (1): 24; J. G. Burggraf to Eliza, April 14, 1862, John G. Burggraf Letters, Willamette University; Vaughan, *Personal Record,* 16; Skaptason, "Chicago Light Artillery," 87; Reed, *Battle of Shiloh,* 14; Samuel Latta to Mary, April 10, 1862, Samuel Rankin Latta Papers, TU.

33. OR 1, 10 (1): 115, 139–141, 144, 249, 273, 277, 446, 450, 591; OR 1, 52 (1): 24; Stanley, *Autobiography,* 194.

34. OR 1, 10 (1): 249–250, 255, 270, 276, 416; Gordon, "Graphic Picture"; Benjamin D. Fearing to sister, April 13, 1862, Ephraim C. Dawes Papers, NL; Medrick, "Skirmishing in Sherman's Front," 1:537; Timothy Blaisdell to unknown, April 12, 1862, CWTI Collection, USAMHI; Robert H. Wood to father, April 14, 1862, Bills Family Papers, TSLA; Sherman, *Memoirs,* 1:230; Americus V. Rice to William Gribben, April 13, 1862, Ohio Memory Community Collection, OHS; Hughes, *Battle of Belmont,* 102–105, 124, 143; Ephraim Dawes to Marshal, April 21, 1862, Ephraim C. Dawes Papers, NL; John B. Rice to wife, April 15, 1862, Rice Family Collection, RBHPC; Samuel Latta to Mary, April 10, 1862, Samuel Rankin Latta Papers, TU.

35. OR 1, 10 (1): 404, 532, 549; Lockett, "Surprise and Withdrawal," 1:604.

36. Johnston, *Life of Gen. Albert Sidney Johnston,* 597; OR 1, 10 (1): 386, 404, 532, 549; Lockett, "Surprise and Withdrawal," 604; Roman, *Military Operations of General Beauregard,* 1:286–287, 291, 529; Richard Walpole to friends, April 12, 1862, Bomar Family Letters, EU.

37. Augustus Hervey Mecklin Diary, April 6, 1862, MDAH; Binford, "Recollections of the Fifteenth Regiment of Mississippi Infantry, CSA," 25.

CHAPTER 8: "WE'VE GOT TO FIGHT AGAINST TIME NOW"

1. OR 1, 10 (1): 257; Smith, *Life and Letters,* 195; I. P. Rumsey Memoir, undated, I. P. Rumsey File, SNMPRF, 15.

2. OR 1, 10 (1): 260; Cunningham, *Shiloh and the Western Campaign,* 207, 212; *Story of the Fifty-fifth,* 73.

3. OR 1, 10 (1): 257; Lawrence, "Stuart's Brigade at Shiloh," 491.

4. OR 1, 10 (1): 257–258.

5. John P. Wheeler, "The Fifty-fifth Illinois at Shiloh," *National Tribune,* May 3, 1883.

6. OR 1, 10 (1): 454; Sykes, "Walthall's Brigade," 1:581–582; R. F. Learned to D. W. Reed, March 22, 1904, Series 1, Box 13, Folder 152, SNMPAF (copy in 10th Mississippi File, SNMPRF).

7. OR 1, 10 (1): 532, 536, 548, 552; Robert A. Smith Report, April 9, 1862, Robert A. Smith Papers, MDAH; Reed, *Battle of Shiloh,* 74; unknown to editors, April 11, 1862, Shiloh Subject File, ADAH.

8. OR 1, 10 (1): 532–533, 554; Wheeler, "Battle of Shiloh," 119–131.

9. OR 1, 10 (1): 404, 533, 624; Bradford Nichol Memoir, February 14, 1862, TSLA; Reed, *Battle of Shiloh,* 85; Lockett, "Surprise and Withdrawal," 1:604–605; William Preston Diary, April 6, 1862, NARA.

10. Johnston, *Life of Gen. Albert Sidney Johnston,* 608; Sword, *Shiloh,* 170; OR 1, 10 (1): 558; Dudley Hayden Diary, May 3, 1862, Richmond *Dispatch,* WS; unknown to editors, April 11, 1862, Shiloh Subject File, ADAH; Hughes, *Pride of the Confederate Artillery,* 29; Davis, *Breckinridge,* 305; Baylor, "With Gen. A. S. Johnston at Shiloh," 610–611; Wheeler, "Battle of Shiloh," 122; Johnston, "Albert Sidney Johnston at Shiloh," 1:565; Roman, *Military Operations of General Beauregard,* 1:292.

11. OR 1, 10 (1): 206, 246, 257–258; John R. Woodward to Ellen, April 13, 1862, 71st Ohio File, SNMPRF.

12. OR 1, 10 (1): 407.

13. Ibid., 258, 554; John R. Woodward to Ellen, April 13, 1862, 71st Ohio File, SNMPRF; James J. Garver Scrapbook, undated, James J. Garver Papers, USAMHI; Lawrence, "Stuart's Brigade at Shiloh," 491; unknown to editors, April 11, 1862, Shiloh Subject File, ADAH.

14. OR 1, 10 (1): 258.

15. Ibid., 258–259, 533, 549; Robert A. Smith Report, April 9, 1862, Robert A. Smith Papers, MDAH; Smith, *Life and Letters,* 18–19, 195–196; Lawrence, "Stuart's Brigade at Shiloh," 492–495; William F. Mosier to D. W. Reed, December 11, 1912, Series 1, Box 14, Folder 161, SNMPAF (copy in 52nd Tennessee File, SNMPRF); Thomas Latimer to parents, April 11, 1862, Thomas P. Latimer Papers, USAMHI; *Story of the Fifty-fifth,* 96–97, 444; Jacob Fink, "The Fifty-fifth Illinois at Shiloh," *National Tribune,* May 3, 1883.

16. OR 1, 10 (1): 258–259, 533, 549; Smith, *Life and Letters,* 18–19, 195–196; Fink, "Fifty-fifth Illinois at Shiloh"; Lawrence, "Stuart's Brigade at Shiloh," 492–495; Thomas Latimer to parents, April 11, 1862, Thomas P. Latimer Papers, USAMHI; *Story of the Fifty-fifth,* 96–97, 444.

17. OR 1, 10 (1): 533, 549.

18. Ibid., 184; OR 1, 10 (2): 95–96; Catton, *Grant Moves South,* 223; Walter Q. Gresham to wife, April 8, 1862, Walter Q. Gresham Papers, LC.

19. Grant, "Battle of Shiloh," 1:468; Gresham, *Life of Walter Quintin Gresham,* 1:182.

20. Alex Oliphant to mother, April 8, 1862, 24th Indiana File, SNMPRF.

21. Cunningham, *Shiloh and the Western Campaign,* 159.

22. Lew Wallace to James Grant Wilson, November 6, 1896, William P. Palmer Collection, WRHS; Fuller, *Generalship of Ulysses S. Grant,* 111–113; Badeau, *Military History of Ulysses S. Grant,* 1:79; OR 1, 10 (1): 170, 185; "March of Lew Wallace's Division," 1:607.

23. Hillyer, "Hillyer on Grant at Shiloh"; Hickenlooper, "Battle of Shiloh—Part II," 5:481; Richardson, *Personal History of Ulysses S. Grant,* 248.

24. OR 1, 10 (2): 95.

25. OR 1, 10 (1): 292, 323, 331–332, 337, 352; Hannaford, *Story of a Regiment,* 280; Buell, "Shiloh Reviewed," 492; Maurice J. Williams Diary, April 6, 1862, 36th Indiana File, SNMPRF; Horace N. Fisher, "A Memory of Shiloh," undated, Horace N. Fisher File, SNMPRF; Horace N. Fisher to father, April 10, 1862, Horace N. Fisher Papers, MAHS.

26. OR 1, 10 (1): 292, 297–298; Buell, "Shiloh Reviewed," 492; Will to mother, April 13, 1862, 6th Ohio File, SNMPRF; Williams, *Historical Sketch,* 16; Wardner, "Reminiscences of a Surgeon," 3:186; T. J. Bryant, "The Story of Shiloh," *National Tribune,* May 10, 1883; "The Battle of Pittsburg Landing," April 15, 1862, Henry Van Ness Boynton Papers, MAHS; Karl Donitz to brother, April 2 (?), 1862, Karl Donitz Letters, Civil War Correspondence Collection, MCM; John Travis to brother, April 10, 1862, Travis Family Papers, UMB.

27. Grant, "Battle of Shiloh," 474–476; Buell, "Shiloh Reviewed," 492–494, 507; W. W. Jackson, "The Battle of Shiloh," *National Tribune,* December 24, 1885; Stone, "Battle of Shiloh," 7:75; OR 1, 10 (1): 292, 333; Stephen A. Hurlbut, "Pittsburg Landing and Shiloh," undated, WS, 20.

28. Charles M. Scott to Anna, April 6, 1862, Charles M. Scott Papers, UWS.

29. OR 1, 10 (1): 386.

30. Richardson, "War as I Saw It," 99.

31. OR 1, 10 (1): 408, 465–466, 569.

32. Reed, *Battle of Shiloh,* 80.

33. OR 1, 10 (1): 465.

CHAPTER 9: "WHERE THE FIGHT IS THE THICKEST"

1. Kiper, *Major General John Alexander McClernand,* 24–25.

2. OR 1, 10 (1): 141, 143; unknown to Sadie, April 21, 1862, Sarah V. Elder Dicken Papers, BGSU.

3. OR 1, 10 (1): 133, 137, 220, 263; OR 1, 52 (1): 22–23; Huffstodt, *Hard Dying Men,* 91.

4. OR 1, 10 (1): 123–124, 126, 128, 130–131; SOR 1, 1:628; Daniel Harmon Brush Diary, April 6, 1862, ALPL; Gould D. Molineaux Diary, April 6, 1862, AUG; "Memorandum of Co. F 11th Iowa 1862," undated, Isaac N. Carr Papers, SHSI.

5. OR 1, 10 (1): 250, 255–256.

6. Ibid., 130, 159, 203, 223, 232; Daniel Clark to sister, May 1, 1862, Woods Family Papers, NL; Willaim L. Wade Diary, April 6, 1862, Willaim L. Wade Papers, CWD, USAMHI; Balzar Grebe, "Autobiography and Civil War Diary," Balzar Grebe Papers, LC, 7; James C. Veatch, "The Battle of Shiloh," *National Tribune,* March 15, 1883; Camm, "Col. William Camm War Diary," 843–844; John L. Harris to parents, March 21, 1862, John L. Harris Correspondence, ALPL.

7. OR 1, 10 (1): 250; Cunningham, *Shiloh and the Western Campaign,* 185; J. L. Bieler to "President and Comrades," undated, 6th Indiana Battery File, SNMPRF; S. E. Barrett to D. W. Reed, August 11, 1903, Series 1, Box 11, Folder 96, SNMPAF.

8. Henry Hole to sister, April 22, 1862, Henry F. Hole Papers, ALPL.

9. Daniel Clark to sister, May 1, 1862, Woods Family Papers, NL; OR 1, 10 (1): 582.

10. OR 1, 10 (1): 408, 421, 427, 465; Regimental History, 5th Tennessee Infantry, undated, Civil War Collection, TSLA.

11. OR 1, 10 (1): 574, 578.

12. Ibid., 115, 423, 430, 465, 489, 592, 598, 600, 605–606; Reed, *Battle of Shiloh,* 81; Richardson, "War as I Saw It," 99; Kendall, "Recollections of a Confederate Officer," 1,061–1,062; Hughes, *Brigadier General Tyree H. Bell,* 39; E. S. Drake to sister, April 13, 1862, E. Steel Drake Papers, HCWRT, USAMHI; T. C. Robertson to mother, April 9, 1862, Thomas Chinn Robertson Papers, NC (copy in LSU).

13. OR 1, 10 (1): 255–256, 271, Reed, *Battle of Shiloh,* 56; Henry H. Wright, "An Iowa Soldier's Story of Shiloh," *National Tribune,* May 3, 1883; Byers, *Iowa in War Times,* 139; Worthington, *Report of the Flank March;* "Francis Markoe Cummins," undated, Francis M. Cummins Papers, AC, USAMHI; D. Shrait to John Rawlins, May 12, 1862, John A. McDowell Papers, AC, USAMHI; Wright, *History of the Sixth,* 78–80; Oliver Boardman to family, April 24, 1862, Oliver Boardman Correspondence and Journals, UI.

14. "Journal of the Orleans Guard," April 6, 1862, HNOC; Livaudais, *Shiloh Diary,* 28–29; OR 1, 10 (1): 626; J. L. Bieler to "President and Comrades," undated, 6th Indiana Battery File, SNMPRF.

15. OR 1, 10 (1): 517, 521, 527; Johnston, "Albert Sidney Johnston at Shiloh," 1:62; Hughes, *Pride of the Confederate Artillery,* 26.

16. OR 1, 10 (1): 250, 267, 447, 497; Bering and Montgomery, *History of the Forty-eighth,* 22; R. P. Buckland to L. G. Rawson, June 6, 1862, Rawson

Family Papers, RBHPC; Henry Buckland to parents, April 10, 1862, Henry Buckland Papers, RBHPC; J. L. Bieler to "President and Comrades," undated, 6th Indiana Battery File, SNMPRF.

17. OR 1, 10 (1): 408–409, 416.

18. Ibid., 115, 139–141, 144, 146–147, 249; Bouton, *Events of the Civil War,* 31; "Anti-dyspeptic," *National Tribune,* May 1, 1879; George Carrington Diary, April 6, 1862, CHS.

19. OR 1, 10 (1): 116, 133, 137, 568, 592, 597; Payson Shumway to wife, April 13, 1862, Payson Z. Shumway Papers, ALPL; Henry Hole to sister, April 22, 1862, Henry F. Hole Papers, ALPL; D. J. Benner to uncle, April 9, 1862, untitled article, *Warren Independent,* April 22, 1862, and undated obituary from *Warren Independent,* Luther Howard Cowan Papers, TSLA.

20. OR 1, 10 (1): 568, 592, 598, 601, 605–606, 608.

21. Ibid., 116, 409, 411, 423, 427, 432, 436, 605; T. C. Buck to sister, April 13, 1862, Stanford's Battery File, SNMPRF; T. M. Page to D. W. Reed, November 3, 1898, Series 1, Box 14, Folder 166, SNMPAF; George W. Jones Diary, April 5 and 6, 1862, Stanford's Battery File, SNMPRF; Stephenson, "First Thunder," 45; Murray, *New Yorkers in the Civil War,* 6:48–50; SNMP Tablet 319; John E. Magee Diary, April 5, 1862, DU.

22. OR 1, 10 (1): 124, 126–128, 132, 162, 578; SOR 1, 1:629; Daniel Harmon Brush Diary, April 6, 1862, ALPL; Thomas C. Watkins Diary, April 6, 1862, CWTI, USAMHI (copy in 18th Illinois File, SNMPRF).

23. OR 1, 10 (1): 130, 205, 220, 222–223, 226, 230; Daniel Clark to sister, May 1, 1862, Woods Family Papers, NL; Payson Shumway to wife, April 13, 1862, Payson Z. Shumway Papers, ALPL; Downing, *Downing's Civil War Diary,* 40; Camm, "Col. William Camm War Diary," 845; John L. Harris to parents, March 21, 1862, John L. Harris Correspondence, ALPL.

24. Taylor, "Reminiscences," 7; Abbott, "Negro in the War of the Rebellion," 3:382; *Report of the Proceedings of the Society of the Army of the Tennessee,* 53.

25. OR 1, 10 (1): 497; "Cobb's Battery Not Captured at Shiloh," 68; Daniel Parvin to wife, April 14, 1862, Daniel J. Parvin Letters, Muscatine Art Center.

26. OR 1, 10 (1): 116, 142, 270–271, 275, 417, 423, 430–431, 447–448, 513; OR 1, 52 (1): 23; George Carrington Diary, April 6, 1862, CHS.

27. Thomas McFadden to unknown, undated, 46th Ohio File, SNMPRF; George Carrington Diary, April 6, 1862, CHS.

28. OR 1, 10 (1): 147, 276; "The Battle at Pittsburgh," *Chicago Tribune,* April 17, 1862; untitled article, *Warren Independent,* April 22, 1862, Luther Howard Cowan Papers, TSLA; Timothy Blaisdell to unknown, April 12, 1862, CWTI, USAMHI.

29. Foster, *War Stories,* 63; Reed, *Battle of Shiloh,* 45; OR 1, 10 (1): 221, 231, 250; George Carrington Diary, April 6, 1862, CHS.

30. OR 1, 10 (1): 133, 137, 140, 228; Charles Peck to brother, April 12, 1862, Haerle Collection, USAMHI.

31. OR 1, 10 (1): 465.

32. Ibid., 117, 130, 134, 137, 228, 250, 256, 276, 432; Downing, *Downing's Civil War Diary,* 41; George Carrington Diary, April 6, 1862, CHS.

33. OR 1, 10 (1): 614–615; Davis, *Orphan Brigade,* 84; Thompson, *History of the Orphan Brigade,* 100; John C. Caldwell Diary, April 6, 1862, CWTI, USAMHI; Reed, *Battle of Shiloh,* 86; Johnston, *Life of Gen. Albert Sidney Johnston,* 604; W. E. Coleman to parents, May 5, 1862, Civil War Collection, TSLA.

34. OR 1, 10 (1): 615; A. H. Duncan Statement, undated, Series 1, box 13, Folder 131, SNMPAF; 6th Kentucky Report, April 14, 1862, Edwin Porter Thompson Papers, FHS; John C. Caldwell Diary, April 6, 1862, CWTI, USAMHI.

35. W. E. Coleman to parents, May 5, 1862, Civil War Collection, TSLA; OR 1, 10 (1): 252, 255–256, 417–419, 421, 615; O. H. Lowry to cousin, April 15, 1862, O. H. Lowry Papers, NC; John C. Caldwell Diary, April 6, 1862, CWTI, USAMHI; Hart, *History of the Fortieth,* 89; Wright, *History of the Sixth,* 84; Oliver Boardman to family, April 24, 1862, Oliver Boardman Correspondence and Journals, UI.

36. OR 1, 10 (1): 117, 134, 137–138, 227; Wright, *History of the Sixth,* 83.

37. OR 1, 10 (1): 124.

38. Ibid., 117, 130–131, 134, 140, 145, 228, 250.

39. Ibid., 288; J.S. to friend, April 17, 1862, Rombauer–Becker Family Papers, HUS; Day, "Fifteenth Iowa at Shiloh," 2:178; E. Bouton to Cornelius Cadle, June 10, 1895, Series 1, Box 12, Folder 107, SNMPAF (copy in Taylor's Battery File, SNMPRF). For numerous records of the 15th Iowa, see the Job Throckmorton Papers, SHSI.

40. OR 1, 10 (1): 286–289; Boyd, *Civil War Diary,* 28–29; Belknap, *History of the Fifteenth,* 188–191; Francis M. Harmon to brother, April 11, 1862, 15th Iowa File, SNMPRF; William Nicholls to friend, April 18, 1862, 15th Iowa File, SNMPRF. For the controversy over when and where the regiments went into action, see the 15th and 16th Iowa Controversy Files, Series 1, Box 15, Folders 409–411, SNMPAF.

41. Edward H. Reynolds Diary, April 6, 1862, CWTI, USAMHI; OR 1, 10 (1): 117, 130–131, 134, 140, 145, 228, 250, 582, 616; Grant, "Battle of Shiloh," 1:473; Connelly, *History of the Seventieth,* 23; Thompson, *History of the Orphan Brigade,* 102.

42. OR 1, 10 (1): 124, 127, 132, 423, 428; Wright, *History of the Sixth,* 87.

CHAPTER 10: "I SHALL HAVE TO PUT THE BAYONET TO THEM"

1. OR 1, 10 (1): 203.

2. Thompson, *Recollections,* 206, 210; Rerick, *Forty-fourth Indiana Volunteer Infantry,* 45; F. Y. Hedley, *Marching through Georgia,* 46–47.

3. OR 1, 10 (1): 203, 208, 211, 214, 217, 219, 243; OR 1, 52 (1): 24; Hobart, *Truth about Shiloh,* 102; Jesse Connelley Diary, April 9, 1862, ISL; Connelly, "Hoosier at Shiloh," 80; Felix H. Robertson to D. W. Reed, August 1, 1909, Robertson's Battery File, SNMPRF; Olney, *Shiloh as Seen by a Private Soldier,* 15; Skaptason, "Chicago Light Artillery," 80; L. W. Mills to editor, April 12, 1862, 2nd Michigan Battery File, SNMPRF; George A. Reaves, "A Report to Determine the Size and Condition of the Peach Orchard at the Intersection of the Sunken Road and Pittsburg Landing Road on April 6, 1862," undated, SNMPVF.

4. OR 1, 10 (1): 203, 206, 207–211, 214, 217, 234, 243–244; McEathron, *Letters and Memoirs,* 5; Isaac Pugh to wife, March 22, 1862, Isaac C. Pugh Papers, University of California, Riverside (copy in 41st Illinois File, SNMPRF).

5. OR 1, 10 (1): 203, 206, 207–211, 214, 217, 234, 243–244; Clinton to Eason Johnson, April 25, 1862, 41st Illinois File, SNMPRF.

6. OR 1, 10 (1): 203, 208–211, 245; SOR 1, 1:639–641; Felix H. Robertson to D. W. Reed, August 1, 1909, Robertson's Battery File, SNMPRF; S. H. Dent to wife, April 9, 1862, and Felix H. Robertson to S. H. Dent, April 25, 1909, both in Stouton Hubert Dent Papers, ADAH; L. W. Mills to editor, April 12, 1862, 2nd Michigan Battery File, SNMPRF; "The Battle of Pittsburg as Seen by One of the Third Iowa," *Missouri Daily Democrat,* April 24, 1862 (copy in 3rd Iowa File, SNMPRF). For the 28th Illinois, see also Howard, *Illustrated Comprehensive History.*

7. OR 1, 10 (1): 155; Cockerill, "Boy at Shiloh," 6:19; Cunningham, *Shiloh and the Western Campaign,* 214; Charles Cowell Diary, April 6, 1862, Charles Cowell Papers, USAMHI; Morrison, *History of the Ninth,* 29; Wardner, "Reminiscences of a Surgeon," 3:184.

8. OR 1, 10 (1): 161; Reed, *Battle of Shiloh,* 15; Isaac Yantis, "The 41st Ill. at Shiloh," *National Tribune,* August 22, 1907; James Oates, "The Ninth Illinois at Shiloh," *National Tribune,* May 10, 1883; Hubert, *History of the Fiftieth Regiment Illinois,* 90.

9. OR 1, 10 (1): 259; Stephen A. Hurlbut, "Pittsburg Landing and Shiloh," undated, WS, 17; Thompson, *Recollections,* 215–216; Olney, *Shiloh as Seen by a Private Soldier,* 17.

10. OR 1, 10 (1): 259, 261; SOR 1, 1:641.

11. OR 1, 10 (1): 533, 549–550.

12. Ibid., 261, 554, 558, 561; Thompson and Thompson, *Seventeenth Alabama Infantry,* 48; John R. Woodward to Ellen, April 13, 1862, 71st Ohio File, SNMPRF; W. H. McClure, "The 71st Ohio at Shiloh," *National Tribune,* June 6, 1907.

13. OR 1, 10 (1): 259.

14. Ibid., 259, 261; John R. Woodward to Ellen, April 13, 1862, 71st Ohio File, SNMPRF; *Story of the Fifty-fifth,* 110, 125; Smith, *Life and Letters,* 193–196.

15. OR 1, 10 (1): 155, 533.

16. Ibid., 550, 553, 555, 558; J. F. Gaines to editor, April 9, 1862, Shiloh Subject File, ADAH.

17. OR 1, 10 (1): 550.

18. Ibid., 203, 621; Wynne, *Hard Trip,* 76–77; L. W. Mills to editor, April 12, 1862, 2nd Michigan Battery File, SNMPRF; Jordan, "Notes of a Confederate Staff-Officer," 1:601; Augustus Hervey Mecklin Diary, April 6, 1862, MDAH; Worsham, *Old Nineteenth,* 39; Eugene F. Falconnet Diary, April 6, 1862, Eugene Frederic Falconnet Papers, TSLA; McMurray, *History of the Twentieth,* 125; Presley Judson Edwards Autobiography, 1898, CHS; John W. Taylor to parents, April 11, 1862, Clyde Hughes Collection, UNC.

19. Thompson, *Recollections,* 219; Stephen A. Hurlbut, "Pittsburg Landing and Shiloh," undated, WS, 16; George Crosley to Edna, April 10, 1862, George Crosley Papers, CWD, USAMHI.

20. Binford, "Recollections of the Fifteenth Regiment of Mississippi Infantry, CSA," MDAH, 27.

21. OR 1, 10 (1): 610; Stephen A. Hurlbut, "Pittsburg Landing and Shiloh," undated, WS, 17; Fred True to sister, April 10, 1862, 41st Illinois File, SNMPRF; E. S. Drake to sister, April 13, 1862, E. Steel Drake papers, HCWRT, USAMHI.

22. OR 1, 10 (1): 204, 212, 215, 218, 233, 235, 238–239, 245, 610; McMurray, *History of the Twentieth,* 126; "The Battle of Pittsburg as Seen by One of the Third Iowa," *Missouri Daily Democrat,* April 24, 1862; Jacob Lauman to son, March 26, 1862, Jacob Lauman Papers, CHS; William F. Hinkle Diary, undated, IHS; Samuel Kennedy Cox Diary, April 6, 1862, 17th Kentucky File, SNMPRF; Stillwell, *Personal Recollections,* 14; Rerick, *Forty-fourth Indiana Volunteer Infantry,* 53; Clinton to Eason Johnson, April 25, 1862, 41st Illinois File, SNMPRF; Fred True to sister, April 10, 1862, 41st Illinois File, SNMPRF; Richardson, "War as I Saw It," 102.

23. D. J. Benner to uncle, April 9, 1862, Luther Howard Cowan Papers, TSLA; Stephen A. Hurlbut, "Pittsburg Landing and Shiloh," undated, WS, 17; Richard Gapen to sister, April 17, 1862, Richard Gapen Papers, CHS.

24. Beauregard, "Campaign of Shiloh," 1:588; Roman, *Military Operations of General Beauregard,* 1:340; Woodworth, *Shiloh,* 144.

25. OR 1, 10 (1): 404; Johnston, *Life of Gen. Albert Sidney Johnston,* 608, 611.

26. OR 1, 10 (1): 621, 624; Johnston, *Life of Gen. Albert Sidney Johnston,* 611–613; McMurray, *History of the Twentieth,* 126; "More 'Shiloh' Alleged

History," *New Orleans Daily City Item,* May 1887 (copy in Samuel W. Richey Confederate Collection, MIAU).

27. OR 1, 10 (1): 621, 624; Dudley Hayden Diary, *Richmond Dispatch,* May 3, 1862, WS; Johnston, *Life of Gen. Albert Sidney Johnston,* 611–613; Pippen, "Concerning Battle of Shiloh"; Alfred Cox Smith to mother, April 10, 1862, Alfred Cox Smith Collection, MDAH.

28. Johnston, *Life of Gen. Albert Sidney Johnston,* 611–613; OR 1, 10 (1): 546, 610, 621, 624; Cochran, "Vivid Story," 66; Wills, *Confederacy's Greatest Cavalryman,* 68; McMurray, *History of the Twentieth,* 126; Braxton Bragg to wife, April 9, 1862, Braxton Bragg Papers, MHS.

29. OR 1, 10 (1): 155–158, 212, 215, 554; Morrison, *History of the Ninth,* 30; Cockerill, "Boy at Shiloh," 22.

30. Hubert, *History of the Fiftieth Regiment Illinois,* 91–92, 96, 101; Mason, "Shiloh," 1:99; Thompson and Thompson, *Seventeenth Alabama Infantry,* 47; unknown to editors, April 11, 1862, Shiloh Subject File, ADAH; Surgeon Statement, April 13, 1862, John McArthur Papers, NARA.

31. Kimbell, *History of Battery "A,"* 43; Enoch Colby to father, April 14, 1862, Francelia Colby Reminiscences, CHS.

32. OR 1, 10 (1): 206, 212, 215, 247; Hedley, *Marching through Georgia,* 49; Van Winkle, "Incidents and Inquiries."

33. OR 1, 10 (1): 439, 453–454; Fowler, *Mountaineers in Gray,* 64–65.

34. OR 1, 10 (1): 442, 455, 622; Worsham, *Old Nineteenth,* 41, 45.

35. OR 1, 10 (1): 387; Rufus B. Parkes Diary, April 6, 1862, Civil War Collection, TSLA; Bradford Nichol Memoir, April 6, 1862, TSLA; Augustus Hervey Mecklin Diary, April 6, 1862, MDAH.

36. Pippen, "Concerning Battle of Shiloh," 344; Johnston, *Life of Gen. Albert Sidney Johnston,* 613–614, 718; OR 1, 10 (1): 439; Johnston, "Albert Sidney Johnston at Shiloh," 1:564.

37. Binford, "Recollections of the Fifteenth Regiment of Mississippi Infantry, CSA," MDAH, 27; Daniel, *Cannoneers in Gray,* 36; Alfred Hudson Compiled Service Record, NARA; Smith, "Secession at Shiloh."

38. Isham G. Harris to William Preston, April 6, 1862, 1, 13, 140, SNMPRF; Johnston, *Life of Gen. Albert Sidney Johnston,* 614.

39. Johnston, *Life of Gen. Albert Sidney Johnston,* 614; Isham G. Harris to William Preston, April 6, 1862, 1, 13, 140, SNMPRF.

40. Johnston, *Life of Gen. Albert Sidney Johnston,* 614–615; William Preston Diary, April 6, 1862, NARA (copy in SNMPRF); Isham G. Harris to William Preston, April 6, 1862, 1, 13, 140, SNMPRF; OR 1, 10 (1): 404.

41. Johnston, *Life of Gen. Albert Sidney Johnston,* 614–615; William Preston Diary, April 6, 1862, SNMPRF; Baylor, "With Gen. A. S. Johnston at Shiloh," 611; Sehlinger, *Kentucky's Last Cavalier,* 136–137; Lee Wickham Statement, undated, Albert Sidney Johnston Papers, TU; Isham G. Harris Statement,

March 8, 1878, Albert Sidney Johnston Papers, TU; Isham G. Harris to William Preston, April 6, 1862, 1, 13, 140, SNMPRF.

42. OR 1, 10 (1): 465, 469–470, 569; Reed, *Battle of Shiloh,* 18; Grant, "Battle of Shiloh," 1:473; Sherman, *Memoirs,* 1:247; Johnston, "Albert Sidney Johnston at Shiloh," 565; Beauregard, "Campaign of Shiloh," 589; Chisolm, "Shiloh Battle-Order," 1:606; Jordan, "Notes of a Confederate Staff-Officer," 601; Roman, *Military Operations of General Beauregard,* 1:551; McDonough, *Shiloh,* 154.

43. Johnston, *Life of Gen. Albert Sidney Johnston,* 566, 569; "The Battle of Shiloh: The First Day's Fight," *Southern Watchman,* April 23, 1862.

44. Grant, "Battle of Shiloh," 483; William R. Stimson to family, April 10, 1862, William R. Stimson Papers, LC; OR 1, 10 (1): 167, 204, 234–235, 533, 537–538, 544–545; OR 1, 52 (1): 24; Thompson, *Recollections,* 223; Skaptason, "Chicago Light Artillery," 90; Rerick, *Forty-fourth Indiana Volunteer Infantry,* 53; J. W. Powell to Cornelius Cadle, May 15, 1896, Powell's Battery File, SNMPRF.

45. OR 1, 10 (1): 204, 234–236, 238, 241, 550; Cluett, *History of the 57th,* 19; Civil War Diary, April 6–7, 1862, VCPL; David W. Stratton Diary, April 6–7, 1862, VCPL (copy in 31st Indiana File, STRI); 44th Indiana Regiment Association Records, 1861–1938, IHS; Leonard H. Mahan Diary, April 6, 1862, ISL.

46. J. W. Powell to Cornelius Cadle, May 15, 1896, Powell's Battery File, SNMPRF; Reed, *Battle of Shiloh,* 61; Dolnick, *Down the Great Unknown;* Connelly, "Hoosier at Shiloh," 80; OR 1, 10 (1): 168, 204, 212–213, 219; Hobart, *Semi-history,* 8; Kimbell, *History of Battery "A,"* 43; Cluett, *History of the 57th,* 20; Skaptason, "Chicago Light Artillery," 91; Stephen A. Hurlbut, "Pittsburg Landing and Shiloh," undated, WS, 19; Clinton to Eason Johnson, April 25, 1862, 41st Illinois File, SNMPRF; OR 1, 52 (1): 24; Saul Howell Diary, April 6, 1862, SHSI; D. J. Benner to uncle, April 9, 1862, Luther Howard Cowan Papers, TSLA; "Iowa Infantry 3rd Regiment losses at Shiloh," undated, Civil War Collection, UI.

CHAPTER 11: "AT ALL HAZARDS"

1. Wallace, *Life and Letters,* 192.
2. T. W. Holman, "The Story of Shiloh," *National Tribune,* September 14, 1899.
3. OR 1, 10 (1): 150; SOR 1, 1:635; W. M. Sweeny, "Man of Resource," *National Tribune,* September 5, 1895; De Hass, "Battle of Shiloh," 686; Reed, *Battle of Shiloh,* 48; Thomas, *Soldier Life,* 41; Edwin A. Bowen to D. W. Reed, undated, 52nd Illinois File, SNMPRF; James H. Guthrie Diary, April 6,

1862, SHSI; *Eighth Reunion of the 12th Iowa Vet. Vol. Infantry,* 55; Sumbardo, *Glimpses of the Nation's Struggle,* 32–34.

4. George to wife, April 9, 1862, 58th Illinois File, SNMPRF; Jonathan B. LaBrant Diary, April 6, 1862, CWD, USAMHI; Elsie Caroline Duncan Hurt Diary, undated, MSCPL, 37; Thomas, *Soldier Life,* 42; OR 1, 10 (1): 150, 153, 164; SOR 1, 1:635, 638; Byers, *Iowa in War Times,* 129; Reed, *Battle of Shiloh,* 61; J. W. Powell to Cornelius Cadle, May 15, 1896, Series 1, Box 14, Folder 169, SNMPAF (copy in Powell's Battery File, SNMPRF); William K. Kay, "The Sunken Road: A Study," January 1957, Sunken Road, SNMPVF. Sweeny's original report is in the Thomas W. Sweeny Papers, HL.

5. Thomas, *Soldier Life,* 42; J. W. Cotes, "The Iowa Brigade on Shiloh's Field," *National Tribune,* December 28, 1893. Charles A. Van Riper Diary, April 6, 1862, UMB; Joseph Harper to wife, April 9, 1862, John W. Gillette Collection, UMB.

6. OR 1, 10 (1): 151, 153, 166–167, 278, 281–282, 284, 291; Oliver Newberry to mother, April 13, 1862, Oliver Perry Newberry Papers, NL; Charles McKay to sister, March 15, 1862, Charles McKay Papers, CWTI, USAMHI; *Report of the Proceedings of the Society of the Army of the Tennessee,* 64; Seth Crowhearst, "Reminiscences of a Union Soldier," undated, Seth Crowhearst Papers, CWD, USAMHI; Peter Bagley Diary, April 6, 1862, 23rd Missouri File, SNMPRF; Ray H. Mattison, "The Vegetative Cover of the Hornet's Nest Area During the Battle of Shiloh," SNMPVF; Morton, "Boy at Shiloh," 63; E. W. Herman Diary, April 6, 1862, 7th Iowa File, SNMPRF; James B. Weaver to wife, April 9, 1862, James Baird Weaver Papers, UI.

7. Wallace, *Life and Letters,* 20.

8. Reed, *Battle of Shiloh,* 70.

9. OR 1, 10 (1): 438, 453, 574; Reed, *Battle of Shiloh,* 16.

10. OR 1, 10 (1): 453; "A Complete List of Absentees from the 6th Tennessee Regiment," undated, 6th Tennessee File, TSLA.

11. Henry George, "Seventh Kentucky at Shiloh," 7th Kentucky File, SNMPRF; Reed, *Battle of Shiloh,* 84–85; OR 151, 280, 438, 453; Losson, *Tennessee's Forgotten Warriors,* 47. For the claims of a second Stephens assault, see SNMP Tablet 337 and W. J. Stubblefield Diary, April 6, 1862, MU, 4.

12. OR 1, 10 (1): 178, 279, 438–439; Grant, "Battle of Shiloh," 1:473; Buell, "Shiloh Reviewed," 1:536; Sherman, *Memoirs,* 1:245; Thomas McFadden to unknown, undated, 46th Ohio File, SNMPRF; E. W. Herman Diary, April 6, 1862, 7th Iowa File, SNMPRF; Moses McCoid to Helen, April 11, 1862, Moses A. McCoid Papers, HL.

13. OR 1, 10 (1): 574.

14. Ibid., 391, 428, 574; Reed, *Battle of Shiloh,* 17, 49; D. C. Govan to Shiloh Park Commission, April 4, 1900, Series 1, Box 13, Folder 139, SNMPAF

(copy in 2nd Arkansas File, SNMPRF); Robert D. Smith Diary, April 6, 1862, 2nd Tennessee File, SNMPRF.

15. OR 1, 10 (1): 428, 574, 576.

16. Ibid., 389, 466, 574; Porter, "Gen. Braxton Bragg at Shiloh," 45, 70, 73; Braxton Bragg to wife, April 9, 1862, Braxton Bragg Papers, MHS.

17. "An Incident of the Battle of Shiloh," undated, Shiloh Subject File, ADAH; David Urquhart to Thomas Jordan, August 25, 1880, David Urquhart Letter Book, UNC.

18. OR 1, 10 (1): 466; Reed, *Battle of Shiloh,* 76; Richardson, "War as I Saw It," 100.

19. OR 1, 10 (1): 153, 165–166, 278; Johnston, *Life of Gen. Albert Sidney Johnston,* 605; John Elwell to family, May 22, 1862, Folsom Collection, University of Colorado at Boulder; James H. Guthrie Diary, April 6, 1862, SHSI; "Funeral of Gen. J. L. Geddes," *Vinton Eagle,* February 25, 1887.

20. OR 1, 10 (1): 151, 153, 480, 488, 491–492; Ray H. Mattison, "The Vegetative Cover of the Hornet's Nest Area during the Battle of Shiloh," SNMPVF; Donald F. Dosch, "The Hornet's Nest at Shiloh," SNMPVF; Dosch, "Hornet's Nest at Shiloh"; Smith, *Battle of Shiloh*, 27–40; Reed, *Battle of Shiloh,* 77; Richardson, "War as I Saw It," 100; McGrath, "In a Louisianan Regiment," 114; Johnston, *Life of Gen. Albert Sidney Johnston,* 604; T. C. Robertson to mother, April 9, 1862, Thomas Chinn Robertson Papers, NC.

21. OR 1, 10 (1): 151, 153, 166, 480, 483, 488, 491–493; Richardson, "War as I Saw It," 101; Byers, *Iowa in War Times,* 131; Kendall, "Recollections of a Confederate Officer," 1,064; G. W. Baylor to Daniel Ruggles, April 2, 1862, WS.

22. OR 1, 10 (1): 151, 153, 466, 480, 484, 487–489, 491–493; Giles B. Cooke Report, undated, Giles B. Cooke Papers, VHS; McBride and McLaurin, *Randall Lee Gibson,* 77; Bevens, *Reminiscences,* 69–71; Alex Morgan to Fanny, April 13, 1862, Alexander Morgan Letters, Baylor University; T. C. Robertson to mother, April 9, 1862, Thomas Chinn Robertson Papers, NC; Miles G. Turrentine to Bettie Waite, April 14, 1862, WS.

23. Kendall, "Recollections of a Confederate Officer," 1066; Braxton Bragg to wife, April 9, 1862, Braxton Bragg Papers, MHS.

24. OR 1, 10 (1): 482–483; Lockett, "Surprise and Withdrawal," 1:605; Richardson, "War as I Saw It," 100; Kendall, "Recollections of a Confederate Officer," 1,065.

25. Giles B. Cooke Report, undated, Giles B. Cooke Papers, VHS; Reed, *Battle of Shiloh,* 70; OR 1, 10 (1): 486; Richardson, "War as I Saw It," 102; Braxton Bragg to wife, April 9, 1862, Braxton Bragg Papers, MHS; T. C. Robertson to mother, April 9, 1862, Thomas Chinn Robertson Papers, NC.

26. OR 1, 10 (1): 149, 574–576, 578–579; William T. Shaw to D. W. Reed, April 6, 1896, Series 1, Box 14, Folder 180, SNMPAF (copy in 14th Iowa File, SNMPRF); Thomas, *Soldier Life,* 42.

27. Sandidge, "Battle of Shiloh," 176; OR 1, 10 (1): 162–164, 428, 472, 497–498, 523; Reed, *Battle of Shiloh,* 18; unknown to Jose, April 9, 1862, Henry D. Mandeville and Family Papers, LSU.

28. OR 1, 10 (1): 162–164, 428, 498; Ambrose, *History of the Seventh,* 50–51; Thomas Stuart Birch Diary, April 6, 1862, EU; Reed, *Battle of Shiloh,* 18; George to wife, April 9, 1862, 58th Illinois File, SNMPRF.

29. OR 1, 10 (1): 466, 597.

30. Ibid., 477; Sandidge, "Battle of Shiloh," 176; Smith Bankhead to R. M. Howe, December 16, 1862, Bankhead Battery File, SNMPRF; Shoup, "How We Went to Shiloh," 139; Daniel, *Cannoneers in Gray,* 29–30. David W. Reed first tabulated the number of guns as sixty-two, although he probably did not take into account earlier attrition in some batteries. Reed, *Battle of Shiloh,* 18; S. H. Dent to wife, April 9, 1862, Stouton Hubert Dent Papers, ADAH.

31. Reed, *Battle of Shiloh,* 18–19, 50, 76; OR 1, 10 (1): 149, 475, 477, 483, 498; Morton, "Boy at Shiloh," 64.

32. Thomas, *Soldier Life,* 42.

33. Reed, *Battle of Shiloh,* 18–19, 50; OR 1, 10 (1): 149, 291, 538–540, 622; SOR 1, 1:662; H. W. H. to parents, April 10, 1862, Shiloh Subject File, ADAH; Dawson, "One Year at War," 192; T. B. Anderson, "Boy's Impression at Shiloh," 72; "The Battle of Shiloh: The First Day's Fight," *Southern Watchman,* April 23, 1862; James Cooper to Farley, April 22, 1862, James Cooper Papers, NC.

34. Lockett, "Surprise and Withdrawal," 605.

35. OR 1, 10 (1): 154, 166, 281, 286, 291, 622; SOR 1, 1:636; Thompson, *Recollections,* 226.

36. OR 1, 10 (1): 162–164; SOR 1, 1:636, 638; Wallace, *Life and Letters,* 193, 214; Thomas Stuart Birch Diary, April 6, 1862, EU; George Sawin to wife, March 23 and April 9, 1862, George Sawin Letters, CHS.

37. OR 1, 10 (1): 149–152, 166–167, 179; Thomas, *Soldier Life,* 43; *Report of the Proceedings of the Society of the Army of the Tennessee,* 68; E. W. Herman Diary, April 6, 1862, 7th Iowa File, SNMPRF; James H. Guthrie Diary, April 6, 1862, SHSI; Hickenlooper, "Battle of Shiloh—Part I," 5:422; Sumbardo, *Glimpses of the Nation's Struggle,* 36–37; Matson, *Life Experiences,* 80; John Elwell to family, May 22, 1862, Folsom Collection, University of Colorado at Boulder.

38. Wallace, *Life and Letters,* 196, 198, 213, 216; I. P. Rumsey Memoir, undated, I. P. Rumsey File, SNMPRF, 11; T. Lyle Dickey to Ann, May 17, 1862, 4th Illinois Cavalry File, SNMPRF.

39. Unknown to editors, April 11, 1862, Shiloh Subject File, ADAH.

40. I. P. Rumsey Memoir, undated, I. P. Rumsey File, SNMPRF, 12; OR 1, 10 (1): 472, 498, 550, 558, 562, 577, 616; Houston, "Shiloh Shadows," 331; Dawson, "One Year at War," 193; SOR 1, 1:662; Reed, *Battle of Shiloh,* 74.

41. *Report of the Proceedings of the Society of the Army of the Tennessee,* 69; "The Life of Elias Perry," undated, Civil War Collection, MHS; Madison Miller Diary, April 6, 1862, Madison Miller Papers, MHS; Searle, "Personal Reminiscences," 1:334–335.

42. OR 1, 10 (1): 154, 279, 409, 418, 478, 523, 533, 550, 555, 592, 597, 603, 616; John D. Thomas Diary, April 1862, UM; unknown to Jose, April 9, 1862, Henry D. Mandeville and Family Papers, LSU; Cunningham, *Shiloh and the Western Campaign,* 303; Reed, *Battle of Shiloh,* 74; "Reminiscences of Shiloh," *National Tribune,* January 28, 1882.

43. OR 1, 10 (1): 410, 439, 459–461; Arndt, "Reminiscences of an Artillery Officer," 1:4–5; W. W. Worthington to parents, April 10, 1862, L. P. Wulff Collection, UT.

CHAPTER 12: "THEY CAN NEVER CARRY THIS LINE IN THE WORLD"

1. P. G. T. Beauregard to Isham G. Harris, March 9, 1880, Pierre Gustave Toutant Beauregard Papers, DU; Johnston, *Life of Gen. Albert Sidney Johnston,* 614–615, 699; Terry, "Record of the Alabama State Artillery," 316; John D. Thomas Diary, April 1862, UM; OR 1, 10 (1): 387, 402, 523; Reed, *Battle of Shiloh,* 67; Roman, *Military Operations of General Beauregard,* 1:297, 350, 537; Isham G. Harris to P. G. T. Beauregard, May 27, 1876, Samuel Richey Confederate Collection, MIAU; Beauregard, "Campaign of Shiloh," 1:590.

2. Johnston, *Life of Gen. Albert Sidney Johnston,* 614–615, 699; OR 1, 10 (1): 404–405, 409; William Preston Diary, April 6, 1862, NARA; Preston, "At the Moment of Victory," 334–335.

3. Roman, *Military Operations of General Beauregard,* 1:525, 531; Sullins, "Heroic Deed"; Cunningham, "Reminiscence of Shiloh."

4. Connelly, *Army of the Heartland,* 167.

5. Shaw, "Battle of Shiloh," 1:183; OR 1, 10 (1): 279; *Third Reunion of the 12th,* 20.

6. Jacob Lauman to son, April 13, 1862, Jacob Lauman Papers, CHS; Samuel Kennedy Cox Diary, April 7, 1862, 17th Kentucky File, SNMPRF; F. Y. Hedley, *Marching through Georgia,* 49; Henry Halleck to Edwin Stanton, April 13, 1862, William T. Sherman Papers, LC; *Complete History of the 46th Illinois Veteran Volunteer Infantry,* 46; Edwin A. Bowen to D. W. Reed, undated, 52nd Illinois File, SNMPRF; OR 1, 10 (1): 118; Buell, "Shiloh Reviewed," 1:511, 536; Erasmus D. Ward to sister, April 12, 1862, Erasmus D. Ward Letters, ALPL.

7. Grant, "Battle of Shiloh," 1:473–474, 481.

8. OR 1, 10 (1): 110.

9. Ibid., 109; "From Pittsburg," *Chicago Times,* April 29, 1862; Camm,

"Col. William Camm War Diary," 853; Reed, *Battle of Shiloh,* 19, 61. At least one Iowan also mentioned mortars. See Gustavus H. Cushman to brother, April 13, 1862, Gustavus Cushman Letters, SHSI (copy in 3rd Iowa File, SNMPRF).

10. OR 1, 10 (1): 131, 265, 274–275; Cunningham, *Shiloh and the Western Campaign,* 306; OR 1, 52 (1): 24–26; Reed, *Battle of Shiloh,* 21, 61; Downing, *Downing's Civil War Diary,* 42.

11. OR 1, 52 (1): 24; Hubbard, "Minnesota in the Battle of Corinth," 483.

12. W. H. McClure, "The 71st Ohio at Shiloh," *National Tribune,* June 6, 1907; Richardson, *Personal History of Ulysses S. Grant,* 251.

13. Smith, *Timberclads,* 299–301.

14. *Report of the Proceedings of the Society of the Army of the Tennessee,* 55; Buell, "Shiloh Reviewed," 511, 521; Thomas C. Watkins Diary, April 6, 1862, 18th Illinois File, SNMPRF; Thomas Stuart Birch Diary, April 6, 1862, EU; Bouton, *Events of the Civil War,* 21; Edwin A. Bowen to D. W. Reed, undated, 52nd Illinois File, SNMPRF; OR 1, 10 (1): 158, 204, 250, 263, 267; D. J. Benner to uncle, April 9, 1862, Luther Howard Cowan Papers, TSLA; Clinton to Eason Johnson, April 25, 1862, 41st Illinois File, SNMPRF; Richard Gapen to sister, April 17, 1862, Richard Gapen Papers, CHS; Stephen A. Hurlbut, "Pittsburg Landing and Shiloh," undated, WS, 20; Hubert, *History of the Fiftieth Regiment Illinois,* 93; "The Battle of Pittsburg as Seen by One of the Third Iowa," *Missouri Daily Democrat,* April 24, 1862.

15. OR 1, 10 (1): 439–440, 466, 616; Lockett, "Surprise and Withdrawal," 1:605; Robert H. Wood to father, April 14, 1862, Bills Family Papers, TSLA.

16. Edwin A. Bowen to D. W. Reed, undated, Edwin A. Bowen Papers, HL (copy in 52nd Illinois File, SNMPRF); OR 1, 10 (1): 118, 132, 161, 461–462, 569, 626; Swaddling, *Historical Memoranda,* 4–5; George Carrington Diary, April 6, 1862, CHS; Alphonso Barto to sister and friends, April 27, 1862, Alphonso Barto Letters, ALPL; Rood, *History of Company "A,"* 29; Reed, *Battle of Shiloh,* 50; Beauregard, "Campaign of Shiloh," 588; A. R. Chisolm Report, April 14, 1862, SNMPRF; Henry P. Andrews to wife, April 12, 1862, Henry P. Andrews Papers, ALPL.

17. OR 1, 10 (1): 118, 132.

18. Ibid., 517; Livaudais, *Shiloh Diary,* 30; L. M. Pipkin to "Sir," March 17, 1909, Series 1, Box 14, Folder 168, SNMPAF (copy in 18th Louisiana File, SNMPRF).

19. OR 1, 10 (1): 118, 221; Camm, "Col. William Camm War Diary," 849; SOR 1, 1:636; Edwin A. Bowen to D. W. Reed, undated, 52nd Illinois File, SNMPRF; Alphonso Barto to sister and friends, April 27, 1862, Alphonso Barto Letters, ALPL; Edwin A. Bowen Diary, April 6, 1862, Edwin A. Bowen Papers, HL.

20. Camm, "Col. William Camm War Diary," 849; OR 1, 10 (1): 118, 129, 161–162, 517, 521; SOR 1, 1:637; "Journal Belongs to Hugh T. Carlisle of

Fremont Sandusky County Ohio," undated, Hugh T. Carlisle Papers, CWD, USAMHI, 65; "Random War Reminiscences of Hugh T. Carlisle," undated, Hugh T. Carlisle Papers, CWD, USAMHI, 54; Chamberlain, *History of the Eighty-first,* 17–18; Wright, *Corporal's Story,* 35; Edwin A. Bowen to D. W. Reed, undated, 52nd Illinois File, SNMPRF; Alphonso Barto to sister and friends, April 27, 1862, Alphonso Barto Letters, ALPL. Mouton's original report is in Clinton Haskell Civil War Collection, UMCL.

21. OR 1, 10 (1): 517–518, 520; Livaudais, *Shiloh Diary,* 31; Aymond, "History of the 16th Louisiana Infantry Regiment"; "Journal of the Orleans Guard," April 6, 1862, HNOC.

22. Alfred Roman Memoir, August 20, 1878, Alfred Roman Memoirs, University of Louisiana, Lafayette.

23. OR 1, 10 (1): 118–119, 124–125, 142, 149, 221, 224, 227; SOR 1, 1:637; Camm, "Col. William Camm War Diary," 849–851; Reed, *Battle of Shiloh,* 18; Edwin A. Bowen to D. W. Reed, undated, 52nd Illinois File, SNMPRF.

24. OR 1, 10 (1): 246–247, 499; Robert A. Smith Report, April 9, 1862, Robert A. Smith Papers, MDAH; Reed, *Battle of Shiloh,* 19, 87; Grant, "Battle of Shiloh," 1:475; McMurray, *History of the Twentieth,* 127.

25. OR 1, 10 (1): 534, 555, 562; Reed, *Battle of Shiloh,* 19; H. W. H. to parents, April 10, 1862, Shiloh Subject File, ADAH.

26. OR 1, 10 (1): 147, 205, 552, 562; T. Lyle Dickey to Ann, May 17, 1862, 4th Illinois Cavalry File, SNMPRF; Eugene F. Falconnet Diary, April 6, 1862, Eugene Frederic Falconnet Papers, TSLA; James H. Kerr to father, April 12, 1862, James H. Kerr Papers, NC; Ephraim Dawes to Kate, April 13, 1862, Ephraim C. Dawes Papers, NL; D. J. Benner to uncle, April 9, 1862, Luther Howard Cowan Papers, TSLA.

27. OR 1, 10 (1): 551; SOR 1, 1:653; Terry, "Record of the Alabama State Artillery," 318; Robert A. Smith Report, April 9, 1862, Robert A. Smith Papers, MDAH; Charles P. Gage to James R. Chalmers, April 16, 1862, James R. Chalmers Papers, NARA; Reed, *Battle of Shiloh,* 75; John E. Magee Diary, April 5, 1862, DU; L. D. G. to parents, April 8, 1862, Gage's Battery File, SNMPRF; Camm, "Col. William Camm War Diary," 852.

28. OR 1, 10 (1): 134, 410, 550–551; William Burge, "Through the Civil War and Western Adventures," undated, William Burge Papers, CWD, USAMHI, 2.

29. OR 1, 10 (1): 386–387, 534, 555, 616–617; Force, *From Fort Henry to Corinth,* 156–157; Beauregard, "Campaign of Shiloh," 591; Roman, *Military Operations of General Beauregard,* 1:529; Smith, *Reminiscences of the Civil War,* 3; Johnston, *Life of Gen. Albert Sidney Johnston,* 629; Clifton Smith to P. G. T. Beauregard, August 5, 1880, Clifton H. Smith Papers, CHS; J. R. Chalmers to D. W. Reed, April 3, 1895, Series 1, Box 13, Folder 117, SNMPAF.

30. George W. Jones Diary, April 6, 1862, Stanford's Battery File, SNMPRF; OR 1, 10 (1): 410, 467; Johnston, "Albert Sidney Johnston at Shiloh," 565,

568; Chisolm, "Shiloh Battle-Order," 1:606; Lockett, "Surprise and With-drawal," 605; Roman, *Military Operations of General Beauregard*, 1:535–536, 551; "The Battle of Shiloh: The Second Day's Fight," *Southern Watchman*, April 30, 1862 (copy in E. Merton Coulter Collection, University of Geor-gia); Randall, "General W. H. C. Whiting," 277; David Urquhart to Thomas Jordan, August 25, 1880, David Urquhart Letter Book, UNC; Burress, "Who Lost Shiloh to the Confederacy?"; Le Monnier, "Who Lost Shiloh to the Con-federacy" (1913); Le Monnier, "Who Lost Shiloh to the Confederacy" (1914); Spenser B. Talley Memoir, 1918, TSLA, 9; P. G. T. Beauregard to William Preston Johnston, March 9, 1877, P. G. T. Beauregard Papers, MDAH; Eugene F. Falconnet Diary, April 6, 1862, Eugene Frederic Falconnet Papers, TSLA; Clifton Smith to P. G. T. Beauregard, August 5, 1880, Clifton H. Smith Papers, CHS; Braxton Bragg to wife, April 9, 1862, Braxton Bragg Papers, MHS. See also McWhiney, "General Beauregard's 'Complete Victory.'"

31. McWhiney, *Braxton Bragg*, 1:244; George W. Jones Diary, April 6, 1862, Stanford's Battery File, SNMPRF; OR 1, 10 (1): 410, 467; Johnston, "Albert Sidney Johnston at Shiloh," 565, 568; Chisolm, "Shiloh Battle-Order," 606; Lockett, "Surprise and Withdrawal," 605; Roman, *Military Operations of Gen-eral Beauregard*, 1:535–536, 551; Randall, "General W. H. C. Whiting," 277; Castel, "Savior of the South?," Spenser B. Talley Memoir, 1918, TSLA, 9; Thomas Jordan to P. G. T. Beauregard, December 6, 1868, Atcheson L. Hench Collection, UVA; P. G. T. Beauregard to William Preston Johnston, March 9, 1877, P. G. T. Beauregard Papers, MDAH; Eugene F. Falconnet Diary, April 6, 1862, Eugene Frederic Falconnet Papers, TSLA.

32. Hannaford, *Story of a Regiment*, 257; "The Shiloh Campaign," *National Tribune*, July 24, 1884; Moore, *Rebellion Record*, 4:415; Wallace, *Life and Letters*, 187; Smith, *Personal Reminiscences*, 10.

33. Reed, *Battle of Shiloh*, 63; "The Shiloh Campaign," *National Tribune*, July 24, 1884.

34. OR 1, 10 (1): 292, 323, 328; "Advance Guard of Gen. Buell," *Phila-delphia Enquirer*, April 18, 1862; George to mother, April 10, 1862, 6th Ohio File, SNMPRF; E. W. Herman Diary, April 6, 1862, 7th Iowa File, SNMPRF; Robert Hammond, "Army of the Ohio at Shiloh," *National Tribune*, July 4, 1907; A. J. Eldred to Sir, April 16, 1862, 12th Michigan File, SNMPRF; un-known to friend, April 8, 1862, Stibbs Family Papers, TU (copy in 12th Iowa File, SNMPRF); Fred True to sister, April 10, 1862, 41st Illinois File, SN-MPRF; George to wife, April 9, 1862, 58th Illinois File, SNMPRF; Putnam, "Reminiscences," 3:203; James Shepard to brother, April 1862, James Shep-ard Correspondence, ISL; McEathron, *Letters and Memoirs*, 6; "The Battle of Pittsburg Landing," April 15, 1862, Henry Van Ness Boynton Papers, MAHS; M. G. Reeves, "Where the Blunder Was," *National Tribune*, April 19, 1883; "The Battle of Pittsburg as Seen by One of the Third Iowa," *Missouri Daily*

Democrat, April 24, 1862; Thomas F. Miller to Benjamin Newton, April 20, 1862, Thomas F. Miller Letters, ALPL; William H. Ross to Father, April 10, 1862, William H. Ross Papers, CHS; William C. Caldwell to parents, April 10, 1862, William C. Caldwell Papers, RBHPC.

35. Camm, "Col. William Camm War Diary," 852; Johnston, *Life of Gen. Albert Sidney Johnston,* 626; Daggett, "Thrilling Moments," 450.

CHAPTER 13: "LICK 'EM TO-MORROW, THOUGH"

1. OR 1, 10 (1): 109.

2. Samuel Kennedy Cox Diary, April 6, 1862, 17th Kentucky File, SNMPRF.

3. Alvin P. Hovey, "Pittsburg Landing," *National Tribune,* February 1, 1883; Buell, "Shiloh Reviewed," 1:534; W. R. Rowley to William T. Sherman, July 12, 1881, William Reuben Rowley Papers, ALPL; Lew Wallace to James Grant Wilson, November 6, 1896, William P. Palmer Collection, WRHS; "March of Lew Wallace's Division," 1:607; OR 1, 10 (1): 170, 175, 180–181; Grant, "Battle of Shiloh," 1:468–469; Allen, "If He Had Less Rank," 73–74. For Wallace, see Stephens, *Shadow of Shiloh.*

4. OR 1, 10 (1): 170, 175, 193, 200; Stevenson, *History of the 78th,* 146; Williams, *Historical Sketch,* 15; John Travis to brother, April 10, 1862, Travis Family Papers, UMB.

5. Poulter, "Second Courier"; Fletcher, *History of Company "A,"* 50–51; OR 1, 10 (1): 176, 179–180, 185–186; Wallace, *Lew Wallace,* 1:467; Lew Wallace to John P. Nicholson, April 11, 1896, Lew Wallace Papers, LC.

6. OR 1, 10 (1): 169, 176, 179–182, 187–188, 191, 199; Wallace, *Lew Wallace,* 467; Atwell Thompson to Cornelius Cadle, August 2, 1895, Third Division File, SNMPRF; "March of Lew Wallace's Division," 610; Lew Wallace to John P. Nicholson, April 11, 1896, Lew Wallace Papers, LC; Force, *From Fort Henry to Corinth,* 163; Alex Oliphant to mother, April 8, 1862, 24th Indiana File, SNMPRF; Charles Kroff Diary, April 6, 1862, Sheery Marie Cress Collection, UO. For an example of postwar writing on the issue, see "General Lewis Wallace's Division at Shiloh," Mortimer Dormer Leggett Papers, WRHS.

7. OR 1, 10 (1): 169, 187–188, 191, 199; Alex Oliphant to mother, April 8, 1862, 24th Indiana File, SNMPRF; Charles Kroff Diary, April 6, 1862, Sheery Marie Cress Collection, UO; William Rhoads to sister, April 15, 1862, Johnston–Rhoads Family Correspondence, ND; Putnam, "Reminiscences," 3:201; Rich, "General Lew. Wallace"; Rich, "Battle of Shiloh"; Lew Wallace to John P. Nicholson, April 11, 1896, Lew Wallace Papers, LC; Lew Wallace to U. S. Grant, August 13, 1873, Lew Wallace Papers, UVA; Hanson, *Ripples of Battle,* 137–140. See also Ferraro, "Struggle for Respect."

8. Hannaford, *Story of a Regiment,* 281; Saul Howell Diary, April 7, 1862, SHSI; OR 1, 10 (1): 292, 323, 328, 332, 333, 337; Kimberly and Holloway, *Forty-first Ohio,* 21; Will to mother, April 13, 1862, 6th Ohio File, SNMPRF; George to mother, April 10, 1862, 6th Ohio File, SNMPRF; Horace N. Fisher, "A Memory of Shiloh," undated, Horace N. Fisher File, SNMPRF; Buell, "Shiloh Reviewed," 518; George Parsons to parents, May 17, 1862, George W. Parsons Papers, IHS; Charles M. Scott to Anna, April 6, 1862, Charles M. Scott Papers, UWS.

9. OR 1, 10 (1): 170, 201; George O. Smith, "Brief History of the 17th Regiment of the Illinois Volunteer Infantry, Dec. 25, 1913," ALPL, 3; Charles M. Scott to Anna, April 6, 1862, Charles M. Scott Papers, UWS.

10. OR 1, 10 (1): 205, 324, 339; Hartpence, *History of the Fifty-first,* 34–44; Fisher, *Staff Officer's Story,* 15; James R. Zearing to wife, April 8, 1862, James R. Zearing Papers, CHS; A. S. Bloomfield to sister, April 15, 1862, A. S. Bloomfield Letters, OHS.

11. OR 1, 10 (1): 292, 296, 298, 354–355, 363–364, 372; Newton, *Wisconsin Boy in Dixie,* 14; William Brown to wife, April 10, 1862, William Brown Papers, SHSW; Richard Henry Pratt Memoir, undated, Richard Henry Pratt Papers, LC, 8; Hillyer, "Hillyer on Grant at Shiloh"; Reed, *Battle of Shiloh,* 64; unknown memoir, July 14, 1906, 59th Ohio File, SNMPRF; Charles H. Brush to father, April 6, 1862, Brush Family Papers, ALPL; Rufus A. Peck Diary, April 6 and 8, 1862, IHS; Rufus A. Peck to wife, April 17, 1862, Peck Family Papers, IHS.

12. OR 1, 10 (1): 292, 302–303, 305, 307, 310, 315, 321, 376–377; Ed to unknown, April 13, 1862, Edwin W. Payne Papers, ALPL; William Robinson to Charlie, April 19, 1862, William Culbertson Robinson Papers, ALPL; Lucien to folks, April 13, 1862, Edwin W. Payne Papers, ALPL; B. H. Brown to family, April 12, 1862, 29th Indiana File, SNMPRF; unidentified Union diary, April 5, 1862, ALPL; James A. Price to brother, April 21, 1862, Price–Moore Family Papers, IHS; John A. Gillis Memoir, April 24, 1862, OHS.

13. OR 1, 10 (1): 119, 147, 239, 241, 250; Reed, *Campaigns and Battles of the Twelfth,* 64; "From the 12th Regiment," undated newspaper clipping, W. W. Warner Collection, SHSI; unknown to E. M. Stanton, undated, W. W. Warner Collection, SHSI; David B. Henderson to George, June 13, 1862, David B. Henderson Papers, Dubuque County Historical Society.

14. Harry Watts Reminiscences, undated, ISL, 35; A. Newton, "An Incident of Shiloh," *National Tribune,* August 19, 1882; Hobart, *Semi-history,* 8; Camm, "Col. William Camm War Diary," 163; OR 1, 10 (1): 119, 134, 144, 147, 159, 251, 324, 387, 434, 455, 466, 506, 616, 622; George Lemon Childress Diary, April 7, 1862, ALPL; SOR 1, 1:629–630; Clark, *Notorious "Bull" Nelson,* 107; William Rhoads to sister, April 15, 1862, Johnston–Rhoads Family Correspondence, ND; Charles J. Cling Memoir, undated, 43rd Illinois File,

SNMPRF. Naval historian Gary D. Joiner has an interesting thesis that the gun-boats fired ricocheting shot off the sides of Dill Branch ravine to reach greater distances. See Joiner, *Mr. Lincoln's Brown Water Navy,* 52–54, and Joiner, "Soul-Stirring Music to Our Ears," 105; Enoch Colby to father, April 14, 1862, Francelia Colby Reminiscences, CHS; Smith, "Brief History of the 17th Reg-iment," 3; William Rhoads to sister, April 15, 1862, Johnston–Rhoads Family Correspondence, ND.

15. OR 1, 10 (1): 250; Maurice J. Williams Diary, April 6, 1862, 36th Indiana File, SNMPRF; E. W. Herman Diary, April 6, 1862, 7th Iowa File, SNMPRF; Horace N. Fisher to father, April 10, 1862, Horace N. Fisher Papers, MAHS.

16. Hickenlooper, "Battle of Shiloh—Part I," 5:435; Billings, *Hardtack and Coffee,* 405; James K. Kelly to comrade, undated, James K. Kelly Papers, UNC.

17. Grant, "Battle of Shiloh," 1:477; Briant, *History of the Sixth,* 104–105; Thomas McFadden to unknown, undated, 46th Ohio File, SNMPRF.

18. Shoup, "Art of War," 8; Andreas, "'Ifs and Buts' of Shiloh," 1:115; Buell, "Shiloh Reviewed," 504–505; Stephen A. Hurlbut, "Pittsburg Landing and Shi-loh," undated, WS, 5; William C. Caldwell to parents, April 10, 1862, William C. Caldwell Papers, RBHPC; Thomas, *Soldier Life,* 42; SOR 1, 1:642; Grant, "Battle of Shiloh," 1:476; OR 1, 52 (1): 559; Roman, *Military Operations of General Beauregard,* 1:338.

19. Buell, "Shiloh Reviewed," 493; OR 1, 10 (1): 186; Stillwell, *Personal Recollections,* 16; Sherman, *Memoirs,* 1:246; Putnam, "Reminiscences," 3:205; Dan MacAuley, "Chesnut Grove," *Washington Post,* December 17, 1893.

20. For specific texts on Grant's leadership, see Laver, *General Who Will Fight;* Ballard, *U. S. Grant.*

21. SOR 1, 1:641–642; OR 1, 10 (1): 109; Chetlain, "Recollections of Gen-eral U. S. Grant," 1:26; Horace N. Fisher to D. W. Reed, March 27, 1905, Series 1, Box 13, Folder 136, SNMPAF; Fisher, *Staff Officer's Story,* 15; Badeau, *Military History of Ulysses S. Grant,* 1:87; Putnam, "Reminiscences," 3:206; Charles M. Scott to Anna, April 6, 1862, Charles M. Scott Papers, UWS.

22. J. M. Thurston Journal, April 6, 1862, MAHS; OR 1, 10 (1): 109; Alex Oliphant to mother, April 8, 1862, 24th Indiana File, SNMPRF; Horace N. Fisher to father, April 10, 1862, Horace N. Fisher Papers, MAHS.

23. OR 1, 10 (1): 387, 410; Braxton Bragg to wife, April 9, 1862, Braxton Bragg Papers, MHS; Worsham, *Old Nineteenth,* 42; Beauregard, "Campaign of Shiloh," 1:591; Roman, *Military Operations of General Beauregard,* 1:305, 308, 539; Van Winkle, "Incidents and Inquiries"; P. G. T. Beauregard to Corinth commander, April 6, 1862, P. G. T. Beauregard Papers, NARA; P. G. T. Beau-regard Special Order, April 6, 1862, Orders and Circulars of the Army of the Mississippi, 1861–1865, NARA.

24. Richardson, "War as I Saw It," 103; OR 1, 10 (1): 384, 387, 402, 432, 467, 565, 599, 622; Jordan, "Notes of a Confederate Staff-Officer," 1:602; Dawson, "One Year at War," 193; William S. Dillon Diary, April 6 and 7, 1862, UM; Thomas Jefferson Crowder Memoir, undated, TSLA, 2.

25. Augustus Hervey Mecklin Diary, April 6, 1862, MDAH; Spenser B. Talley Memoir, 1918, TSLA, 9; Bradford Nichol Memoir, April 8, 1862, TSLA; Schaller, *Soldiering for Glory,* 84; Eugene F. Falconnet Diary, April 6, 1862, Eugene Frederic Falconnet Papers, TSLA; H. W. H. to parents, April 10, 1862, Shiloh Subject File, ADAH; "Bloody Pond," SNMPVF; Alfred Cox Smith to mother, April 10, 1862, Alfred Cox Smith Collection, MDAH; Andrew Devilbliss to Mary, April 16, 1862, Andrew Devilbliss Letter, TU; Joseph D. Thompson to Mary, April 10, 1862, Joseph D. Thompson Papers, TSLA; Thompson, "Battle of Shiloh"; Camm, "Col. William Camm War Diary," 851; Houston, "Shiloh Shadows," 332; Stevenson, *Thirteen Months in the Rebel Army,* 165.

26. Alfred Tyler Fielder Diary, April 6, 1862, TSLA; Eugene F. Falconnet Diary, April 6, 1862, Eugene Frederic Falconnet Papers, TSLA.

27. William S. Dillon Diary, April 6, 1862, UM; Chisolm, "Shiloh Battle-Order," 1:606; Dinkins, "Battle of Shiloh," 314; Roman, *Military Operations of General Beauregard,* 1:305–307; Hughes, *General William J. Hardee,* 109; Johnston, *Life of Gen. Albert Sidney Johnston,* 637; R. F. Learned to D. W. Reed, March 22, 1904, 10th Mississippi File, SNMPRF; OR 1, 10 (1): 410–411, 440, 467, 518, 534, 617, 622; Force, *From Fort Henry to Corinth,* 160; Reed, *Battle of Shiloh,* 20, 73, 75, 78, 81; Johnston, "Albert Sidney Johnston at Shiloh," 1:568.

28. Chisolm, "Shiloh Battle-Order," 606; Jordan, "Notes of a Confederate Staff-Officer," 602–603; A. R. Chisolm Report, April 14, 1862, SNMPRF; Clifton Smith to P. G. T. Beauregard, August 5, 1880, Clifton H. Smith Papers, CHS. For a detailed account of the Beauregard and Prentiss conversation, see "The Battle of Shiloh: The First Day's Fight," *Southern Watchman,* April 23, 1862.

29. OR 1, 10 (1): 473, 499, 518, 522, 555; Reed, *Battle of Shiloh,* 86.

30. OR 1, 10 (1): 418, 583; Eugene F. Falconnet Diary, April 6, 1862, Eugene Frederic Falconnet Papers, TSLA; "The Battle of Shiloh: The First Day's Fight," *Southern Watchman,* April 23, 1862; Shoup, "How We Went to Shiloh," 139.

CHAPTER 14: "ON MONDAY MORNING THE THING CHANGED"

1. Buell, "Shiloh Reviewed," 1:519.

2. Ibid., 524–525, 529; OR 1, 10 (1): 518, 520; Durham, *Three Years with Wallace's Zuuaves,* 89. For the Army of the Ohio's complaints, see the Army of the Ohio Files, Series 1, Box 12, Folders 88–95, SNMPAF.

3. OR 1, 10 (1): 170, 518, 526, 528; Livaudais, *Shiloh Diary,* 32; Clarke, *Diary of the War for Separation,* 151; Roman, *Military Operations of General Beauregard,* 1:316; "Journal of the Orleans Guard," April 7, 1862, HNOC; Joseph D. Thompson to Mary, April 9, 1862, Joseph D. Thompson Papers, TSLA; Thompson, "Battle of Shiloh."

4. OR 1, 10 (1): 170; Robert F. Looney Report, April 25, 1862, H. H. Price Papers, DU; Israel N. Prince to sister, April 13, 1862, Israel N. Prince Letters, HL.

5. OR 1, 10 (1): 170, 528; William Rhoads to sister, April 15, 1862, Johnston–Rhoads Family Correspondence, ND.

6. J. S. Fogle to brother, April 15, 1862, Bartholomew County Historical Society (copy in 9th Indiana Battery File, SNMPRF); OR 1, 10 (1): 161, 170, 193, 201; Henry Otis Dwight Memoir, undated, OHS, 31.

7. OR 1, 10 (1): 161, 170, 193, 201.

8. Ibid., 518–519.

9. Ibid., 170.

10. Ibid., 171, 190, 201; Alvin Hovey to Essie, April 21, 1862, Alvin P. Hovey Papers, IU; Alex Oliphant to mother, April 8, 1862, 24th Indiana File, SNMPRF; J. S. Fogle to brother, April 15, 1862, 9th Indiana Battery File, SNMPRF; Alvin P. Hovey Autobiography, undated, Alvin P. Hovey Papers, IU, 25; William Rhoads to sister, April 15, 1862, Johnston–Rhoads Family Correspondence, ND; Charles Kroff Diary, April 7, 1862, Sheery Marie Cress Collection, UO.

11. OR 1, 10 (1): 134–135, 205, 221, 237, 251.

12. Ibid., 110, 119, 253, 263.

13. Ibid., 119, 135, 251; Camm, "Col. William Camm War Diary," 854; Ephraim Dawes to Marshal, April 21, 1862, Ephraim C. Dawes Papers, NL; Charles J. Cling Memoir, undated, 43rd Illinois File, SNMPRF.

14. Jordan, "Notes of a Confederate Staff-Officer," 1:603; W. A. Howard to family, April 10, 1862, 33rd Tennessee File, SNMPRF; unknown to friend, April 8, 1862, Stibbs Family Papers, TU.

15. OR 1, 10 (1): 293, 324, 328, 335; Engle, *Don Carlos Buell,* 231; Horace N. Fisher to father, April 10, 1862, Horace N. Fisher Papers, MAHS.

16. E. W. Herman Diary, April 7, 1862, 7th Iowa File, SNMPRF; Hazen, *Narrative of Military Service,* 25.

17. OR 1, 10 (1): 303, 307, 311, 355; Hosea, "Regular Brigade," 5:331–332; Lucien to folks, April 13, 1862, Edwin W. Payne Papers, ALPL; Lee, *Kentuckian in Blue;* Levi Wagner, "Recollections of an Enlistee, 1861–1865," undated, Levi Wagner Papers, CWTI, USAMHI; "The Old Madison Band," *Madison Courier,* May 9, 1883 (copy in Phelix Adair Articles, ISL); George to father, April 22, 1862, John P. Sanderson Papers, OHS.

18. OR 1, 10 (1): 324, 328, 335; Fisher, *Staff Officer's Story,* 15.

19. OR 1, 10 (1): 324, 335; Beauregard, "Campaign of Shiloh," 1:592; Hannaford, *Story of a Regiment,* 263.

20. OR 1, 10 (1): 293, 355–357, 366.

21. Wallace, *Life and Letters,* 197, 199.

22. OR 1, 10 (1): 303, 308; Buell, "Shiloh Reviewed," 498.

23. OR 1, 10 (1): 147, 149, 167–168, 276.

24. Grose, *Story of the Marches, Battles, and Incidents,* 108.

25. OR 1, 10 (1): 337.

26. Unknown memoir, July 14, 1906, 59th Ohio File, SNMPRF.

27. OR 1, 10 (1): 149–150, 293.

28. Ibid., 418, 583; unknown memoir, July 14, 1906, 59th Ohio File, SNMPRF.

29. OR 1, 10 (1): 473, 518.

30. Vaughan, *Personal Record,* 17.

31. Johnston, *Life of Gen. Albert Sidney Johnston,* 637.

32. T. C. Robertson to mother, April 9, 1862, Thomas Chinn Robertson Papers, NC; William Stephen Ray Memoir, 1915, UA, 15; Lockett, "Surprise and Withdrawal," 1:605; Robert H. Wood to father, April 14, 1862, Bills Family Papers, TSLA.

33. Baylor, "With Gen. A. S. Johnston at Shiloh," 612; OR 1, 10 (1): 387, 402, 462–463, 467, 612; Alfred Tyler Fielder Diary, April 7, 1862, TSLA; Reed, *Battle of Shiloh,* 21; Clarke, *Diary of the War for Separation,* 150; Beauregard, "Campaign of Shiloh," 590; Roman, *Military Operations of General Beauregard,* 1:308, 313, 532; King and Derby, *Camp-Fire Sketches,* 458.

34. OR 1, 10 (1): 473, 480, 491, 499–500; 15th Mississippi Memoir, undated, Gore Collection, USM, 36; R. H. Wood to Mary, April 9, 1862, R. H. Wood Letter, UVA; Giles B. Cooke Report, undated, Giles B. Cooke Papers, VHS.

35. OR 1, 10 (1): 418, 421, 539.

36. Ibid., 440–443, 449, 452, 595, 604; Beauregard, "Campaign of Shiloh," 591; Roman, *Military Operations of General Beauregard,* 1:313.

37. A. R. Chisolm Report, April 14, 1862, SNMPRF.

38. OR 1, 10 (1): 579, 583, 599; Johnston, *Life of Gen. Albert Sidney Johnston,* 644.

39. A. R. Chisolm Report, April 14, 1862, SNMPRF; OR 1, 10 (1): 572.

40. OR 1, 10 (1): 467, 514.

41. There is some discrepancy concerning Breckinridge's deployment, obviously stemming from the lack of reports. In fact, there are no reports whatsoever from Statham's brigade. David W. Reed even contradicted himself. In the tablets marking the park, he has Statham in the center and Martin on the right. On his battle maps, they are opposite.

42. OR 1, 10 (1): 575.

43. John C. Caldwell Diary, April 7, 1862, CWTI, USAMHI; C. S. Stewart to Julia, April 12, 1862, CWTI, USAMHI.

44. Henry George, "Seventh Kentucky at Shiloh," 7th Kentucky File, SNMPRF; OR 1, 10 (1): 391, 429, 434–435, 570; Reed, *Battle of Shiloh,* 20–21; Lockett, "Surprise and Withdrawal," 605; Roman, *Military Operations of General Beauregard,* 1:315; A. R. Chisolm Report, April 14, 1862, SNMPRF.

45. Thomas Barnett to Fanny, April 10, 1862, Thomas Barnett Papers, ALPL.

CHAPTER 15: "VERY HOTLY ENGAGED AT AN EARLY HOUR"

1. OR 1, 10 (1): 387.

2. Warner, *Generals in Gray,* 46.

3. OR 1, 10 (1): 534, 551.

4. Ibid., 449, 534, 551; Robert A. Smith Report, April 9, 1862, Robert A. Smith Papers, MDAH.

5. OR 1, 10 (1): 546, 559, 563; Dyer, *From Shiloh to San Juan,* 33; Longacre, *Soldier to the Last,* 23, 30; C. S. Stewart to Julia, April 12, 1862, CWTI, USAMHI.

6. OR 1, 10 (1): 340, 434, 442, 449, 456–457, 551; Witham, *Shiloh, Shells,* 55; J. S. Grammar Diary, April 7, 1862, Swett's Battery File, Vicksburg National Military Park (copy in Swett's Battery File, SNMPRF).

7. OR 1, 10 (1): 294, 456; Smith, *Personal Reminiscences,* 12.

8. Moore, *Rebellion Record,* 4:415; Daniel, *Days of Glory,* 82; Bierce, *Collected Works,* 1:257. For more on Bierce, see Coleman, "Ambrose Bierce in Civil War Tennessee."

9. OR 1, 10 (1): 324, 342, 348, 456, 551; A. R. Chisolm Report, April 14, 1862, SNMPRF; Robert A. Smith Report, April 9, 1862, Robert A. Smith Papers, MDAH.

10. OR 1, 10 (1): 342, 551, 559; S. H. Dent to wife, April 9, 1862, Stouton Hubert Dent Papers, ADAH.

11. OR 1, 10 (1): 301, 324, 373–374; SOR 1, 1:647; King and Derby, *Camp-Fire Sketches,* 50.

12. OR 1, 10 (1): 294, 301, 321, 325, 339; Hannaford, *Story of a Regiment,* 267–270; Moore, *Rebellion Record,* 415.

13. OR 1, 10 (1): 293, 328; Grose, *Story of the Marches, Battles, and Incidents,* 109.

14. OR 1, 10 (1): 341, 349–350; David J. Jones to mother, April 9, 1862, David J. Jones Papers, CIN.

15. OR 1, 10 (1): 467, 534; C. S. Stewart to Julia, April 12, 1862, CWTI, USAMHI.

16. OR 1, 10 (1): 341, 343.

17. Ibid., 294.

18. Ibid., 467, 534.

19. Ibid., 338, 551, 556, 570; Robert A. Smith Report, April 9, 1862, Robert A. Smith Papers, MDAH; Wheeler, "Battle of Shiloh," 125; Smith, *Reminiscences of the Civil War,* 3; Houston, "Shiloh Shadows," 333; Chance, *Second Texas Infantry,* 40; C. S. Stewart to Julia, April 12, 1862, CWTI, USAMHI (copy in 21st Alabama File, SNMPRF).

20. OR 1, 10 (1): 563–564, 570–573; Rogers, "Diary and Letters," 286.

21. OR 1, 10 (1): 563–564, 570–573.

22. Ibid., 449, 456, 551.

23. Ibid., 551–552.

24. Ibid., 337, 552.

25. Ibid., 149, 294, 301, 322, 325, 338, 552; Force, *From Fort Henry to Corinth,* 166; Reed, *Battle of Shiloh,* 21; Hart, *History of the Fortieth,* 90; Grose, *Story of the Marches, Battles, and Incidents,* 109; Hannaford, *Story of a Regiment,* 265; Will C. Holden to father, April 10, 1862, Will C. Holden Letter, Soldiers' Letters Collection, Lincoln Memorial Shrine.

26. OR 1, 10 (1): 338–340; Grose, *Story of the Marches, Battles, and Incidents,* 109–110; Moore, *Rebellion Record,* 415.

27. OR 1, 10 (1): 351–352.

28. Smith, *Personal Reminiscences,* 14.

29. David J. Jones to mother, April 9, 1862, David J. Jones Papers, CIN.

30. S. H. Dent to wife, April 9, 1862, Stouton Hubert Dent Papers, ADAH.

31. OR 1, 10 (1): 294, 341–342; Hazen, *Narrative of Military Service,* 26; David J. Jones to mother, April 9, 1862, David J. Jones Papers, CIN.

32. OR 1, 10 (1): 325–326, 328; SOR 1, 1:649.

33. OR 1, 10 (1): 570, 583.

34. Ibid., 570.

35. Robert H. Wood to father, April 14, 1862, Bills Family Papers, TSLA.

36. Unknown to Jose, April 9, 1862, Henry D. Mandeville and Family Papers, LSU.

CHAPTER 16: "UP TO THE MOUTHS OF THE GUNS"

1. Davis, *Breckinridge,* 1–290.

2. A. R. Chisolm Report, April 14, 1862, SNMPRF.

3. OR 1, 10 (1): 617–618.

4. A. R. Chisolm Report, April 14, 1862, SNMPRF.

5. Ibid.; OR 1, 10 (1): 583.

6. Warner, *Generals in Blue,* 225–226.

7. Smith, *Golden Age,* 14.

8. OR 1, 10 (1): 355.

9. Ibid., 293, 325, 348; Reinhart, *History of the 6th,* 65–70.

10. OR 1, 10 (1): 324, 343, 349–350; SOR 1, 1:647; Hazen, *Narrative of Military Service,* 27, 44.

11. OR 1, 10 (1): 294; Opdycke, *To Battle for God and the Right,* 27.

12. OR 1, 10 (1): 357, 366. For the 14th Wisconsin, see *Fourteenth Wisconsin Infantry Corinth and Shiloh.*

13. OR 1, 10 (1): 355; Reed, *Battle of Shiloh,* 22.

14. OR 1, 10 (1): 341–347, 355, 524, 622; Bierce, *Collected Works,* 1:264; Chalaron, "Battle Echoes from Shiloh," 218; unknown to Jose, April 9, 1862, Henry D. Mandeville and Family Papers, LSU.

15. Opdycke, *To Battle for God and the Right,* 27–28; Reed, *Battle of Shiloh,* 22.

16. OR 1, 10 (1): 429, 494, 514, 524, 534, 551; unknown to Jose, April 9, 1862, Henry D. Mandeville and Family Papers, LSU.

17. Frank Jones to mother, April 16, 1862, Johnston–Jones Family Papers, CIN.

18. OR 1, 10 (1): 341; Kimberly and Holloway, *Forty-first Ohio,* 24.

19. Jones, "Personal Recollections," 6:121–122.

20. OR 1, 10 (1): 368–369, 372.

21. Ibid., 348; Hazen, *Narrative of Military Service,* 44; Opdycke, *To Battle for God and the Right,* 28.

22. OR 1, 10 (1): 325; Hazen, *Narrative of Military Service,* 27.

23. Kimberly and Holloway, *Forty-first Ohio,* 23.

24. Ibid., 125.

25. Hazen, *Narrative of Military Service,* 41–42.

26. OR 1, 10 (1): 341–342, 370, 515; Hazen, *Narrative of Military Service,* 27; R. M. Nichols to family, April 13, 1862, 6th Kentucky File, SNMPRF.

27. OR 1, 10 (1): 294, 341, 355.

28. Ibid., 389, 429, 431, 524, 622–623; SOR 1, 1:662–663; Force, *From Fort Henry to Corinth,* 165; Bevier, *History of the First and Second Missouri Confederate Brigades,* 81.

29. Frank Jones to mother, April 16, 1862, Johnston–Jones Family Papers, CIN; unknown to Jose, April 9, 1862, Henry D. Mandeville and Family Papers, LSU; Hazen, *Narrative of Military Service,* 28, 37; OR 1, 10 (1): 343, 349–350, 370, 494, 514, 524; SOR 1, 1:648.

30. OR 1, 10 (1): 343, 349–350, 370, 494, 514, 524; SOR 1, 1:648; Frank Jones to mother, April 16, 1862, Johnston–Jones Family Papers, CIN; Fisher, *Staff Officer's Story,* 15–16; unknown to Jose, April 9, 1862, Henry D. Mandeville and Family Papers, LSU.

31. Unknown to Jose, April 9, 1862, Henry D. Mandeville and Family Papers, LSU; Clarke, *Diary of the War for Separation,* 153.

32. OR 1, 10 (1): 346; Cooper, *William Babcock Hazen,* 47–48.

33. Hazen, *Narrative of Military Service,* 30–31.

34. OR 1, 10 (1): 357, 366–370, 429, 431, 524.

35. Ibid., 357, 366–370, 429, 431, 524; Van Horne, *History of the Army of the Cumberland,* 1:112; Hazen, *Narrative of Military Service,* 27–29; Louis Buford to Charles Buford, April 21, 1862, Charles Buford Papers, LC.

36. Ibid., 367; Frank Jones to mother, April 16, 1862, Johnston–Jones Family Papers, CIN; Almon F. Rockwell Diary, April 7, 1862, LC.

37. OR 1, 10 (1): 294, 355, 362, 456; Magdeburg, "Fourteenth Wisconsin Infantry"; Newton, *Wisconsin Boy in Dixie,* 15; William Brown to wife, April 10, 1862, William Brown Papers, SHSW.

38. Newton, *Wisconsin Boy in Dixie,* 16.

39. Ibid., 15; OR 1, 10 (1): 366.

40. Johnston, *Life of Gen. Albert Sidney Johnston,* 646.

41. OR 1, 10 (1): 456–458; George, "Two Men Sought Water at Shiloh"; Henry George, "Seventh Kentucky at Shiloh," 7th Kentucky File, SNMPRF; George, *History of the 3d,* 31; W. J. Stubblefield Diary, April 7, 1862, MU, 4.

CHAPTER 17: "WE DROVE BACK THE LEGIONS OF THE ENEMY"

1. Prokopowicz, *All for the Regiment,* 111–112.

2. OR 1, 10 (1): 310.

3. Ibid., 295, 364.

4. Warner, *Generals in Blue,* 100. For more on the Crittenden family in war, see Eubank, *In the Shadow of the Patriarch.*

5. OR 1, 10 (1): 357, 362.

6. "Autobiography of Captain Elijah F. Tucker," undated, Elijah Tucker Papers, CWTI; USAMHI, 3.

7. OR 1, 10 (1): 301, 374–375; unknown memoir, July 14, 1906, 59th Ohio File, SNMPRF.

8. OR 1, 10 (1): 315.

9. Ibid., 303, 308; Johnson, *That Body of Brave Men,* 104–106; Hosea, "Regular Brigade," 5:333; Flemming, "Battle of Shiloh as a Private Saw It," 6:198–201.

10. OR 1, 10 (1): 305–306; unknown memoir, July 14, 1906, 59th Ohio File, SNMPRF; "The Old Madison Band," *Madison Courier,* May 9, 1883; Joseph Harper to wife, April 9, 1862, John W. Gillette Collection, UMB.

11. OR 1, 10 (1): 617; McMurray, *History of the Twentieth,* 209.

12. OR 1, 10 (1): 617, "Byrnes Battery," undated, John Joyes Papers, FHS; 6th Kentucky Report, April 14, 1862, Edwin Porter Thompson Papers, FHS.

13. OR 1, 10 (1): 622; Witham, *Shiloh, Shells,* 80.

14. John W. Taylor to parents, April 11, 1862, Clyde Hughes Collection, UNC.

15. Unknown memoir, July 14, 1906, 59th Ohio File, SNMPRF.

16. OR 1, 10 (1): 358, 362–364, 376; Jacob Reep to D. W. Reed, March 30, 1915, 19th Ohio File, SNMPRF.

17. OR 1, 10 (1): 436.

18. Ibid., 358, 363.

19. A. R. Chisolm Report, April 14, 1862, SNMPRF.

20. John W. Taylor to parents, April 11, 1862, Clyde Hughes Collection, UNC; OR 1, 10 (1): 358; King and Derby, *Camp-Fire Sketches,* 51; Wynne, *Hard Trip,* 75; Jacob Reep to D. W. Reed, March 30, 1915, 19th Ohio File, SNMPRF; Augustus Hervey Mecklin Diary, April 7, 1862, MDAH.

21. OR 1, 10 (1): 376, 623.

22. Ibid., 358, 363; unknown memoir, July 14, 1906, 59th Ohio File, SNMPRF; "Battlefield Memories," undated, Chelsey Davis Bailey Papers, IHS.

23. OR 1, 10 (1): 360, 364–365, 376, 623, 625; unknown to father, April 15, 1862, 9th Kentucky File, SNMPRF.

24. Augustus Hervey Mecklin Diary, April 7, 1862, MDAH; McMurray, *History of the Twentieth,* 127; Isaac E. Hirsch Memoir, undated, Isaac E. Hirsh Papers, MSU; Schaller, *Soldiering for Glory,* 84; John W. Taylor to parents, April 11, 1862, Clyde Hughes Collection, UNC.

25. OR 1, 10 (1): 436; McMurray, *History of the Twentieth,* 127–128; William A. Brown Diary, April 7, 1862, Stanford's Battery File, SNMPRF; Augustus Hervey Mecklin Diary, April 7, 1862, MDAH.

26. Horatio to Josie, April 11, 1862, 22nd Alabama File, SNMPRF; A. R. Chisolm Report, April 14, 1862, SNMPRF; Daniel, *Shiloh,* 264; J. J. Davis to wife, April 18, 1862, Davis-Bills Civil War Letters, UMEM.

27. OR 1, 10 (1): 295, 311; Fanebust, *Major General Alexander M. McCook,* 94.

28. OR 1, 10 (1): 120, 308, 311; Dodge, *History of the Old Second Division,* 186; Briant, *History of the Sixth,* 108; Stephen A. Hurlbut, "Pittsburg Landing and Shiloh," undated, WS, 25; T. T. Crittenden to Henry Halleck, undated, T. T. Crittenden Papers, NARA.

29. OR 1, 10 (1): 308–309, 311; 6th Kentucky Report, April 14, 1862, Edwin Porter Thompson Papers, FHS.

30. Thompson, *History of the Orphan Brigade,* 102.

31. OR 1, 10 (1): 500–501.

32. Ibid., 618–619; 6th Kentucky Report, April 14, 1862, Edwin Porter Thompson Papers, FHS; Edgar R., Kellogg, "Recollections of Civil War Service With the Sixteenth United States Infantry," undated, Edgar R. Kellogg Papers, CWD, USAMHI, 9.

33. OR 1, 10 (1): 120, 295, 303, 313; Mason, "Shiloh," 1:102; Dodge, *His-*

tory of the Old Second Division, 188; Edgar R. Kellogg, "Recollections of Civil War Service With the Sixteenth United States Infantry," undated, Edgar R. Kellogg Papers, CWD, USAMHI, 9.

34. OR 1, 10 (1): 618, 620; "Pittsburg Landing," *National Tribune,* May 3, 1883; George to father, April 22, 1862, John P. Sanderson Papers, OHS.

35. Davis, *Orphan Brigade,* 94; Thompson, *History of the Orphan Brigade,* 103.

36. OR 1, 10 (1): 389, 618; Johnston, *Life of Gen. Albert Sidney Johnston,* 651.

37. OR 1, 10 (1): 346, 365, 369.

38. William Richardson to Thomas Jones, April 16, 1862, 25th Indiana File, SNMPRF.

CHAPTER 18: "THE TABLES ARE TURNING"

1. Stephens, *Shadow of Shiloh.*

2. Reed, *Battle of Shiloh,* 90–110.

3. OR 1, 10 (1): 387–388; Alex Oliphant to mother, April 8, 1862, 24th Indiana File, SNMPRF; Harry Watts Reminiscences, undated, ISL, 36; Alvin P. Hovey Autobiography, undated, Alvin P. Hovey Papers, IU, 26.

4. George to wife, April 9, 1862, 58th Illinois File, SNMPRF.

5. OR 1, 10 (1): 422, 506, 519, 522, 526; J. J. Cox Report, April 18, 1862, and J. Robins Report, undated, H. H. Price Papers, DU; "Journal of the Orleans Guard," April 6, 1862, HNOC; Giles B. Cooke Report, undated, Giles B. Cooke Papers, VHS.

6. OR 1, 10 (1): 583.

7. Ibid., 575, 579, 593, 597.

8. Ibid., 565.

9. Ibid., 538; Giles B. Cooke Report, undated, Giles B. Cooke Papers, VHS.

10. OR 1, 10 (1): 543; Terry, "Record of the Alabama State Artillery," 314; Giles B. Cooke Report, undated, Giles B. Cooke Papers, VHS.

11. OR 1, 10 (1): 473.

12. August Schilling Diary, April 6, 1862, BCHS.

13. OR 1, 10 (1): 387–388; Hobart, *Semi-history,* 8; Garrett Smith Ainsworth Diary, April 7, 1862, Garrett Smith Ainsworth Papers, USM.

14. OR 1, 10 (1): 192, 251; Roman, *Military Operations of General Beauregard,* 1:314; Charles J. Cling Memoir, undated, 43rd Illinois File, SNMPRF; Enoch Colby to father, April 14 and 26, 1862, Francelia Colby Reminiscences, CHS.

15. OR 1, 10 (1): 119, 389; Roman, *Military Operations of General Beauregard,* 1:314; Spence, "Services in the Confederacy," 500.

16. OR 1, 10 (1): 575; Clarke, *Diary of the War for Separation,* 156; Stanley, *Autobiography,* 200–201; Roman, *Military Operations of General Beauregard,* 1:313; unknown diary, April 7, 1862, 6th Arkansas File, SNMPRF.

17. OR 1, 10 (1): 593–594, 599–602, 608.

18. Ibid., 205, 234, 236, 238; Jesse Connelley Diary, April 9, 1862, ISL.

19. OR 1, 10 (1): 119, 135, 145, 162, 222, 229, 236, 265–266, 575–577; Murray, *New Yorkers in the Civil War,* 6:45; SOR 1, 1:633; J. S. to friend, April 17, 1862, Rombauer–Becker Family Papers, HUS; Wright, *Corporal's Story,* 42–43; Adair, *Historical Sketch of the Forty-fifth Illinois Regiment,* 6; "Journal Belongs to Hugh T. Carlisle of Fremont Sandusky County Ohio," undated, Hugh T. Carlisle Papers, CWD, USAMHI, 67–68; Chamberlain, *History of the Eighty-first,* 19; Ephraim Dawes to Marshal, April 21, 1862, Ephraim C. Dawes Papers, NL.

20. Wright, *Corporal's Story,* 42–43; Chamberlain, *History of the Eighty-first,* 19; Adair, *Historical Sketch of the Forty-fifth Illinois Regiment,* 6; Ephraim Dawes to Marshal, April 21, 1862, Ephraim C. Dawes Papers, NL; OR 1, 10 (1): 119, 135, 145, 162, 222, 229, 236, 265–266, 575–577; Murray, *New Yorkers in the Civil War,* 6:45; "Journal Belongs to Hugh T. Carlisle of Fremont Sandusky County Ohio," undated, Hugh T. Carlisle Papers, CWD, USAMHI, 67–68; SOR 1, 1:633; J. S. to friend, April 17, 1862, Rombauer–Becker Family Papers, HUS.

21. "Random War Reminiscences of Hugh T. Carlisle," undated, Hugh T. Carlisle Papers, CWD, USAMHI, 55.

22. Edward H. Reynolds Diary, April 7, 1862, CWTI, USAMHI; OR 1, 10 (1): 432–433; SOR 1, 1:653; John E. Magee Diary, April 7, 1862, DU.

23. OR 1, 10 (1): 120, 135, 158, 212–213, 219, 221, 224, 229, 247, 422, 480, 488, 491; Camm, "Col. William Camm War Diary," 854; J. S. to friend, April 17, 1862, Rombauer–Becker Family Papers, HUS; Salling, *Louisianans in the Western Confederacy,* 32; Stephen A. Hurlbut, "Pittsburg Landing and Shiloh," undated, WS, 12; Kendall, "Recollections of a Confederate Officer," 1068; T. C. Robertson to mother, April 9, 1862, Thomas Chinn Robertson Papers, NC.

24. OR 1, 10 (1): 583.

25. Ibid., 583–584, 590.

26. Ibid., 468, 500, 511.

27. Ibid., 120; Stephen A. Hurlbut, "Pittsburg Landing and Shiloh," undated, WS, 25.

28. OR 1, 10 (1): 120; Stephen A. Hurlbut, "Pittsburg Landing and Shiloh," undated, WS, 25; S. D. Thompson, *Recollections,* 236–238.

29. OR 1, 10 (1): 120, 457; D. J. Benner to uncle, April 9, 1862, Luther Howard Cowan Papers, TSLA; Richard Gapen to sister, April 17, 1862, Richard Gapen Papers, CHS.

30. OR 1, 10 (1): 171, 190, 195, 197, 627; "Morgan's Cavalry Was at Shi-

loh"; Walter J. Hardin to sister, April 27, 1862, Adelia H. Hardin Collection, Brigham Young University; William Rhoads to sister, April 15, 1862, Johnston–Rhoads Family Correspondence, ND.

31. Force, *From Fort Henry to Corinth,* 170, 176.

32. OR 1, 10 (1): 171, 201; Ephraim Shay Diary, April 7, 1862, UMB; James Peckham to mother, April 10, 1862, WS, USAMHI.

33. OR 1, 10 (1): 200; Manning F. Force to Robert W. Lee, April 22, 1862, Robert W. Lee Papers, LC.

34. OR 1, 10 (1): 418, 424–425, 441, 449, 452, 539–543; Alex Oliphant to mother, April 8, 1862, 24th Indiana File, SNMPRF; "List of Rebel Prisoners Taken by 20th Ohio Volunteers, USA, April 7th, 1862," undated, Manning F. Force Papers, UW (copy in LC).

35. Alfred Tyler Fielder Diary, April 7, 1862, TSLA.

36. OR 1, 10 (1): 171, 192, 200, 441, 608.

37. Ibid., 171, 192, 200, 441, 608; Garrett Smith Ainsworth Diary, April 7, 1862, Garrett Smith Ainsworth Papers, USM.

38. OR 1, 10 (1): 192, 501; Samuel Kennedy Cox Diary, April 7, 1862, 17th Kentucky File, SNMPRF.

39. OR 1, 10 (1): 190; Alfred Tyler Fielder Diary, April 7, 1862, TSLA.

40. OR 1, 10 (1): 387, 402; L. W. Mills to editor, April 12, 1862, 2nd Michigan Battery File, SNMPRF; Cluett, *History of the 57th,* 23.

CHAPTER 19: "MAKING THEM PAY DEARLY FOR THEIR PURCHASE"

1. 15th Mississippi Memoir, undated, Gore Collection, USM, 37.

2. OR 1, 10 (1): 349.

3. Ibid., 350–351.

4. Ibid., 294, 325, 353.

5. Ibid., 325, 336, 339, 352, 449, 452, 514.

6. Unknown to father, April 15, 1862, 9th Kentucky File, SNMPRF.

7. OR 1, 10 (1): 429–431.

8. Ibid., 158, 295, 303, 309; Johnston, *Life of Gen. Albert Sidney Johnston,* 659; Fisher, *Staff Officer's Story,* 15.

9. OR 1, 10 (1): 120, 212–213, 221, 224, 229, 251.

10. Ibid., 251, 309; Briant, *History of the Sixth,* 108; Stephen A. Hurlbut, "Pittsburg Landing and Shiloh," undated, WS, 26; Charles G. Mount Diary, April 7, 1862, OHS.

11. OR 1, 10 (1): 303, 309; William Robinson to Charlie, April 19, 1862, William Culbertson Robinson Papers, ALPL; George to father, April 22, 1862, John P. Sanderson Papers, OHS.

12. OR 1, 10 (1): 275, 303, 309, 315, 317–318, 418–424, 437; OR 1, 52 (1):

26; Payne, *History of the Thirty-fourth,* 20; Reinhart, *August Willich's Gallant Dutchmen,* 76–77, 79; Hosea, "Second Day at Shiloh," 6:205; Hosea, "Regular Brigade," 5:237; Worsham, *Old Nineteenth,* 43; A. P. Dysart to brother, April 21, 1862, 34th Illinois File, SNMPRF; Samuel B. Franklin, "Memoirs of a Civil War Veteran," undated, Samuel B. Franklin Papers, HCWRT, USAMHI, 2.

13. William Robinson to Charlie, April 19, 1862, William Culbertson Robinson Papers, ALPL.

14. B. H. Brown to family, April 12, 1862, 29th Indiana File, SNMPRF.

15. Widney, *Campaigning with Uncle Billy,* 67–74; William Robinson to Charlie, April 19, 1862, William Culbertson Robinson Papers, ALPL.

16. OR 1, 10 (1): 303–306, 315, 317; Otis, "Second Day at Shiloh," 7:192; Truxall, *"Respects to All,"* 71–72; Cope, *Fifteenth Ohio Volunteers,* 123; K. A. Moore to unknown, April 22, 1862, Pennsylvania Save Flags Collection, USAMHI; Cyrus F. Leasher to uncle, April 11, 1862, MC, USAMHI; Samuel T. Evans Diary, April 3–7, 1862, OHS.

17. OR 1, 10 (1): 304, 311, 315; OR 1, 52 (1): 26; Johnston, *Life of Gen. Albert Sidney Johnston,* 653.

18. OR 1, 10 (1): 315–316, 319; OR 1, 52 (1): 26.

19. A. P. Dysart to brother, April 21, 1862, 34th Illinois File, SNMPRF; OR 1, 10 (1): 158, 594; S. A. M. Wood to Jefferson Davis, June 20, 1862, S. A. M. Wood Papers, ADAH; unidentified Union diary, April 6, 1862, ALPL.

20. OR 1, 10 (1): 304–305; Ed to unknown, April 13, 1862, Edwin W. Payne Papers, ALPL; Payne, *History of the Thirty-fourth,* 20–21; William Robinson to Charlie, April 19, 1862, William Culbertson Robinson Papers, ALPL.

21. William Robinson to Charlie, April 19, 1862, William Culbertson Robinson Papers, ALPL.

22. OR 1, 10 (1): 304–305, 315, 320; McMurray, *History of the Twentieth,* 88, 209, 211; Adams, "My First Company," 297–298; William Stahl Diary, April 7, 1862, MC, USAMHI; N. D. Starr to Henrietta, June 13, 1862, AC, USAMHI; Edwin Witherby Brown, "Under a Poncho with Grant and Sherman," 1914, MIAU, 39.

23. OR 1, 10 (1): 120, 125–129, 149, 206, 221, 225, 311, 318–320, 620; Briant, *History of the Sixth,* 109; Barber, *Army Memoirs,* 58; Camm, "Col. William Camm War Diary," 855; Thomas C. Watkins Diary, April 6, 1862, 18th Illinois File, SNMPRF; "Seventh Iowa Volunteer Infantry Regiment in the Civil War," undated, Charles Thomas Ackley Civil War Letters, UI, 2.

24. OR 1, 10 (1): 251–253, 259, 268, 270–271.

25. Ibid., 206, 251.

26. Ibid., 171, 194, 419, 426, 501, 528, 543.

27. Ibid., 172, 191–192; Alex Oliphant to mother, April 8, 1862, 24th Indiana File, SNMPRF; Harry Watts Reminiscences, undated, ISL, 36; Alvin Hovey to Essie, April 21, 1862, Alvin P. Hovey Papers, IU.

28. OR 1, 10 (1): 194, 196, 202, 529–531, 627; Blackburn, Giles, and Dodd, *Terry Texas Ranger Trilogy,* 23–26, 111–122.

29. OR 1, 10 (1): 194.

30. Ibid., 172, 194, 200, 418–419, 424, 481, 488, 519–522, 618; Reed, *Battle of Shiloh,* 87; Richardson, "War as I Saw It," 104.

31. OR 1, 10 (1): 627; Force, *From Fort Henry to Corinth,* 170, 176; Richardson, "War as I Saw It," 105; Kendall, "Recollections of a Confederate Officer," 1069.

32. Ibid., 172, 194, 200, 418–419, 424, 481, 488, 519–522, 618; Reed, *Battle of Shiloh,* 87; Richardson, "War as I Saw It," 104.

33. OR 1, 10 (1): 325, 336, 339, 352, 449, 452, 514, 535.

34. S. H. Dent to wife, April 9, 1862, Stouton Hubert Dent Papers, ADAH.

35. OR 1, 10 (1): 294–295, 301, 360, 362, 365, 371–373, 376, 611; E. S. Drake to sister, April 13, 1862, E. Steel Drake Papers, HCWRT, USAMHI.

36. OR 1, 10 (1): 413, 437; SOR 1, 1:654; John E. Magee Diary, April 7, 1862, DU; George W. Jones Diary, April 7, 1862, Stanford's Battery File, SNMPRF; Augustus Hervey Mecklin Diary, April 7, 1862, MDAH.

37. OR 1, 10 (1): 294, 301, 322.

38. Ibid., 120, 125–129, 149, 206, 221, 225, 311, 318, 320, 620; Briant, *History of the Sixth,* 109; Barber, *Army Memoirs,* 58; Camm, "Col. William Camm War Diary," 855; Thomas C. Watkins Diary, April 6, 1862, 18th Illinois File, SNMPRF; "Seventh Iowa Volunteer Infantry Regiment in the Civil War," undated, Charles Thomas Ackley Civil War Letters, UI, 2.

39. Lew Wallace to wife, April 9, 1862, Lew Wallace Collection, IHS.

40. OR 1, 10 (1): 295; S. A. M. Wood to Jefferson Davis, June 20, 1862, S. A. M. Wood Papers, ADAH. It is extremely difficult to determine the exact timing and sequence of Wood's attack. Numerous authors provide differing accounts, and the original sources, compounded by the lack of any reports from Kirk's brigade, do not provide a clear picture.

41. OR 1, 10 (1): 594–595, 599, 606, 608; S. A. M. Wood to Jefferson Davis, June 20, 1862, S. A. M. Wood Papers, ADAH.

42. OR 1, 10 (1): 594, 602; S. A. M. Wood to Jefferson Davis, June 20, 1862, S. A. M. Wood Papers, ADAH.

CHAPTER 20: "GET AWAY WITH WHAT WE HAVE"

1. Livaudais, *Shiloh Diary,* 33.

2. William Bradford to wife, April 10, 1862, William Bradford Papers, ISL; William Bradford Diary, April 7, 1862, ISL; OR 1, 10 (1): 255–256, 295, 302–304, 377–381; Hight and Stormont, *History of the Fifty-eighth,* 54; Robert C. Lane Diary, April 7, 1862, ALPL.

3. William McKinney to cousin, April 19, 1862, Wallace Family Papers, WSU; Andrew F. Davis to T. D. Davis, April 21, 1862, Andrew F. Davis Papers, CWTI, USAMHI.

4. William Bradford to wife, April 10, 1862, William Bradford Papers, ISL; OR 1, 10 (1): 255–256, 295, 302–304, 377–381; Thomas Tompkins to Jessie, February 7, 1915, Thomas Tompkins Papers, HCWRT, USAMHI; Kerwood, *Annals of the Fifty-seventh,* 56–57; William H. Kemper Diary, April 6 and 7, 1862, OHS; Genco, *To The Sound of Musketry,* 28; Hight and Stormont, *History of the Fifty-eighth,* 54, 59; Lee, *Thomas J. Wood,* 58; A. S. Bloomfield to sister, April 15, 1862, A. S. Bloomfield Letters, OHS; James O'Halligan to wife, May 21, 1862, James O'Halligan Letters, OHS; Robert C. Lane Diary, April 7, 1862, ALPL; William H. H. Hutton to aunt, April 11, 1862, Wiley Collection, John A. Logan Museum (copy in SIU); Villeroy A. Tambling Diary, April 7, 1862, SIU; John W. Tuttle Diary, April 1–10, 1862, University of Kentucky; Andrew F. Davis to wife, April 17, 1862, Andrew F. Davis Papers, UI; Wills, *George Henry Thomas,* 146–147; Edward Morrow Diary, April 1–10, 1862, MIAU; John T. Wilder to wife, April 16, 1862, John T. Wilder Collection, University of Tennessee at Chattanooga; partial letter, undated, William Leontes Curry Papers, UMCL.

5. OR 1, 10 (1): 158; Force, *From Fort Henry to Corinth,* 170, 176.

6. OR 1, 10 (1): 402, 421, 481, 490–491, 508, 511, 522, 528, 555; Livaudais, *Shiloh Diary,* 32, 37; McGrath, "In a Louisianan Regiment," 119; Reed, *Battle of Shiloh,* 20.

7. A. R. Chisolm to "Aunty," April 22, 1862, Alexander Robert Chisolm Papers, NYHS; OR 1, 10 (1): 402, 419, 481, 501, 506, 522, 539, 579, 602, 619; Clarke, *Diary of the War for Separation,* 158; Beauregard, "Campaign of Shiloh," 1:593; T. C. Robertson to mother, April 9, 1862, Thomas Chinn Robertson Papers, NC; Livaudais, *Shiloh Diary,* 32; Roman, *Military Operations of General Beauregard,* 1:317, 320, 532.

8. Jordan, "Notes of a Confederate Staff-Officer," 1:603; John Adams to P. G. T. Beauregard, April 7, 1862, P. G. T. Beauregard Papers, LC; OR 1, 10 (1): 109, 316, 388, 391, 402, 467–468, 501, 507, 579, 594, 600–602, 627; Sam to cousin, April 9, 1862, Eglantine Agours Letters, DU; Roman, *Military Operations of General Beauregard,* 1:318–323; Horatio Wiley to Josie, April 11, 1862, Shiloh Subject File, ADAH; Beauregard, "Campaign of Shiloh," 593; A. R. Chisolm Report, April 14, 1862, SNMPRF; W. W. Worthington to parents, April 10, 1862, L. P. Wulff Papers, UT.

9. Reed, *Battle of Shiloh,* 22, 79; Jordan, "Notes of a Confederate Staff-Officer," 603; Joseph D. Thompson to Mary, April 9, 1862, Joseph D. Thompson Papers, TSLA; Charles Swett Memoir, April 7, 1862, Swett's Battery File, SNMPRF; Giles B. Cooke Report, undated, Giles B. Cooke Papers, VHS; Cole, "John Cabell Breckinridge," 335; OR 1, 10 (1): 316, 388, 460, 524–526,

619–620; Shoup, "How We Went to Shiloh," 140; Roman, *Military Operations of General Beauregard,* 1:320; Camm, "Col. William Camm War Diary," 860.

10. OR 1, 10 (1): 388, 460, 524, 619–620; Jordan, "Notes of a Confederate Staff-Officer," 603; Roman, *Military Operations of General Beauregard,* 1:320; Braxton Bragg to wife, April 9, 1862, Braxton Bragg Papers, MHS; Sandidge, "Battle of Shiloh," 177; I. A. Stone Memo, April 6–7, 1896, Series 1, Box 14, Folder 185, SNMPAF.

11. OR 1, 10 (1): 388, 501, 535; Oliver, "Your Affectionate Husband," 10; Terry, "Record of the Alabama State Artillery," 319; Alfred Cox Smith to mother, April 10, 1862, Alfred Cox Smith Collection, MDAH; John S. Jackman Diary, April 7, 1862, LC.

12. E. C. Haydel to sister, April 13, 1862, Rosemonde E. and Emile Kuntz Collection, TU; Shoup, "How We Went to Shiloh," 140; Thomas Jordan to James R. Chalmers, April 8, 1862, James R. Chalmers Papers, NARA; unknown diary, April 7, 1862, 6th Arkansas File, SNMPRF; Jordan and Pryor, *Campaigns of Lieut.-Gen. N. B. Forrest,* 145; Oliver, "Your Affectionate Husband," 11; OR 1, 10 (1): 388–389, 457, 502, 531, 566, 595, 619; SOR 1, 1:655; John E. Magee Diary, April 8 and 10, 1862, DU.

13. Hosea, "Second Day at Shiloh," 6:206; Dodge, *History of the Old Second Division,* 205–206; Edwin A. Bowen to D. W. Reed, undated, 52nd Illinois File, SNMPRF; OR 1, 10 (1): 173, 295, 309, 316–318, 325, 360–363; SOR 1, 1:649; Fisher, *Staff Officer's Story,* 16; Harry Watts Reminiscences, undated, ISL, 37; Alvin P. Hovey Autobiography, undated, Alvin P. Hovey Papers, IU, 26.

14. W. R. Rowley to William T. Sherman, July 12, 1881, William Reuben Rowley Papers, ALPL; William S. Hillyer to Lew Wallace, April 8, 1862, Lew Wallace Collection, IHS; Enoch Colby to father, April 14, 1862, Francelia Colby Reminiscences, CHS; Harry Watts Reminiscences, undated, ISL, 37.

15. Camm, "Col. William Camm War Diary," 857, 859; Otis, "Second Day at Shiloh," 7:192.

16. Joseph D. Alison Diary, April 5, 1862, Holloway's Cavalry Company File, SNMPRF; OR 1, 10 (1): 109, 202, 295; OR 1, 10 (2): 97; Grant, "Battle of Shiloh," 1:478–479; Buell, "Shiloh Reviewed," 519; Avery, *History of the Fourth Illinois Cavalry Regiment,* 62; Otis, "Second Day at Shiloh," 7:193.

17. OR 1, 10 (2): 398–400; Joseph D. Alison Diary, April 5, 1862, Holloway's Cavalry Company File, SNMPRF; John McElroy, "Shiloh and After," *National Tribune,* April 19, 1906; Avery, *History of the Fourth Illinois Cavalry Regiment,* 62; Henry N. Peters to family, April 23, 1862, Peters Family Papers, UAR; Arthur and George Wansbrough to parents, April 14, 1862, George and Arthur Wansbrough Letters, OHS; George to father, April 22, 1862, John P. Sanderson Papers, OHS.

18. OR 1, 10 (1): 125–126, 145, 232–233; 269, 271, 276–277; SOR 1, 1:630;

N. H. Hardgrove to William Hardgrove, April 26, 1862, Hardgrove Family Papers, UVA; George Carrington Diary, April 7, 1862, CHS; John R. Woodward to Ellen, April 13, 1862, 71st Ohio File, SNMPRF; Joseph Harper to wife, April 9, 1862, John W. Gillette Collection, UMB; Downing, *Downing's Civil War Diary*, 43; Blanchard, *I Marched with Sherman*, 58; *Report of the Proceedings of the Society of the Army of the Tennessee*, 54; George O. Smith, "Brief History of the 17th Regiment of the Illinois Volunteer Infantry, Dec. 25, 1913," ALPL, 3; William J. Kennedy to mother, April 20, 1862, William J. Kennedy Papers, ALPL; Charles G. Hunt to Miss Herrett, April 17, 1862, Charles G. Hunt Letter, UMB; Ephraim Dawes to Kate, April 13, 1862, Ephraim C. Dawes Papers, NL; Samuel D. Lougheed to wife, April 20, 1862, Samuel D. Lougheed Papers, UWS; Virgil Moats to Eliza, April 9, 1862, Virgil Henry Moats Papers, UMCL; L. S. Willard to brother, April 8, 1862, L. S. Willard Letters, NL.

19. Saul Howell Diary, April 8, 1862, SHSI; OR 1, 10 (1): 109, 147, 149–151, 163, 196, 336, 369, 378; William Bradford to wife, April 10, 1862, William Bradford Papers, ISL; OR 1, 10 (2): 104; William Robinson to Charlie, April 19, 1862, William Culbertson Robinson Papers, ALPL; Oliver Boardman to family, April 24, 1862, Oliver Boardman Correspondence and Journals, UI.

20. Almon F. Rockwell Diary, April 8, 1862, LC; OR 1, 10 (1): 108, 169, 268, 295, 378, 640; Kerwood, *Annals of the Fifty-seventh*, 59.

21. OR 1, 10 (1): 263, 620, 640; Roman, *Military Operations of General Beauregard*, 1:322; Johnston, *Life of Gen. Albert Sidney Johnston*, 653; Henry N. Peters to family, April 23, 1862, Peters Family Papers, UAR.

22. Jordan and Pryor, *Campaigns of Lieut.-Gen. N. B. Forrest*, 146–148; Wills, *Confederacy's Greatest Cavalryman*, 70; Benjamin D. Fearing to sister, April 13, 1862, Ephraim C, Dawes Papers, NL; Ephraim Dawes to Marshal, April 21, 1862, Ephraim C. Dawes Papers, NL; OR 1, 10 (1): 263, 620, 640, 923–924; Avery, *History of the Fourth Illinois Cavalry Regiment*, 63; Issac F. Harrison, "Civil War Reminiscences," undated, J. F. H. Claiborne Papers, UNC.

23. Alfred Cox Smith to mother, April 10, 1862, Alfred Cox Smith Collection, MDAH.

24. *Report of the Proceedings of the Society of the Army of the Tennessee*, 57.

25. Augustus Hervey Mecklin Diary, April 7, 1862, MDAH; OR 1, 10 (1): 263, 266, 640; McCormick, "Sixteen Months a Prisoner of War," 5:69–78; Karl Donitz to brother, April 2 (?), 1862, Karl Donitz Letters, Civil War Correspondence Collection, MCM.

26. OR 1, 10 (1): 402, 502, 522, 556, 566, 590; SOR 1, 1:654–655; John E. Magee Diary, April 7 and 8, 1862, DU; "Journal of the Orleans Guard," April 8, 1862, HNOC; William Wallace Fergusson Diary, April 11, 1862, Fergusson Family Papers, TSLA; C. J. Johnson to son, April 9, 1862, Charles J. Johnson Papers, LSU.

27. OR 1, 10 (1): 627; P. G. T. Beauregard Order, April 8, 1862, P. G. T. Beauregard Papers, NARA.

28. W. A. Howard to family, April 10, 1862, 33rd Tennessee File, SNMPRF; George Cotton to Kemp, June 6, 1862, George Cotton Letters, LSU. For Bragg's original report and that of his subordinates, see the Braxton Bragg Papers, WRHS; Braxton Bragg to wife, April 9, 1862, Braxton Bragg Papers, MHS (copy in LC); Jacob Reep to D. W. Reed, March 30, 1915, 19th Ohio File, SNMPRF; Maurice J. Williams Diary, April 9, 1862, 36th Indiana File, SNMPRF; William N. Mitchell to Rachel, May 11, 1862, William N. Mitchell Letter, SIU; H. F. Huffer to family, April 10, 1862, Henry F. Huffer Papers, HCWRT, USAMHI.

29. OR 1, 10 (1): 140, 150, 232, 254, 280, 285, 290, 298–299, 325–326, 346, 356, 503–504, 557; OR 1, 52 (1): 22; OR 1, 10 (2): 99; Collection Guide, November 14, 1994, George Harvey Papers, IHS; James R. Zearing to wife, April 8, 1862, James R. Zearing Papers, CHS; William C. Caldwell to parents, April 10, 1862, Caldwell Family Papers, RBHPC (see also the William Clinton Caldwell Papers, UMB); Charles M. Scott to Anna, April 6, 1862, Charles M. Scott Papers, UWS; John L. Harris to father, May 21, 1862, John L. Harris Correspondence, ALPL; Alex Morgan to Fanny, April 13, 1862, Alexander Morgan Letters, Baylor University; A. S. Andrews to brother, April 11, 1862, A. S. Andrews Letter, UT; Henry Spaulding to uncle, April 16, 1862, Henry S. Spaulding Papers, DU; Billings, *Hardtack and Coffee,* 301; Fahey, "Fighting Doctor"; Enoch Colby to father, April 14, 1862, Francelia Colby Reminiscences, CHS; Eli Clampitt to brother, April 20, 1862, Eli Clampitt Letter, ISL; Breakey, "Recollections and Incidents," 2:122; Anna S. Webb-Peck, "A Sketch of Hospital Life and Work," undated, Mary Ann Bickerdyke Papers, Kansas Historical Society; unknown to Mr. Moore, 1867, United States Sanitary Commission Records, 1861–1867, NYHS; William J. Kennedy to unknown, April 17, 1862, William J. Kennedy Papers, ALPL; Thomas F. Miller to B. W. Newton, March 29, 1862, Thomas F. Miller Letters, ALPL; Payson Shumway to wife, April 13, 1862, Payson Z. Shumway Papers, ALPL; O. A. Bridgeford to family, April 20, 1862, 45th Illinois File, SNMPRF; C. A. Kuhl, "Pittsburg Landing," *National Tribune,* May 3, 1883; "Reminiscences of the Civil War," Sara Jane Full Hill Papers, LC, 44–45; Barton, *Angels of the Battlefield,* 71–86.

30. OR 1, 10 (1): 298–299; Saul Howell Diary, April 9, 1862, SHSI; B. H. Brown to family, April 12, 1862, 29th Indiana File, SNMPRF.

31. George W. Jones Diary, April 8, 1862, Stanford's Battery File, SNMPRF; SOR 1, 1:660; Oliver, "Your Affectionate Husband," 11; William Doll Memoir, undated, William Henry Harrison Doll Papers, ISL, 74; Henry O. Beasley to wife, April 8, 1862, Henry Oscar Beasley and Family Papers, MDAH; John A. Morgan to sister, April 10, 1862, John A. Morgan Papers, LSU; Francis Terry Leak Diary, April 17, 1862, UNC; Eugene F. Falconnet Diary, April 6, 1862,

Eugene Frederic Falconnet Papers, TSLA; Alfred Tyler Fielder Diary, April 8, 1862, TSLA; J. W. Cullom to Mary, April 10, 1862, 24th Tennessee File, SNMPRF; Houston Huling Parker Diary, April 9 and 11, 1862, MDAH.

32. Barrow, "Civil War Diary," 722; George Hamman Diary, April 8, 1862, ALPL; Grant, "Battle of Shiloh," 1:480; E. W. Herman Diary, April 13, 1862, 7th Iowa File, SNMPRF; Fred True to sister, April 10, 1862, 41st Illinois File, SNMPRF. See also the various original documents from the bodies in Series 4, SNMPAF.

33. Alex Oliphant to mother, April 8, 1862, 24th Indiana File, SNMPRF; *Annals of the War,* 683; Francis M. Harmon to brother, April 11, 1862, 15th Iowa File, SNMPRF; Eli Combs to family, April 10, 1862, 31st Indiana File, SNMPRF; George to mother, April 10, 1862, 6th Ohio File, SNMPRF; Gustavus H. Cushman to brother, April 13, 1862, Gustavus Cushman Letters, SHSI; Livaudais, *Shiloh Diary,* 29; E. C. Alft, "Unknown Here, Shiloh's 'Bloody Sunday Battle Raged," *Elgin Daily Courier-News,* April 5, 1962; Edward H. Reynolds Diary, April 7, 1862, CWTI, USAMHI; William H. Kemper Diary, April 9, 1862, OHS; George Thomas to wife, April 27, 1862, Thomas Family Correspondence, ND; Camm, "Col. William Camm War Diary," 861; Fred True to sister, April 10, 1862, 41st Illinois File, SNMPRF; John R. Ziegler to Nell, April 16, 1862, John R. Ziegler Papers, ALPL; J. S. Fogle to brother, April 15, 1862, 9th Indiana Battery File, SNMPRF; Charles J. Cling Memoir, undated, 43rd Illinois File, SNMPRF; William Richardson to Thomas Jones, April 16, 1862, 25th Indiana File, SNMPRF; Barber, *Army Memoirs,* 60; Garrett Smith Ainsworth Diary, April 9, 1862, Garrett Smith Ainsworth Papers, USM; Alvin P. Hovey Autobiography, undated, Alvin P. Hovey Papers, IU, 27; Mungo Murray to Jenny, May 1862, Mungo Murray Papers, CWTI, USAMHI; Cadle, "Adjutant's Recollections," 5:385; Crute, *Confederate Staff Officers,* 185; E. B. Whitman to J. L. Donelson, April 29, 1866, RG 92, E 576, Box 53, NARA.

34. OR 1, 10 (1): 111; SOR 1, 1:655; John E. Magee Diary, April 10, 1862, DU; Eli Combs to family, April 10, 1862, 31st Indiana File, SNMPRF; Will to mother, April 13, 1862, 6th Ohio File, SNMPRF; Oliver Newberry to mother, April 13, 1862, Oliver Perry Newberry Papers, NL; Charles Cowell Diary, April 25, 1862, Charles Cowell Papers, USAMHI.

35. Calvin Shedd to family, April 19, 1862, Calvin Shedd Papers, University of Miami; OR 1, 10 (1): 100–108, 110, 411–413; Reed, *Battle of Shiloh,* 90–110; James Robertson Diary, May 1, 1862, Iowa State University; David P. Bunn Diary, April 10, 1862, ALPL; A. O. Lowe to Miss R. Porter, April 13, 1862, A. O. Lowe Letter, MDAH.

36. Greg Williams, unpublished Confederate casualty study; Grant, "Battle of Shiloh," 1:481, 1:485; Bouton, *Events of the Civil War,* 31–34; "Report of Killed, Wounded and Missing of the 2d Corps, Army of the Mississippi,

at the Battle of Shiloh, 1862," RG 109, E 103, NARA; OR 1, 10 (1): 136, 212, 327; Grant, "Battle of Shiloh," 1:480–481; Allen, "Shiloh! Grant Strikes Back," 48.

37. Payson Shumway to wife, April 13, 1862, Payson Z. Shumway Papers, ALPL.

CHAPTER 21: "FINISH THE JOB WHILE WE ARE AT IT"

1. J. W. Cullom to Mary, April 10, 1862, 24th Tennessee File, SNMPRF; George Sawin to wife, April 9, 1862, George Sawin Papers, CHS (copy in 58th Illinois File, SNMPRF); Williams, *From that Terrible Field,* 53, 55; W. H. Hook to cousin, July 28, 1862, David C. Turnbull Papers, ISL; C. J. Johnson to wife, April 11, 1862, Charles James Johnson Papers, LSU.

2. Hyde, "Battle of Shiloh"; W. H. Gilligan to parents, April 13, 1862, W. H. Gilligan Letters, ALPL; J. W. Cullom to Mary, April 10, 1862, 24th Tennessee File, SNMPRF; H. W. H. to parents, April 10, 1862, Shiloh Subject File, ADAH; A. Hickenlooper to family, April 11, 1862, Andrew Hickenlooper Papers, CWTI, USAMHI; Eli Combs to family, April 10, 1862, 31st Indiana File, SNMPRF; Samuel Kennedy Cox Diary, April 6, 1862, 17th Kentucky File, SNMPRF; Lew Wallace to wife, April 9, 1862, Lew Wallace Collection, IHS; Enoch Colby to father, April 4, 1862, Francelia Colby Reminiscences, CHS; Virgil E. Reed to brother, September 23, 1863, Virgil E. Reed Letters, Civil War Correspondence Collection, MCM; OR 1, 10 (1): 120; W. L. Patterson to mother, April 10, 1862, Patterson Family Papers, WSU; Alex Oliphant to mother, April 8, 1862, 24th Indiana File, SNMPRF; Torah W. Sampson to mother, April 12, 1862, Torah W. Sampson Papers, FHS; James Scully to wife, April 7, 1862, James Hall Scully Papers, DU.

3. Polk, *Leonidas Polk,* 114; Alfred Tyler Fielder Diary, April 7, 1862, TSLA.

4. Louis Arns to parents, April 14, 1862, 49th Illinois File, SNMPRF; Charles W. Beal to brother, April 18, 1862, Charles W. Beal Papers, ALPL; Enos P. Brobson to friends, April 20, 1862, Enos P. Brobson Letter, TSLA; Crawford, "Saline Guard," 71; D. M. McCullum to father, June 13, 1862, McCullum Family Papers, TSLA; Riley, "Confederate Col. A. C. Riley," 265; T. Otis Baker to son, April 10, 1862, T. Otis Baker Papers, MDAH; Ogden E. Edwards to brother, June 29, 1862, Robert S. Edwards Papers, ND; Thomas Rex King Diary, undated, TSLA; Joseph D. Alison Diary, April 5, 1862, Holloway's Cavalry Company File, SNMPRF; Terrah W. Sampson to mother, April 12, 1862, FHS; William Barnard to friend, April 11, 1862, Simon Peterson Papers, UMCL.

5. "Personal Interview with Mr. Aleck McDaniel," July 22, 1938, in Milligan, *Seeing Shiloh.*

6. Joseph Harper to daughter, April 27, 1862, John W. Gillette Collection, UMB; Elsie Caroline Duncan Hurt Diary, undated, MSCPL, 37; Smith, "Forgotten Inhabitants," 43; Helweg, *Lone Survivor,* 45–47; Lossing, *Pictorial History,* 2:286–287.

7. Unknown to Uncle Josiah, April 6, 1862, Josiah Knighton Family Papers, LSU; Samuel A. Agnew Diary, April 3, 1862, UNC; Mrs. James Ferguson McDougal Diary, April 7, 1862, Elizabeth Porter Pitts Collection, TSLA; Hettie Irwin Hardin Memoir, undated, TSLA; Mary Van Meter Diary, April 6, 1862, University of Kentucky.

8. John H. Gates to Eliza, April 6, 1862, John Hooper Gates Papers, TSLA; Susan P. Gaston, "Reminiscences of the War," undated, in "History of Old Tishomingo County," 1, Alcorn County Chancery Clerk Archives, Corinth, Mississippi; Inge, "Corinth, Miss., in Early War Days," 444; C. J. Johnson to wife, April 4, 1862, Charles James Johnson Papers, LSU; Gervais D. Grainger, *Four Years with the Boys in Gray,* 7 (copy in 6th Kentucky File, STRI).

9. Elsie Caroline Duncan Hurt Diary, undated, MSCPL, 33.

10. Ibid., 39; Charles Marshall, "Miscellaneous Incidents of the Civil War," Historical Reports: Research Reports on Army Units in the Army of the Tennessee, SNMPVF, 1–2; Fisk Gore to sister, April 12, 1862, Civil War Collection, MHS.

11. "The Fall of Shiloh Church," *Cincinnati Daily Times,* June 13, 1862; "The Fall of Shiloh Church," *Sacramento Daily Union,* July 29, 1862; John Paul Howell to Ronnie Brewington, September 26, 1990, Rhea and Howell Family, SNMPVF.

12. Smith, "Forgotten Inhabitants," 43–45; "The Shiloh Log Church House," Shiloh Church, SNMPVF. See Helweg, *Lone Survivor,* for a history of the cabin.

13. "Post Return of US Troops Stationed at Pittsburg Landing," July 20, 1862, in "Returns From Military Posts, 1800–1916," Microfilm 617, Roll 1532, NARA; Marshall, "Miscellaneous Incidents of the Civil War," 1–2.

14. Smith, *Untold Story of Shiloh,* 85–86; William H. Blake to brother, undated, William H. Blake Letter, UT.

15. Thomas Tulley to W. H. Harrison, April 14, 1862, William H. Harrison Papers, UMB; John H. Bills Diary, April 12 and 15, 1862, UNC.

16. Thompson, *Recollections,* 248; John H. Bills Diary, April 7, 1862, UNC; Turner S. Bailey Diary, April 14, 1862, UI; Ed Embly to family, April 28, 1862, HCWRT, USAMHI; L. W. Cantrell to P. G. T. Beauregard, November 17, 1864, Hardin County Letter, SNMPVF; Wright, *Corporal's Story,* 51; Thomas to Josephine, April 15, 1862, Wyckoff Family Papers, MHS.

17. Elliott, *Isham G. Harris of Tennessee,* 111; Cunningham, *Shiloh and the Western Campaign,* 329; Inge, "Corinth, Miss., in Early War Days," 444; OR 1, 10 (1): 390; Johnston, *Life of Gen. Albert Sidney Johnston,* 688, 699.

18. Duke, *Reminiscences,* 102; Johnston, *Life of Gen. Albert Sidney Johnston,* 635, 658; "Lines on the Death of the Confederate Gen. Albert Sidney Johnston, of Ky.," 1862, Confederate Broadside Poetry Collection, Wake Forest University; William H. Browning to brother, April 10, 1862, John Crittenden Papers, AU; Steen's Brigade Morning Report, April 23, 1862, Frederick M. Dearborn Collection, HU.

19. Stanley, *Autobiography,* 202–203, 205–207; Benjamin D. Fearing to sister, April 13, 1862, Ephraim C. Dawes Papers, NL; George to wife, April 9, 1862, 58th Illinois File, SNMPRF; Matson, *Life Experiences,* 83; OR 1, 10 (1): 499; Peter Bagley Diary, April 4, 1862, 23rd Missouri File, SNMPRF; Levi Minkler Diary, April 6, 1862, 18th Wisconsin File, SNMPRF.

20. Levi Minkler Diary, April 7–15, 1862, 18th Wisconsin File, SNMPRF; Peter Bagley Diary, April 7, 1862, 23rd Missouri File, SNMPRF; Henry O. Beasley to wife, April 8, 1862, Henry Oscar Beasley and Family Papers, MDAH; Charles A. Van Riper Diary, April 10, 1862, UMB; Seth Crowhearst, "Reminiscences of a Union Soldier," undated, Seth Crowhearts Papers, CWD, USAMHI; Chambers, "My Journal," 223; J. J. Little to parents, April 13, 1862, J. J. Little Collection, UM.

21. "The Life of Elias Perry," undated, Civil War Collection, MHS; "Letter from Col. Geddes," *Vinton Eagle,* July 16, 1862; E. M. Van Duzee to brother, May 28, 1862, Van Duzee Family Papers, University of Wyoming; Horace McLean to Mary, May 4, 1862, Horace McLean Papers, AU; J. M. Meek to wife, June 20, 1862, Meek Family Correspondence, ND; "Facts That Need to be Explained," *National Tribune,* April 19, 1883; Kiner, *One Year's Soldiering,* 61–153; Watson, "Turkeytown CSA," 301; "Gen. Prentiss at Washington," *Washington Herald,* October 20, 1862; "Gen. Prentiss at the Board of Trade," *Chicago Tribune,* October 21, 1862; "The Captivity of Gen. Prentiss," *Quincy Whig,* November 1, 1862. See the Willard W. Felton Diary, April 1862, WHS, for a good itinerary of the trip southward. For a good account of the 12th Iowa's prisoners, see Genoways and Genoways, *Perfect Picture of Hell.*

22. "Diary of a Rebel Officer," April 18, 1862, *Philadelphia Enquirer;* OR 1, 10 (1): 379; "Battlefield Memories," undated, Chelsey Davis Bailey Papers, IHS.

23. C. J. Johnson to son, April 9, 1862, Charles J. Johnson Papers, LSU; Jim T. Blankinship to Livie, April 18, 1862, 3rd Kentucky File, SNMPRF; unknown to wife, April 14, 1862, Civil War Soldier's Letter, UT; Lucien to folks, April 13, 1862, Edwin W. Payne Papers, ALPL; George F. Lanphear to sister, April 16, 1862, Lanphear Family Letters, UT; unknown to father, April 15, 1862, 9th Kentucky File, SNMPRF; Horace N. Fisher to father, April 2, 1862, Horace N. Fisher Papers, MAHS; William Bradford to wife, April 10, 1862, William Bradford Papers, ISL; Walter Keeble to Fanny, April 10, 1862, Walter Keeble Papers, USAMHI; John Ruckman to John Kinsel, April 12, 1862,

57th Ohio File, SNMPRF; Alex Oliphant to mother, April 8, 1862, 24th Indiana File, SNMPRF; William A. Huddard to father, April 16, 1862, William A. Huddard Papers, UT; Shelton to friend, April 21, 1862, Buel's Battery File, SNMPRF.

24. John Vogel Diary, undated, Frank L. Vogel Collection, Archives of Michigan, 4; William K. Strong to Henry W. Halleck, April 25, 1862, William Kerley Strong Papers, ALPL; John Q. Adams to Sarah, May 11, 1862, John Q. Adams Letters, USM; H. H. Bellamy to parents, undated, Henry H. Bellamy Papers, UMB.

25. OR 1, 10 (1): 375–376; Thompson, *Recollections,* 246; E. C. Sackett to family, April 13, 1862, Sackett Family Letters, ALPL; Orin Miner to Harry, June 10, 1862, Orin H. Miner Papers, ALPL; Eli Clampitt to brother, April 20, 1862, Eli Clampitt Letter, ISL; George Walkington to brother, April 26, 1862, HC.

26. Magdeburg, *14th Wis. Vet. Vol. Infantry,* 11; Briant, *History of the Sixth,* 127; Hurst, "Great Battle of Shiloh," 180; Camm, "Col. William Camm War Diary," 861; "Journal of Company 'A,' May 25, 1861–September 23, 1863," April 14, 1862, ALPL.

27. E. W. Herman Diary, April 11, 1862, 7th Iowa File, SNMPRF; Fisk Gore to sister, April 12, 1862, Civil War Collection, MHS; Garrett Smith Ainsworth Diary, April 12, 1862, Garrett Smith Ainsworth Papers, USM; J. M. Thurston Journal, April 12, 1862, MAHS; Henry Halleck to wife, April 14, 1862, Civil War Letters and Documents Collection, UMCL.

28. William S. Morgan Map, undated, Michael K. Lawler Papers, SIU; "Military Biography of Leon Joseph Fremaux," Leon Joseph Fremaux Papers, Civil War Collection, TU; Leon J. Fremaux, "Map of the Battlefield of Shiloh, April 6 & 7, 1862," LC; Shiloh and Corinth Map, undated, Jeremy Francis Gilmer Papers, UNC; Daniel, *Days of Glory,* 84; Engle, *Struggle for the Heartland,* 164.

29. Fisk Gore to sister, April 12, 1862, Civil War Collection, MHS; E. W. Herman Diary, April 13, 1862, 7th Iowa File, SNMPRF; William Richardson to Thomas Jones, April 16, 1862, 25th Indiana File, SNMPRF; Lennard, "Give Yourself No Trouble about Me," 35; "The Battle of Pittsburg as Seen by One of the Third Iowa," *Missouri Daily Democrat,* April 24, 1862; Charles Foster to S. J. Kirkwood, April 10, 1862, WS; Daniel L. Miles to wife, April 16, 1862, Daniel Lindly Miles Papers, ALPL; Payson Shumway to wife, April 13, 1862, Payson Z. Shumway Papers, ALPL; J. M. Bemis to brother, April 13, 1862, Bemis Family Papers, MHS; Henry Hole to sister, April 22, 1862, Henry F. Hole Papers, ALPL; Daniel Clark to sister, May 1, 1862, Woods Family Papers, NL; Mary Crowell to cousin, April 28, 1862, Mary Crowell Letter, ND; M. D. Leggett to "My Dear Leverett," April 27, 1862, Mortimer D. Leggett Letters, Lincoln Memorial Shrine; Cherry, "Gen. Grant at Shiloh."

30. OR 1, 10 (1): 110; William T. Sherman to John Sherman, April 16 and 22, 1862, William T. Sherman Papers, LC; Henry Hole to sister, April 22, 1862, Henry F. Hole Papers, ALPL; Boynton, *Sherman's Historical Raid,* 28–29; William T. Sherman to William G. Eliot, February 7, 1886, William Greenleaf Eliot Papers, MHS; Schenker, "Ulysses in His Tent"; Benjamin D. Fearing to sister, April 13, 1862, Ephraim C. Dawes Papers, NL. For the Grant/Sherman friendship, see Flood, *Grant and Sherman.*

31. OR 1, 10 (1): 121, 136, 253; George Carrington Diary, April 7, 1862, CHS; OR 1, 10 (2): 100–101, 106; Special Field Order 8, April 16, 1862, and Special Order 19, April 9, 1862, John McArthur Papers, NARA; Samuel D. Lougheed to wife, April 20, 1862, Samuel D. Lougheed Papers, UWS; George E. Armor Discharge, April 19, 1862, George E. Armor Letters, IHS; *First Reunion of the 12th Iowa V. V. Infantry,* 21; B. F. Boring to Will, April 23, 1862, Benjamin F. Boring Collection, VCPL; Wilis to wife, April 20, 1862, Federals Soldiers' Letters, UNC; Samuel Putnam to father, April 18, 1862, Samuel Hildreth Putnam Collection, Marietta College; Lee Ogg to wife, April 9, 1862, Adams Lee Ogg Papers, ISL.

32. Thomas Stuart Birch Diary, April 26, 1862, EU; Sword, *Shiloh,* 443; George to wife, April 9, 1862, 58th Illinois File, SNMPRF; William Parkinson to family, April 19, 1862, William M. Parkinson Letters, EU; James C. Parrott to wife, April 19, 1862, James C. Parrott Papers, SHSI.

33. OR 1, 10 (1): 112–114, 174–190, 297, 358, 379, 381; Magdeburg, *14th Wis. Vet. Vol. Infantry,* 10; *Complete History of the 46th Illinois Veteran Volunteer Infantry,* 46.

34. George B. Wallis to J. G. Bennett, April 28, 1862, George B. Wallis Letter, LSU.

35. Reid, *Radical View,* 1:119–171; Gottlib Probst to Mr. and Mrs. Schneider, April 20, 1862, 32nd Indiana File, SNMPRF; H. R. A. McCorkle Journal, April 6, 1862, TSLA; Magnus Brucker to unknown, April 10, 1862, Magnus Brucker Papers, IHS; J. A. Williston to Elizabeth Tillitson, April 13, 1862, 41st Ohio File, SNMPRF; Emilie Quiner Diary, April 9, 1862, WHS; Ruston Maury to Ann, April 21, 1862, Maury Family Papers, College of William and Mary; Thomas Griffin to wife, April 23, 1862, Thomas Griffin Letter, UT; J. F. Owen to M. M. Owen, April 10, 1862, Owen Family Papers, TSLA; unknown to Mrs. M. Brayman, April [mislabeled March] 7, 1862, Bailhache–Brayman Family Papers, ALPL; M. D. L. Stephens Diary, April 5–8, 1862, UMEM; John Jones to Jefferson Patterson, April 12, 1862, Patterson Family Papers, WSU; Dewalt Shuster to brother, April 10, 1862, Dewalt Shuster Letter, Hamilton College; Edward Fulk to cousin, August 13, 1862, Edward Fulk Letter, Hamilton College; J. M. Stevens to wife, April 8, 1862, Shiloh Subject File, ADAH; Zillah Haynie Brandon Diary, May 8, 1862, ADAH; Eben Weston to Mary, April 27, 1862, Henry S. Weston Papers, CWD, USAMHI;

Albert Forbes to parents, April 16, 1862, Albert M. Forbes Civil War Letters, University of California, Irvine; Daniel Stout to wife, April 12, 1862, Stout Civil War Letters, UMEM; James H. Dobbins to Robert M. Banta, April 22, 1862, Robert M. Banta Papers, IHS; W. F. Grimsley to M. M. Owen, April 10, 1862, Owen Family Papers, TSLA; Robert H. Cartmell Diary, April 8, 1862, TSLA; Noah L. Gebbart to family, April 20, 1862, Noah L. Gebbart Papers, DU; W. H. Hardy to wife, May 3, 1862, William H. and Sallie J. Hardy Papers, USM; Mary Crowell to cousin, April 28, 1862, Mary Crowell Letter, ND.

36. Albert to mother, April 14, 1862, 16th Wisconsin File, SNMPRF; E. J. Nash to cousin, April 14, 1862, E. J. Nash Letter, MSU; OR 1, 10 (1): 122; James Butterfield to Kate, April 13, 1862, James A. B. Butterfield Correspondence, ALPL; Enos P. Brobson to friends, April 20, 1862, Enos P. Brobson Letter, TSLA; James E. Love to Molly, April 22, 1862, James Edwin Love Papers, MHS.

37. Chambers, "My Journal," 232; McDonough, "Glory Can Not Atone"; McEathron, *Letters and Memoirs,* 6; *Harvard Memorial Biographies,* 1:166; Neal, *Illustrated History,* 127; Finding Aid, Oliver White Peabody Papers, MAHS; Mary Crowell to cousin, April 28, 1862, Mary Crowell Letter, ND; "Col. Julius Raith" and "Funeral of Col. Raith," both in undated *Bellville Weekly Democrat;* Adolph Engelmann to Leonard F. Ross, April 12, 1862, and Ross, McClernand, and Grant approval endorsements, David Raith Collection; John A. Andrew letter, April 10, 1862, and E. Kirby to Frank Peabody, April 14, 1862, Amelia Peabody Papers, MAHS; Thomas Stuart Birch Diary, April 11, 1862, EU; Wallace, *Life and Letters,* 198; E. D. Townsend to T. L. Dickey, August 11, 1862, W. H. L. Wallace Papers, NARA; "Arrival of the Remains of Capt. Strong," *Monroe (MI) Commercial,* April 17, 1862; Walter Q. Gresham to wife, April 8, 1862, Walter Q. Gresham Papers, LC.

38. Thomas Stuart Birch Diary, April 11, 1862, EU.

39. F. M. Hereford Report, April 17, 1862, WS; Parks, *General Leonidas Polk,* 236; Young, *Reminiscences,* 35; Simeon C. Wilkerson to wife, November 4, 1862, Wilkerson Family Letters, AU; W. A. Howard to family, April 10, 1862, 33rd Tennessee File, SNMPRF; A. R. Chisolm to "Aunty," April 22, 1862, Alexander Robert Chisolm Papers, NYHS; Charles J. Cling Memoir, undated, 43rd Illinois File, SNMPRF; Thomas McFadden to unknown, undated, 46th Ohio File, SNMPRF.

40. Grant, "Battle of Shiloh," 1:485–486; Simpson, *Ulysses S. Grant,* 140–141; Thomas J. Harrison to wife, April 13, 1862, Thomas Joshua Harrison Civil War Letters, IHS; Sword, *Shiloh,* 459; Seeley Jayne to Lottie, April 14, 1862, Seeley Jayne Letters, ISL; William Innes to wife, April 26, 1862, Jean Simmonds Papers, ISL; Francis M. Harmon to brother, April 11, 1862, 15th Iowa File, SNMPRF; Dawson, "One Year at War," 194; Daniel Horn to wife,

May 1, 1862, Daniel Horn Papers, HL; John A. Gilmore to parents, May 15, 1862, John A. Gilmore Correspondence, HL.

41. George Lemon Childress Diary, April 15, 1862, ALPL; James A. Price to brother, April 21, 1862, Price–Moore Family Papers, IHS; Edward Hoopes to Lizzie, April 25, 1862, Hoopes Family Papers, MDAH. See also Smith, *Corinth 1862.*

42. Chillon C. Carter to family, May 9, 1862, Chillon Conway Carter Papers, Western Kentucky University (copy in 9th Kentucky File, STRI); General Order 47, May 1, 1862, John Mills Kendrick Papers, CHS; John Adams to father, May 14, 1862, Adams Family Collection, CWTI, USAMHI; James E. Slaughter to Braxton Bragg, April 20, 1862, HC; Norman Smith to Cousin, June 8, 1862, Norman Smith Papers, CWTI, USAMHI.

43. OR 1, 10 (1): 120–121.

44. Z. Coleman, "A Discourse on the Death of Gen'l W. H. L. Wallace: Who fell at the Battle of Shiloh, April 6, 1862," April 13, 1862, CHS; Sermon on Shiloh, April 20, 1862, William Weston Patton Papers, CHS; Peter Michals, "Shiloh," undated, Henry C. Marsh Diary, April 6 and 7, 1862, ISL; "Shilo Hill," undated, Richard M. Sandifer Papers, LSU. See also the poem in Catherine Diaden Pearson Papers, Western Kentucky University; SOR 1, 1:643.

45. Camm, "Col. William Camm War Diary," 861; OR 1, 10 (1): 290, 379.

46. J. S. to friend, April 17, 1862, Rombauer–Becker Family Papers, HUS; George Carrington Diary, April 8, 1862, CHS.

Epilogue

1. George Read Lee Diary, April 6, 1863, ALPL; Lorenzo A. Barker Diary, April 7, 1863, Archives of Michigan; Shanks, *Personal Recollections,* 247; Special Order 356, November 20, 1862, Don Carlos Buell Papers, NARA; Sherman, *Memoirs,* 1:244; Jesse Connelley Diary, April 9, 1862, ISL; OR 1, 52 (1): 559; *Second Reunion of the 12th Iowa,* 49.

2. Smith, "Handsomest Cemetery"; E. B. Whitman to J. L. Donelson, April 29, 1866, RG 92, E 576, Box 53, NARA; "A Visit to the Battle-Field of Shiloh—Appalling Picture," *Oxford Falcon,* May 24, 1866; "Shocking Condition of the Confederate Dead at Shiloh," *Talladega Reporter and Watchtower,* January 2, 1878; Ellis, "Who Lost Shiloh to the Confederacy," 313; Shoup, "How We Went to Shiloh," 138. For the national cemetery, see Series 4, SNMPAF.

3. Funeral instructions, undated, Jesse B. Drake Papers, CWD, USAMHI; Shiloh Association Survivors Certificate, 1922, William S. Mead Collection, IHS; *Annals of the War,* 690–692; Smith, *This Great Battlefield;* D. C. Buell to Robert F. Looney, June 9, 1895, Robert F. Looney Collection, MSCPL; Robert F. Looney to D. C. Buell, March 11, 1896, Don Carlos Buell Papers, FHS;

Reaves, *History and Guide;* McCutchen, "Of Monuments and Remembrance"; McCutchen and Smith, *Shiloh National Military Park.*

4. Rice, *Story of Shiloh;* Eisenschiml, *Story of Shiloh;* Rich, *Battle of Shiloh;* Martin, *Campaign of Shiloh,* 105; Nevin, *Road to Shiloh,* 130–135; "First Reunion of Iowa Hornet's Nest Brigade," October 12–13, 1887, Series 3, Box 4, Folder 216, SNMPAF, 12; *Manual of the Panorama of the Battle of Shiloh,* 5, 14; De Thulstrup, *Battle of Shiloh Lithograph;* Smith, "David Wilson Reed"; Smith, "Historians and the Battle of Shiloh." For Reed's papers, see Series 3, SNMPAF.

5. McDonough, *Shiloh,* 98; Castel, "Dead on Arrival," 37; "Shiloh," undated, Lewis E. Sisson Papers, LC.

6. Johnston, *Life of Gen. Albert Sidney Johnston,* 584.

BIBLIOGRAPHY

MANUSCRIPTS

Abraham Lincoln Presidential Library, Springfield, Illinois
Jacob Ammen Papers
Henry P. Andrews Papers
Bailhache-Brayman Family Papers
Henry H. Baltzell Memoir and Diary
Thomas Barnett Papers
Alphonso Barto Letters
John B. Beach Memoir
Charles W. Beal Papers
James A. Black Diary
Brush Family Papers
Daniel Harmon Brush Diary
David P. Bunn Diary
James A. B. Butterfield Correspondence
George Lemon Childress Diary
David McKee Claggett Diary
James F. Drish Papers
Engelmann-Kircher Family Papers
Charles H. Floyd Letters
W. H. Gilligan Letters
Ulysses S. Grant Letters
George Hamman Diary
Douglas Hapeman Diary
John L. Harris Correspondence
Henry F. Hole Papers
Albert Sidney Johnston Special Orders No. 8
"Journal of Company 'A,' May 25, 1861–September 23, 1863"
William J. Kennedy Papers
Robert C. Lane Diary

George Read Lee Diary
John A. McClernand Papers
Daniel Lindly Miles Papers
Thomas F. Miller Letters
Orin H. Miner Papers
Edwin W. Payne Papers
William Culbertson Robinson Papers
Felix Ross Diary
William Reuben Rowley Papers
Sackett Family Letters
Payson Z. Shumway Papers
George O. Smith, "Brief History of the 17th Regiment of the Illinois
    Volunteer Infantry, Dec. 25, 1913"
William Kerley Strong Papers
Unidentified Union Diary
Abram J. Vanauken Diary
Wallace Dickey Papers
Erasmus D. Ward Letters
John R. Ziegler Papers

Alabama Department of Archives and History, Montgomery, Alabama
Zillah Haynie Brandon Diary
Stouton Hubert Dent Papers
Shiloh Subject File
    "An Incident of the Battle of Shiloh"
    "The Death of Gen. Gladden"
    J. F. Gaines Letter
    H. W. H. Letter
    J. M. Stevens Letter
    Horatio Wiley Letter
    Unknown Letter
S. A. M. Wood Papers

Alcorn County Chancery Clerk Archives, Corinth, Mississippi
History of Old Tishomingo County

Archives of Michigan, Lansing, Michigan
Lorenzo A. Barker Diary
Frank L. Vogel Collection

Arkansas History Center, Little Rock, Arkansas
Rufus W. Daniel Diary

Auburn University, Auburn, Alabama
John Crittenden Papers
Horace McLean Papers
Liberty Independence Nixon Diary
Horace Palmer Papers
Wilkerson Family Letters

Augustana College, Rock Island, Illinois
Gould D. Molineaux Diary

Bartholomew County Historical Society, Columbus, Indiana
J. S. Fogle Letter

Baylor University, Waco, Texas
Alexander Morgan Letters

Bowling Green State University, Bowling Green, Ohio
Sarah V. Elder Dicken Papers

Brigham Young University, Provo, Utah
Adelia H. Hardin Collection

Brown County Historical Society, New Ulm, Minnesota
August Schilling Diary

Chicago Historical Society, Chicago, Illinois
John C. Breckinridge Papers
George Carrington Diary
Francelia Colby Reminiscences
Z. Coleman, "A Discourse on the Death of Gen'l W. H. L. Wallace: Who Fell
    at the Battle of Shiloh, April 6, 1862"
Presley Judson Edwards Autobiography
Richard Gapen Papers
Albert Sidney Johnston Papers
John Mills Kendrick Papers
Jacob Lauman Papers
James Lawrence Papers
William Weston Patton Papers
William H. Ross Papers
George Sawin Letters
Clifton H. Smith Papers
Lewis Wallace Collection
James R. Zearing Papers

Cincinnati Historical Society, Cincinnati, Ohio
Johnston–Jones Family Papers
Sobieski Jolly Papers
David J. Jones Papers

College of William and Mary, Williamsburg, Virginia
Maury Family Papers

Corinth Civil War Interpretive Center, Corinth, Mississippi
W. L. Culberson Letter, 19th Louisiana File
Alexander Livaudais Diary, 18th Louisiana File

Delta State University, Cleveland, Mississippi
Charles C. Jacobs Papers

Dubuque County Historical Society, Dubuque, Iowa
David B. Henderson Papers

Duke University, Durham, North Carolina
Eglantine Agours Letters
Pierre Gustave Toutant Beauregard Papers
Clement Clay Papers
Noah L. Gebbart Papers
Robert W. Honnell Papers
John E. Magee Diary
William Massie Papers
Pope–Carter Family Papers
H. H. Price Papers
James Wall Scully Papers
Henry S. Spaulding Papers

Emory University, Atlanta, Georgia
Thomas Stuart Birch Diary
Bomar Family Letters
William M. Parkinson Letters

Filson Historical Society, Louisville, Kentucky
Don Carlos Buell Papers
Johnny Green Diary
Albert Sidney Johnston Papers
John Joyes Papers
Joseph Maas Papers

Torah W. Sampson Papers
Edwin Porter Thompson Papers

Florida State University, Tallahassee, Florida
James Patton Anderson Papers

Hamilton College, Clinton, New York
Edward Fulk Letter
Dewalt Shuster Letter

Harvard University, Houghton Library, Cambridge, Massachusetts
Frederick M. Dearborn Collection

Harvard University, Schlesinger Library, Cambridge, Massachusetts
Rombauer–Becker Family Papers

Van Hedges Collection, Corinth, Mississippi
B. F. Batchelor Letter
A. R. Belser Letter
Braxton Bragg Letter
"Charges and Specifications against Col. S. S. Heard, 17th Regiment
    Louisiana Volunteers"
Thomas Jordan Letter
J. H. Miller Letter
Daniel Ruggles Letter
James E. Slaughter Letter
George Walkington Letter
Freeman Williams Letter
William Letter

Historic New Orleans Collection, New Orleans, Louisiana
P. G. T. Beauregard Letter
Journal of the Orleans Guard

Huntington Library, San Marino, California
Edwin A. Bowen Papers
John A. Gilmore Correspondence
Daniel Horn Papers
Moses A. McCoid Papers
Israel N. Prince Letters
Thomas Kilby Smith Papers
Thomas W. Sweeny Papers

Indiana Historical Society, Indianapolis, Indiana
George E. Armor Letters
Chelsey Davis Bailey Papers
Robert M. Banta Papers
Magnus Brucker Papers
Sylvester Wellington Fairfield Civil War Letters
44th Indiana Regiment Association Records, 1861–1938
Thomas Joshua Harrison Civil War Letters
George Harvey Papers
William F. Hinkle Diary
William S. Mead Collection
George W. Parsons Papers
Peck Family Papers
Price–Moore Family Papers
Lew Wallace Collection

Indiana State Library, Indianapolis, Indiana
Phelix Adair Articles
William Bradford Papers
Eli Clampitt Letter
Jesse Connelley Diary
William Henry Harrison Doll Papers
Seeley Jayne Letters
Leonard H. Mahan Diary
Henry C. Marsh Diary
Adams Lee Ogg Papers
James Shepard Correspondence
Jean Simmonds Papers
David C. Turnbull Papers
Harry Watts Reminiscences
Aurelius M. Willoughby Diary

Indiana University, Bloomington, Indiana
Alvin P. Hovey Papers
W. A. Howard Manuscripts

Iowa State University, Ames, Iowa
James Robertson Diary

Kansas Historical Society, Topeka, Kansas
Mary Ann Bickerdyke Papers
Fred L. Haywood Letter

Library of Congress, Washington, DC
P. G. T. Beauregard Papers
Alpheus S. Bloomfield Papers
Joshua Taylor Bradford Diary
Braxton Bragg Papers
Charles Buford Papers
Samuel Henry Eells Papers
Harry S. Elseffer Papers
John N. Ferguson Diary
Manning F. Force Papers
Leon J. Fremaux, "Map of the Battlefield of Shiloh, April 6 & 7, 1862"
Greene Chandler Furman Papers
Balzar Grebe Papers
Walter Q. Gresham Papers
Isham G. Harris Papers
Sara Jane Full Hill Papers
John S. Jackman Diary
Albert Sidney Johnston Papers
Robert W. Lee Papers
Todd Oliphant Diary
Leonidas Polk Papers
Richard Henry Pratt Papers
Reed Family Papers
Almon F. Rockwell Diary
Alfred Roman Papers
Bela T. St. John Papers
William T. Sherman Papers
Lewis E. Sisson Papers
William R. Stimson Papers
Lew Wallace Papers
Elihu Washburne Papers

Lincoln Memorial Shrine, Redlands, California
Lincoln Memorial Shrine Manuscript Collection
Mortimer D. Leggett Letters
Soldiers' Letters Collection
Will C. Holden Letter

John A. Logan Museum, Murphysboro, Illinois
Wiley Collection
    William H. H. Hutton Letter

Louisiana State University, Baton Rouge, Louisiana
William J. Christie Letters
George Cotton Letters
Gras–Lauzin Family Papers
Arthur W. Hyatt Papers
Charles James Johnson Papers
Josiah Knighton Family Papers
Henry D. Mandeville and Family Papers
John A. Morgan Papers
Thomas Richardson Letter
Thomas Chinn Robertson Papers
Richard M. Sandifer Papers
Peter John Sullivan Letters
George B. Wallis Letter

Louisiana Tech University, Ruston, Louisiana
Roland Oliver Papers

Marietta College, Marietta, Ohio
Samuel Hildreth Putnam Collection

Massachusetts Historical Society, Boston, Massachusetts
Henry Van Ness Boynton Papers
Elizabeth Boyle Everett Diaries
Horace N. Fisher Papers
Amelia Peabody Papers
Oliver White Peabody Papers
J. M. Thurston Journal

McLean County Museum, Bloomington, Illinois
Civil War Correspondence Collection
    Karl Donitz Letters
    Virgil E. Reed Letters

Memphis Shelby County Public Library, Memphis, Tennessee
Elsie Caroline Duncan Hurt Diary
Robert F. Looney Collection

Miami University, Oxford, Ohio
Edwin Witherby Brown, "Under a Poncho with Grant and Sherman"
Edward Morrow Diary
Samuel Richey Confederate Collection

Minnesota Historical Society, St. Paul, Minnesota
Christie Family Letters
Allyn K. Ford Collection

Mississippi Department of Archives and History, Jackson, Mississippi
Francis Marion Aldridge Papers
T. Otis Baker Papers
Henry Oscar Beasley and Family Papers
P. G. T. Beauregard Papers
John A. Cato Papers
5th Mississippi Infantry Papers
45th Mississippi Infantry Papers
Jobe Foxworth Diary
Patrick Henry Papers
Hoopes Family Papers
Jesse R. Kirkland Papers
A. O. Lowe Letter
William H. McCardle Papers
Augustus Hervey Mecklin Diary
Mississippi Governor, John J. Pettus, Correspondence and Papers, 1859–1863
Walter A. Overton Diary
Houston Huling Parker Diary
6th Mississippi Infantry Papers
Alfred Cox Smith Collection
Robert A. Smith Papers
Thomas Smith Manuscript
William Yerger Papers

Mississippi State University, Starkville, Mississippi
Isaac E. Hirsh Papers
Samuel Rankin Latta Papers
E. J. Nash Letter

Missouri Historical Society, St. Louis, Missouri
Bemis Family Papers
Braxton Bragg Papers
James Edwin Love Papers
Civil War Collection
    Fisk Gore Letter
    S. F. Martin Letter
    "The Life of Elias Perry"

William Greenleaf Eliot Papers
Madison Miller Papers
Wyckoff Family Papers

Murray State University, Murray, Kentucky
W. J. Stubblefield Diary

Muscatine Art Center, Muscatine, Iowa
Daniel J. Parvin Letters

National Archives and Records Administration, Washington, DC
RG 29—Records of the Bureau of the Census, 1790–2007
    Entry 293—1860 Census
        Agricultural and Manufacturing Schedule, 1860, Hardin County,
            Tennessee
        Population Schedule, 1860, Hardin County, Tennessee
        Slave Schedule, 1860, Hardin County, Tennessee
RG 92—Records of the Office of the Quartermaster General, 1774–1985
    Entry 576—E. B. Whitman Report
RG 94—Records of the Adjutant General's Office, 1762–1984
    Entry 63—Returns From Military Posts, 1800–1916
    Entry 159—Generals' Papers
        Don Carlos Buell Papers
        T. T. Crittenden Papers
        Ulysses S. Grant Papers
        Stephen A. Hurlbut Papers
        Jacob Lauman Papers
        John McArthur Papers
        John A. McClernand Papers
        Benjamin Prentiss Papers
        Lew Wallace Papers
        W. H. L. Wallace Papers
    Entry 286—William Preston Diary
RG 109—War Department Collection of Confederate Records, 1825–1900
    Entry 116—P. G. T. Beauregard Papers
    Entry 117—James R. Chalmers Papers
    Entry 121—Thomas C. Hindman Papers
    Entry 123—Bushrod Johnson Papers
    Entry 133—Leonidas Polk Papers
    Entry 286—William Preston Diary
    Entry 103—Correspondence of the Western Department and the Army of
        the Mississippi, 1861–1862

Entry 3—Letters, Telegrams Received and Sent by General Breckinridge's Command, December 1861–January 1863
Entry 97—Orders and Circulars of the Army of the Mississippi, 1861–1865
Entry 103—Report of Killed, Wounded and Missing of the 2d Corps, Army of the Mississippi, at the Battle of Shiloh, 1862
Entry 193—Compiled Service Records
Alfred Hudson
John J. Thornton

Navarro College, Corsicana, Texas
P. G. T. Beauregard Papers
James Cooper Papers
George H. Hash Papers
James H. Kerr Papers
O. H. Lowry Papers
Dempsey Neal Diary
Thomas Chinn Robertson Papers

Newberry Library, Chicago, Illinois
Ephraim C. Dawes Papers
Oliver Perry Newberry Papers
I. P. Rumsey Papers
Hiram Scofield Papers
L. S. Willard Letters
Woods Family Papers

New York Historical Society, New York, New York
Alexander Robert Chisolm Papers
United States Sanitary Commission Records, 1861–1867

Ohio Historical Society, Columbus, Ohio
A. S. Bloomfield Letters
Henry Otis Dwight Memoir
Samuel T. Evans Diary
John A. Gillis Memoir
William H. Kemper Diary
Charles G. Mount Diary
James O'Halligan Letters
Ohio Memory Community Collection
    Americus V. Rice Letter
John P. Sanderson Papers
David Harrison Thomas Papers
George and Arthur Wansbrough Letters

David Raith Collection, Colorado Springs, Colorado
Adolph Engelmann Letter

Rutherford B. Hayes Presidential Center, Fremont, Ohio
Henry Buckland Papers
Caldwell Family Papers
William C. Caldwell Papers
Rawson Family Papers
Rice Family Collection

Shiloh National Military Park, Shiloh, Tennessee
Monuments and Tablets

Shiloh National Military Park Administrative Files
Series 1—Administrative Files
    Army of the Ohio File
    Samuel E. Barrett File
    Edward Bouton File
    James R. Chalmers File
    A. H. Duncan Statement
    15th and 16th Iowa Controversy File
    "First Reunion of Iowa Hornet's Nest Brigade"
    Horace N. Fisher File
    Daniel C. Govan File
    Landowner Chains of Title
    "List of Houses on Shiloh Battlefield Mentioned in Reports"
    R. F. Learned File
    William F. Mosier File
    T. M. Page File
    Frank E. Peabody File
    L. M. Pipkin File
    John W. Powell File
    Reed Map, First Day
    Reed Map, Second Day
    William T. Shaw File
    I. A. Stone Memo
    Charles Swett File
    A. C. Waterhouse File
Series 3—David W. Reed Papers
Series 4—National Cemetery Records

Shiloh National Military Park Regimental Files
Albert Letter, 16th Wisconsin File
Joseph D. Alison Diary, Holloway's Cavalry Company File
Louis Arns Letter, 49th Illinois File
Peter Bagley Diary, 23rd Missouri File
James Balfour Letter, 45th Illinois File
Smith P. Bankhead Letter, Bankhead's Battery File
"The Battle of Pittsburg As Seen by One of the Third Iowa," 3rd Iowa File
J. L. Bieler Letter, 6th Indiana Battery File
Joseph Blackburn Letter, 70th Ohio File
Jim T. Blankinship Letter, 3rd Kentucky File
Edward Bouton Letter, Taylor's Battery File
Edwin A. Bowen Letter, 52nd Illinois File
Alex Boyd Letters, 9th Arkansas File
O. A. Bridgeford Letter, 45th Illinois File
A. H. Brown Letter, 29th Indiana File
William A. Brown Diary, Stanford's Battery File
T. C. Buck Letter, Stanford's Battery File
John C. Caldwell Diary, 9th Kentucky File
A. R. Chisolm Report
Charles J. Cling Memoir, 43rd Illinois File
Clinton Letter, 41st Illinois File
Eli Combs Letter, 31st Indiana File
Samuel Kennedy Cox Diary, 17th Kentucky File
J. W. Cullom Letter, 24th Tennessee File
A. N. Currier Letter, 8th Iowa File
Gustavus Cushman Letters, 3rd Iowa File
T. Lyle Dickey Letter, 4th Illinois Cavalry File
William S. Dillon Diary, 4th Tennessee File
A. P. Dysart Letter, 34th Illinois File
A. J. Eldred Letter, 12th Michigan File
Horace N. Fisher, "A Memory of Shiloh," Horace N. Fisher File
J. S. Fogle Letter, 9th Indiana Battery File
F. S. Gates Letter, 72nd Ohio File
George Letter, 58th Illinois File
George Letter, 6th Ohio File
Henry George, "Seventh Kentucky at Shiloh," 7th Kentucky File
D. C. Govan Letter, 2nd Arkansas File
J. S. Grammar Diary, Swett's Battery File
Leroy Guthrie Letter, 18th Missouri File
Francis M. Harmon Letter, 15th Iowa File
Isham G. Harris File

M. Harvey Diary, 57th Illinois File
E. W. Herman Diary, 7th Iowa File
Horatio Letter, 22nd Alabama File
W. A. Howard Letter, 33rd Tennessee File
George W. Jones Diary, Stanford's Battery File
Jonathan B. LaBrant Diary, 5th Illinois File
Edward Larkin Letter, 7th Illinois File
Samuel Rankin Latta Letters, 13th Tennessee File
L. D. G. Letter, Gage's Battery File
R. F. Learned Letter, 10th Mississippi File
Henry C. McArthur Diary, 15th Iowa File
Alexander McEathron Letters, 15th Illinois File
Thomas McFadden Letter, 46th Ohio File
L. W. Mills Letter, 2nd Michigan Battery File
Levi Minkler Diary, 18th Wisconsin File
T. W. Morgan Letter, 49th Illinois File
William F. Mosier Letter, 52nd Tennessee File
William Nicholls Letter, 15th Iowa File
R. M. Nichols Letter, 6th Kentucky File
Alex Oliphant Letter, 24th Indiana File
L. M. Pipkin Letter, 18th Louisiana File
J. W. Powell Letter, Powell's Battery File
Gottlib Probst Letter, 32nd Indiana File
Isaac Pugh Letter, 41st Illinois File
Jacob Reep Letter, 19th Ohio File
William Richardson Letter, 25th Indiana File
William Richardson Letter, 7th Iowa File
Felix H. Robertson Letter, Robertson's Battery File
John Ruckman Letter, 57th Ohio File
I. P. Rumsey Memoir, I. P. Rumsey File
George Sawin Papers, 58th Illinois File
Philip Shaw Diary, 32nd Illinois File
William T. Shaw Letter, 14th Iowa File
Shelton Letter, Buel's Battery File
William Skinner Letter, 71st Ohio File
Robert D. Smith Diary, 2nd Tennessee File
Charles S. Stewart Letter, 21st Alabama File
Stibbs Family Papers, 12th Iowa File
Charles Swett Letter, Swett's Battery File
Neh. C. Thomas Letter, 58th Ohio File
Atwell Thompson Letter, 3rd Division File
Fred True Letter, 41st Illinois File

Unknown Diary, 6th Arkansas File
Unknown Letter, 18th Wisconsin File
Unknown Letter, 31st Indiana File
Unknown Letter, 9th Kentucky File
Unknown Memoir, 59th Ohio File
Unknown Memoir, USS *Tyler* File
V. F. Vail, "Company K, of the 16th Wisconsin, at the Battle of Shiloh,"
    16th Wisconsin File
Charles Van Adder, "Colonel Aaron B. Hardcastle," 3rd Mississippi Battalion
    File
Thomas C. Watkins Diary, 18th Illinois File
Maurice J. Williams Diary, 36th Indiana File
J. A. Williston Letter, 41st Ohio File
Will Letter, 6th Ohio File
Witness Letter, 12th Michigan File
John R. Woodward Letter, 71st Ohio File
Christian Zook Letter, 46th Ohio File

Shiloh National Military Park Vertical Files
Bearss, Edwin C. "Artillery Study—Shiloh NMP"
Bearss, Edwin C. "Historical Base Map: Shiloh National Military Park,
    April 6–7,1862"
Bloody Pond
Donald F. Dosch, "The Hornet's Nest at Shiloh"
Hardin County Letter
Historical Reports: Research Reports on Army Units in the Army of the
    Tennessee
    Charles Marshall, "Miscellaneous Incidents of the Civil War"
William K. Kay, "The Sunken Road: A Study"
Land Owners at the Battle of Shiloh
Ray H. Mattison, "The Vegetative Cover of the Hornet's Nest Area During the
    Battle of Shiloh"
George A. Reaves, "A Report to Determine the Size and Condition of the
    Peach Orchard at the Intersection of the Sunken Road and Pittsburg
    Landing Road on April 6, 1862."
Rhea and Howell Family
Shiloh Church
    "How Bloody Shiloh Got its Name"
    Mary E. Stricklin, "Shiloh Church"
    Mary E. Stricklin, "The Shiloh Log Church House"
    Mary E. Stricklin, "Shiloh School Property Deed"
Significance of the Upper Landing on the Tennessee River
Tillman Cemetery

Southern Illinois University, Carbondale, Illinois
Ulysses S. Grant Collection
William H. H. Hutton Letter
Michael K. Lawler Papers
William N. Mitchell Letter
Isaac Parks Letter
Amos Sanford Papers
Villeroy A. Tambling Diary

State Historical Society of Iowa, Des Moines, Iowa
Isaac N. Carr Papers
Gustavus Cushman Letters
James H. Guthrie Diary
Saul Howell Diary
Henry C. McArthur Diary
James C. Parrott Papers
Job Throckmorton Papers
W. W. Warner Collection

Stones River National Battlefield, Murfreesboro, Tennessee
Jesse P. Bates Letters, 9th Texas File
Chillon Conway Carter Papers, 9th Kentucky File
Joseph O. Freeman Letter, 51st Tennessee File
David W. Stratton Diary, 31st Indiana File

Tennessee State Library and Archives, Nashville, Tennessee
Bills Family Papers
Enos P. Brobson Letter
Robert H. Cartmell Diary
W. A. Caruthers Diary
Civil War Collection
      Jesse P. Bates Letters
      A. M. Clayton Letter
      W. E. Coleman Letter
      5th Tennessee Infantry Papers
      Rufus Parkes Diary
      6th Tennessee File
      Marcus J. Wright Diary
Luther Howard Cowan Papers
Thomas J. Crowder Memoir
Eugene Frederic Falconnet Papers
Fergusson Family Papers

Alfred Tyler Fielder Diary
John Hooper Gates Papers
Hettie Irwin Hardin Memoir
Thomas Rex King Diary
Samuel Rankin Latta Papers
Lindsley Family Papers
H. R. A. McCorkle Journal
McCullum Family Papers
Bradford Nichol Memoir
Owen Family Papers
Elizabeth Porter Pitts Collection
Alfred Roman Memoirs
Spenser B. Talley Memoir
Joseph D. Thompson Papers

Tulane University, New Orleans, Louisiana
Andrew Devilbliss Letter
Army of Tennessee Papers
Civil War Collection
    Leon Joseph Fremaux Papers
Albert Sidney Johnston Papers
Rosemonde E. and Emile Kuntz Collection
Samuel Rankin Latta Papers
Stibbs Family Papers

United States Army Military History Institute, Carlisle, Pennsylvania
Anders Collection
    Francis M. Cummins Papers
    John A. McDowell Papers
    N. D. Starr Letter
Timothy Brookes Collection
Henry Burrell Papers
Civil War Documents Collection
    Rufus Bates Papers
    Alex Boyd Letters
    William Burge Papers
    Hugh T. Carlisle Papers
    John A. Cato Papers
    Leroy Crockett Papers
    Thomas O. Crockett Papers
    George Crosley Papers
    Seth Crowhearst Papers

Rufus Daniel Diary
Jesse B. Drake Papers
David Helmick Papers
Jason Hurd Papers
Edgar R. Kellogg Papers
Jonathan B. LaBrant Diary
Levi Losier Papers
Charles Lutz Papers
William M. McCarty Papers
Spencer Family Papers
Johnston Vandiver Papers
Willaim L. Wade Papers
Henry S. Weston Papers
Christian Zook Papers
Civil War Times Illustrated Collection
Adams Family Collection
Charles Bivens Papers
Timothy Blaisdell Letters
John C. Caldwell Diary
Andrew F. Davis Papers
Richard F. Eddins Papers
Fulton-Lenz Collection
Adley Gladden Papers
Andrew Hickenlooper Papers
Isaac Longnecker Letter
Charles McKay Papers
Mungo Murray Papers
Edward H. Reynolds Diary
Norman Smith Papers
A. S. Stewart Papers
Elijah Tucker Papers
Levi Wagner Papers
Thomas C. Watkins Diary
Thomas Webber Papers
Civil War Soldiers' Letters Collection
Charles Bacon Papers
Charles Cowell Papers
James J. Garver Papers
Haerle Collection
Charles Peck Letters

Earl Hess Collection
    Simeon McCord Papers
Harrisburg Civil War Roundtable Collection
    E. Steel Drake Papers
    Ed Embly Letters
    Henry M. Erisman Papers
    Samuel B. Franklin Papers
    Henry F. Huffer Papers
    Thomas Tompkins Papers
Hathaway Family Papers
Walter Keeble Papers
Thomas P. Latimer Papers
Lowry Hinch Papers
Mann Collection
    Cyrus F. Leasher Papers
    William Stahl Diary
Jacob Miller Papers
Northwest Corner Civil War Roundtable Collection
    John Dance Papers
Pennsylvania Save Flags Collection
    K. A. Moore Papers
Steele–Boyd Family Papers
Wiley Sword Collection
    James Peckham Letter

University of Alabama, Tuscaloosa
V. M. Elmore Letters
Benjamin J. Gaston Letters
Peters Family Papers

University of Arkansas, Fayetteville
William Stephen Ray Memoir

University of California, Irvine
Albert M. Forbes Civil War Letters

University of California, Riverside
Isaac C. Pugh Papers

University of Colorado, Boulder
Folsom Collection
    John Elwell Letter

University of Florida, Gainesville
James Patton Anderson Papers

University of Georgia, Athens
E. Merton Coulter Collection

University of Iowa, Iowa City
Charles Thomas Ackley Civil War Letters
Turner S. Bailey Diary
Oliver Boardman Correspondence and Journals
Civil War Collection
    "Iowa Infantry 3rd Regiment losses at Shiloh"
Andrew F. Davis Papers
James Baird Weaver Papers

University of Kentucky, Lexington
John W. Tuttle Diary
Mary Van Meter Diary

University of Louisiana, Lafayette
Alfred Roman Memoirs

University of Memphis, Memphis, Tennessee
Davis–Bills Civil War Letters
Griffin A. Stanton Journal
M. D. L. Stephens Diary
Stout Civil War Letters

University of Miami, Miami, Florida
Calvin Shedd Papers

University of Michigan—Bentley Library, Ann Arbor, Michigan
Henry H. Bellamy Papers
William Clinton Caldwell Papers
Folsom Collection
John W. Gillette Collection
James H. Hall Papers
William H. Harrison Papers
Charles G. Hunt Letter
Ephraim Shay Diary
Travis Family Papers

Charles A. Van Riper Diary
Walter Weener Papers

University of Michigan—Clements Library, Ann Arbor, Michigan
Wilson S. Beckley Papers
Civil War Letters and Documents Collection
    Henry Halleck Letter
    Jacob Thompson Letter
William Leontes Curry Papers
Clinton Haskell Civil War Collection
Virgil Henry Moats Papers
Simon Peterson Papers

University of Mississippi, Oxford
William S. Dillon Diary
J. J. Little Collection
Lockwood Collection
John D. Thomas Diary

University of Missouri, Columbia
John Tyler Jr. Letter

University of North Carolina, Chapel Hill
Samuel A. Agnew Diary
Taylor Beatty Diary
John H. Bills Diary
J. F. H. Claiborne Papers
Archie K. Davis Papers
Federals Soldiers' Letters
Jeremy Francis Gilmer Papers
Clyde Hughes Collection
James K. Kelly Papers
Francis Terry Leak Diary
Peters Family Papers
John Kennedy Street Papers
Isaac Barton Ulmer Papers
David Urquhart Letter Book
John Thomas Wheat Papers

University of Notre Dame, South Bend, Indiana
Mary Crowell Letter
Robert S. Edwards Papers

Johnston–Rhoads Family Correspondence
Meek Family Correspondence
Parks Family Correspondence
Thomas Family Correspondence

University of Oklahoma, Norman
Sheery Marie Cress Collection

University of South Carolina, Columbia
A. H. Gladden Papers

University of Southern Mississippi, Hattiesburg
John Q. Adams Letters
Garrett Smith Ainsworth Papers
John C. Breckinridge Dispatch
Garner/Ruggles Message
Gore Collection
William H. and Sallie J. Hardy Papers

University of Tennessee, Chattanooga
John T. Wilder Collection

University of Tennessee, Knoxville
A. S. Andrews Letter
William H. Blake Letter
Civil War Soldier's Letter
Nathan Crawford Letter
Thomas Griffin Letter
William A. Huddard Papers
Lanphear Family Letters
John E. Thompson Letter
T. J. Walker, "Reminiscences of the Civil War"
L. P. Wulff Collection

University of Tennessee, Martin
William B. Bate Papers

University of Texas, Austin
Samuel Houston Jr. Papers

University of Virginia, Charlottesville
Hardgrove Family Papers
Atcheson L. Hench Collection

Lew Wallace Papers
R. H. Wood Letter

University of Washington, Seattle
Manning F. Force Papers
Samuel D. Lougheed Papers
Charles M. Scott Papers

University of Wyoming, Laramie
Van Duzee Family Papers

Vicksburg National Military Park, Vicksburg, Mississippi
J. S. Grammar Diary, Swett's Battery File

Vigo County Public Library, Terre Haute, Indiana
Benjamin F. Boring Collection
Civil War Diary
David W. Stratton Diary

Virginia Historical Society, Richmond, Virginia
Giles B. Cooke Papers

Wake Forest University, Winston-Salem, North Carolina
Confederate Broadside Poetry Collection

Western Kentucky University, Bowling Green, Kentucky
Chillon Conway Carter Papers
Catherine Diaden Pearson Papers

Western Reserve Historical Society, Cleveland, Ohio
Braxton Bragg Papers
Mortimer Dormer Leggett Papers
William P. Palmer Collection

Wiley Sword Collection, Suwanee, Georgia
G. W. Baylor Letter
James R. Chalmers Letter
Charles G. Field Letter
Charles Foster Letter
James J. Fraley Letter
Dudley Hayden Diary
F. M. Hereford Report

Stephen A. Hurlbut, "Pittsburg Landing and Shiloh"
Martin V. Miller Letter
J. W. Parker Letter
Wiley Sword, "Shiloh: The Untold Story. New Information about the Battle"
Pitts Tucker Letter
Miles G. Turrentine Letter
Benjamin D. Wall Letter

Willamette University, Salem, Oregon
John G. Burggraf Letters

Stephen E. Williams Collection, Palmyra, Pennsylvania
F. M. Posegate, "The Sunday Battle at Shiloh"

Wisconsin Historical Society, Madison, Wisconsin
William Brown Papers
Willard W. Felton Diary
Emilie Quiner Diary
E. B. Quiner Scrapbooks

Wright State University, Dayton, Ohio
Patterson Family Papers
Wallace Family Papers

NEWSPAPERS

Bellville Weekly Democrat
Chicago Times
Chicago Tribune
Cincinnati Daily Times
Elgin Daily Courier-News
Madison Courier
Memphis Commercial Appeal
Memphis Press Scimitar
Missouri Daily Democrat
Monroe (MI) Commercial
New Orleans Daily City Item
New Orleans Picayune
Niles Republican
Oxford Falcon
Philadelphia Enquirer

Quincy Whig
Richmond Dispatch
Sacramento Daily Union
Southern Watchman
St. Louis Republic
Talladega Reporter and Watchtower
Vinton Eagle
Warren Independent
Washington Herald
Washington Post

PUBLISHED PRIMARY AND SECONDARY SOURCES

Abbott, Abial R. "The Negro in the War of the Rebellion." In *Military Essays and Recollections: Papers Read before the Commandery of the State of Illinois, Military Order of the Loyal Legion of the United States,* 372–384. Chicago: Dial Press, 1899.

Adair, John M. *Historical Sketch of the Forty-fifth Illinois Regiment, with a Complete List of the Officers and Privates and an Individual Record of Each Man in the Regiment.* Lanark, IL: Carroll County Gazette, 1869.

Adams, Robert N. "My First Company." In *Glimpses of the Nation's Struggle, Sixth Series,* 285–298. Minneapolis: Aug. Davis, 1909.

Allardice, Bruce S. *Confederate Colonels: A Biographical Register.* Columbia: University of Missouri Press, 2008.

Allen, Stacy D. "'If He Had Less Rank': Lewis Wallace." In *Grant's Lieutenants: From Cairo to Vicksburg,* edited by Steven E. Woodworth, 63–89. Lawrence: University Press of Kansas, 2001.

———. "Shiloh! The Campaign and First Day's Battle." *Blue and Gray* 14, no. 3 (February 1997): 6–64.

———. "Shiloh! Grant Strikes Back." *Blue and Gray* 14, no. 4 (April 1997): 6–55.

Ambrose, D. Leib. *History of the Seventh Regiment Illinois Volunteer Infantry, from Its First Muster Into the US Service, April 25, 1861, to Its Final Muster Out, July 9, 1865.* Springfield: Illinois Journal, 1868.

Anders, Leslie. *The Eighteenth Missouri.* Indianapolis: Bobbs-Merrill, 1968.

———. *The Twenty-first Missouri: From Home Guard to Union Regiment.* Westport, CT: Greenwood Press, 1975.

Anderson, Patton. "Autobiography of Gen. Patton Anderson." *Southern Historical Society Papers* 23 (1895): 57–70.

Anderson, T. B. "A Boy's Impression at Shiloh." *Confederate Veteran* 19, no. 2 (February 1911): 72.

Andreas, Alfred T. "The 'Ifs and Buts' of Shiloh." In *Military Essays and Recollections,* 105–124. Chicago: A. C. McLurg, 1891.

The Annals of the War Written by Leading Participants North and South. Philadelphia: Times Publishing, 1879.

"Anti-dyspeptic." *National Tribune,* May 1, 1879.

Arndt, A. F. R. "Reminiscences of an Artillery Officer." In *War Papers Read before the Commandery of the State of Michigan, Military Order of the Loyal Legion of the United States,* 3–15. Detroit: Winn & Hammond, 1893.

Avery, P. O. *History of the Fourth Illinois Cavalry Regiment.* Humboldt, NE: Enterprise, 1903.

Aymond, Wayne, Jr. "A History of the 16th Louisiana Infantry Regiment, CSA." MA thesis, Southeastern Louisiana University, 2006.

Badeau, Adam. *Military History of Ulysses S. Grant, from April, 1861, to April, 1865.* Vol. 1. New York: D. Appleton, 1881.

Ballard, Michael B. *U. S. Grant: The Making of a General.* Lanham, MD: Rowman & Littlefield, 2005.

Ballard, Michael B., and Thomas D. Cockrell. *Chickasaw, a Mississippi Scout for the Union: The Civil War Memoir of Levi H. Naron as Recounted by R. W. Surby.* Baton Rouge: Louisiana State University Press, 2005.

Barber, Lucius W. *Army Memoirs of Lucius W. Barber Company 'D,' 15th Illinois Volunteer Infantry, May 24, 1861, to Sept. 30, 1865.* Chicago: J. M. W. Jones Stationery and Printing, 1894.

Barrow, William Micajah. "The Civil War Diary of William Micajah Barrow, September 23, 1861–July 13, 1862." Edited by Wendell Holmes Stephenson and Edwin Adams Davis. *Louisiana Historical Quarterly* 17, no. 4 (October 1934): 712–723.

Barton, George. *Angels of the Battlefield: A History of the Labors of the Catholic Sisterhoods in the Late Civil War.* Philadelphia: Catholic Art Publishing, 1897.

Bassham, Ben. "'Through a Mist of Powder and Excitement': A Southern Artist at Shiloh." *Tennessee Historical Quarterly* 47, no. 3 (Fall 1988): 131–141.

Bates, Toby G. "'Without Doubt, History Will Do the Gallant Hero Justice': Benjamin Mayberry Prentiss and the Failure of American History." MA thesis, University of Mississippi, 2002.

Baylor, George W. "With Gen. A. S. Johnston at Shiloh." *Confederate Veteran* 5, no. 12 (December 1897): 609–613.

Beauregard, P. G. T. "The Campaign of Shiloh." In *Battles and Leaders of the Civil War,* 1:569–593. New York: Century, 1884–1887.

Belknap, William W. *History of the Fifteenth Regiment, Iowa Veteran Volunteer Infantry, from October, 1861, to August, 1865, When Disbanded at the End of the War.* Keokuk: R. B. Ogden and Son, 1887.

Bering, John A., and Thomas Montgomery. *History of the Forty-eighth Ohio Vet. Vol. Inf.* Hillsboro, OH: Highland News Office, 1880.

Berrien, John. *The Military Annals of Tennessee.* Nashville: J. M. Lindsley, 1886.

Bevens, W. E. *Reminiscences of a Private Company "G" First Arkansas Regiment Infantry, May 1861 to 1865.* Newport, AR: William E. Bevens, 1914.

Bevens, William E. *Reminiscences of a Private: William E. Bevens of the First Arkansas Infantry, CSA.* Edited by Daniel E. Sutherland. Fayetteville: University of Arkansas Press, 1992.

Bevier, Robert S. *History of the First and Second Missouri Confederate Brigades, 1861–1865, and from Wakarusa to Appomattox—A Military Anagraph.* St. Louis: Bryan, Brand, 1879.

Bierce, Ambrose. *The Collected Works of Ambrose Bierce.* 12 vols. New York: Neale Publishing, 1909.

Billings, John D. *Hardtack and Coffee, or The Unwritten Story of Army Life.* Boston: George M. Smith, 1888.

Black, Robert C., III. *The Railroads of the Confederacy.* Chapel Hill: University of North Carolina Press, 1952.

Blackburn, J. K. P., L. B. Giles, and E. S. Dodd. *Terry Texas Ranger Trilogy.* Austin: State House Press, 1996.

Blanchard, Ira. *I Marched with Sherman: Civil War Memoirs of the 20th Illinois Volunteer Infantry.* San Francisco: J. D. Huff, 1992.

Bouton, Edward. *Events of the Civil War.* n.p., n.d.

Boyd, Cyrus F. *The Civil War Diary of Cyrus F. Boyd: Fifteenth Iowa Infantry, 1861–1863.* Edited by Mildred Throne. Des Moines: State Historical Society of Iowa, 1953.

Boynton, Henry Van Ness. *Sherman's Historical Raid: The Memoirs in the Light of the Record.* Cincinnati: Wilstach, Baldwin, 1875.

Brazelton, B. G. *A History of Hardin County.* Nashville: Cumberland Presbyterian Publishing House, 1885.

Breakey, William F. "Recollections and Incidents of Medical Military Service." In *War Papers Read before the Michigan Commandery of the Military Order of the Loyal Legion of the United States,* 120–152. Detroit: James H. Stone, 1898.

Brewer, James D. *Tom Worthington's Civil War: Shiloh, Sherman, and the Search for Vindication.* Jefferson, NC: McFarland, 2001.

Briant, C. C. *History of the Sixth Regiment Indiana Volunteer Infantry: Of Both the Three Months' and the Three Years' Services.* Indianapolis: William B. Burford, 1891.

Bryant, T. J. "The Story of Shiloh." *National Tribune,* May 10, 1883.

Buell, Don Carlos. "Shiloh Reviewed." In *Battles and Leaders of the Civil War,* 1:487–536. New York: Century, 1884–1887.

Burress, L. R. "Who Lost Shiloh to the Confederacy?" *Confederate Veteran* 21, no. 9 (September 1913): 443.

Byers, S. H. M. *Iowa in War Times.* Des Moines: W. D. Condit, 1888.

Cadle, Cornelius. "An Adjutant's Recollections." In *Sketches of War History, 1861–1865,* 384–401. Cincinnati: Robert Clarke, 1903.

Camm, William. "Col. William Camm War Diary, 1861–1865." Edited by Fritz Hashell. *Journal of the Illinois State Historical Society* 18, no. 4 (January 1926): 793–969.

Castel, Albert. "Dead on Arrival." *Civil War Times Illustrated* 36, no. 1 (March 1997): 30–37.

———. "Savior of the South?" *Civil War Times Illustrated* 36, no. 1 (March 1997): 38–40.

Catton, Bruce. *Grant Moves South, 1861–1863.* Boston: Little, Brown, 1960.

Chalaron, J. A. "Battle Echoes from Shiloh." *Southern Historical Society Papers* 21 (1893): 215–224.

Chamberlain, William H. *History of the Eighty-first Regiment Ohio Infantry Volunteers during the War of the Rebellion.* Cincinnati: Gazette Steam, 1865.

Chambers, William P. "My Journal." In *Publications of the Mississippi Historical Society, Centenary Series,* 5:221–386. Jackson: Mississippi Historical Society, 1925.

Chance, Joseph. *The Second Texas Infantry: From Shiloh to Vicksburg.* Austin: Eakin Press, 1984.

Cherry, Mrs. W. H. "Gen. Grant at Shiloh." *Confederate Veteran* 1, no. 2 (February 1893): 44–45.

Chetlain, Augustus L. "Recollections of General U. S. Grant, 1861–1863." In *Military Essays and Recollections,* 1:9–31. Chicago: A. C. McLurg, 1891.

Chisolm, Alexander R. "The Shiloh Battle-Order and the Withdrawal Sunday Evening." In *Battles and Leaders of the Civil War,* 1:606. New York: Century, 1884–1887.

Clark, Donald A. "Buell's Advance to Pittsburg Landing: A Fresh Look at an Old Controversy." *Tennessee Historical Quarterly* 68, no. 4 (Winter 2009): 355–390.

———. *The Notorious "Bull" Nelson: Murdered Civil War General.* Carbondale: Southern Illinois University Press, 2011.

Clark, Robert T., Jr. "The New Orleans German Colony in the Civil War." *Louisiana Historical Quarterly* 20, no. 4 (October 1937): 990–1,015.

Clarke, H. C. *Diary of the War for Separation, a Daily Chronicle of the Principal Events and History of the Present Revolution, to Which is Added Notes and Descriptions of All the Great Battles, Including Walker's Narrative of the Battle of Shiloh.* Augusta: Steam Press of Chronicle and Sentinel, 1862.

Cluett, William W. *History of the 57th Regiment Illinois Volunteer Infantry, from Muster In, Dec. 26, 1861, to Muster Out, July 7, 1865.* Princeton: T. P. Streeter, 1886.

"Cobb's Battery Not Captured at Shiloh." *Confederate Veteran* 13, no. 2 (February 1905): 68.

Cochran, J. A. "Vivid Story of A. S. Johnston at Shiloh." *Confederate Veteran* 6, no. 2 (February 1898): 66.

Cockerill, John A. "A Boy at Shiloh." In *Sketches of War History, 1861–1865,* 6:14–34.

Cole, J. R. "John Cabell Breckinridge." *Confederate Veteran* 26, no. 8 (August 1918): 334–336.

Coleman, Christopher Kiernan. "Ambrose Bierce in Civil War Tennessee: Nashville, Shiloh, and the Corinth Campaign." *Tennessee Historical Quarterly* 68, no. 3 (Fall 2009): 250–269.

Complete History of the 46th Illinois Veteran Volunteer Infantry. Freeport, IL: Bailey & Ankeny, 1866.

Connelly, Jesse B. "A Hoosier at Shiloh, April, 1862." *Indiana History Bulletin* 32 (April 1955): 77–82, 95–97.

Connelly, T. W. *History of the Seventieth Ohio Regiment from Its Organization to Its Mustering Out.* Cincinnati: Peak Bros., n.d.

Connelly, Thomas Lawrence. *Army of the Heartland: The Army of Tennessee, 1861–1862.* Baton Rouge: Louisiana State University Press, 1967.

Cooling, Benjamin Franklin. *Forts Henry and Donelson: The Key to the Confederate Heartland.* Knoxville: University of Tennessee Press, 1987.

Cooper, Edward S. *William Babcock Hazen: The Best Hated Man.* Madison, NJ: Fairleigh Dickinson University Press, 2005.

Cope, Alexis. *The Fifteenth Ohio Volunteers and Its Campaigns: War of 1861–5.* Columbus, 1916.

Cotes, J. W. "The Iowa Brigade on Shiloh's Field." *National Tribune,* December 28, 1893.

Cox, T. B. "Sixth Mississippi Regiment at Shiloh." *Confederate Veteran* 18, no. 11 (November 1910): 509.

Crawford, William Ayers. "A Saline Guard: The Civil War Letters of Col. William Ayers Crawford, CSA, 1861–1865." Edited by Charles G. Williams. *Arkansas Historical Quarterly* 32, no. 1 (Spring 1973): 71–93.

Crute, Joseph H., Jr. *Confederate Staff Officers: 1861–1865.* Powhatan, VA: Derwent Books, 1982.

Cudworth, Darius A. "Memories of Fifty Years Ago." In *Glimpses of the Nation's Struggle, Sixth Series,* 223–237. Minneapolis: Aug. Davis, 1909.

Cunningham, John. "Reminiscence of Shiloh." *Confederate Veteran* 16, no. 11 (November 1908): 577.

Cunningham, O. Edward. *Shiloh and the Western Campaign of 1862.* New York: Savas Beatie, 2007.

Daggett, George H. "Thrilling Moments." In *Glimpses of the Nation's Struggle. Fifth Series. Papers Read before the Minnesota Commandery of the Military Order of the Loyal Legion of the United States, 1897–1902,* 440–480. St. Paul, MN: Review Publishing, 1908.

Daniel, Larry J. "'The Assaults of the Demagogues in Congress': General Albert Sidney Johnston and the Politics of Command." *Civil War History* 37, no. 4 (December 1991): 328–335.

———. *Cannoneers in Gray: The Field Artillery of the Army of Tennessee.* Rev. ed. Tuscaloosa: University of Alabama Press, 2005.

———. *Days of Glory: The Army of the Cumberland, 1861–1865.* Baton Rouge: Louisiana State University Press, 2004.

———. *Shiloh: The Battle that Changed the Civil War.* New York: Simon & Shuster, 1997.

———. *Soldiering in the Army of Tennessee: A Portrait of Life in a Confederate Army.* Chapel Hill: University of North Carolina Press, 1991.

Davis, Jefferson. *The Rise and Fall of the Confederate Government.* 2 vols. New York: D. Appleton, 1881.

Davis, William C. *Breckinridge: Statesman, Soldier, Symbol.* Baton Rouge: Louisiana State University Press, 1974.

———. *The Orphan Brigade: The Kentucky Confederates Who Couldn't Go Home.* New York: Doubleday, 1980.

Dawes, Ephraim C. "The Battle of Shiloh—Part I." In *Campaigns in Kentucky and Tennessee, Including the Battle of Chickamauga, 1862–1864,* 7:101–142. Boston: Cadet Armory, 1908.

———. "The Battle of Shiloh—Part II." *Campaigns in Kentucky and Tennessee, Including the Battle of Chickamauga, 1862–1864,* 7:143–171. Boston: Cadet Armory, 1908.

———. "My First Day Under Fire at Shiloh." In *Sketches of War History, 1861–1865,* 4:1–22. Cincinnati: Robert Clarke, 1896.

Dawson, George Washington. "One Year at War: Letters of Captain Geo. W. Dawson, CSA." Edited by Riley Bock. *Missouri Historical Review* 73, no. 2 (January 1979): 165–197.

Day, James G. "The Fifteenth Iowa at Shiloh." In *War Sketches and Incidents,* 2:173–187. Des Moines, 1898.

De Hass, Wills. "The Battle of Shiloh." In *The Annals of the War Written by Leading Participants North and South,* 677–692. Philadelphia: Times Publishing, 1879.

De Thulstrup, Thure. *Battle of Shiloh Lithograph.* L. Prang, 1888.

Dillard, H. M. "Beauregard–Johnston–Shiloh." *Confederate Veteran* 5, no. 3 (March 1897): 99–101.

Dinkins, James. "The Battle of Shiloh, April 6, 1862." *Southern Historical Society Papers* 31 (1903): 298–320.

Dodge, William Sumner. *History of the Old Second Division, Army of the Cumberland.* Chicago: Church and Goodman, 1864.

Dolnick, Edward. *Down the Great Unknown: John Wesley Powell's 1869 Journey of Discovery and Tragedy through the Grand Canyon.* New York: Harper Collins, 2001.

Dosch, Donald F. "The Hornet's Nest at Shiloh." *Tennessee Historical Quarterly* 37, no 2 (Summer 1978): 175–189.

Downing, Alexander G. *Downing's Civil War Diary.* Edited by Olynthus B. Clark. Des Moines: Historical Department of Iowa, 1916.

Duke, Basil W. *Personal Recollections of Shiloh, Read Before the Filson Club, April 6, 1914.* Louisville: Filson Club, 1914.

———. *Reminiscences of General Basil W. Duke, CSA.* New York: Doubleday, Page, 1911.

Duncan, Thomas D. *Recollections of Thomas D. Duncan.* Nashville: McQuiddy, 1922.

Durham, Thomas Wise. *Three Years with Wallace's Zuuaves: The Civil War Memoirs of Thomas Wise Durham.* Edited by Jeffrey L. Patrick. Macon: Mercer University Press, 2003.

Dyer, John P. *From Shiloh to San Juan: The Life of "Fightin' Joe" Wheeler.* Baton Rouge: Louisiana State University Press, 1961.

Eddins, R. F. "Four Years in the Confederate Infantry: The Civil War Letters of Private R. F. Eddins, 19th Louisiana Volunteers." Edited by Ralph A. Wooster. *Texas Gulf Coast Historical and Biographical Record* 7 (1971): 11–37.

Eighth Reunion of the 12th Iowa Vet. Vol. Infantry. Fayette: Reporter Publishing House, n.d.

Eisenschiml, Otto. *The Story of Shiloh.* Chicago: Chicago Civil War Roundtable, 1946.

Elliott, Sam Davis. *Isham G. Harris of Tennessee: Confederate Governor and United States Senator.* Baton Rouge: Louisiana State University Press, 2010.

———. *Soldier of Tennessee: General Alexander P. Stewart and the Civil War in the West.* Baton Rouge: Louisiana State University Press, 1999.

Ellis, A. W. "Shiloh." *National Tribune,* October 12, 1882.

Ellis, W. B. "Who Lost Shiloh to the Confederacy." *Confederate Veteran* 22, no. 7 (July 1914): 313–314.

Engle, Stephen D. "Don Carlos Buell: Military Philosophy and Command Problems in the West." *Civil War History* 41, no. 2 (June 1995): 89–115.

———. *Don Carlos Buell: Most Promising of All.* Chapel Hill: University of North Carolina Press, 1999.

———. *Struggle for the Heartland: The Campaign from Fort Henry to Corinth.* Lincoln: University of Nebraska Press, 2001.

———. "'Thank God, He Has Rescued His Character': Albert Sidney Johnston, Southern Hamlet of the Confederacy." In *Leaders of the Lost Cause: New Perspectives on the Confederate High Command,* edited by Gary W. Gallagher and Joseph T. Glatthaar, 133–163. Mechanicsburg, PA: Stackpole Books, 2004.

Eubank, Damon K. *In the Shadow of the Patriarch: The John J. Crittenden Family in War and Peace.* Macon: Mercer University Press, 2009.

"Facts That Need to be Explained." *National Tribune,* April 19, 1883.

Fahey, John H. "The Fighting Doctor: Bernard John Dowling Irwin in the Civil War." *North and South* 9, no. 1 (March 2006): 36–50.

Fanebust, Wayne. *Major General Alexander M. McCook, USA: A Civil War Biography.* Jefferson, NC: McFarland, 2013.

Ferguson, J. F. "The Army Surprised or the Commanders Careless." *National Tribune,* May 10, 1883.

Ferraro, William M. "A Struggle for Respect: Lew Wallace's Relationships with Ulysses S. Grant and William Tecumseh Sherman after Shiloh." *Indiana Magazine of History* 104, no. 2 (June 2008): 125–152.

Fink, Jacob. "The Fifty-fifth Illinois at Shiloh," *National Tribune,* May 3, 1883.

First Reunion of the 12th Iowa V. V. Infantry, Held at Manchester, Iowa. Dubuque: Times Printing House, 1880.

Fisher, Horace Cecil. *A Staff Officer's Story: The Personal Experiences of Colonel Horace Newton Fisher in the Civil War.* Boston: n.p., 1960.

Flemming, Robert H. "The Battle of Shiloh as a Private Saw It." In *Sketches of War History, 1861–1865,* 6:132–146. Cincinnati: Monfort, 1908.

Fletcher, Samuel H. *The History of Company "A," Second Illinois Cavalry.* n.p., n.d.

Flood, Charles Bracelen. *Grant and Sherman: The Friendship that Won the Civil War.* New York: Farrar, Straus and Giroux, 2005.

Force, Manning F. *From Fort Henry to Corinth.* New York: Charles Scribner's Sons, 1881.

Foster, John Watson. *War Stories for My Grandchildren.* Washington, DC: Riverside Press Cambridge, 1918.

The Fourteenth Wisconsin Infantry Corinth and Shiloh, 1862–1895. Indianapolis: F. E. Engle and Son, 1895.

Four Years with the Boys in Gray. Franklin, KY: Favorite Office, 1902.

Fowler, John D. *Mountaineers in Gray: The Nineteenth Tennessee Volunteer Infantry Regiment, CSA.* Knoxville: University of Tennessee Press, 2004.

Frank, Joseph Allan, and George A. Reaves. *"Seeing the Elephant": Raw Recruits at the Battle of Shiloh.* Westport, CT: Greenwood Press, 1989.

Fuller, J. F. C. *The Generalship of Ulysses S. Grant.* Bloomington: Indiana University Press, 1958.

Fullwood, Ronnie. *Shiloh: House of Peace: The Church That Named the Battle.* Selmer: G. and P. Printing Services, 2003.

Gay, C. L. "Death of a Union Soldier at Shiloh." *Confederate Veteran* 10, no. 4 (April 1902): 163.

Genco, James G. *To The Sound of Musketry and Tap of the Drum: A History of Michigan's Battery "D" through the Letters of Artificer Harold J. Bartlett, 1861–1864.* Detroit: Detroit Book Press, 1990.

Genoways, Ted, and Hugh H. Genoways, eds. *A Perfect Picture of Hell: Eyewitness Accounts by Civil War Prisoners from the 12th Iowa.* Iowa City: University of Iowa Press, 2001.

Gentsch, James F. "A Geographic Analysis of the Battle of Shiloh." MA thesis, Memphis State University, 1994.

———. *History of the 3d, 7th, 8th and 12th Kentucky, CSA.* Louisville: C. T. Dearing, 1911.

George, Henry. "Two Men Sought Water at Shiloh." *Confederate Veteran* 19, no. 9 (September 1911): 452.

Gibson, Charles Dana, and E. Kay Gibson. *Assault and Logistics: Union Army Coastal and River Operations, 1861–1866.* Camden, ME: Ensign Press, 1995.

Gleeson, Ed. *Illinois Rebels: A Civil War Unit History of "G" Company 15th Tennessee Regiment Volunteer Infantry.* Carmel, IN: Guild Press, 1996.

Gordon, Ed A. "A Graphic Picture of the Battle of Shiloh." *National Tribune,* April 26, 1883.

Grant, Ulysses S. "The Battle of Shiloh." In *Battles and Leaders of the Civil War,* 1:465–486. New York: Century, 1884–1887.

———. *The Papers of Ulysses S. Grant.* Edited by John Y. Simon and John F. Marszalek. 31 vols. to date. Carbondale: Southern Illinois University Press, 1967–present.

———. *Personal Memoirs of U. S. Grant.* New York: Charles L. Webster, 1885.

Gresham, Matilda. *Life of Walter Quintin Gresham, 1832–1895.* 2 vols. Chicago: Rand McNally, 1919.

Grimsley, Mark, and Steven E. Woodworth. *Shiloh: A Battlefield Guide.* Lincoln: University of Nebraska Press, 2006.

Groom, Winston. *Shiloh, 1862.* Washington, DC: National Geographic, 2012.

Grose, William. *The Story of the Marches, Battles, and Incidents of the 36th Regiment Indiana Volunteer Infantry.* New Castle, IN: Courier, 1891.

Gudmens, Jeffrey J. *Staff Ride Handbook for the Battle of Shiloh, 6–7 April 1862.* Fort Leavenworth, KS: Combat Studies Institute Press, 2004.

Hammond, Robert. "Army of the Ohio at Shiloh." *National Tribune,* July 4, 1907.

Hannaford, Ebenezer. *The Story of a Regiment: A History of the Campaigns, and Associations in the Field, of the Sixth Regiment Ohio Volunteer Infantry.* Cincinnati, 1868.

Hanson, Victor Davis. *Ripples of Battle: How Wars of the Past Still Determine How We Fight, How We Live, and How We Think.* New York: Doubleday, 2003.

Harbert, P. M. *Early History of Hardin County, Tennessee.* Memphis: Tri-State Printing & Binding, 1968.

Hardee, William J. "Biographical Sketch of Major-General Patrick R. Cleburne." *Southern Historical Society Papers* 31 (1903): 151–163.

Hart, E. J. *History of the Fortieth Illinois Inf. (Volunteers).* Cincinnati: H. S. Bosworth, 1864.

Hartpence, William R. *History of the Fifty-first Indiana Veteran Volunteer Infantry: A Narrative of Its Organization, Marches, Battles and Other Experiences in Camp and Prison, from 1861 to 1866.* Cincinnati: Robert Clarke, 1894.

Harvard Memorial Biographies. 2 vols. Cambridge, MA: Sever and Francis, 1867.

Hawes, Maria Jane Southgate. *Reminiscences of Mrs. Maria Jane Southgate Hawes: Daughter of James Southgate and Jane Smith, born Nov. 30, 1836.* n.p., 1918.

Hazen, W. B. *A Narrative of Military Service.* Boston: Ticknor, 1885.

Hedley, F. Y. *Marching through Georgia: Pen-Pictures of Every-Day Life in General Sherman's Army, from the Beginning of the Atlanta Campaign until the Closing of the War.* Chicago: Donohue, Henneberry, 1890.

Helweg, Duane. *Lone Survivor at Shiloh.* San Angelo, TX: Rimrock Writings, 2008.

Hess, Earl J. *The Civil War in the West: Victory and Defeat from the Appalachians to the Mississippi.* Chapel Hill: University of North Carolina Press, 2012.

Hickenlooper, Andrew. "The Battle of Shiloh—Part I." In *Sketches of War History, 1861–1865,* 402–438. Cincinnati: Robert Clarke, 1903.

———. "The Battle of Shiloh—Part II." In *Sketches of War History, 1861–1865,* 439–483. Cincinnati: Robert Clarke, 1903.

Hicks, Brian, and Schuyler Kropf. *Raising the "Hunley": The Remarkable History and Recovery of the Lost Confederate Submarine.* New York: Ballantine, 2002.

Hight, John J., and Gilbert R. Stormont. *History of the Fifty-eighth Regiment Indiana Volunteer Infantry: Its Organization, Campaigns and Battles from 1861 to 1865.* Princeton: Press of the Clarion, 1895.

Hillyer, W. S. "Hillyer on Grant at Shiloh." *Confederate Veteran* 1, no. 10 (October 1893): 298–299.

Hobart, Edwin L. *Semi-history of a Boy-Veteran of the Twenty-eighth Regiment Illinois Infantry Volunteers, in a Black Regiment.* n.p., 1909.

————. *The Truth about Shiloh: A Compilation of Facts and Figures*. Denver, 1909.

Holman, T. W. "The Story of Shiloh." *National Tribune,* September 14, 1899.

Horn, Stanley F. *The Army of Tennessee*. Indianapolis: Bobbs-Merrill, 1941.

Horsely, A. S. "Reminiscences of Shiloh." *Confederate Veteran* 2, no. 8 (August 1894): 234.

Hosea, Lewis M. "The Regular Brigade of the Army of the Cumberland." In *Sketches of War History, 1861–1865,* 328–360. Cincinnati: Robert Clarke, 1903.

————. "The Second Day at Shiloh." In *Sketches of War History, 1861–1865,* 195–218. Cincinnati: Monfort, 1908.

Houston, Sam, Jr. "Shiloh Shadows." *Southwestern Historical Quarterly* 34, no. 4 (April 1931): 329–333.

Hovey, Alvin P. "Pittsburg Landing." *National Tribune,* February 1, 1883.

Howard, Samuel Meek. *The Illustrated Comprehensive History of the Great Battle of Shiloh*. Gettysburg, SD, 1921.

Howell, H. Grady. *Going to Meet the Yankees: A History of the "Bloody Sixth" Mississippi Infantry, CSA*. Jackson: Chickasaw Bayou Press, 1981.

Hubbard, Lucius F. "Minnesota in the Battle of Corinth." In *Glimpses of the Nation's Stuggle, Sixth Series,* 479–496. Minneapolis: Aug. Davis, 1909.

Hubert, Charles F. *History of the Fiftieth Regiment Illinois Volunteer Infantry in the War of the Union*. Kansas City: Western Veteran Publishing, 1894.

Huffstodt, Jim. *Hard Dying Men: The Story of General W. H. L. Wallace, General T. E. G. Ransom, and Their "Old Eleventh" Illinois Infantry in the American Civil War (1861–1865)*. Bowie, MD: Heritage Books, 1991.

Hughes, Nathaniel Cheairs, Jr. *The Battle of Belmont: Grant Strikes South*. Chapel Hill: University of North Carolina Press, 1991.

————. *Brigadier General Tyree H. Bell: Forrest's Fighting Lieutenant*. Knoxville: University of Tennessee Press, 2004.

————. *General William J. Hardee: Old Reliable*. Baton Rouge: Louisiana State University Press, 1965.

————. *The Pride of the Confederate Artillery: The Washington Artillery in the Army of Tennessee*. Baton Rouge: Louisianan State University Press, 1997.

————. *Sir Henry Morton Stanley: Confederate*. Baton Rouge: Louisiana State Univ. Press, 2000.

Hurst, T. M. "The Great Battle of Shiloh." *Confederate Veteran* 1, no. 6 (June 1893): 179–181.

Hurter, Henry S. "Narrative of the First Battery of Light Artillery." In *Minnesota in the Civil and Indian Wars, 1861–1865,* 640–649. 2nd ed. St. Paul, MN: Pioneer Press, 1891.

Hyde, Anne Bachman. "The Battle of Shiloh." *Confederate Veteran* 31, no. 4 (April 1923): 129–132.

Inge, Mrs. F. A. "Corinth, Miss., in Early War Days." *Confederate Veteran* 17, no. 9 (September 1909): 442–444.

———. "Corinth, Miss., in War Times." *Confederate Veteran* 23, no. 9 (September 1915): 412–413.

Isbell, Timothy T. *Shiloh and Corinth: Sentinels of Stone.* Jackson: University Press of Mississippi, 2007.

Jackson, W. W. "The Battle of Shiloh." *National Tribune,* December 24, 1885.

Jessee, James W. *Civil War Diaries of James W. Jessee, 1861–1865.* Edited by William P. LaBounty. Normal, IL: McLean County Genealogical Society, 1997.

Johnson, Mark W. *That Body of Brave Men: The US Regular Infantry and the Civil War in the West.* Boston: Da Capo Press, 2003.

Johnston, William Preston. "Albert Sidney Johnston at Shiloh." In *Battles and Leaders of the Civil War,* 1:540–568. New York: Century, 1884–1887.

———. *The Life of Gen. Albert Sidney Johnston: His Service in the Armies of the United States, the Republic of Texas, and the Confederate States.* New York: D. Appleton, 1879.

Joiner, Gary D. *Mr. Lincoln's Brown Water Navy: The Mississippi Squadron.* New York: Rowman & Littlefield, 2007.

———. "'Soul-Stirring Music to Our Ears': Gunboats at Shiloh." In *The Shiloh Campaign,* edited by Steven E. Woodworth, 96–109. Carbondale: Southern Illinois University Press, 2009.

Jones, D. Lloyd. "The Battle of Shiloh." In *War Papers Read before the Commandery of the State of Wisconsin, Military Order of the Loyal Legion of the United States,* 51–60. Milwaukee: Burdick & Allen, 1914.

Jones, Frank J. "Personal Recollections and Experience of a Soldier during the War of the Rebellion." In *Sketches of War History, 1861–1865,* 6:111–131. Cincinnati: Monfort, 1908.

Jones, James A. "About the Battle of Shiloh." *Confederate Veteran* 7, no. 12 (December 1899): 556.

Jordan, Thomas. "The Battle of Shiloh." *Southern Historical Society Papers* 35 (1907): 204–230.

———. "Notes of a Confederate Staff-Officer at Shiloh." In *Battles and Leaders of the Civil War,* 1:594–603. New York: Century, 1884–1887.

———. "Recollections of General Beauregard's Service in West Tennessee in the Spring of 1862." *Southern Historical Society Papers* 8 (1880): 404–417.

Jordan, Thomas, and J. P. Pryor. *The Campaigns of Lieut.-Gen. N. B. Forrest and of Forrest's Cavalry, with Portraits, Maps, and Illustrations.* New Orleans: Blelock, 1868.

Jorgensen, Jay A. "Scouting for Ulysses S. Grant: The 5th Ohio Cavalry in the Shiloh Campaign." *Civil War Regiments* 4, no. 1 (1994): 44–77.

Journal of the State Convention and Ordinances and Resolutions Adopted in January, 1861, with an Appendix. Jackson: E. Barksdale, 1861.

Kelly, R. M. "Not Surprised, but Unprepared." *National Tribune,* April 19, 1883.

Kelsey, Jasper. "The Battle of Shiloh." *Confederate Veteran* 25, no. 2 (February 1917): 71–74.

Kendall, John Irwin. "Recollections of a Confederate Officer." Edited by John Smith Kendall. *Louisiana Historical Quarterly* 29, no. 4 (October 1946): 1,041–1,071.

Kerwan, A. D. *Johnny Green of the Orphan Brigade: The Journal of a Confederate Soldier.* Lexington: University of Kentucky Press, 1956.

Kerwood, Asbury L. *Annals of the Fifty-seventh Regiment Indiana Volunteers: Marches, Battles, and Incidents of Army Life by a Member of the Regiment.* Dayton: W. J. Shuey, 1868.

Kimbell, Charles B. *History of Battery "A" First Illinois Light Artillery Volunteers.* Chicago: Cushing, 1899.

Kimberly, Robert L., and Ephraim S. Holloway. *The Forty-first Ohio Veteran Volunteer Infantry in the War of the Rebellion, 1861–1865.* Cleveland: W. R. Smellie, 1897.

Kiner, F. F. *One Year's Soldiering, Embracing the Battles of Fort Donelson and Shiloh.* Lancaster: E. H. Thomas, 1863.

King, W. C., and W. P. Derby, eds. *Camp-Fire Sketches and Battle-Field Echoes.* Springfield, MA: King, Richardson, 1886.

Kiper, Richard L. *Major General John Alexander McClernand: Politician in Uniform.* Kent, OH: Kent State University Press, 1999.

Kuhl, C. A. "Pittsburg Landing." *National Tribune,* May 3, 1883.

Lash, Jeffrey N. *A Politician Turned General: The Civil War Career of Stephen Augustus Hurlbut.* Kent, OH: Kent State University Press, 2003.

Laver, Harry S. *A General Who Will Fight: The Leadership of Ulysses S. Grant.* Lexington: University Press of Kentucky, 2012.

Lawrence, Elijah C. "Stuart's Brigade at Shiloh." *Civil War Papers Read before the Commandery of the State of Massachusetts, Military Order of the Loyal Legion of the United States,* 489–496. Boston, 1900.

Lee, Dan. *Kentuckian in Blue: A Biography of Major General Lovell Harrison Rousseau.* Jefferson, NC: McFarland, 2010.

———. *Thomas J. Wood: A Biography of the Union General in the Civil War.* Jefferson, NC: McFarland, 2012.

Lee, W. H. "Maj. John C. Thompson, of Mississippi." *Confederate Veteran* 11, no. 11 (November 1908): 585.

Le Monnier, Y. R. "Who Lost Shiloh to the Confederacy." *Confederate Veteran* 21, no. 11 (November 1913): 533.

———. "Who Lost Shiloh to the Confederacy." *Confederate Veteran* 22, no. 9 (September 1914): 415–416.

Lennard, George W. "Give Yourself No Trouble about Me: The Shiloh Letters of George W. Lennard." Edited by Paul Hubbard and Christine Lewis. *Indiana Magazine of History* 76, no. 1 (March 1980): 21–53.

Livaudais, Emmond Enoul. *The Shiloh Diary of Emmond Enoul Livaudais.* Edited by Stanley J. Guerin, Earl C. Woods, and Charles E. Nolan. New Orleans: Archdiocese of New Orleans, 1992.

Lockett, Samuel. "Surprise and Withdrawal at Shiloh." In *Battles and Leaders of the Civil War,* 1:604–606. New York: Century, 1884–1887.

Longacre, Edward G. *A Soldier to the Last: Maj. Gen. Joseph Wheeler in Blue and Gray.* Washington, DC: Potomac Books, 2007.

Lossing, Benson J. *Pictorial History of the Civil War in the United States of America.* 3 vols. Hartford, CT: T. Belknap, 1868.

Losson, Christopher. *Tennessee's Forgotten Warriors: Frank Cheatham and His Confederate Division.* Knoxville: University of Tennessee Press, 1989.

Luvaas, Jay, Stephen Bowman, and Leonard Fullenkamp, eds. *Guide to the Battle of Shiloh.* Lawrence: University Press of Kansas, 1996.

Magdeburg, F. H. "The Fourteenth Wisconsin Infantry at the Battle of Shiloh." *War Papers Read before the Commandery of the State of Wisconsin, Military Order of the Loyal Legion of the United States,* 176–187. Milwaukee: Burdick & Allen, 1903.

———. *14th Wis. Vet. Vol. Infantry at the Battle of Shiloh, Tenn., April 7th, 1862.* n.p., n.d.

Manual of the Panorama of the Battle of Shiloh. Chicago: A. T. Andreas, 1885.

"The March of Lew Wallace's Division to Shiloh." In *Battles and Leaders of the Civil War,* 1:607–610. New York: Century, 1884–1887.

Marszalek, John F. *Commander of All Lincoln's Armies: A Life of General Henry W. Halleck.* Cambridge, MA: Harvard University Press, 2004.

———. *Sherman: A Soldier's Passion for Order.* New York: Free Press, 1993.

Martin, David G. *The Campaign of Shiloh, March–April, 1862.* New York: Fairfax Press, 1987.

Mason, George. "Shiloh." In *Military Essays and Recollections,* 93–104. Chicago: A. C. McLurg, 1891.

Matson, Daniel. *Life Experiences of Daniel Matson.* Fowler, CO: Tribune Print, 1924.

Maury, Dabney H. *Recollections of a Virginian.* New York: Charles Scribner's Sons, 1894.

McBride, Mary Gorton, and Ann Mathison McLaurin. *Randall Lee Gibson of Louisiana: Confederate General and New South Reformer.* Baton Rouge: Louisiana State University Press, 2007.

McClure, W. H. "The 71st Ohio at Shiloh." *National Tribune,* June 6, 1907.

McCormick, Andrew W. "Sixteen Months a Prisoner of War." In *Sketches of War History, 1861–1865,* 5:69–87. Cincinnati: Robert Clarke, 1903.

McCutchen, Brian Keith. "Of Monuments and Remembrance: A History and Structural Analysis of the Monuments of Shiloh." MA thesis, Southeast Missouri State University, 1995.

McCutchen, Brian Keith, and Timothy B. Smith. *Shiloh National Military Park.* Charleston: Arcadia Publishing, 2012.

McDonough, James L. "Glory Can Not Atone: Shiloh—April 6, 7, 1862." *Tennessee Historical Quarterly* 35, no. 3 (Fall 1976): 279–295.

————. *Shiloh: In Hell before Night.* Knoxville: University of Tennessee Press, 1977.

McEathron, Alexander. *Letters and Memoirs of Alexander McEathron during the Civil War.* n.p., n.d.

McElroy, John. "Shiloh and After." *National Tribune,* April 19, 1906.

McGrath, John. "In a Louisianan Regiment." *Southern Historical Society Papers* 31 (1903): 103–120.

McKnight, Brian D. "Brig. Gen. James Morrison Hawes." In *Kentuckians in Gray: Generals and Field Officers of the Bluegrass State,* edited by Bruce S. Allardice and Lawrence Lee Hewitt, 131–137. Lexington: University Press of Kentucky, 2008.

McMurray, W. J. *History of the Twentieth Tennessee Regiment Volunteer Infantry, CSA.* Nashville, 1904.

McPherson, James M. *Battle Cry of Freedom: The Civil War Era.* New York: Oxford University Press, 1988.

McWhiney, Grady. *Braxton Bragg and Confederate Defeat,* vol. 1, *Field Command.* New York: Columbia University Press, 1969.

————. "General Beauregard's 'Complete Victory' at Shiloh: An Interpretation." *Journal of Southern History* 44, no. 3 (August 1983): 421–434.

Medrick, Robert W. "The Skirmishing in Sherman's Front." In *Battles and Leaders of the Civil War,* 1:537. New York: Century, 1884–1887.

Milligan, Mancil A. *Seeing Shiloh 1862 and Today.* Indianapolis: Jobbers Publishing, 1940.

Moore, Frank, ed. *The Rebellion Record: A Diary of American Events, with Documents, Narratives Illustrative Incidents, Poetry, etc.* 11 vols. New York: D. Vann Nostrand, 1861–1868.

Moore, Marquerites. "A Study of Early Crump, Tennessee." *Hardin County Historical Quarterly* 9, no. 1–2 (January–June 1992): 28–37.

Moore, Robert A. *A Life for the Confederacy: As Recorded in the Pocket Diaries of Pvt. Robert A. Moore, Co. "G" 17th Mississippi Regiment Confederate Guards Holly Springs, Mississippi.* Edited by James W. Silver. Jackson, TN: McCowat-Mercer Press, 1959.

"Morgan's Cavalry Was at Shiloh." *Confederate Veteran* 13, no. 5 (May 1905): 206.

Morrison, Marion. *A History of the Ninth Regiment Illinois Volunteer Infantry.* Monmouth, IL: John S. Clark, 1864.

Morton, Charles. "A Boy at Shiloh." In *Personal Recollections of the War of the Rebellion,* 52–69. New York: G. P. Putnam's Sons, 1907.

———. "Opening of the Battle of Shiloh." *Military Order of the Loyal Legion of the United States, War Papers 88* (1912): 1–20.

Murray, R. L., ed. *New Yorkers in the Civil War: A Historic Journal.* Wolcott, NY: Benedum Books, 2006.

Neal, W. A. *An Illustrated History of the Missouri Engineer and the 25th Infantry Regiments: Together with a Roster of Both Regiments and the Last Known Address of All that Could Be Obtained.* Chicago: Donohue and Henneberry, 1889.

Nevin, David. *The Road to Shiloh: Early Battles in the West.* Alexandria: Time-Life Books, 1983.

Newton, A. "An Incident of Shiloh." *National Tribune,* August 19, 1882.

Newton, James K. *A Wisconsin Boy in Dixie: The Selected Letters of James K. Newton.* Edited by Stephen E. Ambrose. Madison: University of Wisconsin Press, 1961.

Niles, F. A. "Several Surprises at Shiloh." *National Tribune,* March 29, 1883.

Nixon, Liberty Independence. "An Alabamian at Shiloh: The Diary of Liberty Independence Nixon." Edited by Hugh C. Bailey. *Alabama Review* 11, no. 2 (April 1958): 144–155.

Oates, James. "The Ninth Illinois at Shiloh." *National Tribune,* May 10, 1883.

Official Journal of the Proceedings of the Convention of the State of Louisiana. New Orleans: J. O. Nixon, 1861.

The Official Records of the Union and Confederate Navies in the War of the Rebellion. 30 vols. Washington, DC: Government Printing Office, 1894–1922.

Oliver, R. A. "'Your Affectionate Husband': Letters from a Catahoula Parish Confederate Soldier, September 1861–May 1862." Edited by William M. Cooper and Donald M. Fowler. *Journal of the North Louisiana Historical Association* 14, no. 1 (Winter 1983): 1–13.

Olney, Warren. *Shiloh as Seen by a Private Soldier.* n.p., 1889.

Opdycke, Emerson. *To Battle for God and the Right: The Civil War Letterbooks of Emerson Opdycke.* Edited by Glenn V. Longacre and John E. Haas. Urbana: University of Illinois Press, 2003.

Otis, Ephraim A. "The Second Day at Shiloh." In *Campaigns in Kentucky and Tennessee, Including the Battle of Chickamauga, 1862–1864,* 173–202. Boston: Cadet Armory, 1908.

Parks, Joseph H. *General Leonidas Polk, CSA: The Fighting Bishop.* Baton Rouge: Louisiana State University Press, 1962.

Paxton, William Edwards. "'Dear Rebecca': The Civil War Letters of William Edwards Paxton, 1861–1863." Edited by Ken Durham. *Louisiana History* 20, no. 2 (Spring 1979): 169–196.

Payne, Edwin W. *History of the Thirty-fourth Regiment of Illinois Volunteer Infantry, September 7, 1861–July 12, 1865.* n.p., n.d.

Peebles, T. H. "From Participant in Battle of Shiloh." *Confederate Veteran* 16, no. 6 (June 1908): 281–282.

Peterson, Lawrence K. *Confederate Combat Commander: The Remarkable Life of Brigadier General Alfred Jefferson Vaughan Jr.* Knoxville: University of Tennessee Press, 2013.

Pippen, W. B. "Concerning Battle of Shiloh." *Confederate Veteran* 16, no. 7 (July 1908): 344.

"Pittsburg Landing." *National Tribune,* May 3, 1883.

Plummer, Mark A. *Lincoln's Rail-Splitter: Governor Richard J. Oglesby.* Urbana: University of Illinois Press, 2001.

Polk, W. M. "The Concentration before Shiloh—Reply to General Ruggles." *Southern Historical Society Papers* 9 (1881): 178–185.

———. "Facts Connected with the Concentration of the Army of the Mississippi Before Shiloh, April, 1862." *Southern Historical Society Papers* 8 (1880): 457–463.

———. *Leonidas Polk: Bishop and General.* 2 vols. New York: Longmans, Green, 1915.

Porter, George C. "Gen. Braxton Bragg at Shiloh." *Confederate Veteran* 18, no. 2 (February 1910): 62–63.

Poulter, Keith. "The Second Courier." *North and South* 4, no. 2 (January 2001): 38–39.

Preston, William. "'At the Moment of Victory': The Battle of Shiloh and General A. S. Johnston's Death as Recounted in William Preston's Diary." Edited by Peter J. Sehlinger. *Filson Club History Quarterly* 61, no. 3 (July 1987): 315–345.

Prichard, James M. "Glory Denied: The Hard Fate of George B. Crittenden." In *Confederate Generals in the Western Theater: Essays on America's Civil War,* edited by Lawrence Lee Hewitt and Arthur W. Bergeron Jr., 2:1–22. Knoxville: University of Tennessee Press, 2001.

Prokopowicz, Gerald J. *All for the Regiment: The Army of the Ohio, 1861–1862.* Chapel Hill: University of North Carolina Press, 2001.

Putnam, Douglas, Jr. "Reminiscences of the Battle of Shiloh." In *Sketches of War History, 1861–1865,* 3:197–211. Cincinnati: Robert Clarke, 1890.

Rafuse, Ethan Sepp. "McClellan and Halleck at War: The Struggle for Control of the Union War Effort in the West, November 1861–March 1862." *Civil War History* 49, no. 1 (2003): 32–51.

Randall, James R. "General W. H. C. Whiting." *Southern Historical Society Papers* 23 (1895): 274–277.

Reaves, Stacy W. *A History and Guide to the Monuments of Shiloh National Park.* Charleston: History Press, 2012.

Reed, David W. *The Battle of Shiloh and the Organizations Engaged.* Washington, DC: Government Printing Office, 1909.

———. *Campaigns and Battles of the Twelfth Regiment Iowa Veteran Volunteer Infantry from Its Organization, September 1861, to Muster Out, January 20, 1866.* n.p., 1903.

Reeves, M. G. "Where the Blunder Was." *National Tribune,* April 19, 1883.

Reid, Whitelaw. *A Radical View: The "Agate" Dispatches of Whitelaw Reid, 1861–1865.* 2 vols. Edited by James G. Smart. Memphis: Memphis State University Press, 1976.

Reinhart, Joseph R. *A History of the 6th Kentucky Volunteer Infantry US: The Boys Who Feared No Noise.* Louisville: Beargrass Press, 2000.

Reinhart, Joseph R., ed. *August Willich's Gallant Dutchmen: Civil War Letters from the 32nd Indiana Infantry.* Kent: Kent State University Press, 2006.

Reinoch, Henry. "Surprised at Company Inspection." *National Tribune,* April 19, 1883.

"Reminiscences of Shiloh." *National Tribune,* January 28, 1882.

Report of the Proceedings of the Society of the Army of the Tennessee at the Fourteenth Annual Meeting, Held at Cincinnati, Ohio, April 6th and 7th, 1881. Cincinnati: Society of the Army of the Tennessee, 1885.

Rerick, John H. *The Forty-fourth Indiana Volunteer Infantry: History of Its Services in the War of the Rebellion and a Personal Record of Its Members.* LaGrange, IN, 1880.

Rice, DeLong. *The Story of Shiloh.* Jackson, TN: McCowat-Mercer, 1924.

Rich, Joseph W. "The Battle of Shiloh." *Iowa Journal of History and Politics* 7, no. 4 (October 1909): 503–581.

———. *The Battle of Shiloh.* Iowa City: State Historical Society of Iowa, 1911.

———. "General Lew. Wallace at Shiloh: How He Was Convinced of an Error after Forty Years." *Iowa Journal of History and Politics* 18, no. 2 (April 1920): 301–308.

Richardson, Albert D. *A Personal History of Ulysses S. Grant.* Hartford, CT: American Publishing, 1868.

Richardson, Frank L. "War as I Saw It, 1861–1865." *Louisiana Historical Quarterly* 6 (January 1923): 89–106.

Riley, A. C. "Confederate Col. A. C. Riley, His Reports and Letters, Part II." Edited by Riley Bock. *Missouri Historical Review* 85, no. 3 (April 1991): 264–287.

Rogers, William P. "The Diary and Letters of William P. Rogers, 1846–1862." Edited by Florence Damon Pace. *Southwestern Historical Quarterly* 32, no. 4 (April 1929): 259–299.

Roland, Charles P. *Albert Sidney Johnston: Soldier of Three Republics*. Austin: University of Texas Press, 1964.

Roman, Alfred. *The Military Operations of General Beauregard in the War Between the States, 1861–1865: Including a Brief Personal Sketch of His Services in the War with Mexico, 1846–8*. 2 vols. New York: Harper & Brothers, 1883.

Rood, R. H. *History of Company "A," Thirteenth Iowa Veteran Infantry, from September 12th, 1861, to July 21st, 1865*. Cedar Rapids: Daily Republican Printing and Binding House, 1889.

Rowland, Dunbar, and H. Grady Howell Jr. *Military History of Mississippi, 1803–1898, Including a Listing of All Known Mississippi Confederate Military Units*. Madison, MS: Chickasaw Bayou Press, 2003.

Ruggles, Daniel. "The Concentration before Shiloh—Reply to Captain Polk." *Southern Historical Society Papers* 9 (1881): 49–63.

Salling, Stuart. *Louisianans in the Western Confederacy: The Adams–Gibson Brigade in the Civil War*. Jefferson, NC: McFarland, 2010.

Sandidge, L. D. "The Battle of Shiloh." *Southern Historical Society Papers* 8 (1880): 173–177.

Schaller, Frank. *Soldiering for Glory: The Civil War Letters of Colonel Frank Schaller, Twenty-second Mississippi Infantry*. Edited by Mary W. Schaller and Martin N. Schaller. Columbia: University of South Carolina Press, 2007.

Schenker, Carl R., Jr. "The Grant–Halleck–Smith Affair." *North and South* 12, no. 1 (February 2010): 11–12.

———. "Ulysses in His Tent: Halleck, Grant, Sherman, and 'The Turning Point of the War.'" *Civil War History* 56, no. 2 (June 2010): 175–221.

———. "Who Failed to Fortify Pittsburg Landing." *North and South* 13, no. 1 (May 2011): 46–53.

Searle, C. P. "Personal Reminiscences of Shiloh." In *War Sketches and Incidents,* 326–339. Des Moines: P. C. Kenyon, 1893.

Second Reunion of the 12th Iowa V. V. Infantry, Held at Manchester, Iowa. Dubuque: C. B. Dorr Press, 1884.

Sehlinger, Peter J. *Kentucky's Last Cavalier: General William Preston, 1816–1887*. Lexington: Kentucky Historical Society, 2004.

Shanks, William F. G. *Personal Recollections of Distinguished Generals*. New York: Harper & Brothers, 1866.

Shaw, William T. "The Battle of Shiloh." In *War Sketches and Incidents,* 1:183–207. Des Moines: P. C. Kenyon, 1893.

Shedd, Charles E. *A History of Shiloh National Military Park, Tennessee*. Washington, DC: Government Printing Office, 1954.

Sherman, William T. *Memoirs of General William T. Sherman, Written by Himself.* 2 vols. New York: D. Appleton, 1875.

"The Shiloh Campaign." *National Tribune,* July 24, 1884.

"The Shiloh Campaign." *National Tribune,* March 27, 1884.

Shoup, Francis A. "The Art of War in '62—Shiloh." *United Service* 11 (July 1884): 1–13.

———. "How We Went to Shiloh." *Confederate Veteran* 2, no. 5 (May 1894): 137–140.

Simpson, Brooks D. *Ulysses S. Grant: Triumph over Adversity, 1822–1865.* Boston: Houghton Mifflin, 2000.

Skaptason, Bjorn. "The Chicago Light Artillery at Shiloh." *Journal of the Illinois State Historical Society* 104, no. 1–2 (Spring–Summer 2011): 73–96.

———. "Retreat and Save Yourselves: A Study in Union Leadership Failure at Shiloh." MA thesis, Loyola University, Chicago, 2010.

Smith, B. "What Another Soldier Thinks About It." *National Tribune,* March 29, 1883.

Smith, G. S. "One Brigade That Was Not Surprised." *National Tribune,* April 19, 1883.

Smith, H. I. *History of the Seventh Iowa Veteran Volunteer Infantry during the Civil War.* Mason City, IA: R. Hitchcock, 1903.

Smith, Jacob H. *Personal Reminiscences Three Weeks Prior, During, and Ten Days After the Battle of Shiloh.* Detroit: Winn & Hammond, 1894.

Smith, John Thomas. *A History of the Thirty-first Regiment of Indiana Volunteer Infantry in the War of the Rebellion.* Cincinnati: Western Methodist Book Concern, 1900.

Smith, Myron J. *The Timberclads in the Civil War: The "Lexington," "Conestoga," and "Tyler" on the Western Waters.* Jefferson, NC: McFarland, 2008.

Smith, Ralph J. *Reminiscences of the Civil War and Other Sketches.* Waco, TX: W. M. Morrison, 1911.

Smith, Robert D. *Confederate Diary of Robert D. Smith.* Edited by Jill K. Garrett. Columbia, TN: UDC, 1975.

Smith, Timothy B. *Corinth 1862: Siege, Battle, Occupation.* Lawrence: University Press of Kansas, 2012.

———. "David Wilson Reed: The Father of Shiloh National Military Park." *Annals of Iowa* 62, no. 3 (Summer 2003): 333–359.

———. "The Forgotten Inhabitants of Shiloh: A Case Study in a Civilian–Government Relationship." *Tennessee Historical Quarterly* 67, no. 1 (Spring 2008): 36–55.

———. "'Gallant and Invaluable Service': The United States Navy at the Battle of Shiloh." *West Tennessee Historical Society Papers* 58 (2004): 18–36.

———. *The Golden Age of Battlefield Preservation: The Decade of the 1890s and the Establishment of America's First Five Military Parks.* Knoxville: University of Tennessee Press, 2008.

———. "'The Handsomest Cemetery in the South': Shiloh National Cemetery." *West Tennessee Historical Society Papers* 56 (2002): 1–16.

———. "Historians and the Battle of Shiloh: One Hundred and Forty Years of Controversy." *Tennessee Historical Quarterly* 63, no. 4 (Winter 2003): 338–339.

———. *Mississippi in the Civil War: The Home Front.* Jackson: University Press of Mississippi, 2010.

———. *Rethinking Shiloh: Myth and Memory.* Knoxville: University of Tennessee Press, 2013.

———. "Secession at Shiloh: Mississippi's Convention Delegates and Their State's Defense." *Hallowed Ground* 13, no. 1 (Spring 2012): 28–35.

———. *This Great Battlefield of Shiloh: History, Memory, and the Establishment of a Civil War National Military Park.* Knoxville: University of Tennessee Press, 2004.

———. *The Untold Story of Shiloh: The Battle and the Battlefield.* Knoxville: University of Tennessee Press, 2006.

Smith, Timothy B., ed. *The Battle of Shiloh: Tennessee in the Civil War.* Nashville: Tennessee Historical Society, 2012.

Smith, Walter George. *Life and Letters of Thomas Kilby Smith: Brevet Major-General United States Volunteers, 1820–1887.* New York: G. P. Putnam's Sons, 1898.

Spence, Philip B. "Services in the Confederacy." *Confederate Veteran* 8, no. 11 (November 1911): 500–501.

Stanley, Henry Morton. *The Autobiography of Sir Henry Morton Stanley.* Edited by Dorothy Stanley. Boston: Houghton Mifflin, 1909.

Starr, N. D., and T. W. Holman. *The 21st Missouri Regiment Infantry Veteran Volunteers. Historical Memoranda.* Fort Madison, IA: Roberts & Roberts, 1899.

Stephens, Gail. *Shadow of Shiloh: Major General Lew Wallace in the Civil War.* Indianapolis: Indiana Historical Society Press, 2010.

Stephenson, Jon G. "First Thunder at Shiloh." *Civil War Times Illustrated* 36, no. 1 (March 1997): 42–55.

Stevenson, Thomas M. *History of the 78th Regiment O. V. V. I., Its "Muster-in" to Its "Muster-out": Comprising Its Organization, Marches, Campaigns, Battles and Skirmishes.* Zanesville, OH: Hugh Dunne, 1865.

Stevenson, William G. *Thirteen Months in the Rebel Army: Being a Narrative of Personal Adventures in the Infantry, Ordinance, Cavalry, Courier, and Hospital Services.* New York: A. S. Barnes & Burr, 1862.

Stillwell, Leander. *Personal Recollections of the Battle of Shiloh.* n.p., 1892.

Stone, Henry. "The Battle of Shiloh." In *Campaigns in Kentucky and Tennes-see, Including the Battle of Chickamauga, 1862–1864,* 7:31–99. Boston: Cadet Armory, 1908.

The Story of the Fifty-fifth Regiment Illinois Volunteer Infantry in the Civil War, 1861–1865. n.p., 1887.

Sullins, D. "Heroic Deed at Shiloh." *Confederate Veteran* 5, no. 1 (January 1897): 10.

Sumbardo, Charles L. *Glimpses of the Nation's Struggle.* New York: D. D. Merrill, 1893.

Supplement to the Official Records of the Union and Confederate Armies. 100 vols. Wilmington, NC: Broadfoot Publishing, 1994.

Surby, R. W. "Fighting Them Over." *National Tribune,* March 29, 1883.

"Surprise at Shiloh." *National Tribune,* April 5, 1883.

Swaddling, John. *Historical Memoranda of the 52nd Regiment Illinois Infantry Volunteers from Its Organization, Nov. 19th, 1861, to Its Muster Out, by Reason of Expiration of Service, on the 6th Day of July, 1865.* Elgin, IL: Gilbert and Post, 1868.

Sweeny, W. M. "Man of Resource." *National Tribune,* September 5, 1895.

Sword, Wiley. "General G. T. Beauregard's Role at the Battle of Shiloh: Hero or Villain?" In *Confederate Generals in the Western Theater: Essays on America's Civil War,* edited by Lawrence Lee Hewitt and Arthur W. Bergeron Jr., 3:39–59. Knoxville: University of Tennessee Press, 2001.

———. *Shiloh: Bloody April.* Rev. ed. Dayton, OH: Morningside, 2001.

Sykes, E. T. "Walthall's Brigade—A Cursory Sketch with Personal Experiences of Walthall's Brigade, Army of Tennessee, CSA, 1862–1865." In *Publications of the Mississippi Historical Society, Centenary Series,* 1:477–616. Jackson: Mississippi Historical Society, 1916.

Symonds, Craig L. *Stonewall of the West: Patrick Cleburne and the Civil War.* Lawrence: University Press of Kansas, 1997.

Taylor, John T. "Reminiscences of Services as an Aide-de-Camp with General William Tecumseh Sherman." *Military Order of the Loyal Legion of the United States,* 1892.

Terry, James G. "Record of the Alabama State Artillery from It's Organization in May 1836 to the Surrender in April 1865 and from It's Re-organization Jan'y 1872 to Jan'y 1875." *Alabama Historical Quarterly* 20, no. 2 (Summer 1958): 141–447.

Third Reunion of the 12th Iowa V. V. Infantry, Held at Waterloo, Iowa. Manchester, IA: Manchester Press, 1888.

Thomas, B. F. *Soldier Life: A Narrative of the Civil War.* n.p., 1907.

Thompson, Ed Porter. *History of the First Kentucky Brigade.* Cincinnati: Caxton Publishing House, 1868.

———. *History of the Orphan Brigade.* Louisville: Lewis N. Thompson, 1898.

Thompson, Illene D., and Wilbur E. Thompson. *The Seventeenth Alabama Infantry: A Regimental History and Roster.* Bowie, MD: Heritage Books, 2001.

Thompson, Joseph Dimmit. "The Battle of Shiloh: From the Letters and Diary of Joseph Dimmit Thompson." Edited by John G. Biel. *Tennessee Historical Quarterly* 17, no. 3 (September 1958): 250–274.

Thompson, S. D. *Recollections with the Third Iowa Regiment.* Cincinnati, 1864.

Truxall, Aida Craig, ed. *"Respects to All": Letters from Two Young Brothers Fighting in the Civil War.* Pittsburgh: University of Pittsburg Press, 1962.

Ulmer, J. B. "A Glimpse of Albert Sidney Johnston through the Smoke of Shiloh." *Southwestern Historical Quarterly* 10, no. 4 (April 1907): 285–296.

Van Horne, Thomas B. *History of the Army of the Cumberland: Its Organization, Campaigns, and Battles.* 2 vols. Cincinnati: Robert Clarke, 1875.

Van Winkle, Alexander. "Incidents and Inquiries about Shiloh." *Confederate Veteran* 16, no. 3 (March 1908): 102.

Vaughan, Alfred J. *Personal Record of the Thirteenth Regiment, Tennessee Infantry.* Memphis: S. C. Toof, 1897.

Veatch, James C. "The Battle of Shiloh." *National Tribune,* March 15, 1883.

Villard, Henry. *Memoirs of Henry Villard: Journalist and Financier, 1835–1900.* 2 vols. Boston: Houghton, Mifflin, 1904.

Wallace, Isabel. *Life and Letters of General W. H. L. Wallace.* Carbondale: Southern Illinois University Press, 2000.

Wallace, Lewis. *Lew Wallace: An Autobiography.* 2 vols. New York: Harper & Brothers, 1906.

Wardner, Horace. "Reminiscences of a Surgeon." In *Military Essays and Recollections: Papers Read before the Commandery of the State of Illinois, Military Order of the Loyal Legion of the United States,* 173–191. Chicago: Dial Press, 1899.

Warner, Ezra J. *Generals in Blue: Lives of the Union Commanders.* Baton Rouge: Louisiana State University Press, 1964.

———. *Generals in Gray: Lives of the Confederate Commanders.* Baton Rouge: Louisiana State University Press, 1959.

War of the Rebellion: A Compilation of the Official Records of the Union and Confederate Armies. Washington, DC: Government Printing Office, 1880–1901.

Watkins, Sam R. *"Co. Aytch," Maury Grays, First Tennessee Regiment, or A Side Show of the Big Show.* Nashville: Cumberland Presbyterian Publishing, 1882.

Watson, Elbert. "Turkeytown CSA." *Alabama Historical Quarterly* 23 (1961): 300–302.

Welch, Paul D. *Archeology at Shiloh Indian Mounds, 1899–1999.* Tuscaloosa: University of Alabama Press, 2006.

Wheeler, John P. "The Fifty-fifth Illinois at Shiloh." *National Tribune,* May 3, 1883.

Wheeler, Joseph. "The Battle of Shiloh." *Southern Historical Society Papers* 23 (1895): 119–131.

Widney, Lyman S. *Campaigning with Uncle Billy: The Civil War Memoirs of Sgt. Lyman S. Widney, 34th Illinois Volunteer Infantry.* Edited by Robert I. Girardi. Bloomington, IN: Trafford Publishing, 2008.

Wilkie, Franc B. *Pen and Powder.* Boston: Ticknor, 1888.

Williams, James M. *From that Terrible Field: Civil War Letters of James M. Williams, Twenty-first Alabama Infantry Volunteers.* Edited by John Kent Folmar. Tuscaloosa: University of Alabama Press, 1981.

Williams, T. Harry. "Beauregard at Shiloh." In *Confederate Generals in the Western Theater: Essays on America's Civil War,* edited by Lawrence Lee Hewitt and Arthur W. Bergeron Jr., 1:25–43. Knoxville: University of Tennessee Press, 2001.

———. *P. G. T. Beauregard: Napoleon in Gray.* Baton Rouge: Louisiana State University Press, 1954.

Williams, Thomas J. *An Historical Sketch of the 56th Ohio Volunteer Infantry During the Great Civil War from 1861 to 1865.* Columbus, OH: Lawrence, 1899.

Williamson, David. *The Third Battalion Mississippi Infantry and the 45th Mississippi Regiment: A Civil War History.* Jefferson, NC: McFarland, 2004.

Wills, Brian Steel. *The Confederacy's Greatest Cavalryman: Nathan Bedford Forrest.* Lawrence: University Press of Kansas, 1992.

———. *George Henry Thomas: As True as Steel.* Lawrence: University Press of Kansas, 2012.

Wingfield, Marshall. *General A. P. Stewart: His Life and Letters.* Memphis: West Tennessee Historical Society, 1954.

Witham, George F. *Shiloh, Shells and Artillery Units.* Memphis: Riverside Press, 1980.

Wood, D. W. *History of the 20th OVVI Regiment and Proceedings of the First Reunion at Mt. Vernon, Ohio, April 6, 1876.* Columbus, OH: Paul and Thrall, 1876.

Woodworth, Steven E. *Decision in the Heartland: The Civil War in the West.* Westport, CT: Praeger, 2008.

———. *Jefferson Davis and His Generals: The Failure of Confederate Command in the West.* Lawrence: University Press of Kansas, 1990.

———. *Nothing but Victory: The Army of the Tennessee, 1861–1865.* New York: Knopf, 2005.

———. *Shiloh: Confederate High Tide in the Heartland.* Santa Barbara, CA: Praeger, 2013.

————. "When Merit Was Not Enough: Albert Sidney Johnston and Confederate Defeat in the West, 1862." In *Civil War Generals in Defeat,* edited by Steven E. Woodworth, 9–27. Lawrence: University Press of Kansas, 1999.

Worsham, W. J. *The Old Nineteenth Tennessee Regiment, CSA, June, 1861–April, 1865.* Knoxville: Paragon, 1902.

Worthington, Thomas. *A Brief History of the 46th Ohio Volunteers.* n.p., n.d.

————. *Report of the Flank March to Join on McClernand's Right, at 9 A. M., and Operations of the 46th Reg't Ohio Vols., 1st Brigade, 5th Division, on the Extreme Union Right, at Shiloh, April 6, 1862.* Washington, DC, 1880.

————. *Shiloh: The Only Correct Military History of Ulysses S. Grant and the Missing Army Records for Which He Alone Is Responsible, to Conceal His Organized Defeat of the Union Army at Shiloh, April 6, 1862.* Washington City: M'Gill and Witherow, 1872.

Wright, Charles. *A Corporal's Story: Experiences in the Ranks of Company "C," 81st Ohio Vol. Infantry, during the War for the Maintenance of the Union, 1861–1864.* Philadelphia: James Beale, 1887.

Wright, Henry B. *A History of the Sixth Iowa Infantry.* Iowa City: State Historical Society of Iowa, 1923.

Wright, Henry H. "An Iowa Soldier's Story of Shiloh." *National Tribune,* May 3, 1883.

Wynne, Ben. *A Hard Trip: A History of the 15th Mississippi Infantry, CSA.* Macon: Mercer University Press, 2003.

Yantis, Isaac. "The 41st Ill. at Shiloh." *National Tribune,* August 22, 1907.

Young, John Russell. *Around the World with General Grant.* 2 vols. New York: Subscription Book Department, 1879.

Young, L. D. *Reminiscences of a Soldier of the Orphan Brigade.* Paris, KY, n.d.

INDEX

Jackson, Tennessee, 23, 27, 405
Jefferson, Thomas, 1
Jenkins, T. F., 105
John J. Roe, USS, 332
Johnson, Amory K., 195, 223
Johnson, Bushrod R. 53, 62, 108–109, 131–132, 151, 158, 160, 165, 271, 299, 429
Johnson, Charles, 33
Johnson, George W., 30, 169, 344
Johnson, Roxana, 78
Johnson, R. W., 374
Johnston, Albert Sidney, xi, 19, 22–26, 28–32, 35–37, 267, 287, 289, 291, 304–306, 330, 344, 374, 389, 407, 409–410, 418, 420–422, 428
and Confederate march to Shiloh, 59–65, 67–70, 72–76
and death, 186–188, 190–194
and first day, 82, 84, 90–92, 95, 104, 125, 129–131, 133–141, 143, 149–152, 155–156, 158–160, 168, 174, 197, 200–203, 205, 209, 217–219, 233
and Forts Henry and Donelson, 4–7
Johnston, Joseph E., 104
Johnston, Robert A., 344
Johnston, William Preston, 24, 41, 61, 70, 76, 130, 160, 218, 233, 374
Joiner, Gary D., 482n14
Jomini, Antoine-Henri, 5
Jones, Charles, 70, 107, 348
Jones, David, 310
Jones, Dudley, xvii
Jones, Frank, 320
Jones, Frederick C., 309
Jones, James M., xvi
Jones, Lloyd, 78
Jones Field, 49, 154, 156, 167, 169, 171–173, 203, 254–255, 257, 267–268, 270–271, 273–274,

316, 349–350, 352, 354–356, 358–359, 361, 375
Jordan, Thomas, 59–60, 62–63, 72, 75, 90, 101, 139, 183, 205, 250, 259, 268, 389

Kelley, Louis D., 164
Kelly, John H., 32, 356, 385
Kendrick, Mills, 148
Kentucky, 4, 22, 24–26, 30–31, 47, 67, 72, 150, 169, 185, 229, 241, 272, 313, 329–331, 344, 370, 418
Kentucky Troops (CS)
3rd Infantry, 432
4th Infantry, 31, 169–170, 342–344, 360, 432
5th Infantry, 169–170, 343–344, 393, 432
6th Infantry, 169–170, 334, 342, 432
7th Infantry, 32, 73, 201, 328, 429
Lyon's (Cobb's) Battery, 169, 273, 384, 432
Morgan's Squadron Cavalry, 225, 432
Thompson's Company Cavalry, 432
Kentucky Troops (US)
1st Infantry, 303–304, 310, 317, 324, 427
2nd Infantry, 303, 309–310, 368, 427
5th Infantry, 333, 343–344, 361, 427
6th Infantry, 302, 316, 320, 322, 324–325, 427
9th Infantry, 336, 338, 383, 428
11th Infantry, 317, 320, 326, 383, 428
13th Infantry, 327, 331, 336, 383, 428
17th Infantry, 356, 425
20th Infantry, 303, 317, 368, 427
24th Infantry, 387–388, 428
25th Infantry, 14, 177, 356, 425